Applying Sport Psychology

FOUR PERSPECTIVES

Jim Taylor, PhD

Gregory S. Wilson, PED

University of Evansville

Editors

Human Kinetics

Cataloging-in-Publication Data

Applying sport psychology : four perspectives / Jim Taylor, Gregory S.
   Wilson, editors.
      p. ; cm.
   Includes bibliographical references and index.
   ISBN 0-7360-4512-0 (soft cover)
   1. Sports--Psychological aspects.   I. Taylor, Jim, 1958-   .
II. Wilson, Gregory S. (Gregory Scott), 1960-   .
   [DNLM: 1. Sports-psychology.   2. Psychology, Applied.   QT 260
A6485 2005]
GV706.4.A68 2005
796.01--dc22   2005018528

ISBN: 0-7360-4512-0

The Web addresses cited in this text were current as of May 20, 2005, unless otherwise noted.

Acquisitions Editors: Amy N. Clocksin and Myles Schrag; **Developmental Editor:** Renee Thomas Pyrtel; **Assistant Editors:** Ann M. Augspurger and Maureen Eckstein; **Copyeditor:** Julie Anderson; **Proofreader:** Pam Johnson; **Indexer:** Betty Frizzéll; **Permission Manager:** Dalene Reeder; **Graphic Designer:** Fred Starbird; **Graphic Artist:** Yvonne Griffith; **Photo Manager:** Kelly J. Huff; **Cover Designer:** Robert Reuther; **Photographer (cover):** Comstock, Stockbyte, Photodisc; **Photographs (interior):** © Human Kinetics, unless otherwise noted; **Art Manager:** Kelly Hendren; **Illustrator:** Al Wilborn; **Printer:** Versa Press

Printed in the United States of America   10 9 8 7 6 5 4 3 2 1

Human Kinetics
Web site: www.HumanKinetics.com

United States: Human Kinetics
P.O. Box 5076
Champaign, IL 61825-5076
800-747-4457
e-mail: humank@hkusa.com

Canada: Human Kinetics
475 Devonshire Road Unit 100
Windsor, ON N8Y 2L5
800-465-7301 (in Canada only)
e-mail: orders@hkcanada.com

Europe: Human Kinetics
107 Bradford Road
Stanningley, Leeds LS28 6AT, United Kingdom
+44 (0) 113 255 5665
e-mail: hk@hkeurope.com

Australia: Human Kinetics
57A Price Avenue
Lower Mitcham, South Australia 5062
08 8277 1555
e-mail: liaw@hkaustralia.com

New Zealand: Human Kinetics
Division of Sports Distributors NZ Ltd.
P.O. Box 300 226 Albany
North Shore City, Auckland
0064 9 448 1207
e-mail: info@humankinetics.co.nz

Contents

Preface

Legendary U.S. collegiate and Olympic swimming coach James "Doc" Counsilman wrote nearly 20 years ago that "future improvements in swimming may come, not from better physical preparation, but from better mental or psychological preparation for both practice and competition" (1977, p. 266). Since then, there has been a growing awareness and appreciation of the significant impact that the mind has on athletic performance. With this increased recognition, researchers in sport psychology have focused on identifying the specific mental factors that play a pivotal role in athletic performances. In turn, sport psychology consultants have developed intervention methods based on this research and their own experiences working with coaches and athletes. Somewhat apart from this formal exploration of sport psychology, coaches and athletes have conducted their own "research" derived from their direct experience with athletic performance and have developed their own techniques for maximizing sport performance.

This divergence of information gathering between those who study sport psychology—researchers and consultants—and those who experience sport psychology—coaches and athletes—has resulted in a chasm of our understanding of how the mind affects sport performance.

To help bridge that gap, *Applying Sport Psychology: Four Perspectives* is the first book to integrate the views of researchers, consultants, coaches, and athletes in a wide-ranging and in-depth exploration of the essential mental areas that influence sport performance.

This book is designed to benefit a diverse audience. It will appeal to researchers who want to gain a full understanding of the latest theoretical and empirical investigations in the field. This book will be a useful textbook in academia—for professors and students alike—as a comprehensive source of information about the mental aspects of sport performance. Consultants will value *Applying Sport Psychology: Four Perspectives* for the depth and breadth of knowledge and strategies they can learn from researchers and other

consultants and from coaches and athletes who are "in the trenches" using sport psychology every day. Coaches will benefit from this book for its diverse points of view in their work with athletes. Finally, athletes will learn practical information and tools from leading researchers, consultants, and coaches that they can use to enhance their sport performances.

Each chapter in *Applying Sport Psychology* contains four integrated discussions of relevant issues. Within each chapter, a sport psychology researcher provides the theoretical and empirical foundation of the topic, which reviews the latest conceptual and scientific research in the area. Supporting this theoretical perspective, a sport psychology consultant integrates the research findings with hands-on experience to provide an overview of intervention knowledge and strategies aimed at enhancing sport performance. The consultant acts as the bridge between the research and the "real-world" applications of sport psychology. Integrated throughout each chapter are salient comments from successful coaches and athletes. Providing personal insights, these observations describe both the coach's and athlete's perspective and experiences dealing with the issue at hand. This unique approach allows the reader to fully grasp the many layers of each topic addressed in *Applying Sport Psychology*.

The book is divided into four parts, each dealing with important issues in applied sport psychology. Part I, Psychological Factors in Athletic Performance, describes the most essential mental factors associated with sport performance. The topics discussed are motivation, confidence, intensity, focus, and emotions. Part II, Enhancing Athletic Performance, addresses the intervention strategies that are most commonly studied by researchers and used by consultants, coaches, and athletes. The techniques that are most often used to enhance performance are psychological assessment, goal setting, mental imagery, and routines. Part III, Psychology and the Coach, considers areas that are most relevant to coaching effectiveness: the coach–athlete relationship and team cohesion.

Part IV, Psychological Problems of Athletes, focuses on serious mental and physical issues that athletes may confront. Although performance enhancement is most often associated with applied sport psychology, there is a growing awareness of areas beyond athletic performance that can affect athletes as people. Topics addressed are injuries, eating disorders, substance abuse, and career transitions.

Sir Roger Bannister (1981), in *The Four Minute Mile*, observed, "Experiments in the laboratory are not of much practical value to athletes" (p. 133). Unfortunately, many athletes, coaches, and some consultants share this attitude. We suggest that this perception is based largely on the fact that coaches and athletes have had few opportunities to interact in a collaborative way with the scientific community. Furthermore, even sport psychology consultants have not always been included in the development and implementation of research that could have practical value to coaches and athletes. We hope that *Applying Sport Psychology: Four Perspectives* acts as a bridge to span the chasm that we spoke of earlier and encourages the producers, conveyors, and consumers of applied sport psychology to build meaningful relationships. Only by building this bridge can we hope to gain a more complete understanding of the impact of mental factors on sport performance and expect

to develop more effective tools that will allow athletes to push the limits of what is possible.

A Note on Chapter Authorship

Applying Sport Psychology: Four Perspectives illustrates a process or a flow of information in each of the topic areas that the book covers. As a result, the placement of the titles (researcher, consultant, coach, and athlete) is especially important to the book's purpose. This flow of information highlights the uniqueness of the book and shows how theory is often applied in real-life settings. We want to make it clear that the order of authorship in each chapter is determined by the individual's role in this flow of information, not by relative workload of all the authors, as is customary convention in academic authorship.

Both the editors of this book and Human Kinetics are grateful for the work of all involved, especially the lead contributors that organized the "chapter teams." Specifically, this "team" concept gets at the heart of what the book is about, and offers the reader four very unique insights into sport psychology.

Acknowledgments

I express my deepest gratitude to my coeditor, Dr. Gregory Wilson, whose dedication, professionalism, hard work, patience, and tough love with the contributors made this book possible. Because of the power of the Internet, I have had a wonderful collaboration with someone whom I have never met. Gregg, it has been a pleasure.

I would also like to thank my wife, Sarah, because you complete me.

J.T.

The idea for this book would never have come to fruition if not for Jim's guidance. It is truly amazing what can be accomplished via the Internet. Jim, thanks for keeping my feet on the ground throughout this project. It has been my privilege to work with you.

Most important, I thank my wife Roseann, daughter, Jessica, and son, Kyle. Your love, support, and encouragement make all things possible.

G.W.

We would like to thank the researchers, consultants, coaches, and athletes who contributed to *Applying Sport Psychology: Four Perspectives*. Without their expertise and commitment, our vision would never have been realized.

We would also like to express our gratitude to everyone at Human Kinetics, including Rainer Martens, Amy Clocksin, Myles Schrag, and Renee Thomas Pyrtel, for their faith in us and their immense patience in getting this book finished.

J.T., G.W.

I

Psychological Factors in Athletic Performance

Part I begins the exploration of applying sport psychology for researchers, consultants, coaches, and athletes. This section covers five psychological areas (motivation, confidence, intensity, focus, and emotions) that are widely believed to have the most influence on athletic performance. Considerable research is described in the following chapters that has found robust and consistent relationships between these five psychological issues and competitive performance. Our own experience and discussions with many applied sport psychology consultants, coaches, and athletes in many sports from around the world have shown that these five factors also play a significant role in the "real world" of sport.

The five psychological areas, derived from a performance pyramid developed by Taylor (2001), are ordered in a reasoned way, in which they ascend from a general influence on training and preparation to a specific and immediate impact on competitive performance. At the base of the pyramid lies motivation, because without motivation there is no interest or desire to train. Motivation ensures that athletes put in the necessary time and effort to be totally prepared to perform their best. Chapter 1 examines the effect that motivation has on athletes' training and competitive efforts and what consultants, coaches, and athletes can do to maximize motivation.

From motivation and preparation comes confidence in athletes' physical, technical, and tactical capabilities and in their ability to perform their best in important competitions. Confidence gives athletes the desire to compete and the belief that they can achieve their goals. Chapter 2 explores the essential role that confidence plays in all facets of training and competition. Particular emphasis is placed on how confidence evolves naturally through effective preparation and specific strategies that are designed to proactively develop confidence.

From confidence comes athletes' ability to manage their intensity and respond positively to the pressures of competition, which enables athletes to consistently maintain their ideal level of intensity so they are physically capable of performing their best. Chapter 3 describes the relationship that intensity has with competitive performance. Emphasis is placed on how athletes can identify their optimal level of intensity and how they can adjust it before and during competitions.

From intensity comes the ability to focus effectively and avoid distractions during training and competition. Chapter 4 discusses the often misunderstood influence that focus has on competitive performance. The issue of focus is demystified and a practical approach described that offers simple and practical techniques for enhancing focus during competition.

From these four psychological factors comes athletes' ability to master their emotions and ensure that emotions help rather than hurt their competitive performances. Chapter 5 explores what is perhaps the most complex and challenging psychological influence on performance. A discussion of the counterintuitive relationship that emotions have with performance is offered as well as insights into how athletes can best manage their emotions in competition. Having ascended this performance pyramid, athletes will have the tools to achieve their goals and perform to the best of their abilities.

CHAPTER

1

Motivation

Brent Walker, PhD—researcher
Sandra Foster, PhD—consultant*
Scott Daubert, BA—coach
DeDee Nathan, MS—athlete

The objectives of this chapter are

- to arrive at a definition of motivation that is meaningful for coaches, athletes, and consultants;
- to describe how motivation affects athletic performance while integrating the theories of motivation;
- to offer recommendations and resources to help athletes discover their ideal level of motivation; and
- to offer practical suggestions for helping athletes to initiate and sustain motivation at ideal levels during the competition season and beyond.

*Though Brent Walker, the researcher, is listed as the first author for this chapter to maintain consistency with the four perspectives highlighted in this book, the editors credit Sandra Foster, the consultant, as the lead contributor to this chapter.

When watching Olympic athletes compete, viewers may wonder why athletes train so long and hard for the short time during which they put their skills to the test. What is their motivation? Some spectators may be convinced that these athletes are motivated by a hunger for fame or financial reward. Others might suggest that these athletes' motivation is self-oriented, a push to achieve a personal goal or to experience peak performance. Still others might believe that winning a gold medal for one's country is the ultimate drive.

Which of these speculations is most accurate? This chapter provides some answers to this question as it examines motivation, an important topic to applied sport psychology researchers and consultants as well as to coaches and athletes. The next pages focus on situations frequently studied by researchers and encountered by consultants, coaches, and athletes when they must grapple with shifts in athletes' motivation that emerge during a season and those that can occur after significant losses.

Key Issues

Motivation influences both daily progress and competition outcomes from the very moment a young person signs up for Little League or a high school basketball player accepts a scholarship at a Division I university. The impact of a team's collective motivation—its presence or absence—figures prominently in the strategic decisions made by coaches throughout a season, from the opening day of training camp to the playoffs. And a child's motivation, as evidenced by his or her mood and effort exhibited during sport, can be a source of consternation, confusion, or celebration for parents.

Motivation is related to an athlete's level of self-confidence and effectiveness of goal setting, topics described in detail in later chapters (chapters 2 and 7, respectively). Likewise, motivation is intertwined with athletes' emotions (see chapter 5). However, motivation can be considered on its own merit as a crucial element in understanding why athletes compete successfully, persist during training, and choose to remain involved in sport, even after major setbacks.

Chapter Purpose and Author Team

This chapter's intent is to survey theoretical models of motivation and to offer practical recommendations for increasing its positive impact on athletic performance. Dr. Brent Walker, the researcher, provides the empirical basis for the chapter as he weaves both theory and outcomes from specific studies into the recommendations. The consultant, Dr. Sandra Foster, draws on her experiences with athletes whose chosen sport demands both technical prowess and finely tuned mental skills (such as golf, figure skating, and martial arts) to illustrate the role of motivation in training persistently and competing successfully. The coach and athlete contributors, Scott Daubert, a manager of professional mountain bike teams, and DeDee Nathan, a former Olympic heptathlete, share their stories and insights throughout, giving voice to how motivation exerts its impact in real time.

Sport-Specific Definition of Motivation

A fundamental definition of motivation usually refers to the *drive* to engage in an activity. The term *will* is often used interchangeably with *drive* to indicate a mental predisposition to initiate and persist in an endeavor. Other definitions of motivation address the amount of effort exerted and the direction of that effort, that is, whether the person is motivated to pursue desired end results or to avoid painful outcomes.

Motivation also has been defined as the ability to act. However, this reference to ability brings into play concepts such as self-efficacy beliefs, talent, capacities, physical states, and momentary needs—aspects of motivation that will be considered in other chapters. For the sake of clarity, the following sport-specific definition is used throughout the chapter: Motivation is the inclination to pursue and persist in activities related to one's sport.

Impact of Motivation on Athletic Performance

Researchers Ryan and Deci (2000) put their considerable understanding of motivation very succinctly: "Motivation concerns energy, direction, persistence, and equifinality—all aspects of activation and intention. Motivation . . . is at the core of biological, cognitive, and social regulation. Perhaps more important, in the real world, motivation is highly valued because of its consequences: Motivation produces" (p. 69). These last two words help explain why coaches, athletic directors, parents, and even alumni want athletes to be motivated: because this condition leads to much-desired outcomes. Motivation moves an athlete to engage in needed preparation, even when practices are difficult, grueling, and long. Highly motivated athletes will stay focused and defer their involvement in other activities to postseason time off or even until retirement from sport. The degree of an athlete's motivation is reflected in his lifestyle choices—whether he is committed to practicing good eating and sleep habits and refrains from the use of street drugs and alcohol for the sake of attaining the physical conditioning conducive to high performance.

Motivation As a Component Under an Athlete's Control

What perhaps makes motivation so important in the minds of sport psychology consultants is that it can be understood as the factor over which athletes appear to have the most control. An individual, or even a team, can shift motivation, sometimes quickly. We can see evidence of this in wildly different second-half performances, suggesting that the coach or the team captains got the motivation going during halftime. Most football fans can recall a breathtaking "Hail Mary," the ultimate display of a last-minute burst of motivation. Other factors affecting competition performance, such as an athlete's physical attributes or talent or the difficulty of a task, are far less rapidly changed.

Evidence of High Motivation

Motivated athletes exhibit abundant energy and enthusiasm. In a word, they are "on." The gaze of a motivated athlete is purposeful, her movements deliberate. Her posture and walk portray an air of confidence. Think of Venus or Serena Williams striding onto the court at the 2003 Australian Open. In precompetition activities such as warming up, motivated athletes convey their intention to display skill effectively and outplay the competition. Think of the Brazilian soccer team before the final round of the 2002 World Cup. There may be a seriousness or toughness in their interactions with competitors or even the fans that seems to declare, "I have a job to do and will not be distracted by anything."

Evidence of motivation is likewise apparent in comeback situations, when athletes demonstrate resilience and dedication as they return to a competition site to "get it right this time." Croatian skier Janica Kostelic is one example of such motivation. After clinching the 2003 overall World Cup title, she won a fifth World Cup slalom race in Sweden, where she had never before skied well despite several attempts. "It was really nice to finally get a good result here," she told the press afterward. "I gave it everything I had" ("Kostelic Beats Paerson," 2003).

Motivated athletes arrive on time for training sessions, ready to devote their energies to meeting the objectives set by the coach. Their equipment is in good shape. They have taken steps to resolve problems with interests or responsibilities that compete for their time and attention. Their motivation, measured as their overall commitment to their sport, is observable in the effort they expend to master new skills and to memorize important maneuvers and in the interest they show when given corrective feedback by coaches.

Evidence of Low Motivation

Defeat, dejection, and despair are signs of *amotivation* (Ryan and Deci, 2000) or what we would call low motivation. In contrast to motivated athletes, amotivated athletes appear to be uninvolved, disengaged from the action, and distracted. Their participation looks impaired or half-hearted. A slight setback in competitive circumstances and the amotivated athlete will stop whatever effort he had been exhibiting, quite the opposite reaction of the motivated athlete, who will strive even harder to get back in the game when facing a setback.

An amotivated athlete may be late to practice or may not make it at all. Behaviorally, an amotivated athlete may seem listless, slow to respond, and even confused by the coach's instructions. A progressive withdrawal may occur, or the athlete may even quit. Emotionally, an amotivated athlete may manifest flat affect and blunted reactions to others or may seem sad or hopeless.

Evidence of Other Problems With Motivation

Another problem with motivation can be seen in the manifestation known as *excessive motivation*. Although some researchers conclude that overtraining and burnout are conditions resulting from motivation in its extreme (cf. McKenzie, 1999), such conditions can be an understandable yet unhealthy response to the athlete's perception that he lacks the resources needed in the face of high demand. While appearing to be "too motivated," athletes who are overtraining may be responding to a number of forces, for example, coercive coaching, parental pressures, or an over-identification of self-as-athlete, in the absence of any other source of self-worth. One example of excessive motivation was discussed by Krane and her colleagues (Krane, Greenleaf, and Snow, 1997) in their qualitative case study of a young female gymnast who exhibited relentless overtraining. These researchers noted the coach's pressure on the gymnast to win and his impatience with her many injuries. The researchers also described her need for perfection and to outdo others.

In a later section of this chapter, practical recommendations are offered to illustrate ways in which consultants and coaches can help athletes with problems in motivation. Now, we turn to conceptual background and the research on motivation.

Sources of Motivation for Sport Participation

From its beginnings, the field of psychology has been intrigued by the subject of motivation. Influenced by philosophers of ancient Greece as well as 17th- and 18th-century European thinkers, the psychologists of the 20th century readily subscribed to the idea that human beings were motivated to seek pleasure and to avoid pain (Atkinson, 1957; McClelland, 1951; McClelland, Atkinson, Clark, and Lowell, 1953). Early on, theorists Thorndike

(1935) and later Mowrer (1960), in their research on conditioning in animal learning, were influenced by this idea of hedonism. Freud (1920/1950), while making the case for the reality principle controlling the ego, also suggested that the reality principle was still influenced by the drive to seek pleasure and avoid pain. Although sport psychologists agree that motivation is vital to sport success, reasons for individual motivation often vary from athlete to athlete. Each athlete develops a view of motivation, and researchers interested in this issue have built on these previous theories derived from general psychology.

This section examines several key sources of motivation: (1) motivation as a function of an athlete's self-worth; (2) motivational levels in response to what researchers call "motivational climate"; (3) motivation as a function of whether an athlete is "moved" by factors that are outside herself or is driven from within (extrinsic vs. intrinsic motivation); and (4) motivation as a function of social influences, such as the athlete's parents and role models. The research is examined from the point of view of its value to consultants, coaches, and athletes.

Coach's Perspective

I've been closely involved with two cyclists who drew motivation from "crushing" their fellow competitors. Each of them spoke of how they would make their challengers hurt during the competition. These announcements came at race venues or during preparation (sometimes several months in advance of the event). I sometimes felt threatened by the athlete's tone and intentions, although I was not competing against them. Both riders could deliver the punishment they promised, so I suspect that voicing their intent was part of their process.

■ ■ ■ ■ ■

Motivation As a Function of Self-Worth or Social Goals

More recently in psychology, theorists have attempted to explain motivation in terms of self-worth (Harter, 1978) and the human desire to behave competently and receive positive feedback from others in challenging situations—what Harter termed *competence motivation theory* (Harter, 1978, 1981).

Elaborating on the theory of motivation based on competence, Urdan and Maehr (1995) added the dimension of socially oriented goals to the original achievement motivation construct developed by Maehr and Nicholls (1980). Social goals were defined as "the perceived social purposes of success or failure" (Urdan and Maehr, 1995, p. 251) with success resulting in the approval of important others and being admired by one's group.

Motivation As Influenced by Goal Orientations and the Motivational Climate

Similar to the theories of Thorndike and Mowrer, Nicholls' (1984, 1989) achievement goal theory reflects what is known as an *approach–avoidance orientation,* which similarly proposes that people are motivated by the desire to seek success by demonstrating skill and to avoid failure resulting from exhibiting low-ability behavior. Nicholls further posited that there were two distinct goal orientations to which individuals are predisposed, acquired from the socialization they experienced at home, in school, and in physical activity contexts (Ames, 1992; Duda, 1992, 1993; Nicholls, 1984, 1989; Roberts, 1984, 1992, 2001).

These two orientations are known as an *ego orientation,* in which being better than others is important (social comparison), where competence is defined by using external standards or norm-based comparisons; and a *task orientation,* wherein the individual is self-referenced in that he compares his current progress with his own past achievements. He thus is motivated by the desire to master tasks and expand his performance repertoire. Furthermore, whether an individual adopts an ego or a task goal in a given situation depends on his dispositional orientation as well as the motivational climate of the situation (Ames, 1992).

Motivational climate refers to the behavior and attitudes exhibited by important others in a particular situation. Motivational climate affects an individual's motivation and *goal of action* by influencing her interpretations of what types of behaviors are necessary to succeed in that situation (Roberts, Treasure, and Kavussanu, 1997). If the situation is characterized by fierce competition, social comparison of one's results with those of others, and coaches who emphasize winning, then a *performance motivational climate* focused on achievement is said to exist, and individuals are likely to be *ego involved.*

If, instead, the situation is one in which learning is valued for its own sake, the improvement or mastery of skills is emphasized, and coaches exhort athletes to do their best, then a *mastery*

motivational climate (Ames, 1992; Nicholls, 1989) is said to be operating, and individuals are likely to become *task involved.* Hence, success, failure, and achievement are recognized in terms of the individual's goal of action (Nicholls, 1984, 1989).

The definition of success is highly personal. What one athlete defines as success in a sport may not be considered success for another participant in the same sport (Roberts et al., 1997). Research has supported this conclusion by examining the beliefs that individuals develop in achievement situations. For example, Duda (1989) found that ego-oriented individuals linked their sport performance with their evaluation of themselves and with their perceived social status. That is, they were motivated by the desire to outdo others and to be "on top." In contrast, task-oriented athletes perceived links between their sport participation and performance and their level of effort and cooperation. What motivated them was a desire for self-improvement and to be part of a community.

So, an important question arises for coaches and consultants who want to enhance the motivation of sport participants. What type of motivational climate should be emphasized?

This key question has led to a heated debate among researchers (Duda, 1997, 2001; Hardy 1997, 1998; Harwood, Hardy, and Swain, 2000). Several have emphasized the importance of a mastery climate in the development of motivation (Duda, 1997; 2001; Roberts, 2001; Roberts et al., 1997). Others (Hardy 1997, 1998; Harwood et al., 2000) have argued that solely promoting a mastery climate does not correspond to the true dynamics of sport. What coaches and consultants might glean from this controversy is that aspects of both arguments have merit and that considering the developmental level of an athlete or team is crucial.

For example, when an athlete is attempting to learn new skills or hone existing ones, then a mastery climate that promotes task involvement sets the stage for engendering motivation that can help sustain persistence and promote adaptive achievement patterns. This has been especially true with children, as the research has consistently shown (for reviews, see Biddle, 2001; Duda, 1992, 1993; Roberts, 2001; Roberts et al., 1997; Treasure, 2001).

In contrast, at the highest developmental levels of sport where winning is paramount, an athlete's ego involvement is important and, very likely, necessary. Observations of many successful athletes, highlighting their ego-involved behavior, perhaps to an extreme, provide anecdotal support for this assumption. However, several lines of research point to a conclusion that athletes benefit from an ego orientation only if it is accompanied by a task orientation. In fact, research suggests that elite athletes are high in both ego and task orientations (Duda and Whitehead, 1998).

In one example of this research, Steinberg (1996) found that novice golf participants asked to adopt both ego and task involvement goals exhibited higher levels of enjoyment, persistence, and skillful performance in a putting task than those instructed to adopt either a task- or an ego-based goal alone. In another study, Roberts, Treasure, and Kavussanu (1996) found that high-ego- and high-task-oriented individuals showed the same achievement behaviors as the high-task- and low-ego-involved individuals.

This research holds two critical applications for coaches and consultants. First, coaches and consultants should identify how an athlete defines success and his goal of action in a competitive situation. By doing so, coaches gather information about the motivation of their players by pinpointing the "why" of behavior. Coaches can then use this information to cater their approach to the motivational needs of a player. To understand how athletes define success, a coach or consultant can use the questions included in the interview section of this chapter, and to gather information about an athlete's goal of action, coaches and clinicians can use the Perception of Success Questionnaire (Roberts, Treasure, and Balague, 1998). Second, to enhance motivation, coaches and consultants would be well served by creating an environment with both mastery and performance aspects. What coaches and consultants can take away from this research is that promoting an environment with both mastery and task-oriented (performance) aspects may provide the best context for enhancing motivation. Because a mastery climate encourages the demonstration of maximum effort during skill acquisition in training periods, an athlete who adopts a task focus is likely to succeed. In the heat of competition, the one who is focused on mastering the situation while giving it her best effort (demonstrating a combination of ego and task involvement) will most likely prevail, no matter how success is defined in the situation.

Coach's Perspective

In an off year I witnessed a professional cyclist have more "off" days than "on" and therefore struggle with critical comments from the media and his peers. The following year this same rider came to preseason camp charged with new perspectives. He had spent countless quality hours training, he had learned to cook and eat the right foods to complement his training, and he had listened to his body when it needed rest. He went on to quiet his critics and earn his peers' respect with repeated wins and remarkable performances.

■   ■   ■   ■   ■

Intrinsic and Extrinsic Motivation

Many coaches and athletes have heard the terms *extrinsic* and *intrinsic*. Most consultants will recognize the important theoretical contribution of Deci and Ryan (Deci, 1975; Deci and Ryan, 1985, 1991), who explained how people could be extrinsically motivated, intrinsically motivated, or even amotivated, as illustrated later in the chapter by the case of Mike. Their work continues to prompt research interest and also the effort to devise applications for sport performance enhancement. The next few paragraphs describe briefly each type of motivation.

Extrinsic Motivation

Extrinsic motivation refers to many different behaviors that a person exhibits as a means to an end. Three levels of extrinsic motivation have been proposed (Ryan, Connell, and Grolnick, 1990), and have been ordered along a "self-regulation" continuum. The first level, known as external regulation, typifies extrinsic motivation as most people construe it: as action directly influenced by outcomes imposed by external others, either rewards such as approval or punishments like fines and criticism.

Introjection is the second level of extrinsic motivation and describes when the external source of the motivation has been "introjected" or internalized. As a result of this internalization by the person, his anxiety and fear of embarrassment now regulate his behavior, which previously had been directly influenced by others. One example is the athlete who fears her harsh and demanding coach but soon comes to behave as if the coach's demeaning remarks are true and is now motivated by the need to prevent further shaming and teasing.

The third level, called identification, describes extrinsic motivation in which the person has concluded that a certain behavior is valuable and therefore performs it as if this action were internally regulated. This level of extrinsic motivation is exemplified by athletes who declare that their involvement in sport is an important aspect of their identity. Thus, they appear to be acting under their own volition.

Amotivation

This type of motivation, noted earlier, describes a state experienced by people who feel powerless to produce any desired result with their behavior. They feel no sense of control and that it is impossible to make things happen. They can no longer find a good reason to continue to do something and will soon abandon their attempts. An amotivated athlete has decided that his efforts are futile in his quest to become more skillful. He may well quit midseason or give up his sport altogether.

Intrinsic Motivation

Intrinsic motivation is at work when a person performs an action for the pure enjoyment of it, without a primary urge to obtain external rewards and without being excessively burdened by the fear of failure. Intrinsic motivation is operating when an athlete explains his reason for participating in sport as for the fun of it, because it just feels good, or both. Intrinsic motivation has understandably generated a great deal of interest within sport psychology consulting as consultants consider the value in helping athletes develop this type of motivation.

Athlete's Perspective

I have always had an innate drive to achieve goals. I began competing in sports more than 20 years ago, when I decided it was much more enjoyable to play an organized sport after school than go home. It did not take long to discover that I had a talent in athletics. I competed for the fun of it. Competing in sports gave me a sense of accomplishment and completion. I started off competing in team sports and quickly discovered that I did not like losing as a team. I wanted to have more control over whether I won or lost. Track and field was the perfect sport for me. Although I was a part of a team, unless I was on a relay I was responsible for my own performance and could only blame myself if I did not compete well. This mentality has continued throughout my entire career.

■ ■ ■ ■ ■

Deci (1975) and earlier theorists such as White (1959) proposed that there were subcategories of intrinsic motivation just as levels of extrinsic motivation had been designated. Consultants may be most familiar with one of the three types, called *intrinsic motivation toward accomplishments,* also known as mastery motivation or, as noted earlier, task orientation. An example of this subcategory of intrinsic motivation may be observed in an athlete who pursues a sport to experience the feeling of competence and to achieve results that demonstrate to others his mastery of sport-specific skills.

A second subcategory is termed *intrinsic motivation to experience stimulation.* Flow states (Csikszentmihalyi, 1996, 2000), peak experiences, and excitement are the end results sought by the person who is activated by this type of intrinsic motivation. So-called extreme athletes and their "adrenaline rush" feats may be understood in terms of this type of intrinsic motivation.

A third subcategory is called the *intrinsic motivation to know* and describes behavior that is prompted by curiosity, desire for novelty, or the need to understand and make meaning of an experience. Athletes who are fascinated by new techniques and may themselves create innovations are prompted by this subtype of intrinsic motivation. Figure skaters like Axel Paulsen, who created a new jump, or Sasha Cohen, who pushed the envelope to be the first woman to land a quad, may have been influenced by this type of intrinsic motivation.

Self-Determination Theory

In their more recent writings, Ryan and Deci (2000) presented their earlier research in the context of positive psychology under the term *self-determination theory*. They proposed the existence of three innate human needs—to be in relationship with others, to experience competence, and to function with autonomy. These authors argued persuasively for creating conditions that meet these needs and, therefore, help people to function at their best. "Inspired, striving to learn, extend themselves, master new skills, and applying their talents responsibly" (p. 68). They cited numerous studies showing the positive effects of autonomy-supportive teaching (Deci, Nezlek, and Sheinman, 1981; Ryan and Grolnick, 1986) and parenting (Grolnick, Deci, and Ryan, 1997).

The implications for coaches and the consultants who work alongside them are clear. There is value in creating a motivational climate that engenders these elements of intrinsic motivation: freely participating without coercion, an atmosphere where learning and skill mastery are emphasized, and an atmosphere where there is satisfying stimulation in the pursuit of the sport. Athletes participating in such conditions, according to this research, are more likely to expend energy purposefully in their skill acquisition, to persist when training becomes very demanding, to strive during a challenging competition, and to remain resilient in the face of setbacks.

Coach's Perspective

A mountain bike rider I worked with displayed visible changes in motivation during competition. When she used others' comments or suggestions as inspiration, digging deep or rising to the occasion became difficult. If she returned to a self-inspired state of mind where she raced for her own satisfaction, she morphed into a different racer. In a four-lap World Cup race, I saw her jump from somewhere in the high teens to the top five in one 18-minute lap. Afterward she told me she stopped racing for others and started racing for herself. That change of mind pushed her to the front of the race.

■　■　■　■　■

Social Influences and Motivation to Participate in Sport

As Taylor, Baranowski, and Sallis (1994) suggested, parents influence their children's initial participation in sport and physical activity in general through three main mechanisms: role modeling, social influence, and social support processes. Role modeling has been the most frequently investigated aspect of parental influences on children's entrance into the sporting realm. However, the outcomes of this research are equivocal (Anderssen and Wold, 1992; Biddle and Goudas, 1996; Dempsey, Kimiecik, and Horn, 1993; Gottlieb and Chen, 1985; Welk, Wood, and Morss, 2003).

Studies have shown that parents play a more salient role through other social–cognitive processes such as demonstrating encouragement and support. For example, in two separate investigations, Brustad (1993, 1996) found that children's perceptions of competence and levels of desire (i.e., motivation) to participate in physical activity were related to their perceptions of their parents' encouragement of their participation. Similarly, Babkes and Weiss (1999) found that 9- to 11-year-old soccer players who believed that their parents looked on their soccer ability favorably and perceived more frequent positive contingent reinforce-

ment after success showed higher levels of soccer competence and intrinsic motivation than players who perceived lower levels of the same variables in their parents. These studies seem to suggest that a supportive climate offered by parents is likely to lead to greater motivation and continued sport participation by children. Coaches need to identify the young people who do not appear to get enough parental support (e.g., parents do not attend games or parents are overly critical of their child's performance), because these athletes may need extra attention to optimize motivation and their overall sport experience.

Effect of Models on Motivation

Although research has not clearly identified parents as a consistent role model for the initiation of sport behavior, observing others does have a significant impact on the motivational experiences of sport participants. From watching a coach demonstrate a maneuver to imitating one's favorite player, modeling permeates all levels of sport. As Bandura (1986) stated, "Most human behavior is learned by observation through modeling" (p. 47). From a motivational perspective, modeling is considered to be one of the most powerful means of transmitting values, attitudes, and patterns of behavior and thought.

According to Bandura, four processes are essential for successful modeling to occur—attention, retention, production, and motivation. An observer must attend to the appropriate information being modeled, retain the information gathered from the model, be capable of producing the desired movement, and be motivated to carry out the behavior. If any one of these processes is missing, the model's impact will be diminished.

Importance of Model Similarity

Possibly the most important consideration in designing interventions to increase motivation and enhance sport performance is model–observer similarity. As Bandura (1986) asserted, certain model characteristics (e.g., age, gender, race, skill level) influence the impact of the modeling on the observer–learner. It is easier for individuals to believe they can accomplish skills or change behaviors if they see someone similar to them doing these things before making the attempt themselves (Bandura, 1997). Moreover, models who are similar to observers or learners are likely to elicit the observers' undivided attention and increase the learners' motivation by increasing their *self-efficacy*, meaning the "judgments of their capabilities to organize and execute courses of action required to attain designated types of performances" (Bandura, 1986, p. 391).

Peer Modeling in Mastery and Coping Contexts

Although it may be intuitive to coaches to choose a model who can most accurately perform a skill, some research has suggested that choosing model similarity over performance ability (thereby choosing peer models rather than adult models) may increase motivation and, thus, skill acquisition or behavior change. Research in educational psychology has shown that observing peer models leads to higher levels of cognitive skill learning, self-confidence, and motivation (see Schunk, 1987, for a review). Research has further suggested that model similarity be considered not only with respect to physical characteristics but also with respect to psychological considerations such as an observer's confidence or emotional state.

It can thus be argued that it is beneficial for more skilled athletes with high levels of confidence to observe a model demonstrating nearly flawless performance without a lot of "fuss." Thus, a mastery model who demonstrates errorless performance and verbalizes a confident, positive attitude that she possesses high ability and that the task is of low difficulty for her would be appropriate. In contrast, a less experienced athlete or one who may be experiencing fear or doubt may benefit from a coping model who expresses the cognitions, behaviors, and emotions that are consistent with a task perceived as difficult or fear inducing (Schunk, 1987, 1988). Evidence for this latter assertion was demonstrated by Weiss, McCullagh, Smith, and Berlant (1998), who found that a coping model led to higher self-efficacy judgments than a mastery model or a control group for young fearful children learning to swim. Neither the mastery nor coping models produced differences in swimming performance compared with one another, but both led to swimming improvements compared with a control group. Coaches and consultants should become aware of the conditions that may arise when teaching occurs. Are the emotional and psychological characteristics of the learners being taken into account? For example, a coach who is a highly successful former athlete, for whom skills come easily, is advised to have coping models available for learners just tackling a new and challenging skill. These models can assist an athlete in discovering that she can overcome fears and difficulties and learn the technique. An athlete low in confidence may benefit from observing a peer encounter and successfully overcome similar psychological challenges to reach a goal.

Self-Modeling and Feedforward

Capitalizing on modeling similarity as an important component of motivation, Dowrick (1983, 1991, 1999) developed the concept of *self-modeling*. Unlike the traditional method in which coaches use video as a critiquing tool, self-modeling offers an edited video in which a person views only his successful behaviors. Self-modeling is designed to enhance the self-efficacy of an individual as it "provides clear information on how best to perform skills, and it strengthens beliefs in one's capability" (Bandura, 1997, p. 94).

Because past behavior is the strongest predictor of current self-efficacy judgments, by observing oneself executing successful moves, a learner pays greater attention and is provided with the information to continue progressing. Although limited in number, the sport studies that have examined the effect of self-modeling on psychosocial variables such as self-efficacy and performance have yielded encouraging results. For example, Halliwell (1990) found improvements in performance and confidence of professional hockey players coming back from injury or after experiencing slumps when he developed music videos showing only the successful highlights of their games. Likewise, Singleton and Feltz (1999) examined the effect of self-modeling on collegiate hockey players' performance and found that the players exposed to self-modeling experienced greater shooting accuracy and self-efficacy for shooting performance compared with controls.

Finally, in a study of novice adult swimmers, Starek and McCullagh (1999) found that the self-efficacy and performance of adult novice swimmers improved from baseline measures following a self-modeling intervention. Interestingly, though, a peer modeling group did not differ from the self-modeling group in terms of increases in self-efficacy, but the self-modeling group increased swimming performance to a significantly greater degree than the peer modeling group.

A specific mode of self-modeling known as *feedforward* also has the potential to positively influence motivation and performance. Feedforward modeling provides the athlete with information about possible future behavior rather than his past or current behavior. Feedforward is similar to self-modeling in that an athlete views himself performing successfully, but it differs in that the performance shown is a behavior or skill that the athlete has yet to accomplish. Two studies have examined the use of feedforward and found positive results. In the first, Dowrick and Dove (1980) worked with three children (ages 5-10) with spina bifida. The authors created edited videotapes of the children showing them engaged in swimming maneuvers without any assistance—by editing out the therapist providing support. Thus, the children were viewing themselves completing swimming strokes that they were not yet capable of achieving independently. After this feedforward intervention, the children made significant improvements in their swimming skill.

A second study by Maille (cited in Franks and Maille, 1991) further illustrated the exciting benefits and possibilities associated with feedforward modeling. Working with a nationally ranked female powerlifter, Maille created a video of a series of training lifts with the scenes manipulated so that the lifter was lifting more weight than she had currently accomplished. Using this technique, the athlete realized an improvement of 26% over a 25-week intervention. (Experts considered a 10% gain typical during that time period.) It appears that through this technique, the observer's perceptions are transformed so that what was previously viewed as beyond one's capabilities soon becomes part of one's repertoire.

Coaches and consultants may well consider the value of this application for athletes with whom they are working. Sport is replete with stories of records once thought to be unbeatable. Perhaps this creative technique of feedforward can yield even more "unachievable" feats like Roger Bannister running the first sub-4-minute mile or Mark McGwire and then Barry Bonds exceeding Roger Maris' single-season home run record.

Impact of Modeling on Ongoing Motivation

In situations where motivation is ebbing, a coach can call on the "'war stories" of others who have mastered the particular sport to help an individual or team reaffirm their commitment and reactivate themselves for the next few minutes of competition. Of course, these stories can also focus on role models whose acting out or doping cost them dearly. Think of boxer Mike Tyson, basketball star Latrell Spreewell, Canadian sprinter Ben Johnson, and others who attained world-class status but fell from grace. As part of a discussion of lifestyle choices, consultants and coaches can point to a famous athlete's behavior that cost him a loss of money through fines and loss of valuable endorsements, the elimination of his eligibility, a ruined reputation, or the relinquishing of an Olympic gold medal.

In such a discussion, athletes should adequately understand the meaning of the celebrity's downfall. Otherwise, they may conclude that the short-term gains were justified by the illegal or inappropriate behavior—whether gambling, taking steroids for performance improvement, or striking or verbally abusing a referee or coach. Consultants and coaches can help make the impact of modeling exceedingly positive by reminding the athlete of those who have come back successfully from defeat, who have recovered from a sport-related injury and returned to competition, or who have demonstrated responsible behavior by agreeing to drug rehabilitation or sanctions following an incident.

Athlete's Perspective

Over the years, I have often been asked who my role models were. As a young athlete, I did not idolize anyone. As I matured athletically, I realized that there was a lot more to competing in sports than mere athletic ability. I became inspired by anyone who worked hard and pursued excellence in his or her discipline. I respected any athlete who competed with integrity. My college coach often placed me in difficult competitive situations with Olympians and world-class athletes. He understood the dynamics of creating a champion. Competing in sporting events can be more of a mental battle than physical challenge. My college coach understood that for me to reach my greatest athletic potential I had to believe that I could successfully compete with anyone in the world on any given day.

■　■　■　■　■

Identifying and Strengthening Optimal Motivation Levels

Athletes define success in multiple ways, and coaches should take these definitions into account when attempting to help athletes increase their level of motivation. Moreover, the kind of motivation influencing an athlete or team may shift during a season or as one effect of growing older, maturing as an athlete, becoming more skilled, or winning and losing competitions. Although intrinsic motivation appears to be the most important kind for producing enduring effort and resilience, research has shown that elite athletes and, most likely, professional teams are influenced by a combination of extrinsic and intrinsic motivations. A key task for coaches and consultants is to accurately determine what motivates athletes so that consulting interventions can be on target.

Athlete's Perspective

My saga began in 1992 at the track-and-field Olympic trials in New Orleans. I went there to compete to the best of my ability. If I made the team, I made the team. I missed the team by 1.5 seconds and a personal best score of more than 6,200 points. I was neither crushed nor destroyed. I just wanted to compete well. I understood that I was a neophyte heptathlete with only four competitions under my belt. I showed great potential in the event and was excited about my competitive future.

As I prepared for the 1996 track-and-field Olympic trials, my motivation changed. At that point in my career, I had competed on every major track-and-field team possible. The Olympics was the last dance. I had several coaches, family members, and friends supporting my every step. I wanted to succeed not only for myself but also for those who had invested their time and energy in my athletic career. I was in the best shape of my life and training had gone perfectly. As far as I was concerned, I was already on the team and I just had to go through the motions of competing. I competed in the 2-day competition and on the second day I, once again, missed the team by 1.5 seconds. This time I was devastated. I had not achieved my personal goal, and I had let down all the people who had invested in my career. This was unacceptable. I had some decisions to make before I decided to devote another 4 years of my life to training and competing.

I took some time off, sorted it all out, and began preparing for the 2000 track-and-field Olympic trials in Sacramento, California. This time it was more of a struggle for me to train. There was not a lot of money to be made competing in the heptathlon. I was not getting any younger, and pride was definitely not enough to keep me motivated. In 1991, I had become a born-again Christian. As I began to understand that God had purpose for my life, I began to realize that part of my purpose was connected to my track-and-field career. In order for me to continue to train with the same tenacity and discipline as before, I had to gain an understanding of that purpose through prayer.

As I began to focus on my spirituality and being obedient to the Word of God, my career exploded. I set numerous personal records in my event between the ages of 28 and 30. I set an American indoor record at 31 years of age. It kept getting better and better. Finally, it was time to make the Olympic team again. There was no doubt in my mind that I was going to Sydney, Australia. My confidence and motivation did not come from my physical prowess and ability levels like my prior two experiences. My confidence and motivation came from trusting the Word of God. I made the team and competed in Sydney. It was the highlight of my career, and I am glad I invested the 8 years that it took for me to finally achieve my goal.

■　■　■　■　■

Assessing an Individual Athlete's Motivation

Open-ended interviewing methods and validated instruments are available to assist the practitioner in learning what motivates an individual athlete. Coaches and consultants may find useful the following approaches for identifying an individual's motivation.

Interviewing

Consultants can use the motivational interviewing method, which has been found helpful in identifying factors for relapse prevention in chemical dependency settings (Baker et al., 2002; Miller, Yahne, and Tonigan, 2003). This type of structured approach can be modified to suit the age, skill level, and ranking of an athlete. In a similar vein, the following questions may help the consultant comprehensively assess an athlete's type of and level of motivation:

- Go back to your first days of playing [name of sport]. What were the reasons you started? Who got you involved? What did they say to you about the sport and what it would be like for you to play?

- Who were your first role models? How did they affect your wanting to start and to continue playing [name of sport]?

- How has your family responded to your playing [name of sport]? What do they say to you that helps you to feel motivated? What do they do that can sometimes be demotivating or discouraging?

- What were your first experiences with coaches like? How did these first coaches motivate you? What did they say and do that made you want to try harder? Were there ever times when they said or did things that made you upset, angry, or want to quit?

- What were the reasons that you began to compete after being first involved recreationally?

- What motivated you to stay involved in [name of sport] and to keep training to reach your current level of skill?

- What motivates you now to play [name of sport] well? What motivates you and keeps you going when you feel discouraged, have a tough training session and feel frustrated, or get bored when learning a routine? How do you get back in the game after a disappointing loss?

- How do you respond when people around you compare you with others in an unfavorable way or say you should give up playing [name of sport]?

- When things became difficult during your training and maybe even others around you quit, what helped you to continue playing [name of sport]?

- If you have experienced a serious injury, what motivated you to go to your rehabilitation sessions and to follow the instructions of your sports medicine physician, physiotherapist, sport psychologist, or other professional involved in your well-being and recovery? Did any people in particular help you get back to playing?

- What helps you persist when you are learning or polishing a new skill and you get tired or think that you won't be able to master it?

- What words do you say to yourself to get yourself started at the beginning of a training or conditioning session, before a competition, or during a competition at crucial points?

- What imagery or other techniques do you use to motivate yourself?

Using Validated Instruments

Influenced by Deci and Ryan's work on motivation, researchers developed an instrument in the French language for assessing motivation in sport, Echelle de Motivation vis-à-vis les Sports (Briere, Vallerand, Blais, and Pelletier, 1996). Two studies validated a translation of the measure into English (Pelletier et al., 1995). Consultants may find this instrument, known as the Sport Motivation Scale, a useful tool for evaluating an individual athlete's inclination to engage in his or her sport in all the dimensions and subtypes proposed by Deci and Ryan. There are 28 items that measure motivation on seven subscales representing three types of extrinsic motivation, three subcategories of intrinsic motivation, and amotivation.

A newer instrument may also be useful to consultants, the Situational Motivational Scale (Standage, Treasure, Duda, and Prusak, 2003). (This and the previous instrument have not yet been published; for more information, contact the authors.)

Assessing Team Motivation

Although a majority of research and theoretical perspectives have approached the study of motivation from an individual perspective, recent research has begun to examine motivation from a team perspective. This approach has been carried out almost exclusively under an efficacy framework, specifically identified as *collective efficacy*. A team's motivation or collective efficacy involves the identification of a group's shared beliefs in their ability to meet situation-specific demands.

In a sport like gymnastics with little interdependence among team members, aggregating individual efficacy judgments may be sufficient for predicting the group's performance. However, for a highly interactive sport like basketball, a group assessment of motivation may be more appropriate, one that examines the group's belief in the team as a whole rather than as a collection of individuals.

How individuals view the capabilities of the group as a whole is more important than how they view their individual capabilities. Research by Feltz and Lirgg (1998) supported this notion, because they found collective efficacy to be a more accurate predictor of intercollegiate team hockey performance than individual self-efficacy beliefs over a season.

Finding the Ideal Level of Motivation

Using the strategy of recall of optimal states of functioning advocated by Hanin (2000), a practitioner might ask an individual athlete or a team to think back to a time during training or competition when the level of motivation seemed ideal. The conditions to recreate this level of motivation could then be identified. Instructions should be modified to suit the age and maturation of the athletes being assessed, of course. The following format is suggested as a guide:

> After taking a few minutes to relax your mind and body, begin to think back to a time when you were feeling really motivated about [your sport]. Let this be a time during your training when you felt totally committed to mastering your skills (polishing your routine, completing practice successfully with your teammates so you were all completely ready for the upcoming competition). Now notice what comes to mind—the words you were saying to yourself, if any; the images that come up for you, if any. Notice the physical sensations and emotions that you are experiencing now as you think about this time when your motivation to train was ideal.

A second version can ask the athlete to think back to times "when you felt unbeatable (ready to go out and have the performance of your life, ready to set a new personal best record)."

Athlete's Perspective

I have been running for more than 20 years, during which time I experienced numerous highs and lows. As I review my career, I cannot pinpoint any one technique that consistently worked for maintaining motivation. Each year of training brought different challenges. My ability to maintain motivation was directly related to my ability to adjust to various types of changes. For instance, as I prepared for the 2000 Olympic Games, one of my coaches was diagnosed with leukemia and needed to be hospitalized the month before I left. This coach had already purchased his ticket and made plans to support me in Sydney. Although it was a very difficult time, my motivation levels did not decline. I actually became more determined to represent my friends, family, and country well at the games because of my coach and his illness.

■ ■ ■ ■ ■

Reaching and Sustaining Ideal Motivation

Consultants, coaches, and athletes must understand the importance of motivation as it relates to all aspects of performance and become aware that motivation is likely to be the factor over which the athlete has more personal control than any other. Consultants can then assist athletes in recognizing their ideal motivational state for training and competition and finding techniques for shifting from demotivating beliefs, self-talk, and behaviors to those that activate the athlete and direct her efforts to reaching her goals. Consultants can also advise coaches about the motivational climate that is helpful to athletes during training at different points during a season and before and during competition.

Coach's Perspective

As a mountain bike team manager, I was neither the riders' coach nor their agent. I had little influence on a rider's motivation throughout his training and little to do with money he earned. However, I discovered early on that by listening to an athlete's game plan, how he felt, specific goals he had, past experiences, and even events unrelated to sport, together we learned new motivational techniques. In time our casual interviews grew to be beneficial to both the rider and me as we reached new heights by way of brainstorming or varying our viewpoints or even by my playing a friendly devil's advocate.

■ ■ ■ ■ ■

Creating the Climate for Ideal Motivation

It has been argued that in some sports, a coaching culture of toughness and survival of the fittest (e.g., quickly weeding out nonperformers) is imperative to create winning teams and successful individual contributors, particularly in contact sports like American football. Some insiders have criticized this coaching culture (Green, 1997), and outside observers have decried conditions of coercive coaching in sports such as figure skating and gymnastics (e.g., Brennan, 1999; Ryan, 1995).

Space limitations do not permit a full debate of the role of negative motivation in performance enhancement. However, sport psychology researchers such as Krane and her colleagues (Krane et al., 1997) have illuminated the physical and emotional cost to athletes and their loved ones of excessive reliance on extrinsic motivation, particularly punishments such as humiliating social comparisons, other forms of verbal abuse, and physically harmful practices such as coercing an athlete to train or compete when injured. Turman (2003) surveyed coaching techniques and found that certain behaviors were motivating, whereas other tactics like ridiculing an athlete were demotivating.

Stated another way, the overreliance on extrinsic motivation can result in these outcomes for athletes: (1) Athletes essentially give control over to others; (2) their self-worth is adversely affected when they lose because athletic prowess has become the primary source of self-esteem; (3) they can get caught up in overtraining in an effort to gain the approval of hard-driving coaches or parents, and burnout or injury can follow; and (4) emotional mastery is less likely to occur because of the high probability of experiencing frustration and self-blame.

In contrast, there is a place for integrating what researchers Ryan and Deci (2000) proposed—the value of engendering intrinsic motivation by creating environments that support basic human needs for competence, autonomy, and relatedness. Consultants, in their work with coaches, can make the case for building relationships with athletes based on fostering mutual respect, supporting athletes' autonomy while making clear the natural consequences of poor choices, and facilitating competent performance through positive modeling, the use of self-referenced goals (see chapter 7), and corrective feedback that is constructive and focused on fixing the error and not just "'slamming" the person.

Coach's Perspective

During one-on-one talks with riders I worked closely with, I made a point of asking whether they were happy with how things were going. We could have been discussing training or racing, but I always asked how they felt without leading or judging. I encouraged them to ask themselves how they felt about their efforts. When they expressed emotions or situations that were negative, I tried to help them understand why they felt that way and what they could do to make a change. When they displayed positive vibes, I encouraged them to build on their satisfaction by reliving the moment or feeling. I believe that their willingness to discuss helped them learn what to avoid and what to develop on their way to reaching their potential.

■ ■ ■ ■ ■

Noticing First What Is Working

The emerging area of positive psychology is affecting the way that motivating people is practiced in business (Harter, Schmid, and Hayes, 2002; Shatte, Reivich, and Seligman, 2000), in youth development (Larson, 2000), and in many aspects of psychology as a discipline (Diener, 2000; Valliant, 2000). Of relevance to sport are the findings of the "appreciative inquiry" research (Cooperrider, 1995). Appreciative inquiry is a perspective proposing that people in business or other endeavors will be more motivated to correct their mistakes and address problems in general if they focus first on what is working, essentially, what they are doing right.

The impact of this approach has been remarkable (Watkins and Mohr, 2001). Consultants could explore whether coaches would be willing to give positive feedback first if they understood it is more than just a "nice thing to do." Rather, this order of providing information reduces defensiveness and allows athletes to more readily comprehend and act on corrective feedback.

Research in sport supports coaches' use of noticing what is working and providing instruction that supports and encourages athletes while giving the technical information they need to successfully execute the skill (Smith and Smoll, 1990). These researchers developed a 3-hour coach training program based on their preliminary findings with Little League coaches and participants. Despite the brevity of this training, boys coached by those who received instruction reported more enjoyment and showed less performance anxiety and greater self-esteem than did boys whose coaches had not been trained. Moreover, intrinsic motivation appeared to have been generated by the coaches' emphasis on fun and self-referenced progress.

Increasing Motivation With Positive Emotions

Again drawing from the emerging area of positive psychology, growing research evidence demonstrates the value of positive words in business, an approach that is applicable to engendering motivation in sport (see chapter 5). A leader's positive mood was found not only to improve morale in the workplace but actually to affect the bottom line (Goleman, Boyatzis, and McKee, 2002). Frederickson (2000, 2001) found that positive emotions in work settings reduced conflict and increased employee effectiveness. She explained her *broaden-and-build* model in this way: "Positive emotions have a complementary effect. They broaden people's momentary thought-action repertoires, widening the array of thoughts and actions that come to mind" (Frederickson, 2000, p. 133).

Sport psychology research has indicated the value of teaching athletes to interrupt negative self-statements, using so-called thought stoppage (Meyers and Schleser, 1980). Although this is a useful tactic, consultants may wish to go one step further, applying research findings that show the benefit of positive words on performance enhancement. For example, a consultant might assist an athlete in identifying the word or phrase that not only halts a negative thought sequence but also redirects the athlete to more focused and performance-enhancing thoughts. Repeatedly using the word "Stop!" followed by "Switch!" could help an athlete shift focus to positively motivating self-statements that guide his efforts more effectively toward the goal.

The chapter consultant has found in her work (Foster and Prussack, 1999) that the question, "Is this negative thought useful right now?" can redirect the athlete away from the chain of negative ruminations, including self-criticism for thinking so negatively in the first place. "What would be more helpful instead?" is the refocusing question, prompting the athlete to shift to a specified set of key words that activate effort toward the accurate execution of a skill. She also found useful having an athlete script specific positive words to say aloud when emotions surfaced that could derail his skillful performance.

Consultants may also want to teach specific elements of optimistic explanatory style (Abramson, Seligman, and Teasdale, 1978) that can help an athlete remain motivated and better able to recover after a setback and to persist during arduous periods of training. The chapter consultant has found in her work with athletes and business people (Foster, 2002) that the elements of time, pervasiveness, and personalization are particularly useful in enhancing performance in competitive situations:

- My good qualities are enduring (Time) and affect many aspects of my life, including my sport (Pervasiveness).

- Bad things that happen, including tough training sessions, are temporary. I get another chance tomorrow at my next practice (Time).

- When I have a bad day, it does not mean I am having a terrible life or should give up my sport. The negativity is something I can corral. Then I can focus instead on what is going well in my life (Pervasiveness).

- When things are going wrong, I need to take responsibility for my part in fixing the problem and also consider the role of others and external conditions in what happened (Personalization).

- I can correct this mistake. I get another chance in my next practice (Pervasiveness and Personalization).

- I have control over my thoughts. I can switch lousy thoughts to my key words and get back on track (Personalization).

Intervening in Situations of Low Motivation

Consider this scenario describing an athlete showing low motivation:

Mike has been the very last to arrive in 6 out of 10 practices and even missed a key practice before the homecoming game. He began a promising season at his high school full of good-natured jokes and encouragement for his teammates. After four straight losses, he now looks listless and passive on the field and has trouble executing even simple plays. The head coach is so furious with his promising young quarterback that he can't talk to him without ranting. Mike seems alternately defensive and dazed, and it's gotten so bad that the assistant coach has stepped in, trying to get his player back on track. Lectures from the well-meaning principal who doubles as athletic director haven't helped.

What could the coaches and a consultant do to assist Mike in regaining his flagging motivation? First, the consultant could talk with Mike to find out his explanation of events and their causes, his history as quarterback, and any current life situations that could be interfering with his focus. Next, the consultant could help Mike identify what has motivated him in the past, compare his response with what the consultant learns is the motivational style of the head coach, and share this with the coach. The consultant could then guide Mike in recalling his ideal level of motivation, past memories of successful competitions, and positive words that Mike could use to cue effective action when he begins to feel himself sinking. Regarding the team's motivation, the consultant could ask the head coach to recall his most outstanding motivational speeches that appealed to their sense of mastery, personal satisfaction, and community pride. The consultant and coach could also discuss the best ways to involve the assistant coach and principal in generating a winning attitude. Incentives for great practices could be devised, perhaps points accrued collectively that could be traded for a steak dinner sponsored by the alums at the end of the season.

The coach could immediately contact Mike's hero, the former quarterback of the team, who plays for the state university nearby. This role model could be briefed by the coach and consultant and then spend time with Mike practicing passing and sharing comeback stories—his own—and those suggested by the consultant, based on information gleaned from the talks with Mike. After hearing from the consultant about the benefits of refraining from ridiculing his quarterback, the coach could show Mike videotapes of successful past games and point out what he did to execute his passes skillfully.

Consider this second example:

Kim's parents remember vividly all the recruitment calls and letters from the prestigious Ivy League schools and the state universities well known in fencing circles. Kim's outstanding performance in the prior year's tournaments hadn't surprised her club coach and definitely started a buzz about this previously unknown foil fencer. Soon, offers beckoned with respectable scholarship money included. Kim fretted about whether she could handle the change from her urban community college to a "fancy place" in a city hundreds of miles from home. At the urging of her parents and coach, she reluctantly transferred. Despite her talent, superb physical condition, and obvious skill, Kim's new coach found his rookie unable to cut it. Within 3 months of her arrival, he was contemplating how to justify sending her home.

For Kim, the consultant could first talk to the coach to assess the current motivational climate and learn what changes he must see in order for her to stay. If the coach's expectations seem unattainable, the consultant could explore what other results the coach would accept from Kim and within what time frame. The consultant could help Kim think through her motivational history to determine whether she has been relying exclusively on extrinsic reasons for transferring (her club coach's and her parents' urging), when before it was likely she was intrinsically motivated to compete.

The consultant could guide Kim in thinking back to times when she experienced an ideal level of motivation and also remember successful competition memories before she moved. Using the recalled material, Kim and the consultant could then discuss what she could do to rekindle her "drive from inside," which likely has elements of both ego and task orientation. Together, the consultant and coach could think about a person who could be a supportive and inspiring role model for Kim to persist in this situation, whether a member of Kim's new team or another athlete, preferably a fencer. They could also explore what steps she could take to help her feel at home in this environment and a part of her team. With concrete ideas in mind, Kim could then propose to her coach an action plan for becoming a fully functioning athlete.

Key Points

- Motivation is a critical variable in an athlete or a team's performance, influencing the amount of effort expended, the ability to remain resilient after setbacks, how long someone will persist during long and difficult periods of training, and actual competition results.

- Motivation may be the factor over which athletes have the most control.

- An athlete can exert more control over motivation by becoming aware of his or her level of motivation and learning strategies for influencing it.

- Two main types of motivation have been identified—extrinsic and intrinsic. Each may exert a salient influence, depending on the developmental level of the athlete or team. However, research also shows that there is an enduring effect of intrinsic motivation on sport performance.

- Recommendations for consultants and coaches for increasing motivation include these:

  For consultants—teach the value of noticing first what is working well for the athlete or team (recalling strengths and successes) before focusing on problems; help athletes find positive words to use when distressed to shift negative mood state.

  For coaches—build relationships with athletes based on mutual respect that support their autonomy while making clear the natural consequences of poor choices. Increase competent performance through positive modeling, the use of self-referenced goals, and corrective feedback that is constructive, instructive, and not just critical.

Review Questions

1. What various terms are used interchangeably with motivation and what is a good working definition of this important concept?

2. What are the signs of high and low motivation?

3. What are the sources of motivation?

4. What is the key difference between intrinsic and extrinsic motivation, and how does each have a role in the competition results of an athlete or a team?

5. What strategies can consultants and coaches use to help increase motivation for an individual athlete and for a team?

CHAPTER

2
Confidence

Luis G. Manzo, PhD—researcher
Gregory W. Mondin, PhD—consultant
Bobby Clark—coach
Terri Schneider, MA—athlete

The objectives of this chapter are

- to provide an in-depth understanding of confidence and define it in a way that is both scientifically rigorous and practically valuable;
- to examine the relationship between confidence and athlete performance;
- to look at ways confidence can be assessed;
- to consider a variety of strategies for helping athletes develop and maintain confidence; and
- to discuss the powerful role of an optimistic mind-set in building confidence.

onfidence may be the single most influential psychological contributor to success in sports. Athletes may have all the ability in the world to perform well and achieve their goals, but if they don't believe they have that ability, then they won't fully use that ability. For example, a gymnast may be physically and technically capable of executing a double-back somersault with a full twist, but he won't attempt the skill if doesn't have the confidence that he can successfully execute the skill.

Many athletes compete at a high level but are not considered among the best; for example, a basketball player who plays in a European professional league rather than the NBA or a tennis pro who is ranked 200 in the world. These athletes have exceptional physical and technical skills in most facets of their sport, not unlike their more successful peers. What separates these athletes from those who are considered to be the best in their sport if they seem to have similar skills at their disposal? It is often not their physical or technical capabilities but rather their belief in their ability to use those capabilities at a critical time in the most important competition of their lives. The best athletes have the confidence that they will perform their best and be successful when it really counts. The lower-ranked athletes don't have that confidence, so they won't, for example, go for the 3-point shot with the game on the line or try to hit an offensive lob at match point against them.

Key Issues

The goal for all athletes is to ensure that they have a resilient and lasting belief in their ability. This confidence enables them to fully use their ability in the most important competition of their lives, under the most difficult conditions, and against the toughest competitors they have ever faced. Despite its obvious importance, confidence is a fragile quality that takes considerable time to gain and can be lost in seconds. Understanding the role that confidence plays in sport competition is essential for all those involved with athletes—including the athletes themselves—to help them gain and maintain their confidence in the face of common athletic challenges.

Chapter Purpose and Author Team

The purpose of this chapter is to explore the relationship between confidence and sport performance. The complementary views of a sport psychology researcher (Dr. Luis Manzo), an applied consultant (Dr. Gregory Mondin), a coach (Bobby Clark), and an athlete (Terri Schneider) will be integrated to present a broad overview of the influence that confidence has on athletic performance. Particular emphasis will be placed on understanding the nature of confidence, how it affects athletes, and, most important, how athletes can develop confidence that will enable them to consistently perform at their highest level.

Coach's Perspective

The keys to confidence are preparation, being able to see one's experiences from various points of view (such as thinking like a realistic optimist), and having a source of encouragement and support.

■　■　■　■　■

Athlete's Perspective

In many ways confidence has laid the foundation for my athletic life and, almost more significantly, my life outside of sport. It's the essence of self that allows me to keep coming back for more, taking on more risk, increasing my threshold of adventure. It provided the groundwork for my evolution as an athlete.

■　■　■　■　■

Defining Confidence in Sport

Most sport psychology researchers, applied consultants, coaches, and athletes agree that confidence is an essential contributor to optimal sport performance. Research has identified confidence as a characteristic that clearly distinguishes between successful and unsuccessful athletes (Graham and Stabler, 1999; Jackson, 1996; Ravizza, 1977). For example, Mahoney and Avener (1977) found that U.S. Olympic qualifiers in men's gymnastics reported higher levels of self-confidence than nonqualifiers. In interviews with elite sport performers, Jones and Hardy (1990) found that more than 80% associated a high level of confidence with their athletic success. Evidence also suggests that teams with high collective confidence perform at a higher level than teams with low collective confidence (George and Feltz, 1995; Lirgg and Feltz, 1994).

The task of defining confidence is complicated by the use of terms such as *self-efficacy, self-confidence, sport confidence,* and *perceived competence* to represent confidence. Furthermore, there is often considerable overlap between these concepts, and the terms are commonly used interchangeably. A goal of this chapter is to provide a definition of confidence that offers researchers, consultants, coaches, and athletes a common foundation from which they can understand confidence in their own particular setting and in a way that meets their specific needs.

Bandura (1977) coined the term *self-efficacy* and defined it as an individual's belief that he or she has the necessary skills to produce a desired outcome. Self-efficacy is considered to be situation specific; that is, a person can have confidence in one area but not in another, even if they are closely related. Bandura further suggested that self-efficacy influences a person's choice of activities, the effort put forth in attempting to succeed at a task, and the persistence with which the individual will continue after failure. Bandura (1997) later added that the greater a person's self-efficacy, the more success he or she will experience.

Vealey (1986) applied Bandura's (1986) ideas specifically to sport and developed the notion of sport confidence, which she defined as athletes' certainty that they have the ability to be successful in their sport. Initially, Vealey differentiated between state sport confidence (i.e., confidence just before an event) and trait sport confidence (i.e., how confident athletes generally feel about their athletic ability). Later, Vealey (2001) indicated that the distinction between state and trait confidence was unnecessary and suggested that confidence should be viewed as a belief that changes in relation to an athlete's point of reference; for example, an athlete's confidence about her performance in an upcoming race may differ from her confidence for the entire season.

Consultants, coaches, and athletes often use a different language than researchers to describe confidence. Tutko and Tosi (1976) defined confidence as believing in one's ability, having faith in one's talent, accepting challenges that test limits, knowing strengths and weakness, going all out to achieve a desired result, and not engaging in second guessing. These authors added that confidence allows athletes to take risks, be creative, and perform in ways they could not otherwise. More recently, consultants have characterized confidence as a "state of assurance" and a "belief in one's powers" (Zinsser, Bunker, and Williams, 2001). Coaches and athletes use words such as attitude, trust, and certainty.

The perspectives that researchers, consultants, coaches, and athletes have about confidence share common elements related to athletes' fundamental faith in their readiness to perform their best. Drawing on these diverse viewpoints, we define confidence as athletes' belief in their ability to achieve their goals and fully realize their ability. Athletes who have confidence are able to be positive, motivated, intense, focused, and emotionally in control when they need to be. Athletes with this belief are able to stay confident even when they're not performing well. Confident athletes are not negative and uncertain in difficult competitions and they're not overconfident in easy competitions. Confidence also encourages athletes to seek out pressure situations and to view difficult conditions and tough opponents as challenges to pursue (Taylor, 2001).

Athlete's Perspective

As a fledgling athlete, I was told I could have confidence. I was told I could try hard and accomplish things, but I didn't truly believe this until I achieved success. Over the years my successes have nurtured my sense of confidence, but the true test has always been pitting my earned confidence against the negative voices and the perceived failures.

■　■　■　■　■

Coach's Perspective

When athletes get stuck in a rut and seem to lack confidence, I encourage them to change their perspective. I tell them that instead of focusing on their mistakes, they should think about how they can help their teammates play better. This helps the athlete move past mistakes and avoid getting stuck.

■　■　■　■　■

Assessing Confidence

Researchers, consultants, coaches, and athletes all see the value in being able to assess athletes' confidence. For researchers, the development of valid measures of confidence helps them to better understand the concept of confidence and how it influences athletic performance. For consultants, coaches, and athletes, an accurate measure of confidence enables them to judge how confident athletes are and to assess changes in confidence over time. Much like physical testing to determine athletes' physical strengths and weaknesses, measuring confidence offers athletes tangible evidence of their current level of confidence, their need to work on it, and progress they make in developing their confidence (see chapter 6).

Researchers have developed a variety of inventories to assess confidence. The first measure of confidence was a subscale of the Competitive State Anxiety Inventory-2 (CSAI-2; Martens, Vealey, and Burton, 1990). The two most widely used measures are the Trait Sport Confidence Inventory (TSCI) and the State Sport Confidence Inventory (SSCI; Vealey, 1986). The TSCI assesses how confident athletes generally are in sport situations. The SSCI measures confidence just before a competition. More recently, the Carolina Sport Confidence Inventory (CSCI) was developed to measure dispositional optimism and sport competence, which together comprise sport self-confidence (Manzo, Silva, and Mink, 2001). The CSCI correlated significantly with the TSCI and the self-confidence subscale of the CSAI-2. Other developments in the measurement of confidence have included sport-specific instruments, such as the Gymnastic Efficacy Measure (McAuley, 1985), which attempt to account for how unique aspects of a sport affect confidence.

Consultants and authors of applied sport psychology books have developed inventories to facilitate their applied work with athletes. Instruments such as the Tennis Confidence Inventory (Weinberg, 2002) take the rigorous aspects of research-based assessments and modify them for easy administration and evaluation. These measures usually involve asking athletes a series of questions and calculating a confidence score based on their responses.

Performance profiling (Butler and Hardy, 1992) is another instrument that has been adapted from research for applied use (e.g., Taylor, 2001). This tool involves having athletes rate themselves on a 1 to 10 scale on a variety of psychological areas including confidence. In a similar vein, perhaps the simplest and most direct measure of assessing confidence is the "confidence ruler," which was originally developed by Bandura (1977) for research purposes. The confidence ruler is a scale from 0 to 10 with 1-point increments that can be applied to a specific sport, skill, or goal. Athletes are asked, "On a scale from zero to ten, where 0 is not at all confident and 10 is extremely confident, where would you say you are when it comes to [identified skill or task]?" This method gives athletes a visual estimate of their confidence and can then be used as a base point for the implementation of confidence-building strategies.

A significant benefit of all of the assessment tools described here is that they are easily administered and interpreted. These pencil-and-paper instruments have simple directions and can be given to both individuals and groups. Additionally, they generally take less than 15 minutes to complete. Because confidence scores consist of simple additive calculations, they can be readily computed by athletes and a confidence score can be determined by each athlete completing the inventories. Interpretation is also relatively straightforward. Because confidence scores are generally conceived of as linear in nature, that is, low scores indicate a lack of confidence and high scores reflect greater confidence (there has been little empirical consideration of overconfidence), athletes and coaches can readily gain meaning from the scores they obtain from the instruments. Consultants can then use this information as a springboard from which to discuss strategies for increasing confidence.

Developing Confidence

Bandura (1977, 1986, 1997) advocated four general ways in which people can enhance their confidence: (1) performance accomplishment (i.e., past successes); (2) vicarious experience (i.e., watching similar others succeed); (3) verbal persuasion (i.e., encouragement from others); and (4) physiological arousal (i.e., how athletes feel). Bandura suggested that all attempts to build confidence are grounded in these four approaches.

Bandura (1997) also argued that confidence is influenced by how people interpret their experiences. If athletes see their successes as being attributable to external factors such as weak competition or luck, confidence is not likely to increase. Conversely, failure may enhance confidence if athletes interpret the defeat in a way that affirms their ability; for example, they performed well, maintained their effort, and overcame adversity despite the defeat.

Vealey (2001) expanded Bandura's categories of confidence-building experiences to nine sources of sport confidence:

- Mastery
- Demonstration of ability
- Physical and mental preparation
- Physical self-presentation
- Social support
- Seeing others perform well
- Coach's leadership
- Feeling comfortable in competition or environmental comfort
- Situational favorableness

Athlete's Perspective

As a young athlete I found that the more I tried to do, the more I saw myself as confident. So I kept upping the ante athletically and the successes kept coming, feeding the confidence machine and squelching the nay-saying voices.

■ ■ ■ ■ ■

Choosing Confidence

Becoming confident does not happen by accident or chance. It is a process in which athletes must be committed and actively engaged. Similar to any form of athletic training, this involvement must begin with a conscious decision to want to improve. Cook (1992) suggested that confidence is a choice that athletes make: "I am committing myself to becoming a more confident athlete." Dedication to this goal sets in motion athletes' choice to believe in their training and take advantage of performance-enhancement techniques, such as positive self-talk, mental imagery, and goal setting, that foster confidence (Cook, 1992). Each day athletes make numerous decisions about the content and intensity of their preparations that may or may not build their confidence. By choosing to become confident, they are choosing to use the many methods for building confidence.

Increasing one's confidence is a deliberate process that begins with a realization that one's confidence is low and is interfering with the pursuit of competitive goals. This awareness may come from self-exploration, from feedback from coaches or teammates, or through psychological testing. Athletes must come to believe that confidence can be improved (some athletes believe that it cannot be changed). Finally, athletes must actively seek out methods to develop their confidence. Consultants can play a crucial role in helping athletes through this process by fostering self-awareness, convincing them that they have the power to build their confidence, and teaching them about the many ways in which confidence can be enhanced.

Developing Confidence Through Preparation

Over and over we hear coaches and athletes sing the praises of confidence in relation to performance. Frequently, they refer to preparation as the primary tool for developing confidence. For example, collegiate basketball coaching legend John Wooden believes that confidence is simply a natural result of correct preparation (Wooden and Jamison, 1997). Cyclist Lance Armstrong spends hours plotting his training regimen right down to the amount of pasta he will eat after a workout, so that he will feel confident that he has done everything he can to prepare for competition (Armstrong and Jenkins, 2000).

Taylor (2001) wrote that preparation is the foundation of confidence. If athletes believe that they have done everything they can to perform their best, they will have confidence in their ability to perform well. This preparation includes the physical, technical, tactical, and mental parts of their sport. If athletes have developed these areas as fully as they can, they will have faith that they can use those skills gained from preparation to perform as well as they can. The more of these areas athletes cover in their preparation, the more confidence they will breed in themselves.

Coach's Perspective

Many factors contribute to confidence, such as owning your successes and supporting and encouraging athletes, to name a few. However, I have found that the key to confidence is preparation.

Preparing athletes for a competition goes way beyond the basics of conditioning and technical training. To really develop an athlete's confidence, the coach must prepare him for the various challenges and scenarios that he might face in a game. Such preparation also involves learning about one's opponents, respecting their strengths, and planning how to exploit their weaknesses. I have found that one way to build an athlete's confidence is to prepare for games by analyzing videotapes of our previous games as well as scouting tapes of our opponent's performance. During these sessions we point out the strengths and weaknesses of the opponents so that our team knows what to expect. I strongly believe that knowledge of one's opponents is related to confidence.

■   ■   ■   ■   ■

Recognizing Strengths

Identification of specific sport-related strengths is a powerful means for athletes to develop their confidence. This strategy increases confidence by requiring athletes to focus on their strengths and taking their mind off their weaknesses. It is not uncommon for athletes to have difficulty identifying their strengths. Athletic strengths can be identified and acknowledged in several ways. Athletes can take an inventory of their strengths, which helps them clarify their physical, technical, tactical, and mental assets. Athletes can also keep a journal or "confidence log" of their past accomplishments and their ongoing successes in training and competition. This "success focus" acts as a constant reminder of their abilities. When athletes experience failure and begin to lose confidence, they can turn to their inventory and confidence log to remind them of their capabilities and why they should remain confident.

Modeling Confidence

Having confident role models—seeing them succeed and observing how they respond to success—is an influential way athletes can build confidence. Seeing friends, teammates, competitors, and other athletes succeed can gird athletes' belief that they too can succeed. Having confident role models increases confidence in several ways. It enables an athlete to experience success—in this case, vicariously—without the danger of failure. Confident role models help athletes learn what it takes physically, technically, tactically, and mentally to be successful so they are better prepared for competition. A confident role model also shows athletes what success looks and feels like, thus creating positive emotions that reinforce athletes' beliefs about their confidence and that can inspire them to become successful themselves. When choosing models, athletes should select individuals with whom they share some characteristics, for example, age and skill level. The more athletes have in common with potential models, the more easily they will identify with their models and gain

the greatest benefit from the models' actions (Lirgg and Feltz, 1991).

Developing Confidence Through Social Support and Encouragement

Feedback from others can significantly affect an athlete's confidence. Support, in the form of encouragement and constructive feedback from friends, family, teammates, and coaches, can reinforce athletes' confidence and bolster their belief in their capabilities. Research to date has been highly supportive of this view. Coaches from many sports view social support as a useful strategy for enhancing confidence (Gould, Hodge, Peterson, and Giannini, 1989). Additionally, athletes feel more competent and motivated when they receive positive feedback and encouragement from their coaches (Black and Weiss, 1992).

Confidence derived from social support will not, however, instill a lasting and resilient belief. It is often fragile and can be easily invalidated by failure (Bandura, 1977). Additionally, negative feedback from coaches, teammates, and family can hurt confidence. Thus, social support can be a good source of confidence early in athletes' development of confidence, but they should rely on more influential and enduring strategies as they approach competition.

Coach's Perspective

I agree with the importance of social support and encouragement. There are times when an athlete can overanalyze experiences and performance, thus spending too much time in his or her head. In these situations, coaches should help foster confidence by staying positive and encouraging athletes during games and practices. The trick is to encourage athletes with praise that is meaningful and can be used to improve performance.

■   ■   ■   ■   ■

Using Self-Talk

Self-talk is what athletes say to themselves or others about their ability to achieve their competitive goals. Self-talk can either strengthen athletes' confidence by being positive or hurt confidence by being negative. Self-talk that is positive, task oriented, goal directed, and encouraging will bolster their confidence. Conversely, self-talk that is negative, critical, angry, and devaluing will harm confidence. Athletes can use self-talk that draws on support from others, their own strengths, and positive role models, and their preparations can build confidence and help athletes regain their confidence following poor performances.

Positive words and phrases are most effective when they are simple, are positive, and focus on athletes' strengths (Murphy, 1996). To assist athletes in this process, three types of positive self-talk are suggested: (1) emotional (i.e., statements that generate positive emotions, such as excitement, contentment, or joy); (2) technical (i.e., statements that help athletes focus on successful execution); and (3) memory (i.e., statements that recall past successes; Murphy, 1996).

Athlete's Perspective

A few months before the Hawaii Ironman World Championships, 1992, I pulled my calf muscle during the Germany Ironman. I rehabbed the injury and continued to train, deciding to use the down time to run and to work on my mental skills as an athlete, because this was one of my virtues. I visualized pieces of my upcoming race, as well as my finish, seeing myself crossing the finish line, feeling strong and successful.

For Hawaii that year I came up with three words I used in training—patience, strength, and flow. I said them to myself when I needed to be in each particular frame of mind. For instance, if I was trying too hard or felt tight, I would think *flow* and at the same time visualize myself moving in a relaxed and controlled manner. Each time I thought *flow,* I could generate that visual by concentrating on my breath as it moved through my body. The breath, then, became the metaphor for flow. By focusing on my breathing I could generate a flow feeling instantly.

By the time I got to Hawaii, the words had become instant cues for a desired frame of mind. I was a bit apprehensive about how my calf would respond during the race, but I used my words and stayed focused on my task of racing at my potential. I spent time on certain sections of the run course the week before the race, leaving patience, strength, and flow "vibes" and visual cues in the lava fields to "pick up" as I executed on race day.

Training the positive self-talk for a few months allowed me to focus only on myself and what was going on in my body and mind in sync. This reinforced the concept that I only had control over my race and no one else's nor the race conditions. If I executed my race honestly, then success could always be mine. It also put me in a positive frame.

My swim and bike were strong. With favorable wind conditions I was able to clock 5:02 on the bike and it felt effortless (patience and strength). My watch stopped working at some point in the race so during the run, I just paced by intuition and the drive of my newfound tools (patience, strength, and flow).

I noticed that my mind was positive the entire event. If I felt a struggle or negative thought creep in, I would replace it with *patience, strength, or flow.* I checked in with my body constantly, asking "can I go faster given the distance remaining? Yes, you have more to give." And I would open up my stride just a bit for speed and then lock down on my pace. I thought about how much I had put out for this race in my training, and that allowed me to fully own each minute and my entire race. I wanted a strong finish; I earned it, I deserved it, and I owned it.

As I rounded the corner on Alii Drive before the finish line in Hawaii in 1992, I had no idea what my overall time would be. My only motive during the run had been to remain positive and focused on my pace in the moment, use my tools, and then let go of the outcome. I wanted to be in the moment, and the finish line would be what it would be.

A photographer from *Triathlete Magazine* took a photo of me running from behind just as I saw my time on the clock. I had a raised fist in the air for triumph. What I saw at that moment was my best time on that course (9:29). It gave me a fourth place finish for a woman.

The tangible rewards were a huge perk for me, but the real treasures of that race were my newfound ability to use my self-talk tools and remain in the moment in a positive manner the entire race. This showed me that as an athlete I had graduated to a new level of maturity, an evolution to the person I aspired to be. My confidence levels rose once again.

■　■　■　■　■

Gaining Confidence From Adversity

It is one thing for athletes to be confident when they are performing well and things are going their way. It is an entirely different challenge for athletes to maintain their belief in themselves when they are faced with adversity. To more deeply ingrain confidence, athletes can expose themselves to as much adversity as possible and learn to respond positively. Adversity can involve anything that takes athletes out of their comfort zone. Adversity can be environmental obstacles such as bad weather, including rain during a soccer game, or poor competitive conditions, such as an unfriendly crowd at a hockey game. Adversity can also involve an opponent; for example, someone who is a little better than an athlete, an opponent who has a style of play that is frustrating, or someone whom athletes believe they should defeat but who always seems to get the better of them.

Building confidence through adversity begins by having athletes experience adversity in training that they will likely face in competition. This exposure to adversity in training provides several essential benefits. It demonstrates athletes' competence to perform well under difficult conditions. It teaches athletes skills they can use to perform at a higher level in competition. It helps them develop a positive attitude toward adversity, so when they are faced with it in competition, they are motivated to react well to it rather than avoid it. Exposure to adversity during training also prepares athletes for the adversity that they will inevitably experience when they perform in important competitions.

Athlete's Perspective

Once I gained some sense of confidence as an athlete, I realized that I had to check in with it daily. A low-confidence day can lead me to shy away from riding technical single track on my mountain bike or to end a running speed workout early. Or worse, low confidence can leave me gripped with fear on a mountain peak during an adventure race.

When this happens I always try to come back to what I know, what I have control over, and I focus on that to move me through a sketchy section of a race. Experience tells me that some essence of control is always there for the taking, like a tool in your mental tool box. Even after all these years, sometimes finding that tool is not automatic, and I have to look for it.

■ ■ ■ ■ ■

Enjoying Success

All other techniques for building confidence would go for naught if athletes did not then perform well and succeed. Success validates the confidence athletes have developed in their ability. It demonstrates that their belief in themselves is well founded. Success further strengthens confidence, making it more resilient in the face of adversity and poor performance. Finally, success rewards athletes' efforts to build confidence, encouraging them to continue to work hard and develop their abilities.

Using success to build confidence is a progressive process that begins in training with an increased faith in basic skills, strategies, and simple performance execution. Confidence then evolves through successful efforts in mastering more complex technique, tactics, and performance sequences. It continues to grow as athletes have success in simulated competitions such as scrimmages and practice matches. Confidence grows stronger with success in less important competitions and culminates in a high level of confidence when athletes are able to experience success in important competitions, under difficult conditions, and against challenging opposition. An upward spiral of confidence and performance is created in which improved confidence raises subsequent performance, which elevates confidence, which in turn increases performance (McAuley, 1985).

Athletes can foster this benefit in several ways. They can ensure that they maximize the number of successes they have by relying on their strengths and making an effort to reduce their weaknesses. Athletes can also gain ownership of their successes by attributing them to their abilities and efforts rather than to external forces. Finally, they can use mental imagery to repeatedly see and feel themselves succeeding outside of training and competitive settings (for more on mental imagery, see chapter 8).

Defining the Optimistic Mind-Set

Researchers have long known that the attributions athletes make following failure are vastly different than those they may make about success (Biddle, Hanrahan, and Sellars, 2001; Taylor and Riess, 1989) and that confidence appears to influence the types of attributions athletes make. Researchers have found that when confident individuals experience setbacks, they stay positive, focus on their strengths, and look for solutions to the problems. In contrast, less confident individuals are likely to attribute their difficulties to their own shortcomings (Bandura and Wood, 1989).

The attributions that athletes make about their sport experiences can directly affect their current level of confidence, their ability to build their confidence, and how they react when their confidence is challenged. Coaches and athletes can make attributions that foster a sense of confidence by adopting an optimistic mind-set (Seligman, 1990). Thinking like an optimist involves practicing the three P's of positive thinking: personalization, pervasiveness, and permanence.

Personalization

Personalization involves athletes taking responsibility for those factors that are under their control while not blaming themselves for aspects of their performances that are beyond their control. Optimistic athletes strengthen their confidence by making *internal attributions* (e.g., to their ability and effort) for their successes, thereby taking ownership of their successes. They protect their confidence in the face of failure by making *external attributions* for their setbacks either to factors outside of their control (e.g., bad luck or tough opponent) or to factors that are within their control (e.g., poor technique or tactics) that they have the power to change in the future. This optimistic mind-set allows these athletes to interpret their performances—both successful and unsuccessful—in ways that enhance and protect their confidence.

Pessimistic athletes, on the other hand, disown their successes by making external attributions (e.g., luck, poor competition), believing that they were not responsible for their successes. Pessimists sabotage their confidence by attributing their failures to their inadequacies (e.g., lack of ability) and by taking full responsibility for their failures even when their failures may have been caused by factors outside of their control (e.g., better opponent, adverse conditions). This pessimistic mind-set colors these athletes' interpretations of their performances in a way that hurts their confidence whether they succeed or fail.

Coach's Perspective

Confidence also relates to the reasons why athletes compete in athletics. I often say that if you play just to start or be on the field during games, maybe you are playing for the wrong reasons. To be successful in a sport, you need to like it first. You need to like being out there on the field practicing every day with your teammates, regardless of whether it is hot, cold, raining, or snowing. Practicing is what we do day in and day out; you practice a lot more than you play games. If you don't like what we are doing, then maybe you shouldn't be here.

■ ■ ■ ■ ■

Pervasiveness

Pervasiveness is the degree to which individuals believe that the causes of their successes and failures will generalize to all areas of their lives. Optimistic athletes enhance their overall confidence by making *global attributions* for their successes; for example, they were successful because they are great athletes who always handle pressure well rather than they just had a good competition. Optimists make *specific attributions* for their setbacks, in which they attribute their failures to the unique circumstances associated with the present situation rather than to their overall ability.

Pessimistic athletes limit the confidence-building potential of successes by making a specific attribution to their success; for example, they just happened to perform well today and this competition isn't indicative of how they will perform in the future. Pessimists view setbacks as being indicative of their general ability and indicative of how they will perform in the future (Peterson, Maier, and Seligman, 1993).

Permanence

Permanence refers to the belief that the causes of events are either permanent or temporary. Optimistic athletes foster confidence in their ability and efforts by making *stable attributions* for their successes, in which they assume that what enabled them to be successful in the present will continue to ensure success in the future. Optimists safeguard their confidence by making *unstable attributions* for their failures, believing that what caused their failure today will not continue to affect them in the future.

Pessimistic athletes limit their ability to build confidence by making unstable attributions for their successes (e.g., "I was on today, but it won't last"). This impermanence prevents pessimists from internalizing their successes and seeing that those successes reflect their ability to succeed in the future. Pessimists make stable attributions for their failures, in which they assume that the causes of their failures will continue to cause them to fail in the future (Seligman, Reivich, Jaycox, and Gillham, 1995).

Developing an Optimistic Mind-Set

Seligman (1990) argued that pessimists are not destined to a life of negativity and low confidence. Rather, he believes that an optimistic mind-set can be developed through a series of systematic steps. This process involves carefully identifying sources of information that arise out of successes and failures and actively identifying and using feedback that will foster an optimistic mind-set and protect and enhance confidence.

Seeking Positive Feedback

Every training and competitive experience offers information that can either build or harm athletes' confidence. Optimistic athletes are skilled at recognizing positive feedback and distancing themselves from negative feedback, thereby protecting and enhancing their confidence. Pessimistic athletes, in contrast, are highly sensitive to negative feedback that confirms their negative beliefs about their abilities, and they ignore positive feedback that might enhance their confidence.

Athletes can strengthen their confidence by first becoming aware of the many sources of information that build or hurt confidence. The first step involves taking stock of the diverse sources of feedback that are present before, during, and after training and competition, including direct performance feedback, feedback from others, modeling, and athletes' own thoughts, emotions, and behavior. Being able to identify these sources enables athletes to separate positive from negative feedback. This "inventory" also helps athletes become more aware of the kinds of feedback they are most sensitive to and can guide them in better directing their attention to more constructive information. Athletes can then commit to seeking positive feedback that will bolster their confidence before, during, and after their training and competitive performances.

Accepting Feedback

All athletes can recall winning a big game or beating a tough opponent. Athletes also inevitably experience setbacks and failures. Both successful and failing experiences offer feedback that can either help or hurt athletes' confidence. Optimistic and pessimistic athletes differ greatly in the kinds of feedback they more readily accept. Athletes who have an optimistic mind-set are attuned to confidence-building feedback and are able to minimize negative feedback that might hurt their confidence. Optimists recognize and accept the positive feedback as confirmation of their ability and their belief in that ability. In response to failure, optimistic athletes filter the feedback in a way that protects their confidence. Although they accept negative feedback associated with failure, they turn the information into lessons they can use to achieve future success. This way of accepting apparently negative feedback actually increases their confidence because, with this new knowledge, they have a better chance of succeeding in the future.

In contrast, athletes with a pessimistic mind-set are less aware of positive feedback and often miss information that would enable them to build their confidence. Instead, they are highly sensitive to negative feedback, which they use to confirm their already low opinions of themselves as athletes. This pessimistic mind-set has a devastating effect on their confidence because they acknowledge feedback that supports their poor view of themselves and prevent themselves from accepting positive feedback that comes from success.

These differing ways of accepting feedback affect optimistic and pessimistic athletes in the immediacy of competition, where the inevitable ups and downs of competition have a direct influence on confidence, which, in turn, affects subsequent performance. Optimistic athletes focus on positive feedback that raises their confidence and their performances during competition. Pessimistic athletes, because of their ready acceptance of negative feedback and their lack of awareness of positive feedback, often lose confidence easily in competition when they are not performing well or the competition is going against them, which results in a decline in their level of performance.

These divergent styles also influence athletes in the long term. Optimistic athletes, because they acknowledge and accept predominantly positive feedback, make regular "deposits" to their confidence "accounts" that they can then use to maintain their confidence in the face of setbacks and failures. As a result, their confidence account is often replenished and never gets depleted. Over the long term, pessimistic athletes are always in "confidence debt" and are never able to get their confidence account in the plus column.

Framing the Athletic Experience

The final area that distinguishes athletes with optimistic and pessimistic mind-sets involves how they frame their sport experiences. Framing involves the perspective that athletes have about their successes and failures. How athletes frame their competitive experiences colors the lenses through which they look at their performances and directly influences their confidence to achieve their goals.

Athlete's Perspective

I am asked often how I can attempt events like the Eco Challenge, a 7- to 10-day expedition adventure race. How can I execute all of those dangerous activities under physical duress while sleep deprived? If you had told me 15 years ago I would be competing in these events, I'm not sure I would have believed you. Over time, I have gathered more confidence in the form of experiences, taking many small steps that have had a significant effect on my confidence.

A very large part of that confidence has come in the form of mistakes and losses. I learned many years ago that if I take even a moment to reflect on a "bad" race, I can open doors inside myself that can show me who I am as a strong, evolved athlete. The hard lessons force those doors open if I let them. And on the other side is an immense belief in self that stems from surviving the setbacks, picking myself up, and moving on. This basic concept has given me more confidence than all of the wins in my career. In the knowing, the belief in self, the understanding, there stands the basic reason why I engage in sport in the first place: to express myself in a way that I love. We start with that concept, new and shiny, and years of confidence building brings us back to that place.

So now when I look at a 10-day expedition race, I see adventure, and pain and camaraderie, and a microcosm of life stuffed into a short period of time. But the doubt has been muted by the years of experience and built confidence. A perk is that I can carry this confident, positive self into my life and execute without hesitation things that seem to stop many people in their tracks. And I realize that I am lucky to have had these challenges, which have provided me with a sense of confident self that is beyond what I could have gained without sport.

■　■　■　■　■

Optimistic athletes have rose-colored lenses that allow them to clearly see and accept positive feedback and lessen the impact of negative feedback. Their successes are framed in a way that reinforces their belief that they can succeed in the future. Their failures are seen in ways that limit their damaging effects and augment their benefits. The ways in which optimistic athletes frame these experiences ensure that both their successes and failures have a positive effect on their confidence.

Pessimistic athletes have lenses that are dark and murky, allowing them to readily accept negative feedback yet blinding them to positive feedback. Pessimistic athletes frame their athletic experiences in ways that inhibit opportunities for them to build their confidence. They frame their successes in ways that distance themselves from these favorable outcomes and ascribe the causes of the successes to external forces. Their failures are framed to affirm athletes' negative beliefs about themselves. These athletes focus on negative aspects of the setbacks and wallow in their incompetence. In both cases, pessimistic athletes have little chance of gaining confidence in their athletic capabilities.

Coach's Perspective

Preparation is important but without the right perspective can be useless. This relates to the notion of optimism. However, optimism needs to be tempered with realism. Athletes need to be able to evaluate their performance objectively, regardless of wins and losses, to see what they did effectively as well as where their areas of growth lie. We do not talk about winning; instead, we focus on quality performances. If we play our very best, chances are we are going to win. If a better team beats us, we have to own up to this fact. However, there are two ways of looking at such a loss. You can see it as a validation of your weaknesses or as a challenge to improve.

■　■　■　■　■

Key Points

- Confidence may be the most important psychological contributor to athletic performance because it affects performance directly (if athletes don't believe they have the ability to succeed, they won't use that ability) and indirectly (confidence influences other psychological factors including motivation, intensity, focus, and emotions).
- Confidence is defined as athletes' belief in their ability to achieve their goals and succeed.
- Research has demonstrated a clear link between confidence and performance; confident athletes are more successful than less confident athletes.

(continued)

- Confidence can be developed with a variety of techniques, including preparation, recognizing strengths, having confident role models, developing social support, using self-talk, responding positively to adversity, and having successful experiences.
- The way in which athletes attribute their successes and failures has a significant influence on their confidence.
- An optimistic mind-set, with the use of the three P's (personalization, pervasiveness, and permanence), can help athletes make attributions to success and failure that build confidence.
- Athletes can develop an optimistic mind-set by seeking out positive feedback, learning to only accept feedback that will foster confidence, and framing their successes and failures in a way that encourages positive feedback and limits negative feedback.

Review Questions

1. What are various terms used to describe confidence, and how is it commonly defined?
2. What are the ways in which confidence can be developed according to Bandura and Vealey?
3. How is confidence assessed, and what value does it have to researchers, consultants, coaches, and athletes?
4. What strategies can athletes use to increase their confidence?
5. How do attributions affect confidence?
6. What are the three P's of the optimistic mind-set, and how do they influence confidence?
7. What are the three ways that athletes can develop an optimistic mind-set?

3

Intensity

Gregory Wilson, PED—researcher
Jim Taylor, PhD—consultant
Finn Gundersen—coach
Terry Brahm—athlete

The objectives of this chapter are

- to define intensity based on both scientific evidence and practical experience;
- to explain what intensity is and how it influences athletic performance;
- to discuss why athletes have differing levels of optimal intensity and what factors affect intensity; and
- to present practical methods of raising, lowering, or maintaining intensity for high-level performance.

Training has been going well for weeks as the day of competition approaches. Throughout the weeks of training, a feeling of confidence and excitement has been building. Suddenly, just before the competition, the athlete experiences difficulty breathing, muscle tension, butterflies in the stomach, and feelings of uncertainty and apprehension. What has happened?

Intensity has a central role in precompetitive preparation and is the most critical psychological factor before competitive performance. The applied sport psychology consultant can play a significant role in helping athletes learn to control and maintain their precompetition and competitive intensity. Consultants can help athletes identify their optimal level of intensity, recognize situations in which intensity is less than optimal, and determine the possible causes of these changes. Perhaps the most important service a consultant can provide is to teach athletes the skills to monitor and adjust their intensity before and during competition to ensure that their intensity remains at an optimal level throughout the competition.

Key Issues

During both training and competition, athletes experience levels of intensity ranging from deep relaxation to highly energized states. Yet the level of intensity required for optimal athletic performances has often been debated. Moreover, the relationship of intensity to performance is complicated and may involve factors that are as yet unidentified. Regardless of these issues, intensity remains one of the most discussed topics in sport psychology, and the ability to identify an athlete's optimal intensity is important for both coaches and athletes when attempting to maximize athletic performances.

Chapter Purpose and Author Team

The purpose of this chapter is to provide an in-depth understanding of the impact of intensity on athletic performance. Issues that are examined include athlete and sport factors that influence intensity, understanding optimal intensity, and identifying the causes and symptoms of over- and underintensity. This chapter also offers practical information and tools for assessing, achieving, and maintaining optimal intensity. Intensity will be explored comprehensively with insights from a researcher into its theoretical and scientific study, from a consultant into applied concerns, and from a coach and athlete based on their real-life experiences with intensity. The researcher (Dr. Gregory Wilson) integrates recent theoretical and empirical research findings concerning the relationship of intensity to sport performance within the context of the applied issues presented by the consultant. The consultant (Dr. Jim Taylor) describes the important areas in which intensity influences performance based on his applied work with a wide range of athletes. The coach (Finn Gundersen) offers his unique perspective through a successful coaching career in alpine ski racing that included coaching for the U.S. Olympic ski team, whereas the athlete (Terry Brahm) discusses the meaning of intensity in his competitive career that included representing the United States at the Olympics as a 5,000-meter runner.

Sport-Specific Definition of Intensity

The term *intensity* is recommended over other more commonly used terms, such as *arousal, anxiety,* and *nervousness* (Landers and Boutcher, 1986; Silva and Hardy, 1984; Spielberger, 1989). These latter terms have negative connotations that can limit their value. For example, arousal has sexual associations that can distract athletes and anxiety and nervousness are sensations that athletes generally want to avoid. We recommend that *intensity* be used because it has positive associations and athletes typically view intensity as an integral contributor to optimal performance (Taylor, 2001; Taylor and Wilson, 2002).

Zaichkowsky and Takenaka (1993) suggested that intensity has three important qualities that affect performance. First, there exists a physiological activation that includes heart rate, glandular and cortical activity, and blood flow. Second, behavioral responses are evident in terms of the amount of motor redundant activation. Third, cognitive and emotional responses are exhibited in terms of positive or negative perceptions of the physiological and behavioral symptoms of intensity.

Athletes experience a wide range of intensity in training and competition, ranging from very low (e.g., relaxed, calm) to extremely high (e.g., energized, agitated). Intensity may be experienced by athletes positively, leading to increases in confidence, motivation, stamina, strength, endurance, and sensory acuity (Carver and Scheier, 1986), or negatively, leading to fear, dread, muscle tension, breathing difficulty, and loss of confidence, motivation, focus, and coordination (Eysenck and Calvo, 1992). The ability of athletes to monitor and control their intensity will dictate how they perform in training and competition.

During the last decade, the scientific and applied understanding of intensity and its influence on athletic performance has increased dramatically (Cox, 1998; Hanin, 2000; Weinberg and Gould, 1999). These new insights have shown that intensity is a complex attribute that is affected by individual athletes and the sport in which they participate; in turn, intensity acts on athletes in idiosyncratic and sometimes surprising ways.

Intensity Is Multifaceted

Intensity is now seen as being affected by many physical, psychological, and emotional factors. Hardy (1990, 1996), for example, proposed the cusp catastrophe model, which suggests that intensity possesses thought (i.e., worry and apprehension) and somatic (i.e., physiological activity) components. This theory asserts that declines in performance will only occur when high somatic intensity and high cognitive intensity are both present. When this situation arises, "catastrophe" occurs, resulting in a rapid and dramatic deterioration in athletic performance (Cox, 1998). For example, a pole vaulter who is apprehensive over an upcoming meet may experience high levels of cognitive intensity, as expressed by negative thoughts and doubts about his ability to achieve his goals. These worrisome thoughts are manifested in physiological experiences of overintensity, such as muscle tightness and rapid breathing, both of which may

be detrimental to successful performance. The challenge for consultants is to identify the precise reasons for changes in intensity in individual athletes. Only when an athlete can identify the specific causes for changes in intensity can she then learn to control them and, thus, perform her best (Taylor and Wilson, 2002).

Intensity Is Unique to Each Athlete

Consultants' work would be much simpler if all athletes performed their best at the same level of intensity. This, however, is not the case. The earliest theory, the inverted-U hypothesis (Yerkes and Dodson, 1908), suggested that as intensity increases performance will improve, but only to a point, after which more intensity hurts performance (Cox, 1998). From an applied perspective, the inverted-U hypothesis suggests that all individuals should possess moderate levels of intensity, regardless of physiology, skill level, experience, competitive setting, or other factors.

However, the inverted-U hypothesis does not account for the individual differences in the way athletes respond to the stress of competition (Fazey and Hardy, 1988; Raglin and Hanin, 2000) or the unique demands of different sports (Taylor, 1995). Recent research (Raglin and Turner, 1992; Wilson and Raglin, 1997) indicates that a significant proportion of athletes perform better at higher levels of intensity. Further evidence (Raglin and Morris, 1994; Wilson and Raglin, 1997) suggests that the level of competition influences intensity levels within athletes. For example, many athletes exhibit lower intensity levels when competing in "easy" as opposed to "hard" competitions.

The individual zone of optimal functioning (IZOF) model asserts that optimal intensity varies depending on the unique characteristics of the athlete (Hanin, 2000). Hanin (2000) believes that intensity is (1) a part of athletes' responses to the competitive situation, (2) determined by how athletes perceive the situation, and (3) a reflection of their past experiences in similar situations. IZOF research has demonstrated that the optimal level of anxiety may vary greatly across athletes, with between 30% and 45% of athletes performing best when anxiety is high (Raglin and Hanin, 2000).

Another view of the individual nature of intensity was offered by reversal theory (Jones, 1995), which states that the most important factor in understanding the relationship between intensity and performance is athletes' own interpretations of their perceived intensity. For example, high intensity can be beneficial to performance if athletes perceive their high intensity as positive. Conversely, if athletes interpret their intensity negatively, intensity will hurt performance (Kerr, 1997).

Reversal theory further suggests that there can be shifts in the perceptions of intensity throughout the duration of a sporting competition (Kerr, 1989). For example, a golfer may begin a round feeling confident and motivated about her performance and, as a result, interpret the accompanying intensity as positive. However, as the round progresses and she makes several bad shots, her perceptions of her intensity may shift. The same level of intensity that was once viewed as positive is now seen as negative and thus negatively affects her golf performance.

Perceptions of Ability

The perceptions that athletes hold about their ability to succeed in a given competition influence their level of intensity and whether they interpret it as positive or negative. Landers and Boutcher (1986) proposed five areas that affect the perceptions of one's ability: (1) demands of the situation, (2) the individual's resources for effectively managing the demands, (3) consequences of the situation, (4) "meaning" that is attached to the consequences, and (5) recognition of bodily reactions. For example, Eddie, an 18-year-old freshman goalie for a collegiate hockey team, has been named the starter for the championship game. He perceives that the requirements of his starting role in such an important game (demands) are greater than his ability (resources) to perform successfully. He believes that he will fail in his performance (consequences) and it will disappoint his family and ruin his chances at a career in the National Hockey League (meaning). The confluence of these appraisals leads Eddie to experience a dramatic increase in his intensity before the game.

Past Experience

Recent studies have also found past experience to be an important contributor to both an athlete's precompetition and her optimal level of intensity (Wilson, Raglin, and Pritchard, 2001; Wilson and Steinke, 2002). Findings from these studies suggest that when athletes are grouped based on attribution styles (e.g., optimistic, defensive pessimistic, or pessimistic), those athletes labeled as optimistic tend to have lower precompetition and optimal intensity values than athletes who

were more pessimistic in nature. However, no performance differences have been found between optimistic and defensive pessimistic athletes. This lack of performance differences may be explained by how more pessimistic athletes view intensity. It has been suggested that individuals who possess a defensive pessimistic attribution style may actually use these higher levels of intensity as motivation to perform (Sanna, 1998). This research is important for consultants, because lowering the intensity of an athlete who is a defensive pessimist may actually harm performance, whereas raising the level of intensity for an optimistic athlete may harm performance.

Perceptions of Competitive Situation

Taylor (2001) suggested that the specific setting in which an athlete performs may also influence intensity. For example, a gymnast might experience higher intensity while performing on the balance beam than on the floor exercise. Situational factors that are present at competitions also influence intensity. Competitive conditions such as the facility, weather, and crowd size may affect intensity. How familiar athletes are with the competitive situation and conditions will also affect intensity.

It is likely that the level of the competition, such as whether the competition is above, at, or below an athlete's typical level, will influence intensity. Competitions above athletes' usual level would cause an increase in intensity, whereas competitions at a lower level might lead to a decline in intensity. The level of opposition could be expected to have a similar effect on intensity. Csikszentmihalyi (1975) supported this view by suggesting that athletes who perceive that their abilities exceed the demands of a competitive situation (i.e., they are better than their opponents) will experience boredom, which will lower intensity, and if the demands of the situation exceed their abilities, they will become frustrated or fearful and their intensity will increase.

Intensity Is NOT Sport Specific

How intensity affects athletic performance depends on the type of sport in which athletes compete. Oxendine (1970) was the first theorist to suggest that intensity is sport specific. He believed that optimal intensity depended on the motor demands of a sport. For example, sports involving gross motor activities requiring strength and speed (e.g., shot put, football, hockey) require high intensity for optimal performance. In contrast, relatively lower intensity would be needed in sports involving fine muscle movements (e.g., golf, diving, archery). However, despite the intuitive appeal of Oxendine's ideas, research support for this idea has been virtually nonexistent (Fazey and Hardy, 1988; Gould and Krane, 1992; Raglin and Turner, 1992).

Athlete's Perspective

If there are two competitors who are equally prepared in terms of physical training, the competition will always go to the athlete who is the most prepared mentally. That individual will be able to control his intensity level and get the most out of his performance.

For example, several days before the 1988 Olympic Trials, I began to get very anxious and tense. Training had gone perfectly, and I knew that I was physically ready. However, as the event for which I had trained for years approached, I became very nervous. My coach, Sam Bell, sensed this and brought me back to the proper level of intensity by calmly discussing the upcoming trials. He told me to be myself, to simply go out and compete as I had the over the last few months, and I would make the Olympic team. This brief talk made me realize that I was overly intense and that I needed to calm myself in order to run well. I believe that this was the most important factor in my making the Olympic team that year in the 5,000 meter.

■ ■ ■ ■ ■

Coach's Perspective

Alpine skiing by its very nature demands a high level of intensity, or at least that is the mind-set of the athletes and coaches who participate. Because speed measured by time determines the final result, higher speed in any of the four events contested becomes the goal for the athlete, right or wrong. Speed equals excitement and risk taking, while increasing the chances of falling and sustaining an injury. Whether the skier is going 80 miles per hour in a downhill or just missing a turning pole in slalom with the tip of her ski by less than an inch at 25 to 35 miles per hour, ski racing demands that the body be at its most heightened awareness, that all the senses be on maximum alert, and that the brain be fully engaged in competing or in just surviving.

Highly physically stimulating sports demand a similar level of intensity over and over again, which is what most coaches seek in determining optimal arousal. An athlete who is physically ready with lots of adrenaline flowing is preferred over the athlete who is cold and passive and apparently not ready to be athletically explosive.

■ ■ ■ ■ ■

Identifying Optimal Intensity

Optimal intensity refers to the ideal level of physiological and cognitive intensity that will allow athletes to perform their best (Hanin, 2000; Taylor, 2001). There is no one optimal level of intensity for all athletes; rather, optimal intensity is personal for each athlete. Whether athletes attain optimal intensity in a competition is determined by numerous personal, social, athletic, and situational variables over which the athlete may have little awareness and even less control (Schmidt and Wrisberg, 2000).

As indicated in both the IZOF model (Hanin, 2000) and cusp catastrophe theory (Fazey and Hardy, 1988), all athletes have a level of intensity that allows them to perform their best. The first goal of consultants in working with intensity regulation with athletes is to teach them to how to identify their optimal intensity.

Coach's Perspective

I asked a number of United States ski team coaches the following question an hour before the start of a very important international race: "What is the optimal level of intensity for your athletes today?" The answers varied depending on the skill level and start numbers of their athletes, but I have combined them into a number of general responses:

"In the athletes' sport psychology talks in the off-season, we go through a bunch of techniques for arousal regulation and calming methods. It mostly comes from the athletes; they have to be aware of where they are and what at level they need to be. We teach them methods they can use to achieve their optimum levels."

"Today is just like any other race; they have had the right warm-up, they have the right mental focus, and the athletes have reassured themselves that they have done everything they can to have a good race, so they can relax and really charge and not hold back."

Response for athletes stepping down one level—from the World Cup to the North American series: "We told them to not let down because they came from the World Cup to a Nor-Am, because a Nor-Am is where they belong. We are trying to keep the same intensity during a race as a training day, not changing anything. We are actually trying to keep them more focused, more relaxed, not so jazzed that it's a race because they are training so well. They have practiced their ideal arousal level over and over, and today, because the course is so difficult, they can never let up; they must focus and fight all the way to the finish."

■ ■ ■ ■ ■

Identify Relevant Personal Factors

Using a form such as the Intensity Identification Form (form 3.1), consultants can ask athletes the following questions concerning the optimal intensity they have experienced in the past:

- Before and during a successful competition, how did the athlete feel physically? For example, did he have increased heart rate and sweating, or was he calm and at ease? Athletes should be as specific as possible in describing their physiological conditions.

- What were the athlete's thoughts and emotions at the time: positive and excited, neutral, or low key?

- What social influences are typically present or absent during successful performances, such as family, coaches, and friends?

The same questions should also be asked about poor performances. Typically, what emerges from this examination is a consistent pattern of physiological, cognitive, and social activity that is associated with optimal and nonoptimal intensity, as well as the corresponding level of performance. At the bottom of form 3.1, athletes can summarize those factors that are associated with both successful and unsuccessful performances.

The purpose of this exercise is to help athletes understand what their body feels like, what they are thinking and feeling, and with whom they are interacting in performance situations that are both good and poor. The goal of intensity identification is to make athletes aware of these differences before they compete so they can then take proactive steps to reproduce those factors that are associated with good performance through the use of intensity regulation.

Experiment With Different Intensities in Training

Athletes who are unsure of their optimal intensity can use training to experiment with varying intensity levels and their impact on performance. For example, a 400-meter runner can divide a training session composed of six 400-meter timed intervals into three parts in which, using the intensity regulation techniques described later in this chapter, she runs two intervals each at low, moderate, and high levels of intensity (with adequate rest in between). She can then use her feelings during each segment of workout and the times she ran to help her identify her optimal intensity.

Compare Successful and Unsuccessful Performances

Hanin (1986) offered two methods for determining an athlete's optimal intensity range. Initially, Hanin followed athletes through an entire season and measured intensity 1 hour before competition. By comparing precompetitive intensity to individual performances, Hanin was able to determine optimal intensity for each athlete. However, the logistical problems in following an athlete throughout a competitive season can make this method impractical (Hanin and Syrja, 1995; Raglin and Hanin, 2000). It can also be difficult getting athletes to cooperate because of this approach's intrusiveness (McCann, Murphy, and Raedeke, 1992).

In response to this problem, Hanin (1986) developed a retrospective method for assessing an athlete's IZOF. Hanin and others (Morgan and Ellickson, 1989) found that recall of precompetitive intensity remained highly accurate even 18 days after a competition.

An important finding of IZOF research is that athletes can successfully predict precompetitive levels of intensity up to 48 hours before competition (Raglin and Turner, 1992; Wilson and Raglin, 1997). This ability can be used as a reference point for intervention with athletes (Hanin, 2000). With this knowledge, consultants can use significant deviations from optimal intensity to guide the type of interventions (e.g., raising or lowering intensity) they recommend.

Form 3.1 Intensity Identification

Directions: In the space below, indicate the competitive, mental, and physical factors that are related to your best (ideal intensity) and worst (overintensity or underintensity) competitions. At the bottom, summarize the positive and negative factors that distinguish your prime from poor intensity.

	Best competitions	**Worst competitions**
Importance of competition		
Difficulty of opponent		
Competitive conditions		
Thoughts		
Emotions		
Physical feelings		

From *Applying Sport Psychology: Four Perspectives,* by Jim Taylor and Gregory S. Wilson, 2005, Champaign, IL: Human Kinetics.

Athlete's Perspective

Intensity is definitely unique to each athlete. The role of the coach is to observe and communicate with each athlete to find out what makes her tick and then set the environment to allow her to perform at her highest level. The role of the athlete is to pay attention to how she responds to various levels of intensity in practice and competition and then to communicate these feelings to the coach. It must be a two-way line of communication, and the athlete needs to be in touch with her own emotions.

■   ■   ■   ■   ■

General Intensity Control Strategies

With a clear understanding of what optimal and nonoptimal intensity feels like and how it influences performance, athletes can now develop skills to achieve and maintain optimal intensity. This section examines general intensity control techniques that athletes can use to either increase or decrease their intensity. Later sections of this chapter introduce specific strategies to help athletes respond to the causes and symptoms of over- and underintensity.

Precompetitive Management

On the day of the competition, the time immediately before the competition is the most crucial period of competitive preparation. What athletes think, feel, and do before they compete will dictate how they perform. Athletes should have three goals before they compete: Their equipment should be prepared, their bodies should be warmed up and at optimal intensity, and they should be mentally prepared to perform their best. The use of routines in precompetitive management is discussed in detail in chapter 9.

Mental Imagery

Mental imagery, one of the most commonly used mental training strategies by athletes, can be used to adjust their intensity up or down before competition (Caudill, Weinberg, and Jackson, 1983). High-energy images of intense competition, strong effort, and success can raise intensity. Calming images of relaxing scenes, peace, and tranquility can reduce intensity (for more on mental imagery, see chapter 8).

Coach's Perspective

Competition day is all about the day's weather, the variable terrain and snow conditions, and the course that is to be run. On the World Cup circuit, the athletes are given one opportunity to learn the race course (usually 45 minutes) and the accompanying terrain and snow conditions (except downhill—which is the longest and fastest event and entails a number of course inspections and training runs before the day of competition). The athletes memorize the course and conditions from start to finish, with the assistance of coaches who are strategically placed along the course pointing out difficult combinations and terrain. The athletes often stop, close their eyes, and review the course from the start to where they are.

One athlete in particular has developed a reputation for being somewhat "crazy" during inspection because when he stops to review the course with his eyes closed, his arms are wildly flying around as he negotiates each turn he has memorized. Many times his whole body becomes part of the routine, much to the amusement of the athletes and spectators around him. Nonetheless, he is one of the top 10 athletes in the world.

■   ■   ■   ■   ■

Key Words

A common pitfall that many athletes experience is that they become so absorbed in the heat of competition that they forget to do important things to perform optimally, such as monitoring and adjusting their intensity. Athletes can develop key words to remind them of what they need to do to achieve optimal intensity (see form 3.2). Applied consultants can encourage athletes to identify intensity key words that have either an energizing or a calming effect and to use them before and during competition to help maintain optimal intensity (for more on key words, see chapter 4).

Music

Music has a profound emotional and physiological impact on people. Music can create feelings of happiness, sadness, inspiration, or anger. It can excite or calm people. Although this relationship has not been studied in the sports world, many well-known athletes, including Olympic 400-meter champion Michael Johnson, Olympic figure skater Kristi Yamaguchi, and Major League Baseball player Derek Jeter, use music to regulate intensity before competition. Consultants can assist athletes in

Form 3.2   Intensity Key Words

Directions: A variety of intensity key words are listed in the following table. In the spaces provided, identify other intensity key words that you can use.

Psych-Down	
Sample key words	**Your key words**
Breathe	
Loose	
Relax	
Calm	
Easy	
Trust	

Psych-Up	
Sample key words	**Your key words**
Go for it	
Charge	
Attack	
Positive	
Hustle	
Commit	

From *Applying Sport Psychology: Four Perspectives,* by Jim Taylor and Gregory S. Wilson, 2005, Champaign, IL: Human Kinetics.

selecting the appropriate style of music to reach their optimal intensity. For instance, athletes who need to increase their intensity should listen to high-energy music, whereas those needing to reduce intensity should listen to relaxing music.

Athlete's Perspective

Athletes should experiment with different levels of intensity in their training. Certainly the most important skill that is developed is the physical competency in one's sport; however, practice sessions can also be used to develop the mental framework needed to perform at an optimal level. It is helpful to experiment in practice under differing levels of intensity and match these intensity levels to your performance. If you are not sure under which level of intensity you perform the best, practice is the time to find out, not an actual competition.

■　■　■　■　■

Controlling Overintensity

Overintensity is the most common form of nonoptimal intensity. Athletes experience overintensity for a variety of reasons, but the outcomes are the same—physical and psychological discomfort and poor competitive performance. To gain control of their overintensity, athletes must follow several steps: (1) Understand its causes so that they can solve the fundamental problem that is leading to overintensity, (2) recognize its symptoms so that appropriate intensity control techniques can be used, and (3) apply the most effective "psych-down" strategies to achieve and maintain optimal intensity (Taylor and Wilson, 2002).

Causes of Overintensity

Athletes experience overintensity for a reason. At some level, they believe that the upcoming competition is threatening to them. This belief triggers all of the physical and psychological symptoms that lead to poor competitive performance. To relieve their overintensity, athletes must understand what is causing it.

Coach's Perspective

It is not uncommon for an athlete in alpine ski racing to take an additional run on a course in which he is supposed to only run once. This can happen because he was interfered with or because the athlete ahead of him fell and was a potential hazard; in this situation the skier behind the fallen skier would be waved off, stopped, and returned to the start for another attempt on the course. This can cause the athlete a great deal of anxiety, frustration, and even anger, especially if he was having a fast or good run.

Coaches need to help the athlete achieve the necessary perspective to focus again on the task ahead of him, to regain control of his feelings, and to overcome a sense of the rerun being unfair or a bad break. In the very fast events of downhill and super G, there are times when the coach literally has to reassemble the athlete's courage. Some racers have enough fear of the course that they can just gather enough courage to risk it all once a day. There was an unusual incident a few years ago in which a coach had to order an athlete to take the rerun. But the coach knew the athlete thoroughly, and the result was a dramatic success.

■　■　■　■　■

Lack of Confidence

Athletes who lack confidence are placed in a threatening and untenable position; they must perform in a competitive situation for which they have little faith in their ability to succeed. Considered in this light, overintensity—anxiety in its truest sense—is inevitable. A good place for consultants to start in helping athletes lower their intensity is to alter how athletes appraise their upcoming competition (Kerr, 1997). In fact, Edwards and Hardy (1996) reported that athletes whose confidence increased perceived their intensity to be more facilitative to their competitive performances (see chapter 2).

Assuming that athletes are well prepared physically and technically, a lack of confidence is most often caused by negative, inaccurate, or extreme cognitive appraisal of a competitive situation (Landers and Boutcher, 1986). At the heart of this faulty appraisal process is the perception by athletes that they can't cope effectively with the five areas of appraisal (i.e., demands, resources, consequences, meaning, and recognition of bodily reactions). Thus, by developing their confidence, athletes can reduce their overintensity at its source by reevaluating the situation positively and accurately.

Athlete's Perspective

Before entering a competition where I knew the skill level was higher than what I was used to competing against, I would remember my best practice or competition from the past weeks or months. I would recall the feeling mentally, physically, and spiritually that I had when running fast. I would go over those feelings again and again in my mind until I was in that mental frame and I was confident that I would be able to compete at the highest level. If an athlete is not confident, competing at a high level is difficult.

■ ■ ■ ■ ■

Coach's Perspective

Often the spread in age, ability, and experience in a field of 140 competitors is broad. Competitors who just make it into the race at the end of the field are at the upper limits of their abilities and experience. They approach the race having conceded the win and top 15 to the better competitors; their biggest challenge is often the increased difficulty of the terrain and conditions. Steep and very hard snow conditions can intimidate the best of competitors, let alone someone starting at the back. The hardest task for a coach is to convince his or her athletes who are ready for a higher level of competition that they will be successful despite the better competitors and more difficult conditions. Athletes competing for the first time on a very difficult course worry about not the other racers but the mountain. Perception becomes the reality, and negative perception needs to be altered or athletes are defeated before they begin. The coach plays a critical role here.

■ ■ ■ ■ ■

Internal Focus

Nideffer (1989) suggested that athletes who become distracted by thoughts, physical sensations, and emotions, particularly when those distractions lower confidence, are more likely to experience a shift away from optimal intensity. Internal distractions, such as negative thoughts, discomforting emotions, thoughts about past failures, and a preoccupation with technique, can cause athletes to feel threatened and to experience overintensity. Another internal distraction that is common among athletes involves focusing on the outcome of competition rather than on its process. This emphasis causes athletes to feel pressure to achieve the desired outcome and detracts from their focus on performing their best.

External Focus

Athletes who focus on external factors that can interfere with performance increase the likelihood that they will experience overintensity. Social causes of overintensity come primarily from pressure that athletes feel from significant others including parents, coaches, friends, com-

munity, and media. Overintensity results from the perception that if athletes do not live up to the socially derived expectations, they will disappoint people who are important to them, and they will not be loved, respected, or supported (Krohne, 1980; Passer, 1982).

Focusing on environmental factors, such as the setting, competitive conditions, noise, unfamiliarity with the situation, unexpected events, and worry over uncontrollable aspects of the competitive situation, can also cause athletes to feel overintensity. These factors can have an unsettling effect on athletes, cause them to lose confidence, and, as a result, elevate their intensity to a level that may hurt performance (see chapter 4).

Athlete's Perspective

One of the more challenging aspects of competing in the Olympics is controlling both internal and external factors that affect your performance. You cannot dwell on the fact that everyone (friends, family, teammates, coach, media) wants you to win a gold medal. Instead, you need to recognize that although the entire world is watching, you need to stay focused on the simpler processes of your sport (mechanics, stride, pace). In my case, all I needed to do was to focus on running the 5,000 meters as fast as I could. All the other factors just added to the experience, but I did not allow them to distract me from my performance. If I had let these things enter my mind, my level of intensity would have soared, and I would not have been at an optimal level of intensity to compete.

■ ■ ■ ■ ■

Symptoms of Overintensity

Intensity can be manifested in three ways: physically, behaviorally, and psychologically (Hanin, 2000; Jones, 1995; Kerr, 1997). The most apparent physical symptoms include extreme muscle tension, stomach butterflies, shaking muscles, difficulty breathing, and excessive perspiration (Landers and Boutcher, 1986). Other more subtle physical signs include increased heart rate, fatigue, and decreased motor coordination. Behavioral indicators include an increase in pace during competition, generalized agitation, an increase in performance-irrelevant or superstitious behaviors, tense body language, more mistakes, and a decrease in competitive performance (Eysenck and Calvo, 1992). Psychological symptoms of overintensity include negative self-talk, a shift from performance-relevant thoughts to performance-irrelevant thoughts, a decline in motivation, an excessive narrowing of concentration (Nideffer and Sagal, 1998), and emotions such as frustration, anger, and fear (Elko and Ostrow, 1991; Hamilton and Fremouw, 1985).

Cognitive Psych-Down Techniques

Reducing overintensity using psychological psych-down techniques focuses on changing the causes of overintensity. This section addresses a variety of psychological strategies that athletes can use to lower their intensity. These techniques can be used first during training sessions and then before and during competitions to achieve and maintain optimal intensity.

Build Confidence

The most effective way to relieve the psychological and emotional causes of overintensity is to develop athletes' confidence in their ability to achieve their goals. Chapter 2 describes many useful techniques that consultants can teach athletes to improve their confidence, such as positive self-talk, thought stopping, and positive litanies. Most important, confidence should develop progressively out of athletes' experiences in training and competitions. Confidence should be grounded in quality preparation; the consistent use of mental skills in training; positive responses to adversity; support from others, such as coaches, teammates, family, and friends; and daily successes in training. Confidence built in this way will be well founded, deeply ingrained, and resilient in the face of obstacles, mistakes, and failure.

Often athletes, particularly those who are young or less experienced, become so overwhelmed by the approaching competition that they lose perspective and are simply not able to view the situation objectively. This loss of perspective further hurts confidence as the competition approaches. This distortion may lead to irrational thinking, which further increases intensity (Ellis, 1962). The applied consultant can assist athletes in rationally assessing the upcoming competition by discussing the five appraisal areas (discussed earlier), either individually or in a team setting. Typically, by being shown another way of viewing the situation, athletes are able to recognize the extremity of their thinking and accept a more realistic perspective, which then shifts their intensity to an optimal level (Heyman, 1984).

Coach's Perspective

As headmaster of a sports academy specializing in alpine ski racing and Nordic cross-country skiing, I initiated our participation into other high school sports through the state high school association. With only 50 boys and 35 girls in our school facing high schools of 500 to 1,200, soccer and track and field became the classic case of David vs. Goliath. Athlete and team confidence was built by playing to our strengths—our overall conditioning and competitive nature—while downplaying our lack of sport-specific skills and playing time. We proved over and over again that any team can be defeated on any given day, and we won numerous state titles in soccer and fall cross country, because of our commitment to be superior in conditioning, tougher psychologically, and at times smarter players on the field. Before long, our reputation preceded us and we had the psychological advantage at game time. In the end, we raised the level of play and competition throughout the state.

■ ■ ■ ■ ■

Redirect Focus

The ability of athletes to redirect their focus onto cues that will help them to perform their best is essential for relieving overintensity. If athletes are not focused on those things that cause overintensity, such as negative thoughts and emotions, worry about the outcome, and expectations of others, they are less likely to experience increased intensity. By attending to cues that are important to performance, athletes also feel more confident and have a greater sense of control over their efforts, which can also reduce intensity. Chapter 4 offers a more detailed discussion of focus and how it can be used to maximize performance.

Physical Psych-Down Techniques

Although preventing the causes of overintensity is the ideal intervention, there will be times when athletes experience overintensity before and during competition. At these times, they must have the tools to immediately identify its primary symptoms and take active steps to reduce their intensity to an optimal level. Consultants can play an essential role in providing athletes with the information and skills they need to act quickly and effectively when they experience overintensity.

Breathing

When athletes are experiencing overintensity, the respiratory system contracts, so that oxygen intake is inadequate for the demands of competition. Williams and Harris (1998) suggested that breathing is the simplest and most effective technique for reducing overintensity.

Controlled breathing provides oxygen to enrich the blood and allow athletes to give their best efforts. Breathing is also the primary way in which carbon dioxide is removed from the body. A build-up of carbon dioxide in the tissues is associated with muscle fatigue and cramping, both of which can seriously impair athletic performance. Without sufficient oxygen, the body's ability to resynthesize energy is impaired, which also adversely affects performance. Taking deep, rhythmic breaths will allow athletes to replenish their body's oxygen supply and reduce the noticeable symptoms of overintensity.

Controlled breathing also has psychological benefits. A significant problem with overintensity is that athletes tend to become focused on its negative symptoms such as muscle tension, high heart rate, and stomach butterflies. By taking slow, deep breaths, athletes alleviate some of these symptoms, thereby increasing confidence and feelings of control and well-being. Additionally, by focusing on their breathing, athletes will pay less attention to the negative feelings associated with overintensity.

Muscle Relaxation

Muscle tension is one of the most uncomfortable and debilitating symptoms of overintensity (Landers and Boutcher, 1986). Tight muscles inhibit coordination and flexibility, disrupt technique, hurt performance, and increase the likelihood of injury. Consultants can teach athletes practical and easy-to-use techniques of muscle relaxation.

Passive relaxation is a common strategy that works effectively with all but the most overly intense athletes. This technique involves deep breathing and a procedure in which athletes focus on relaxing their muscles and imagine the tension gradually draining from their bodies. For athletes who experience significant muscle tension, *progressive relaxation* will be more effective in relaxing tense muscles. This technique involves alternating tension and relaxation of major muscle groups (head and neck, arms and shoulders, chest and back, and legs). Somewhat counterintuitive, progressive relaxation requires athletes to tense rather than relax their muscles. The procedure involves tensing a muscle group for 5 seconds, releasing the tension for 5 seconds, taking a deep breath, and repeating.

Relaxation training increases athletes' awareness of their muscle tension and how it affects performance. The relaxation process teaches athletes to discriminate between states of complete tension and total relaxation. Once athletes recognize their muscle tension, they have the ability to actively reduce their tension, lower their intensity, and improve their performances (Weinberg and Gould, 1999). Because muscle relaxation takes practice, consultants can foster its use by making it a regular part of training.

Athlete's Perspective

Muscle relaxation is another great way to lower intensity levels when they are too high. On the night before a competition, I often found it very hard to sleep because of prerace tension. I found that if I lay on my back with my arms at my sides, breathed deeply and slowly, and then flexed each muscle group from head to toes, I would often feel like the tension had left my body. At times, I would feel like I was becoming very light and almost lifting off the bed, and at other times I would feel like I was sinking down deep into the mattress. This technique often led to a good night's sleep and let me control my intensity so that mentally I was ready for a big race.

■　■　■　■　■

Smiling

Smiling is a surprising yet effective technique for inducing relaxation in athletes. The value of smiling was discovered several years ago when a consultant was working with a professional tennis player who became frustrated and angry during an on-court practice session as she struggled to improve a part of her game. She became so upset and tense that her game was getting worse rather than better and, on a whim, the sport psychologist told her to smile. As can be easily imagined, smiling was the last thing that she wanted to do, and she expressed her feelings to the consultant. However, simply to appease the consultant, she formed a big smile, and when she did, the consultant told her to hold it. Within 2 minutes, a remarkable transformation occurred. As she held the smile, the tension in her shoulders disappeared and her body, which had been hunched and closed, began to rise and open up. She went on to have a productive practice in which she was able to overcome her earlier difficulties.

The consultant was amazed at the transformation and curious as to why smiling had such a dramatic effect on the athlete. A review of the research on the effects of smiling revealed several causes. First, as people grow up, they learn that smiling is associated with happiness and good feelings. Also, research has demonstrated that smiling actually alters blood flow in the brain, causing the release of neurochemicals that produce a calming effect (Zajonc, 1985). Finally, it is difficult to think and feel in a way that is contrary to one's body language.

Athlete's Perspective

One of the best ways to control overintensity is to simply smile. My coach of 10 years, Sam Bell, had a great ability to make me smile or laugh when I needed it the most. I would always seek out Coach Bell before a race for reassurance and also because I knew that I would come away laughing or smiling at something he would say. The second I smiled, I knew that I was ready to compete.

■ ■ ■ ■ ■

Controlling Underintensity

Because of the inherent pressures associated with competition, underintensity is not common among athletes (Williams and Harris, 1998). However, it may be evident in some athletes and in some competitive situations, such as when an athlete is heavily favored to win or when an athlete has a big lead and feels assured of victory. Consultants can help athletes recognize when a decrease in intensity may happen and how they can respond to it to maintain their optimal intensity.

Causes of Underintensity

Like overintensity, underintensity is caused by an interaction of psychological and situational factors. This relationship is based largely in how athletes perceive themselves relative to the competitive situation and those against whom they will be competing.

• **Overconfidence**. Athletes who are overconfident believe that they will win easily. Overconfidence is caused by athletes' perceptions that

they are far superior to their opponents and that the conditions are ideally suited for them. This overconfidence prevents athletes from preparing fully for competition, giving maximum effort, and marshaling their full psychological and physical capabilities while competing. Because athletes don't feel the need to perform up to their abilities, they lack the motivation and focus. Intensity tends to stay low because athletes don't feel it is necessary to raise their heart rate, respiration, blood flow, adrenaline, and other physical factors to an optimal level.

• **Lack of importance**. Recent research (Wilson et al., 2001; Wilson and Raglin, 1997) indicates that athletes tend to have lower precompetitive intensity before competitions considered as easy or less important by both the coach and athlete compared with those competitions considered hard or difficult. This lower intensity may reflect the athletes' perceptions that the competition they are about to face is not worthy or demanding of their total athletic ability.

• **Low motivation.** A lack of interest in or motivation to compete will also produce underintensity. Athletes who lack the desire to perform will not feel the need to activate themselves physiologically. Additionally, Czikszentmihalyi (1975) suggested that athletes who perceive that their ability exceeds the demands of the competitive situation will experience boredom, which is reflected in underintensity.

• **Physical causes**. Fatigue from overtraining or overcompeting, sleeping difficulties, and competitive stress can cause underintensity. Other physical causes of underintensity include nutritional deficiencies and injuries. In all cases, athletes suffering from these physical causes will simply not have the physiological resources to activate their bodies to perform their best in competition.

Athlete's Perspective

At times, there are competitions in which the opponents are not equal in talent. When this happens, it is important for the higher caliber runner to stay motivated and interested in the race. This can be a time when the athlete experiments with new race tactics or tries new mechanics. A competitive situation should never be wasted because there are significant potential gains to be made from each competition. An athlete should not let her intensity level down or consider a race less important just because the level of talent in the race may not be of the highest caliber.

■ ■ ■ ■ ■

As in most sports, athletes in alpine skiing are often required to step down from a higher level of competition to return home to qualify for their state, regional, or national championships. To perform as an underdog involves one approach, and to perform as a favorite involves an entirely new approach. In the latter case, the challenge is almost always psychological, because the variables of terrain and courses set are easily within the athletes' abilities. Psychologically, favorites fear the underdogs who are gunning for their uniform, their position, and the chance to knock them off. The life of a junior competitor revolves around opportunities to compete against "national" team athletes, wearers of the uniforms they so covet. Coaches go to great lengths to create race-day simulations for their top competitors to ensure no letdown and to instill in their athletes the ability to perform at all levels. For many athletes, qualifying is a big enough carrot to raise the intensity level; however, qualifying is not enough for other athletes. A year after not making a regional championship and performing poorly at the state championships, two boys I coached made the U.S. ski team. There was no better motivation for a hard summer and fall of training than the memory of failing during the past season at a level below them.

■　■　■　■　■

Symptoms of Underintensity

Underintensity may be evident in some athletes and in some competitive situations, such as when an athlete is far superior to her opponent and is expected to win easily or when an athlete has a large and seemingly insurmountable lead in a competition. As with overintensity, underintensity can manifest itself physically, behaviorally, and psychologically. Psychological symptoms include a decline in interest and motivation to compete, difficulty narrowing concentration, an oversensitivity to external distractions, and a generalized feeling of "not being all there." Physical signs of underintensity include low levels of heart rate, respiration, and adrenaline. These changes are experienced as low energy and feelings of lethargy. Behaviorally, underintensity can be seen as a decrease in pace during competition, "let-down" body language, a reduction in performance-relevant behaviors (e.g., routines), an increase in mistakes, and a decline in competitive performance.

Cognitive Psych-Up Techniques

Cognitive psych-up techniques aim to control intensity at its source, by altering the thoughts that trigger the decline in intensity. These strategies change the beliefs and perceptions that cause athletes to lose intensity before and during a competition. By teaching these techniques to athletes, consultants can help them to counter these "let-downs" and maintain optimal intensity that will enable them to perform their best.

• **Raise personal importance of competition**. Athletes' intensity can be affected by how they perceive the importance of the competition and the difficulty of the opponent. Athletes who see little importance in the competition may experience underintensity, and poor performance is likely to follow. In such instances, the athlete needs to raise the personal importance of the competition by finding value in the competition and resetting his competitive goals according to those new perceptions. If the competition isn't seen as important or the opponents aren't viewed as challenging, then athletes need to shift their motivation and focus from the outcome to other aspects of the competition that will maintain intensity and maximize performance, such as working on new technique or tactics. By altering their perceptions about the competition and changing their goals in a way that will challenge and motivate them, athletes can internally elevate their intensity and maintain a high level of performance.

• **Bring confidence back to earth**. Although it is important for athletes to believe they can be successful, overconfidence can often lead to disaster. Confident athletes believe they can be successful if they work hard and perform their best. Overconfident athletes believe that their victory is guaranteed no matter what they do. Athletes need to be reminded of the David versus Goliath effect, in which an overwhelming favorite is beaten because he lacked intensity and didn't expend the necessary effort to win. The emphasis for bringing confidence back down to earth involves helping athletes understand what they need to be successful and maintaining a healthy respect for their opponents.

• **High-energy self-talk**. Let-down self-talk such as "I have this competition won" and "I quit" are commonly associated with feelings of underintensity (Caudill et al., 1983; Williams and Harris, 1998). These types of self-talk produce a physiological decline in intensity that directly interferes with effective performance. In a sense, athletes tell their bodies that there is no longer need to perform, so their bodies shut down and lose their intensity. This self-talk needs to be replaced with high-energy self-talk that will raise physiological intensity to an optimal level (Edwards and Hardy, 1996). For example, the statements described previously should be replaced with "Finish strong" and "Keep at it."

Physical Psych-Up Techniques

The benefit of physical psych-up techniques is that they act directly on the intensity that athletes experience before and during a competition. Whereas other psych-up techniques may take time to influence performance, physical psych-up strategies have an instantaneous effect on performance. When consultants teach these methods to athletes, the athletes learn to recognize and act immediately on the lower intensity, enabling them to regain their optimal intensity and to return a high level of performance.

• **Physical activity**. Intensity is partially the result of the amount of physiological activity athletes experience before a competition. The most direct way to increase intensity in athletes is through vigorous physical activity. The type of physical activity will largely depend on the sport, but many times any type of running, jumping, or active movement will be beneficial. The point is to elevate the athlete's heart rate and blood flow.

• **High-energy body language**. High-energy body language is another effective means of raising intensity. Techniques such as athletes pumping their fists, slapping their thighs, and giving high-fives to their teammates increase intensity by combining energetic physical action, quick and forceful movement, positive thinking, and strong and positive emotions. In addition to the physical increase in intensity, high-energy body language has the powerful effect of drawing athletes' focus into the present, sharpening awareness of their goals, increasing their motivation and resolve, and making them excited about competing. If there are fans present, high-energy body language also can incite a similar increase in intensity among spectators, which athletes can feed on to further heighten their intensity.

Athlete's Perspective

There comes a point when every athlete has the opportunity to take her performance to the next level. This often can be predicted in practice but only realized in competition. How athletes handle this opportunity is connected to how they perceive their abilities. If they feel that they don't belong in the competition (because it is either too hard or too easy), then they are not likely to have a positive experience. An athlete has to view each competition as an opportunity to grow, and when she does, she is more likely to grow along with it as well.

■   ■   ■   ■   ■

Key Points

- Intensity is the physiological reactions (e.g., heart rate, respiration, blood flow, adrenaline) that athletes experience before and during a competition and whether they perceive that intensity as helpful or harmful.
- Athletes' level of intensity will determine how well they perform in competition.
- Overintensity is often characterized by muscle tension, shallow breathing, rapid heart rate, and doubts about an athlete's ability to succeed.
- Underintensity typically is characterized by lethargy accompanied by a loss of motivation and difficulty focusing.
- Because optimal intensity is personal, athletes must determine their own ideal level of intensity.
- There are four major theories aimed at explaining the relationship between intensity and athletic performance.

- To determine ideal intensity, athletes can recall past competitions in which they have performed well and poorly and examine the competitive situation and their thoughts, emotions, and physiological experiences.
- Athletes can use a variety of strategies to raise or lower their intensity to an optimal level.

Review Questions

1. List several common symptoms of overintensity.
2. What are the causes of overintensity?
3. If an athlete is overly nervous before a competition and the coach perceives that her level of intensity is above what is needed for optimal performance, what suggestions might the coach make that would allow the athlete to control her overintensity?
4. List several common symptoms of underintensity.
5. What are the causes of underintensity?
6. An athlete is having a hard time preparing mentally for an upcoming contest. The athlete appears flat and unemotional before the game, and the coach knows that this athlete typically performs best when intensity is high. What strategies might be used to raise the level of intensity for this athlete?

4

Focus

Richard K. Stratton, PhD—researcher
Kim Cusimano, PhD—consultant
Chuck Hartman—coach
Nicole DeBoom, BA—athlete

The objectives of this chapter are

- to review the latest theories and research and examine the key components of focus;
- to describe how focus can be assessed;
- to discuss the influence that focus styles have on the ability to focus; and
- to detail a variety of strategies for developing, maintaining, and regaining focus.

Maintaining focus during competition is essential to achieving optimal performance. If athletes are unable to focus on relevant information and avoid the numerous distractions that are a regular part of sport competition, athletes have little chance of performing at their highest level and achieving their goals.

Despite this importance, focus may be the most misunderstood psychological contributor to performance, and this lack of understanding causes coaches and athletes to use focus in ways that actually hinder rather than help performance. Most athletes think of focus as concentrating on one thing for a long time. In fact, a number of years ago, former Australian Open tennis champion Hana Mandlikova said that she improved her game by staring at a tennis ball for 10 minutes a day. Although this exercise might have helped her become more skilled at staring at a stationary ball for long periods of time, it is not likely to have helped her tennis (Taylor, 2001).

Focus in most sports is a much more complex process that involves myriad cues on which athletes must focus. Each sport has qualities and conditions that make it unique and that require a specific understanding of optimal focus. Researchers and consultants are responsible for studying and fully understanding the complexity of focus. Coaches and athletes must then draw on their own experiences and apply this knowledge to their particular sports to ensure that athletes have the tools to maintain an optimal focus and maximize their competitive performances.

Key Issues

A significant challenge for athletes in training and competition is to maintain an effective focus and avoid distractions that can interfere with optimal performance. Because of its complexity, researchers have been challenged to understand focus, and consultants and coaches have struggled with how they can help athletes improve their ability to focus in training and competition. Clarifying what focus is, how it affects performance, and the ways it can be developed is an essential step for athletes to optimize their ability to focus and maximize their competitive performances.

Chapter Purpose and Author Team

The purpose of this chapter is to provide an in-depth understanding of the influence that focus has on sport performance. This objective will be accomplished by offering readers four perspectives. The latest theory and research are integrated to provide a solid scientific foundation on which coaches and athletes can draw (by Dr. Richard Stratton). The chapter is structured around the primary applied concerns that consultants address in their work with athletes (by Dr. Kim Cusimano). Throughout the chapter, a coach (Chuck Hartman) and an athlete (Nicole DeBoom) describe their experiences with focus in relation to performance and provide perspective on the role that focus plays in the real world of sport competition.

Understanding Focus in Sport

Previous writers have used various terms to describe the phenomenon of focus including *attention, concentration,* and *cognitive effort.* Kahneman (1973) discussed the relationship between attention and cognitive effort. Variations in cognitive effort are related to a person's ability to carry out multiple activities within the same time frame. Moran (1996) used the term *concentration* as he explored the relationship between attention and sport performance. He described concentration as the capacity to exert mental effort on a task while ignoring distractions. Moran further suggested that the terms *attention* and *concentration* can be used interchangeably. Jackson and Csikszentmihalyi (1999) stated that "flow is about focus" (p. 5), noting that focus is essential to a state of consciousness in which athletes are totally absorbed in the activity in which they are engaged.

These terms, however, are not used in this chapter because they lack the clarity and depth to adequately describe the phenomenon. *Attention* lacks precision and is often thought of in terms of "pay attention." *Concentration* is too often thought of as attending to only one thing at a time and, thus, lacks the flexibility to include a wider range of attentional phenomena. *Cognitive effort* is unclear and largely unfamiliar to the lay population. For the sake of consistency and clarity, we use the term *focus* in this chapter to describe the phenomenon of attending to particular internal and external cues that positively or negatively influence athletic performance. This definition of focus is drawn from the latest theoretical and empirical research yet is sufficiently simple, clear, and practical for use by consultants, coaches, and athletes.

Focus is essential to competitive success because it acts as the "director" of athletes' competitive efforts. Optimal focus enables athletes to attend to relevant cues, evaluate competitive conditions, acquire pertinent information, plan strategies, make sound decisions, and act in ways that will maximize competitive performance. Poor focus directs attention away from beneficial information and onto cues that distract athletes from these processes.

Athlete's Perspective

Focus is probably the most important aspect of triathlon racing. It can either guarantee success or trigger failure. Triathletes need to practice focus every day in training so they can rely on it in a race. Swimming, cycling, and running all require great amounts of internal focus. In many cases, the clock is your only competitor, so you need to be very in tune with yourself to push to your limits. When I was racing as an amateur, I was often racing against people who started in a different wave (which could be an hour before or after me), so I wouldn't know who won the overall title until the end of the race. I had to stay focused the entire time, so that I would not make mistakes in the transition area or forget to consume enough calories.

■ ■ ■ ■ ■

An evolution of theory, research, and practical knowledge has led to dramatic advancements in our understanding of the function of focus and the sophisticated way in which it influences athletic performance. This increased insight has involved collaboration from many fields, including psychology, physiology, sensation, perception, and sport science.

Early discussions of attention were built around what were known as single-channel models, which suggested that individuals are only able to perform one task within a given time frame (Keele, 1973). Single-channel models were based primarily on an understanding of how the central nervous system functions; specifically, that sensory or motor neurons are only capable of transmitting one piece of information at a time (Shea, Shebilske, and Worchel, 1993).

However, the applicability of the single-channel models of attention to human performance has been questioned (Allport, Antonis, and Reynolds, 1972; Kahneman, 1973). Although examples exist honoring single-channel processing in sports (e.g., execution of rudimentary skills), most would agree that single-channel processing cannot adequately account for the myriad cues that athletes must focus on and respond to in order to perform in most sports. It has been argued that the human body contains thousands of neural pathways, which allow for simultaneous parallel processing of information and, thus, the potential for performing multiple tasks at the same time (Kahneman, 1973).

As criticism of the single-channel models of attention grew (Magill, 2001), other models were proposed. As a group, these alternatives are known as capacity models of attention (Magill, 2001), which posit that individuals have the ability to focus on and perform multiple tasks simultaneously. A person's attention is considered flexible but not unlimited. Kahneman (1973), in describing such a model, suggested that the notion of flexible attention is akin to a balloon in which air—attentional demands—can be added up to a point, beyond which additional air will cause the balloon to burst. Applied to sports, these models indicate that athletes are capable of focusing on and responding to significant amounts of information but will reach a point where they can neither attend nor react to more information.

There are several critical constraints to a person's attentional flexibility. First, athletes must attain an optimal level of intensity to have all attentional resources available to them (see chapter 3). Variations in intensity cause athletes to redirect their attention to nonessential information that hinders their ability to achieve optimal focus and maximum performance. Second, skill acquisition must be maximized to free up attentional resources. The less athletes need to focus on during the execution of skills, the more they can focus on optimizing their performances. Third, performance that is automated and requires little conscious effort enhances athletes' attentional abilities (Kahneman, 1973). For example, research has shown that in a task that involved both skill execution and information gathering, experts were better at focusing on and searching for visual cues than were novices (Abernethy and Russell, 1987), and attempts to improve the novices' focus and search skills were unsuccessful (Abernethy, 1999). These findings indicate that novices, because they must devote so much of their attention to performing the skill, lack the capacity to effectively focus on and engage in the visual search.

Coach's Perspective

Intensity and focus are directly related. Our players with the best levels of focus also had high levels of intensity. But, in baseball, because we play so often, this intensity is not the "psyched up" type of intensity but rather a persistent desire to play well and win. Players who lack this consistent intensity seem to have difficulty maintaining their concentration.

■   ■   ■   ■   ■

Athlete's Perspective

In triathlons, you need to be mentally flexible. Many external factors can cause an athlete to lose her focus and throw in the towel. It's amazing how many professionals will quit a race if they get a flat tire or a penalty. I think they are not prepared to deal with something that might throw a wrench into their race plan. In triathlons, it's so important to continually reassess the situation. Too many people let emotions take over when they could salvage their race by staying calm. You cannot predict what will happen out there. You cannot control anyone's actions except your own.

■   ■   ■   ■   ■

Components of Focus

Focus consists of several essential components. The overall notion of focus can be thought of as a complete machine, and individual components can be thought of as the parts of the functioning machine.

Voluntary or Involuntary Focus

Attention has been described in the literature in two distinct ways: (1) controlled or conscious information processing and (2) involuntary or unconscious processing (Nideffer, 1995; Schiffrin and Schneider, 1997; Wegner, 1994). Controlled processing is the act of consciously focusing atten-

tion and is effortful in nature. Athletes use this type of focus when learning a new skill, rehearsing a performance mentally, or using imagery. During unconscious processing, athletes become completely immersed in the sport task without conscious effort and yet experience clear and precise focus. The conscious effort and repetition that are necessary early in skill development and performance execution, and the increased learning that comes from repetition, allow athletes to later engage in involuntary focus and automatic movement (Huey, 1968).

Orienting Response

An orienting response refers to athletes' tendencies to automatically focus on anything new that comes into awareness (Pavlov, 1927). For example, when a cyclist in a peloton crashes, other riders will automatically focus on it and respond accordingly.

Athletes' ability to focus optimally may influence the accuracy of their orienting response (Reeve, 1976). If athletes are distracted from the competition, they may miss cues that are important to their performance. To return to the cycling example, if a cyclist behind the crash is distracted (e.g., by cheering fans on the side of the road), he may take too long to process and react to this highly relevant cue and have insufficient time to avoid the accident.

Attention Span

Attention span is defined as how long an athlete can focus on a task (Kauss, 2001). The duration that athletes can focus on a particular set of cues is influenced by their personal characteristics and the nature of the activity. Attention span is an individual trait, and athletes will vary in the length of time they are able to maintain focus (Butler and McKelvie, 1985). In addition, attention span is influenced by athletes' interest in the task. Athletes who are highly engaged in an activity are better able to focus effectively than those uninterested or bored by the activity. Attention span is also affected by the demands of the sport. Some sports require that athletes maintain focus for only a few seconds (e.g., 100-meter dash), whereas other sports demand that focus be kept for several hours (e.g., a marathon). To focus effectively, athletes must understand their focus capabilities, their interest in the sport, and the focus demands of the sport.

Infielders and outfielders are constantly struggling to maintain their focus because most of the action involves the pitcher and the catcher. We try various strategies to keep them in the game so they don't get caught by surprise when a ball is hit to them. Our strategy for this is to remind them to play as if every ball is coming to them.

■　■　■　■　■

Selective Attention

Selective attention is the ability of athletes to focus on certain cues to the exclusion of others (Wrisberg and Shea, 1978). Athletes can selectively attend to internal or external cues. Internal cues refer to any information that athletes could focus on inside of themselves, for example, thoughts, emotions, physiological activity, and kinesthetic feedback. External cues involve information that athletes could attend to outside of themselves, for instance, sights, sounds, smells, touch, and other sensory feedback.

Every sport has relevant cues, which help athletes perform optimally, and distracting cues, which keep athletes from performing their best. Athletes' ability to focus depends on how well they are able to selectively attend to relevant internal and external cues and ignore distracting cues.

Relevant Cues

Performance-relevant cues help athletes to perform their best (Nideffer, 1995). Internal-relevant cues include positive thinking, helpful emotions, information about athletes' intensity and physiology, kinesthetic feedback related to technique, and analysis, integration, and decision making related to competitive information. External-relevant cues consist of competitive conditions, communication between teammates, scrutiny of opponents, physical contact with other competitors, awareness of sports equipment, observation of competitive tactics, and recognition of the score and time left in the competition. Performance-relevant cues are sport specific, meaning the sport that athletes participate in will dictate what is relevant.

Distracting Cues

The second component important to maintaining focus is athletes' ability to ignore cues that distract them from performing their best. The ability to focus on relevant cues while not attending to distracting cues is essential for optimal sport focus.

There are two types of distracting cues: interfering and irrelevant (Taylor, 2001).

Interfering cues are internal or external cues that hinder performance directly, for example, negative thoughts, other competitors, crowd noise, and thinking about past mistakes (Nideffer, 1995). Focusing on interfering cues reduces motivation, lowers confidence, raises intensity, generates negative emotions, and hinders athletes' ability to focus on relevant cues. This interference, and the associated mental and physical deterioration, ensure a less than optimal performance.

Irrelevant cues take athletes' minds away from an effective focus but do not directly hurt performance, for example, social plans for that evening, work that is due the following day, or what athletes will eat after the competition. By focusing on such irrelevant information, the athlete loses optimal focus and performance declines. For instance, a runner, in the last mile of a half marathon, starts thinking about the meal he will have at his favorite restaurant that evening. While he is engaged in this thought, his pace slackens and he is unaware of another runner catching up to him before the finish. By attending to the irrelevant cue of food, he wasn't able to maintain his focus on his pace and he missed the more important cue of the approaching runner's footsteps, which would have given him a chance to respond quickly and perhaps hold off the charging competitor.

Perceptual Narrowing

Perceptual narrowing defines a relationship between attention and physiological arousal. Easterbrook (1959) and Landers (1980) described a model in which the processing of relevant and irrelevant cues varies depending on athletes' level of arousal. At low levels of arousal, athletes process both relevant and irrelevant information in a mostly unfocused manner. An increase in arousal results in more effective focus, where relevant cues are processed more readily and irrelevant information is more easily ignored. However, as arousal progresses to even higher levels, focus and arousal assume a curvilinear relationship, whereby athletes' focus narrows to a point at which even relevant cues are missed—the tunnel-vision effect.

Hebb (1976) suggested that this narrowing of attention at high levels of arousal is attributable to the operation of the central nervous system (CNS). The CNS functions much like a household electrical system. At high levels of arousal, the CNS detects potential for overload and, like an electrical system, begins to shut down less important systems with the goal of protecting the core functions of the human body. For athletes, increased arousal may signal a perceived threat, causing the CNS to narrow focus onto the immediate threat to ensure that the athletes pay attention to and avoid the danger. Unfortunately, this action often results in a less effective focus and a decline in performance.

Athlete's Perspective

I have a great example in my husband, Tim, the current Ironman world champion, and his ultimate level of focus while racing. The 2001 Hawaii Ironman World Championship was a terrible day as far as conditions go. It's always hot and windy in Kona, but in 2001, it had rained the night before and as the winds picked up to hurricane force, the sun came out and created a sauna effect to add to the athletes' misery.

Tim had been pulled over early in the bike ride for a questionable position penalty. He had to get off his bike, effectually breaking his rhythm, and then get back into his groove knowing that he would be spending 3 minutes in the "sin bin" before he was allowed to start the run. He needed all the focus he could muster to continue to push within his limits for the remaining 4 hours of the bike ride. The Ironman requires more than 8 hours of racing, and if Tim had lost focus and pushed beyond his limits to make up for his impending penalty, he would have probably suffered serious consequences later in the run.

Tim rode into transition and stood in the penalty box for 3 minutes while watching his toughest competitors head onto the run ahead of him. It was like watching a caged lion; Tim was calm and cool (a.k.a. focused!), but he was rearing to go. Once he got out onto the run, no one stood a chance. Tim never lost his focus. In fact, he was so focused that he blocked out most external distractions. When I crossed paths with Tim (I was on my way to a 13th-place finish for the women), he had about 2 miles left and he was winning by almost 15 minutes! I stopped, stood in the middle of the road, and waved my arms, so excited to see my husband in first! Tim, however, didn't see me. He ran right by me. He later said, "You wouldn't believe how many people are cheering out there. You can't expend energy acknowledging everyone who cheers for you. You have to stay focused." I think Tim was experiencing a bit of the tunnel-vision effect. If his tunnel vision had narrowed much more, he may have missed some important cues. This shows how much focus is needed to win a race like the Ironman.

■　■　■　■　■

Focus Style

There is considerable evidence that athletes focus on and are distracted by different cues (Nideffer, 1976; Van Schyock and Grasha, 1983). Some athletes are highly sensitive to internal cues whereas others respond more readily to external cues. This difference in the ways that athletes focus is referred to as focus style (Nideffer and Sagal, 2001; Taylor, 2001). Understanding athletes' focus styles helps them to become aware of their attentional strength and weaknesses, recognize why they have difficulties focusing, and develop appropriate interventions to enhance their ability to focus.

Focus style is considered an athlete's preference for attending to certain cues (Taylor, 2001). Depending on their focus style, athletes are more comfortable focusing on some cues and avoiding or ignoring other cues. All athletes have a particular style that influences their ability to focus in their sport. This focus style is most evident when athletes are under pressure. Although focus styles are not readily amenable to change, the goal is for athletes to maximize their focus strengths and reduce the impact of their focus weaknesses in training and competitive performance.

Focus styles involve how athletes focus along two dimensions in response to the attentional demands of a sport: direction and width (Nideffer, 1990). Direction refers to whether athletes are focusing on cues inside or outside of themselves. Width relates to whether they are required to focus on just a few cues or a wide range of cues. Athletes' focus styles can be determined on the basis of which type of information along these two dimensions they attend to most comfortably.

• **Broad-external.** The broad-external focus style involves athletes' ability to attend to a wide range of cues outside themselves (Nideffer, 1990). Athletes must focus on and process a diverse array of external cues, such as their own field position, placement of teammates and opposing players on the field, and plays that unfold in front of them. Athletes who must have a broad-external focus style to perform well include football quarterbacks, basketball point guards, and soccer players.

• **Broad-internal.** Analysis of strategies and problem solving during competitive situations are associated with a broad-internal focus style (Nideffer, 1990). This focus style requires athletes (and coaches) to analyze and integrate large amounts of information, make decisions, and produce solutions and courses of actions based on those analyses. Coaches in team sports and athletes such as chess players, baseball catchers, and golfers must have a broad-internal focus style to perform their best.

- **Narrow-external.** A narrow-external focus style involves athletes directing their attention to one or two cues outside of themselves that are essential for performance (Nideffer, 1990). This focus style requires athletes to identify and attend to a few external cues while eliminating the imposition of both internal and external cues that could hurt that singular focus. Athletes who need to have a narrow-external focus include shooters and baseball pitchers.

- **Narrow-internal.** The ability to narrow focus and direct it to one or two internal cues is associated with a narrow-internal focus style. Athletes with a narrow-internal focus style are adept at organizing information and mentally rehearsing their performance (Nideffer, 1990). Sports that require a narrow-internal focus include weightlifting, sprinting, and shot put. This very narrow focus helps athletes block out distractions and confine focus to only the most relevant internal cues (e.g., positive thoughts, technique, intensity).

Athlete's Perspective

In triathlons, listening to your body is probably the most important part of racing up to your potential. You need to know the signs that precede breakdown. Many people find themselves going along just fine, and suddenly they bonk. They don't simulate race situations in practice, so they don't know what signs to look for to avoid a breakdown. For me, internal cues are mostly nutrition oriented. When I am riding and I suddenly start feeling very crabby and negative, I know I need to consume some calories. If I reach "crabby stage," I know I've got to be really smart if I want to salvage the race.

■ ■ ■ ■ ■

Assessing Focus

Given the importance of focus to athletic performance, it is incumbent on researchers, consultants, coaches, and athletes to develop the means to assess athletes' focus capabilities and the focus demands of the sports in which they compete. This first step is necessary for athletes to develop the tools to use their focus style. Their knowledge of the focus demands of their sport helps them develop skills that will maximize their focusing capabilities to perform optimally.

Test of Attentional and Interpersonal Style

The Test of Attentional and Interpersonal Style (TAIS; Nideffer, 1976) is a 144-item test designed to assess 17 different ways that individuals focus and interact with others. Subjects are asked to indicate on a 4-point Likert scale, ranging from "not at all" to "very much so," how they feel at the moment. Nideffer suggested that athletes' ability to focus effectively based on the demands of the sport will have a significant influence on the quality of their performances. Abbreviated and sport-specific versions of the TAIS have been developed to more accurately and efficiently assess athletes' ability to focus.

Systematic Recall

Because most athletes do not have access to the TAIS, a simpler and more direct means of assessing focus style is needed. Systematic recall is a useful tool for helping athletes to determine their attentional strengths and weaknesses. This process begins by having athletes recall past training and competitive situations when they performed well. Athletes then determine what cues they were focused on and how they altered their focus as needed. They then recall past training and competitions when they performed poorly and consider what they were focusing on in these situations and how it hurt performance. Most athletes will find that a pattern emerges in which they tend to perform best when they focus a particular way—using their natural focus style—and perform poorly when they focus another way (Taylor, 2001).

Athletes must understand their focus style to manage it effectively. To perform optimally, athletes must understand how they focus best and learn to actively focus in a way that is consistent with their focus style. Managing their focus style well becomes particularly important in competitive pressure situations. Athletes under pressure tend to revert back to a focus style that will hinder rather than help their performance (Nideffer, 1990).

Demands of Sport

The demands of particular sports play an essential role in how athletes focus during training and competition. Different sports require different kinds of focus, and athletes must understand the specific demands of a sport to focus effectively. The goal is for athletes to use their focus style and skills to focus optimally, which means attending to relevant cues and ignoring distracting cues specific to that sport.

To gain this understanding, athletes must scrutinize their sport, looking for cues that will facilitate performance and those that will interfere with performance. These cues should include internal and external as well as broad and narrow cues. Once athletes understand these cues, they can explore the focusing sequence that will enable them to perform their best. For example, a baseball shortstop begins with a narrow-internal focus in which he focuses on the hitting report he received from his coach about the batter at the plate. He then shifts to a broad-internal focus whereby that information is integrated with the current game situation, he decides where he should position himself, and he analyzes how he should respond to different scenarios with this batter. The player then moves to a broad-external focus to see the entire field of play. As the pitcher begins his wind-up, the shortstop shifts to a narrow-external focus to see the batter hit the ball and reacts accordingly. Understanding their focus style and the demands of their sport gives athletes the knowledge to develop focus skills and adapt to the unique requirements of their sport.

Focus Strategies

Once athletes understand their focus style and the focus demands of their sport, they can develop the skills to maximize their focus strengths, minimize their focus weaknesses, and adjust to the unique focus challenges that their sport presents to them. At the heart of effective focusing is the ability to shift focus according to needs of the particular competitive situation. If athletes have a focus style that is optimal for the sport scenario, they will focus effectively and perform well. If the competitive situation has focus demands that are different than their natural focus style, problems in performance may arise. All sports require a variety of shifts in focus during the course of training and competition. The ability to shift focus on demand is a skill that can be learned and, with practice, mastered. This section examines a variety of focus techniques that athletes can use to facilitate the development of optimal focus.

Mindfulness: Being in the Moment

Performance in sport is greatly influenced by athletes' ability to be "mindful"; to remain in the present, and to be centered and relaxed regardless of what is happening in the competitive situation. Many athletes possess characteristics such as perfectionism, high expectations, anxiety, and an outcome orientation, which are incongruent with the notion of mindfulness. These athletes associate mindfulness with inaction and loss of control, which seem counterproductive to optimal performance.

Mindfulness, however, is vastly different than the way many athletes conceive it, and it offers many benefits to focusing and athletic performance. Mindfulness teaches athletes to focus on the present rather than dwelling on past mistakes or future results. This present focus enables athletes to be more alert to relevant performance cues and allows them to more easily disregard distracting cues. Mindfulness produces a relaxed physiological state that enables the body to perform in competition what it has learned in training. This calm demeanor comes from having athletes focus on the physiological symptoms of a relaxed body: low heart rate, relaxed muscles, slow and deep breathing (for more on relaxation, see chapter 3). In this state, athletes become more confident because they are controlling these symptoms and working toward a desired goal. Mindfulness can be achieved using various forms of meditation (e.g., transcendental meditation, Zen meditation, the relaxation response; Benson, 1977) as well as different types of muscle relaxation (e.g., progressive and passive relaxation; Jacobson, 1930).

Process Focus

Perhaps the greatest obstacle to effective focus is having an outcome focus during a competition. Outcome focus involves athletes focusing on the possible results of a competition: winning, losing, rankings, or whom they might lose to or defeat. Many athletes believe that by focusing on the outcome, they are more likely to achieve that outcome. In fact, the result of an outcome focus is usually the exact opposite of the outcome athletes want, specifically, performing their best in competition. What most athletes do not realize is that having an outcome focus hurts performance because if athletes are focused on the outcome, they are not focused on performing well to achieve their goal.

When athletes use an outcome focus, performance declines for a couple of reasons. First, athletes are no longer focusing on cues that will help them perform well. Second, an outcome focus, and the preoccupation with results, can cause athletes to feel pressure and become anxious, which will hurt competitive performance.

Coach's Perspective

We teach our players to not focus on outcome. We don't want them to let the fear of losing prevent them from playing well. When things start to go bad, players may begin to lose focus. Interventions such as quick team meetings on the field or in the dugout are important to break this misdirected focus.

■　■　■　■　■

The way to achieve success in a competition is to focus on the process of the event. A process focus—the "how" of performing well—involves athletes attending to cues that are necessary for optimal performance. An essential question for athletes to ask themselves to achieve a process focus is, "What do I need to do now to perform my best?" This question takes athletes away from a poorly focused state, such as dwelling on past mistakes or future worries, and directs their attention to the present and what they can control to perform their best.

To foster a process focus, athletes find the best answer to the previous question: "What do I need to do now?" They can benefit from having specific cues that, when they lose focus, bring them back to the process. Cues can be found in technical, tactical, psychological, physiological, social, and environmental components of sport. From the many cues on which athletes could focus, they must filter out irrelevant options and narrow their focus to the most relevant cues to achieve optimal performance. Additionally, the answer to the preceding question will change during the course of competition, and athletes must be able to adapt their responses to the unique demands of the particular competitive situation (Taylor, 2001).

Reset Procedure

For most sports, maintaining focus for an entire event is virtually impossible because it is mentally and physically draining to focus continuously throughout a competition. Athletes then need to be able to "release" their focus periodically and yet regain focus on demand. A reset procedure is the process of using focusing techniques to redirect athletes' attention on performance-enhancing cues after a break or when distracted (Pacelli, 1997). There are two components of a reset procedure: Identify one's vulnerabilities, and create a process for redirecting focus onto performance-relevant cues.

First, to identify their vulnerabilities, athletes must understand what they find most distracting. For example, an athlete with a narrow-internal focus style may find that she is easily distracted if there is a great deal of activity around her. This awareness will enable her to recognize when she is faced with a competitive situation that causes focusing problems. Second, this understanding allows her to use previously identified and practiced focusing techniques to redirect her focus when lost and improve performance. All of the techniques described in the section on focusing strategies can be used as part of athletes' reset procedures.

Coach's Perspective

I have two examples of this type of problem: We had an infielder who made 43 errorless fielding attempts. He made an error on the 44th attempt and then missed his next two straight fielding attempts. We had a pitcher who, after giving up a home run, would throw four straight balls to the next batter. We tried to break this pattern by teaching him a cue (see following section on key words), PEP, which stood for "play every pitch." We also teach our players to separate the different aspects of their game. We don't want problems they may be having with their hitting to carry over to their fielding or vice versa.

■　■　■　■　■

Key Words

Key words are powerful tools athletes can use to focus more effectively in training and competition (Loehr, 1994). Key words are verbal cues that remind athletes on what they need to focus. Key words can relate to any area that influences performance, including technique, tactics, physiology, thoughts, emotions, behavior, and conditions. The value of key words is that, when athletes lose focus, repeating a predetermined key word will redirect their focus back onto performance-relevant cues.

For example, a triathlete developed a set of key words to help her focus during her races. For the swim, she knew that she tended to get nervous before the start, which caused her to go out too fast and tire quickly, so her swim key words were "composed and patient" to remind her to stay calm and not to rush. During her rides, she often forgot to eat and drink enough, so her bike key words were "fuel is cool" to make sure she paid attention to her nutrition. Finally, on the run, she would often tighten up late in the race, so her run key words were "long and loose" to remind her to stay relaxed and to keep her stride long.

Key words have value in several ways. First, they can be used to establish focus at the start of the competition. By repeating their key words just before a competition, athletes can actively shift focus in preparation for the event, turn away from distractions, and narrow their focus on performance-relevant cues. Second, athletes can use key words to consistently maintain their focus. Using key words regularly during the course of competition, athletes can constantly remind themselves of what will enable them to focus effectively. Third, because athletes will inevitably lose focus during competition, key words can be used as a reset procedure to help them regain focus.

Athlete's Perspective

Running is not as natural for me as other sports. Although I was a very fast runner when I was growing up, I did not compete throughout high school and college. I missed those reminders and reprimands from coaches that would have ingrained what to do when I'm tired and my form starts to crumble. Now, as a professional triathlete, I need to focus on key words and positive thinking the entire time during my runs, whether I'm practicing or racing. Things will be going along great, and then suddenly I feel terrible and I realize that my shoulders are no longer relaxed and I'm leaning forward too much. I have to think, "Shoulders loose!" and, "Stay upright!"

■　■　■　■　■

Simulation Training

Training and competition are vastly different experiences for athletes. Training typically emphasizes skill development and tactical rehearsal. Competition introduces demands and pressures beyond those normally found in training, which place a greater burden on athletes' abilities to focus. Simulation training is useful for improving athletes' ability to focus in competition. Simulation training involves making practice as "real" as possible by helping athletes to train like they compete. For example, a cross country running team could simulate a race among team members that would require them to respond to common race challenges such as weather, course conditions, opponents, tactics, and pace. The value of this practice is that it approximates the demands and pressures of competition and allows athletes to respond positively to the focusing challenges of competition before they actually compete.

Simulation training enables athletes to develop and master the skills they will need to maintain optimal focus and perform their best in competition. In simulated competitions, athletes become aware of what they will confront in actual competition—what they need to focus on, what the potential distractions are—and can then practice an effective focus for competition. During competition, athletes will be more confident that they have the ability to focus effectively and avoid distractions because they have practiced these skills repeatedly in simulation training.

Athlete's Perspective

Simulation training can help so much in triathlon racing, because you know what to expect when you get to the race. My first triathlon was a hilarious debacle. Because I was fresh off my collegiate swimming career, I was one of the first people out of the water. I had borrowed a bike from a friend and didn't really know how to use his pedals and bike shoes. I spent almost 10 minutes trying to get on the bike. I finally got out there, did the bike ride, and tried to start running. I felt like I had no butt. I had absolutely no muscle memory for that sequence of activities. Needless to say, I was not "hooked" on triathlon from my first race. However, my competitive drive said, "I know I can do better than that," which kept me going. Now I do brick workouts at least twice a week, where I combine two or three disciplines into one workout. Sometimes I do bike–run workouts, sometimes I do swim–bike workouts, and sometimes I swim, bike, and run. Now in a race, I *know* I'm going to feel awful, so I expect it and I push through it with the confidence that things will get better.

■　■　■　■　■

Focus Routines

As stated earlier, in most sports, it is not easy to maintain a process focus through its entire duration. It is only natural that athletes' minds will wander, regardless of mental strength. Fortunately, few sports require uninterrupted focus for the length of the competition. Rather, many sports are actually a series of shorter performances with breaks in between, for example, tennis, golf, gymnastics, and cricket. Even for sports that appear to involve nonstop performance, such as long-distance running and cycling, there are opportunities for athletes to take brief mental breaks, for instance, at water stations and on descents. Taylor (2001) suggested a "focus routine" that is designed specifically to help athletes maintain focus during competition and also takes into account the importance of breaks in competition. Routines are addressed in great detail in chapter 9.

Being well-prepared for the early stages of a competition is not enough for athletes to ensure success. One thing that separates the great athletes from the good ones is their ability to be consistently focused and ready for every performance and to perform consistently to the conclusion of the competition. What athletes think, feel, and do between performances often dictates whether they are focused and prepared to perform their best consistently. Focus routines can be invaluable in helping athletes reach that state of total preparedness. The three-step focus routine—rest, regroup, refocus—allows athletes to fully use these competitive breaks to maximize focus and performance.

Rest

Immediately after the conclusion of a performance or when the opportunity for a mental break arises, athletes should take a few moments to recover physically. Particularly after a long or physically demanding performance in which they become fatigued, athletes should take active steps to rest by taking deep breaths and letting their muscles relax. This phase of the focus routine is especially important near the end of a long competition in which athletes are tired, have difficulty focusing because of their fatigue, and need to recover as much as possible to be ready for the next performance. Deep breathing and relaxing also help athletes center themselves and better prepare for the next performance.

Regroup

This phase of the focus routine addresses athletes' focus on their emotions between performances (see chapter 5). Particularly when they are not performing well or the competition is at a critical juncture, athletes can experience and

become overly focused on a variety of emotions, including excitement, joy, frustration, or anger. Regrouping allows athletes to gain awareness of how their emotions are influencing them and, if this influence is negative, to redirect focus away from the emotions and back to the process. Regrouping helps athletes to let go of unhealthy emotions so they don't adversely affect focus and performance. Because of the powerful influence emotions have on athletes, their ability to "get their act together" between performances may be the most important thing they can do to prepare for the next performance.

Athlete's Perspective

As my coach told me before Wildflower Half Ironman this year, "Don't be negative. Not once." I know people like to keep any negative words out of their routine, but this worked for me. I got my first-ever flat only 1 minute into the bike ride, but I stayed positive and focused on my effort, and I turned the race into a good experience. My result was much better than I had hoped for, but I stayed within myself and didn't get rattled. It was just another tough day on the job.

■   ■   ■   ■   ■

An important realization that can make regrouping easier is that performances in a competition are not directly related to each other. In other words, the chances of being successful in the next performance are in no way associated with how athletes performed in the last performance. For example, a poor uneven parallel bars routine by a gymnast has no direct bearing on how he performs on the pommel horse.

Past and future performances only become connected when athletes dwell on the last performance. For example, if a softball pitcher is focusing on the frustration and anger she feels from having walked the last batter to load the bases, she increases her chances of pitching poorly in the next performance because her negative focus will interfere with her focusing on the next batter. Using the time between performances to regroup will enable athletes to replace the negative emotions with positive ones, thereby increasing their chances of performing well in the future.

Refocus

If athletes have lost focus at the conclusion of a performance, they must regain their focus during the refocus phase. Following rest and regrouping, refocusing involves athletes redirecting their focus on what they need to do in the next performance. This refocusing can involve attending to any performance-relevant cues, including technique, tactics, physiology, psychology, or conditions. Athletes must begin the next performance with a clear focus on what they need to do to perform their best.

Mental Imagery and Other Focusing Techniques

Mental imagery is a powerful focusing tool that can help athletes identify and attend to relevant competitive cues. By using mental imagery, athletes are able to practice focusing on important competitive cues, enabling them to improve their focusing skills before they arrive at the competition. The practice and improved use of their focus skills gained from mental imagery will then allow athletes to better use these skills to maximize their focus and performances in competition. Mental imagery is discussed in greater detail in chapter 8.

Many of the issues that are discussed in other chapters can interfere with effective competitive focus. Internal and external cues, such as loss of motivation, negative thinking, over- or underintensity, harmful emotions, conflict between coaches and athletes, team dynamics, injuries, eating disorders, substance abuse, and concerns about career, can cause athletes to lose focus.

The strategies discussed in each chapter can help athletes improve their focus by clearing their minds of distracting cues. Essential techniques for facilitating focus include goal setting, positive self-talk, relaxation training, emotional control, communication, and support from others. To achieve an effective and consistent focus, athletes must recognize the cause of their focus difficulties and find the most effective method for overcoming the focus challenges they face.

Athlete's Perspective

The best way to guarantee focus while racing is to practice it during every workout so that in a race situation it will be instinctive. Of course, some activities are more natural to a person than others. For example, I am a very natural swimmer. I started swimming when I was 6 years old and have been a competitive swimmer ever since. I have spent countless hours learning technique and constantly being reminded (or reprimanded!) when my stroke would fall apart. By now, at 31 years old, I don't have to think too much about my technique. I have a few key words that I use like "high elbows" and "press the T," but I rarely need to use them, especially in a race. When I'm swimming in a race, the main thing I need to focus on is my breathing, in other words, keeping my effort under control. Because I spent so much time on technique over the years, it is ingrained enough that I can focus on the effort when I'm racing. I believe that helps my performance because I'm not thinking about too many things at once. I'm not overloaded.

■ ■ ■ ■ ■

Focus on the Ultimate Goal

Athletes know what it feels like to achieve optimal focus. Their minds seem empty of unnecessary thoughts. Focus comes naturally and without any effort. Their senses are especially sharp and attuned to the competition. All aspects of their competitive experience—technical, tactical, physical, and mental—come together and work as one. The result is a consistently high level of performance and great satisfaction in their efforts. Many terms are used to describe this phenomenon: peak performance (Williams and Krane, 2001), flow (Csikszentmihalyi, 1990), and being in the zone (Nideffer, 1992). Regardless of what this state is called, the information and strategies discussed in this chapter can help athletes develop the skills to maintain an effective focus so that they can perform their best and achieve that unique experience.

Key Points

- Focus is a complex and often misunderstood contributor to athletic performance.
- Research indicates that individuals have the ability to focus on and perform multiple tasks simultaneously, but that capacity is limited.
- Focus involves athletes attending to relevant cues and ignoring distracting cues during training and competition.
- Key components of focus include voluntary or involuntary focus, the orienting response, attention span, selective attention, and perceptual narrowing.
- Athletes can attend to either internal or external cues and either relevant or distracting cues.
- Athletes appear to possess preferred focus styles that predispose them to be more receptive to certain information and less sensitive to other information.
- Athletes' focus strengths and weaknesses can be assessed by using the Test of Attentional and Interpersonal Style, by systematic recall, and by understanding the demands of their sport.
- Strategies that athletes can use to improve their ability to focus include mindfulness, process focus, reset procedures, key words, simulation training, focus routines, and mental imagery.

Review Questions

1. How does focus influence sport performance?
2. What are the essential components of focus?
3. What are some internal and external cues (both relevant and distracting) that athletes may focus on during competition?
4. What is a focus style and why is it helpful to have a flexible focus style?
5. What are three strategies commonly used to improve focus?

5

Emotions

Marc Jones, PhD—researcher
Jim Taylor, PhD—consultant
Miyako Tanaka-Oulevey, MA—coach
Mary Grigson Daubert, RN—athlete

© Eyewire

The objectives of this chapter are

- to define and operationalize emotions in a way that is scientifically rigorous enough to meet the precision expected by researchers and consultants yet simple and practical enough to be of use to coaches and athletes;
- to explore both scientifically and practically the influence of emotions on athletic performance;
- to discuss why athletes have divergent emotional reactions to competition; and
- to explain how athletes can gain emotional mastery and use emotions to their advantage during competition.

Emotions are as much a part of the competitive sports experience as physical conditioning, equipment, technique, strategy, and teamwork. It could be argued that emotions are the raison d'être of sport competition. The emotions that athletes connect to their sport experiences act as the initial and ongoing impetus to train and compete, whereas the emotions they feel following competition can influence their future motivation, goals, and efforts.

Taylor (2001) suggested that emotions are the ultimate determinants of how athletes perform in competition. The impact of emotions on athletic performance is so powerful and pervasive because they affect every aspect of an athlete's performance: physical, psychological, technical, and tactical. Yet many in the sports world, from researchers and consultants to coaches and athletes, hold misconceptions about how emotions arise, how they affect performance, and whether athletes are capable of altering the emotions they experience.

Key Issues

During training and competition, athletes can experience a broad spectrum of emotions that range from negative emotions, such as frustration and disappointment, to positive emotions, such as excitement and satisfaction. The relationships of these diverse emotions with athletic performance are complex and often counterintuitive, yet these connections have only recently begun to be explored in the sport psychology community. Emotions are clearly an important topic, because the ability of researchers and consultants to understand these interactions and the capacity for coaches and athletes to incorporate the resulting insights and tools into competitive preparation and performance determine whether emotions facilitate or interfere with athletes' performances.

Chapter Purpose and Author Team

The purpose of this chapter is to offer readers a broad and in-depth exploration of the role that emotions play in athletic performance. The researcher (Dr. Marc Jones) integrates the latest theoretical and empirical findings about emotions in the context of the issues raised by the consultant. The consultant (Dr. Jim Taylor) describes the essential areas in which emotions influence performance based on his applied experience working with a wide range of athletes in many sports. The coach (Miyako Tanaka-Oulevey) gives her perspective on how emotions affect athletes. Last, the athlete (Mary Grigson Daubert) discusses the meaning and impact of emotions on her competitive performances.

Athlete's Perspective

Shedding a tear or two during training was not tolerated. My coach didn't stand for any emotional outbursts. He expected his athletes to do as he requested without comment. How you felt was not relevant to him. Besides, on competition day you had to race no matter how you felt. So I tuned out to how my body felt and never analyzed my emotions.

Occasionally, though, I would pop like a shaken champagne bottle. Frustrations, tears, and feelings of total devastation would gush out. Sometimes I was so mad at myself I couldn't ride my bike properly. I would make many mistakes and fight my bike with stiff arms and shoulders. I looked as if I had forgotten how to ride.

After many years of working through my inner responses to situations, I have come to appreciate how much my emotions can affect my athletic performance.

In my 10-year career I won two World Cup races. The races involved very different terrains and different circumstances. But one thing was the same—the way I rode. On those two occasions I felt relaxed and in control of my bike. In fact, the bike was like an extension of my body. I could put it anywhere on the technical trail. My thoughts were clear and focused on the tasks that lie ahead. I had no time for negative thoughts or to daydream. In both instances I only acknowledged irrelevant or negative thoughts and mentally moved back to the task at hand.

■　■　■　■　■

I totally agree that emotions are the raison d'être of sport competition. As a Japanese synchronized swimming national team coach and as a former Olympic medalist, I have experienced many kinds of emotions in many different degrees both in competition and in training.

■　■　■　■　■

Defining Emotions and Emotional Experiences

Arriving at a single definition of emotion is challenging given that it must account for the breadth of influence emotion has on human functioning and must describe diverse experiences such as anger, excitement, embarrassment, guilt, and happiness. At the same time, emotions, however dissimilar they may appear to be, share some common characteristics. From these unifying qualities, Deci (1980) developed a definition that has been used widely in sport psychology research (Jones, 2003; Vallerand, 1983, 1987; Vallerand and Blanchard, 2000):

> An emotion is a reaction to a stimulus event (either actual or imagined). It involves change in the viscera and musculature of the person, is experienced subjectively in characteristic ways, is expressed through such means as facial changes and action tendencies, and may mediate and energize subsequent behaviors. (p. 85)

Although this definition offers a precise and thorough description of emotions, it nevertheless does not do justice to the impact that emotions have on athletes nor does it adequately portray the richness and depth of emotional experience that athletes feel. Suffice it to say that despite our inability to fully describe emotions, all athletes know what emotions feel like and their importance in athletes' sporting lives.

Some emotions influence outcome positively and others negatively. When I was young, I used to try to reduce negative emotions as much as possible. However, the more I tried to dismiss the negative emotions, the stronger they became. I finally decided not to fight with negative emotions; rather, I tried to focus on accepting them, coping with them, and turning them into positive emotions. Because emotions occur in sports, no matter what, we need to recognize the emotions we have in competition or training, realize which emotions influence our outcome positively or negatively, and then to learn how to cope with these emotions.

■　■　■　■　■

Emotion As a Response to Competition

Athletes may respond emotionally to many different internal or external events. For example, a 1,500-meter runner may feel excited as she walks into the stadium to warm up, nervous before her race because she lacks confidence in her ability, and angry after the race because she performed below her expectations. How individuals interpret situations has been given a central role in explaining emotional reactions, and several researchers suggest that athletes only respond emotionally to events that they perceive to have personal relevance (Clore, 1994; Lazarus, 1991, 2000a, 2000b). For example, almost every athlete would feel tremendous pride if he or she won an Olympic gold medal because such an achievement typically carries considerable personal significance.

Influence of Emotions on Athletes

Emotions affect athletes at many levels of personal and sport functioning, including physiological, psychological, and behavioral levels. Understanding the ways in which emotions affect athletes is essential in helping them gain mastery over their emotions during competition.

Emotions lead to physical changes that can have a powerful role in the emotional experience. For example, when we feel happy we are physically relaxed and we smile, when we feel embarrassed we blush, and when we feel sad we cry. Of particular relevance to athletic performance are changes that result from activity of the sympathetic nervous system. These changes are often referred to as the "fight-or-flight response" and are associated with a perception of threat to one's well-being. Emotions that are often associated with this reaction include anger and fear, and the physiological changes that athletes report include a dry mouth, rapid breathing, increased heart rate, increased blood pressure, and muscle tension. These physiological changes are also an important part of the emotional experience because they influence the intensity of the emotions that are felt (Zillmann, 1971). For example, heightened levels of these physiological changes may increase an athletes' level of anger.

However, not all emotions are accompanied by an overt physiological response, and individuals may experience a range of more subtle emotions with less pronounced physiological shifts such as guilt or pride. As a result, the subjective feelings that an athlete experiences must also be recognized as important and are typically assessed in sport psychology research through the administration of self-report inventories (Jones, 2004).

A primary reason why emotions are so important in sport is because of the potential impact they have on athletes and their competitive performances. Taylor (2001) suggested that emotions affect the intensity, motivation, confidence, and focus of athletes. Because the effect of intensity on athletic performance is addressed in chapter 3, we will discuss here how emotions affect the other three psychological factors.

Vallerand and Blanchard (2000) pointed out that many theorists consider emotions to serve a motivational function that can mobilize athletes to channel extra physical and mental resources into their sports. Hanin (2000a) suggested that optimal emotions for sport performance motivate athletes to initiate and maintain the required amount of effort for successful performance, whereas dysfunctional emotions decrease motivation and effort expended in performance. Thus, emotions can lead athletes toward a goal (e.g., excitement) or away from a goal (e.g., fear). Certain emotions can have either effect depending on the individual and the situation. For example, an athlete feeling embarrassed about missing an easy shot in basketball may try to stay away from the ball to avoid further opportunities. Another athlete, by contrast, may respond to her embarrassment by being motivated to take the next big shot.

The relationship between emotion and confidence is particularly pertinent to success in sport. If an athlete is experiencing an emotion that he perceives as counterproductive to optimal performance, such as fear or frustration, he may lose confidence in his ability to succeed and hurt his performances by reducing effort and persistence. Conversely, experiencing an emotion perceived to be beneficial to athletic performance may bolster confidence, thereby increasing motivation and effort (Bandura, 1997; Kerr, 1997; see chapter 2).

Coach's Perspective

As an athlete, I understood that emotions influenced my performance. However, when I started coaching, I didn't know how to help athletes with mental training. When I started coaching at the age of 21, I didn't have my own coaching philosophy. At the beginning, I thought the real work of being a coach was in coaching technical and tactical skills. Of course, the coach has to motivate athletes and make them work hard, but I thought that this part of coaching would be easy. In the first few years, I would always yell at athletes to pump them up before the competition. When they looked nervous, I yelled at them not to be nervous. When they looked anxious or worried, I told them to be confident. I found out that the more I told them not to be nervous, the more nervous they became. I also found out that the athletes didn't gain confidence without being told *how* to gain confidence or how to decrease their anxiety. As I continued coaching, I realized the importance of mental training in coaching. Coaches must know what emotions occur in sports, how much emotions influence athletes, and ways to cope with emotions.

■ ■ ■ ■ ■

Finally, emotions may affect athletes' focus during competition. Increased physiological arousal—caused by fear or anger, for example—can narrow an athlete's focus, which may enhance performance by helping the athlete concentrate on relevant cues and avoid distractions. However, if arousal is too high, focus can become overly narrow, causing athletes to miss task-relevant cues (Easterbrook, 1959) (see chapter 4). In addition, athletes who are experiencing optimal emotions may have fewer distractions and be able to attend more easily to sport-related cues. Hanin (2000a) suggested that optimal emotions for performance ensure efficient use of available resources until task completion. For example, Eysenck and Calvo (1992) indicated that worry may facilitate performance because an individual who is worried about something may allocate extra mental resources to the task. In contrast, dysfunctional emotions may lead to an inappropriate use of resources. For example, a tennis player may be playing well when a questionable line call results in her losing the point. The tennis player becomes angry and, as a result, dwells on the unfairness of the call rather than directing her attention to the next point, which causes her to play poorly and lose the game. Some athletes prefer to experience few emotions because they find any emotions—even pleasant ones—to be distracting and would rather remain calm and emotionally detached during competition (Uphill and Jones, 2004; see chapter 4 for more on focus).

Athlete's Perspective

Over time I noticed small things about how I felt and how I performed. For instance, if I was feeling so happy that I joked around in the morning of competition, I tended to have a fast race with intense focus. The bike was easy to handle and I would try to do wheelies and skids. Pushing myself during the race came naturally. Hurting was fun; it was good. If I had a problem I was able to overcome it smoothly and resume racing. Good results always reflected my good mood. So I realized that to help myself get top results I needed to work on happiness within myself.

Competitions are usually several laps of a circuit with approximately 2 hours of riding. During the 2 hours, many things happen. Not only do you ride among 50 to 80 others, attempting to be first onto the narrow single track, but you also need to stay on top of your machine. Steep ascents, tricky downhills, corners, holes, mud, tree roots, and the occasional wandering spectator keep you busy. For me to win or be a contender I have to concentrate, make myself hurt, use the correct gearing, steer correctly, be assertive, make quick decisions, and anticipate other riders' moves. Last, I need to believe in myself. I need to believe I can do it. As simple as this may sound, it is not easy. I often question my motivation, and it is rare to have a competition where I do everything perfectly and have no doubts. But the less time I spend questioning myself the more focused I am on the race. And good focus produces better results.

■　■　■　■　■

Emotions and Athletic Performance

Emotions can consume all aspects of an athlete's performance by affecting how athletes think, feel, and behave during competition (Hanin, 2000a; Jones, 2003; Lazarus, 2000b; Vallerand and Blanchard, 2000). Research has shown that a wide range of emotions are associated with changes in performance. Jones, Mace, and Williams (2000) examined the relationships between the emotions experienced by international hockey players before and during competition and their performance levels. When the players performed well, they reported feeling more nervous and quick, alert, or active before the game and more confident and relaxed during games than when they played poorly. Research has also shown that the emotions that affect performance may be specific to individual athletes. Hanin and Syrjä (1995a) reported that junior-elite ice hockey players selected 44 positive emotions (e.g., alert, active) and 39 negative emotions (e.g., tense, angry) as being relevant to their performances. All the emotions were either helpful or harmful depending on their idiosyncratic meaning and intensity to the athletes.

Coach's Perspective

Each athlete reacts differently in the same situation. For example, in synchronized swimming, some athletes take excitement, such as that gained by looking at the tremendous number of people in the audience, as a positive stimulus, but some athletes experience excitement as fear. Because each athlete perceives the same situation in different ways, a coach must understand the perceptions of each athlete.

■　■　■　■　■

Pleasant Versus Unpleasant Emotions

Athletes usually describe the emotions they experience as either positive or negative. Positive emotions that athletes may feel include the excitement of competition, the joy of optimal performance, and the exhilaration of success. Negative emotions may include the frustration of poor performance, the anger at a losing effort, the fear of injury, and the disappointment at a failed performance.

Athletes often refer to how these emotions make them feel rather than how the emotions influence their performances. For example, excitement and satisfaction are pleasant (positive) emotions, and anger and disappointment are unpleasant (negative) emotions. Yet, counterintuitively, positive emotions don't always lead to improved performance and negative emotions don't always hurt performance. To the contrary, some positive emotions, such as satisfaction about one's level of performance, can cause complacency and a decrease in performance. Conversely, frustration and anger can increase intensity and raise the quality of performance. For example, Terry and Slade (1995) found that winners in a karate tournament reported higher levels of anger than did losers.

Helpful Versus Harmful Emotions

Athletes cannot just seek positive emotions that make them feel good; rather, they must create emotions that enhance competitive performance. Thus, emotions must be looked at in terms of whether they are helpful or harmful to performance rather than just how good or bad the emotions feel. Athletes, coaches, and sport psychology consultants must also decide whether it is worth experiencing unpleasant emotions if they are also helpful and feeling pleasant emotions if they are harmful. For example, anger may improve the quality of an athlete's performance, but the consequences of being angry may be so unpleasant that it is not worth experiencing for the sake of athletic success.

◤ *Athlete's Perspective*

North of Quebec city is a ski resort called Mt. St. Anne. I first went there in 1998 and found it hot and humid with millions of bugs. Heat I can deal with but not humidity and biting insects. I couldn't wait to leave the place. That year, I crashed out on the course and broke my shoulder.

Two years later I returned to compete. Days before my competition, my parents called to say that they were separating after 30 years of marriage. I was devastated by this news and struggled to focus on racing. In 2002 when I returned yet again to compete, I found I couldn't focus. I wanted to leave. There were so many bad memories associated with the area that I felt really sad. Out on the course I was distracted. I found I couldn't ride my bike very well and made constant mistakes. In practice I crashed heavily twice, injuring my hip and legs. When I finally did race, I was far from my best.

It would be nice if you could choose the weather conditions for race day: About 80 °F, cloudy, with a dry race course that has been wet recently to keep the dust down would be perfect. But these conditions are scarce more than common. On one course it rained so heavily that a 1-mile stretch of narrow wooded trail became a knee-deep sloppy mud pool. By the time I arrived to this section, my bike had doubled in weight with sticky mud so carrying it was a chore. So I slipped, tripped, and skated my way through the mud bog for 1 mile, absolutely hating it. It was no fun. I couldn't believe the race organizers could be so stupid to think that something like this would be fun; after all, isn't that why I do this in the first place? For fun! Well, it wasn't fun, so I allowed myself to hate it, to be angry, and to feel these feelings as long as I kept running (not walking) with my bike. Once back on firm ground I let my anger go, remounted my bike, and rejoined my usual race-style focus. Looking back I still smile. It wasn't fun but I still went fast!

■　■　■　■　■

Emotion Matrix

The dimensions of positive–negative and helpful–harmful emotions lead to a 2×2 emotion matrix with four quadrants that illustrates the experience and influence of emotions on athletes (see figure 5.1). This matrix is consistent with Hanin's individual zones of optimal functioning model, which outlines the complex and often counterintuitive relationship between emotions and performance (e.g., Hanin and Syrjä, 1995a, 1995b, 1996; D'Urso, Petrosso, and Robazza, 2002; or see Hanin, 2000a, 2000b, for a review). A key element of this matrix is that the relationships between specific emotions and performance are fluid rather than fixed and that both pleasant and unpleasant emotions can be helpful or harmful to performance.

Individual differences in how an athlete interprets his emotions may determine their influence on performance. For example, some athletes perform well when they are calm and happy whereas others perform best intense and agitated. The nature of the sport may mediate the relationship between emotions and performance. McGowan and Shultz (1989) reported that defensive players on American football teams used anger as a strategy to increase motivation, intensity, and performance. This relationship was not found, however, among offensive players, who are generally required to perform more complex tasks during competition. Finally, emotions that are initially helpful can later become harmful; for example, frustration and anger may initially increase motivation and intensity but eventually may cause athletes to try too hard and hinder technical and tactical execution. Indeed, a number of authors have advocated greater research into the temporal patterning of emotions and their relationship with performance (Cerin, Szabo, Hunt, and Williams, 2000; D'Urso et al., 2002; Hanin, 2000a; Jones, 1991).

- **Pleasant-helpful.** Pleasant-helpful emotions are considered optimal emotional states because they feel good and they lead to improved performance. These emotions usually include excitement, exhilaration, and joy. Pleasant-helpful emotions motivate athletes to pursue their goals,

	Pleasant	Unpleasant
Helpful	Excitement Exhilaration Joy Happiness Pride	Frustration Anger
Harmful	Satisfaction Contentment	Fear Desperation Panic Rage Despair Embarrassment Shame Guilt Distress Sadness

Figure 5.1 Emotion matrix.

increase their confidence in their ability to succeed, regulate intensity to a facilitating level, direct focus more effectively, and reduce the experience of pain.

• **Pleasant-harmful.** Pleasant-harmful emotions, such as satisfaction and contentment, may feel good but usually hurt performance. These emotions harm motivation by causing a sense of completion of goals, reduce intensity required for optimal performance, and decrease athletes' ability to stay focused and avoid distractions. Pleasant-harmful emotions often occur when athletes are leading a competition and are pleased with their performance, causing them to feel complacent and self-satisfied.

• **Unpleasant-helpful.** Unpleasant-helpful emotions do not feel good to athletes, but these emotions can enhance the quality of performance, at least temporarily. Frustration, anger, and, in some cases, fear can provide impetus to athletes, particularly when they are performing poorly.

Unpleasant-helpful emotions may trigger motivation to clear the obstacles that have caused these emotions, increase efforts to attain goals, elevate intensity, and distract athletes from competitive pain. Although these emotions may improve performance, they are not the first choice of emotions to improve performance. Unpleasant-helpful emotions are often only beneficial for a short time, after which they hurt performance. Additionally, unpleasant-helpful emotions draw on feelings that are counterproductive to athletes' overall happiness and well-being.

• **Unpleasant-harmful.** Unpleasant-harmful emotions are the worst emotions that athletes can experience because these emotions not only cause athletes to feel bad but also lead to declines in performance. These emotions can influence athletes in two ways. Some of these emotions, such as desperation or panic, may be harmful because they raise intensity to interfering levels, cause athletes to try too hard, and hinder technical and tactical execution. Other emotions, such as despair, triggered by the perception that the situation is hopeless, can cause a complete physical and psychological shutdown of everything that influences performance. When athletes experience these emotions, motivation to perform, confidence in their ability to succeed, physical intensity, and focus all decline to a point at which performance ceases. Also, unpleasant-helpful emotions can turn harmful when they persist or become too intense and consuming. For example, some anger can improve performance, but if that anger turns to rage, athletes will lose the ability to think clearly, intensity will rise to a level that interferes with physical functioning, and the thorough absorption in the anger will preclude athletes from focusing effectively on their performances.

Coach's Perspective

It is interesting to see the emotion matrix in figure 5.1. It is true that there are some unpleasant yet helpful emotions. I usually explain to athletes that it is okay or even natural to have unpleasant emotions during training or in competition. When athletes are angry (unpleasant-helpful), I tell them to keep being angry, hold the energy of anger in mind, and then explore how to turn that energy into positive energy in competition. Anger is not a good emotion for maintaining motivation in sports, but it is good to use the energy of anger in competition. On the other hand, when athletes are scared or panicked (unpleasant-harmful), I tell them that it is normal to feel that way in an important competition. I even praise them when they can specify what kinds of emotions they are experiencing in competition. Of course, it is hard to cope with the harmful emotions, but coping with any adversity is one of the most important mental skills in sports.

■　■　■　■　■

Negative Emotional Chain

The emergence of unpleasant-harmful emotions typically follows a predictable course referred to as "the negative emotional chain" (Taylor, 2001). This sequence begins during a period of poor performance. At this time, frustration, an emotional reaction that occurs when athletes' efforts toward a goal are thwarted, is often the first negative emotion to arise. Initially, frustration acts as an unpleasant-helpful emotion by motivating athletes to clear the obstacles with which they are presented (e.g., technical difficulties, ineffective tactics). However, if the athletes are unable to resolve the cause of the frustration, the intensity of the frustration will grow and the emotion will shift to being harmful because the frustration will begin to interfere with their ability to think clearly, focus effectively, and maintain optimal intensity. As a result, performance is likely to continue to deteriorate.

If frustration goes unresolved, the next stage of the negative emotional chain is anger. At first, anger may act as an unpleasant-helpful emotion by further motivating athletes to resolve their performance difficulties. However, this benefit is usually short lived because the anger overwhelms athletes during the heat of competition. Although their physical and mental efforts may increase, they are typically not well directed or effective because of anger's negative influence on thinking, focus, and intensity.

In some cases, athletes may experience a sort of panic in which they maintain their efforts but express them in a frenzied, disorganized, and, ultimately, fruitless attempt to alter the course of the competition. In this panic, athletes try anything to improve their performances and produce a change in the competition, but their efforts are doomed to fail.

In other cases, as the anger proves to be ineffective, athletes come to believe that they cannot do anything to alter their performance or the tide of the competition. At this point, athletes experience despair and a feeling akin to learned helplessness (Seligman, 1975), appraising the situation as having no hope for change. Athletes then resign themselves to failure, accept defeat, give up all efforts in the competition, and experience disappointment and sadness.

Coach's Perspective

When I was an Olympic athlete, the most harmful emotions I experienced were contentment, satisfaction, and overconfidence. As a coach, I think that athletes limit their potential when they become satisfied with their ability or performance. I always tell athletes that pleasant-harmful emotions are much worse than unpleasant-harmful emotions. Elite athletes are never satisfied with themselves. As long as the pursuit of excellence is the goal of sports competition, athletes must stay motivated and guard against complacency.

■　■　■　■　■

Why Athletes Respond Emotionally

Athletes experience particular emotions depending on their appraisal of competitive situations (Cerin et al., 2000; Kerr, 1997; Vallerand, 1983, 1987), which is affected by their relationship to their sport, their attitude toward their athletic participation, and their perceptions of their ability to effectively manage the demands placed on them.

Appraisal Patterns As Triggers of Emotional Responses

The evaluation of competitive situations that trigger emotions is considered by Lazarus' cognitive–motivational–relational theory to comprise primary and secondary appraisal (see Lazarus, 1991, 2000a, 2000b, for detailed reviews). Primary appraisal is concerned with how important a situation is to an athlete in terms of his or her goals. For example, a rugby player who is tackled heavily in a match and knocked backward may feel ashamed because he failed to live up to his view of himself as being a physically dominant player. In contrast, his teammate, for whom being perceived as skillful is more important, does not feel ashamed because he accepts being tackled as a normal part of rugby. Secondary appraisal concerns athletes' perceptions of their ability to cope with the situation. Athletes who are confident they can produce a beneficial change in the competitive situation will experience pleasant-helpful emotions, whereas a belief that they cannot improve things will lead to unpleasant-harmful emotions.

The types of primary and secondary appraisals that athletes make determine the emotions they experience and the spectrum of psychological contributors to their sport performance. Consulting experience suggests that part of the appraisal process outlined by Lazarus, which is particularly relevant to competitive sports, is whether an event is appraised as actually (or potentially) harmful or beneficial: in other words, whether athletes appraise the competitive situation as a threat of anticipated loss or a challenge of anticipated gain. The more confident athletes are of their ability to overcome obstacles, the more likely they are to feel challenged rather than threatened (Lazarus, 1999).

In competitive sport, a threat appraisal arises from the perception that winning is all-important, failure is unacceptable but likely, and the outcome of the competition is a significant reflection on the worth of the athlete as a competitor and as a person. This threat is most often associated with too great an emphasis on winning, results, and rankings. Pressure to win from parents, coaches, media, and the athletes themselves is also common. The threat appraisal produces "defensive" emotions that may be helpful at first, for example, marshaling anger to avoid the threat of failure, but, in time, the persistent threat will likely lead to unpleasant-harmful emotions such as panic and despair.

A threat appraisal can trigger a vicious cycle in which the appraisal hurts essential psychological contributors to performance (Taylor, 2001). The threat appraisal can reduce the motivation to perform and compete because of the wish to avoid the threat, especially when the threat (e.g., losing) is imminent. For example, when an athlete is behind in a competition, she may give up (i.e., a significant loss of motivation). The threat appraisal also suggests to athletes that they're incapable of overcoming the situation that is causing the threat, so their confidence is hurt and they experience strong unpleasant-harmful emotions, such as fear, desperation, panic, despair, and sadness. The threat appraisal also causes anxiety and all of the negative physical symptoms associated with overintensity. These negative changes caused by the threat appraisal make it difficult for athletes to focus effectively because there are many distractions pulling athletes' focus away from a useful process focus. The culmination of a threat appraisal is that athletes inevitably perform poorly and gain little enjoyment from their sport.

A challenge appraisal in competitive sport is associated with the perception that, although obstacles and setbacks are inevitable, success is likely with patience and persistence. Failure, although not desirable, is tolerable and, in fact, may have value to athletes in their sport participation (Taylor, 2001). With a challenge appraisal, there is less emphasis on the outcome of competitions and greater emphasis on athletes enjoying the process of their sport regardless of whether they win or lose. The challenge appraisal leads athletes to emphasize the fun aspect of sport and experience competition as exciting and enriching. Sports, when perceived as a challenge, are experiences that are relished and sought out at every opportunity. Thus, a challenge appraisal is highly motivating, to the point where athletes love being in pressure situations and perform their best in them. The challenge appraisal results in athletes experiencing pleasant-helpful emotions, such as excitement, joy, and exhileration. It also stimulates athletes to achieve optimal intensity, where they are relaxed, energized, and physically capable of performing their best. Athletes also have the ability to attain an ideal focus, in which they are totally focused on what enables them to perform their best. All aspects of the challenge appraisal lead athletes to a higher level of performance and greater enjoyment in their sport.

Athlete's Perspective

Part of my attraction to mountain bike racing is the culture. The environment is informal and friendly and draws many different types of people, from young to old. My favorite part is listening to postrace stories. Competitors gather at the finish line at the end of each event. Bikes are cast aside as the sweaty, grubby riders swap yarns. Some measure their performance by their placing, others by how they felt. Some are disappointed and others thrilled. My judgment of a good race is based on how hard I tried and whether I enjoyed it. I have won many races hating almost every second of the race. During such a race, I may have battled with negativity and self-loathing. It was hard to be happy despite winning. At other times, I have finished fifth, given every portion of myself, worked hard, dug deep to be competitive, and felt ecstatic.

■   ■   ■   ■   ■

Investment in Performance

The investment that athletes have in their sport participation is a primary contributor to their emotional reactions in competition. This connection refers to how important their sport involvement is to them. The degree to which athletes' self-identities are highly interwoven with their athletic successes and failures influences how pleasant or unpleasant their emotions are, the intensity of those emotions, and whether they are helpful or harmful to the athletes' sport performances. For example, athletes who are overly invested in their sport may find losing unpalatable, so when they are in a losing situation, they may make a threat appraisal and experience strong unpleasant-helpful emotions, such as frustration or anger, as a means of altering their losing path. If those

emotions do not turn the tide of the competition, unpleasant-harmful emotions may arise. In contrast, if their investment is balanced and healthy, athletes are more likely to make challenge appraisals and experience pleasant-helpful emotions.

Performance Consequences

How athletes perceive the possible consequences of their competitive performances influences their emotional reactions to competition (Lazarus, 2000a). For example, if athletes believe that their participation will most likely lead to failure and that failure will have unpleasant consequences such as thinking less of themselves or being criticized by others, unpleasant-harmful emotions will arise. Conversely, if athletes have confidence that they will be successful and that their success will have positive consequences, the success will validate their years of training or they will be rewarded financially, athletes will experience pleasant-helpful emotions.

Athlete's Perspective

Racing is never easy. Some days pushing myself is easier, but other days it's hard. Some days I can suffer with ease, and other times suffering is impossible. My best races are the days when I don't really feel too much. My focus on the task at hand is extremely strong. Memories of a good race are minimal. I can only recall thinking about the upcoming track, mile by mile or kilometer by kilometer. When remembering the race, I only can recall small segments, usually when I made a crucial decision.

■   ■   ■   ■   ■

Demands and Resources

As Lazarus (1991, 2000a, 2000b) suggested, emotions during competition are influenced significantly by the athletes' perceptions of the resources they have available to effectively manage the demands of the competitive situation. In general, if the demands exceed the perceived resources of athletes, unpleasant-harmful emotions, such as distress, rage, panic, or despair, are likely to arise. These emotions occur because athletes believe they have little ability to master the demands of the competitive situation. For example, if an athlete is competing against an opponent who has beaten her three previous times and, in the early stages of the competition, the athlete is faring no better than before, she will likely become frustrated in her efforts. At some point during this competition, she will experience despair and may give up because she sees no way out of this repeatedly uncontrollable situation. Conversely, if athletes perceive that they have the capacity to overcome the demands of the situation, they will likely respond with pleasant-helpful emotions because they have confidence that they will prevail.

Outside Influences

External forces can play a substantial role in the emotional reactions that athletes have during competition. Common outside influences include encouragement, expectations, pressure, or criticism from others, such as teammates, family, friends, media, and community. Athletes who feel supported by others will likely experience pleasant-helpful emotions such as excitement and joy in their sport participation. In contrast, athletes who feel burdened by unrealistic expectations from others may respond with unpleasant-helpful emotions, such as anger, to help them avoid the outside pressures. If, however, they either do not believe they can live up to those expectations or actually fail to meet those expectations, they will succumb to unpleasant-harmful emotions, such as sadness and despair, as the weight of the external influences grows.

Gaining Emotional Mastery

The goal for the researcher, consultant, and coach is to help athletes gain mastery over their emotions so that emotions help rather than hurt their competitive performances. To accomplish this objective, athletes must first understand the ways in which they respond emotionally to competitive situations. Then, they can identify those circumstances that cause harmful emotions. Finally, athletes need to develop the skills that will enable them to use their emotions to their advantage in competition.

For athletes to be truly successful, they must have *emotional mastery* (Taylor, 2001). Athletes can gain control of their emotions with awareness and practice. They can develop healthy and productive emotional habits. Their emotions can facilitate their competitive efforts and help them achieve their athletic goals. Qualities that Goleman (1995) associated with emotional mastery include

the abilities to stay motivated and persist in the face of frustration, to control urges and the need for immediate gratification, to be able to adjust mood, and to keep negative emotions from interfering with the ability to think clearly and act appropriately. All of these assets converge to enable athletes who have emotional mastery to be their own best allies. These athletes have the ability to ensure that the energy they put into their competitive efforts—and the positive and negative emotions they feel as part of those efforts—help them progress toward their goals.

Athlete's Perspective

Ten years of crashing off my mountain bike has left me with many scars. The initial injuries have healed, but occasionally I develop a dull ache from an old torn ligament, broken bone, or muscle strain. Before competitions, it's not unusual to feel physically stiff or achy from old injuries. Rarely does the ache develop into anything more serious. Experience has taught me to acknowledge the ache and mentally move on, focusing on the upcoming event. And 10 minutes after the start of the competition, the problem usually disappears.

The same applies to the regular toilet stops the morning of a competition. I could spend a good majority of my warm-up time in the restroom. Needing to constantly go to the restroom can be a good sign. It means that I am ready to race or suitably nervous (I prefer to call this feeling "worried"). It's good to be worried or a little nervous, because that is what pushes me to ride fast. But to warm up properly, I need to keep on schedule so I need to limit how many times I visit the restroom. Interestingly again, once in the competition the urge to go to the restroom completely disappears.

■ ■ ■ ■ ■

Maintaining Emotional Perspective

When athletes gain a healthy perspective on the meaning of their sport participation, they are less likely to become overly invested in their efforts and their self-identity is not likely to become too connected with their successes and failures. Athletes, regardless of their level of competition, should care about their sport participation. Why should they work hard to reach their goals if they don't really care about attaining that high level? So, some level of investment is normal, healthy, and necessary. However, athletes with emotional mastery understand that ups and downs are a natural part of sports. This attitude keeps them from getting overly upset about setbacks and takes the pressure off of them to have a big success every time. These athletes are able to stay positive and motivated even when they are not at their best and, most important, they never give up; they keep working hard, no matter how bad it gets. They look for the cause of their difficulties and then find a solution. With this perspective, athletes with emotional mastery respond positively to the obstacles they face, minimize the severity of the difficulties, clear the barriers that arise, and find success again. Both success and failure are recognized as essential and inevitable parts of the process of achievement. Success validates their efforts and confirms their belief in themselves. Failure provides meaningful lessons and valuable information that further their athletic efforts and increase the chances of future success.

Making Effective Emotional Choices

At the heart of emotional mastery is athletes' ability to objectively evaluate their self-perceptions as well as their emotions and reactions during participation in sports. Taylor (2001) suggested that emotions are a simple, but not easy, choice. They are a simple choice because if athletes have the option to feel bad and perform poorly or feel good and perform well, they will certainly choose the latter option. However, emotions are not an easy choice because past emotional experiences and unhealthy emotional habits can lead athletes to respond emotionally in competitive situations in ways that are harmful and result in poor performance. The best choices are made when athletes are aware of when old emotional habits will arise and choose a positive emotional response that will lead to good feelings and successful performance.

Mastering Emotions Through Prevention and Intervention

Emotional mastery can occur in two forms: prevention and intervention. Prevention, the ideal form of emotional mastery, involves the capacity to stop emotions from occurring in the first place. Although clearly not realistic in many cases, preventive measures can, at minimum, limit the negative impact of emotions on performance and,

at best, stop the emotions from arising at all. Prevention emphasizes that athletes recognize beforehand situations in which harmful emotions may arise and alter the situation or their perception of the situation so that unhealthy emotions don't emerge. Intervention involves athletes' responding in a constructive way when detrimental emotions do appear in competition. Because it may be impossible to keep harmful emotions from occurring, intervention stresses that athletes develop the ability to step back from an intensely emotional experience and apply strategies that they learned in training to halt the incursion of harmful, destructive emotions during competition.

Before specific techniques can be used to gain control of emotional reactions during competition, athletes must first make several observations that act as the foundation of emotional mastery.

The first step to emotional mastery is self-awareness. Athletes need to become familiar with their emotions during competition. They should ask themselves (or have a sport psychology consultant or coach ask them), "What is this feeling I (you) have?" Athletes can keep a written record of their emotional reactions during competition, or this monitoring can be done by a coach or trusted third party, such as a sport psychology consultant. Athletes can easily distinguish between positive and negative emotions, but only with experience can they learn the differences between helpful and harmful emotions, particularly in the heat of competition. When athletes feel bad and are performing poorly, they need to judge whether they are, for example, fearful, angry, frustrated, or disappointed and whether those emotions are helping or hurting them. Athletes can begin this awareness process in training by identifying practice situations that trigger emotions.

An increased awareness of both the situations in which these emotions arise and the consequences of such responses can lead to more helpful emotional responses and improved performance. For example, during a practice match, a tennis player can record her emotions and how they affect her play on changeovers. After the match, she can see more clearly how her emotions influenced her level of play and the outcome of the match. Research has shown that increasing awareness can be an effective strategy in dealing with unpleasant-harmful emotions. In a study examining the impact of self-awareness strategies in controlling anger among competitive soccer players, Brunelle, Janelle, and Tennant (1999) found that self-awareness was effective in reducing angry behaviors.

Once athletes become adept at identifying their emotions and recognizing whether they are helpful or harmful, the athletes can then understand that they will continue to feel bad and perform poorly if they allow their current harmful emotional state to persist. This awareness will show them that they need to do something different to reverse the harmful trend and motivate them to action.

With this increased understanding of their emotional states, athletes can search themselves and their environment for possible causes of their emotional reactions. Understanding the reasons why athletes react a certain way during competition provides them with further information about the emotional experience and gives them greater understanding and control over what they are feeling. This process also encourages athletes to step back from their emotions, which offers a different perspective and often lessens the intensity and impact of the emotions. This approach also interrupts the negative emotional chain and provides athletes with the opportunity to reverse its course.

With this more detached and objective outlook toward the competitive situation and the emotional reactions they are experiencing, athletes can begin to consider courses of action that will serve them best and choose the path that feels better and that will lead to success. These options can include different ways of thinking (e.g., being positive, motivated, focusing on the process rather than on the outcome), feeling (e.g., excited, psyched up), and acting (e.g., having more energy, putting in greater effort). Finally, athletes can choose and commit to a positive course of action directed at altering their current emotional state and the competitive situation that caused the emotions. The ultimate goal of this emotional mastery process is for athletes to be able to choose an emotional path that will help them achieve their competitive goals.

Not all athletes have the ability or the willingness to approach emotional mastery in such a deliberate way. Some athletes' emotional experiences during competition are overwhelming and stepping back from intense emotions is not possible, even those that hurt performance. Consultants must give these athletes the tools to distract themselves from the emotions, thereby reducing their negative impact on performance, or to direct emotions in a way that is helpful. Such an approach is not ideal, but any effort to rein in emotions during a competition is better than uncontrolled emotions.

Techniques for Emotional Mastery

Emotional mastery is acquired with awareness, control, and practice. Athletes can facilitate the development of emotional mastery by adopting the foundation of emotional mastery previously discussed. These steps are the basis for applying emotional mastery skills to emotional situations that arise during competition.

Developing specific emotional mastery skills is the next step in gaining complete mastery of emotions. These strategies focus primarily on changing the way athletes think about the competitive situations in which they find themselves. Additionally, physiological techniques are also used to address the visceral aspects of the emotions (see chapter 3).With time and practice, these emotional mastery skills can be internalized and athletes will be able to use them to their advantage whenever they are faced with emotionally demanding situations in their sport participation. Additionally, athletes can learn to use emotional mastery preventively. They can learn to recognize common competitive situations in which harmful emotions arise; for example, when their strategy is not working or when they are going through a period of poor performance. Then they can initiate the emotional mastery process before harmful emotions appear, thereby stopping the negative emotional chain before it starts and allowing themselves to improve their level of performance.

Reappraisal

Challenging the way athletes appraise events can alleviate harmful emotions and generate helpful ones. Helping athletes gain a different, and more positive, perspective on the competitive situation lies at the heart of reappraisal. Athletes react with harmful emotions because they appraise the situation as a threat. Reappraisal by athletes themselves, a coach, a teammate, or a sport psychology consultant is aimed at offering them other perspectives on the situation that will alter their appraisal to one of challenge, thereby replacing harmful appraisals with perceptions that will generate pleasant-helpful emotions.

For example, a gymnast was experiencing frustration because she was unable to master a skill in the first few days she had been practicing a new routine. She expected to learn the skill quickly and to use it in an upcoming competition.

Seeing that these emotions were hurting her, her coach explained that the skill was difficult, that it would take several weeks to master, and that she would not allow the gymnast to use the skill in the upcoming meet anyway. The coach told her about an older and more experienced gymnast who struggled with the skill for months before she was able to use it in competition and that she was well ahead of the other gymnast in learning the new skill. This new perspective helped the gymnast to relax and be more positive, patient, and persistent in the ensuing weeks as she practiced the skill, and she even felt excitement at the progress she was making toward incorporating the skill into her competitive floor exercise routine.

Reframing is a particular type of reappraisal that helps athletes gain a new and healthier view of the situation that is causing harmful emotions. The aim of reframing is for athletes to alter the meaning of an event, thereby changing their emotional reactions to it. For example, when a water polo player felt ashamed because he had missed several good chances to score during a match, the coach pointed out that the player continued to play aggressively, got into good positions to score, and still took shots when scoring opportunities arose. In addition, the coach affirmed his continued faith in the player and his belief that the player's ongoing efforts would pay off with a goal very soon. This reframing of the competitive situation removed the appraisal that caused the shame and replaced it with an appraisal that produced helpful emotions such as pride, inspiration, and satisfaction.

Athlete's Perspective

My perception of my body has always been a little off. As a teen I struggled with how I viewed myself, and I associated negative thoughts with being overweight. Even though I am far from overweight, when I am having trouble with negative thoughts I feel heavy and slow. I tend to look down at my front tire and rock my upper body. In mountain biking, looking down at the front wheel is not helpful. You need to look up the trail so you can ride safely and fast among the dirt and rocks. Rocking your upper body alters your balance on the bike, and this is not helpful because the edges of the tracks sometimes drop yards down a hillside. So on those days when I battle with negativity, I also have a rough day on the bike.

■　■　■　■　■

Problem Solving

Problem solving is an essential tool for athletes to reappraise the circumstances that may cause harmful emotions. Problem solving alters athletes' appraisals of the emotional situation itself, their appraisals of their ability to effectively cope with its demands, and their actual ability to handle the demands that initially trigger a harmful emotional reaction. Problem solving involves generating alternative responses to the current circumstances, considering the potential consequences of the various choices, and selecting the response that will best solve the problem (Platt, Prout, and Metzger, 1986).

Problem solving benefits athletes who are struggling emotionally in several ways. It requires athletes to step back from their emotions and the situation that is causing them, resulting in the emotions losing some of their intensity and influence. Problem solving can increase athletes' ability to effectively cope with the current situation by giving them tools they can use to overcome the demands. Problem solving also gives athletes a sense of control over a situation that previously felt out of their control. Finally, problem solving gives athletes tangible steps they can take to resolve the emotionally unsettling problem.

For example, a 100-meter high hurdler was frustrated because she kept hitting the hurdles with her trail leg. Instead of getting upset about it, she decided to do some detective work. Her coach videotaped her on several practice runs through the hurdles and they watched the video of each performance. After careful scrutiny, they saw that her torso was too erect over the hurdle, causing her trail leg to drop. At the following practice session, she tried several different body positions until she came up with the one that was both comfortable and enabled her trail leg to clear the hurdles. Problem solving allowed this athlete to resolve the difficulty that could have become a significant "hurdle" to her development and a cause of unpleasant-harmful emotions. Finding a solution was also emotionally beneficial because she was excited to have overcome an obstacle that was holding her back, and this excitement motivated her to continue to work hard.

Self-Talk

There is evidence to support the use of positive self-talk to control emotions in sport. In their analysis of coping strategies used by elite figure skaters, Gould, Finch, and Jackson (1993) reported that 76% of the sample used rational thinking and self-talk to cope with the stress of competition. Jones and Mace (1998) described how self-talk that focused on preshot preparation helped a professional golfer avoid dwelling on self-doubts, alleviated the unpleasant-harmful emotions he had been experiencing, and improved his play (for more on self-talk, see chapter 2).

Mental Imagery

Mental imagery is another strategy that has been shown to help athletes gain control of their emotions in sport settings (Mace, 1990). Imagery can be used to generate pleasant-helpful emotions, such as excitement or joy, by having athletes see and feel themselves experiencing those emotions in competitive situations. Imagery can also be used to replace negative images that may be causing negative emotions. In addition, imagery of effective coping and mastery of demanding competitive situations can enhance athletes' perceptions of their ability to cope in a competitive situation, resulting in a more pleasant-helpful emotional state. For example, a soccer player who experiences fear when faced with taking a penalty kick can use imagery in several ways. The player can imagine himself going through a preshot routine that focuses on deep breathing, positive self-talk, and a process focus. He can also imagine a successful penalty kick and the feelings of excitement and joy he will experience.

According to Martin, Moritz, and Hall (1999), imagery that focuses on regulating intensity in competition can be an effective tool for emotional control. Other research has found mental imagery to be beneficial to athletes by increasing excitement, enabling them to maintain composure during competition (Munroe, Giacobbi, Hall, and Weinberg, 2000), and reducing distress in high-risk sports (Jones, Mace, Bray, MacRae, and Stockbridge, 2002; for more on mental imagery, see chapter 8).

Athlete's Perspective

In the days leading up to a major event, I would become very nervous. My apprehension would engulf my every thought, and I would verge on the point of panic. During these moments my heart rate would increase and I would sweat. After a day of nervousness at this level, I would feel very tired. So to reduce my anxiety about the unknown result of the upcoming race, I would think about things over which I had power. Closing my eyes, I would think about the race track. Where were my strengths? Where was I going to have to find extra effort? Where could I make up time? I would imagine myself riding tricky parts of the trail smoothly, almost floating and putting my bike where I wanted it to go. I would remind myself that I had done the hard work and the race was the fun part. My thoughts brought me back to the things that were in my control. This would keep my nervous tension at a healthy level that enabled me to race well.

■ ■ ■ ■ ■

Intensity Regulation

The intensity with which athletes experience emotions affects the impact that those emotions have on sport performance. One way to reduce the influence of harmful emotions is to change the intensity that athletes feel during competition. For example, a shooter who is angry—and overly intense—because of a poor scoring round can use relaxation techniques, such as deep breathing and muscle relaxation, to lower his intensity and feelings of anger. Conversely, a speed skater who is disappointed and close to despairing of qualifying for the national championships can use motivating self-talk and engage in positive high-intensity body language to replace the harmful emotions associated with low intensity with helpful emotions and higher intensity.

However, caution is warranted when athletes use these intensity-altering techniques to manage emotions. Increasing or decreasing intensity can have a blanket effect on the range of emotions experienced by the athletes and their overall physiological functioning. Consequently, although a technique may alter the intensity of a harmful emotion, such as frustration, it may also change the intensity of helpful emotions, such as excitement, and the intensity needed to meet the physical or technical demands of the sport. Coaches and athletes should take care in developing appropriate strategies to master emotions to ensure that the unwanted effects are removed and the beneficial effects are maintained. A number of strategies are described in chapter 3 that aim to raise or lower the physiological arousal (intensity) of athletes.

Training Success

Emotional mastery cannot be learned in competitive settings. The pressure and intensity of competition make it nearly impossible for athletes to focus on performing their best and trying to develop new emotional skills at the same time. Just as technical skills are first practiced and mastered in training, emotional skills must also be tried and tested in training before they can be used effectively in competition.

Emotions that are experienced during competition, such as frustration, anger, or despair, will almost inevitably arise in training, although perhaps with less intensity. At the same time, because training is not as important as competition and there are usually frequent breaks, athletes are in a better position to focus on and take steps to change their emotional reactions. For these reasons, training is an ideal setting in which athletes can practice emotional mastery.

The involvement of a coach or sport psychology consultant can facilitate the development of emotional skills during practice. When athletes begin to react with harmful emotions, the coach or consultant can step in, point out the emotion and how it is affecting performance, and suggest a strategy for altering the emotion. For example, a baseball pitcher was getting angry at himself in practice because his curveball wasn't working for him. As his anger grew, he tried harder and harder, which caused him to throw several wild pitches. Having talked to him about his anger before and having suggested some techniques he could use, the pitching coach reminded him of these strategies. Heeding his coach's advice, the pitcher took several minutes to regroup, did some deep breathing and relaxed his body, and focused on the proper technique for his curveball. Immediately, his pitches improved and his anger was replaced with excitement and satisfaction of having regained control over both his emotions and his pitching. After he repeated this process in subsequent practices, these new emotional mastery skills became ingrained and he was able to use them successfully in games when he began to get frustrated with his play.

Emotional Mastery in Action

Frustration is often the first unpleasant-harmful emotion that athletes experience in a competition. For example, if their goal is to perform well and win a competition, athletes may experience frustration if they are making mistakes, are performing poorly, or are behind in a competition. As discussed earlier, frustration can initially be an unpleasant-helpful emotion that pushes athletes to find a way to remove the obstacles to their goal. However, if the frustration is not relieved, athletes may get caught in the negative emotional chain.

If athletes can learn to respond positively to frustration when it first occurs, they can prevent other stronger unpleasant-harmful emotions from arising and they can stop the negative emotional chain before it starts. Their goal is to react positively to the first indications of unpleasant-harmful emotions. This pleasant-helpful emotional reaction starts with recognition that frustration is starting to build and that continued frustration will hurt their performances (self-awareness).

The next step in reversing the negative emotional chain is for athletes to regain perspective about the meaning of the competitive situation, most notably in how they appraise mistakes and poor performance (reappraisal). Recognizing that these "failures" are a normal and inevitable part of sport reduces the threat appraisal and acts as the foundation for stopping the negative emotional chain (reframing). With a challenge appraisal in place, athletes are in a position to take practical steps to counter the frustration they will periodically experience.

The next step toward emotional mastery is for athletes to step back from the emotions that are interfering with their performances. Relaxation techniques that directly lower athletes' intensity are useful tools to encourage this detachment (intensity regulation). Reducing the intensity associated with frustration lowers the experience of the frustration itself, which makes it easier for athletes to gain mastery over the frustration.

When athletes begin to experience the negative emotional chain, their thinking can become clouded with negativity, which can further drive them down an unhealthy and unproductive road during competition. Athletes can alter their thinking by becoming aware of what they say to themselves and others and shifting it in a helpful direction with positive thinking (self-talk). They can also combat all aspects of the negative emotional chain by generating positive and motivating images in which they see and feel themselves overcoming the frustration, performing well, and succeeding (mental imagery).

With the influence of the initial unpleasant-harmful emotions reduced, athletes are in a better position to make conscious choices in how they respond to their emotions. However, athletes may not always be able to figure out for themselves the best way to relieve their frustration, so they can look to other, more experienced athletes for guidance. They can observe other athletes to see how they react when they get frustrated. They can also talk to a coach or sport psychology consultant to help them develop alternative ways of responding to their frustration.

Athletes can learn to identify when frustration usually begins for them. Frustration typically occurs in response to a pattern of mistakes or poor performance, for example, after an athlete has made the same mistake three times. The next step is to recognize a pattern before frustration arises. If athletes make the same mistake several times in a row, they know that if they keep repeating the mistake they will become frustrated. Having realized that frustration is just around the corner, athletes can find a solution to the problem so the pattern doesn't continue, for example, make a technical or tactical correction that will enable them to stop making that same mistake (problem solving). Having found a solution to the problem, they can then rehearse their positive responses to frustration in practice so that these responses become ingrained and

can be used effectively in competition (training success).

Coach's Perspective

I believe that it is best for athletes not to have any negative emotions in competition. To prevent them from having negative emotions, I usually tell them to focus on the quality of their performance, not the outcome. When athletes start focusing on the outcome, they experience harmful emotions such as fear and distress. I tell athletes to "focus on right now" and "just do what you can do now." By focusing on "now," athletes find it easier to reduce their negative emotions and focus on performance itself. Last, I tell athletes that "there is no emotion that you can't control by yourself." There must always be a reason why an athlete becomes anxious or worried in a competition, and likewise there must be a reason why an athlete is satisfied. If athletes understand what they are really thinking and how they perceive their situation, they can control their emotions more easily.

■ ■ ■ ■ ■

Key Points

- Athletes react in particular emotional ways depending on their appraisal of competitive situations.
- Changes in emotional states can have both positive and negative impacts on sport performance.
- The relationship between specific emotions and performance can be counterintuitive in that pleasant emotions may sometimes be harmful to performance and unpleasant emotions may sometimes be helpful to performance.
- Developing emotional mastery enables athletes to maintain performance during competition and prevent the emergence of unpleasant-harmful emotions, which typically follow a predictable c ourse referred to as the negative emotional chain.
- Athletes can use a number of techniques (e.g., reappraisal, self-talk, mental imagery) to gain emotional mastery.

Review Questions

1. Why is the impact of emotions so powerful and pervasive?
2. How do emotions physiologically and psychologically influence athletes?
3. What are the components of the emotion matrix, and what are examples of emotions that could be located in each quadrant?
4. What is the difference between a threat appraisal and a challenge appraisal?
5. What are some causes of emotional reactions in competition?
6. What are some techniques for developing emotional mastery?
7. What is the negative emotional chain and how can it be stopped?

II

Enhancing Athletic Performance

Part II focuses on mental "tools" that athletes can use to improve their training and competitive performances. Unlike the many techniques that are described in part I to develop specific psychological areas (i.e., motivation, confidence, intensity, focus, and emotions), the strategies discussed in part II have a more global influence, with the ability to enhance any or all of these factors.

Chapter 6 examines the value of psychological assessment in athletic preparation and performance. The chapter describes how athletes can gain a better understanding of themselves as athletes and as people by using a variety of formal and informal measurement strategies. Self-understanding shows athletes, as well as coaches and consultants, their strengths and areas in need of improvement and enables athletes to learn more about how they react in certain situations. This self-understanding then leads to more efficient change and more focused and better quality training.

Chapter 7 explores goal setting, perhaps the most widely used technique in applied sport psychology. The chapter explains how goal setting is essential for athletes to perform at their highest level possible. Goal setting provides direction for athletes' motivation. Goals increase athletes' commitment and motivation and provide deliberate steps toward their competitive aspirations.

Chapter 8 discusses the value of mental imagery in enhancing all aspects of performance. It demystifies this somewhat intangible technique and shows how athletes can use imagery to improve technical, tactical, and mental skills as well as training and competitive performance. The chapter offers a clear and practical approach to developing a comprehensive mental-imagery program.

Chapter 9 describes the universal value of routines in enhancing the quality of training and precompetitive preparations. Although most consultants, coaches, and athletes are familiar with using routines to get ready for competitions, this chapter shows how routines can be used before and during training and between performances in sports that involve a series of short performances (e.g., tennis and golf). The chapter offers a detailed plan for developing routines for all sport settings.

6
Psychological Assessment

Thad R. Leffingwell, PhD—researcher
Natalie Durand-Bush, PhD—consultant
Dean Wurzberger—coach
Petra Cada—athlete

© Empics

The objectives of this chapter are

- to provide a comprehensive overview of different types of psychological assessment;
- to discuss the characteristics of psychometrically sound measures of psychological skills, such as validity, reliability, and practicality;
- to provide insight into commonly used questionnaires for assessing psychological skills in sport; and
- to discuss the use of critical thinking skills for the evaluation, selection, and appropriate use of psychological assessment tools in research and applied contexts.

Psychological assessment is an important component of sport psychology consulting, as it is in other areas of applied psychology. Applied sport psychologists may use assessment in every aspect of their work to assess individual athletes' attributes and skills, coaches' behaviors, reactions to events like retirement or injury, team "chemistry," and the effectiveness of interventions.

One of the more controversial uses of psychological assessment in sports is personnel selection. Recently, the *Washington Times* (Hruby, 2000) reported that the New York Giants professional football team requires all draft prospects to answer a 400-item questionnaire that assesses their mental and emotional states. Many other professional teams use different assessment tools that measure such traits as aggressiveness and leadership skills as well as cognitive abilities (cf. Merron, 2002). Often teams may not select a physically gifted athlete simply because of the perception that he will not be a "team player." Some studies have been able to discriminate between more and less successful athletes using psychological tests. For example, personality tests were able to correctly predict approximately 75% of athletes who would make the U.S. Olympic rowing team (Morgan, Brown, Raglin, O'Connor, and Ellickson, 1987).

However, the effectiveness of psychological assessments for personnel selection is less well documented in the literature, and the ultimate effectiveness of these tests is unknown.

Despite the widespread use of psychological assessment in the sports world, concerns exist about its practical and ethical use with athletes. Specifically, questions are raised about its validity outside of the research realm, its appropriateness in athlete selection, and whether current assessment tools are sensitive enough to measure changes in athletes engaged in mental training programs.

Key Issues

Regardless of debates regarding the use of tests in certain situations, it is difficult to imagine an interaction in applied sport psychology that does not involve the use of psychological assessment. The available evidence suggests that a majority of applied sport psychology consultants use some sort of psychological assessment in their work (Gould, Tammen, Murphy, and May, 1989; Vealey and Garner-Holman, 1998). Consultants ask a number of questions when working with athletes or teams: "What are this athlete's psychological strengths and weaknesses?" "How motivated or confident are team members?" "What are the athletes like when performing at their best?" "Is the team improving as a result of the consultation?" Attempts to answer questions like these involve psychological assessment. Every observation that consultants make of athletes, whether based on behavioral observations, responses to interview questions, or paper-and-pencil questionnaires, constitutes a psychological assessment. Furthermore, assessments can contribute to the consulting process in many ways, for example, by helping to profile athletes or teams, select and design appropriate interventions, or evaluate the outcomes of one's consulting.

Chapter Purpose and Author Team

The purpose of this chapter is to provide a broad overview of psychological assessment in sport. As previously mentioned, psychological assessment includes a variety of approaches, such as behavioral observations, physiological monitoring, self-monitoring, and interviewing techniques (Vealey and Garner-Holman, 1998). Excellent manuals on psychological assessment (Duda, 1998; Nideffer and Sagal, 2001) and an online directory of more than 350 sport and exercise psychology assessment instruments (www.fitinfotech.com) are available.

Although general psychological assessment tools may occasionally be useful to applied sport psychologists, the emphasis in this chapter is on sport-specific measures that can be used to evaluate athletes' psychological strengths and weaknesses relative to their sport. This chapter is structured around the primary applied issues that consultants face in their assessment work with athletes (Dr. Natalie Durand-Bush). Recent empirical research will be linked to these issues (Dr. Thad Leffingwell), and throughout the chapter, a coach (Dean Wurzberger) and an athlete (Petra Cada) provide their perspectives on the role of psychological assessment in sport.

Coach's Perspective

Most coaches place a high value on determining the psychological strengths and weaknesses of the athletes they are coaching. In my experience, motivation and confidence are especially big areas of interest for soccer coaches. From a practical standpoint, many coaches would find psychological testing to be similar to physical fitness testing. It can help us identify each individual's psychological strengths and weaknesses and then act on that knowledge by implementing an appropriate training program.

■　■　■　■　■

Athlete's Perspective

When I was asked to join the Canadian national table tennis team in 1989, I had just won the title as the under-10-year-old Canadian national champion. At the time, I was representing Nova Scotia at the nationals and I was "spotted" by the national coaches. To join the national team, I did not have to undergo any psychological testing. In my sport in Canada, there is not an oversupply of players, so none of us ever has to be tested or screened for potential or for individual strengths and weaknesses. The standard procedure that the coaches use for personnel selection is based on observation. However, I believe that if we had used a variety of psychological assessments, we could have identified certain skills or lack of skills and saved some time. Not all of the athletes who joined the national team in the same year that I did are competing today!

■　■　■　■　■

Characteristics of Sound Measures

The fundamental value of any psychological assessment instrument lies in how well it measures what it is supposed to measure. A number of different inventories are typically available for a given type of assessment (e.g., for the measurement of motivation or confidence). Consultants should keep three issues in mind when evaluating whether a particular assessment tool is appropriate for their needs: validity, reliability, and practicality. However, a word of caution: Even the most reliable and valid psychometric measure must be interpreted in the context of all other available information. Although measures can provide valuable bits of information, these bits must be qualified by and informed by other sources of information in practice. Furthermore, self-report measures can be prone to biases (e.g., socially desirable responding, malingering, or cultural or language differences) that must be factored in when using psychometric measures. Establishing trust and rapport, ensuring confidentiality, and informing athletes that the results of any assessment are only used to help them improve can reduce some of the common biases associated with self-report measures.

Validity

The validity of an assessment tool indicates the degree to which it measures what it purports to measure (DeVellis, 1991). There are different types of validity, each addressing different questions that may arise about the value of an inventory. *Content validity* addresses the adequacy of the content of the measure. Questions to be asked about content validity include, "Does the instrument adequately assess the behavior of interest?" and "Would experts agree that the items in the test measure the construct of interest?" Content validity is usually evaluated by experts in the area who look at whether the items in the test appear to reflect what the test developers are trying to measure. However, consultants trained to use and teach different psychological skills (e.g., self-confidence, motivation, goal-setting) can determine if an instrument includes sufficient items relevant to the skills of interest.

The second type of validity is termed *construct validity*, which refers to whether an inventory truly assesses the constructs of interest. Test developers use a number of approaches to assess construct validity, such as determining whether a new inventory is correlated with other instruments that measure the same construct (*convergent validity*) or is not correlated with unrelated constructs (*divergent validity*). Ideally, a good measure of a construct would show a moderate to high correlation with similar measures and would not correlate with unrelated measures. Finally, and perhaps most important to applied sport psychology consultants, a measure should have *predictive validity*, such that the measure empirically predicts some outcome of interest (e.g., performance, satisfaction, or enjoyment).

Evaluating the validity of a measure is never really complete. When evaluating measures, test users must consider whether there is evidence to support the validity of a measure for the intended purpose with the identified population. This process requires that sport psychologists be familiar with the scientific literature to be able to make informed choices about the use and administration of psychometrically sound measures. When in doubt, consultants should discuss their concerns with measurement experts in order to provide the best service to their clients and remain ethical in the process.

Reliability

Reliability refers to the consistency or repeatability of an assessment tool (DeVellis, 1991). In other words, a measurement tool that is reliable will provide the same results regardless of who administers it or how many different times it is taken. With standard paper-and-pencil assessments, two types of reliability are of primary concern: internal consistency and test–retest reliability. Internal consistency refers to how well all of the items in a scale correspond or "hang together." If a number of items are supposed to be measuring the same thing, they should be responded to in a similar fashion. When reading about the internal validity of items, look for values above .80, because they usually reflect acceptable internal consistency (Vincent, 1999).

Test–retest reliability refers to how stable the measure is when completed by the same person over time. If the assessment is intended to measure something expected to be relatively stable (e.g., psychological skills or personality traits), then repeated measures by the same individual should yield similar results. Test developers usually assess test–retest reliability by administering the measure to a sample of individuals twice over a short time period, usually within 2 weeks. Of course, test–retest reliability is not relevant for measurement of factors that are expected to change based on the situation (e.g., state anxiety).

Practicality

A measure may be adequately reliable and valid but impractical for its intended use. For example, someone interested in assessing the relationship between mood and performance could follow athletes throughout an entire competitive season and use the Profile of Mood States (POMS) to correlate their mood before each competition with their competitive performance. However, the logistics of following athletes for such a long period of time often prohibit this approach, and, as a result, it is not practical for many athletes. Applied sport psychology consultants must be mindful of the demands and competing agendas of athletes and coaches when selecting measures and choose the most practical instruments available (Vealey and Garner-Holman, 1998). Often this requires that measures be short and concise. Fortunately, abbreviated versions of a number of measures including the POMS have been developed, and evidence of their reliability and validity is available.

A few of these brief measures are highlighted in the chapter. In general, applied consultants should carefully select psychological assessment tools to get the highest quality and most relevant information in the most efficient way possible.

Coach's Perspective

The validity of testing is a huge concern for coaches. What is the assessment tool really telling us? To be most useful to us, the test must tell us something related to performance and areas that could be improved by focused training. Sometimes athletes simply tell us what we want to hear on psychological tests. On my teams, we have handled that by having a sport psychology consultant do assessments and keep the results confidential between the athlete and consultant. That way the athlete can feel free to answer honestly, without having to expose a weakness to the coaches.

■　■　■　■

Athlete's Perspective

The validity and reliability of psychological testing can be improved by verifying that athletes are comfortable with the sport psychologist. When I first started working with a sport psychologist, my coach liked to come to the meetings. However, I was not comfortable with this arrangement, and now I am finally meeting with the sport psychologist alone. I feel more at ease with this increased confidentiality and do not feel that I have to answer in a way that my coach would like me to.

■　■　■　■

Uses of Psychological Assessment

Psychological measures can be used in a variety of ways by applied consultants working with athletes. Vealey and Garner-Holman (1998) referred to these uses as the "what" and "why" of assessment in applied sport psychology. Although there are many possible uses of psychological assessment and a number of possible measures for any given use, we have chosen to focus on a few common applications and measures.

Coach's Perspective

Anxiety, motivation, confidence, and cohesion are all very important to coaches because these elements are important to individual and team performance. As with physical assessment and training methods, coaches need to be open to using any technological advances, including psychological assessment, that could improve performance.

■ ■ ■ ■

Athlete's Perspective

I strongly believe that psychological assessments are very useful and that not enough focus is given to them in my sport. The importance of these types of assessments is underestimated, but this kind of testing can only work if the athlete understands what is being done and the reasons for it. It is also important that the athlete is willing to participate.

■ ■ ■ ■

Evaluation of Psychological States and Traits

Applied sport psychology consultants are interested in the psychological states that athletes experience before or during competition or their traits or general predispositions to experience certain states. These states and traits have important effects on performance and can be improved through psychological skills training (Williams, 2001). For example, mental skills play an important role in the management of stress and anxiety by providing athletes with more positive and adaptive responses to potentially disturbing situations or events (Anshel and Anderson, 2002). Athletes who mentally prepare to more efficiently regulate their arousal level and the intensity of their emotional experiences have been shown to demonstrate more consistency in their performance (Williams, 2001). However, before people can learn and practice self-regulatory techniques, they first need to become aware of their emotional and psychological states (Ravizza, 2001). According to Ravizza, awareness is a key element for improving self-control. As athletes gain awareness, they can better control their emotions, thoughts, and physiological responses and integrate them into optimal performances. Conversely, a lack of awareness in the present moment typically has been associated with an excessive focus on the outcome. Enhanced awareness should thus be encouraged because it allows athletes to become mindful of their ideal performance states as well as the everyday behaviors in which they engage to achieve these states (Ravizza, 2001). One way to increase this awareness is by inviting athletes to complete psychological tests to evaluate a number of attributes and skills.

Anxiety

Competitive anxiety is one psychological attribute that has received a tremendous amount of research attention (see chapter 3 for a discussion of the relationship of athletic performance and intensity). Although debate continues about the precise nature of the relationship between competitive anxiety and sport performance, it is considered an important psychological contributor to athletic performance. In contemporary approaches, competitive anxiety is conceptualized as having somatic and cognitive components (Martens, Vealey, and Burton, 1990). Although variability exists across sports, settings, and individual athletes, most researchers agree that every athlete has an optimal level of physiological activation (i.e., somatic anxiety) and that under- or overactivation is detrimental to performance (Woodman and Hardy, 2001). Because a major goal of applied consultants is to help athletes achieve an optimal level of intensity, consultants must be able to accurately assess activation.

One popular measure of state anxiety and perhaps one of the most researched sport-specific inventories available is the Competitive State Anxiety Inventory (CSAI-2; Martens, Burton, Vealey, Bump, and Smith, 1990). This 27-item tool includes three subscales: cognitive anxiety, somatic anxiety, and self-confidence. The CSAI-2 was rigorously developed, and a large body of literature supports its validity and reliability.

Despite its meticulous development, challenges to the validity of the CSAI-2 have arisen as a result of more sophisticated analyses. One recent study questioned its factorial structural validity because indexes of inadequate fit resulted when it was subjected to confirmatory factor analyses (Lane, Sewell, Terry, Bartram, and Nesti, 1999). Others have also challenged the construct validity of the CSAI-2 by questioning whether the measure, particularly the somatic anxiety subscale, measures anxiety as a negative affect akin to fear or non-specific arousal that may be experienced as a positive emotion like excitement (Jones, 1991, 1995). Jones and Swain (1992) developed a modified version of the CSAI-2 that measures symptom intensity with the original response scale, and they included an interpretation scale that asks athletes to evaluate the symptom as facilitative or debilitative to performance. Because several studies have found the interpretation of symptoms to be as good as or better than symptom intensity as a predictor of performance (Woodman and Hardy, 2001), applied sport psychologists should consider using this modified version to get a better account of the emotional state of athletes before competition.

Brief measures of competitive state anxiety have been developed that may be more practical for use in applied settings. For example, a consultant may be interested in accumulating precompetition state anxiety measures from an athlete over several occasions to try to understand the ideal state for that athlete. Even a relatively brief 21-item measure may be too cumbersome for this task, but a measure with only a few items would be ideal. The Mental Readiness Form (Krane, 1994) and the Anxiety Rating Scale (Cox, Russell, and Robb, 1998, 1999) both use single items to assess state somatic anxiety, cognitive anxiety, and self-confidence. Both have also demonstrated adequate concurrent validity when statistically compared with the CSAI-2 and could be considered as reasonable alternatives to the longer CSAI-2 in applied settings. However, to date, these measures have only been evaluated using intensity response scales. Additional versions that include a directional interpretation scale are not yet available.

Applied consultants are also interested in assessing psychological traits that influence sport performance. Measures that examine traitlike predispositions to experience competitive anxiety (i.e., trait anxiety) are available. The unidimensional Sport Competition Anxiety Test (Martens et al., 1990) has been supplanted by a measure consistent with the current multidimensional conceptualization of anxiety, that is, the Sport Anxiety Scale (SAS; Smith, Smoll, and Schutz, 1990). The 21-item SAS consists of three subscales measuring trait somatic anxiety, cognitive anxiety, and cognitive disruptions. Although one recent study raised questions about the structural validity of the measure (Dunn, Dunn, Wilson, and Syrotuik, 2000), the measure has demonstrated acceptable psychometric properties (Smith, Smoll, and Wiechman, 1998).

Finally, one of the more popular and well-supported theoretical models depicting the relationship between anxiety and performance is Hanin's individualized zones of optimal functioning (IZOF) model (Raglin and Hanin, 2000). Hanin recently expanded this model to include emotions other than anxiety (Hanin, 2000). According to this model, each athlete has a unique profile of multidimensional positive and negative mood states that is associated with best and worst performances. Each of these positive and negative mood states can help or inhibit performance. The approach to assessing mood constructs is idiographic in that individual athletes identify the most personally relevant emotional states and then rate the positive or negative tone of these states relative to performance. Because of the idiographic nature of this type of assessment, traditional psychometric properties are unknown, but the approach has great intuitive and practical appeal for applied consulting with athletes. An example of a multidimensional IZOF profile of emotional states for successful and poor performances can be found in figure 6.1.

Athlete's Perspective

One of the most important things to know about athletes is their optimal level of physiological activation. Everyone is different, and what works for your teammates may not work for you. For example, I have a teammate who is always underactivated. For me, this state would be detrimental to my performance. I also know that it is impossible to always be at your optimal level of activation, but through assessments, you should know what works best for you in different situations. I have been in competitive situations where I have felt underactivated; that is, too calm and relaxed, and the results were not good.

■   ■   ■   ■   ■

Motivation

Another concept that can be measured in terms of traits or states is motivation. More than 20 tests exist to assess motivation, but some have been more commonly recognized and used. Measurement of motivation is far from straightforward, and one must think carefully about what construct is to be measured. For example, motivation can be thought of as either situational (statelike, immediate motivation to engage in or pursue a specific task now) or contextual (traitlike, general motivation to engage in a general class of behaviors over time, like play a certain sport). A second aspect to be considered is the nature of motivation to be assessed, which could include intrinsic or extrinsic factors or both (Vallerand and Fortier, 1998). Finally, one may be interested in a more abstract conceptualization of motivation. Goal orientation theory relates motivation to the general orientation of individuals to define success in terms of competence (task goals) or self-worth (ego goals; Duda and Hall, 2001). From a consultant's perspective, if you work with athletes who report that they compete in their sport to please their parents or to win medals at all costs, for example, it might

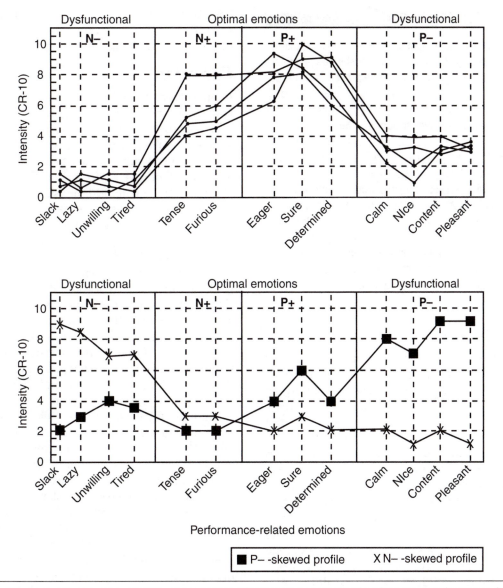

Figure 6.1 Emotion profiles based on Hanin's zones of optional functioning and emotional profiling measure for successful (top) and unsuccessful (bottom) javelin throw performances (Hanin, 2000).

Reprinted, by permission, from Y.L. Hanin, 1999, *Emotions in sport* (Champaign, IL: Human Kinetics), 315, 316.

be beneficial to ask them to complete a few tests to evaluate their levels of intrinsic and extrinsic motivation as well as their task and ego orientation. The results could be used to support your observations and to educate the athletes on the value of intrinsic motivation and task orientation. Once again, if you are a skilled interviewer, you could likely do this type of assessment without the use of questionnaires.

The Situational Motivation Scale (Guay, Vallerand, and Blanchard, 2000) is a valid and reliable multidimensional measure of intrinsic or extrinsic situational motivation. The Sport Motivation Scale (Pelletier et al., 1995) is a sound inventory that assesses various components of intrinsic and extrinsic motivation and amotivation in sport, but at a more contextual level. Other instruments like the Exercise Motivations Inventory (Markland and Hardy, 1993) and the Personal Incentives for Exercise Questionnaire (Duda and Tappe, 1989) evaluate motives for participating in exercise settings. Finally, the Task and Ego Orientation Questionnaire (Duda, 1989) and the Perceptions of Success Questionnaire (Roberts, Treasure, and Balague, 1998) are useful measures of the general motivational orientation of individuals.

Athlete's Perspective

Psychological assessment should be used in addition to other methods. It is equally as important as physical testing, and even if athletes are negative toward it at the beginning, they will eventually realize that a variety of questions may prompt them to think about aspects of sport that they never thought about before. For example, at one period of my training, I was not highly enthusiastic about going to practice every day. I completed different tests relating to motivation, was able to determine what was causing this problem, and worked to change it immediately. These types of assessments can be very useful to screen motivational problems in athletes. However, it is just as important to know how to proceed once a motivational problem is discovered. The coach, sport psychologist, and the athlete need to sit down together and discuss the results.

■   ■   ■   ■   ■

Confidence

Another variable requiring constant assessment is confidence. Confidence can vary substantially from one competition to the next depending on past results (Durand-Bush, 1995). Several tests are available to measure confidence or related constructs such as self-efficacy and self-esteem in both sport and exercise contexts; however, it might not be practical to administer a questionnaire before each competition. For some athletes, it could be intrusive and even disrupt their focus, and in such cases verbal checks are efficient and just as effective. For consultants who will use scales to assess confidence at opportune moments, note that scales have been developed specifically for children, adults, athletes, and coaches. The Trait Sport-Confidence Inventory and State Sport-Confidence Inventory (Vealey, 1986) assess beliefs regarding one's ability to be successful in sport. It could be useful to administer these inventories early in a season to get an idea of an athlete's level of confidence. On the other hand, the Physical Self-Efficacy Scale (Ryckman, Robbins, Thornton, and Cantrell, 1982) measures perceived physical ability and confidence in physical self-representation in social situations. This scale could be administered to athletes or individuals who have concerns about their physical ability and image in the presence of others. Finally, the CSAI-2 described earlier includes a subscale that assesses state self-confidence (Martens et al., 1990). Consequently, a consultant could be more efficient by assessing both anxiety and confidence at the same time with one questionnaire. The draw-back is that there might not be as much depth in the results if the scale contains fewer items than other scales focusing solely on self-confidence.

Cohesion

Another type of psychological state related to team sport performance is perceptions of team cohesiveness. Coaches and applied sport psychology consultants involved with teams are often interested in enhancing team chemistry or cohesion in an attempt to improve performance. Group cohesion is a dynamic and multidimensional process that takes into account instrumental goals or task cohesion as well as social and affective needs or social cohesion (Carron, Brawley, and Widmeyer, 1998). Although available data suggest that the effect of performance on subsequent cohesion may be stronger than the influence of cohesion on performance (Mullen and Cooper, 1994), there is enough evidence suggesting that monitoring and enhancing cohesion are worthwhile tasks (Carron, Colman, Wheeler, and Stevens, 2002). Consequently, several questionnaires have been developed to assess group cohesion. Carron, Widmeyer, and Brawley (1985) created the Group Environment Questionnaire, a tool commonly used for assessing task and social aspects of group cohesion. The Multidimensional Sport Cohesion Instrument (Yukelson, Weinberg, and Jackson, 1984) is another instrument that was designed to assess group cohesion based on task-related and social factors in basketball. To examine interpersonal working relationships, group success, and attraction to sport groups, one can use the Team Cohesion Questionnaire (Gruber and Gray, 1981). Discussing the results of a group cohesion questionnaire with a sports team can be enough to create change. The exercise allows the members to become aware of issues affecting the team and provides an opportunity for them to openly discuss and find solutions as a group.

Evaluation of Psychological Skills and Attributes

In addition to studying traits and states, sport psychologists are interested in helping athletes enhance specific psychological skills that, in turn, allow athletes to better control their thoughts, emotions, and behaviors during performance. To this end, it is worthwhile to assess the athletes' level and frequency of use of psychological skills to identify strengths and weaknesses (Murphy and Tammen, 1998). Furthermore, adequate assessments of psychological skills can be used to give feedback to athletes and evaluate progress and outcomes of psychological skills training efforts.

Assessment of Single Skills and Attributes

Numerous inventories have been developed to evaluate single psychological skills including attention, imagery, and leadership. In fact, one can use several tests to measure the same skill. Because so many are available, consultants must carefully determine and justify what they want to measure and, of course, consider the validity and reliability of the instruments. The following section describes some assessment instruments that are often used to evaluate specific psychological skills.

Attention

In terms of attention, the Test of Attention and Interpersonal Style (TAIS; Nideffer, 1976) is perhaps the most widely used and cited in the literature. This test allows one to examine two dimensions of attention: width (broad–narrow) and direction (internal–external) (see chapter 4). The TAIS has been used to predict sport performance based on attention characteristics and capacities. Although Nideffer (1976) found the instrument to be valid and reliable, some researchers evaluated the factorial validity of the TAIS and found that many of its subscales had insufficient factorial validity as well as poor discriminant validity (Ford and Summers, 1992). Sport-specific versions of the TAIS have been developed to examine attention in baseball (Albrecht and Feltz, 1987), riflery (Etzel, 1979), tennis (Van Schoyck and Grasha, 1981), and soccer (Fisher and Taylor, 1980). However, the psychometric properties of these tests are unknown. Some consultants have found that attention is often misunderstood by athletes. Athletes often report that they need to focus better, but they do not know how to do this. Educating them about the dimensions of attention and helping them break down challenging sport tasks to determine the type of focus they need to perform those tasks can be very useful. Also, assessing athletes' attentional style makes them aware of their strengths and weaknesses. The TAIS can serve this assessment purpose; however, individuals must take a course to be able to administer the TAIS, and the fees can be expensive.

Imagery

Imagery is another skill that is commonly assessed by researchers and sport psychology consultants. The Imagery Use Questionnaire (Hall, Rodgers, and Barr, 1990) examines factors related to using imagery in sport and appears to have acceptable psychometric properties. Hall, Pongrac, and Buckholz (1985) also developed the Movement Imagery Questionnaire to assess visual and kinesthetic imagery of movements, but the validity of this questionnaire is not clear. For athletes who are not familiar with imagery or have never used it, consultants can assess the athletes' skill level using a paper-and-pencil questionnaire. It is sometimes difficult for athletes to articulate the vividness and control of their imagery; thus, they feel guided and can be more specific when they respond to questions on an assessment tool. (See chapter 8 for a full discussion of mental imagery.)

Leadership

Evaluating leadership is valuable in sport settings, and consequently several instruments have been developed to gain insight into athletes' and coaches' leadership qualities and behaviors. Chelladurai (1990) has made a significant contribution to the research on leadership in sport. Chelladurai and Saleh (1980) developed the Leadership Scale for Sports (LSS), which examines three specific aspects of leadership: (1) athletes' preferences for specific leader behaviors of coaches, (2) athletes' perceptions regarding actual leader behaviors of their coaches, and (3) coaches' perceptions of their own leadership behaviors. This questionnaire is particularly interesting if a consultant wants to evaluate and compare the perceptions of both coaches and athletes. It is not uncommon for these two parties to have diverging perceptions regarding a given situation. If the communication is not optimal, this can easily result in tension or conflict and can potentially compromise the relationship between coaches and their athletes. Clarifying perceptions and trying to improve the communication between both parties is an important role for a consultant in many instances. Asking coaches and athletes to complete a questionnaire like the LSS and discussing the results with both the coaches and athletes is an objective way to improve communication. Another test, the Sport Leadership Behavior Inventory (Glenn and Horn, 1993), was developed to assess leadership tendencies in soccer athletes; however, little is known about the validity of this instrument.

Staleness

Some sports involving high levels of aerobic fitness require intense training during which athletes stress their bodies to improve performance. Typical training regimens include sustained periods of high volume and high intensity, followed by a tapering period during which training loads are reduced and athletes are able to recover. Optimal training requires that a balance be maintained between training loads that result in adaptive compensation, which increase performance, and training loads that result in maladaptive responses, which hurt performance. For the majority of athletes, this type of training schedule improves performance. However, some athletes do not respond this way and their performance plateaus or declines (Morgan et al., 1987; Raglin, 1993; Raglin and Wilson, 2000). If athletes suffer significant and prolonged performance decreases that cannot be overcome by short-term rest, they may be suffering from what is known as the *staleness syndrome* (Raglin, 1993). Staleness is a psychobiological reaction involving both psychological and biological symptoms, such as depression and neuroendocrine changes (Raglin and Wilson, 2000).

An optimal training load appears to be individual to each athlete, which has rendered the task of predicting and detecting the early onset of staleness more difficult (Raglin and Wilson, 2000). Although a variety of physiological, neurological, and psychological measures have been used in attempts to accurately predict staleness, psychological changes that result from overtraining have been found to be the most stable and reliable (Raglin, 1993; Raglin and Wilson, 2000). Most notably, The Profile of Mood States (POMS; McNair, Lorr, and Droppleman, 1971) is a reliable 64-item questionnaire that assesses tension, depression, anger, fatigue, confusion, and vigor. These mood factors are then combined to provide an overall assessment of an athlete's total mood state. Mood changes detected by the POMS have been found to be relatively sensitive and specific predictors of staleness when objective indicators of staleness are known. However, the ability of the POMS to reliably differentiate athletes likely to experience staleness is less known (Raglin and Wilson, 2000). Two uncontrolled studies in which the POMS was used to quantify training loads resulted in the prevention of staleness in two small samples (Berglund and Säfström, 1994; Raglin, 1993). Nevertheless, less supportive results were found in another study (Martin, Andersen, and Gates, 2000). A shortened 37-item version of the POMS has also been developed and shown to be highly correlated to results obtained with the longer version (Curran, Andrykowski, and Studts, 1995; Shacham, 1983).

More recently, Kellman and colleagues attempted to develop a sport-specific measure of staleness to provide a more precise analysis of the stress-recovery process and more accurate predictions of staleness. Kellman (2002) framed the problem of staleness as one of *underrecovery* to training demands and developed the Recovery-Stress Questionnaire for Athletes (RESTQ-Sport; Kellman and Kallus, 2001) to measure both stressors and recovery states of athletes. According to Kellman and Kallus (2001), the development of staleness is determined by more than simply increased training loads. It is a function of the complex interaction of physical stress, psychological stress, and use of recovery or coping strategies. Consequently, the RESTQ-Sport includes measures of general, emotional, and social stress; recovery processes used; and psychological indicators of staleness.

The 12 subscales of the RESTQ-Sport have been found to have adequate internal consistency and test–retest reliability over short periods of time (Kallus and Kellman, 2000). Some data also suggest that the recovery scales of the RESTQ-Sport are predictive of performance, with less recovery yielding poorer performance (Kellman, Kallus, and Kurz, 1996). It also appears that the RESTQ-Sport is comparable to the POMS in evaluating the psychological impact of overtraining (Kellman, Altenburg, Lormes, and Steinacker, 2001). Controlled experiments have not been conducted to test the utility of the RESTQ-Sport for monitoring athletes to prevent the onset of staleness; however, case studies have been presented that provide some, albeit weak, evidence that this measure may be useful for staleness prevention (Kallus and Kellman, 2000; Kellman and Kallus, 2001).

One significant advantage of using the RESTQ-Sport over the POMS is that it assesses not only the psychological impact of training but also the perceived sources of stress and recovery resources of athletes. This information is of great value to applied consultants, coaches, and athletes for taking preventive and proactive steps in response to staleness. Interventions might include reductions in training load (i.e., physical stress) as well as strategies to reduce overall stress levels and improve recovery resources, such as improved sleep quality and social interactions. The RESTQ-Sport can also serve the important functions of enhancing communication between athletes, coaches, and applied consultants and increasing overall performance and well-being. An example of an athlete's scores on the RESTQ-Sport at two different times in her training cycle can be found in figure 6.2.

Of interest to applied consultants who prefer brief assessments, Kellman and colleagues also

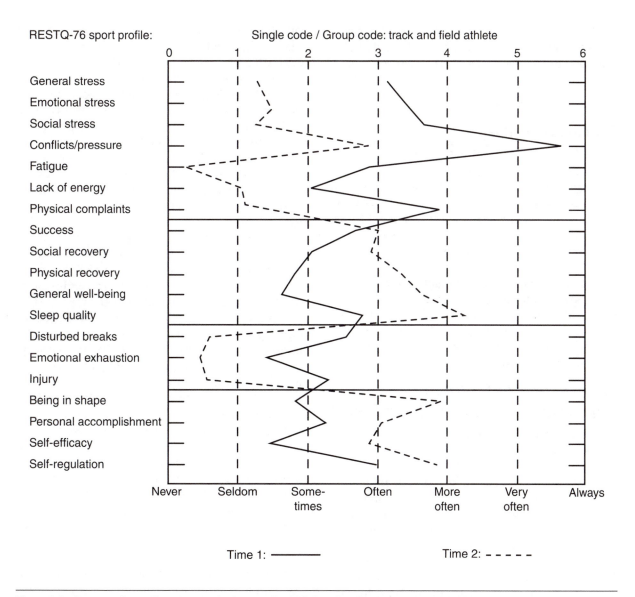

RESTQ-76 sport profile: Single code / Group code: track and field athlete

Figure 6.2 Recovery-Stress Questionnaire for Athletes (RESTQ-Sport) profiles for a female track athlete following the intense overload phase of training (Time 1, solid line) and after a planned taper to enhance recovery (Time 2, dashed line).

Reprinted, by permission, from M. Kellman et al., 2002, The recovery-cue and its use in applied settings: Practical suggestions regarding assessment and monitoring of recovery. In *Enhancing recovery: Preventing underperformance in athletics* (Champaign, IL: Human Kinetics), 224.

developed a concise measure of stress and recovery, the Recovery-Cue (Kellman, Botterill, and Wilson, 1999; Kellman, Patrick, Botterill, and Wilson, 2002), a seven-item inventory of what are believed to be the most critical dimensions of stress and recovery. It was designed to be used frequently over longer periods of time, for example, over an entire season. Relatively little data on the psychometric properties of the Recovery-Cue are available, but it is a promising new measure that may maximize the practical benefits of assessing stress and recovery.

Athlete's Perspective

Being able to evaluate staleness during training is extremely important. In the national training center here in Ottawa, there are both male and female players and we all train on the table the same amount of hours per week. However, we are all different ages, ranging from 16 to 45 years old! Obviously, we are also at different levels of physical fitness. How is a coach to detect staleness? To make things even worse, every player has a different pain threshold, which makes it hard for the coach to determine if we are being excessively sensitive or if we are genuinely overtrained. I think assessment of staleness would be helpful, and I wish we could use this type of psychological testing in our sport.

■ ■ ■ ■ ■

Readiness to Engage in Psychological Skills Training

Sport psychology consultants may at times be interested in the motivational readiness of athletes to engage in psychological skills training (PST). Some athletes may be interested in PST as a way to enhance performance, whereas others may be reluctant or disinterested. A reliable and valid brief measure of readiness to use PST is the Stages of Change for Psychological Skills Training (Leffingwell, Rider, and Williams, 2001). Awareness of an athlete's readiness to use PST can be helpful to consultants who are wondering whether they should spend more time creating interest in PST or proceed with interventions.

Assessment of Multiple Psychological Skills and Attributes

Although many inventories have been developed to assess one particular skill, others can evaluate multiple psychological skills. The advantage of using such tests is that one can obtain an overall profile of skills at once, rather than administering multiple single-skill tests, which can take considerable time for clients or participants. The disadvantage of using multiple-skill tests is that some of the skills included might lack some depth. Nevertheless, researchers and sport psychology consultants find merit in using them. Following are examples of multiple-skill tests.

Ottawa Mental Skills Assessment Tool

The Ottawa Mental Skills Assessment Tool (OMSAT-3*; Durand-Bush, Salmela, and Green-Demers, 2001) is a psychometrically sound test that includes 48 items and 12 mental skill scales grouped under three broader conceptual components: (1) foundation skills (goal setting, self-confidence, commitment), which are believed to be essential for high-quality performance in sport and are considered the building blocks for the development of other mental skills; (2) psychosomatic skills (stress reactions, fear control, relaxation, activation), which influence variations in physiological activation as well as mental and physical intensity and can be used for their regulation; and (3) cognitive skills (imagery, mental practice, focusing, refocusing, and competition planning), which rely on thinking processes and activities that include sensation, perception, learning, memory, and reasoning. The OMSAT-3* is user-friendly in that it contains clear, comprehensive items that target general behaviors as well as behaviors more specific to both training and competition. After completing the questionnaire, individuals can immediately obtain a summary profile that includes their scores on the 12 different scales, a visual graph, and an interpretation of their scores based on each skill (see figure 6.3 for an example).

The OMSAT-3* has acceptable psychometric properties. A first-order confirmatory factor analysis (CFA) revealed that the OMSAT-3* scales have a sound factorial structure (Durand-Bush et al., 2001). An important feature of the OMSAT-3* is that its scales are regrouped under three broader conceptual components. A second-order CFA assessing the validity of the three broader conceptual components also yielded adequate indexes of fit. The OMSAT-3* can significantly discriminate between competitive and elite level athletes, thus displaying discriminant validity. In terms of reliability, the OMSAT-3* scales generally reflected acceptable internal consistency, with values ranging from .68 to .88. Intraclass reliabilities ranged from .78 to .96 and yielded a mean temporal stability score of .86, indicating that the OMSAT-3* scales are generally stable over time.

Previous experiences with the OMSAT-3* have shown that it is useful for generating discussion, confirming current training and competitive behaviors, and determining what is beneficial for each athlete. When a consultant is working with a large group of athletes, it is often difficult to meet with all of them individually. One way to respect time constraints and to obtain a holistic view of a team's strengths and weaknesses is to have the athletes complete a multiple-skill inventory like the OMSAT-3* and calculate team and individual scores. These scores can be visually displayed and discussed in a team session to target areas of intervention. They can also be used to help develop appropriate mental skills training programs for both teams and individual athletes. Finally, the development and maintenance of mental skills can be monitored by administering an inventory like the OMSAT-3* at different times throughout a season. These results can indicate that interventions need to be altered or increased based on the changing needs and interests of the athletes involved.

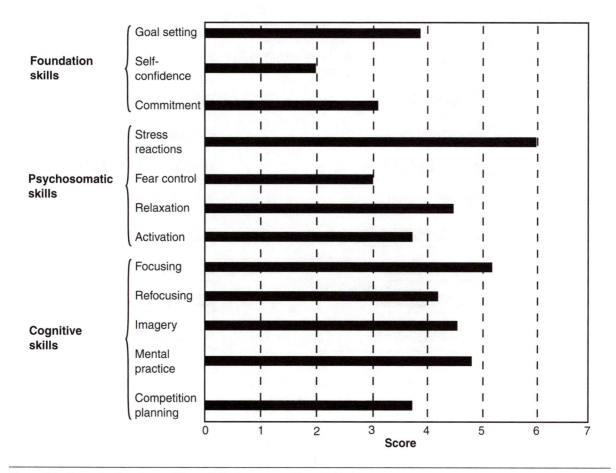

Figure 6.3 Example of an Ottawa Mental Skills Assessment Tool (OMSAT-3*) summary profile that includes an athlete's scores on the 12 different scales.

We have a fairly big team here in Ottawa. Outside of actual table tennis practice, everyone has different schedules and times of availability. It is almost impossible to get all of us together at the same time. One thing you want to avoid is discouraging an athlete by piling on too many psychological tests. A good solution to this problem is to assess multiple skills.

■ ■ ■ ■ ■

Test of Performance Strategies

The Test of Performance Strategies (TOPS; Thomas, Murphy, and Hardy, 1999) is a 64-item questionnaire that assesses a total of nine self-regulation and performance enhancement skills including self-talk, emotional control, automaticity, goal setting, imagery, activation, relaxation, negative thinking, and attentional control. The structural validity of the measure has only been established using exploratory factor analysis, but the measure has demonstrated adequate internal consistency (α = .66-.81). Test–retest reliability estimates are not reported, but the measure has been found to discriminate among athletes of different competitive levels (Thomas et al., 1999).

Two features distinguish the TOPS from other measures. First, the TOPS assesses the frequency of use of psychological skills rather than the level of agreement with characteristics more akin to measures of personality. Second, the measure includes subscales for both practice and competition, which can be quite useful. Only moderate correlations have been observed for the practice and competition scales for the same strategy, suggesting somewhat differential use of strategies in competition and training (r = .25-.69; Thomas et al., 1999). Normative data are available for athletes at different competitive levels, which can be valuable when providing comparative feedback to athletes regarding their use of psychological skills

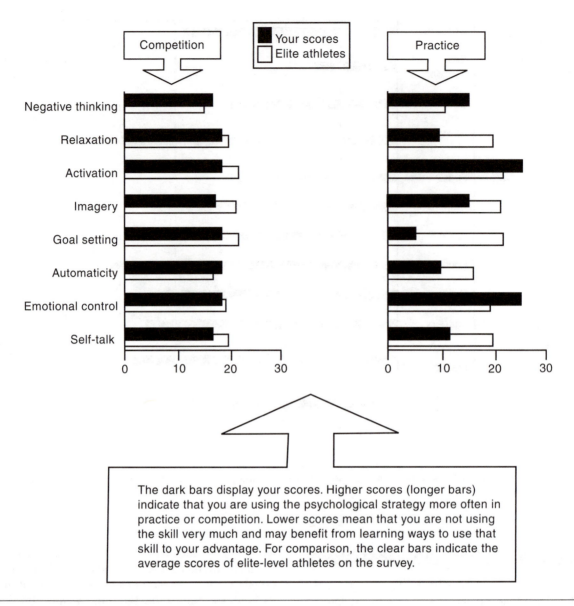

The dark bars display your scores. Higher scores (longer bars) indicate that you are using the psychological strategy more often in practice or competition. Lower scores mean that you are not using the skill very much and may benefit from learning ways to use that skill to your advantage. For comparison, the clear bars indicate the average scores of elite-level athletes on the survey.

Figure 6.4 Normative feedback comparing an intercollegiate athlete's reported use of psychological skills as measured by the Test of Performance Strategies (TOPS) with elite athletes' normative scores on the same measure.

compared with that of athletes at similar or higher levels of competition (see figure 6.4). This kind of normative feedback can help to identify relative strengths and weaknesses and motivate athletes to gain a competitive edge over athletes at the same or higher levels.

Athletic Coping Skills Inventory-28

Another multiple skills assessment tool is the Athletic Coping Skills Inventory (ACSI)-28, which was developed by Smith, Schutz, Smoll, and Ptacek (1995). According to the authors, a confirmatory factor analysis justified seven underlying subscales: (1) coping with adversity, (2) peaking under pressure, (3) goal setting and mental preparation, (4) concentration, (5) freedom from worry, (6) confidence and achievement motivation, and (7) coachability. Smith and colleagues retested after 1 week and reported reliability coefficients ranging from .47 to .87. Although the ACSI-28 appears to be an acceptable instrument, some questions can be raised. For example, why are goal setting and mental preparation part of one scale when mental preparation is a broad concept encompassing several requisite skills and strategies, including goal setting (Orlick, 1996)? The same question can be posed regarding the confidence and achievement motivation scale. The literature suggests that confidence and achievement motivation are two distinct constructs (Duda and Hall, 2001), yet they were incorporated in the same scale. Statistically, it might have been the best option; however, from a theoretical point of view, it is suspect. Finally, some specific items might be more difficult to interpret because they concurrently ask two questions; however, if consultants follow up with a face-to-face interview, they could clarify with athletes the information obtained from the test.

Coach's Perspective

Psychological skills can be taught to athletes with the intent of improving athletic performance. The most useful measures would be able to identify strengths and weaknesses and would be sensitive to improvements over time. Attention, imagery, and leadership are all important to coaches.

■ ■ ■ ■ ■

Additional Assessment Methods

Many traditional paper-and-pencil assessment tools are available to applied sport psychology consultants to provide a better understanding of the individuals with whom they work. However, as previously mentioned, there is value in using a combination of methods not only to gain the most accurate and in-depth picture of clients but also to satisfy their personal assessment needs. Aside from using paper-and-pencil tests, consultants frequently use verbal communication or interviewing when working with athletes. Effective interviewing requires training and to a great extent can be considered the art of a consultant's

work (Ivey and Ivey, 2003). It is therefore important that consultants develop a variety of interviewing skills to evaluate psychological skills and develop personalized interventions to help their clients.

Observation is another method used to gather important information. Although consultants can informally spend time on the field with their clients to make observations about their behaviors and interactions, consultants can engage in more systematic observation by using specific instruments to document information. In one particular study, Lloyd and Trudel (1999) used an adapted version of the Flanders Interaction Analysis in the Classroom instrument to analyze the content of verbal interactions between a consultant and several of his clients. This instrument is only one among several that can be adapted and used to observe athletes and coaches in action. Several instruments exist and have been documented (Darst, Zakrajsek, and Mancini, 1989); consultants need appropriate training to engage in systematic observation and to adapt instruments for use in sport psychology.

Another method that is increasingly being used by consultants in their work with athletes is videotaping. Coaches have long used this method to discuss performances with their athletes. Trudel, Gilbert, and Tochon (2001) wrote an interesting article to describe the use of video to study pedagogical interactions in sport. Although filming can be used for research purposes, there is much to be gained from using videos with athletes in consultation to improve performance. Videotaping and debriefing can be done by consultants in a more informal manner; however, debriefing can take the form of a structured stimulated recall session to provide specific feedback (Gilbert, Trudel, and Haughian, 1999).

Key Points

- Researchers, applied consultants, coaches, and athletes are becoming increasingly more aware of the importance of psychological assessment for improving athletic performance, at both the individual and team level.

- Psychological assessment tools must have acceptable psychometric properties (i.e., validity and reliability) and be practical.

- A number of psychological states and traits relevant to sport performance (e.g., anxiety, motivation, confidence, team cohesion) can be reliably and validly measured.

- A number of tools are available to evaluate specific psychological skills and attributes perceived to be important for optimal sport performance (e.g., attention, imagery, leadership, staleness, readiness to engage in PST).

(continued)

- Global measures (e.g., OMSAT-3*, TOPS, ACSI-28) can be used to assess multiple psychological skills at once.

- Because many psychological inventories are available, consumers must determine their objectives for psychological assessment and must choose the most appropriate tools for achieving their objectives.

- Applied sport psychology consultants should use a variety of assessment methods (e.g., observation, interviews, paper-and-pencil tests, videotaping) when attempting to evaluate and monitor athletes' psychological skills and attributes.

Review Questions

1. Why is psychological assessment important in sport, exercise, and health psychology?

2. How can psychological assessment be used to enhance sport performance?

3. What does the term *validity* mean when used in statistical reference to a test?

4. What is the difference between construct and content validity?

5. What does the term *reliability* mean with regard to psychological assessment?

6. How are psychological states different from traits?

7. How is Hanin's ZOF assessment method different from other types of assessment of psychological states?

8. Why is the assessment of mood states important in the training of athletes?

9. How are the OMSAT-3*, TOPS, and ACSI-28 different from each other?

10. Why should consultants be critical when reviewing and selecting psychological assessment tools?

11. Why should consultants use multiple methods of assessment when working with athletes?

CHAPTER

7
Goal Setting

Robert S. Weinberg, PhD—researcher
Robert J. Harmison, PhD—consultant*
Ric Rosenkranz, MS—coach
Stacia Hookom, RN—athlete

© Photodisc

The objectives of this chapter are

- to review research regarding the relationship between goal setting and sport performance;
- to discuss how goal setting regulates behavior and performance in sport;
- to present goal-setting principles to help coaches and athletes set goals; and
- to describe the details of a goal-setting program that helps athletes plan, execute, and evaluate learning and performance.

*Though Robert Weinberg, the researcher, is listed as the first author for this chapter to maintain consistency with the four perspectives highlighted in this book, the editors credit Robert Harmison, the consultant, as the lead contributor to this chapter.

For years, coaches, athletes, and applied sport psychology consultants have alluded to the importance of goal setting in achieving athletic success. Anecdotal reports by coaches and athletes commonly indicated the use of goal setting as a means to enhance motivation and improve performance. The first order of business for most consultants working with athletes was to have them identify their competitive goals. Despite this interest, and although many studies were conducted in industrial and organizational settings, little empirical research was conducted in sport settings before 1985 to support the use of goal setting by athletes. Since then, as Burton, Naylor, and Holliday (2001) noted in their chapter in the *Handbook of Sport Psychology,* "an exponential explosion of goal setting research in sport has occurred" (p. 497), and Kyllo and Landers (1995) conducted the first meta-analysis on goal setting in sport settings. Hence, by the mid-2000s, although there has been a tremendous amount of goal-setting research in the sport psychology literature supporting its value to athletes and coaches, there is often a disconnect between what researchers have empirically discovered and what applied consultants, coaches, and athletes actually do in sport settings.

Key Issues

Athletes must maintain high levels of motivation to achieve competitive success. Athletes need strategies to focus their efforts and regulate their behaviors during training and competition to consistently perform their best. Goal setting is often viewed as one of the most effective means to motivate and direct athletic behavior (Burton et al., 2001; Gould, 2001). Typically, coaches do not have a problem getting athletes to set goals. However, many coaches experience difficulty getting athletes to set goals that enhance the quality of their training and competitive performances. Athletes generally do not need to be convinced that goals are important; rather, they need to be instructed concerning the best goals to set and the most effective way to apply them to their training and competitive efforts.

Chapter Purpose and Author Team

The purpose of this chapter is to integrate empirical findings from the goal-setting literature with an applied sport psychology consultant's perspective regarding how this information is best incorporated into sport settings. The researcher (Dr. Robert Weinberg) reviews goal-setting theory and research in industrial, organizational, and sport settings and provides insights into the types of goals athletes should set and the most effective way to set them. Drawing on his experiences working with elite athletes, the consultant (Dr. Robert Harmison) describes goal-setting strategies that are consistent with the goal-setting principles identified in the research to help athletes increase their motivation for sport and enhance the self-regulation of their sport behaviors. The coach (Ric Rosenkranz) offers his views on the importance of goal setting in coaching athletes. Finally, the athlete (Stacia Hookom) shares her perspective on the use of goal setting and its impact on the learning and performing of sport skills required to be a World Cup snowboarder.

Understanding Goal Setting and Sport Performance

Goal setting is a complex process that is used by many coaches and athletes, but it is also frequently misused. Ineffective application of goal setting often results from incomplete knowledge of the essential components of goal setting and how it is used with athletes. The value of goal setting depends on how well applied consultants, coaches, and athletes grasp the intricacies of goal setting and its relationship to sport performance.

The term *goal* refers to attaining a specific level of proficiency on a task, usually within a specified time limit (Locke, Shaw, Saari, and Latham, 1981). Goals can sometimes be objective and quantifiable, such as improving one's tennis first-serve percentage from 55% to 60%. Goals also can be subjective and more difficult to measure, such as increased satisfaction with teammates.

In sport settings, applied sport psychology consultants have distinguished between outcome, performance, and process goals. *Outcome goals* refer to the desired result of a competition, for example, finishing first in a swim meet or winning the state golf championship. Thus, achieving an outcome goal depends, at least in part, on the ability and performance of other athletes. *Performance goals* refer to athletes' actual performance in relation to their own standard of excellence (e.g., improve their high jump from 5 feet 9 inches to 6 feet) and are under athletes' control. *Process goals* are concerned with how athletes perform particular skills or execute certain strategies. They are typically the focus in practice or training (e.g., in basketball, following through on a foul shot). Although outcome goals are a necessary part of goal setting, process and performance goals are particularly important for athletes because these goals are within the control of athletes and because achievement of process and performance goals often leads to attainment of outcome goals.

Goals regulate human action by providing an internal standard by which people can compare and evaluate their performances (Locke and Latham, 1990). Goals influence how we behave, and they help us judge how well we are doing as we strive for a predetermined level of performance. In addition, goals mediate how performance is affected by degree of commitment, knowledge of results, personality factors, monetary incentives, time limits, participation in decision making, and competition.

More than 600 goal-setting studies have been conducted testing the goal setting–performance relationship. This research has explored issues such as goal proximity, goal commitment, goal type, goal specificity, and goal difficulty. Indicative of the findings, of the 201 studies involving more than 40,000 participants that were reviewed by Locke and Latham (1990), goal-setting effects were evident in 183 studies, a remarkable 91% success rate. This influence of goal setting on performance has been robust in its consistency and magnitude, with this effect being present across a wide variety of tasks, settings, performance criteria, and types of participants.

Goal specificity has been one of the most studied aspects of goal setting, and research findings have repeatedly demonstrated that specific, challenging goals enhance performance and productivity in industrial and organizational settings more effectively than "do your best" goals or no goals at all. Another oft-studied aspect of goals, goal difficulty, has produced equally compelling results, finding that the more difficult the goal, the better the performance (Chidester and Grigsby, 1984; Mento, Steel, and Karren, 1987; Tubbs, 1991). The only exception to this rule is when participants reach the limits of their ability and are simply unable to perform at a higher level.

Considerable goal-setting research has combined goal specificity and goal difficulty. These studies produced equally robust findings. In sum, specific, difficult goals consistently lead to higher levels of performance than do-your-best goals, easy goals, or no goals (Locke and Latham, 1990).

In 1985, Locke and Latham suggested that goal setting might be even more effective in sports than in business because the measurement of performance is typically more objective in sports than in organizational settings. Goal-setting research in sport settings has focused on goal specificity, goal difficulty, and goal proximity. Research that surveyed consultants who had worked with Olympic and collegiate athletes indicated that consultants believed that goal setting was one of the most frequently used, and most effective, psychological interventions in both individual athlete–coach and group consultations (Gould, Greenleaf, Guinan, and Chung, 2002; Gould, Tammen, Murphy, and May, 1989; Sullivan and Nashman, 1998; Orlick and Partington, 1988; Weinberg, Burton, Yukelson, and Weigand, 1993, 2000).

Although applied consultants, coaches, and athletes strongly believe in the effectiveness of goal setting in enhancing performance, the sport psychology literature offers less impressive support than that found in the industrial and organizational literature. For example, Burton and colleagues (2001) conducted a review using 56 goal-setting studies (combining goal specificity and goal difficulty) and found that 44 studies demonstrated moderate or strong effects, a 78% effectiveness rate. Interestingly, in an earlier review, Burton (1993) only found 14 empirical sport-related studies, with positive effects occurring in approximately 66% of these studies. It appears that as more studies have been conducted in sport settings, the strength of goal-setting effects is increasing. However, the robustness of the goal setting–performance relationship is still less than that found in the industrial and organizational literature (see Burton et al., 2001, for a detailed review).

Goal-Setting Interventions in Sport

Although the research discussed to this point has demonstrated a significant relationship between goal setting and sport performance, other investigations have explored the effects of different types of goal-setting interventions on performance. For example, several intervention studies conducted across an entire athletic season indicated that setting specific, obtainable, moderately difficult goals led to higher levels of performance than equivalent control conditions (Kingston and Hardy, 1997; Swain and Jones, 1995; Weinberg, Stitcher, and Richardson, 1994). In addition, recent studies with athletes (e.g., Burton, Weinberg, Yukelson, and Weigand, 1998; Filby, Maynard, and Graydon, 1999; Weinberg, Burke, and Jackson, 1997; Weinberg, Burton et al., 2000) also found positive performance effects for different goal-setting interventions. Although the specific type of goal-setting intervention varied, the results reveal consistencies across sport settings:

- Goals should be moderately difficult, challenging, and realistic.

- Long-term goals provide athletes with direction, and short-term goals provide them with motivation as well as make long-term goals seem more achievable.

- Action plans (i.e., specific ways that goals will be accomplished) facilitate the implementation of goal-setting strategies, although athletes often do not have action plans for how to reach their goals.

- Goal acceptance and commitment are important in keeping motivation high over time.

- Athletes using multiple goal strategies exhibit the best performance.

- Goals plus feedback produce better performance than either goals or feedback alone.

- Athletes and coaches are not systematic in writing down their goals, although they think about and image their goals.

- Major barriers to achieving goals include lack of time, stress, fatigue, academic pressures, and social relationships.

Coach's Perspective

Coaches and athletes generally do not place enough emphasis on the mental aspects of their sports, choosing instead to focus on hard physical training or tactical aspects alone. Although this pattern may be changing as coaches and athletes are increasingly exploring the various avenues of performance enhancement, very few coaches or athletes make the mental side of sport a high priority of their programs. Beyond performance enhancement, setting and achieving goals can greatly increase the athlete's satisfaction and enjoyment of the sport.

One of the most user-friendly mental aspects of sport is the process of setting goals. Athletes need to determine what they want from their athletic endeavors and formulate these often nebulous wishes into concrete goals, which should be put on paper. Coaches should provide direction and motivation in the goal-setting process, but the athletes should determine what they want to achieve. Coaches who simply give athletes goals to work for are failing to tap into the synergy created by athletes and coaches collaboratively working toward shared athletic success.

Proper goal setting facilitates an athletes' development and achievements. Athletes without goals are like tumbleweeds, moving in ever-changing directions with an uncertain destination. These tumbleweeds never end up at the top of the world or even in a desirable place. More likely, they eventually get hung up on some obstacle or just disappear from the sport.

Before athletes can set effective goals, they must determine their current level of ability in relevant aspects of the sport. From there, athletes and coaches can specify desired abilities to achieve within a given time frame and determine how large the gap is between the current and desired abilities. A goal or series of goals will serve as a bridge to cross that gap.

■ ■ ■ ■ ■

Athlete's Perspective

I am a natural goal setter. I started out with goals of getting straight A's and making State in ski racing. Those goals and visions of success motivated me and taught me the path of a goal-oriented lifestyle. As I became a more experienced athlete, the paths toward achieving my goals became more refined.

Obtaining my goals was very rewarding. My successes taught me to dream exceptionally big, in some cases too big. I set specific and difficult goals as I realized that I could accomplish them. The goals that were realistic I was able to reach, whereas others I am still working on. At times, some goals had to take priority over others, a sacrifice for my greater desires. Today, I set goals constantly. They require specific actions to get them done, but I apply them to everything: time management, conditioning, snowboard training, and snowboard racing.

■ ■ ■ ■ ■

Why Goals Work

Whether goals are effective in enhancing sport performance is one important question. Another equally compelling question is why goals work. This understanding is essential for researchers and consultants to devise the most effective goal-setting interventions and for coaches and athletes to apply this knowledge to the specific demands of their sport.

Goals Provide Motivation

The most often discussed account of how goal setting works, the mechanistic explanation, proposes that goals influence performance in several distinct ways (Locke, 1968). First, goals influence performance by directing an individual's attention to the task and to relevant cues in the athletic environment. Collegiate and Olympic athletes have reported that the most important reason they set goals is to help them focus on the task at hand (Weinberg, Burton et al., 1993, 2000). Second, goals mobilize effort and enhance persistence by providing a standard necessary to achieve other goals and by offering feedback in relation to performance. For example, a long-distance runner may not feel like putting in the required mileage day after day or may feel bored with the repetitiveness of training. By setting short-term goals and seeing progress toward her long-term goal, she can maintain her motivation daily as well as over time. Finally, goals influence performance through the development of relevant learning strategies. For example, if a basketball player has a goal to improve his free-throw shooting percentage from 70% to 75%, then he might invoke the strategies of shooting an extra 100 free throws each day, changing his preshot routine, or altering his shooting mechanics.

Goals Regulate Behavior

Goals also work because they help regulate athletes' behavior. Self-regulation involves generating thoughts, emotions, and behaviors that are planned and adapted to the achievement of personal goals (Zimmerman, 2000). Self-regulation can be structured into three cyclical phases. The planning phase consists of goal-planning activities before athletes begin their efforts to learn or perform sport skills. The execution phase involves self-observation and self-control behaviors that athletes use to facilitate the execution of their goals. During the evaluation phase, athletes complete the self-regulatory cycle by evaluating their learning and performance efforts in relation to their goals, setting the stage for a new self-regulatory cycle to begin.

The importance of goals in regulating behavior is demonstrated by the finding that expert athletes use self-regulation more than nonexperts and novices (Cleary and Zimmerman, 2001; Kitsantas and Zimmerman, 2001). Experts have been found to (1) plan for their goal-achievement efforts more effectively by selecting more specific process goals during practice, (2) choose more technique-related strategies to achieve their goals and monitor their technique and performance outcomes more often, and (3) evaluate their performances more and attribute their failure more to faulty strategies. Not only do these self-regulatory skills enhance these athletes' development, but expert athletes experience greater satisfaction with their learning efforts. The self-regulation profile of experts seems particularly important given that research has revealed that the development of expertise is related more to people's ability to self-regulate their efforts than to their innate talent (Ericsson, 1997, 2002; Ericsson, Krampe, and Tesch-Romer, 1993; Ericsson and Lehmann, 1996).

Coach's Perspective

Individual athletes can differ greatly in terms of what motivates them to perform in practice and competition. Whereas some love to train and derive great pleasure from hard workouts, others only tolerate the workouts so that they can succeed in competition. One athlete may see sport as the means to make money, another may view sport as a way to stay lean, and yet another may plan her lifestyle around sport. With all these potential differences in motivation, the coach must strive to match a style of setting goals with each athlete's motivational orientation. Some athletes will need to set goals daily, whereas others seem to run on auto-pilot toward their season goal in an almost obsessive manner. Some athletes have difficulty focusing on process goals, whereas others don't seem to care about specific outcomes. Regardless of such differences, proper goals will provide direction to the athlete's time and energy. Goals serve as a frequent reminder of why the athlete is working hard and help to determine what he or she should and should not do, both in training and in life. Sometimes an athlete has all the necessary talent, motivation, and work ethic but has a lifestyle that is not conducive to achieving his goals. Simply put, if something (in training and in life) isn't going to help the athlete reach his goals, the coach and athlete should question whether this element is necessary.

■ ■ ■ ■ ■

Athlete's Perspective

Initially, goals worked because they directed my focus and motivated me to work hard. The feelings of success I felt from accomplishing a goal were addictive. They made me want to set greater goals and achieve those as well. The goals that I have not accomplished continue to be goals in progress; any failure is only temporary. When I do not reach a goal, I decide I just have to work harder, learn more, or, perhaps, apply a different strategy. The only time I fail is when I quit trying. Therefore, I have a lot of emotional conflict when I consider retirement. Part of me doesn't want to let go of my sport, because that would mean letting go of my set goals, almost accepting failure. Yet, it is actually impossible for every goal to be accomplished. Goal setting is a constantly evolving cycle. As a goal-oriented person, I always want to do better the next time.

■　■　■　■　■

Goal-Setting Principles

Although the discussion so far has provided strong evidence of the effectiveness of goals in enhancing sport performance, it would be an error to think that all goals are equally effective. For example, research has shown that the most effective goals are specific, difficult, and realistic (Filby et al., 1999; Kingston and Hardy, 1997; Weinberg, Burton et al., 2000). Additionally, the climate created by the coach also affects goal-setting effectiveness. Specifically, climates that are more adaptive should be encouraged, where the focus is on increased effort and performance against one's own standard of excellence.

The discussion so far has demonstrated the complexity of goal setting and the importance of different components in creating an optimally effective goal-setting program. The effectiveness of goal setting depends on understanding how athletes' personalities influence goal setting and the situations in which they find themselves. The following 10 goal-setting principles clarify how these diverse influences can contribute to effective goal setting.

1. **Set specific goals.** One of the most consistent findings from the goal-setting literature is that specific goals produce higher levels of task performance than no goals or general do-your-best goals (Locke and Latham, 1990). Contrary to popular belief, telling athletes to "go out and do your best" is not as powerful in enhancing motivation and performance as encouraging athletes to achieve a specific, measurable goal.

2. **Set realistic yet challenging goals**. Another frequently reported finding is that goals should be difficult and challenging, yet attainable (Locke and Latham, 1990). Goals that are too easy do not present a challenge to athletes, which leads to less than maximum effort. Setting goals that are too difficult and unrealistic will often result in failure and can cause frustration, lowered self-confidence and motivation, and decreased performance.

3. **Set long- and short-term goals.** Many coaches and athletes focus on long-term goals, such as winning the state championship or making an Olympic team. Long-term goals provide the final destination for athletes but do not show them how to reach that destination. Additionally, long-term goals direct the athlete's focus on the future rather than the present. Short-term goals show athletes what they need to accomplish to achieve their long-term goals and provide feedback concerning progress toward the long-term goals. This feedback is both motivational and self-regulatory, allowing adjustment of goals either upward or downward. Short-term goals also help athletes to view their long-term goals as more attainable by giving them smaller and more manageable goals to achieve as they progress toward their long-term goals.

4. **Set competition and training goals**. One mistake that athletes often make in setting goals is focusing solely on competition goals. Although competition goals are important because they guide athletes in their preparation for upcoming events, training goals are of equal value. Most athletes report that it is easier to "get up for" and be motivated for a competition, whereas additional motivation is often needed for daily training (Gould, 1998). Daily training involves more time and greater effort with fewer immediate rewards, so training goals can provide athletes with inducements to continue their efforts.

5. **"Ink it, don't think it."** Several applied sport psychology consultants (Gould, 1998; Weinberg, Burton et al., 2000) have emphasized the importance of recording goals. Unfortunately, coaches and athletes do not typically write down their goals, at least not systematically (Weinberg, Butt, and Knight, 2000; Weinberg, Butt, Knight, and Perritt, 2001). Recording goals in a public place seems to be of added benefit, for example, posting goals on a bulletin board outside a swimming pool with a graph recording the number of yards swimmers have completed each week. This public recording appears to encourage social comparison, which can be a very potent motivational tool.

6. **Develop goal-achievement strategies**. As stated earlier, one mechanism underlying the effectiveness of goals in enhancing performance is the development of relevant learning strategies (Locke, 1968). Unfortunately, athletes often neglect this aspect of goal setting, as goals are set without a defined set of strategies to achieve these goals. Setting goals without also developing appropriate strategies for achieving them is like setting a goal to drive from New York to Los Angeles without having a map to direct you; you know where you want to go but not how to get there. A softball player who sets a goal to improve her batting average 0.25 points from last season needs to develop specific strategies to accomplish this goal (e.g., change her stance, lift weights to improve her strength, develop a routine before and during batting to help her focus). These learning strategies need to be identified and incorporated into her practice efforts so that she can actively pursue the goal of improving her batting average.

7. **Prioritize process, performance, and outcome goals**. Given the emphasis society places on competition and winning, athletes often feel compelled to focus on the outcome of a competition. Unfortunately, a preoccupation with outcome goals actually interferes with athletes' achieving the desired outcome. By focusing on the outcome that occurs at the conclusion of a competition, athletes do not pay sufficient attention to the process, which will hinder their ability to perform their best and achieve their outcome goals. The irony is that the best way to achieve a particular outcome is to focus on performance or process goals (Kingston and Hardy, 1997; Orlick and Partington, 1988). Process and performance goals ensure that athletes develop the necessary skills and strategies, and perform at the required level, to achieve their outcome goals.

8. **Set individual and team goals**. Coaches of team sports often ask, "Should I have my players set individual goals in addition to team goals?" There is a place for individual goals within a team sport, as long as the individual goals do not take precedence over team goals (Weinberg, Burton et al., 2000). Ideally, individual goals should coincide with and support team goals just as team goals should bolster individual goals. However, because team success is the priority, individual goals should always be secondary to team goals.

9. **Provide support for goals**. Social support is an important factor in keeping people motivated and persistent, especially when obstacles prevent goal attainment (Albrecht and Adelman, 1984; Cohen, 1988). Research (Hardy, Richman, and Rosenfeld, 1991) has reinforced the critical role that significant others can play in helping individuals achieve their goals. Thus, support and encouragement from coaches, teammates, family, and friends can foster athletes' motivation and help them maintain their commitment to their goals. An athlete who doesn't achieve an important goal may be discouraged and lose motivation to continue to pursue her goals. A "pep talk," a vote of confidence, some perspective, and a refocusing on future goals from others can help to allay her discouragement and reinvigorate the athlete to continue her efforts.

10. **Provide feedback**. Evaluative feedback is essential for effective goal setting because it provides athletes with information about their efforts. This feedback either affirms athletes' goal-related efforts or offers them information that they can use to adjust their goals or their goal strategies to maximize the value of the goals. Evaluative feedback should be ongoing and incorporated into the formal goal-setting program. Periodic goal-evaluation meetings between athletes and coaches or athletes and the applied consultant can be scheduled to evaluate current performance in relation to individual and team goals, allowing for goals to be regularly reevaluated and adjusted to provide new motivation and commitment for athletes.

Coach's Perspective

Coaches can play a very important role in helping athletes set goals. Often, athletes have difficulty formulating a goal that is realistic, yet difficult. The coach can provide an objective viewpoint of the athlete's current ability and potential. Sometimes, the athlete will need a vote of confidence to help her realize she is capable of more or that her secret dream goal isn't absurd at all. Other times, the athlete needs to be reminded that she has just started the sport and that the elite athletes have been training in their sport for many years. There's often a gender difference, such that males tend to be overconfident and females underconfident, although sometimes the opposite is true.

Coaches can enhance the goal-setting process in a number of other ways. First, the coach should ensure that the training and competition program supports the goals of the athlete or team. Also, the coach should provide the athlete with frequent evaluations of where he or she is in the process of working toward a goal. Along with providing this evaluation, the coach needs to give honest feedback of whether the athlete is on track to achieve the goal. If not, the coach and athlete should modify the goal or action plan. When a goal is achieved, the coach needs to congratulate the athlete, make the success well known to others, and make sure that time is taken to celebrate that success. From there, it's time to refocus and get to work on setting new and higher goals.

Things rarely go exactly as planned, so athletes need to set flexible goals and be ready to reevaluate the situation if something unexpected comes up. When an athlete is injured or his athletic preparations are disrupted, he must refocus and go to plan B. It may be helpful to set goals for getting back to health or normalcy, after which the athlete can then work toward the original goals.

■ ■ ■ ■ ■

Athlete's Perspective

It is hard for me to recognize when a goal is difficult, too difficult, or too easy. A lot of that has to do with my confidence. I believe in my heart that I can win, but the question is when that will be. I don't want to set goals that are too high or too fast, for fear of frustration. Still, when I do set loftier goals, I am usually able to reach them.

When I set a tough goal, I need to plan actual steps toward achieving it. At first, my dreamlike goal will seem so overwhelming that I can't even picture myself doing it. But I go through my planned steps, and with each one I gain more confidence in the possibility of achieving the goal. Around the final steps, in a sudden moment, I will know I can do it. I can see it in my mind and I believe it.

■ ■ ■ ■ ■

Goal-Setting Program

Athletes, coaches, and applied sport psychology consultants agree that goal setting is an important strategy to enhance athletes' motivation and increase performance. The information presented in this chapter provides a firm theoretical and empirical foundation for the inclusion of goal setting in athletes' psychological preparation for training and competition. Yet, athletes and coaches do not always use goal setting to their fullest advantage. Coaches and applied consultants must help athletes set the right kind of goals. Perhaps the greater challenge is getting athletes to effectively motivate and regulate their athletic behavior by controlling, observing, and evaluating their goal achievement efforts.

To successfully implement a goal-setting program, athletes must accept several essential self-motivational beliefs (Zimmerman, 2002). First,

athletes must believe that they are capable of learning and performing the skills they identify as important for competitive success. For example, if a baseball pitcher has confidence that he can improve his flexibility and strength, he will set more challenging training goals and increase his efforts if he falls short of these goals. Second, athletes need to believe that mastering their sport skills and executing their task strategies will result in achieving their outcome goals. To maintain his motivation toward his goal of leading the league in earned run average, the same baseball pitcher must believe that remaining committed to improving his pitching technique, physical conditioning, and psychological skills will allow him to attain his goal. Third, athletes should be encouraged to adopt a task orientation as they attempt to achieve their goals. If this baseball pitcher is able to see the achievement of his outcome goals as milestones in a lifelong learning process and if he values the process of learning and performing, then he will set more goals focused on self-improvement rather than comparison with other pitchers in the league. In addition, he will be motivated to participate by his intrinsic interest rather than by external rewards, which are often outside of his control.

A goal-setting program is presented next to help athletes and coaches effectively set goals and observe, evaluate, and direct their goal-achievement efforts. The goal-setting program is organized according to the three phases of self-regulation discussed previously (i.e., planning, execution, and evaluation) and is designed to be consistent with the goal-setting principles described earlier. *Goal planning* helps athletes set effective goals and identify strategies to achieve these goals. *Goal execution* helps athletes monitor and control the learning and performance of their sport skills. Finally, *goal evaluation* allows athletes to assess the adequacy of their goal-achievement efforts.

A concern that coaches and athletes may have is the time commitment required to create and maintain a goal-setting program given the amount of time that needs to be devoted to physical and technical training. Fortunately, after an initial investment in developing the program, goal setting not only is not time consuming but can actually increase the efficiency and effectiveness of training and competitive efforts.

With the proper worksheets, most athletes can prepare a preliminary goal-setting plan in less than 1 hour. A follow-up session of another 30 minutes with coaches can help refine the program. As the season progresses, athletes can spend less than 15 minutes each week recording progress and modifying goals in terms of difficulty and time needed for attainment. Monthly meetings of 20 to 30 minutes with coaches can ensure ongoing communication, coordinated effort, and appropriate goals.

When time should be allotted to goal setting depends on individual athletes and teams. To encourage adherence, it can be helpful to incorporate goal setting into the structure of practice sessions, for example, mandatory goal planning during the final 15 minutes of the last practice of the week. However, because of the unique nature of individual and team training and competitive schedules, coaches and athletes should examine their schedules and find a time that encourages continuing commitment to and ongoing focus on goal setting.

Goal Planning

Before attempting to learn sport skills or perform in competition, athletes must engage in planning that sets the stage for their action and efforts (Zimmerman, 2002). *Setting goals* and *strategic planning* are two key activities of the planning phase, both of which evolve from athletes' analysis of their current capabilities and what they need to do to improve their skills and performance. In the goal-planning phase, athletes identify the direction goals should take them and the specific means by which their goals can be achieved. This provides athletes with a clear vision of what they want to accomplish and active steps to attain their goals. Creating a mission statement, identifying outcome goals, and strategic planning are three steps in the goal-planning process.

Mission Statement

Covey (1989) described the importance of beginning with the end in mind, which means that people should know their goal destination, allowing all goal-achievement behavior to be pointed in that direction. This perspective serves as a frame of reference by which people can examine whether their behaviors are in line with what they want to accomplish. Athletes must also ensure that they keep the end in mind to prevent the attainment of empty successes.

Athletes can initiate the goal-planning process by developing a mission statement (Covey, 1989). Creating a mission statement begins with the use of imagery to see and feel themselves achieving their ultimate goals (see chapter 8 for more on imagery). The following exercise, adapted from

Covey (1989), can help athletes identify the characteristics, contributions, and achievements for which they would like to be remembered:

> Imagine that a banquet is being held in your honor at the end of your season (or career) to celebrate your accomplishments in your sport. A large number of people attend to pay tribute to you, including family, friends, coaches, teammates, and even some of your fiercest competitors. During the ceremonies, several people, whom you have selected, speak to the group on your behalf, extolling you, what you contributed, and your accomplishments. What would you like each of these speakers to say about you, your life, and your athletic career? What kind of athlete or person would you want their words to describe? What qualities would you want to be remembered by? For what achievements would you like to be best remembered?

The second part of developing a mission statement entails transferring ideas and thoughts generated by this exercise into a written mission statement (Covey, 1989). Athletes start by completing the statement: "My mission is to. . . ." Next, they identify the set of characteristics that they possess that will allow them to fulfill their mission. For example, "I outwork everyone" or "I respect and care for my teammates" or "I am coachable." Finally, athletes think of the various roles they play in life, such as team captain, wife, daughter, and friend. Athletes identify who they are in these roles, what is important to them in each role, and what they need to do in each role to fulfill their mission. For example, "As a team captain I will lead by example and challenge my teammates to push themselves beyond their limits every day."

Outcome Goals

The next step in implementing a goal-setting program is to identify dream (or career), seasonal, and competition outcome goals. These goals provide athletes with a clear vision of what they want to ultimately accomplish and will help them decide on the best process and performance goals to achieve their outcome goals. Setting outcome goals without supplemental performance or process goals is not recommended because of the potential negative motivational effects of outcome goals, such as increased anxiety and lower confidence (Burton, 1989, 1992, 1993; Hall and Byrne, 1988). However, the motivational benefits of setting outcome goals include providing athletes with long-term direction and short-term inspiration for their goal-achievement efforts (Hardy, Jones, and Gould, 1996). Another benefit of outcome goals is that they provide an important means of evaluating goal-achievement progress (Zimmerman, 2000).

Athletes should first identify and record their dream or career goals. These goals specify what athletes would ultimately like to accomplish in their sport. Dream goals encourage athletes to "think big" and to remove any limits that they may place on their ability. These goals provide athletes with the inspiration to work hard, overcome adversity, and pursue their goals with passion and commitment.

Athletes can then identify and write down the results they want to achieve in the upcoming competitive season. Seasonal goals specify what athletes want to accomplish that season in terms of placings, rankings, team selection, and other desired outcomes. These outcome goals become a set of standards toward which athletes aim throughout the season. These goals also serve as end results that provide direction at the beginning of the season for goal-achievement behaviors as well as inspiration during long and grueling training periods and performance slumps. In addition, seasonal goals supply an important measure for athletes to judge the adequacy of their competitive performances as the season progresses.

Finally, athletes can set competition goals that identify how athletes want to perform in particular competitions during the season. Competition goals are beneficial in several ways. First, they provide athletes with more proximal goals to pursue to help them maintain their motivation and training efforts during a long season. Second, competition goals guide athletes in their training emphases and schedules at different points during the season. Third, competition goals specify results that athletes must achieve to attain their seasonal goals. Competition goals can include accumulation of points in a season-long series of competitions (e.g., World Cup ski racing circuit), rankings (e.g., state wrestling placement), or team selection (e.g., three top-five finishes during the cross country running season to qualify for the national championships).

Athlete's Perspective

My ultimate goal always seemed to be an outcome goal, like an Olympic medal or overall title. I viewed those ends as the definition of success. That vision actually was counterproductive, resulting in frustration and impatience. Through conversations I learned that I had to find success daily and feel successful at each moment in what I had already accomplished. I began to pride myself on overcoming my multiple injuries, major ones that would have retired a lot of athletes. I felt successful because each day I was working hard and learning. When I learned to focus on these smaller successes I began to realize the importance of strategic planning, like setting short-term goals and using training regimens that gradually increase in difficulty. These items in the superstructure led to confidence and acquired ability so that I was capable of reaching my dream by achieving goals.

■ ■ ■ ■ ■

Strategic Planning

Strategic planning regarding the achievement of goals is fundamental to successful goal planning (Zimmerman, 2000). Most athletes are aware of the importance of setting goals, and many are able to set outcomes goals for themselves. However, rarely do athletes devote a sufficient amount of time and energy to determining how they will achieve their goals. Athletes need suitable strategies to allow them to master and perform their sport skills, and these strategies will work best if they are focused specifically on areas relevant to performance, including technique, physical fitness, and mental preparedness. In addition, athletes need to continually make adjustments when planning and selecting their strategies given that no single strategy will work equally well on all tasks, for every occasion, and across time (Zimmerman, 2000). A goal-setting tool that aids in effective strategic planning is performance profiling (Butler and Hardy, 1992; Jones, 1993).

Performance Profiling

A performance profile is a visual map of performance areas that athletes identify as important to achieving their goals (Butler and Hardy, 1992). Goal-based performance profiling helps athletes to identify performance areas, evaluate their strengths and weaknesses in these areas, plan for and engage in goal-based strategies, and monitor progress in these areas (Jones, 1993). Performance profiles can be easily modified so that athletes can adjust their training and performance strategies to meet the demands presented by new tasks and situations.

The first step in creating a goal-based performance profile involves identifying physical (e.g., strength, speed, stamina), technical (e.g., sport-specific techniques and skills), tactical (e.g., competitive strategies and game plans), and psychological (e.g., confidence, focus, imagery) areas that athletes need to develop to achieve their seasonal goals. For example, a baseball pitcher may identify the need to develop a split-finger fastball and the ability to throw first-pitch strikes (technical), to increase his shoulder flexibility and lower-body strength (physical), to get ahead of a hitter in the count (tactical), and to learn how to stay focused and relaxed in pressure situations (psychological). Then, athletes can designate the 10 most important areas they need to work on. Finally, they can rate their ability in each of these 10 areas on a scale from 1 (low) to 10 (high) to provide a specific and measurable assessment of their abilities (see figure 7.1 for a sample performance profile). The results of the performance profile provide a set of goals under the athletes' control that should help them achieve their outcome goals.

Coaches can complete the performance profile for their athletes and provide ratings of the performance areas. By doing so, coaches can gain awareness of what areas are most important to their athletes, allowing coaches to provide the necessary feedback and support their athletes' achievement efforts. The coaches' ratings also offer athletes a reality check of their own perceptions.

Training Goals

Outcome goals clarify where athletes want to go in their sport participation. Performance profiling provides athletes with the physical, technical, tactical, and psychological areas that influence performance and with athletes' strengths and weaknesses in those areas. Training goals specify how athletes will develop the areas that affect performance and how they will accomplish their outcome goals. Athletes should establish training goals for physical conditioning, technical and tactical development, and mental preparation. All training goals should specify the area to be addressed, the means by which the training goal will be accomplished, and a reasonable time frame for achieving the goals. Training goals also act as the superstructure for goal execution and the development of daily goals.

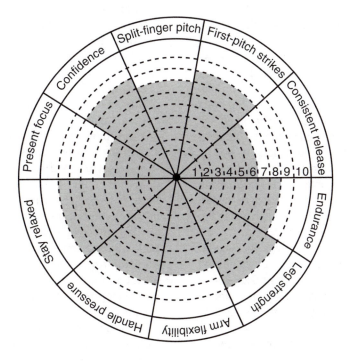

Figure 7.1   Sample goal-based performance profile for a baseball pitcher.

Coach's Perspective

Athletes should set one or two major goals for the season, usually defining some desired placing, qualification, or performance standard at an event. From there, I ask them to consider all the possible ways they could work toward this goal. Some of these ways involve practice and training, but many have more to do with recovery, diet, health, mental approach, and time management. Within each of these domains, I encourage the athlete to set goals, which could be considered process goals, to make the outcome goal more easily achieved. The athlete ends up with numerous mini-goals, which support and lead to the big goals of the season. Athletes who take this holistic approach to goal setting gain an appreciation for the little things that contribute to success, and they leave fewer things to chance. Not all the goals will be achieved. However, athletes have more chances for success with this process, both in terms of the number of goals they achieve and in terms of reaching their biggest goals.

■ ■ ■ ■ ■

Athlete's Perspective

My mission statement was a personal decision about what kind of athlete I was going to be. I wanted coaches to enjoy working with me because of my work ethic and my focus. I wanted a relationship of mutual respect; I work hard for you and you work hard for me.

I realized through experience that this mission statement could not apply to everything in my life. If I wanted to reach my dream goal, I had to sacrifice. As I continued to reach higher levels in my sport, I had to make more choices. First, I had to focus on one sport. I tried to be good at two in particular, but I was average at both. I had to focus on snowboarding, my sport of choice. Eventually, I had to choose between snowboarding and my higher education, as well as my relationships. To be my best at one thing, I had to channel all of my energy into that. No distractions were allowed. It became an agreement with myself. Everything I had was required to fulfill my role as the athlete who was dedicated and focused.

The superstructure involves strategic planning for the athlete, including conditioning, mental training, and sport-specific training. The whole picture makes a successful athlete. It is what takes a goal from a dream to something attainable. I worked with my coaches to create a plan so that I could reach my dream. My coaches enabled me and our plan allowed me to improve and achieve my goals.

My mental improvements have been made through a relationship with my sport psychologist. I learned to take control of my race day situations. On race day I can control things around me that had previously seemed uncontrollable. We began with simple experienced emotions and progressed to character improvement. Now, I attempt to actively make each competition my competition rather than waiting for my competition to come.

On the hill, I focus on one snowboarding technique at a time. One summer, I spent an entire off-season of snowboard training on arm position. It was a large time commitment, but now I automatically have good arms.

I became my best when I quit relying on myself for everything and used experts to help me out. Now, my focus is directed to my goal. As my conditioning coach is saying "30 more seconds," I can visualize my gold medal rather than looking at the clock. My whole support system helps me develop and is my superstructure. My supporters know I am going all out, so they are willing to help me take steps to make the big dream goal happen.

■ ■ ■ ■ ■

Goal Execution

When attempting to execute their goals, athletes should use a number of strategies to control the learning and performance of their sport skills (Zimmerman, 2002). Self-control methods help athletes to optimize their focus and efforts geared toward accomplishing their goals. The effectiveness of these methods, however, depends on the athletes' ability to observe their own efforts as well as the events taking place in the athletic environment around them (Zimmerman, 2002).

Athletes need to use specific strategies to increase the likelihood of accomplishing the goals that they identified during their goal planning. One such method, *self-instruction,* involves athletes describing to themselves, out loud or in writing, the steps to be taken to execute a sport task (Zimmerman, 2000). A second method, the identification and use of *task strategies,* helps athletes break down the learning and performing of their sport skills into their fundamental parts (Zimmerman, 2000), thus allowing athletes to more efficiently and systematically accomplish their goals. Setting daily training goals and establishing critical performance keys for competition are two goal-setting strategies that assist athletes with these self-control processes.

Athlete's Perspective

I learned performance keys early, to stop my nervousness. I would get so many butterflies on race day that I would crash immediately. I read *The Mental Edge for Alpine Ski Racing* (Taylor, 1995), in which the author discussed creating a race day routine. My routine involved running up the hill chanting my keys and then down the hill chanting a different key. The keys I used helped me focus on technique so that I wouldn't get so nervous. I mastered that routine and used it for a long time. But later I ran into a downward cycle. With some evaluation I realized that my keys had changed. I had become a veteran who rarely got nervous, so I needed to get fired up rather than calmed down. My keys changed to incorporate more motivators. I also learned to use my keys during the actual race. When I was really scared I would chant them all the way through the course, so that I wouldn't forget to go fast. I had a lot of success with that, so I began to use it each race. Then, I started using my keys at the start gate. I say them out loud so I don't forget to think about them and so they have more impact. When I start my race, I repeat the most important key through the racecourse. Sometimes, I may even use two keys, like "move, look ahead." One time though, my key was, "I don't want to go home; I don't want to go home." My sport is single elimination and on that day, not going home was my motivator.

Now, I try to make each training day like race day. I am trying to incorporate my vocal performance keys into my training as a motivator. It is tough with the distracting nature of noncompetition day. But this is my action step toward my next performance and outcome goals.

■ ■ ■ ■ ■

Daily Goals

After creating the goal-based performance profile, athletes now are in a position to instruct themselves and identify specific, daily training strategies to work on the various skills they need to master. This goal-setting technique involves athletes daily verbalizing or writing down the specific training behaviors in which they will engage to improve the physical, technical, tactical, and psychological skills they identified while goal planning. Athletes should select no more than three skills to work on during each training day. Once the skills for that day are identified, athletes can select specific strategies to use during that day's training session to improve their identified skills. For example, a basketball player might single out her rebounding technique for that day and choose the strategy of working on additional rebounding drills with one of her assistant coaches after practice. By doing so, this athlete is able to break down her goal of improving her rebounds per game into a more specific, behaviorally based process goal of the number of successful block-outs in a rebounding drill. Athletes should consult with their coaches to design task strategies to help them learn and perform their most important sport skills.

Performance Keys

Whereas the purpose of setting daily goals is to help athletes instruct themselves and select specific strategies for training, identifying critical performance keys is aimed at helping athletes control their performance during competition. The primary objective for this goal-setting strategy is help athletes break down their performances into a small number of behaviors under their control. If athletes are able to execute these critical behaviors, they are more likely to perform their best and achieve their outcome goals. For example, a golfer enters the final round of a tournament that he is leading with the following performance keys: (1) hit 16 of 18 greens in regulation with approach shots, (2) swing with my body and not with my hands, and (3) replay in my mind the best shot from the previous hole before playing the next hole. By verbalizing or recording their critical performance keys before the start of a competition, athletes instruct themselves on what they need to do and identify their task strategies to achieve their performance results.

Observation and Recording

Athletes' success in controlling the learning and performing of their sport skills requires that they observe their goal-achievement efforts. *Self-observation* is defined as the monitoring of specific characteristics of an individual's performance, the surrounding conditions, and the consequences of the performance (Zimmerman, 2000). Four features contribute to effective self-observation. First, feedback gained from self-observation should allow athletes to take corrective action at an appropriate time, such as a ski racer reviewing her videotaped training runs immediately after her runs rather than after training. Second, performance feedback needs to provide athletes with relevant information, and training sessions and settings should be structured to promote access to this useful data. For example, only practicing tennis serves in low-pressure situations does not provide players with information about how they might serve when their opponent is two points away from victory. Third, for their actions to be modified appropriately, athletes need to perceive their behaviors accurately and without distortion or confusion. Fourth, self-feedback must focus on accomplishments and not just deficits to maintain athletes' motivation and minimize self-criticism.

Zimmerman (2000) described *self-recording* as a common form of self-observation that can greatly enhance the timeliness, informativeness, accuracy, and positive quality of self-feedback. Keeping records related to athletes' training and performances allows for the most meaningful personal information to be acquired, maintains the accuracy of athletes' self-observations, and provides a log of evidence related to the athletes' mastery of their most important sport skills. Performance profiling and sport journals are two effective strategies.

• **Periodic use of performance profiling**. Performance profiling can be used periodically during a competitive season for athletes to record their progress toward mastering their most important sport skills. At designated times during the season, athletes and coaches can complete a performance profile and observe progress in the areas identified in the profiles. This goal-setting technique provides athletes with evidence of improvement in their skills. It also allows coaches to give feedback to athletes regarding their goal progress. Athletes can modify their profiles to replace areas that have been mastered with new areas of focus. With periodic use and modification of their profiles throughout the season, athletes can provide themselves with up-to-date, accurate, useful, and positive feedback.

• **Sport journals**. A sport journal is another effective way for athletes to monitor and record their goal-achievement efforts. By recording their training and performance efforts daily, athletes can maintain accurate self-observations of their progress and accumulate an ongoing history of athletic development. A sport journal also provides opportunities for athletes to monitor their thoughts and emotions during the course of a season. With consistent recording of all aspects of their athletic lives, athletes can notice recurring

patterns in their training and performance efforts, identify significant features in their sport environment, and take appropriate corrective actions in pursuit of their goals (Zimmerman, 2000). See Ravizza (2001) for helpful guidelines for keeping a sport journal.

Coach's Perspective

Training logs are an essential tool for tracking an athlete's progress. A good training log reads like a recipe book, with enough detail to replicate the menu at a later time. Whether a goal is reached or not, good records in the training log can provide clues about why things went the way they did. The log can also reveal the degree of discrepancy between the prescribed training plan and the actual training completed. Frequently entering information in the training log allows athletes to reflect on what they are doing to become better, to feel good about their effort and work, and to track the immediate effects of their training and competitions. Also, one can use the information to repeat successes or avoid failures.

In endurance sports, performance keys are very useful for keeping the effort going when the body wants to quit. Often, there are times in the competition when energy levels and motivation decrease. Performance keys can help to get athletes through these "bad patches" until they regain their energy and motivation. Similarly, oftentimes an athlete is challenged by opponents and must choose between trying to increase the pace and effort or backing off. Appropriate performance keys can help athletes make the right call in those situations by allowing them to focus on relevant messages regarding things they can control that can ensure their success, rather than focus on what their opponent is doing, which is outside of the athlete's direct control. In some cases, performance keys can be chanted or repeated until they become ingrained and replace distracting or negative thoughts. When this occurs, the body responds to the repeated message and is able to push through pain, fatigue, and other obstacles. One athlete I coached used the chant "feet light, legs strong, I can do this all day long" to power him successfully through the marathon portion of the Ironman triathlon.

■　■　■　■　■

Goal Evaluation

After their initial goal-related efforts, athletes should assess their efforts and plan goals for future learning and performance of sport skills

(Zimmerman, 2002). Athletes can evaluate their development, determine what has and has not worked, identify what changes need to be made, and modify their training and performances to more effectively pursue their goals.

Self-Evaluation

Zimmerman (2000) defined *self-evaluation* as comparing self-monitored information with a standard or goal. Self-evaluation is a key process in goal evaluation, and athletes can choose from several criteria by which to evaluate the adequacy of their learning and performances: mastery, previous performance, and normative information.

- **Mastery criteria**. Athletes who use mastery to evaluate their learning and performance can place themselves on a continuum ranging from novice to expert (Zimmerman, 2000). As athletes master new skills, they will incrementally progress along the continuum to higher levels of competence. The use of mastery for self-evaluation is recommended because it focuses on individual improvement over which athletes have control. Goal-based performance profiling allows athletes to use mastery to identify specific process goals and task strategies aimed at developing their sport skills. Using daily goals for training and critical performance keys for competition also encourages athletes to use mastery as a point of reference, allowing them to judge the adequacy of their learning and performance independent of results.
- **Previous performance criteria**. Using previous performance criteria involves comparing current performance with earlier performance (Zimmerman, 2000). For example, a volleyball player can evaluate her success in improving her serve by comparing her serve percentage over the first 10 games of the season with her percentage from last season. Keeping records of ongoing performances in a sport journal allows athletes to readily compare past and current performance, highlight progress or stagnation in performance, and adjust goals and strategies to ensure that goals are being pursued in the most effective way.
- **Normative criteria**. Whereas mastery and previous performance criteria rely on intrapersonal comparisons, normative criteria involve comparisons with others (Zimmerman, 2000). Because most athletes' primary motivation in sport is competitive success, they place great emphasis on normative criteria in judging their athletic progress. How well athletes accomplish their outcome goals, such as winning an Olympic medal, is an important source of information when they evaluate their progress and one that most athletes will use to determine the effectiveness of their goals and efforts. However, using normative criteria alone for self-evaluation is not recommended because athletes have less control over normative criteria and they can become overly focused on their perceived failures rather than progress they are making toward their long-term goals (Zimmerman, 2000). To be most effective in the goal-setting process, athletes should use normative criteria as only one of several means of evaluating their development.

Attributions

As part of evaluating their progress toward their goals, athletes should consider why they succeeded or failed to achieve their goals. The attributions that athletes make to explain their performances relative to their goals have a significant impact on future motivation, goal setting, and effort. If athletes focus on executing their task strategies and use mastery and previous performance criteria to judge their goal-based efforts, they are more likely to attribute any failure to accomplish their goals to poor strategy choice (Zimmerman and Kitsantas, 1996, 1997). For example, a golfer with the performance key of landing her tee shots in 12 out of 14 fairways could attribute her failure to achieve her outcome goal of a top-10 finish in a tournament to her lack of attention to her putting. This attribution to controllable factors allows athletes to increase their motivation, adjust their goals, and maintain their commitment to their goals because they conclude that they can succeed in the future by either altering their task strategies (e.g., working on putting in practice) or modifying their performance keys during competition (e.g., focusing on putting during the next tournament). In contrast, if athletes attribute their failure to achieve their goals to a lack of ability (which they cannot control), they are likely to experience frustration, lose motivation, lower their goals, or give up completely. Thus, effort, strategy, or technical attributions, as opposed to ability, opponent, conditions, or luck attributions (over which athletes have no control), allow athletes to use their failures to achieve their goals as positive experiences from which they can learn lessons to help them reach their goals in the future. This type of self-evaluation marks the conclusion of the goal-setting cycle and sets the stage for a return to the beginning of the goal-setting process and future goal planning and goal-achievement efforts.

Key Points

- The term *goal* refers to a specific level of proficiency on a task, usually within a specified time limit.
- Goals regulate human action by providing an internal standard by which people can compare and evaluate their performances.
- Three types of goals are commonly set to enhance motivation and performance: outcome, performance, and process.
- The influence of goal setting on athletic performance has been robust in its consistency and magnitude, with this effect being present across a wide variety of tasks, settings, performance criteria, and types of participants.
- Goal setting is effective because it increases motivation and regulates behavior directed toward achievement of goals.
- Goal setting is most effective when a particular set of principles is applied: Goals should be specific, realistic, and challenging; long- and short-term goals should be set for training and competition; goals should be written down; strategies for achieving goals must be identified and implemented; outcome, performance, and process goals should be set for individuals and teams; and goals should be supported by others and evaluated regularly.
- An effective goal-setting program must include goal planning, goal execution, and goal evaluation.

Review Questions

1. What are the three primary types of goals that should be set?
2. According to the industrial–organizational and sport psychology literatures, how effective is goal setting in enhancing performance?
3. How does goal setting enhance performance?
4. What are 5 of the 10 key principles related to goal-setting effectiveness?
5. What are the three stages of a goal-setting program?
6. Of what value is goal-based performance profiling in developing a goal-setting program?
7. What are two ways that athletes can ensure that they execute their goals?
8. What are two ways that athletes can observe and record their goal-based efforts?
9. What three types of criteria can athletes use to evaluate their goals?

8

Mental Imagery

Bruce D. Hale, PhD—researcher
Lynn Seiser, PhD—consultant
E.J. McGuire—coach
Eric Weinrich—athlete

© Sport the Library

The objectives of this chapter are

- to provide a precise and thorough definition of mental imagery;
- to explain what imagery is and how it affects performance;
- to describe factors that influence the effectiveness of mental imagery;
- to explore the variety of areas in which imagery can enhance performance;
- to present a model that will facilitate the creation of quality imagery; and
- to show how effective imagery scripts can be developed to maximize the value of mental imagery.

It's the last game of the Stanley Cup finals. Steve Yzerman of the Detroit Red Wings gets ready to take a critical face-off in the left face-off circle in the Carolina Hurricanes' defensive zone. Here's an example of an imagery script that Steve Yzerman might have written:

The referee has blown his whistle for a face-off in the opponent's left circle. It's the last game of the Stanley Cup Finals with the score tied 2 to 2 with less than 2 minutes in the third period. Before I move into the circle, I quickly notice where the red-sweatered Carolina Hurricane defenders are lined up outside the circle and that my right defenseman is crouched in center ice inside the blue line. I quietly call "play 4" to a circle of teammates so they know the puck is going back to the defenseman to slap a shot on goal. I cannot hear the noise of the crowd anymore. As I slide into the face-off circle, I take a quick deep breath and think "quick snap" to myself. I position myself for the drop with my eyes glued on the black disk in the ref's hand. I anticipate the drop, forcefully slide into the other center with my left hip, and tie up his white-taped stick with mine. As the puck is dropped, it seems to be in slow motion. I quickly and effortlessly reach up with my stick to pick the black puck out of the air with my white stick blade and feel my wrists snap powerfully backward as the puck shoots back to the blue line. I storm the net and try to block the goalie's vision as the puck rockets low and hard toward the stick side of the net. I see the red light go on, hear the crowd erupt in a loud scream, and jump up and down on the ice with my arms and stick saluting the goal.

Mental imagery is a fundamental tool used by most serious athletes to enhance their performance. Almost every sport psychology self-help book includes a chapter on mental imagery (Bull, 1992; Williams, 1998). Mental imagery is also one of the most studied areas in sport psychology, with research beginning in the early 20th century (Feltz and Landers, 1983; Hinshaw, 1991; Jacobson, 1931; Richardson, 1967; Washburn, 1916). For almost a century, research has shown that imagery may enhance sport performance.

Key Issues

All athletes imagine themselves performing in their sport, whether running a personal record or serving an ace at match point. But they may not necessarily know how to gain the most benefits from using imagery. A quick perusal of self-help books shows that most athletes and coaches don't understand how imagery can be used in training and competition, how to incorporate imagery into training routines, or how to use imagery to maximize the "transfer of training" effects from practice to games.

Chapter Purpose and Author Team

This chapter explores the value of mental imagery in improving athletic performance and discusses ways to maximize the benefits of imagery and organize a structured mental-imagery program. The researcher, Dr. Bruce Hale, describes the theoretical underpinnings and empirical support for imagery in sport. The consultant, Dr. Lynn Seiser, offers a detailed discussion on how imagery can be taught to coaches and athletes and used to facilitate training and competitive efforts. The coach, E.J. McGuire, provides his perspective on the use of mental imagery in professional hockey. Finally, the athlete, professional hockey player Eric Weinrich, describes how he uses imagery to enhance his play on ice.

Coach's Perspective

I have witnessed (and facilitated) imagery practice in some way with every hockey player I've coached, at any level. In the most rudimentary way, any exchange of videotape, a daily occurrence between assistant coaches and NHL players, is a start at getting the players to "see themselves" as they are currently performing.

Understandably, players are usually fairly pragmatic in their requests for visual aids. Star goal scorer Jeremy Roenick, for example, is more apt to request footage of himself performing that role perfectly. His teammate on the Flyers, second-year player Justin Williams, by contrast, facilitates his imagery sessions with footage of good positional play.

If indeed the prevailing attitude toward imagery use in pro hockey is changing, it has been recent, perhaps best espoused by the NHL's 2000 best defenseman award winner, St. Louis Blues' captain Chris Pronger. He said, "I think most of the players do some visualization. I visualize myself making the plays and doing positive things on the ice" (Miller, 2001, p. 68). This was not the case more than 10 years ago, according to Dave "Tiger" Williams, who played the last of his 14 years in the big leagues in 1988. "I don't think many guys do it," he said. "And as for the coaches teaching it, they don't. At least it never happened to me, and I played for a dozen coaches in the macho pro atmosphere of the NHL" (Miller, 1991, p. 68).

An NHL player's resistance to admit imagery or visualization habits might simply be a throwback to these macho traditions of ice hockey, where use of sport psychology concepts could be perceived among peers as admitting weakness. This prevailing machismo is spawned in the rough-and-tumble mentality of many of hockey's development leagues. Unlike the other three "major" professional men's team sports in North America, the National Hockey League's primary "feeder" system for incoming talent is not an academic institution. Candidates on a fast track to the NHL can be said to be professionalized in their full-time occupation well before 20 years of age, and the rigid demands do not lead to an inquisitive, broad-thinking, instructive setting, as is more prevalent in academic institutions. Hence, a hockey player's exposure to the concept of mental imagery would vary widely in frequency and quality in those formative years.

Change is occurring from within at a rather glacierlike pace. Performance enhancement interventions are now gaining acceptance as providing an edge, an incentive in developing amateur and minor pro players to reach the "bigs." Simply by dreaming about attaining their goal of playing in the NHL, these aspiring athletes are already on the right path. Our goal as coaches is to refine this mental exercise of imagery and direct it toward individual personal improvement.

■ ■ ■ ■ ■

Understanding the Use of Mental Imagery in Sport

Confusion has abounded among researchers, consultants, coaches, and athletes alike about what terms best describe this powerful mental training tool. Is it imagery, visualization, mental practice, or mental rehearsal? Terms were often used interchangeably in the wrong fashion (Corbin, 1972; Richardson, 1967; Suinn, 1980). Historically, *mental practice* and *mental rehearsal* were the terms used to describe the technique, but they really only describe the general strategy of rehearsing a skill mentally before completion of the physical task without clarity on how it is rehearsed or what sensory or cognitive modalities are used. Many athletes and coaches call this process *visualization,* which is a type of mental imagery that emphasizes the visual aspects of imagery, but this term does not adequately describe the influence of imagery on athletes. At present, most practitioners use the broader term *mental imagery* to describe various structured mental practice techniques that use many senses to recreate an athletic performance as a means of enhancing performance in training and competition (Hale, 1998; Holmes and Collins, 2001; Vealey and Greenleaf, 1998).

Mental imagery is best described as a process of internalized rehearsal involving precise multisensory representation of the athletic experience (Vealey and Greenleaf, 1998). It is more than just creating pictures in your mind's eye (this better describes visualization); it involves an actual neurological representation of yourself in action. Mental imagery can involve sight, sound, touch, movement, smell, and taste as well as emotions, thoughts, and actions. The goal of mental imagery is to reproduce the athletic experience so accurately that athletes feel as if they are actually performing the sport (Hale, 1998; Holmes and Collins, 2001).

Mental imagery is not simply imagining oneself spontaneously. Rather, the value of imagery lies in its use as a structured program that uses scripts designed to address areas that athletes want to improve. Imagery scripts are detailed training and competitive scenarios that athletes prepare before they begin imagery sessions that guide them in the physical setting, competitive context, specific performances, and particular areas that will be emphasized. Imagery scripts provide the "stage" on which the imagery is acted out.

How Does Mental Imagery Work?

There is still considerable debate about how mental imagery works and why it can influence athletic performance. Some explanations emphasize mental benefits such as motivation, confidence, and focus. Other views suggest that mental imagery has a learning effect on performance, in which the body can't discriminate between imagined and actual movement (Hale, 1998; Murphy and Jowdy, 1992).

One view proposes that mental imagery enhances performance by improving key mental factors that influence athletic performance. Some researchers have found that imagery increases the amount of time devoted to practice and that players are more motivated and confident as a result (Callow and Hardy, 2001; Feltz and Landers, 1983; Paivio, 1985). Moritz, Hall, Martin, and Vadocz (1996) suggested that imagery can improve performance when athletes rehearse

- general tactics and overall performance;
- specific skills and plays;
- the successful use of particular mental skills, for example, using self-talk or being focused;
- effective reactions to competitive stress and emotions; and
- the feelings of a successful performance and achieving a desired goal.

Another explanation that stresses the mental benefits of imagery, termed *symbolic learning,* proposes that imagery helps performers learn and focus on key aspects of the skill and may reduce distractions before and during execution (Sackett, 1934). Some researchers (Hale, 1994) suggest that external mental imagery may be particularly helpful in early learning of new skills (especially cognitive tasks) because it helps the performer to develop a clear picture of the whole movement and then creates learning cues in muscle memory that speed up learning (Feltz and Landers, 1983; Hird, Landers, Thomas, and Horan, 1991; Ryan and Simons, 1983).

Coach's Perspective

Most players, especially the elite ones, perform imagery naturally, without even knowing what they're doing. Wayne Gretzky's most striking quality was not his skating speed and agility, his passing ability, or the speed and accuracy of his shot but rather his unmatched ability to "see the ice." His oft-described trait of being able to anticipate the play before it occurred and his ability to "disappear" into the surrounding environs of the play sequence and reappear at precisely the opportune playmaking or scoring moment may be consistent with a biological or information-processing explanation. Or it can be attributed to patterns and movements mentally rehearsed in his typical game preparation routine.

At the opposite end of the scale from the aesthetic skill of a Gretzky is the oft-demeaned "tough guy" role, which exists on each team. This player's "skill" contribution to a team might most often come after the whistle has blown to stop play, with his stick and gloves cast aside, knuckles bared in preparation for a fistfight. One such player of this ilk whom I had the opportunity to coach was Donald Brashear of the Philadelphia Flyers.

Admirably, Donald was astute enough to know that he must maintain an above-minimal on-ice skill level to stay in the NHL. To that end, he was a willing participant in postpractice, extra skill development work as well as a regular visitor to the assistant coaches' offices for feedback and discussions on positional responsibilities within the team's playing system (i.e., the "'cognitive task" component alluded to by Feltz and Landers, 1983).

Yet Donald's other off-ice activity, imagery, is well documented in conversation with a sport psychologist who worked with him on the Vancouver Canucks (Miller, 1991, pp. 73-74):"The main thing I do to keep control is visualize before the game what's going to happen and how the game is going to unfold, I think about what kind of players they have and which guys are going to be thrown at me. The main thing is anticipation . . . Being in control requires a lot of focus—a lot of work with your mind just before the game, and also the day before the game. I think about it a lot."

As an assistant coach charged with a number of pregame preparation duties that had me passing through the dressing room, I have seen what I believe to be imagery in action before every contest. The blank stares, the silent rocking mantras of players seated in their dressing cubicles, hands grasping and regrasping their game sticks are all parts of the individual players' routines before games.

■   ■   ■   ■   ■

Another perspective that suggests a direct physical benefit of mental imagery on performance, termed *psychoneuromuscular feedback,* argues that when athletes imagine themselves performing a skill, the brain sends innervations—muscle movement commands—to the same muscles used in the actual movement (Bakker, Boschker, and Chung, 1996; Hale, 1982; Jacobson, 1931). This view contends that the value of mental imagery comes from the production of low-level muscular activity in the muscles and joints, from which feedback is sent back to the brain and analyzed to improve future motor programs for the same action. There is, however, no research to fully support this explanation (Feltz and Landers,

1983; Kohl and Roenker, 1983; Slade, Landers, and Martin, 2002).

Perhaps the most complex explanation of the benefits of mental imagery comes from Lang's (1979) bioinformation theory of emotional imagery. Lang proposed that imagery consists of an organized set of propositions—learned scripts that contain certain objects, actions, and meanings—stored in the brain that are accessed and processed when you imagine. He presented three types of propositions that contribute to the value of imagery: stimulus propositions, response propositions, and meaning propositions.

Stimulus propositions are pieces of sensory information that provide the content of the imagery, for example, the shape and color of a basketball, the feel of a hockey stick, and the sounds of an arena. Response propositions influence how athletes react physiologically, emotionally, and kinesthetically in the imagery, for instance, a pregame increase in intensity, feelings of frustration or anger, and the motion of a tennis serve. According to Lang, response propositions determine whether behavioral changes occur when athletes imagine certain scenarios; for example, a runner who gets anxious before races would need to imagine becoming relaxed if improvement were to occur. Beneficial response propositions must be present, modified, or strengthened for mental imagery to enhance performance (Hecker and Kaczor, 1988). Research to date (Bakker et al., 1996; Hale, 1982; Slade et al., 2002) supports the notion that images that contain specific response propositions will evoke concurrent physiological and emotional responses. One preliminary study reported that response-laden imagery scripts improved field hockey shooting performance better than stimulus-laden scripts (Smith, Holmes, Whitemore, Collins, and Devonport, 2001).

Meaning propositions—often ignored by practitioners—make the mental imagery significant to the individual imager. Meaning propositions might include the importance of the competition to the athlete, the time in the game, and the criticalness of an imagined play.

Another current neuroscience explanation of imagery effects suggests that motor imagery and motor preparation and execution are "functionally equivalent"; that is, they both use many of the same neural mechanisms (Decety and Grezes, 1999; Jeannerod, 1997). This theory implies that many of the same learning procedures used in physical practice should also be applied to mental practice. Several decades of research (Holmes and Collins, 2001) have provided central, peripheral, and behavioral evidence of this process. These authors have offered a seven-point functional equivalence checklist to be used by sport psychologists and coaches who are using imagery to enhance performance.

Impact of Mental Imagery

Mental imagery has been shown to influence sport performance on many levels and in many ways. Researchers, consultants, coaches, and athletes have found ways in which mental imagery can benefit athletes in training and competition. Imagery can be of value in improving physical, technical, tactical, psychological, and perceptual aspects of performance (Vealey and Walter, 1993).

Enhancing Physical Skills

A fundamental way in which imagery enhances sport performance is by improving the learning of skills and their execution in competition. Imagery has been found to provide benefits beyond those accrued through traditional physical practice. In fact, research indicates that combining physical and mental practice offers athletes greater skill acquisition than physical practice alone (Corbin, 1972; Feltz and Landers, 1983).

• **Skill learning.** Two of the most important ways in which athletes acquire new skills is through observation and practice. Mental imagery can use both these means to enhance the learning of new skills. Athletes can watch the proper execution of a skill by a coach or another athlete and then use that image to see themselves performing the skill properly. Athletes can then practice the skill repeatedly in imagery and ingrain the feeling of correct execution of the skill in the brain's motor plan of the action (Feltz and Landers, 1983; Murphy and Jowdy, 1992).

• **Performance execution.** Imagery can be a valuable tool for improving overall competitive performance. Athletes can repeatedly see and feel themselves performing in competitions, for example, a gymnast performing her floor exercise routine. Imagining performances before a competition can further ingrain the physical and technical skills necessary for competitive success. Mental imagery enables athletes to rehearse these skills by incorporating them into a vivid and accurate re-creation of the competitive setting.

• **Error correction.** All athletes make mistakes during competitive performances. Imagery can help athletes identify and correct technical errors, maintain focus and rebuild confidence, and allow for a return to proper technical execution. When athletes make a mistake—particularly when it is repeated—they often dwell on it, overanalyze it, stop trusting their bodies, and continue to make the same mistake rather than correct it. This downward spiral not only hurts the physical execution of the skill but also damages confidence, increases anxiety, causes frustration, and distracts focus.

Imagery can be used to correct errors in several ways. Athletes can use external imagery, perhaps based on videotape feedback, to see how they are performing the skill incorrectly. They can also use internal imagery to further understand their technical problem by examining the kinesthetic differences between performing the skill incorrectly and correctly. Once the problem has been identified, athletes can then use external imagery based on videotape feedback or instruction from their coach to see themselves correcting mistakes and executing the skill properly. Athletes can also use internal imagery to remind themselves of the feelings associated with good execution of the skill. Once athletes regain the proper image and feeling, they can continue to use internal imagery to repeatedly rehearse proper execution until the error has been corrected and proper execution has returned.

Enhancing Perceptual Skills

Mental imagery can be used to improve the "thinking" part of sport performance, such as reading critical game cues, making quick decisions, and rehearsing automatic correct responses to complex game situations. Imagery enables athletes to develop these perceptual skills in a setting that is often simpler than actual performance, which allows them to focus directly on areas to be improved without distraction from the many other aspects of sport performance.

• **Learning and practicing strategy.** Imagery can be used by coaches to help their athletes efficiently learn new competitive strategies during practice sessions. For example, a hockey coach could have players imagine different "break-away" strategies against various fore-checking defenses.

Players could decide which teammate to pass to based on the defensive configuration of the opposing team and which teammate is open. Imagery affords athletes this benefit because they are able to attend to the relevant tactical information without the presence of cues that occur in actual practice that can detract from the initial learning of new strategies.

• **Problem solving.** Imagery is often used by coaches to decide on new attacking or defending strategies during a competition. Coaches can scout their opponent's formations and then imagine countering them with their own strategy to gain a competitive advantage. Players can be taught to imagine new offensive strategies or plays against the new defense that they are likely to face in competition. Imagery allows coaches and players to replay competitive situations and solve problems that arise without having to actually perform those scenarios. Performance reviews and adjustments can also be done with imagery during breaks in the competition.

Enhancing Psychological Skills

Athletes can use mental imagery to improve their mental skills to create positive mind-sets that allow them to perform their best. Imagery can enhance mental skills in two ways. First, imagining successful performances is motivating, instills confidence, helps ingrain optimal intensity, reinforces ideal focus, and creates positive emotions. Second, athletes are able to incorporate mental skills, such as goal reminders, positive self-talk, relaxation exercises, and focus cues, in imagery, thereby further locking these skills into their competitive repertoires.

• **Motivation.** During arduous practices and difficult competitions, imagery can help athletes stay motivated by seeing and feeling themselves perform well and succeeding (Paivio, 1985). Imagery can reignite their passion for their sport and the desire and determination to keep going in the face of pain, frustration, and disappointment. Athletes can imagine themselves performing their best, achieving their short- and long-term goals, and realizing their dreams. Examples of motivating imagery might include imagining ideal execution of a new skill, completion of a difficult routine, or a sought-after performance in a critical competition (Martin, Moritz, and Hall, 1999) (see chapter 1).

• **Confidence.** Imagery can enhance confidence in several ways (Callow and Hardy, 2001). Athletes can imagine themselves practicing coping responses to difficult competitive situations such as bad weather, poor field conditions, or an unfriendly crowd. Mastery imagery builds confidence by allowing athletes to see and feel themselves performing well before the actual competition. Athletes can conjure up memories of past successful performances to generate confidence for an upcoming competition. Finally, athletes can include positive self-talk in their imagery to improve confidence for future performances (see chapter 2).

• **Intensity.** Imagery can be a valuable part of intensity training where athletes learn to adjust their intensity to a level that fosters successful performances. Athletes can use imagery to induce a more relaxed state in sports such as golf or archery (e.g., imagining being at ease in a safe, warm place) or to raise intensity in sports such as rugby and basketball (e.g., imagining being aggressive and explosive like a tiger). Most commonly, athletes can use "coping" imagery in which they use relaxation techniques to see and feel themselves calming down in stressful competitive situations, for example, before a lacrosse player plays in the most important game of her life (see chapter 3).

• **Focus.** Mental imagery is a powerful tool for improving focus. The very act of imagery enhances focus because, during imagery, athletes are required to maintain attention on the images they generate. The better athletes can focus on their imagery, the better they will be able to focus during competition. During imagery, athletes also focus on particular cues that are important for competition, such as the ball in baseball, opponents in field hockey, and the terrain in a ski race. They can also include key words, for example, *smooth, attack,* or *strong,* in their imagery to instill essential cues that will help competitive performance. Imagery can increase awareness of competitive cues that can contribute to faster decision making and improved execution of individual or team tactics (see chapter 4).

• **Emotions.** Mental imagery can have a powerful, positive impact on athletes' emotions. Because effective imagery is more than just a "'thinking" experience, but rather one in which athletes experience competitive situations in a very immediate way, emotional reactions to the imagery commonly emerge. Athletes often feel the same emotions in their imagery as they do in actual competitions including uncomfortable emotions such as fear, frustration, and anger (see chapter 5).

Athletes can use imagery to foster positive emotions in two ways. First, athletes can use coping imagery to imagine themselves in difficult competition situations in which negative emotions usually arise and to see and feel themselves dealing with the situation effectively and replacing the interfering emotions with positive ones. Second, athletes can generate facilitating emotions, such as anticipation, excitement, and joy, in their imagery from the start to establish a positive emotional atmosphere throughout an imaged competitive scenario.

• **Interpersonal and life skills.** Although not often considered, mental imagery can help coaches and athletes improve their interpersonal skills in areas such as coach–athlete interactions, team relationships, and contact with media, and their life skills, for example, preparing for an exam or a job interview. Social and life situations are as much performances as sport performances, both requiring many of the same skills to be successful, for example, motivation, confidence, calmness, focus, and positive emotions. All of the issues that have been discussed here can be applied to interpersonal and life skill development to enhance the quality of athletes' personal interactions and their ability to succeed in the challenges they will face in their lives.

• **Injury rehabilitation.** Surgical and rehabilitative technologies over the past 20 years have enabled athletes to fully recover from injuries that were once considered career ending. Yet, despite the return to full physical functioning, athletes do not always return to or surpass their previous level of competitive performance. This deficit is often attributed to psychological damage that is inflicted by the physical injury and the lack of full recovery of the mental aspects of the injury (Taylor and Taylor, 1997). Considerable research has demonstrated the value of mental imagery in the rehabilitation of sport injury. Imagery can enhance the healing process by reducing muscle tension, increasing blood flow, and stimulating strength gain (Smith, Holmes and Collins, 1998). Injured athletes can also use imagery to manage the inevitable pain that occurs during rehabilitation. Finally, imagery can be used to help athletes maintain their sport skills and competitive sharpness by continuing to train and compete in their mind's eye (see chapter 12).

Maximizing the Value of Mental Imagery

A number of factors contribute to the quality of the mental imagery that athletes generate. Paying attention to these factors increases the likelihood that athletes gain the maximum benefits and improve their athletic performance. Hale (1998) suggested the following four principles ("four R's") to maximize the value of mental imagery: relaxation, realism, regularity, and reinforcement.

Relaxation

Most consultants recommend relaxation as a useful precursor to mental imagery. A deep state of relaxation, it is believed, helps athletes generate better quality images and makes them more open and receptive to the images and feelings they are trying to experience. However, some researchers have suggested that relaxation strategies may be unnecessary for imagery rehearsal to be effective (Holmes and Collins, 2001). They add that preimagery relaxation may be most beneficial for sports that require a low level of intensity for optimal performance, such as golf, archery, and riflery. However, for sports that demand high intensity, for example, powerlifting, wrestling, and sprinting, being relaxed before and during imagery might interfere with a complete reproduction of the actual sport performance. The experiences of consultants, coaches, and athletes indicate that it is probably useful to incorporate some kind of relaxation strategy before an imagery session.

Realism

This principle states that athletes should make their images as realistic as possible so that imagery transfers maximally to sport performance. Athletes should use as many senses as possible and create imagery that is as vivid as possible. Some athletes who have generated very realistic imagery indicate that they feel as if they are actually competing. The imagery script at the beginning of this chapter is an example of the role of realism in imagery. The script describes the setting of a hockey game; sounds and colors associated with the game; the position of teammates and opposing players; psychological factors, such as intensity, focus, and emotions; and the physical sensations associated with the action.

Imagery Perspective

Imagery perspective refers to where the "imagery camera" is when athletes engage in mental imagery (Mahoney and Avener, 1977). The internal perspective involves athletes seeing themselves from inside their body looking out, as if they were actually performing. The imagery camera is inside their head looking out through their eyes. It has been argued that internal imagery may be most effective because it replicates the perspective of athletes when they are actually performing (Hale, 1998; Holmes and Collins, 2001). One particular benefit that has been associated with internal imagery is the use of more kinesthetic imagery, which involves athletes generating the same muscular activity and actually feeling the imagined movements (Bakker et al., 1996; Hale, 1982; Holmes and Collins, 2001).

The external perspective involves athletes seeing themselves from outside their body like on video. The imagery camera follows their performance from the outside. Athletes can benefit from external imagery when they are trying to correct errors or when they are first learning a sport skill because it allows them to see themselves in the proper position and executing the correct movement.

Athletes often use both perspectives. Although early research attempted to show that internal imagery was preferred by elite athletes and was superior to external imagery (Mahoney and Avener, 1977), most later research (Hardy, Jones, and Gould, 1996) found that both types of imagery can be helpful, particularly at different stages of training and competitive cycles (Collins, Smith, and Hale, 1998) and with different types of sport tasks (Hardy and Callow, 1999). Many athletes report switching perspectives (Holmes and Collins, 2001) and still are able to experience kinesthetic imagery. It is recommended that athletes use the perspective that is most natural for them and experiment with the other perspective to see if it helps them in a different way for different skills (Holmes and Collins, 2001; Taylor, 2001). The introductory imagery script appears to use the internal perspective, with an emphasis on the player seeing his teammates and opposing players around him and all of the action emanating from his tactics during the face-off.

Vividness

A widely held belief among researchers, consultants, coaches, and athletes is that the more vivid the images that athletes can generate, the more valuable the imagery will be in enhancing sports performance (Lang, 1979). Vividness involves creating images that are clear and accurate—a good metaphor might be adjusting the focus on a camera until the image has shifted from blurry and indistinct to crisp and clear. Vividness is also gained by incorporating as many senses, thoughts, and feelings into the imagery as possible so the imagined scenes seem as realistic as the actual performance. The precise portrayal of the game situation that is described in the imagery script at the beginning of this chapter provides the richness necessary for vivid imagery. The color of the opposing team's jerseys, the exact position of the right defenseman, and the specific scenario once the puck is dropped are examples of clear and detailed images.

Less experienced athletes often find it difficult to create vivid imagery because their sensory and motor images are not fully ingrained. With practice, imagery vividness can be enhanced through the creation and repetition of athlete-generated response propositions involving physiological, emotional, and kinesthetic feelings and actions of the actual performance (Holmes and Collins, 2001; Lang, 1979).

Controllability

As mentioned earlier, athletes will imprint the images and feelings that they generate in their imagery. If athletes imagine themselves performing well, then positive images will be learned. However, if they imagine poor performances, then those negative images will take root (Murphy and Wookfolk, 1987). For imagery to be beneficial, athletes must create imagery that portrays proper technical and tactical execution and successful performances. The hockey player described in the opening imagery script creates a scenario that is conducive to highly controlled images. His use of familiar tactics, precise actions, and slow motion when the puck is dropped provides the player with exacting cues that guide him through the script.

It is not uncommon for athletes to perform poorly in their imagery. For example, a basketball player will imagine the ball sticking to the floor when he dribbles or a soccer player will inadvertently imagine missing a penalty kick. This experience can be frustrating, because if athletes cannot imagine good performances, they are going to have a difficult time performing well in real life.

These uncontrolled images are usually attributable to one of two causes. First, athletes may lack imagery experience. In time, as they practice imagery more, athletes will become more adept at controlling the images they generate. Second, the uncontrolled images reflect a fundamental lack of confidence in their ability to successfully execute certain skills or produce desired outcomes. This underlying lack of faith unconsciously causes athletes to generate images that mirror those doubts (for ways to build confidence, see chapter 2).

Imagery control is a skill that develops with practice. If mistakes occur in athletes' imagery, they should not just let the poor images go by. If they do, athletes will replay the negative images and feelings, which will hurt their actual performances. Instead, when athletes perform poorly in their imagery, they should immediately break the skill into parts and imagine each part successfully. With time and repetition, athletes can put the parts together, gain control over their imagery, and gain its maximum benefits.

Multiple Senses

To generate the highest quality and most beneficial mental imagery, athletes must create imagery that is multisensory. As athletes develop their imagery skills, they should emphasize the various senses that might be used during actual competition, including sights, sounds, touch, smell, and taste. The more senses that can be generated, the more realistic and vivid the imagery experience will be. The introductory imagery script is a truly multisensory experience. It incorporates the sound of the referee's whistle, the colors of the puck and the blade of the player's hockey stick, and the feeling of sliding his left hip into the opposing player. This sensory detail brings the written script to life and makes readers feel like they are experiencing the face-off.

Thoughts and Emotions

What athletes think during a competition often dictates their intensity, their emotions, and their performance. Mental imagery gives athletes the ability to learn new and better ways of thinking during competitions. They can generate competitive situations in their imagery in which they have displayed negative self-talk and body language. Drawing on the techniques described in chapter 3, athletes can replace the negative self-talk and body language with positive expressions that will improve their performance. When mental rehearsal is positively structured to match desired competitive outcome, athletes will feel that they have been there before, and the familiarity of the situation will breed confidence and success.

Emotions also play an important role in athletes' ability to gain the most benefit from their mental imagery. Incorporating emotions that athletes normally experience during competition can be useful at several levels. Including emotions in imagery enhances the realism and vividness of the imagery. Creating positive emotions during imagined competitions can help program constructive emotions that will help athletes to perform their best. Imagining competitive scenarios that have evoked negative emotions in the past gives athletes the opportunity to practice and instill different ways of responding to the stresses of competition that caused the negative emotions. The hockey player who describes the imagery script at the start of the chapter includes thoughts and emotions throughout the scenario. The tension from the end of a tied fifth game, choosing to call play 4, thinking "quick snap," and describing his excitement over the goal being scored create a greater depth of image that bolsters its value.

Speed of Imagery

Athletes should learn to imagine skills and strategies at "real-time" speed (Etnier and Landers, 1996). This practice enables athletes to imprint the thoughts, feelings, and actions necessary to prepare them for real-time performance. "Slow-motion" imagery (Holmes and Collins, 2001) can be used in the early stages of learning, during error correction to ensure proper execution of a skill, or to provide focus on a specific component of an imagined performance. At the face-off in the opening imagery scenario, the player imagines the drop of the puck and his reaction to it in slow motion, creating a set of images that are clear, precise, and compelling. At the conclusion of slow-motion imagery, athletes are encouraged to end their imagery session with imagery at normal performance speed.

Duration of Imagery Sessions

Most research (Feltz and Landers, 1983; Hinshaw, 1991; Murphy and Jowdy, 1992) indicates that athletes should spend no more than 15 minutes rehearsing each particular image. One study (Driskell, Copper, and Moran, 1994) suggested that task type may determine the duration of practice, with motor-oriented tasks (e.g., a high jumper imagining the approach, takeoff, and landing of a high jump) requiring more repetition than cognitive tasks (e.g., a baseball pitcher imagining pitch selection).

Regularity

The regularity principle states that, like any athletic skill, mental imagery only has benefits if it is practiced consistently. Athletes would not get stronger if they lifted weights once a week, and they would not improve technically if they only worked on technique every few weeks. Improvement of any sort—whether physical, technical, or mental—comes from a commitment to regular and directed efforts toward specific goals.

One way to optimize the value of mental imagery is for athletes to alternate periods of actual physical practice with imaged practice (Corbin, 1972; Murphy and Jowdy, 1992; Richardson, 1967). Research clearly shows that athletes who combine imagery and physical practice maximize motor learning and performance. In fact, one study (Etnier and Landers, 1996) suggested that the best time to use imagery is immediately before execution of a task.

Coach's Perspective

Following are some ways that a coach can help the sport psychology consultant:

1. Support the sport psychology consultant. A tone of respect by the coach when introducing the sport psychology consultant to the team goes a long way in ensuring acceptance of the consultant and paving the way for good rapport. To subtly remind players that coaches are in tune with the topics discussed by the consultant, coaches could use the language of the domain (e.g., "parking" of bad plays or bad breaks in a game, "focusing in" on the task at hand in a game, "loving the challenge" of an approaching critical situation in a game). A believable excerpt from a "tuned in" coach making postpractice closing comments might include this: "During your imaging of what to expect from tomorrow's opponent, guys, keep in mind that . . ."

2. Acknowledge players' efforts. Coaches should give a general "thanks" to players in a group setting for the individual time they are taking to make themselves better under the guidance of the sport psychology consultant. For example, "As each individual player gets better, our team collectively gets mentally tougher." "Our break-out plays are working better; I think imaging each of your roles is making a difference."

3. Specify roles. Coaches need to be explicit with the sport psychology consultant about his or her role with the team. For example, where is the line between accessibility and overkill (for example, being too much of a looming presence)? Is the locker room off limits for imagery sessions? Should the consultant be present on game day? Is athlete–consultant contact best made over the phone and apart from the players' daily sport-specific activities?

■ ■ ■ ■ ■

Reinforcement

The reinforcement principle states that athletes should use visual and kinesthetic aids to improve the vividness, control, and quality of their images. The use of videotape, detailed explanations of skills, and effective demonstrators can aid in developing clear and positive images (Smith and Holmes, 2002). Videotapes of proper execution can allow athletes to identify and focus on critical performance cues and movements that can be incorporated into imagery. Videotape can also be used to replay game action and pinpoint errors that can be corrected in imagery.

Demonstrations by coaches and veterans in which effective execution of skills or tactics is explained and shown can further provide valuable visual cues that athletes can use in their imagery. These observations can enhance athletes' understanding of key aspects of their sport, which can then be transferred to imagery.

A variety of other tools can provide feedback and reinforcement for athletes in their use of mental imagery. Hand-held and helmet-mounted video cameras offer real-life visual perspectives to improve internal imagery. Virtual-reality video games can also augment internal imagery. Biofeedback and biomechanical analysis can help athletes develop kinesthetic imagery. Finally, using actual sports equipment during imagery, for example, holding a tennis racket, can facilitate tactile and kinesthetic imagery (Holmes and Collins, 2001).

Contributors to Effective Imagery

Holmes and Collins (2001) offered a framework for maximizing mental imagery application, termed PETTLEP:

Physical
Environment
Task
Timing
Learning
Emotion
Perspective

The emphasis of imagery, according to PETTLEP, is on its motor and kinesthetic elements; imagery is a "representation of the self in action from a first person (internal) perspective" (Jeannerod, 1997, p. 15). Imagery and actual physical execution of a movement involve the same cognitive and motor systems (i.e., they have "functional equivalence"; Decety and Grezes, 1999). The key difference is that in imagery, actual physical movement is blocked or suppressed, whereas in physical execution, overt action occurs (Bonnet, Decety, Jeannerod, and Requin, 1997). PETTLEP asserts that if physical practice and mental practice are equivalent, then many of the procedures that optimize physical practice should also be used for mental practice.

• **Physical.** The physical component of PETTLEP suggests that imagery should closely mirror the physical movements during motor preparation and execution. Athletes are encouraged to use relevant sports equipment and simulated movements (what has been called "'dynamic kinesthetic imagery"; Gould and Damarjian, 1996) to closely replicate the sensations associated with actual movement. This perspective calls into question the traditional practice (Miller, 1991) of using relaxation exercises before imagery in sports that require a high level of intensity.

• **Environment.** According to PETTLEP, creating an environment in mental imagery that precisely replicates the actual competitive setting is essential for effective imagery. The competitive environment can be recreated with videotapes of athletes' past performances in familiar training and competitive venues, photographs, and detailed descriptions of specific competitive settings, all of which enable the athlete to personalize his or her imagery scripts (Lang, 1979). Recent research has provided initial support for the use of personal videotapes to enhance environmental cues in imagery (Smith and Holmes, 2002).

• **Task.** This aspect of PETTLEP suggests that imagery may differ along a number of dimensions, such as skill level of athletes, stage of learning, and complexity of the skills being rehearsed in imagery. For imagery to be most effective, it should be consistent with the particular requirements of sport and the specific nature of the athlete generating the imagery. For example, skills that emphasize form would benefit from imagery that uses an external perspective so athletes could see the proper positioning and simulate correct kinesthetics to recreate the feelings associated with correct execution (Callow and Hardy, 1997).

• **Timing.** PETTLEP asserts that the timing of an imagined performance should approximate the time needed to execute the actual performance (Landers et al., 2002; Vogt, 1995). For example, in figure skating, a 4-minute long program should take approximately that long in imagery. Holding sports equipment (e.g., ski poles for a slalom ski race) during imagery has been found to enhance the timing of performance (Holmes, Collins and Saffery, 2000). Additionally, slow-motion imagery may actually be detrimental to performance because it interferes with temporal rhythm in tasks where timing is critical, for example, a golf swing or a baseball swing.

• **Learning.** The learning component of PETTLEP involves changing the content of the imagery over time to accommodate the acquisition of skills that occurs during the learning process. As the execution of a skill becomes more refined and automatic, different imagery may be needed, for example, imagining use of the skill in the context of an overall sport performance. External imagery may be more useful in early learning where a visual perspective is necessary, and later learning will benefit from an internal perspective emphasizing kinesthetic feelings once the performer is well acquainted with the actual movement sensations and basic skill components (Hale, 1994).

• **Emotion.** According to PETTLEP, athletes are encouraged to include emotional response propositions in their imagery to create similar emotional reactions as those experienced in actual competition. Emotions can be generated in imagery by including meaning propositions (Lang, 1979), which create investment in the images and the emotions that are often associated with increased significance (e.g., excitement, frustration). Once again, the use of relaxation techniques is cautioned for emotionally laden imagery because low levels of intensity may negate the emotional response propositions that are introduced into the imagery. Only in target sports where low intensity is nec-

essary (e.g., shooting, golf) should nonemotional imagery be used (Holmes, 1996).

• **Perspective.** Although some evidence indicates that internal imagery may be more beneficial than external imagery (Hinshaw, 1991), PETTLEP suggests that the differences in perspective may depend on the interaction between the athlete and the demands of the sport (Collins et al., 1998; Smith and Holmes, 2002). For example, sport skills that are more cognitively based (e.g., shot selection in golf, reading defenses in American football) may benefit more from internal imagery, whereas those that have a stronger technical focus (e.g., a tennis serve, gymnastic skill) may profit from external imagery (Feltz and Landers, 1983). In an accuracy task like golf putting, Lutz, Landers, and Linder (2001) found that an internal "form focus" was less beneficial than an internal "outcome focus." PETTLEP recommends considering the individual athlete's preference and experience when choosing a perspective for a particular image.

Structuring Mental Imagery

Anecdotal evidence from consultants, coaches, and athletes indicates that successful athletes use mental imagery in a variety of settings to enhance their training and competitive performances (Mahoney and Avener, 1977; Orlick and Partington, 1988). An examination of these experiences identifies four settings (Hardy and Fazey, 1990) in practice and competition in which many athletes and coaches successfully incorporate mental imagery into their traditional physical, technical, and tactical efforts (see table 8.1 for an example).

Enhancing the Quality of Training

Imagery can be a valuable complement to physical practice before and after physical execution of a skill or performance. Before athletes practice, they can imagine themselves performing correctly. The preperformance imagery reinforces a positive image and feeling of the skill, narrows focus, highlights relevant cues, instills confidence, and generates positive emotions. After execution of a skill or performance, athletes can benefit from imagery in two ways. If their performance was successful, imagery can help athletes deepen the image and feeling associated with a success-

Table 8.1

Critical Moments to Use Imagery

When	Critical moment	Purpose
Before, during, and after practice	Performance rehearsal	To rehearse skill learning and performance
Before competition	Quick preview	To provide relaxing images, repetition of simple and advanced skills, competitive strategies, past successes, goal programming
During competition	Competition preview	To provide an example of actual skill execution, strategies and plays; to rehearse action movement and events before they occur
	Instant imagery	To imagine the feeling of a movement or play after successful execution; to commit to memory; to identify or correct an error
After competition	Competition review	To evaluate good and bad aspects of performance after a competition to assist in planning training and to reward good performance

Adapted, by permission, from B. Hale and B. Howe, 1999, Visualizing the perfect match. In *Rugby tough,* edited by B. Hale and B. Howe (Champaign, IL: Human Kinetics), 66.

ful performance and enhance its acquisition and execution. If mistakes were made, the poor image and feeling can remain. Corrective imagery can help athletes to clear out the unsuccessful image and feeling and replace them with ones that are effective. This editing process facilitates future skill or performance execution.

Athlete's Perspective

I use imagery in every aspect of my sport—during the pregame skate, during games, between periods, and before and after games. I imagine different game situations constantly.

Training

Much of the training athletes do involves a lot of repetition. When you have trained year after year, you need a way to keep motivated to train hard. I try to imagine myself in a race or think of a game situation where the exercise I am doing can help my performance next season. When I ride the stationary bike, I imagine what Lance Armstrong must go through in his training routines. As much as it hurts, it is nothing compared with what he endures. If I can push myself harder on a ride each day, then in overtime in a game I may be able to outskate or outperform a better player because I'm

better conditioned. I use images of battling Eric Lindros on a face-off or another player for the puck in front of the crease to motivate me to work harder with weights and plyometric training. I also think of images from last season to motivate me to work harder. When I imagine Taylor Pyatt of the Sabres tossing me around in the corner last season, it motivates me to do one more pull-up. This type of mental imagery has helped me every summer in training camp to stay motivated.

Practice

Practice time may be the best time for imagery use. I use almost every practice drill or exercise as a "pretend" game situation. Every time I carry the puck around a cone or do a two-on-one drill, the image of a game situation goes though my head. I use images from the last game to keep me focused in drills.

For example, I know that when Mark Messier is in the off-wing position as a left-hand shot, his favorite position on a rush, he can hit another player with a pass easier or has a better angle to shoot on goal. How did I play this situation the last time it arose, and what will I do differently or the same the next time it occurs? Each time I face a two-on-one in practice, these images flash through my mind. The more I concentrate on making the right decision with this image in practice, the better I will be the next time it happens in a game. In practice situations, I always imagine competing against a Messier, Lemieux, or Jagr. Even though our players may do something different in practice than these great players, I feel that if I can imagine playing well against these top players, I can handle any play that occurs in a game.

In training camp, we practice power play setups. It's a perfect example of a live game situation. I try to focus on what penalty killers (players whose role it is to protect the puck and safely allow time to pass while a team is short-handed because of a teammate being in the penalty box) do in this situation because they usually act more cautiously in a game. Because of modern technology and in-depth pregame preparation, we know each team's system and their personnel for penalty killing. For example, if we are preparing for a team like Dallas, we know that their forwards and defense players like to block shots on the ice. I know that when I visualize getting the puck to shoot at the point on a power play, I may see two bodies sliding at me. I mentally rehearse my options to this defensive style and practice imagining either shooting, moving to shoot, or passing. I incorporate these different choices into our actual power play practice during the week. Sometimes you only get one chance in a game, and making the right decision depends on your preparation.

■ ■ ■ ■ ■

Preparing for Competition

Many athletes incorporate mental imagery into their precompetitive routines as a means of ensuring total physical, technical, tactical, and mental preparation. Before the competition, athletes can see and feel themselves executing skills or tactics correctly and imagine successful performances to build confidence and generate positive emotions about the impending competition. Imagery of upcoming competitive situations can also help athletes prime their focus and intensity to competitive levels. For example, shortly before a 100-meter freestyle swim race, a swimmer can imagine himself in the blocks, having a good start, experiencing a fast swim, and having a strong finish to enhance his confidence and direct all of his energy toward having a good race.

Athlete's Perspective

For me, game day has always started the night before. I always imagine myself making a big play or scoring a goal. If we have played a team before, I always review a specific play or event to imagine what I could have done better defensively or offensively.

I imagine myself making the correct decision quickly or being more aggressive tying up my opponent in front of the crease. Because I know most of the goalies in the league, I try to imagine where I want to shoot on the goalie playing tomorrow; I try to remember where past shots have beaten him before, and I imagine myself shooting a goal past him. I also try to review the tendencies of the opponent's top offensive threats. Do I have to be ready to position myself in front of the net to battle a goal scorer or will I have to skate into the corners to tie him up? I recall what has worked on a player before, and I imagine myself using the same strategy successfully again.

During the pregame skate, I review our game strategies and my positioning on offense and defense. I imagine our breakout plays, our penalty kills, and power play positions. I try to actually practice some of the shots I have mentally rehearsed that I want to take against the goalie. I talk positively to myself and I think positive thoughts. I know all the hard work I have done in training camp and practice will help me succeed.

■ ■ ■ ■ ■

Using Imagery During Competition

In sports that have brief bursts of performance and breaks in between (e.g., tennis, American football), athletes can use mental imagery to maintain optimal performance or to remedy ineffective performance. During breaks in a competition, such as time-outs, injuries, and penalties, athletes can briefly engage in imagery to help in several areas. Athletes can review their prebreak performance to identify areas that are working and those that need to be changed. If athletes lose confidence, lose their intensity, become distracted, or feel negative emotions, they can use imagery to redirect their thoughts and feelings. Imagery can also be used to review and rehearse skill or tactical execution for the return to competition. For example, the coaches and players on a basketball team during a time-out discuss the set of plays they will run and then review the plays in their mind's eye.

Coach's Perspective

An assistant coach on the bench during an NHL contest can make a difference by directing his attention to an overlooked team member, the backup goalie. Imagery is a key component in this reliever's ability to be at peak readiness to contribute his best at a moment's notice. This same ongoing imagery practice (e.g., playing the game in his head as it unfolds on the ice in front of him) is what can turn a 3-hour block of time from a spectator event into a performance enhancement session.

The assistant coach does not need to be well versed in the technical "goalie-speak" of the goaltenders' subculture to keep him on task throughout the game. In the minors, staff may require this "extra" player to compile notes or take statistics on a clipboard as a means to stay on task. At the pro level, in-game conversation, asking opinion, and other acts of attention are the more common approach. How about asking this goalie to wear his catching glove, complete with a game puck in the pocket or webbing, and mentally see every on-ice shot coming right into that squeezed pocket? How about asking your pro backup goalie to add to his game simulation by wearing his mask? Additionally, speaking with him during the two intermission sessions, something that is taboo with the goalie who is actually playing in the game, is one more method of keeping the backup ready for an impromptu insertion into the current game and for making productive use of his bench time.

Last, all the imagery support talk from the assistant coach on the bench during the game does not have to be directed at the backup goaltender. All coaches would do well to spice their running commentary with verbiage supportive of the team's sport psychology consultant. Replace the profanity with comments like, "Let's imagine some solutions from here on the bench, guys, not focus on the mistakes being made! Take those solutions out there on your next shift!" "Let's look for that puck to come right to our stick blade and imagine our options! If we really want it, we won't be taken by surprise when it arrives!" "Let's be ready for your teammate's shot to come right off (opposition goalie's name) big blue leg pads and onto your stick. Visualize beating the goalie and burying it in the back of the net!"

■ ■ ■ ■ ■

Athlete's Perspective

During the game I don't visualize much when I am on the bench. All the work should have been done ahead of time. I just try to stay focused and react automatically to what happens. Players and coaches might talk about things we can do differently on the next shift, but we don't make big changes to our game plan. In between periods, our team might make some small changes in strategy that I will imagine, but usually I try to stay positive and keep working hard during the game. I trust in my ability and my experience to get the job done. If you do the practice and mental rehearsal regularly beforehand, your performance in the game will be fine.

■ ■ ■ ■ ■

Reviewing Competitive Performances

Mental imagery can be a useful tool for reviewing and evaluating competitive performances. Instead of thinking and talking about how they performed, athletes can "replay" important parts of the competition with imagery to reveal aspects of the performance that were successful and those that need improvement. This review imagery can identify physical, technical, tactical, and psychological areas that provide valuable lessons to athletes about what worked, what didn't, and what changes need to be made. This postcompetitive review can direct immediate practice plans, facilitate preparation for the next competition, and guide long-term development.

Coach's Perspective

Coaches, you should practice imagery too!

Want to improve your coaching? Imagery work practiced away from the bench can help you as much as it helps your star center. I've rehearsed situations where I've been the model of composure under stress (quite the opposite, many would testify, from what has been the actual case!).

The norms of elite hockey allow for a degree of animation and verbal protest in response to a rule interpretation that a coach feels has slighted his team. Frequently, reports emerge from players that the coach "completely lost it behind the bench," that the focus of the game disintegrated into a verbal sparring match between bench and referee. At that point, strategy, instruction, and game outcome too often take second or third priority. Such a situation is counterproductive if the players view it but is even more detrimental if they're allowed to participate.

On game days, in addition to a vigorous run or workout to deplete any stores of physical energy, it's just as critical for a coach to spend a few quiet moments in an imagery session. Pick a portion of your coaching style or demeanor that you identify as in need of some refinement, then "see it" occurring just as you would like during the contest. I find it helpful to mentally scan the arena first and imagine some of the smells of the moment, the temperature, and other stage-setting characteristics of the environment. Then, in my most frequent scenario, I resurrect some of the most protest-worthy officiating decisions from my memory bank of past games. I try to give them present-day believability by putting tonight's officials' faces atop the striped shirts and tonight's opponent's uniform color on the subsequent power play. Last, in my best fairy tale mode, I am producer, director, and scriptwriter for the movie that shows the power play being successfully killed off as a result of some calmly delivered instructions from me. Mission accomplished (at least for the imagery session)!

Seeing your planned strategies play themselves out successfully in your mind's eye in a big game is a start. Yet, don't stop there, coach! Before that game scenario, see yourself in practice outlining the specific parts of the entire success in segmented drills. See yourself giving crisp verbal instruction to the "left brainers" on your team; clear chalkboard diagrams to the "visual learners"; providing great drill performance instruction, execution, and corrections to all your kinesthetic learners; and, for your "right brained" integrators, providing an understandable postpractice rational explanation, synthesizing how it will all come together. Who said coaching in this modern era would get easier?

■ ■ ■ ■ ■

Developing a Mental-Imagery Program

The value of mental imagery lies in the quality of the images that athletes generate and, much like physical and technical training, the repetition of the imagery. A mental-imagery program allows athletes to consistently address key areas they need to improve. Athletes can use mental imagery to systematically develop technical, tactical, and mental aspects of their sport performance.

Setting Mental-Imagery Goals

The first step in developing a mental-imagery program is to set goals. These goals could be technical, such as improving execution of a skill; tactical, such as being more patient early in a competition; mental, such as increasing confidence or reducing intensity; or related to overall performance, such as improving consistency. Goals that address areas in need of improvement provide athletes with a clear purpose in their imagery efforts and guide them in developing their imagery (see chapter 7).

Working Up the Mental-Imagery Ladder

The next step involves creating a mental-imagery performance ladder. Athletes would not begin to change a part of their performance in an important competition. Rather, they would start off practicing new skills in a practice situation where mistakes do not matter. Similarly, athletes do not want to begin their mental-imagery program in a major imagined competition but rather start their imagery in a familiar and comfortable practice setting. Athletes can create a five-step ladder of practice and competitive situations in which they can imagine themselves performing. The ladder should start with the least important practice situation and progress to the most important competition in which they will perform. For example, a low rung of the mental-imagery ladder for a tennis player could have her hitting with a teammate, a middle rung might involve playing a practice match in front of her coach, and high rung could have her playing in the finals of an important tournament. This ladder enables athletes to work on areas they have identified in increasingly more demanding situations.

Athletes should begin their mental-imagery program at the lowest rung of the ladder and work their way up to the highest rung. They should not move up to the next rung until they can perform the way they want at the current rung. Once athletes feel good at a particular rung, they should stay there for several imagery sessions to reinforce the positive images, thoughts, and feelings.

Creating Imagery Scripts

Once athletes have established their goals and built their mental-imagery ladder, they are ready to create practice and competitive scenarios that they will follow in their mental-imagery sessions. These scenarios are actual practice or competitive situations in which athletes can work on their technical, tactical, mental, and performance goals.

If athletes perform in a sport in which competitive performances last at most a few minutes, such as figure skating and gymnastics, they can imagine themselves in an entire performance. If, however, they perform in a sport that lasts a long time, such as hockey or baseball, it would be unrealistic for them to imagine an entire performance. Instead, athletes should identify four or five brief performance situations that are realistic. For example, a running back in American football might imagine running a variety of plays in practice in which he is the ball carrier. As he moves up the mental-imagery ladder, he can imagine running those plays in practice, scrimmages, and increasingly important games.

Athletes' imagery scenarios should be practice or competition specific. Athletes should not just imagine themselves performing in a nonspecific location and event, under undefined conditions. Rather, athletes should imagine a practice or competition scenario in which they perform at a particular site, in a specific event, against an identifiable opponent. Also, the events, locations, conditions, and opponents should be appropriate to their level of ability. For example, if a soccer player is competing at a regional level, she should not imagine herself competing against American World Cup and Olympic star Brandi Chastain.

Individualized imagery scripts can maximize the use of imagery in enhancing performance (Smith, Holmes, Whitemore, Collins, and Devonport, 2001). Personalized rather than generic imagery scenarios help create stimulus, response, and meaning propositions (Lang, 1979) that are most relevant to an individual athlete. The creation of individualized imagery scripts involves a three-step process (Hale, 1998; see table 8.2) that should result in greater quality images and more benefit to performance.

Telling the Story

Select a competitive scenario or a specific skill to be worked on and outline the basic imagery story line. For example, returning to the example introducing this chapter, Steve Yzerman might break his face-off actions into the following components: (1) check the positions, (2) call a play, (3) visualize and feel an effective face-off, (4) breathe and repeat cue, (5) tie up his stick and step into circle, (6) win face-off, and (7) storm the net and see a goal. Write down the components of your skill in sequential order.

Adding the Details

This next step involves adding appropriate adjectives and descriptors to each component. Athletes should incorporate stimulus propositions from

Table 8.2

Writing an Imagery Script (Yzerman Script)

Step 1: Telling the basic story (list the components)	Step 2: Adding the details (add descriptors or action or emotional words)	Step 3: Refining the script (write stimulating sentences into a paragraph)
1. Check the positions	Red-sweatered 'Cane' defenders; right-defenseman crouched	I quickly notice where the red-sweatered defenders lined up outside the circle.
2. Call the play	Quietly call play 4 to teammates; cannot hear noise of the crowd	I quietly call play 4 to a circle of teammates so they know where the puck is going.
3. Breathe and repeat cue	Slide into the circle; take a deep breath; think "quick snap"	I take a quick deep breath and think "quick snap" to myself.
4. Step in the circle and tie up his stick	Slide into the other center; tie up his white-taped stick	I anticipate the drop, slide into the other center, and tie up his white-taped stick with mine.
5. Visualize and feel a successful face-off	My stick effortlessly swiping the puck	Then I quickly visualize my stick effortlessly swiping the puck out of the air and how strong my right wrist and hand feel.
6. Win face-off	Pick black puck out of air; feel my wrists snap powerfully backward	I quickly and effortlessly reach up with my stick to pick the black puck out of the air.
7. Storm the net and see a goal	Storm the net; hear the crowd erupt; jump up and down on the ice	I see the red light go on, hear the crowd erupt in a loud scream, and jump up and down on the ice.

Adapted, by permission, from B. Hale and B. Howe, 1999, Visualizing the perfect match. In *Rugby tough,* edited by B. Hale and B. Howe (Champaign, IL: Human Kinetics),85.

practice and competitive settings (e.g., colors, tactile aspects of equipment, sounds, smells, and feelings) to enhance the vividness and accuracy of the imagery. They can then integrate meaning and response propositions that ensure realistic emotions and corrective reactions to the imagined scenarios. Imagined settings, emotions, and actions that are most vivid will be most beneficial to enhancing performance. Athletes should use familiar words and expressions (Lang, 1979) that produce clear multisensory images and that evoke strong emotion and kinesthetic reactions.

Refining the Script

This step involves having athletes combine the story and the details into a clear, easily readable script that will replicate that actual sport experience. They should use a first-person perspective and describe the thoughts, feelings, and actions that they would normally experience. Athletes can either memorize the script or make an audiotape to guide them during an imagery session.

For example, in item 5, Win the face-off, Yzerman might write, "I am zoned in on the black puck and can anticipate its drop from the hand of the referee. As it is dropped, I quickly pick the puck out of the air with my white stick blade and feel my wrists snap powerfully backward as the puck shoots back to the blue line."

Using a Mental-Imagery Log

Because mental imagery is not tangible like, for example, the amount of weight lifted or the time to run a sprint, it is useful for athletes to keep a log of their mental-imagery sessions. By recording their mental-imagery sessions, athletes are able to see improvement as they make their way up the ladder.

The first piece of information athletes should record is the rung of the mental-imagery ladder. They should record a number between one and five to indicate where they are in their climb up the ladder. They can rate the quality of the imagery session on a 1 to 10 scale. How clear were the images, how well did they perform, how did they feel about the imagery session?

Athletes can describe their performance, that is, what they worked on and what they actually imagined during the imagery session. They can specify the number of mistakes they made in the imagery session. Athletes can then indicate what type of mistakes they made most frequently.

Athletes can rate the quality of their senses in the imagery session. They can assign themselves a score of 1 to 10 for the clarity of the visual, auditory, and physical imagery they experienced. Last, athletes can evaluate the mental aspects of their imagery by briefly describing relevant thoughts and emotions they had during the imagery session. The emphasis of this area should be on the positive or negative quality of their thoughts and emotions.

Considering Practical Concerns

A mental-imagery program is best executed in an organized and scheduled way. Athletes should structure their mental-imagery sessions into their daily routines. If they schedule these sessions for the same time every day, they are more likely to adhere to the program. Athletes should find a quiet, comfortable place where they will not be disturbed. Each session should last no longer than 10 minutes. Athletes should do mental imagery three to four times a week. Like any form of training, if they do it too much, they may get tired of it. Finally, athletes should begin their mental-imagery sessions with one of the relaxation procedures described in chapter 3. The deep state of relaxation will help athletes generate better quality images and will make them more receptive to the images and feelings they are trying to ingrain.

Key Points

* Various imagery-based terminology has been used interchangeably by researchers, consultants, coaches, and athletes over the last few decades, including visualization, mental imagery, mental practice, and mental rehearsal. For the sake of consistency and accuracy, mental imagery has been chosen to best describe this powerful mental training tool.

- A number of theories have been proposed to explain how mental imagery influences sport performance, including motivational theory, symbolic learning, psychoneuromuscular feedback, bioinformational theory, and functional equivalence, but no evidence has been found that supports any theory unequivocally. To date, the bioinformational and functional equivalence explanations remain the most promising attempts to understand the relationship between imagery and sport performance.

- Imagery has been found to be beneficial in physical, perceptual, and psychological skill enhancement before, during, and after competition.

- The PETTLEP model offers practical ways to maximize and structure mental imagery to ensure optimal benefit.

- The value of mental imagery is enhanced when athletes prepare individualized imagery scripts that take into account the unique aspects of the athlete and the particular demands of the sport.

Review Questions

1. Define the following terms and show how they are similar and different: mental imagery, mental practice, mental rehearsal, motor imagery, visualization.

2. What are the basic tenets of each of the following theories: motivational theory, symbolic learning, psychoneuromuscular feedback, bioinformational theory, functional equivalence?

3. What are the various ways that imagery can be used to enhance physical skills, perceptual skills, and psychological skills?

4. What does each letter of the PETTLEP model represent, and what principle does each term signify?

5. What are Hale's (1998) "four R's," and what are some ways they can be used to improve the value of imagery?

6. Prepare an individualized imagery script using the three-step process for a sport skill or performance.

9

Routines

Thomas Schack, PhD—researcher
Blair Whitmarsh, PhD—consultant
Ron Pike—coach
Chrissy Redden—athlete

The objectives of this chapter are

- to discuss the importance of routines in preparing athletes;
- to demonstrate how routines can be used in a variety of settings to enhance performance;
- to explain how and why routines work;
- to discuss when to use routines;
- to list the important elements of a routine; and
- to show coaches and athletes how to develop effective routines.

A basketball player approaches the free throw line and gets ready to take a potentially game-winning shot. As he approaches the line, he assumes the same stance and uses the same breathing pattern that he always uses. He bounces the ball the same way and the same number of times.

A tennis player lines up her feet in the exact same way as she prepares to serve. She bounces the ball three times, takes a deep breath, and then places the ball against her strings. Looking over at her opponent and then back to the racket, she is now ready.

A competitive swimmer finds a quiet corner of the aquatics facility 10 minutes before his race. Taking out his portable CD player, he listens to his favorite music and visualizes the long, powerful strokes that he needs to swim his best. He will be ready to compete because he is following the same pattern of success that always works for him.

Most athletes understand the importance of mental preparation and, more important, they understand that consistent behavior before and during a performance is the best way to ensure that they are totally prepared to perform their best. A routine can be defined as a series of pre-performance behaviors organized into a comprehensive plan aimed at maximizing the performance. Routines are one of the most effective ways to systematically plan for success. Routines have been shown to be invaluable in helping athletes achieve their competitive goals.

Key Issues

Routines can be viewed as a mental skill that athletes must develop to enhance their performances. When athletes try to create a routine without fully understanding the mechanisms that make a routine successful, the routine may be ineffective. Applied consultants and coaches can help athletes maximize the value of their routines by sharing research findings about routines. The more athletes understand about routines, the more effective their routines will be.

Routines play a critical role in athletes' preparation for competition and have been shown to be effective before, during, and after competition (Boutcher, 1990; Cohn, 1990; Schack, 1997). Most coaches and athletes recognize the value of competitive routines, but they often are unaware of the importance of routines in training. Athletes who develop routines for all aspects of their athletic experience and adapt them to the specific settings and situations in which they perform give themselves the best chance of success.

Chapter Purpose and Author Team

The purpose of this chapter is to provide a general overview of routines and how they can be developed and applied to any athletic setting. The consultant (Dr. Blair Whitmarsh) provides the structure of the chapter by introducing readers to the essential ways in which routines influence athletic performance. The researcher (Dr. Thomas Schack) describes the theoretical and empirical findings related to routines that support their value to athletes. Compared with other areas of sport psychology, the topic of routines has received relatively less attention. As a result, this chapter relies on the research that is available, as well as the experiences of the consultant, coach, and athlete. The coach (Ron Pike) explains how he uses routines to help prepare his athletes for competition. Finally, the athlete (Chrissy Redden) describes how she uses routines in training and competition to ensure she is prepared to perform her best.

Understanding the Rationale for Routines

The need for consistency in training and competition as the foundation of optimal performance is well understood by applied sport psychology consultants, coaches, and athletes. A number of factors, however, can interfere with athletes' ability to perform at a consistently high level in training and competition, including their physical, psychological, and emotional states, the significance of the event, and environmental and social influences. Routines can ensure that all positive influences on performance are supported and all negative influences are minimized by controlling the ways in which these factors affect performance.

Routines form the physical, psychological, and environmental foundation on which technical skills, physical conditioning, and mental skills can be optimally developed in training and used in competition. Between-performance routines (for sports that involve a series of short performances, such as tennis, golf, and baseball) enable athletes to maintain a high level of performance consistency throughout a competition. Postcompetition routines allow athletes to evaluate their performances, learn important lessons from the competition, and use that information to prepare for future training and competitions.

Routines connect physical, technical, tactical, and mental strategies aimed at enhancing performance, for example, physical and technical warm-up, intensity control, self-talk, mental imagery, focusing, and optimal performance. Routines become as essential to performance as proper equipment, good technique, and effective tactics. Routines allow athletes to control every area that influences training and competitive performance and to take specific responsibility for those aspects of their preparation. Athletes become aware of how routines prepare them and affect their performances. Athletes are then motivated to reproduce their routines before every performance because the routines enable athletes to use their training and competitive time to their benefit.

A number of explanations have been offered to clarify the precise mechanisms that make routines effective. Each explanation provides a different perspective on how routines work. Some of the accounts complement each other, whereas others are in sharp contrast, yet each increases our understanding of the value of routines.

Coach's Perspective

Volleyball, like many other team sports, requires individuals to work cohesively as a unit. Athletes and coaches need to be prepared to meet the many challenges of competition and to adjust and react to variations in the competitive environment to function most efficiently. Routines are a key component to accomplish this.

When I began coaching, I was very conscious of the need for routines in precompetition, particularly as they related to individual athlete mental preparation. Athletes set up prematch routines considering all the elements of preparation from the timing and content of meals to the last minute mental or tactical prepara-

tion. In contrast, team preparation was for the most part left to the common warm-up protocols that were a part of volleyball culture, and there was little if any intentionality in terms of developing or implementing team routines.

Over the years I began to notice that we started matches slowly, often losing the first set, and took a lot of time to get into the match flow as a group. Although most of the athletes did a great job of preparing themselves individually, it became evident that certain individual routines the athletes had conflicted with the corporate routines developing within the group. Not only did this negatively affect our team's overall preparation and performance, but it also had a detrimental effect on other team members' preparation because they didn't understand why some athletes were off on their own. In essence, individual routines were superseding the loosely defined corporate routines, resulting in a poor team flow early in matches.

At this point I realized we needed well-defined team routines that provided structure and a common thread necessary for individuals to prepare as a group. Although the need for individual routines was not diminished, the construction of team routines was much more deliberate in both practice and competition, allowing individual routines to be fully integrated into the team environment and ensuring a greater likelihood of success.

■ ■ ■ ■ ■

Athlete's Perspective

In my sport, cross-country mountain biking, we travel extensively around the world. Sometimes we compete at familiar venues, but we often are in unfamiliar venues. Each time I compete at a new venue, I scout the area for good places to buy food and water, and I study the new terrain and weather patterns. With all this change happening regularly (sometimes as often as each week), reverting to my routines helps me stay grounded and keep my goals in mind. It makes the world smaller and therefore more manageable.

My routines on race day definitely help me maintain my attention and avoid negative distractions. For example, I like to stay at the team accommodations the morning of the race for as long as possible. If my race is at 10 A.M., I would aim to be at the race site at 8:50 A.M. This gives me ample time to get my bike and myself organized, have a little chat with the support staff, and then have a sufficient warm-up. Certain circumstances have disrupted this pattern, and on those days when I've found myself at the race site hours ahead of time, the result is always the same: I get distracted, lose my focus, and ultimately end up with a less than sufficient warm-up.

My race day warm-up can also be considered a routine. When I do all aspects of my warm-up, I feel confident that I can start fast and without hesitation. I can then also put large demands on my legs and heart and they will respond positively. For example, I like to ride a small portion of the course during my warm-up. This gives me the confidence of knowing how the terrain looks that morning, I am confident that my bike is working perfectly, and it's a natural aerobic warm-up.

I have also found that having routines in my physical and psychological training helps me stay mentally focused and helps reduce the negative impact of important competitions. With my sport, we often find accommodations that allow us to cook our own food. This allows me to follow my diet and also helps me to maintain my daily routine.

■　■　■　■　■

Attention Control Theory

Sport competition places significant demands on athletes' attentional capabilities. Fans, expectations, past competitive experiences, and competitive stress are just a few of the distractions that athletes must contend with in their competitive efforts, preventing them from focusing on internal and external cues that are necessary for optimal performance. Attention-control theory (Boutcher, 1990) suggests that the value of routines is that they help athletes to avoid distractions and maintain focus by organizing athletes' attentional demands and providing clearly defined cues that athletes can attend to before and during competition. This explanation argues that if athletes are focused on their routines, they are less susceptible to internal or external distractions (see chapter 4).

Activation Set Hypothesis

Being properly "primed" for competition is essential for optimal performance, and insufficient warm-up is a common explanation for competitive performance failure. Although this initially was explained as "forgetting" by Adams (1961), a more recent interpretation of this phenomenon (Schmidt, 1988; Schmidt and Lee, 1998) suggests that, without adequate preparation, the "activation set" (i.e., the physical, psychological, and technical contributors to performance) may not be triggered before the start of a competition. The activation set hypothesis (Schmidt and Lee, 1998) asserts that routines activate these performance sets by guiding athletes through various physical, psychological, and technical strategies

designed to ensure they are properly warmed up in all relevant performance areas.

Mental Rehearsal Theory

All athletes would agree that a significant part of pre-performance preparation involves mentally rehearsing how they want to perform in competition. Yet athletes may forget to engage in this rehearsal because they are so focused on other aspects of their preparation. The mental rehearsal theory (Cohn, 1990; Schmidt, 1988) posits that mental rehearsal of future performance is an essential part of routines, ensuring that athletes take time to review the physical, technical, and mental demands that the competition will place on them and to rehearse strategies that will enable them to overcome those challenges before they perform (see chapter 8).

Mental Calibration Model

Being mentally prepared to perform their best is essential for athletes to achieve their competitive goals. All of the physical preparation by athletes would go for naught if they were not also mentally ready. The mental calibration model (Schack, 2002) suggests that adequate physiological activation is presumed to exist as a basic requirement of competitive performance and, as a result, the mental components are the most influential contributors to performance. Additionally, most problems that arise during competition are more likely caused by a mental breakdown rather than physiological difficulties. Moreover, physiological problems that arise are often attributed to failures in athletes' mental functioning. The best way for athletes to affect physiological functioning is to direct mental skills strategies to resolve the cause of the physiological deterioration, for example, change the negative thinking that causes anxiety during competition.

Routines enable athletes to evaluate competition conditions. For example, bouncing a ball in a volleyball service routine supplies the server with information about the ball, the floor, and the state of her muscles. This information can then be used to optimally prepare for her serve. Routines also enable athletes to adjust and fine-tune their preparations based on those evaluations or in pursuit of a particular competitive goal. This adaptation can involve adjustment to the conditions, opponents, competitive situation, or internal influences that can affect performance. Just like adjusting a race-car engine to the conditions of the track, air temperature, and weather, routines calibrate all competitive components to achieve optimal performance.

An important task of routines is creating a mind-set that will initiate optimal physiological preparation and foster athletes' best performances. Examples of a positive mind-set include establishing a performance goal, generating positive mental rehearsal, and identifying mental tools (e.g., self-instruction) that athletes can use to trigger beneficial performance reactions. This mind-set acts as the foundation for all actions related to competitive performance.

The mind-set, however, only sets the tone for optimal performance. Routines must also include mental tools, for example, cue words, that put the mind-set into action. Research on routines indicates that cue words have a stabilizing effect on performance (Boutcher, 1990). Cue words are tools that athletes can use to facilitate an effective focus in training or competition by directing attention to essential task-relevant information, thus ensuring proper execution. (See chapter 4 for a complete discussion on cue words.)

The significance of a competition is another common cause of performance failure because of its added pressure and the associated anxiety that can result (see chapter 3, Intensity). This effect is clearly seen in the differences in quality of performances for many athletes between training and competition. These variations in performance are attributable to the increased investment that athletes have in the outcome of competitions compared with training (i.e., competitions matter). In important competitions, this stress can hurt athletes physiologically in the form of muscle tension, breathing difficulties, and a loss of coordination and psychologically by creating doubt and fear.

Expectations that athletes have about their performances are closely linked to the significance of a competition. Typically, the more important the competition, the higher the expectations athletes have about their performance. These expectations, unfortunately, often interfere with rather than foster optimal performance because athletes place great weight on meeting the expectations for such an important competition and these beliefs cause precompetitive doubt and anxiety. Expectations have their place (e.g., as a motivator), but exclusive emphasis on expectations can cause athletes to become preoccupied with the results of the competition and distracted from the performance (see chapter 4, Focus).

Routines can help reduce the negative impact of important competitions and their associated expectations in several ways. First, routines communicate to athletes that, regardless of its importance, this is just another competition for which to prepare. Second, routines create feelings of familiarity and comfort because athletes have engaged in the components of the routine many times in the past. Third, by focusing on the elements of the routine, athletes are better able to keep their mind off of the stressful aspects of the competition. Finally, because routines have deliberate and active steps, athletes feel more in control and, as a result, feel less stress about the upcoming competition.

Measuring the Effects of Routines on Performance

Numerous studies have been conducted exploring the role of routines in athletic performance. These investigations have examined a number of questions about the value of routines, including whether they are commonly used by athletes, whether they enhance performance, and what components of routines are most important. Much of this research has focused on pre-performance routines, particularly the use of cognitive and behavioral strategies in routines. Little attention has been directed toward between-performance, post-competition, and coach routines (Bloom, Durand-Bush, and Salmela, 1997).

Initial studies examined whether routines were common among athletes. One study of female professional golfers found that their pre-putt and pre-shot behavior was consistent and stable over the course of a round of golf (Crews and Boutcher, 1987). For example, the golfers took the same number of practice swings and glances at the target before playing each shot. Other studies noted that routines possessed overt behavioral components and an underlying structure and that the frequency and the timing of routines were essential contributors to their value (Boutcher and Zinsser, 1990; Cohn, Rotella, and Lloyd, 1990).

Initial studies on the efficacy of routines in enhancing performance were supportive of their value. Research on golfers and tennis, volleyball, and basketball players revealed, for instance, that athletes who used a pre-performance routine performed significantly better than those who did not use a routine (Crews and Boutcher, 1986; Heishman, 1989; Lobmeyer and Wasserman, 1986; Moore, 1986).

Other research explored how different strategies that comprised a routine influence performance. A variety of cognitive strategies that were included in pre-competitive routines were found to enhance performance, including self-talk (Bunker and Owens, 1985; Bunker and Rotella, 1982; Schack, 1997), focus (Ravizza and Rotella, 1982), mental imagery (Mahoney and Avener, 1977), and psyching up (Caudill, Weinberg, and Jackson, 1983; Shelton and Mahoney, 1978).

Most of the research looking at routines has included both cognitive and behavioral strategies. Cognitive strategies often include techniques such as those just mentioned. Behavioral strategies might include practice swings in golf or bouncing a basketball before a free throw. Studies conducted in a number of sports, including diving (Highlen and Bennett, 1983), golf (Cohn et al., 1990; Rotella and Bunker, 1981), tennis (Moore, 1986), gymnastics (Mahoney and Avener, 1977; Schack, 1997), and volleyball (Schack, 2002), demonstrated that routines that include both cognitive and behavioral strategies are effective in improving performance.

Coach's Perspective

One of the greatest benefits of routines is enhancing an athlete's ability to perform under pressure. Good players abound, but it is the great players who are capable of performing under pressure. For the last 5 years I have worked with two equally skilled athletes who have had considerably different views on individual routines as they related to practice and pre-match preparation. For the purposes of discussion we will call them Mark and Paul. Mark was very committed to routines both in training and in pre-competition. He diligently worked on tactics and strategies in practice each day, religiously watched videotape each week on our next opponent and on our match plan, and planned and analyzed cues necessary to make good decisions in the match. Paul, on the other hand, who was an exceptional player, had a more laissez-faire approach to the game. Although he maintained the team routines (e.g., warm-up, video, team meals), he refused to create personal routines designed to uniquely meet his needs during competition. In most competitions it was hard to distinguish between these two athletes, because both were gifted athletes who performed at a high level. The distinction, however, became very evident when pressure was introduced and they needed

to perform. Under pressure, Mark was able to read and react to the situation and, based on his knowledge and preparation, adjust and perform admirably. Paul, on the other had, became consumed with the moment, and if errors were made or adjustments were needed, it was evident by his diminished level of play that he was not prepared to handle the situation. Although Paul had a good career with some improvement, Mark, thanks to the routines he had developed over 5 years, became an All-Canadian performer.

■ ■ ■ ■ ■

Athlete's Perspective

I frequently find that including my self-talk, focus, and mental imagery routines into my prerides on the racecourse enhance that particular performance. I like to preride courses solo and practice the gearing and thought processes that I want to have during the race. I think of it as brainwashing myself, but it works!

My season is so long that I will also avoid doing my routines just to get a little break. This break allows me to be excited and fresh for the important competitions.

■ ■ ■ ■ ■

Convincing Athletes of the Benefits of Routines

Research supporting the value of routines demonstrates their importance for athletes in their training and competitive preparations. Despite this evidence, athletes may not be convinced of the worth of routines. To persuade athletes that developing and using routines are to their advantage, it is worthwhile to illustrate the many benefits that routines offer athletes.

Athlete's Perspective

When I first read this chapter, I didn't think I could comment because I honestly didn't think I had any routines. But in reality I have many! And the more I use them, the better I perform. When I use routines, I can definitely feel increased confidence, focus, and preparedness, though I can't explain why. I used to get really flustered when I would miss a "feed." (My sport is an endurance race and usually lasts 2 to 2 1/2 hours, so it is essential that our support personnel give us water and an energy drink. This is called a feed. It's against our rules to take any "feeds" from anyone other than your own support person. So, missing a feed could detrimentally affect the outcome of the race.

I remember one particular race where my support person was off somewhere and totally missed me. I couldn't get my mind back on the race and ended up losing about 10 spots. I was really angry at the finish and blamed my support person fully. In the next year, there were probably a couple more similar instances. I realized that no one was perfect and allowing somebody else's mistake to affect me negatively was silly. I started to mentally rehearse missing feeds, or any other challenge, during the race. I was then able to allow the situation to occur and allow my focus to be undisturbed. My theory was that I could win no matter what! This small example shows that I have many routines, some that I use daily, others that I only use for major competitions like Games or Worlds.

It is important to allow flexibility to adjust to unpredictable or uncontrollable circumstances. For example, earlier I mentioned that I like to do a portion of my warm-up on the course. In the uncontrollable event of heavy rain, it's better not to get on the course any earlier than the start pistol. Riding in heavy rain would only make the bike dirty and slow me down. I therefore have a "rain option" warm-up that still allows me to fully prepare and stay dry and warm.

■　■　■　■　■

Preparation

An essential function of routines is to help athletes fully prepare for their training and competitive performances. Routines enable athletes to adapt to performance situations in a nonthreatening environment over which they have control. Routines help athletes to transfer what they developed in training and to use those skills optimally in competition. This transfer process is often difficult for athletes because of the pressures, demands, and complexities present in competition that are not evident in training. Routines help athletes to feel a sense of familiarity, predictability, and control over their competitive environments. This comfort increases the chances that athletes will be able to fully use the skills they acquired in training.

Routines enhance preparation in several ways. First, physical aspects of the routine help athletes to achieve an optimal level of intensity through warm-up, relaxation, or psyching-up strategies, so when they begin their performance they are physically prepared to perform from the first movement.

Second, psychological elements of the routine ensure that athletes are mentally prepared to perform their best. Mental areas that athletes should address in their routines include motivation, confidence, and focus. Strategies that are often incorporated into a routine include goal setting, self-talk, cue words, and mental imagery. Inclusion of these and other mental techniques help athletes start their performance in a frame of mind that will result in optimal performance.

Third, routines assist athletes in preparing themselves technically and tactically for their performance. An essential part of routines is a precompetitive review of relevant techniques or tactics that they need to execute correctly. With use of mental imagery, discussion with a coach or teammate, or step-by-step review or practice of necessary technique or tactics, athletes ingrain these techniques, which increases athletes' chances of proper execution.

Fourth, routines help athletes ensure that their equipment is ready for performance. Athletes who compete in sports that involve equipment, like ski racing, tennis, and triathlon, often experience failure because they have not prepared their equipment adequately. This neglect often occurs simply because athletes forget to prepare their equipment. Routines minimize the chances of this oversight if equipment preparation is incorporated into the routine.

Control

Many aspects of performance are outside of athletes' control. At the same time, for athletes to perform successfully, they must be able to gain control over important aspects of their performances, and routines offer a way of gaining that control. Control refers to those situations and conditions that affect performance that athletes can influence before and during competition.

The first step in understanding the role of control in routines is for athletes to recognize what they cannot control, for example, weather, competitive conditions, opponents, and officiating. After accepting things over which athletes have no control, they can then direct their attention and efforts toward those areas that they can control, for example, their physiology (e.g., muscle tension, breathing, heart rate), mind (e.g., attitude, expectations, emotions, decisions), and behavior (e.g., actions, interactions). Having identified the areas that are controllable, athletes can then include strategies in their routines that will maximize those areas for performance. Also, the defined and structured nature of routines can give athletes a greater sense of control, calm, and comfort, even when the environment that they are in is out of their control. This sense of control alone can often be the difference between optimal and subpar performance.

Flexibility

The competitive arena is, by its very nature, difficult, unpredictable, and uncontrollable. Despite their best efforts, athletes can never prepare for every eventuality that may occur in competition or control everything that may influence their performances. Routines offer a structure within which to prepare for performance and the flexibility to adjust to the uncertain nature of competition. Because routines are not inviolate, but rather provide a guide for athletes to follow, they can also be readily altered to fit the demands of a unique or unexpected competitive environment. Unforeseen changes in the competitive setting, such as weather, unexpected opponents, late arrival, insufficient warm-up space, and broken or lost equipment, can have a disturbing and disruptive effect on athletes before a competition. Athletes often perform below expectations because they are unable to respond appropriately to these occurrences or become unsettled mentally (e.g., lose motivation or confidence, get distracted, or experience anxiety). Athletes with well-organized yet flexible routines will be better able to respond positively to these challenges, keep their composure, and maintain a high level of performance.

Self-Awareness

Internal and external influences on performance can interact in training and competitive situations. Particularly in competitions, external factors can interfere with athletes' performances, for example, time schedules, delays, postponements, antagonistic fans, and adverse weather. Because these external influences almost always affect all competitors, these demands in and of themselves do not determine who is successful or unsuccessful; rather, success is often determined by how individual athletes respond to the challenges. Those athletes who can respond positively to these difficulties are more likely to achieve their goals.

Routines help athletes to gain self-awareness that will enable them to respond better to these external forces. Developing routines helps athletes to gain insight into what areas influence their performances. This understanding enables athletes to recognize when difficulties arise and what their effects might be. Without this self-awareness, athletes may not recognize the occurrence of these

interfering factors soon enough to respond, and because athletes also may not have routines available to them, they will not know how to react in a positive way. Routines also give athletes the structure and the tools to respond to adversity, enabling athletes to respond immediately and positively to these difficulties, thus minimizing their influence on performance.

Integration

Routines integrate physical, psychological, and behavioral contributors to performance, ensuring that each area influences the others in a positive and supportive way. For example, deep breathing is an important physical strategy aimed at relaxing the body. Breathing is also an effective psychological tool for enhancing focus. Incorporating deep breathing into a routine offers athletes the integrated benefits of increased physical awareness, reduced intensity, and improved focus (see chapter 3).

Routines also integrate behavioral contributors whose physical and psychological influences can help athletes execute important actions and skills. For example, golfers can facilitate their shot preparations by incorporating deep breathing into their practice swings. The breathing relaxes their bodies and narrows their focus, which allows them to engage in better quality practice swings. This integration results in improved physical, psychological, and technical preparation, which will result in optimal performance.

Types of Routines

Athletes must be physically and psychologically prepared to perform their best in training and competition. Complete preparation for training is essential for athletes to ensure quality training efforts and to fully develop and ingrain the physical, technical, tactical, and mental skills that are necessary for competitive success. Total readiness for competition is fundamental to athletes' performing their best consistently and achieving their goals in competition. Given all the areas that athletes must address in their training and the importance of effective preparation, attempts at preparing these areas in an unstructured or haphazard way can only result in less than total readiness. Routines provide athletes with the structure and the process to fully prepare every contributor to performance so that when they begin their training session or competition they are ready to perform at their highest level.

Many applied sport psychology consultants, coaches, and athletes use the term *ritual* in place of *routine*. Rituals are typically rigid, have a ceremonial aspect to them, and can contain superstitious elements that have no real influence on performance. Athletes can develop the belief that if the ritual is not performed, their competitive performances are doomed. Routines, in contrast, are flexible and include only those elements that have a clear impact on performance. Athletes believe that a routine will help them get prepared to compete, but they also understand that precompetitive activities can sometimes interfere with the routine. Whereas rituals often control athletes, athletes always control their routines. For example, one soccer goalie may believe that not washing the jersey she wore when she last won will enable her to play well. But if the jersey is inadvertently laundered, then she may believe that the "luck" of the jersey has been washed away and that she is doomed to play poorly. Clearly, whether her jersey is clean or not has no real bearing on the quality of her play. In contrast, the opposing goalie follows a routine that includes physical warm-up, shots on goal by her teammates, and imagery of making saves during the game. These useful steps prepare her to play optimally.

Routines become a purposeful "microenvironment" for athletes to create optimal performance patterns. This controlled environment within a training or competitive setting enables athletes to direct every contributor to performance. For example, physiological and psychological processes, such as muscle tension and focus, become attuned to each other. Thus, routines help to regulate and fine-tune athletes' performances.

Coach's Perspective

Challenges in sport and competition are presented in numerous ways with countless variations. Although trying to anticipate and prepare for all possibilities in a dynamic sport environment is virtually impossible, having well-established individual and team routines enhances the likelihood of success and helps the athlete make decisions. When coaches improve team and individual responses to likely scenarios, certain components of the game become very automatic, allowing athletes more time to deal with the variations and nuances in the competitive environment. Conversely, if an athlete doesn't have sufficient time to develop these routines, she will often struggle to solve challenges presented in the competitive environment, thereby resulting in diminished performance levels.

A couple of years ago we were training a team to compete at the World University Games in Beijing, China. At the time the national team coach had recognized a lack of International-level players in the country at a certain position and was trying to increase the pool by training some of the more talented players from other positions. During the initial rounds of the competition, the athletes appeared in control of their skills and their performances were quite admirable given that they were in a new position. However, as the demands of the competition increased, it became evident that the routines these athletes had spent so many years developing and honing were not meeting the challenges that were being presented. Although their volleyball skills and routines were well trained through countless practices and competitions, the slight differences presented to them by playing a new position at the International level resulted in considerable frustration and reduced performance levels. This was not necessarily because of a lack of talent but because the routines and preparation they were relying on did not adequately meet their needs in competition. Essentially most, if not all, of the routines these athletes had developed through the years were honed playing a different position and, although some of the skills transferred, it was evident that these athletes would need considerably more time training the routines of their new position. Ironically, in the end our best player in that position, although arguably not the most talented, was the one who had played that position for the greatest number of years. Although the demands of the competition were higher than he was used to, the well-defined set of routines he had developed over the years transferred well to the competition. These routines allowed him to more adequately deal with the demands placed on him.

■ ■ ■ ■ ■

Training Routines

Too often, athletes arrive for training with little thought given to the upcoming training session or a clear purpose of what they want to accomplish. Their focus is on anything but learning new skills, gaining fitness, improving team play, or aggressively working through the drills that might be presented by the coach. Athletes also often begin their training without a proper physical warm-up. Most athletes simply fail to prepare for training sessions, and the result is the inability to gain the fullest benefit from training. This failure to maximize the benefits of training is important because athletes are only as good in competition as what they gained in training.

The primary purpose of a training routine is to ensure complete readiness, thereby enabling athletes to get the most out of their training efforts. These efforts are directed toward integrating the mind and body so that athletes can learn new technical skills, improve their physiological functioning, and learn to work effectively with teammates. Training routines need only last a few seconds but will help athletes to get the most out of their training. Routines will also lay the foundation for developing competition routines.

Mental Preparation

The competitive sport environment places tremendous psychological demands on athletes. Athletes' ability to effectively meet these demands is essential to achieving their competitive goals. The place where these challenges are first faced, rehearsed, and overcome is in training. Additionally, the quality of athletes' training, for example, developing sound technical and tactical skills, is often determined by their mental preparedness for training. Mental areas such as motivation, confidence, intensity, focus, and emotions all play essential roles in developing effective skills and practicing the demands of competition.

Training routines can help athletes develop these important mental areas. Instilling important mental skills for the two purposes discussed previously can best be accomplished in a structured and systematic way. Athletes who incorporate these mental areas into their training will enhance their mental skills and learn and ingrain technical and tactical skills necessary for competitive success. Training routines that include mental preparation help athletes to train at a level of motivation, intensity, and focus that more closely simulates competitive levels.

Training routines designed to regulate mental readiness need to consider the mental areas that influence performance, as mentioned previously. Athletes must be aware of their motivation, confidence, intensity, focus, and emotions before and during training sessions. Specific areas that athletes need to be aware of include their determination before training, the effort they expend during training, their self-talk, their level of intensity, their focus, and the emotions they are experiencing. Once this accounting has taken place, athletes can build specific mental skills into their training routines, for example, goal setting, positive self-talk, psyching up or calming down, cue words, and letting go of emotions, to ensure that these areas positively influence their training efforts.

Athlete's Perspective

I really enjoy my mental preparation and skill development routines in my training. They make the training so much more meaningful. They also bring "home" to the race site!

Whereas training routines give me a solid base of mental, technical, and physical ability, competition routines have an instant result on race day. I sometimes think of them as more important, but without the training base, I would be lost at the race.

The postcompetition routines are definitely the most forgotten routines! I try to remind myself to do an equipment analysis with the team mechanic. It's so important, but after a successful result, we sometimes think everything went perfectly. This is seldom the case, and I like to reflect and learn.

Thank you for the reminder that I should evaluate my routines to ensure that they are still optimally preparing me for competition! After reading this chapter, I am examining my physical and technical warm-up, precompetition nutrition, equipment, interactions, and mental preparation.

■　■　■　■　■

Skill Development

A principal goal of training is to develop the skills necessary to perform optimally in competition. Despite this obvious importance, athletes are often not prepared to train effectively and, as a result, their skill development is slowed. Training routines help athletes facilitate their skill development in several ways. First, training routines identify what athletes want to accomplish in the training session. This objective gives athletes a clear direction and purpose to their training. Second, with this goal in mind, athletes can direct their focus on specific aspects of the goal before and during a training sequence, thereby increasing the quality of the training session and the likelihood that the relevant skills will be learned. Third, having this goal and focus, athletes can adjust their intensity to a level that is most conducive to skill development. Unlike in competition, where intensity is often higher, skills are best learned at lower levels of intensity, where the mind and the body are more receptive.

Competition Routines

Significant demands are placed on athletes at every point of a competition. Athletes' abilities to meet those demands will determine their success and how their performance affects them in future training and competition. Competitive routines can be used before the start of competition, between performances (for sports such as tennis, baseball, and golf that consist of a series of short performances), and at its conclusion. Each type of routine helps athletes prepare themselves at different stages of the competition.

Precompetitive Routines

Everything that athletes do before a competition must be directed toward their total preparation for competitive success. Precompetitive routines are designed to help athletes achieve that complete state of readiness that will allow them to perform their best. These routines also ensure that athletes have the proper mind-set for the competition and that their mind and body are in sync. This integration allows athletes to fully use the physical, technical, tactical, and mental skills that they gained in training.

Precompetitive routines include every area that influences athletes' performances, such as physical, technical, tactical, mental, equipment, and team, and give athletes specific strategies for preparing each area. Precompetitive routines should include an extensive physical and technical warm-up, review of essential tactics, preparation of equipment, discussion with teammates, and mental preparation that consists of goal setting, positive self-talk, intensity regulation, focusing, and mental imagery.

Precompetitive routines also help athletes to deal with the internal and external stressors of competition. These routines allow athletes to put the stress into proper perspective and enable them to focus their mental and physical energies on the task at hand. Precompetitive routines help athletes to block out external distractions and reduce interfering internal "static" that can hurt performance. Successful athletes are not those who eliminate competitive stress but rather those who recognize the stressors and respond to them in a positive way. Precompetitive routines allow athletes to fully marshal their resources and direct them toward meeting the challenges of competition in a structured and effective way.

Typically, when athletes are asked if they use routines as part of their competitive repertoire, they usually think first of precompetitive routines. Preparing for a big competition is probably the most common use of routines by coaches and athletes. Aside from the benefits of improved preparation, precompetitive routines offer athletes a sense of familiarity, stability, comfort, and

control, which is so essential amidst the many unknowns and stresses of the competitive arena.

There is no one ideal precompetitive routine. For every athlete, there is a different routine, but all will have common elements. Each athlete must decide what exactly to put into his or her routine and how to structure it. Developing an effective precompetitive routine is a process that will take time (Taylor, 2001).

The first step for athletes in designing a precompetitive routine is to list everything they need to do before a competition to be completely prepared. Some of the common elements athletes should include are meals, review of competitive tactics, physical warm-up, technical warm-up, equipment check, discussion with teammates (for team sports), and mental preparation. Other more personal elements that might go into a precompetitive routine include going to the rest room, changing into their competition clothing, and using mental imagery.

Athletes must then decide in what order they want to engage in the components of their list as they approach the start of the competition. Athletes should consider competition activities that might need to be taken into account. For example, time limitations for their precompetitive meal or use of a practice area can influence when they perform different parts of their precompetitive routine.

Athletes must also specify where each step of their routine can best be completed. They should use their knowledge of competitive sites at which they often perform to figure this part out. For example, if an athlete likes to be alone before a competition, is there a quiet place where she can get away from people?

Finally, athletes must establish a time frame for completing their precompetitive routine. In other words, how much time do athletes need to get totally prepared, and when do they need to begin their routine to be ready for the competition? Some athletes like to get to the competition site only a short time before they begin. Others like to arrive hours before. All of these decisions are personal, and athletes need to find out what works best for them.

Once athletes have organized their precompetitive routine, they can try it out at competitions. Some things may work and others may not. In time, athletes will be able to fine-tune their routines until they find the one that is most comfortable and best prepares them for competition. Athletes must remember that precompetitive routines only have value if they're used consistently. If athletes use their routine before every competition, in a short time they will not even have to think about doing it. The precompetitive routine will simply be what athletes do before each competition to ensure that they are totally prepared to perform their best (Taylor, 2001).

Between-Performance Routines

In sports that involve a series of short performances (e.g., American football, diving, wrestling), the time between performances often determines whether athletes maintain a high level of performance or turn around poor performance. For these sports, being well prepared for the first performance is not enough. What athletes think, feel, and do between performances often dictates how they perform. Athletes must take control of the time between performances to ensure that they are totally prepared for every performance in a competition.

Between-performance routines can be invaluable in ensuring that athletes are prepared for every performance within a competition. What separates the great athletes from the good ones is not their ability to perform well once but rather their ability to be ready for every performance and to perform consistently well throughout a competition. By being totally prepared for every performance, athletes can be sure that they do not give their opponents "free points" because they are not ready. Taylor (2001) offered a simple and useful structure, the four R's, for helping athletes use the time between performances to their greatest benefit (Note: These four R's for routines should not be confused with the four R's for mental imagery offered by Hale [see chapter 8]).

The first R is *rest*. Immediately after the conclusion of the previous performance, athletes should take several slow, deep breaths and let their muscles relax. This is especially important after a long or demanding performance in which athletes may be out of breath or fatigued. Recovering from the last performance is particularly important near the end of a long competition where the competition may be on the line and athletes are tired and need to rest as much as possible to be ready for the next performance. Deep breathing and relaxing also help athletes center themselves and better prepare them for the next R.

The second R is *regroup*. This phase of the between-performance routine addresses athletes' emotions between performances. Particu-

larly when they are not performing well or the competition is at a critical juncture, athletes may feel a variety of emotions such as excitement, frustration, anger, or depression. Regrouping allows athletes to gain awareness of how their emotions are influencing them and, if emotions are affecting them negatively, to master these emotions so that they help rather than hurt the next performance. If athletes feel frustrated, angry, or disappointed following a poor performance, they are more likely to perform poorly in the next performance. To prevent this downward spiral, athletes need to give themselves more time to regroup and let go of the unhealthy emotions. Because of the powerful influence emotions have on athletes' performances, athletes' ability to "get their act together" emotionally between performances may be the most important thing they can do to prepare for the next performance (see chapter 5 for more about emotions).

The third R is *refocus*. During competitions, especially in high-pressure situations, athletes tend to focus on the last performance or the outcome of the competition, neither of which will help them perform well. This is a form of outcome focus. When this happens, athletes need to return to a process focus for the next performance. During the refocus phase of the between-performance routine, athletes should first evaluate their present situation, for example, the score, how they are performing, and tactics. Then they should focus on what they need to perform well in the next performance. Their focus may be technical, tactical, or mental. The important thing is for athletes to begin the next performance with a clear focus on what they want to do to perform their best (see chapter 4 for more about focus).

The fourth R is *recharge*. For athletes to perform their best, their bodies must be at an optimal level of intensity. Just before beginning the next performance, athletes should check and adjust their intensity. If they need to lower their intensity, they should slow their pace, take deep breaths, and relax their muscles. If athletes need to raise their intensity, they should increase their pace, take short, intense breaths, and jump up and down (see chapter 3 for more about intensity).

Postcompetition Routines

The conclusion of a competition is either an exciting time to relish a successful performance or a time of disappointment about a failed performance. Athletes who are successful usually want to just enjoy the experience, and athletes who fail to achieve their goals often prefer to forget about the competition as soon as possible. Yet, the time following a competition is essential to help athletes achieve their season-long goals and prepare for the next competition.

Postcompetition routines provide athletes with the opportunity to fully benefit from the competitive experience, whether a success or failure, and to use the experience to help them succeed in the future. Postcompetition routines include physical, mental, and equipment closure on the competition. These routines should start with a physical cool-down in which athletes assess their physical state, determine the presence of injuries, stretch, get a massage, and rehydrate and refuel themselves. Next, athletes can check and clean their equipment and prepare it for travel. Finally, athletes can engage in a mental and emotional cool-down. This part of the postcompetition routine allows athletes to experience, express, and let go of their emotions (e.g., frustration, anger, and sadness following a poor performance). Once athletes have addressed their feelings about the competition, they can then thoroughly analyze their performance, including a review of all aspects of their performance, identification of its strengths and weaknesses, and lessons learned about their performance. This information enables athletes to better plan their upcoming training schedules to address any concerns that may have arisen in the just-concluded competition and to better prepare themselves for the next competition.

Practical Concerns

Athletes change and mature physically, technically, and mentally, and their competitive preparation needs often evolve as well. Yet, athletes can become comfortable with the routines they have been using for years and assume that, because their routine was effective at one time, it is still effective now. Using routines is an ongoing process, and athletes should examine their routines periodically to ensure that they continue to optimally prepare athletes for competition. Additionally, as athletes search for new strategies to improve their performances, they should experiment with new ways to prepare themselves for competition.

Athletes should evaluate in detail their competitive preparations and consider other approaches that might enhance performance. Areas that athletes should consider include physical and technical warm-up, precompetition nutrition, equipment, interactions, mental preparation, and length and location of their preparation efforts. As athletes progress up the competitive ladder, they will find that improvements in performance become smaller and more difficult to achieve. Fine adjustments to their competitive routines that elevate their level of competitive readiness can facilitate performance gains and continued competitive success.

Regardless of the sport in which athletes participate, adhering to competitive routines can be difficult because of the venue, competition schedules, weather conditions, and other uncontrollable factors. Athletes who compete in team sports have additional challenges related to their routines that athletes from individual sports never have to face. Not only must team players adapt the execution of their routines to the specific competition, but they must also fit it into the structure of team preparations. Given the time constraints during a competition and the obvious priority that must be given to team activities, athletes can find it difficult to perform their personal routines and get optimally prepared for a competition. Precompetitive team routines often consist of team meetings, subteam meetings (e.g., offense, defense), organized physical warm-up, and rehearsal of competition strategies, and they establish a clear timetable to which team members must adhere to the team routine.

Allowing individual as well as team routines can be facilitated in several ways. First, coaches must appreciate that members of the team have different needs precompetitively, between performances, and postcompetition. If coaches respect individual needs, they will give team members the time and space they need to prepare within the structure of the team routine. Second, coaches should communicate to the athletes the need and value of both team and individual routines and how both can be accomplished. Third, individual athletes must learn the team routine and build their own routines around them. Fourth, teammates must respect each other's unique needs in preparation and not interfere with individual athletes as they engage in their precompetitive routines. Fifth, athletes must be flexible and modify their routines based on the team routine and the current competitive situation.

Key Points

- Complete physical, technical, tactical, mental, and equipment preparation is essential for athletes to achieve optimal competitive performance.
- Routines are an effective way to ensure that athletes prepare fully for competition.
- A number of explanations have been offered for how routines enhance performance, including improved attention, better warm-up, use of mental rehearsal, and the integration of all mental aspects of performance.
- Research has found that routines are commonly used by athletes and are effective in improving performance.
- Benefits of the use of routines include better preparation, greater control over influences on performance, more flexibility, increased self-awareness, and more integration between physical, technical, and mental contributors to performance.
- Four types of routines are most useful to athletes: training, precompetitive, between-performance, and postcompetition.
- Training routines encourage athletes to be optimally prepared for their practice efforts by ensuring physical warm-up, instilling motivation, engendering confidence, creating ideal intensity, and allowing effective focus.
- Routines for every phase of a competition, including precompetitive, between-performance, and postcompetition, help athletes maintain a high level of performance throughout a competition and assist them in learning valuable lessons about their performance for future training and competitions.

Review Questions

1. Why are routines so beneficial for athletes?
2. What are two explanations for how routines influence performance?
3. What are three benefits of routines?
4. What are the two ways that training routines help athletes in their practice efforts?
5. What are some key issues that athletes must consider in planning their precompetitive routines?
6. What are Taylor's four R's of between-performance routines?
7. What purpose do postcompetition routines serve?

III

Psychology and the Coach

Part III explores the role that coaches and teams play in athletic performance. Almost every sport, whether individual or team, has a coach, who affects athletes in many ways (e.g., physical, technical, tactical, psychological, and social). In addition to typical team sports, even most individual sports are organized around teams (e.g., track and field, tennis), so the influence of athletes on one another can be profound.

Chapter 10 focuses on the coach–athlete relationship. Issues to be addressed include the leadership, interpersonal dynamics, education, and ethics that underlie this relationship. The goal of this chapter is to provide insights into the coach–athlete relationship and offer suggestions on how it can be developed so that the relationship is mutually rewarding, fosters healthy personal development in athletes, and facilitates their competitive success.

Chapter 11 examines the roles of coaches and athletes in the larger context of teams. A coaching staff and diverse athletes create a complex dynamic that must be balanced for teams and individual athletes to fully realize their goals. This chapter looks at how a team is created, roles are identified, and cohesion is developed. It offers a variety of approaches to foster team cohesion and maximize individual and team performance.

10
Coach–Athlete Relationship

Sophia Jowett, PhD—researcher

Geoff Paull, PhD, and Anne Marte Pensgaard, PhD—consultants

Per Mathias Hoegmo, MS—coach

Hege Riise—athlete

The objectives of this chapter are

- to discuss the theoretical and conceptual models that have been developed to examine the dynamics between coaches and athletes;
- to examine factors that influence the quality of the coach–athlete relationship;
- to consider conflict in the coach–athlete relationship;
- to discuss ethical issues that pertain to the coach–athlete relationship;
- to review strategies that contribute to the development of healthy athletic relationships; and
- to consider the role of consultants in developing optimal coach–athlete relationships in different sport contexts.

This chapter explores how interpersonal dynamics, relationships, leadership, communication, and education influence the quality of coach–athlete relationships. Effective coach–athlete relationships enable coaches to influence athletes in a positive way. The complex dynamics between coaches and the athletes with whom they work are affected by personality styles, the status of coaches and athletes, maturity, and familial, cultural, and other factors. The ability of coaches and athletes to understand these dynamics and use them to their advantage will determine whether the coach–athlete relationship facilitates or interferes with athletic training and will determine the benefits that both coaches and athletes gain from the relationship.

Key Issues

The coach–athlete relationship is an essential contributor to effective coaching, the development of an athlete, and successful competitive performances. Enhancing our knowledge of the psychological and social foundations of healthy and effective coach–athlete relationships has several important benefits. Greater insights into this relationship help coaches and athletes ensure that they are making optimal contributions to the relationship. These insights also help consultants to enhance the relationship. Thus, researchers must continue to explore and refine their understanding of these relationships.

The need to examine the development of optimal coach–athlete relationships is emphasized by administrators and officials in sport institutions and associations as well as by sport psychology researchers and consultants (Jowett and Cockerill, 2003; Jowett and Ntoumanis, 2004; Poczwardowski, Sherman, and Henschen, 1998). Recognition of the role that the coach–athlete relationship plays, and more generally the role of psychosocial issues, in achieving competitive success is reflected in the emphasis placed on coaching-education programs worldwide (e.g., the Australian Sports Commission, the Coaching Association of Canada, the American Sport Education Program, and Sports Coach UK).

Despite this focus, researchers and consultants have observed a gap between the scientific understanding of coach–athlete relationships in sport and the value of this knowledge to coaches and athletes (Coppel, 1995; Iso-Ahola, 1995). A common concern is that research on coach–athlete relationships has little practical value to consultants in their efforts to develop positive coach–athlete relationships (Poczwardowski et al., 1998). This disconnection between research and application may be attributable to a lack of both clear scientific delineation of the coach–athlete relationship and valid instrumentation to assess such relationships (Wylleman, 2000). Research that advances knowledge and understanding of coach–athlete relationships at both scientific and practical levels is necessary to bridge this gap.

Chapter Purpose and Author Team

The purpose of this chapter is to examine in depth the importance of the coach–athlete relationship to the sporting and personal lives of athletes. This goal is addressed from the diverse perspectives of a researcher (Dr. Sophia Jowett), two consultants (Drs. Geoffrey Paull and Anne Marte Pensgaard), a coach (Per Mathias Hoegmo), and an athlete (Hege Riise). The ultimate objective of this chapter is to help coaches and athletes work together to build relationships that encourage the highest quality of coaching and the fullest development of the athlete. Another goal is to foster the ongoing observation of best practices in coach–athlete relationships and further develop rigorous explanations, measurement instruments, and empirical evidence to uncover the impact of coach–athlete relationships on the competitive athletic arena.

Understanding the Coach–Athlete Relationship

Coaching has been viewed as an interpersonal process composed of an important relationship that develops between the coach and the athlete (Jowett and Cockerill, 2002; Kalinowski, 1985; Lyle, 1999). The coach–athlete relationship is a complex phenomenon with many key contributors that act both independently and interactively: (1) coaches' and athletes' individual difference characteristics (e.g., age, gender, experiences, personality); (2) athletic environment in which the relationship is embedded (e.g., type and level of sport); and (3) cultural environment, including values, philosophies, norms, and beliefs.

The nexus of these contributors to the coach–athlete relationship has a significant influence on a variety of areas: (1) intrapersonal (e.g., motivation, self-esteem, satisfaction, enjoyment, dropping out); (2) interpersonal (e.g., communication, conflict, decision making); (3) psychosocial (e.g., motivational climate, team cohesion), and (4) sport-specific (e.g., fitness, training quality, skill development, and competitive performance).

Case studies conducted with Olympic athletes and coaches (Jowett, 2003; Jowett and Cockerill, 2003; Jowett and Meek, 2000a) have illustrated how the coach–athlete relationship affects athletes both as sport performers and as human beings. For example, a male sailor explained that the relationship with his coach allowed him to develop love and perseverance for his sport. In contrast, a female athlete stated that her coach "did not understand how I felt and he pushed me, something I could not tolerate at the time . . . I carried on training and competing through the seasons under his instructions resulting in suffering exhaustion, failing to qualify [at a major championship] and injuring myself" (Jowett, 2003, p. 453). Such accounts offer strong support for the notion that the coach–athlete relationship is essential to the development of athletes as competitors and people (Jowett and Cockerill, 2003).

Athlete's Perspective

A coach is important in bringing about performance accomplishments, developing the team's confidence, and organizing training sessions that include challenging tasks and exercises that provide players with mastery experiences. The coach must also be able to instill a philosophy of hard work. I want a coach who expresses enthusiasm, joy, and excitement during practice. I expect a coach who can encourage us when we succeed and can show anger or discontent when we are not performing to the best of our abilities. Both positive and negative feedback is required—however, it should be more positive than negative. A coach should pay attention to everybody in the team—both those who are elected for the lineup and the substitutes. This makes us feel that we are part of the team—during practice and also on match day.

Coach's Perspective

I am particularly concerned about knowing the players as well as possible both on and off the field. I want to know what kind of activities (e.g., school, work) they are involved with outside the soccer field and what they are interested in. This provides me with a more complete understanding of a player, and I strongly believe that this enables me to help the player to perform regularly to his or her optimal level. I use two useful tools when I am working on the coach–athlete relationship: the arena model and the flow model. The arena model provides me with an overview of which arenas (e.g., school, work) the player is involved with during a typical day, whereas the flow model indicates how one arena relates with another. I have found a high correlation between different arenas. For example, a player who has a stressful situation at the university is likely to underperform in training and competition. If the coach and the player can talk openly about these matters, it will create both trust and understanding between the two, and I hope the player will perceive less stress. I find it demanding but absolutely necessary to understand each player as well as I possibly can.

The dynamics of the coach–athlete relationship have been explored from two perspectives, namely, the leadership perspective and the relationship perspective. These perspectives differ in terms of where the greatest influence on the relationship lies. The leadership perspective supposes that the coach's leadership style determines the quality of the coach–athlete relationship. In contrast, the relationship perspective assumes that the quality of the coach–athlete relationship is affected by the continuous interrelating of the coach and the athlete.

Leadership Perspective

The leadership perspective emphasizes coaches' interpersonal behavior, more specifically, the impact of coaches' behaviors and actions on athletes' physical and psychosocial aspects such as performance, satisfaction, and self-esteem. This perspective has largely defined coaches' behaviors or coaches' leadership as "the behavioral process of influencing individuals and groups toward set goals" (Barrow, 1977, p. 232). In essence, leadership is a characteristic of the coach, and leading is what the coach does to the athlete and originates within the coach. Major approaches to the study of coaches' leadership in sport include the multidimensional model of leadership (Chelladurai, 1978, 1993) and the mediational model of coach–player relationship (Smith and Smoll, 1996; Smoll and Smith, 1989; Smoll, Smith, Curtis, and Hunt, 1978).

Multidimensional Model of Leadership

Chelladurai and Carron's (Chelladurai, 1978; Chelladurai and Carron, 1978) multidimensional model focuses on three aspects of coaching behavior: actual leader behavior (i.e., behavior that originates from a leader's personality, ability, and experience), preferred leader behavior (i.e., behavior that reflects characteristics of the members), and required leader behavior (i.e., behavior that is dictated by the demands and constraints of the situation). This approach includes proposed relationships among antecedents, leader behaviors, and consequences. The model suggests that athletes' performance and satisfaction are attributable to the degree of congruence among the three aspects of leader behavior. For example, the greater the consistency among the three aspects of coaches' behaviors, the greater the likelihood that the athlete will experience competitive success and satisfaction.

The Leadership Scale for Sports (LSS; Chelladurai and Saleh, 1978, 1980) was developed to measure five coaching behaviors from both the coach's (perceived) and the athlete's (perceived and preferred) perspectives. According to Chelladurai (1993), the autocratic and democratic behaviors represent the decision style coaches commonly use. The training and instruction behaviors correspond to the task-oriented coach behavior, which aims at improving athletes' performance. The social supportive behaviors correspond to the relationship-oriented behavior, where the coach emphasizes personal concern

for individual athletes. Finally, coaches' positive feedback is focused on providing credit, appreciation, and reward for athletes' good performances, which serves as a motivator.

Challenges have been raised about the LSS as a universal measure of coaches' leadership behavior. In a recent review, Chelladurai and Riemer (1998) showed that the scale's reliability estimates have not been consistent or adequate. Specifically, certain behavioral dimensions (i.e., autocratic behavior, social support, and positive feedback) in both the "athletes' preferences" and "athletes' perceptions" versions have repeatedly failed to record acceptable internal consistency estimates. Furthermore, the moderately low levels of explained variance reported in the original LSS validation suggest that the scale may not measure all or the majority of the aspects involved in the interplay between coaches and athletes. At a conceptual level, other interpersonal aspects such as coaches and athletes' thoughts and feelings need to be examined to yield a more holistic picture of how coaches affect athletes' sport experiences (Bloom, Durand-Bush, and Salmela, 1997). At a measurement level, research should concentrate on improving the LSS by generating new and meaningful items as well as dimensions based on open-ended interviews with athletes and coaches (Chelladurai and Riemer, 1998; Horn, 1992).

Mediational Model of Coach–Player Relationship

Smoll and colleagues' (1978) mediational model focuses on the interrelationships between coaches' overt behaviors and athletes' perceptions of coaching behaviors, as well as athletes' attitudes toward coaches. The model proposes that "players' evaluative reactions to their coaches' behaviors are mediated by their perception and recall of those behaviors" (Smoll et al., 1978, p. 530). Although coaches may foster an environment that develops and nurtures the athlete, the players' perceptions and recall of these behaviors have a direct bearing on the players' evaluations of coaching effectiveness. The mediational model moves away from assessing perceptions of coaching behaviors to assessing actual behaviors as they occur in the field or on the court. This shift is considered an important advancement, especially because research findings have indicated that coaches have little awareness of how frequently they engage in certain behaviors and the effects of behaviors on their athletes (Smith, Smoll, and Curtis, 1978).

This has led to the development of the Coaching Behavior Assessment System (CBAS; Smith, Smoll, and Hunt, 1977). The CBAS enables the direct observation, coding, and analysis of coaches' behaviors during training sessions and competitions. The system consists of 12 behavioral dimensions such as reinforcement, nonreinforcement, punishment, ignoring mistakes, keeping control, general technical instruction, organization, and general communication. In addition to assessing coaches' behaviors, the CBAS assesses players' perceptions of coaching behaviors and their evaluative reactions to coaching behaviors. Such a multimethod approach offers a more detailed description of the complex coach–player interactions. Nevertheless, the CBAS has recently been criticized for its measurement limitations. Brewer and Jones (2002) argued that the CBAS captures a limited and generic number of coaching behaviors. They suggested that, in further developing the specific context of any set of behaviors (i.e., for a type of sport), coaches' education programs and cultural differences should also be considered. Like the multidimensional model of leadership, the mediational model and its instrumentation do not permit exploration of the dyadic nature of the coach–athlete relationship. Both models of sport leadership may be insufficient for identifying, exploring, and explaining the complexity inherent in interpersonal dynamics between a coach and an athlete, because the dynamic two-way interaction that naturally occurs in coach–athlete relationships is often ignored.

Relationship Perspective

Hinde (1997), reviewing interpersonal relationships in general, stated that it is necessary to incorporate behavioral, affective, and cognitive variables in the study of relationships and also to emphasize the bidirectional or reciprocal nature of relationships. In sport, the relationship perspective aims to place equal emphasis on behaviors, feelings, and thoughts of both coaches and athletes. Consequently, this approach reveals how coaches and athletes affect each other, their relationships, and the things they try to achieve independently and together. Jowett and colleagues (e.g., Jowett and Cockerill, 2002; Jowett and Meek, 2000a) described the athletic relationship as a situation in which the coach's and the athlete's emotions, thoughts, and behaviors are mutually and causally interdependent. This definition incorporates both relationship members (coach and athlete) as well as the interplay among their behaviors, feelings, and thoughts.

Closeness, Commitment, and Complementarity: The Three C's

Jowett and colleagues (e.g., Jowett, 2001; Jowett and Cockerill, 2002; Jowett and Ntoumanis, 2004) used the interpersonal constructs of closeness (Berscheid, Snyder, and Omoto, 1989), commitment (Rosenblatt, 1977), and complementarity (Kiesler, 1997) to operationally define coaches' and athletes' emotions, thoughts, and behaviors, respectively. These mutually exclusive constructs have been examined independently in general interpersonal theory and research. However, their incorporation in an integrated relationship model is in line with the definition of the coach–athlete relationship that postulates the interconnectedness of relationship members' feelings, thoughts, and behaviors (see Jowett, 2003; Jowett and Meek, 2000a; Jowett and Ntoumanis, 2004).

Closeness refers to the feelings experienced and perceived by the coach and the athlete in the relationship. A number of case studies have indicated that closeness is a function of interpersonal issues such as liking, trust, and respect (e.g., Jowett and Cockerill, 2003; Jowett and Meek, 2000a, 2000b). Liking is associated with the ability to disclose and share information openly. Trust promotes self-disclosure, permits open channels of communication and voicing of needs, and facilitates effective problem solving. Respect implies a degree of acceptance and appreciation, a positive feeling that the other in the relationship is worthy of credit because of his or her position, knowledge, and actions. Such qualities have been associated with successful coaching and positive coaching (Janssen and Dale, 2002), whereas their absence is associated with less harmonious and less supportive coach–athlete relationships (Douge, 1999). Specifically, lack of trust has been found to increase competitiveness within the relationship by creating an environment where envy and other negative emotions (e.g., distress) are cultivated (Jowett, 2003).

Commitment is defined as an intention to maintain and optimize a coach–athlete relationship (e.g., Jowett and Ntoumanis, 2004). Commitment promotes so-called maintenance acts: tendencies to accommodate rather than retaliate when a relationship member behaves or performs poorly and to think in terms of oneness (Jowett and Cockerill, 2003; Jowett and Meek, 2000a). Perceived commitment is important because it allows greater flexibility in the relationship, especially when change is necessary. Lack of commitment in the coach–athlete relationship can make its appearance in many different disguises such as criticisms and negative feedback, lack of common goals, general communication problems (e.g., disagreements, arguments), and lack of emotional and informational support (Jowett, 2003). Furthermore, its absence has been shown to contribute to relationship dissolution (Jowett, 2003).

Complementarity reflects an environment in which both the coach and the athlete work together to improve performance. This exists when, for example, a coach reacts to her athletes in a reciprocal manner in terms of control (e.g., the coach provides instructions and in turn the athlete follows the instructions) and in a corresponding manner in terms of affiliation (e.g., both the coach and the athlete adapt a friendly stance). Complementary transactions are associated with superior performance and with harmonious and satisfying relationships (Jowett and Cockerill, 2003; Jowett and Meek, 2000a; Jowett and Pearce, 2001). Noncomplementarity has a negative influence on the coach–athlete relationship, its members, and its outcomes. For example, noncomplementary behaviors create a coaching climate of disorder (excessive obedience and discipline) and power struggles (Jowett, 2003; Jowett and Meek, 2002).

Co-Orientation: A Fourth C in the Coach–Athlete Relationship

Co-orientation deals with coaches' and athletes' interperceptions. The way coaches and athletes perceive each other and the way they think others perceive them is an interesting notion. Examining how (and why) people perceive each other the way they do may uncover complexity that exists in the coach–athlete relationship. According to the interperception theory (e.g., Laing, Phillipson, and Lee, 1966; Newcomb, 1953), relationship members such as the coach and the athlete have two perspectives that can be assessed: direct perspective or perceptions and metaperspective or metaperceptions. The direct perspective aims to capture how, for example, the athlete perceives her coach (e.g., I trust my coach), whereas the metaperspective aims to capture how, for example, the athlete imagines her coach to perceive her (e.g., I think my coach trusts me). By comparing coaches' and athletes' direct and metaperspectives, we gain a more intricate picture of the quality of the relationship. For example, a comparison between one person's direct perspective (e.g., coach) and the other person's direct perspective (e.g., athlete) on the same issue indicates a coach–athlete dyad's level of agreement or disagreement. A comparison between one person's metaperspective (e.g., coach) and the other person's direct perspective (e.g., athlete) on the same issue indicates the level of understanding or misunderstanding that is experienced in any given dyadic relationship (see figure 10.1).

These comparisons are possible through the use of two instruments. The Coach–Athlete Relationship Questionnaire (CART-Q; Jowett and Ntoumanis, 2004) is a brief, simple-to-use, self-report instrument that measures affective, cognitive, and behavioral interpersonal aspects in the coach–athlete relationship: closeness (e.g., I trust my athlete), commitment (e.g., I am committed to my coach), and complementarity (e.g., When I coach my athlete, I feel at ease). Although the CART-Q (Jowett and Ntoumanis, 2004) measures

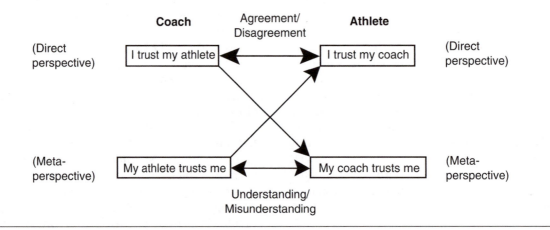

Figure 10.1 Coach's and athlete's interpersonal perception.

Adapted, by permission, from S. Jowett and M. Cockerill, 2002, Incompatibility in the coach–athlete relationship. In *Solutions in sport psychology,* edited by L. Cockerill (Andover, United Kingdom: Thomson Learning), 25.

coaches' and athletes' three C's from a direct perspective (e.g., I trust my coach), a modified version of the CART-Q (see Jowett, 2002) enables the assessment of coaches' and athletes' three C's from a metaperspective (e.g., My coach or athlete trusts me).

The interperception method is particularly useful to applied sport psychology consultants who work with coaches and athletes because it can readily illustrate points of agreement versus disagreement and understanding versus misunderstanding (Jowett and Cockerill, 2002; also see Jowett, 2005, for more information about practical uses of method and instrumentation). Ultimately, levels of agreement and understanding in the coach–athlete relationship reflect the degree to which the coach and the athlete are able to work effectively together and the degree to which potential interpersonal conflict inhibits positive relationship outcomes (e.g., team cohesion, satisfaction, motivation). The use of the closeness, commitment, complementarily, and co-orientation (three C's plus one) model in research and consulting provides a framework from which the interpersonal dynamics in a coach–athlete relationship can be explored.

Influences on the Coach–Athlete Relationship

The coach–athlete relationship is a complex phenomenon that affects and is affected by numerous variables. Such interactivity must be addressed by researchers and consultants regardless of the theoretical or conceptual framework they choose to work with. A practical understanding of this complexity by coaches and athletes will help them develop relationships that maximize performance and satisfaction.

Sport Type

Different types of sports (e.g., team vs. individual sports) place unique demands on the coach, the athlete, and the coach–athlete relationship. For example, coaches and athletes of individual sports (e.g., golf, gymnastics, swimming) have more opportunities to develop deeper and more interdependent relationships. In team sports (e.g., basketball, football, volleyball), the relationships between coaches and athletes are often hierarchical, more formal, less intimate, and more flexible. Salminen and Liukkonen (1996) found that percep-

tions regarding coach behavior (e.g., autocratic behavior) were markedly different when coaches and athletes of team sports were compared with coaches and athletes of individual sports. The difference in perceptions was much smaller between coaches and athletes of individual sports than those of team sports. Drawing on this finding, these researchers concluded that coaches in individual sports have better opportunities to communicate and attend to an athlete's needs than do coaches in team sports. Coaches and athletes, by exchanging information through talk, goal setting, and general dialogue, form a common ground that often aligns their perceptions about performance and other related issues; when differences exist, individuals recognize and accept them. When the relationship between the coach and athlete rarely includes communication, discrepant views are not realized and resolved. Although such an issue is possibly more apparent in team sports, Brewer and Jones (2002) noted that this factor has not been systematically examined, so research cannot offer insight about the impact of discrepant views on performance, satisfaction, motivation, cooperation, and trust or practical guidance to coaches and athletes on how to deal with discrepant views.

Athlete's Perspective

When you have 18 to 20 players who are supposed to pull together in the same direction and they differ when it comes to experience and level, this is clearly a challenge for the coach. There is a strong need for lots of communication with every player, which can take a lot of time and effort.

■ ■ ■ ■ ■

Coach's Perspective

In team sport, there is often fierce competition to be selected to the squad and then to the first team (the start-up team). When a player is not selected, several issues arise such as whether he or she has lost the coach's trust.

■ ■ ■ ■ ■

Athletes' Competitive Level

The level at which athletes compete (e.g., elite vs. novice) can affect the course and conduct of the relationships between coaches and athletes. Limited research has shown that mature and older athletes prefer a relationship-oriented approach (supportive behaviors) from their coaches (Chelladurai and Carron, 1983). Studies have demonstrated an association between coaches' social supportive behaviors and athletes' performance (Rees, Ingledew, and Hardy, 1999) as well as between coach support and recovery from injury and athlete burnout (Udry, Gould, Bridges, and Tuffey, 1997). Moreover, athletes and coaches who operate at the highest level of competitive sports may be more motivated to establish interdependent relationships because the risks are higher than for those participating at lower levels. Empirical evidence indicates that top-level coaches and their athletes who work closely together maximize the opportunities to achieve their shared goals (Jowett and Cockerill, 2003; Jowett and Meek, 2000a).

Youth Sport

Coaches in youth sport are faced with the challenge of working with their athletes' parents. The coach–athlete–parent tripartite consists of dyadic relationships, their effectiveness of which may be impaired when (1) the coach and the parent find themselves battling for control of the athlete or (2) the athlete is too old or independent to be parented any longer (Hellstedt, 1987). Parents have the responsibility to provide their children with the opportunity, means, and support to pursue their goals in an achievement environment. On the other hand, coaches' responsibilities revolve primarily around providing their athletes with training, instruction, and support so that goals, dreams, and aspirations are fulfilled. Although both parents and coaches have a common purpose to support children and to provide the opportunities and challenges so that young athletes' needs are fulfilled, often coaches and parents are confronted with conflict and power struggles. It is not unusual to find athletes themselves entangled in this conflict, causing them to feel distressed and unhappy. Under such conditions, relating and communicating are difficult for all relationship members. Apart from limited research (e.g., Brustad, 1996; Smoll, 1996), the role of parents in relation to the coach and the young athlete has been overlooked by researchers. Consequently, parents are often left to wonder what their role is in their child's sporting experience, and coaches are left unaware of how to approach and guide parents so that they all work together. Without guidance, some parents negatively affect their child's experience by not becoming involved, putting too much pressure on their child to excel in sports, becoming overinvolved in coaching and planning decisions, or engaging in deviant behavior (see Hellstedt, 1990). Research in this area would

provide important information that national governing sport bodies and other relevant authorities could use to help parents and coaches guide the young athlete effectively and successfully.

Gender of the Coach and Athlete

Gender of the coach and athlete (opposite sex: female coach–male athlete, male coach–female athlete; or same-sex: male coach–male athlete, female coach–female athlete) seems to influence the quality of the coach–athlete relationship. However, despite this intuitive observation, to our knowledge, there has been no research into the impact of these gender patterns on coach–athlete relationships. Research in friendships has shown that female–female friendships are more confiding, intimate, and emotionally expressive than male–male friendships (Unger and Crawford, 1992). Because relationships between females are characterized by emotionality (e.g., feelings of attachment or belongingness), female coaches and athletes may be more likely to form highly interdependent and emotionally laden athletic relationships. On the other hand, male coaches' and athletes' relationships may be based on transactions that aim to achieve the performance goals set without the expression of feelings. If this is so, could opposite-sex athletic relationships be less satisfactory or successful because of the different rewards that motivate male and female athletes to stay in the relationship? Whether such gender differences in the coach–athlete relationship have practical ramification for effective coaching, competitive success, interpersonal satisfaction, and communication as well as conflict and incompatibility is open to empirical investigation.

Athlete's Perspective

I have personally gained the most from female coaches. They have been very professional and enthusiastic; they also bring a more "soft" approach. I do not mean that they have fewer demands or are kinder in any sense, but they care more for and value the person, not only the player. They are more observant and tend to detect performance changes (deterioration) at an early stage. This shows that they care about the player (the 24-hour athlete, as we say in Norway). This approach allows the player to open up to the coach if she wants to. Having said that, I also know male coaches who are equally caring.

■　■　■　■　■

Coach's Perspective

As a male coach for a female national team, I think that the personality of the coach is more important than gender when it comes to getting good results. However, there is no doubt that female players prefer a more democratic leadership type than do male players.

■ ■ ■ ■ ■

Longevity of a Coach–Athlete Relationship

The length of time that coaches and athletes have worked together is also an important contributor to the quality of the coach–athlete relationship. A recent small-scale study by Jowett and Gale (2002) investigated newly developed coach–athlete relationships (spanning up to 3 years) as well as well-established relationships (spanning 4 years or more) in track and field. Established coach–athlete relationships demonstrated greater levels of commitment (i.e., people expected to maintain their partnership over time) than newly developed ones. Future research should examine this area in terms of its impact on coaching effectiveness, competitive success, satisfaction, and team cohesion.

Athlete's Perspective

It is very satisfying for players when their coach presents a long-term plan, including both evaluations and short-term goals, covering more than just one season. Coaches need time to determine how to treat each player individually, because this makes each player feel important, and nothing is better than satisfied players! It must be very rewarding for the coach to see the result of his or her work over a period of time, to see that his or her team has become intrinsically motivated and has developed a strong sense of achievement. I think that when a coach is involved with the same club over time, the chances for having success increase.

■ ■ ■ ■ ■

Coach's Perspective

Before the Olympic Games in Sydney, where our team won the gold medal, we had worked together for 4 years. During these 4 years we learned to know the players very well, which plays an important role in getting the best from every player.

■ ■ ■ ■ ■

Cultural Environment

The coach–athlete relationship must be viewed within the context of the national, racial, or ethnic culture in which it exists. Vergeer (2000) stated that culture influences the meaning, purpose, and importance people attach to their relationships, and Duda and Hayashi (1998) cautioned that instruments developed in a specific cultural context should not be uncritically used in different cultures. In addressing the cultural context in which a coach and athlete are located, Jowett and Ntoumanis (2003) developed and validated a culture-specific questionnaire that measures the nature of a relationship established in a predominantly collectivist culture (i.e., Greek). Jowett and Ntoumanis (2003) revealed that Greek coaches and athletes attach somewhat different definitions to the interpersonal constructs of closeness, commitment, and complementarity as opposed to their British counterparts—a predominantly individualist culture (see Jowett and Ntoumanis, 2004). For example, in terms of commitment, the British coaches and athletes emphasize maintaining close ties (interdependence) over time, whereas the Greek coaches and athletes emphasize acceptance and sharing. Although both British and Greek coaches and athletes establish or desire to establish lasting relationships, each cultural group emphasizes different aspects of commitment. This information can be used by applied consultants, coaches, and athletes to enhance relationships, especially relationships between members of different nationalities. Cross-cultural variation in the coach–athlete relationship requires further research to determine how the culture in which a coach–athlete relationship is developed influences the quality and effectiveness of the relationship.

Typical and Atypical Coach–Athlete Relationships

The quality and effectiveness of the coach–athlete relationship are also affected by the type of relationship. Jowett and Meek (2000b) identified two types of coach–athlete relationships: typical and atypical (see figure 10.2).

The typical relationship refers to coaches and athletes who are not related in any way other than their sporting relationship. In this relationship, coaches and athletes have clearly defined roles, and they have no other roles that can blur the purpose of the primary relationship.

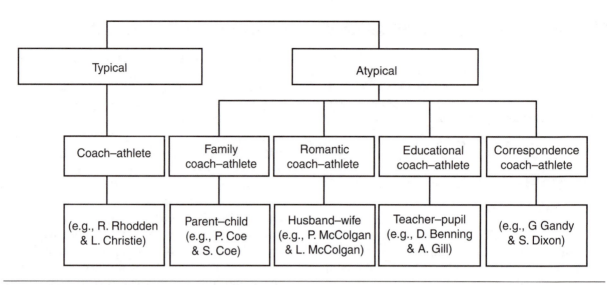

Figure 10.2   A tentative taxonomy of coach–athlete relationship types.

From S. Jowett and G. Meek, 2000, *Outgrowing the family coach-athlete relationship. A case study.* Presented at the International Conference on Sport Psychology at Centre of Sport Science and Halmstad University, Sweden. By permission of S. Jowett.

The atypical relationship is less common and involves a dual role in which the coach and athlete are also related through familial, marital, educational, or career ties and correspondence. Examples of atypical relationships in which the coach and athlete are married to each other include Gabriela Szabo and Zsolt Gyongyossy (Gabriela won a gold medal in 5,000 meters in the 2000 Sydney Games) and Voula Patoulidou and Dimitris Zarzavatsidis (Voula won a gold medal in 100-meter hurdles in the 1992 Barcelona Games). Well-known familial coach–athlete relationships include Venus and Serena Williams and their father Richard (both tennis players reached the Wimbledon singles final in 2000 among other distinguished titles) and Daniel Caines with father Joe (Daniel won a gold in 400 meters in the 2002 European Championships in Munich). An "educational" dyad can be seen between George Gandy, lecturer and athletics coach (Loughborough University) and Chris McGeorge (Chris won a gold medal in 1,500 meters in the World University Games in 1985).

Finally, the correspondence coach–athlete relationship operates interindependently. For example, coaches and athletes communicate through the mail, through e-mail, or by phone, and subsequently athletes execute the training program on their own or with the assistance of others. An example of an atypical correspondence coach–athlete relationship is that of Mary Onyali with Henk Kraayenhof (Mary won a bronze medal in 200 meters in the 1996 Atlanta Games).

The degree to which these apparently different coach–athlete relationships are truly typical or atypical is based on fundamental factors. For example, case studies that have been conducted to investigate marital and familial atypical athletic relationships have revealed that the nature of these relationships is not markedly different from typical relationships; however, the degree to which, for example, closeness is experienced is more intense in the familial and marital athletic relationships (Jowett and Meek, 2000a, 2002). It is neither surprising that coaches and athletes who belong to such atypical athletic relationships experience a stronger emotional connection nor unexpected that both types of relationships endorse common relational properties (like trust, respect, information exchange, disclosure, common goals, cooperation, and compatible goals). That both types of relationships endorse common relational properties indicates that the coach–athlete relationship is underlined by generic qualities that cut across typical and atypical dyads; however, there are differences that make atypical coach–athlete relationships demanding, complex, and by their nature multifaceted. For example, the high level of interdependence that naturally exists in family and marital coach–athlete relationships means that they could experience interpersonal conflict. Consequently, Jowett and Meek (2002) highlighted that in the family coach–athlete relationship, it is important to specify the boundaries of the parent–child and coach–athlete relationships.

Once such dual relationships are separated and their functions are clearly identified, conflict is eliminated as members assume the required roles for the setting.

Level of Motivation

Athletes and coaches invest considerable effort, time, and energy as they strive to reach a specified level of performance. It is crucial to understand the motives behind this engagement to see its impact on the coach–athlete relationship. Coaches, in their effort to nurture their athletes' talent, create a coaching climate that fosters either autonomy (e.g., it allows athletes to express themselves and try new things) or control (e.g., it dictates athletes' decisions and choices; Deci and Ryan, 2000). The creation of one or another climate is affected by coaches' motivation and ultimately affects athletes' motivation positively or negatively. Vallerand (2001) stated that "motivation is not only intrapersonal but also a social phenomenon" (p. 268). The manner in which such climates and coach–athlete relationships are associated is yet to be determined. Furthermore, answers to certain questions would provide us with useful information: For example, in what ways can autonomy or control climates and coach–athlete relationships affect both the athlete's and the coach's confidence, self-esteem, and satisfaction? Limited research has shown that elite-level coaches who focus on process improvement more than outcome and on development of autonomy more than control develop athletes who perform better and who also perceive less stress (Pensgaard and Roberts, 2000; Pensgaard and Duda, 2002). (See chapter 1 for a discussion on motivation.)

Obstacles to Effective Coach–Athlete Relationships

Now that we have discussed what issues influence the quality of coach–athlete relationships, we turn to the areas that interfere with the development of effective relationships. This knowledge will allow applied consultants, coaches, and athletes to take proactive steps to prevent difficulties from arising in a coach–athlete relationship and, should problems emerge, provides directions on how to remove the obstacles so that the relationship can return to a productive level.

Interpersonal Conflict

Scanlan, Stein, and Ravizza (1991) defined interpersonal conflict "as experiencing discord between oneself and significant others" (p. 112). Incompatibility and broken relationship rules are considered among the major reasons for conflict experienced between coaches and their athletes. The following discussion examines the concept of compatibility versus incompatibility and the notion of relationship rules in coach–athlete relationships.

Compatibility Versus Incompatibility

Coach–athlete relationships are characterized by interdependence. Occasionally, such two-way interactions develop conflict in goals, beliefs, values, emotions, or actual behavior. To determine whether a relationship is compatible, it is necessary to examine the influence that relationship members (coach and athlete) have on each other. When athletes are asked what they are looking for in a coach, common answers include a friend, someone they can trust, someone they can cooperate and work with, someone who understands their strengths and weaknesses, someone to help them realize their dreams, and someone with the knowledge and expertise to make them successful (e.g., Jowett and Cockerill, 2003). Similarly, when coaches are asked what they are looking for in an athlete, their response often is motivation, hard work, and determination to improve performance and achieve success. However, even when such attributes exist at one point in time, they may be absent at another. Coaches, athletes, and circumstances change, and compatible relationships may become incompatible (see Jowett, 2003). Thus, achieving and maintaining compatibility are significant challenges to coach–athlete relationships.

Carron and Bennett (1977) stated that "in order to achieve compatibility in a relationship, an equilibrium between the self and others is necessary" (p. 672). They devised a method to examine factors that contribute to compatibility between coaches and athletes based on Schutz's (1966, 1967) theory of interpersonal behavior. According to this perspective, coaches and athletes need to express and receive affection, inclusion, and control. Carron and Bennett's study showed that in compatible relationships, coaches exhibited and received more affection, inclusion, and control behaviors, whereas in incompatible relationships, both coaches and athletes were less likely to act inclusively (i.e., interact, associate, communicate).

Horne and Carron (1985), who examined predictors of compatibility, found that as long as the athlete perceives that the coach provides the preferred amount of a coaching behavior (i.e., positive feedback, autocratic behavior), the relationship is likely to be viewed as compatible.

Compatibility is an important interpersonal construct that has received very little attention. Future research in this area can explore several questions: What personal or situational circumstances may lead to incompatibility? Are compatible relationships always constructive and incompatible relationships destructive? Are compatible relationships more likely to be enduring? What emotions or feelings are associated with compatible and incompatible dyads? What conflict resolution skills may produce compatibility in coach–athlete relationships?

Athlete's Perspective

In a team, everyone must want to work toward the same goal and be prepared to do the job that is needed to reach that goal. But we have to acknowledge that we are all different. So we have to respect one another and use our differences as positive energy. Everybody can contribute something unique and we should be grateful that we are different. To get along out there on the field, regardless of whether we fit together or not off the field, is paramount. It is important that the coach develop a team that fits into his or her play philosophy—in other words, to compose a team of players who play well together and who can make each other better.

■ ■ ■ ■ ■

Coach's Perspective

A great degree of compatibility is important in a team. A degree of compatibility can be reached if everybody is involved in activities such as goal setting and formulation of team rules. These activities will lead to a greater sense of responsibility and pride. Every single player must feel that he or she has a sense of ownership and belongs to the team. I am very concerned about putting together a team—both players and support personnel—who can challenge each other. We have to appreciate that we are different and that these differences can be used to our advantage.

■ ■ ■ ■ ■

Relationship Rules and Broken Rules

Relationship rules are means by which coaches and athletes address goals and attempt to satisfy needs. Rules are defined as expectancies for appropriate behavior and, in turn, relationships can be defined by the rules that operate within them (Honeycutt, Woods, and Fontenot, 1993). Argyle and Henderson (1984) identified a list of friendship rules such as addressing other people by their first name, asking them for personal advice, respecting their privacy, trusting and confiding in each other, volunteering help in time of need, showing emotional support, being tolerant of their other friends, and not being jealous or critical of their other relationships. In sport, relationship rules are expected to assist coaches and athletes in coordinating behaviors, defining desired behaviors, helping enhance stability and predictability, and providing cohesion by setting boundaries on their relationships. In effect, relationship rules aim to help coaches and athletes achieve goals that are commonly sought in these relationships. The application of relationship rules serves two major functions: (1) to regulate behavior to minimize potential conflict that may disrupt the relationship, and (2) to provide an exchange of rewards that motivates the individual to stay in the relationship (Dwyer, 2000; Hinde, 1997). The maintenance of rules in any given relationship is necessary for a high-quality (stable and harmonious) relationship (Argyle and Henderson, 1984; Roloff, Soule, and Carey, 2001).

A research study that examines coaches' and athletes' perceptions of relationship rules is currently under way by Paul Carpenter and Sophia Jowett. Responding to the lack of explicit empirical research in this area, our research intends to explore the shared nature of relationship rules (i.e., identifying the rules shared by coaches and athletes with respect to how they should or should not think, feel, and behave in the coach–athlete relationship). The development of a conceptual model that identifies relationship rules and the role of rules in coach–athlete relationships is a main goal of this study. The development of a relationship rules model will ultimately provide a platform on which substantive research can be conducted in this area. If research can identify the shared rules that lead to a successful coach–athlete relationship, coaches and athletes can establish rules that will enable them to build effective and satisfying relationships.

Athlete's Perspective

It creates a bad atmosphere if one player is always late for practice or meetings and 20 people have to wait for this one person. That is unacceptable. Our team has a large number of individuals, and to avoid chaotic conditions and maintain the morale of the team, we have to have rules of conduct. In addition, these rules must apply on and off the field.

■ ■ ■ ■

Coach's Perspective

Our player guidelines are to a large extent based on ethical and professional grounds. Our guidelines include the following:

1. Help each other improve (try to be accurate when we coach each other, provide constructive feedback, demonstrate care on and off the field, have a positive body language, be generous when others succeed).

2. Show loyalty (avoid public conflicts or arguments, never talk negatively about other players in public).

3. Have a positive attitude on and off the field (develop as a person and as a player, handle different situations like injuries and long trips as a challenge, deal with disagreements or bad referees).

4. Accept and appreciate that players in the team are different (remember that the team is more important than you and that everybody is important!).

■ ■ ■ ■ ■

Ethical Issues

Coaching has undergone great ethical scrutiny over the past 20 years. Awareness of the threats of, and repercussions from, unethical behavior influences the policy and procedures of most sport organizations. Issues such as alcohol and drug use, injuries, racial discrimination, and sexual and other harassment can have a significant and negative impact on the quality of the coach–athlete relationship and on the development of athletes as competitors and people (see, e.g., Brackenridge, 2001; Carr and Murphy, 1995). Because of the significance of these concerns, researchers and consultants must investigate the role of ethics, and coaches and athletes must become educated about ethical issues to ensure that everyone involved in sport is treated with respect and dignity.

Power and Authority

The different uses of power and authority can sometimes lead to ethical concerns. Coaches who seek to rule, control, command, punish, and criticize use their role and position to coerce and influence athletes in their everyday behavior (Janssen and Dale,

2002), but as long as a coach's style is consistent, is agreed to by all parties, and does not take advantage of, deceive, or endanger people, then this use of power and authority is not necessarily unethical. Coaches who seek to relate, communicate, understand, inspire, mentor, motivate, and challenge can be equally at risk for unethical behavior by placing responsibility on athletes and potentially exposing an athlete or team to harm. The line between reasonable use of power and position and abusive and unethical behavior must be continually monitored by appropriate authorities such as national sport governing bodies and sport councils in an attempt to ensure the health and welfare of both athletes and coaches.

Sexual harassment is a problem of growing concern from youth to elite levels. Although the most common abuse scenario involves a male coach and a female athlete, recent research suggests that sexual harassment is not initiated exclusively by male coaches and can occur within same-sex relationships (Sundgot-Borgen, Fasting, Klungland, Berlund, and Brackenridge, in press). Coaches must also be aware of the potential for athletes to initiate a relationship that breaches ethical behavior. An athlete's respect for a coach can become a romantic attraction that places the coach and the athlete in an uncomfortable and potentially harmful situation. Although the athlete's initiation of a romantic relationship might be a mitigating circumstance, coaches are still ultimately responsible for upholding ethical standards and codes of conduct and maintaining appropriate boundaries between themselves and the athletes in their charge.

Another unethical use of coaches' power and authority is in coercing athletes to conform to physical demands of weight and body composition that may be unhealthy. This kind of pressure from coaches is common in women's sports such as gymnastics, swimming, and skating, in which body shape and size can affect performance. Pressure from coaches to lose weight can lead to nutritional deficiencies, injuries, and eating disorders (see chapter 13). Men's sports are no more immune, with coaches using their power and position to force their athletes to take performance-enhancing drugs to gain weight and muscle mass or to use pain killers to enable athletes to play while injured (see chapter 14). Such inappropriate demands destroy the coach–athlete relationship.

Exploitation

The inherent influence of coaches on athletes can provide many opportunities for athletes' exploitation. Particularly in youth sports, exploitation can occur as athletes show promise for future success in a sport. Coaches may see an athlete as their ticket to the "big time." They can become overly invested in their athletes' development and make decisions for the athletes that place the coaches' interests ahead of those of the athletes. This exploitation can occur when a coach continues to work with an athlete even though the coach's ability is no longer sufficient to foster the athlete's development. When the contribution that a coach can make has been exhausted, the ethical course of action is to put the athlete's development above the coach's own interests and assist the athlete in finding another coach who can take the athlete to the next level of performance.

Coaches may also engage in unethical behavior by assuming a dual role, for example, as a talent scout or an agent in recruiting athletes for collegiate or professional teams. These dual roles are highly unethical because coaches have a vested interest that may conflict with what is in the athletes' best interests. Sport organizations must explicitly prohibit this type of dual role among their coaches to safeguard the welfare of athletes. Coaches as individuals must also be cognizant of the allure of these opportunities and make deliberate choices to act ethically and in the best interests of the athletes with whose care and development they have been entrusted.

Facilitating Coach–Athlete Relationships

Because coach–athlete relationships are dynamic, they are capable of flexibility, adaptation, and growth. Changes to these relationships can happen suddenly because of situational circumstances, can evolve over time, or can be consciously and actively initiated by the coach, the athlete, or both in collaboration. Effective changes in coach–athlete relationships are best accomplished by active input and participation of both the coach and athlete.

Communication

Interpersonal communication provides a means for understanding the psychology of coach–athlete relationships and a tool for effective coach–athlete relationships. Two approaches offer different, yet equally useful, ways of examining this influence in coach–athlete relationships.

The role-related behavior perspective (Ellis and McClintock, 1990) illustrates how people adopt various roles in the pursuit of their goals. This approach also looks at how people accept, apply, and perhaps resist various roles. Several kinds of roles in communication processes can affect a coach–athlete relationship. *Assigned* roles are determined by other people, by birth, or by other circumstances over which a person has little control. In terms of sport competition, assigned roles include gender, age, club or national affiliation, and participation factors such as a designated position on a team. *Chosen* roles are those that people have the power to select in a relationship. Coaches might choose to be authoritarian or democratic, for example. Alternatively, coaches might adopt interdependent relationships with their athletes. Similarly, depending on factors like their personality and the value they see in the coach–athlete relationship, athletes may decide to be demanding, resistant, friendly, hostile, or submissive. *Referential* roles include circumstances that are generally outside the sports context but may influence performance in the sport. The term *referential* means that there is an expectation (often stereotypical) of how someone who has a role will behave. Typically, this is seen in power imbalances where the coach, as an expert, has authority over athletes, who are expected to be subservient to the coach's beliefs.

Athlete's Perspective

Communication is just so important! Knowing that the coach really notices how you perform, recognizes the effort you are putting in, and can provide feedback—positive or negative, but constructive, honest, and "to the point"—makes all the difference. If a coach hardly communicates with the players, then it is difficult to be motivated. A coach who talks with his or her players is more likely to know their strengths and weaknesses and thus is more able to create simulated situations during practice and to prepare players for upcoming situations. Talking and communicating do not necessarily require long meetings with players.

Some time ago, one coach decided not to include me in the start-up team for several matches; this was something I had never experienced before, and it was difficult to cope with. I was a regular member of the national team at the time and I did not notice that my performance had declined in any way. If he had talked with me and told me his reasons, the problem could have been solved immediately and a lot of frustration could have been avoided. Regular talks between the coach and the player can make all the difference and should be high on the coach's priority list.

■　■　■　■　■

Coach's Perspective

The relationship between the coach and the athlete is in constant change. I have both formal and informal communications with my athletes. The formal communications consist of three to four personal meetings with a player during a year where we talk about a wide range of things. These meetings primarily aim to highlight performance-related issues. I use a computer-based analytical program to gain very precise information about every player's performance. From a pedagogical perspective, this method really enhances the feedback process and is highly appreciated among the players. Informal communications occur all the time on and off the field. Moreover, we have positive experience from having social activities for the whole group (players and support personnel); this really enhances the cohesion of the group.

■　■　■　■　■

Role conflict can occur when one member in the relationship does not recognize or accept a particular role, whether assigned, chosen, or referential. This is a potential threat to the effectiveness of a coach–athlete relationship and might be characterized by, for example, resistance to conformity, one or another person experiencing unmet or conflicting needs, incongruent attitudes or beliefs, unaccepted relationship rules, and poor performance within the definition or expectations of an agreed role.

The second approach to understanding coach–athlete interactions is described by the transactional analysis model of personality. This suggests that personal ego states stimulate the processes of communication between people (Stewart and Joines, 1987). The model describes the Parent ego-state as behaviors, thoughts, and beliefs that have developed from our experiences with parents or authority figures. An Adult ego state provides logic and rationality around behaviors, thoughts, and beliefs that are directly related to the present. The Child component is largely concerned with behaviors that would be considered either childish (e.g., obstinacy, dependence, or uncontrolled

anger) or childlike (such as free will, a sense of fun, and purposeless enjoyment).

Communication between a coach and an athlete is conveyed through these ego states. For example, a coach might transmit the message that practice will continue for 30 more minutes—possibly an Adult statement about completing goals for a session. An athlete who also assumes an Adult role (the two are complementary) could translate coach's message as an intention to maximize the athlete's development. However, if an athlete assumed the Child role, he could perceive this message judgmentally as "you think I'm not good enough," causing resistance to the well-intended efforts of the coach. Such conflicting positions potentially hurt the coach–athlete relationship and the quality of the athlete's training. Therefore, when coaches and athletes assume noncomplementary roles, confusion and conflict can arise. These examples illustrate possible impacts from adopting states that are inconsistent or in conflict with the best interests of the relationship and how lack of understanding of roles can limit the relationship and the achievement of goals.

The interpersonal dynamics between coaches and athletes popularly described in conventional coaching processes can be appreciated from the transactional analysis perspective, with the following examples.

• A Dominant or Authoritarian Coach often operates as the Parent in demanding respect and obedience from athletes. This can be useful with less mature athletes or where firm leadership is required to achieve goals, but it might restrict the ability of athletes to become self-reliant in their preparation and decision making.

• The Casual Coach comes from Child much of the time as seen in his or her laissez-faire approach to outcomes. The Casual Coach sees fun and fulfillment as acceptable sport goals, perhaps more so than winning, and can be a quite successful style with mature athletes or at the nonelite level.

• Cooperative Coaches often assume the Adult role in their interactions with athletes. The goal of this more rational approach is to empower and instill self-management that will enable athletes to take responsibility for their effort and achievements. This type of coach can typically be successful in developing team cohesion and helping athletes achieve shared goals.

Interpersonal conflict can be reduced both by awareness of the dominant ego styles of an athlete and a coach when a relationship is developing and by self-monitoring of interactions to remove misunderstanding and incompatible ego expressions. A consultant's involvement in this is both educational in raising awareness of communication factors (such as ego states) and also interventional in perhaps observing typical interactions (particularly in stressful situations), interpreting incompatible ego state expressions, helping instill confidence around expression of and challenge to ideas and beliefs, and perhaps exploring the origins of dominant personality styles with coaches and athletes when these are entrenched and negatively affect the ambitions and goals that have been set.

Empowerment

The notion of empowerment involves individuals having perceptions of control over their lives (Rapaport, 1993). Empowerment encourages athletes to participate actively in decision making and to take responsibility for their involvement in sport. Athletes are challenged to generate their own ideas about their training and competitive preparations and are welcomed to respond to coaches' suggestions. Coaches who are accustomed to using an authoritarian leadership style may find empowerment threatening because it requires that they cede some of their power to the athletes. Athletes, in turn, may feel less secure in their sport participation because they can no longer rely on their coaches to make all their decisions and to take responsibility for them. However, these feelings of uncertainty are usually temporary, and empowerment offers long-term benefits including greater independence, increased knowledge, and more confidence because athletes are more actively involved in all aspects of their sporting lives. The benefits for coaches include having athletes who provide useful feedback; who are motivated, interested, and insightful; and who ensure that their coaches also continue to develop.

The work of a consultant in encouraging and supporting empowerment involves a number of factors. Initially these could center simply on the fact that being empowered can be an unusual situation for athletes who have grown up being told what to do by others. Therefore, strategies for minimizing risk and controlling fear of failure might need to be addressed before adjusting areas of responsibility and decision making between an athlete and his coach. A typical technique in these areas would be goal setting—encouraging athletes to set goals that are realistic to them and then encouraging more challenging goals as confidence grows. Communication skills might also be introduced as an athlete is encouraged to explore new sources of information about planning, preparation, and performance. This might include ways to objectively share information with others, to engage in assessment and evaluation with various experts, and perhaps to establish variations in training programs to accommodate changing social situations and needs as young athletes grow into adolescence. Other typical empowerment characteristics are based on developing reflective skills and acceptance of feedback for accurate attributions about performance, identifying intrinsic sources of motivation that facilitate focus and concentration and sustain long-term participation, and learning to manage emotional arousal at performance-enhancing levels.

Role of Sport Psychology Consultants

A healthy coach–athlete relationship is necessary for athletes to perform their best, for them to grow as people, and for both the coach and athlete to derive satisfaction from their work together. In contrast, ineffective coach–athlete relationships can lead to conflict, poor sport performance, and dissatisfaction. Sport psychology consultants can play an important role in the development of healthy coach–athlete relationships. Their ability to help coaches and athletes understand each other, improve communication, and respond positively to conflict can be pivotal, particularly when coaches and athletes do not readily develop a rapport. Although applied consultants can facilitate development, they must also be cautious not to interfere with the natural evolution of the coach–athlete relationship, become a "go-between," or create dependence on themselves for effective communication.

Athlete's Perspective

Having a sport psychology consultant is very useful. During a championship playoff—when a group of 30 persons travel together—there will always be situations where somebody will need some support or inspiration. It is important to have somebody who is not involved in the team selection process with whom you can talk openly and air your frustrations. This is how I have used our sport psychologist (Anne Marte

Pensgaard) when I have been frustrated because of my own performance or other matters. We have also worked on performance-enhancement strategies such as visualization.

■　■　■　■　■

Coach's Perspective

Using a sport psychologist provides several benefits. First, we receive expert knowledge in areas crucial to good results. A sport psychologist with good pedagogical skills can contribute with important perspectives as well as help reinforce success criteria that already have contributed to the positive development of the team. The sport psychologist on our team works independently with each player based on the player's needs, and we also have educational sessions for the whole group where we learn about relaxation techniques and self-confidence training. We map the players' needs in advance. The earlier the player learns about mental preparation, the better! The sport psychologist is a proactive discussant who helps me keep my focus on the important matters. It gives me confidence to know that we have a professional to provide quality control.

■　■　■　■　■

Individual Sports

Consultation with individual-sport athletes and their coaches offers consultants both opportunities and obstacles to effective intervention that are not present in team sports. For example, consultations with individual-sport coaches and athletes have a number of benefits, including fewer coach–athlete relationships to deal with, the ability to observe and intervene immediately, and less chance of role ambiguity. Consultants are also able to devote more time and energy to assessing, understanding, and offering feedback to the coach and athlete. Consultants may have an easier time gaining coach–athlete agreement concerning goals, training approaches, and competitive strategies.

Common challenges include lack of motivation on the part of the athletes, personality conflicts, and power struggles. The intensity and intimacy of one-on-one relationships in individual sports can also present problems. Coaches and athletes often spend inordinate amounts of time together, and that time is often physically and emotionally stressful. Ordinary problems can seem extraordinary in such an intense environment.

After considering such advantages and disadvantages, the sport psychology consultant must diagnose and treat factors that adversely affect the quality and effectiveness of the coach–athlete relationship. The phase of diagnosis may involve interviews with the coach and the athlete separately and together, the use of questionnaires such as the CART-Q and the LSS, and observations during training and competition, which will provide a base for identifying and understanding what factors affect the relationship positively or negatively. The phase of treatment is designed to combat negative factors that cause interpersonal conflict such as arguments, disagreements, hurt feelings, and incompatible roles and behaviors. Consultants often arrange a series of sessions with both the coach and the athlete that aim to discuss and resolve such issues. These sessions provide a means by which channels of communication between the coach and the athlete are reestablished. Furthermore, consultants may choose to enhance the quality and effectiveness of the coach–athlete relationship through the implementation of goal setting, the delivery of educational programs that seek to develop communication skills (including assertive communication), the establishment of relationship rules and social support, the development of role compatibility, and development of a sense of responsibility for successes and failures.

Team Sports

Consultants who work with teams are presented with unique challenges. Consultants in team settings often assume a very different role than those who work in individual sports. Because of the size of a team and number of coaches, the time and energy that consultants can devote to particular issues are diluted. Team-sport consultants are often required to assume a more educational, compared with counseling, role. For example, one of the authors (Anne Marte Pensgaard), who works with the Norwegian national women's soccer team, has one group meeting at each training camp, with the rest of her time divided between individual meetings with the players and coaches and observations at training sessions. In between camps, she follows up with the athletes and coaches via telephone and e-mail.

A significant challenge for consultants working with a team is to find a balance between involvement with the coaches and interaction with the athletes. Consultants can assume essential roles in their work with coaches and athletes. Their work with athletes often involves identifying early signs of dissatisfaction and emerging conflicts. Consultants' work with coaches can involve acting as a sounding board for coaches on issues that they face. Perhaps most essential when working with a team is that the consultant have a positive, collaborative relationship with coaches.

Relationship enhancement programs or approved psychological interventions specifically designed to improve the quality of the coach–athlete relationship in either team or individual sports are almost nonexistent. Applied sport psychology desperately needs to develop programs and interventions and test their effectiveness through scientific research.

Key Points

- Interpersonal dynamics have been examined through leadership and relationship models.
- Leadership models emphasize leaders' (coaches') interpersonal behaviors.
- Relationship models emphasize both relationship members' cognitive, affective, and behavioral relational aspects.
- The coach–athlete relationship is affected by multiple factors (e.g., type and level of sport).
- The coach–athlete relationship is inversely affected by incompatibility and lack of relationship rules.
- Awareness of the ethical issues that surround the coach–athlete relationship is paramount.
- The coach–athlete relationship can be facilitated by communication and empowerment.
- The role of a sport psychology consultant is diverse in individual and team sports.

Review Questions

1. What is the significance of the coach–athlete relationship?
2. What issues are involved in the coach–athlete relationship?
3. Describe the models that study the dynamics between coaches and their athletes.
4. What is the role of relationship rules in preventing interpersonal conflict?
5. In what way does coach–athlete incompatibility affect the coach–athlete relationship?
6. In what ways can a sport psychology consultant enhance the quality of coach–athlete relationships?
7. How is the role of sport psychology consultants affected by the context of sport (team vs. individual sports)?

11

Team Cohesion

Ulf Schmidt, PhD—researcher
Rick McGuire, PhD—consultant
Sue Humphrey and George Williams—coaches
Brian Grawer—athlete

The objectives of this chapter are

- to offer a comprehensive discussion of team cohesion including definitions, terminology, and contributors;
- to discuss the relationship between team cohesion and athletic performance;
- to explore the stages that comprise the life course of a team; and
- to describe practical strategies for building a cohesive team.

The dynamics of a team can play an essential role in how the team functions, how its individual members interact and perform, and how the team as a group performs in the competitive arena. A team that is highly cohesive can often overcome teams with superior talent that lack a good team chemistry (Alberda and Murphy, 1997; Carron 1981, 1982, 1988, 1994; Carron and Chelladurai, 1981; Carron, Hausenblas and Mack, 1996; Rossum and Murphy, 1994; West, 1996).

Because teams are composed of different individuals, roles, and responsibilities, creating a positive team dynamic is a complex and challenging task. It requires more than bringing in the most talented athletes. Rather, building a successful team involves considering not only the athletes' abilities but also their personalities, needs, and goals. A healthy team dynamic is a carefully constructed entity in which the whole is greater than the sum of its parts.

Key Issues

Building a team that gets along well, functions effectively, and performs well as individuals and as a group is the greatest challenge faced by a team's leaders. The ability of coaches, athletes, and applied sport psychology consultants to understand the process and components of creating a positive dynamic is essential to building such a team. Building an effective team begins with an assessment of the kind of team that the leaders wish to build and careful consideration of what talents, personalities, and roles will be needed for the team. Once the team has been brought together, a variety of strategies can be used to foster a team dynamic that will enable it to achieve its goals.

Chapter Purpose and Author Team

The purpose of this chapter is to provide a detailed overview of the influence that team cohesion has on team performance. The researcher (Dr. Ulf Schmidt) provides a foundation of theoretical perspectives and empirical support for the consultant's practical applications. The consultant (Dr. Rick McGuire) describes the practical implications of team cohesion to a team's functioning and performance. The coaches (Sue Humphrey and George Williams) offer a real-world perspective of the importance of team cohesion. Finally, the athlete (Brian Grawer) describes how team cohesion affects his participation, performance, and enjoyment as a member of a team.

Athlete's Perspective

Team building is such an important aspect of sport. Being together and determined allows individuals to rely on their teammates. You can take on bigger challenges and endure tougher situations with the support and trust of your teammates. Effective team-building skills contribute to a successful team!

■ ■ ■ ■ ■

Understanding Team Cohesion

The dynamics of a team are grounded in our understanding of what a team is and what it means for a team to be cohesive. Although it is easy to assume that people involved in sport are talking about the same thing when speaking of *team* and *cohesion,* considerable variation can be found in what researchers, consultants, coaches, and athletes consider a team to be and what makes a team cohesive. Teams can consist of athletes, such as tennis players or golfers, whose members aren't dependent on each other in their performances. These teams are formed for more efficient training or for cumulative scoring of individual competitions. For these teams, whether priority is given to individual or team success can be unclear and a source of conflict. Teams can also consist of athletes who rely on each other's coordinated efforts to achieve success, for example, in rowing and basketball. In these cases, the goals of the team should take precedence over those of its individual members. Cohesion has different meanings as well. For some, cohesion means a team of athletes who get along well. For others, cohesion refers to a team's ability to execute well together. These different meanings have significant implications for how consultants and coaches work to create a cohesive team. Because of this lack of consensus, it is essential to provide clear and unambiguous definitions for these concepts.

Sociologists and sport psychologists (e.g. Russell, 1993) differentiate between a crowd, group, and team. A crowd is defined as a large number of people that forms at random and has no unifying purpose. A group is seen as a gathering of people who congregate on a regular basis with a particular purpose in mind but whose coordinated efforts are not necessary for that purpose. A team is considered an assemblage of people whose express purpose it is to work together toward an agreed-upon goal.

Coach's Perspective

Although most coaches in most settings understand and subscribe to the belief that there is "no I in team," we understand that our team is nearly totally driven by a focus on the individual and on each individual's personal performance achievement. Our athletes are offered very little, if any, incentive or reward for our being a great Olympic team. Their reward comes from being great Olympians, from successful individual achievement in the Olympic arena. For these athletes to experience ultimate success necessarily requires that some of their own teammates must fail.

■　■　■　■　■

Carron (1982) defined cohesion as a dynamic process that is reflected in the tendency of a group to come together in the pursuit of its goals. More recent conceptions (Carron, Brawley, and Widmeyer, 1998) have described cohesion as having two dimensions. The first dimension involves the unity that the team expresses toward a common goal. This element emphasizes the functioning of the group without regard to concerns for its individual members. The second dimension focuses on the particular concerns of individual team members. This component considers the roles and responsibilities of team members and their feelings about their place on the team.

Other factors have also been offered as essential aspects of team cohesion (Carron and Hausenblas, 1998). The reasons for team cohesion vary; some teams place greater emphasis on the quality of the relationships within the team, whereas other teams place more value on achieving common goals. Cohesion can also be characterized by the reason a team comes together, for example, for fun, skill development, or objective success. Finally, cohesion has a temporal dimension, where teams form, function, and disband at different rates (Carron, 1988; Russell, 1993; Tuckman, 1965).

Team cohesion is reflected in its members' perceptions (Carron, Widmeyer, and Brawley, 1985, 1988). Every team member views the team's structure, functions, and relationships differently and develops his or her own unique perceptions and feelings about the team. Although closely linked to the objective characteristics of the team (e.g., size, structure, roles), cohesion is also understood as the sum of the subjective perceptions of the team members (Carron et al., 1985).

According to Carron and his colleagues Brawley and Widmeyer (e.g., Carron et al., 1985, 1998), cohesion can also be differentiated along two dimensions: perspective and reference. Perspective refers to whether cohesion is perceived from the viewpoint of the individual in terms of the individual's attraction to the group or from a more comprehensive perspective estimating cohesion among all group members. Reference relates to whether cohesion is based on an orientation to the task or to social climate. Task-related cohesion can be explained as coordination of the team members' actions toward a common goal. Social climate refers to a greater concern for relationships within the team. These two dimensions create four possible orientations about team cohesion:

1. Group-task: The way the group as a whole functions to achieve its goals
2. Group-social: The general quality of the relationships in the group
3. Individual-task: The extent to which the individual's actions and those of the group as a whole are coordinated to achieve its goals
4. Individual-social: The quality of the individual members' relationships within the team

Coach's Perspective

All of the efforts to build cohesive team relationships and a strong team experience are for moments when the challenges and demands are at their absolute greatest and when nothing short of our best is demanded. And in that moment, we must all understand that we are in it together, that we are one great big family together, and that we are the greatest track-and-field family (team) in the world!

■　■　■　■　■

Relationship Between Team Cohesion and Athletic Performance

The issue of team cohesion has received considerable attention over the years from researchers, consultants, coaches, and athletes alike. This interest is based on the assumption that a cohesive team will perform better and be more successful than a less cohesive team. Considerable research has been conducted to determine whether this belief can be supported under scientific scrutiny (e.g. Russell, 1993; Schmidt and Schleiffenbaum, 2000a, 2000b; Zander, 1994).

The most comprehensive body of work studying the impact of team cohesion on performance has been conducted by Carron and colleagues (Brawley, Carron, and Widmeyer 1987; Carron, Brawley, and Widmeyer 1990; Carron and Chelladurai, 1981; Widmeyer, Brawley, and Carron 1992; Widmeyer, Carron, and Brawley 1992). These researchers have concluded that the influence of cohesion on team sport performance depends on whether the cohesion is based on an orientation to social climate or the task that brought the team together.

From the research examining the impact of social climate, no significant relationship was found between the degree of social cohesion within a team and that team's degree of success. Studies in ice hockey, basketball, and field hockey found no relationship between how attractive team members viewed the team or the quality of relationships among team members and team success (e.g., Carron and Chelladurai, 1981; Carron et al., 1996). In sum, how well team members got along had no impact on how well the team performed. However, not unexpectedly, Carron (1988) found that team success had an influence on social cohesion. Team members got along better when their teams won than when they lost.

Other interesting, and sometimes counterintuitive, results were reported. Research found that teams with low social cohesion, regardless of their competitive level, could still be successful (Carron et al., 1998). Also, the higher the level of competition and the more successful the team, the less important social cohesion was (Widmeyer, Brawley, and Carron, 1992; Widmeyer, Carron, Brawley, 1992). In other words, even teams that had poor social cohesion were able to perform well and achieve their goals.

Rivalry between team members also did not hurt team performance if the team members were not directly dependent on each other (e.g., gym-nastics team) or when only a small degree of coordination between team members was necessary (e.g., baseball). For sports requiring significant team member interdependence (e.g., volleyball), rivalry and team conflict hurt team performance (Carron, 1988, 1994; Carron and Hausenblas, 1998). Although low social cohesion within a team does not hurt team performance, high social cohesion does not hurt team performance either (Schmidt and Schleiffenbaum, 2000a, 2000b).

The research examining the influence of task cohesion on team performance reported vastly different findings (e.g., Carron and Chelladurai, 1981). High task cohesion had a positive influence on the team performance. When a bond between team members was forged based on their commitment to team goals, the team performed better and was more successful (e.g., Carron et al., 1998). According to the findings on the impact of social cohesion on team performance mentioned previously, as a general tendency the influence of task cohesion on team performance was greater for sports that required higher team-member interdependence (Carron, 1982, 1988; Carron and Chelladurai, 1981; Russell, 1993). On the other hand, a high task cohesion also had a positive influence in sports with a rather low team interaction. Carron and Spink (1992, 1993), for example, showed that participants in an exercise and fitness class with a high individual task cohesion had a higher adherence rate than participants with a lower individual task cohesion.

Coach's Perspective

It is our challenge to create an environment and provide an experience that fosters great team cohesion and allows all athletes and staff members to feel totally supported in their role and mission. They must experience an environment filled with safety, security, caring, and trust.

■ ■ ■ ■ ■

Life of a Team

Although there is no guaranteed plan for building a successful team, there is a common set of dynamics, or stages, that all teams experience. Every team has a life course that it follows from inception to dissolution. This life course begins as individuals join others to meet personal needs, build relationships, or pursue common goals. It ends either when the relationships are no longer fulfilling, when the objective has been achieved, or when it becomes clear to team members that the goal will never be accomplished. How efficiently and effectively teams make these transitions influences the quality of the relationships within a team, their performance as a team, and, ultimately, their competitive success.

Understanding this life path of a team can help consultants, coaches, and athletes make positive contributions to the life of a team and either extend or shorten its life, depending on the needs of the team and its individual members. This section presents the key stages of the life of a team relying on two models by Tuckman (1965) and Drexler, Sibbet, and Forrester (1988). Tuckman offered a five-stage model and Drexler and Sibbet presented a seven-stage model. Because there are some unique and shared aspects of the models, each stage of both models will be presented as they fit into the overall description of the life of a team. Both perspectives provide valuable insights into the understanding of the dynamics of a team as it evolves through its life course.

Athlete's Perspective

For our highly ranked NCAA Division I basketball team, it was essential for our success that we had a positive team-building atmosphere. It is important to be able to turn to your teammate during a high-anxiety, high-pressure situation, and know that he is confident not only in his own skills but also in the skills of his teammates.

■　■　■　■　■

Coming Together

The first step in the creation of a team involves disparate individuals coming together as a group with the intention of working together for some agreed-upon purpose. Tuckman (1965) called this stage "forming." Methods through which teams form may vary, but all have the goal of creating a unified and functional team that will achieve the goals that brought the individuals together. Some teams form by a formal tryout (e.g., youth sport teams), some through a structured draft (e.g., professional teams), others by recruitment or invitation (e.g., a regional, national, or college team), others by volunteering or registering (e.g., recreational leagues), and still others by circumstance (e.g., through pick-up games). Regardless of the way in which a team forms, this stage is defined by initial experiences that create the team and identify its membership. This stage is typically an exciting time in the life of the team as team members are glad to have "made the team" and

share in a spirit of new beginnings. Team members experience enthusiasm, anticipation, hope, shared support, positive belief, and an expectation that they will achieve the goals for which they joined the team.

Drexler and Sibbet (1988) referred to this initial stage as "orientation." In this phase, the players answer two questions. First, they ask, "Why am I here?" to find out what they can contribute to the team. Second, they ask, "Why should this team be formed?" and decide what the team may be capable of achieving this season. Once these questions have been answered, every team member will have found his or her basic role and responsibilities in the team.

Coach's Perspective

A rather unique feature of the Olympic track and field team is that we as the head coaches have no input into who is selected to become a member of our team. The other staff members are selected in a variety of ways by various groups within the USA Track and Field organization. In every case, these individuals are chosen because they have demonstrated great leadership qualities in their field. In the case of the assistant coaches and managers, this means that many of them have been recognized as being great head coaches themselves in their own professional setting.

The approximately 150 athletes are selected to the Olympic team based on their performances at the U.S. Olympic Trials and by meeting performance standards established by the International Olympic Committee. This competition occurs 1 month before the Olympic Games, leaving very little time to develop and establish relationships and a sense of team and team cohesion.

■　■　■　■　■

Getting to Know Each Other

This stage of the life of a team involves new teammates getting to know each other. The newly united team members begin their first interactions among themselves and clarify their relationships. During this phase of team building, friendships are forged and rivalries are identified. What is often referred to as "team chemistry" begins to emerge.

Drexler and Sibbet (1988) suggested that "trust building" is essential for team members to get to know each other and that, in this stage, they ask, "Who are you?" to find out about their teammates. During trust building, the players intensify their contact among each other and learn whom they can trust and with whom they may have conflict.

Team members also find out what is expected of them, what they can expect from their teammates, and what level of involvement they must have as a part of this team. If trust grows within the team, players will offer each other support and the foundation of a healthy team dynamic will be laid. However, if conflict arises, mistrust and caution will dominate and may affect the team throughout the season.

Tuckman (1965) less optimistically called this stage "storming," because these initial forays into establishing relationships often involve disagreement and conflict as the team members assert their individual needs, establish their desired position within the team, and test each other.

Storming is usually related to team members' roles within the team or their relationship with the coaches. The controversy may be focused on such issues as starting positions, playing time, attention received, or the nature of the relationship with the coaches. Whether these concerns are real or imagined, they can sow conflict in a team that can slow or halt the development of team cohesion and limit the quality of team performance.

It has been suggested that storming and high levels of team performance are not compatible (McGuire, 1998). Excessive conflict within a team can hurt motivation, reduce confidence, elevate intensity, distract focus, and produce harmful emotions, all of which can detract from team performance. However, there is ample evidence to suggest that storming alone will not necessarily hurt team performance. Many professional sport teams from the past were known for their infighting yet were also successful (e.g., baseball's Oakland A's of the 1970s, basketball's Detroit Pistons of the 1980s, soccer's Manchester United of the 1990s, and the L.A. Lakers from 2000-2004). It could be argued that some conflict can be beneficial to team performance by increasing motivation, raising intensity, and creating an emotionally charged atmosphere. Although it is desirable for teams to be harmonious, when it is not possible because of the personalities of the individuals on the team, storming must be kept to a level at which it does not interfere with individual or team performance.

Coach's Perspective

If nothing else, head coaches must be great communicators. We must ensure that communication with all members of the team is regular, consistent, and thorough. This system of communication must be reciprocal, so that all team members are able and expected to communicate openly and effectively with us and with each other.

We play our role best as the facilitator of others—the caretaker, the custodian, and the steward of others and their opportunities. In this way, we best contribute to the ultimate success of our team and our mission.

■　■　■　■　■

Athlete's Perspective

As a player, I could look into my teammates' eyes and see if they needed building up at that particular moment or day. A simple word of support from a friend can really help to clear an athlete's mind and allow her or him to compete at a high level. If I have the trust and reliance of my teammates and they have that in me, we can pursue and persevere together through the turmoil of a season, the pressures of a game, and the fatigue of a grueling practice.

■　■　■　■　■

Buying Into Goals and Roles

This stage involves team members identifying and buying into their team's goals and the roles that each team member must play. This stage is the first in which the athletes are no longer individual athletes but rather become members of the team with a shared purpose and common goals. It is also the first point in the life of a team when the athletes can truly be called a team.

According to Tuckman (1965), this stage, "norming," indicates the emergence of a maturing team. The team has established its goals, team members learn their roles and responsibilities, and they become comfortable in the team culture. Even when difficulties arise, team members respond to the conflict in a way that helps rather than hurts the team dynamic and team performance. For example, if a substitute wishes to become a starter, the "sub" does the best he or she can in the assigned role, works hard to improve and earn the starting position, and continues to encourage his or her teammates to do the same.

Tuckman believes that a team is fully "normed" when members can look at themselves and every other member of the team and name their role, accept their role, and encourage themselves and others to do their best in that role. When a team is fully normed, it is ready to focus on performing its best (McGuire, 1998).

Similarly, Drexler and Sibbet (1988) suggested that a primary emphasis in this stage involves goal and role clarification, in which the goals for the team are established and roles for each team member are clarified. At this point members should ask, "What are we doing and what do I need to do?" The team must also make clear the tasks that must be accomplished and determine how much each player is willing and able to contribute to achieve the team's goals. If the team can answer these questions with consensus, it will be capable of working together toward common goals. However, if the team cannot agree on answers, then the team may lack clear direction, team members may fail to accept their roles, and team cohesion may not develop.

Drexler and Sibbet (1988) believe that at this point in the development of a team, experimenting, testing, and conflict have to end and a commitment has to be made to the goals and roles of the team. At this point, the question is, "How do we do it?" During the commitment phase, agreement must be reached on how team members will perform their roles and how the team will accomplish its goals. If all team members agree on how to proceed, then all team resources will be united and directed in the most productive way. It is at this point that the team members begin to share a common vision and feel a bond in pursuit of the mission that they have established for themselves.

Drexler and Sibbet (1988) also indicated that the team goes through an implementation phase, during which the goals, roles, and commitments that were made are put into action in practice and initial competitions. The question at this point is, "Who does what, when, and where?" If all team members can answer this question to their satisfaction and can put that answer into action, then the team will begin the process of performing at a high level. If, however, disagreements still arise with regard to the answer, then conflicts will develop and the team will have difficulty fully implementing its goals and roles.

Coach's Perspective

For any team to become a great success, it is critical that all members of the team clearly understand their role and be allowed to play that role to the fullest for the team. This includes our role as the head coaches. We understand that our role, along with the head managers, is to lead, facilitate, organize, and coordinate. We do not have to be everything to everybody, and we don't have to have an answer for every question.

We must have a great resource of talent and expertise to provide support and service as we carry out our mission. We have assistant coaches, assistant managers, medical doctors, chiropractors, athletic trainers,

massage therapists, sport psychologists, nutritionists, travel coordinators, media relations professionals, diplomatic liaisons, security personnel, interpreters, cultural consultants, and administrative and clerical support. And, of course, we have the athletes!

Each of these individuals has a talent, an expertise, a reason for being with the team, and a role to play. It is our role to see that all of these resources and services are used maximally for the ultimate success of the team. It is our role to see that these professionals are provided with the resources necessary for them to be successful as well as the opportunity to play their role effectively.

■　■　■　■

Maximizing Performance

The life of a team reaches its acme when every team member and the team as a whole can direct its full attention to maximizing its competitive performances. At this stage of a team, everyone is committed to team goals and all team members know their roles and responsibilities. What emerges is a group of athletes working as one unit toward their shared goals.

Tuckman called this stage "performing," where a team moves beyond all the preparations (forming, storming, and norming) and can get on with being a great performing team. In the performing stage, teams are characterized by a unity of purpose and great focus. Team members are confident, trusting, and supportive of themselves and of each other (West, 1996). There is great energy, enthusiasm, and effort. The security that team members feel as a part of the team enables them to move out of their comfort zones, take risks, and raise the level of their individual performances (Carron and Hausenblas, 1998). They are able to work together in a synergistic way and help each other perform better. Team members experience great joy, pride, satisfaction, and personal fulfillment in their efforts and performances (West, 1996). This process can become self-regenerating, creating a "luscious cycle" where great performances lead to more great performances (McGuire, 1998).

Drexler and Sibbet (1988) agreed with Tuckman (1965) that the result of the team's efforts so far is "high performance." At this point, the skills and tactics needed to build and maintain a cohesive team are mastered at both individual and team levels. The team is now prepared to perform to its fullest ability and is able to direct its focus, efforts, and energy toward its competitive performances and achievement of its goals.

Athlete's Perspective

Teammates need to be able to lift each other up, in both skill level and mental level. This type of atmosphere will provide your team with the best opportunity to be successful.

■　■　■　■　■

Coming to the End of the Line

The end of the line marks the conclusion of one life of a team. Whether the team has gotten along, functioned effectively, or achieved its goals, every team moves out of the performing stage at some point. The team may have remained in the performing stage for a month, a year, or several years, but sooner or later a time will come when the team is no longer able to perform.

Tuckman (1965) called this stage "adjourning," during which the life of the team ends and the team disperses. But the dissolution of the team can occur in several ways. The entire team can be dissolved and every team member seeks out another team. The team may keep its core members and only replace its supporting cast. The team may cast off central figures who had been the center of the team. Regardless of how the team adjourns, its composition, identity, chemistry, and cohesion are finished. Tuckman (1965) did not, however, suggest that the team is dead. Instead, he believed that the life of a team is a dynamic process and that the end of one life of a team can mean the beginning of a new life and a new team-building process.

Drexler and Sibbet (1988) hold a similar view as Tuckman, labeling this stage "renewal." This last phase of a team's life describes what happens after a team has reached its goals (or failed to achieve its goals). At this point, team members must determine the next step in the life of the team. The question here is, "Why should we continue?" This process of renewal begins with a discussion among team members and consensus on whether the team should renew itself or allow it to end its life. If the team chooses to continue, the entire process of team cohesion starts again. If the team opts not to continue, the team members—now individual athletes again—consider joining other teams and beginning the life course of a new team.

Assessing Team Cohesion

The value of research that studies the relationship between team cohesion and team performance is in providing consultants, coaches, and athletes with the information and tools to develop the team cohesion that will lead to increased team performance and greater team success. Once consultants, coaches, and athletes have a working knowledge of the key issues that influence this relationship, the next step is to provide them with the ability to measure the type and quality of cohesion in a team. To that end, considerable research has been conducted aimed at developing assessment tools that effectively measure team cohesion.

Martens (1972) was the first to create a team cohesion inventory by introducing the Sport Cohesiveness Questionnaire (SCQ). The SCQ contains seven items that measure group cohesion by assessing interindividual relationships, individual influences, amusement or pleasure, teamwork, familiarity among group members, and membership in emotional and cognitive terms. The seven items of the SCQ are conceived as independent dimensions of cohesion. However, more recent research has shown that the SCQ lacks validity (Carron et al., 1985, 1998).

Gruber and Gray (1982) provided the next step in the evolution of the assessment of team cohesion. The Multidimensional Sport Cohesion Instrument (MSCI) was created from a pool of items the authors obtained from previous nonsport cohesion questionnaires, theoretical conceptions of cohesion, research from organizational psychology, and interviews with coaches. A factor analysis of these items yielded scales reflecting quality of teamwork, sense of membership to the group, roles within the group, and strategies of dividing these roles (Gruber and Gray, 1982). According to Carron (1988), the MSCI was the first inventory to differentiate between task and social cohesion.

The Multidimensional Sport Cohesion Inventory, developed by Yukelson, Weinberg, and Jackson (1984), was another instrument that attempted to differentiate the specific components of team cohesion. However, like the Gruber and Gray inventory, it was culled from a wide variety of sources, lacked a firm theoretical foundation, and had questionable validity (Carron et al., 1985, 1998).

The work of Carron and colleagues that was discussed previously represented important progress in the study and assessment of team cohesion (Carron, 1981, 1982, 1988, 1994; Widmeyer, Brawley, and Carron, 1985). Their research led to the development of the most frequently used inventory to date for assessing team cohesion, the Group Environment Questionnaire (GEQ). The GEQ measures and differentiates between social and task cohesion. Both factors are also assessed for individual team members as well as the team as a whole. The GEQ has proven to be a valid instrument that has value in the laboratory and in the field (Carron et al., 1985) and has been adapted for different cultural settings and different languages (Schmidt and Schleiffenbaum, 2000a, 2000b).

The GEQ is a useful tool at several levels when groups of athletes are brought together to form a team. It provides important information that consultants, coaches, and athletes can use to facilitate the creation of a cohesive team. The GEQ educates team members about different aspects of team cohesion, helping them to understand its importance and their role in the building of team cohesion. It shows team members what their priorities are in terms of team cohesion, for example, whether they value social or task cohesion. The GEQ can also be used periodically throughout a season to assess changes in team cohesion.

In addition to using formal team cohesion assessments, such as the GEQ, consultants and coaches can gain considerable information through informal data gathering, for example, watching athletes interact and talking with team members. Relevant information can include potential role assignments within the team, whether a social or task cohesion will be more effective, and possible problem athletes. Consultants and coaches can then use this information to determine what weaknesses or obstacles in team cohesion may exist, where conflicts may arise, and how best to create a cohesion that will lead to the achievement of the team goals.

Enhancing Team Cohesion

The greatest value of the research that has been conducted lies in the use of this knowledge by consultants, coaches, and athletes to enhance the cohesion of teams at all levels of competition. Actively developing team cohesion is a progressive process that requires every member of the team to make a commitment to the team and each member to take responsibility for and deliberate steps toward the team's goals.

To achieve this level of united performance is an exciting and fulfilling experience for everyone involved, but it does not happen easily or by chance. The creation of a cohesive and successful team will only occur as the result of skilled leadership, knowledge and understanding of teams, caring and empathy, and wisdom and patience. In short, the development and maintenance of a great team require application of both the science and the art of coaching (McGuire, 1998).

There is no proven formula, no secret recipe, and no foolproof blueprint for building a group of individual athletes into a team. There are also significant obstacles to building a cohesive team, including traditional models of teams, public opinion, pressure from the media, societal changes, and cultural differences. Building a cohesive and successful team involves understanding the experience of the individual athletes who comprise the team and uncovering the ways in which team members can become personally invested in the team, feel satisfied with the contributions that they are making, and feel responsibility for the team's cohesiveness and success (McGuire, 1998). The following sections present strategies for enhancing team cohesion.

Athlete's Perspective

To be an effective builder, one must be a good listener, very observant, and extremely selfless. Trust during a game or competition must begin off the court. The bond that teammates have must be strengthened in their everyday life. The more you know about a teammate's personality, lifestyle, background, and work ethic, the more able you are to build him up. You need to know what distracts certain teammates and what motivates certain teammates. You need to know how certain teammates respond to adversity and how you can help them to concentrate and respond more efficiently. If athletes are given a chance to do these things for one another, they will excel.

■ ■ ■ ■ ■

Coach As Catalyst

The coach is the definer, shaper, and provider of the sport experience for the members of a team (Vernacchia, McGuire, and Cook, 1996). The impact of the coach is felt in many different ways within the team (Syer, 1986; Syer and Connolly, 1984). Experienced coaches share a mutual understanding and genuine respect for the complex, often subtle, and sometimes mysterious phenomenon known as team. Whatever the level of sport competition, from youth to Olympic to professional, the challenge facing coaches is to take the individual athletes with differing capabilities, temperaments, attitudes, needs, and goals and to lead, shape, teach, nurture, and sometimes will them into becoming a committed, focused, effective, unified, and successful team.

The coach serves the role of team environmental engineer, designing and shaping the environment within which the athletes and team live, train, and compete. This environmental engineering includes both the physical and interpersonal landscapes. The coach determines what goes into the environment and what is acceptable within the environment. The coach's influence on the team environment includes determining and modeling the values, attitudes, and behaviors that are acceptable and encouraged (e.g., mutual support, hard work, communication) as well as those that are discouraged (e.g., tardiness, selfishness, conflict). By carefully defining and engineering the team environment, coaches lay the foundation for the type of team environment they want to engender and begin the process of indoctrinating their athletes into that environment (Syer, 1986; Syer and Connolly, 1984; Vernacchia et al., 1996).

Coaches must realize that they cannot force a group of individual athletes to become a cohesive team. Coaches simply do not have power over how athletes think, feel, behave, and interact with others. Threats and punishment can produce temporary adherence to a team ethic, but these efforts will be short-lived because either the consequences are not applied consistently or the recipients of the consequences react to these strictures with anger and resistance (Syer, 1986; Syer and Connolly, 1984; Vernacchia et al., 1996).

Lacking the power to force athletes to accept the team culture, coaches must rely on their ability to influence their athletes and convince them of the value of buying into the team. This influence is accomplished by what coaches say, how they behave, and the quality of the relationships they build with their athletes. This impact is supplemented by the coaches' ability to influence significant others who may, in turn, influence the athletes (i.e., parents, spouses, peers, fans, other coaches; Syer, 1986; Syer and Connolly, 1984; Vernacchia et al., 1996).

The coach's role involves nurturing and guiding athletes to see the value of creating a cohesive team. The role requires coaches to communicate directly, clearly, and consistently the values, attitudes, and behaviors that are necessary for building a unified team. Ultimately, the coach's job is to "sell" the team to every one of its members so that each feels a sense of ownership and commitment to the team. When this connection is established, team members will put the needs of the team ahead of their own and work together to achieve the team's goals (McGuire, 1998).

Transformational Versus Transactional Leadership

Much can be learned about the influence of the coach on his or her team from business management theory and research examining leadership contributors to building a cohesive team (Schmidt and Schleiffenbaum, 2000a, 2000b; West, 1996; Zander, 1994). One such area involves the distinction between transactional versus transformational leadership (Podsakoff, MacKenzie, and Bommer, 1996). Transactional theory suggests that leaders offer transactions to their team members in the form of specific expectations related to team members' behavior and performance as a means of building team cohesion. If these expectations are met, team members are rewarded. If these expectations are not met, team members either do not receive rewards or are punished. This behavioral approach asserts that team members can be "conditioned" to accept the team values through the administration of appropriate rewards and punishments (Podsakoff et al., 1996).

In contrast, the transformational perspective proposes that a leader actually transforms athletes into more cohesive team members rather than the athletes simply joining the team for the rewards they will receive (Podsakoff et al., 1996) Transformational leadership seeks to fundamentally influence the values, needs, and goals of the team members, so that they accept their team responsibilities because these responsibilities are now consistent with their own values, needs, and goals. Transformational leadership encourages all team members to transcend their own self-interest in the name of the cohesiveness and success of the team. Transformational coaches foster this change by creating a dialogue with their athletes about the meaning of being a part of a team and what will create a cohesive and successful team. They also nurture this team ethic by acting as role models, demonstrating the commitment necessary to achieve team goals. Transformational coaches seek to earn team members' trust by putting the needs of the team ahead of their own, thus encouraging team members to do the same.

Transformational coaches are responsive to each member of the team. They realize that team members have unique abilities, personalities, attitudes, needs, and goals. These coaches seek to understand each team member fully, connect what the team member wants with the expectations and objectives of the team, show team members that team cohesiveness and success are in their best interests, and help all team members realize their ability and fulfill those needs and goals while playing a positive and vital role in the team's success.

Transformational leaders act in six very specific ways that actively and clearly demonstrate to team members what is expected of them and the value in taking ownership of the team: (1) articulate a vision (see and sell the big picture); (2) provide an appropriate model (lead by example); (3) foster the acceptance of team goals (develop a team spirit, encourage collaborative efforts); (4) have high performance expectations (seek excellence in all and for all); (5) provide individualized support (committed to individual team members' development); and (6) provide intellectual stimulation (provide new ways to look at key issues; MacKenzie, Podsakoff, and Rich, 2001).

Coach's Perspective

We establish mechanisms for keeping everyone connected throughout the course of the team's life and tour together, including both regular direct personal communication and a daily team newsletter. This not only allows us to keep every team member informed of necessary team information, daily reports, upcoming events, and schedules but also allows us to engage their minds as well as their bodies. This is how people experience, buy into, and contribute to the concept of team.

■　■　■　■　■

Heart of the Team

The composition and relationships of a team can be characterized by a series of concentric circles emanating from the innermost circle. The center of this configuration can be viewed as the "heart of the team." All team members will place or find themselves somewhere in this series of circles. Those closest to the center will be at the heart of the team, whereas those farther from the center will never feel fully a part of the team. Team members can find themselves on the fringe of the team for a number of reasons, such as being unsatisfied with their role or playing time, experiencing injury, having conflicts with members at the heart of the team, or being a newcomer (McGuire, 1998).

The experiences of those team members at its heart are vastly different than those on the fringe. Players at the heart of the team feel invested in

and connected to the team. There is clear and open communication between team members. Everyone at the heart of the team is "on the same page," and they feel supported and encouraged by their teammates and respond in kind to them. These team members are satisfied with their roles and feel excitement, joy, and fulfillment in their shared experiences. What results is a high degree of satisfaction with the team, high self-regard with respect to players' contributions to the team, personally high performance and success, and gratification in their part of the team's success.

Fringe members feel disconnected from the team. There is little communication with other team members, and the communication that does occur is typically negative and critical. These team members feel unsupported by their teammates and are not able to give support in return. Fringe members are dissatisfied with their role on the team, believe that they are not being given the opportunity to contribute, and believe that they are being treated unfairly. They feel frustrated, angry, disappointed, and sad because their efforts are not producing the results they want. What results is little self-regard or regard for the team, poor individual performance, and little fulfillment in their place on the team.

The goal is to build a team with a "big heart," in which all team members reside at the heart of the team and there are no fringe players. Being at the heart of the team does not require that every team member be a starter or make significant contributions to the team's success. Instead, it means that team members believe that the role they play is important and that they are valued and appreciated for their contributions. Being at the heart involves having supportive relationships with other team members, especially with the coach. Ultimately, being at the heart of a team means that members believe they are an essential part of the team's efforts and its successes.

Athlete's Perspective

I remember a game versus Iowa State University my senior season of competition. The game was about to go into its third overtime period. Our entire team was exhausted. Two teammates in particular, Kareem Rush and Clarence Gilbert, looked as if they had spent all of their energy and could not go on. They each were having a career game, both scoring more than 32 points each, but their body language and their eyes were telling me that they needed help.

I grabbed them each by their jersey, looked intensely into their eyes, and passionately proclaimed, "I will be your energy and your strength! I know you are tired! Turn to me! I will be your energy for as long as you need! Share my energy and use it to strengthen you!" As I said that, their exhausted looks disappeared. A load had been lifted. In the heat of the competition these two had felt like they were on their own. My statements helped them to realize that their teammates were right there with them. They were not alone. We were a unit, a group, a team. And together as one unit we fought through the third overtime, sending it to a fourth overtime as well. We prevailed after four overtimes, 112 to 109!

■　■　■　■　■

Begin With the End in Mind

Consistent with the research (e.g., Carron, 1988; West, 1996) revealing the relationship between task cohesion and team performance, the process of building team cohesion must start with a clear goal of what the team wants to accomplish. Covey (1990) suggested that one of the most fundamental habits of successful people is that they begin with the end in mind. If this maxim is applied to sport, the end shows coaches and teams where they want to go. With the destination clarified, coaches can develop a road map to arrive there. Coaches and the members of their team must have a clear vision of what success means to them, such as getting along well, giving their best effort, or achieving a specific result in competition, and what type of team cohesion will help them to fulfill that vision. Knowing the final objective also helps the team identify the essential values, attitudes, and actions necessary to accomplish the goal. Coaches can understand not only what will be defined as a successful team but also how the team members can make the team experience personally meaningful and satisfying.

Athlete Perception of Team Experience

The ultimate goal of building team cohesion is for athletes to perceive their experience on the team as positive and rewarding. Team members who have this attitude will give their best effort, be supportive team members, and make significant contributions to both the cohesion of the team and the team's pursuit of its goals. As a result, consultants and coaches can take active steps to

ensure that athletes have a positive experience as team members.

MacKenzie and colleagues (1996) suggested that there are 12 critical conditions for team members that determine whether they have a satisfying and fulfilling team experience. The following inventory of 12 questions reflects these critical conditions or factors and focuses on the athletes' evaluations of their experience as team members:

1. Expectations: Do I know what is expected of me by my coaches and team?
2. Resources: Do I have the equipment and supplies that I need to be able to train and compete?
3. Opportunity: Do I have the opportunity to do what I do best regularly?
4. Recognition: In the last week, have I received recognition and praise for doing well?
5. Caring: Do my coaches seem to care about me as a person?
6. Encouragement: Do I have coaches and teammates who encourage my development?
7. Input: Do my opinions seem to count with my coaches and teammates?
8. Value: Does the mission or purpose of this team, and my coaches, make me feel that my role is important?
9. Commitment: Are my teammates committed to quality training and preparation?
10. Relationships: Do I have a best friend on this team?
11. Feedback: In the last month, has a coach talked with me, at practice or away from practice, about my progress?
12. Development: In this past season as a member of this team, have I had the opportunities to learn and grow?

Using this battery of questions, either formally or informally, consultants and coaches can gain essential insights into team members' perceptions about their experience on the team. With this information, consultants and coaches can identify potential areas of dissatisfaction and conflict in team members and prevent problems from arising. Knowing what each team member needs to feel connected to the team, consultants and coaches can also take specific steps to maximize each team member's involvement and experience as a part of the team. At a practical level, these critical conditions can serve as a foundation for the coach's efforts at team building. They can act as a guide for the daily tasks that each team member performs and in which the team as a whole engages in the development of a cohesive and successful team.

Coach's Perspective

Although individual athletic performance is the focus of the team, we don't compete and perform in a vacuum, particularly in the Olympic setting. Coaches must show the team that we have anticipated the many external and internal forces that can be distracting and destructive to great performance and achievement (i.e., competitive environment, injury, disruptive teammates, housing, roommates, travel, food, nutrition, lifestyle, security, event tickets, family and friends, personal coaches, uniforms). This can be addressed up front with the entire team to demonstrate that every effort has been made to eliminate all of the obstacles that we possibly can control. Instructions can be given regarding "expecting the unexpected" and directions provided regarding appropriate responses when confronted with threatening surprises. We must model this same understanding and approach as leaders.

■ ■ ■ ■ ■

Key Points

- The cohesiveness of a team influences individual members' performance, their satisfaction as a team member, and eventual success for the team.
- A team is considered an assemblage of athletes whose express purpose it is to work together toward an agreed-upon competitive goal.
- Current perspectives on team cohesion offer coaches, athletes, and applied sport psychology consultants with valuable tools with which to observe, assess, and understand players and ultimately build a cohesive and successful team.
- A team progresses through a life course that follows clearly defined stages: coming together, getting to know each other, goals and roles, maximizing performance, and end of the line.
- Research has shown that more likely task cohesion, but not social cohesion, has a significant positive influence on team performance.
- Team cohesion can be measured with a variety of instruments, the most widely accepted of which is the Group Environment Questionnaire.
- Coaches, athletes, and applied sport psychology consultants can take active steps to build a cohesive team.
- The coach plays a pivotal role in whether a team develops into a cohesive unit.
- Coaches can use practical strategies during practice and competition to encourage cohesiveness.

Review Questions

1. What are the definitions of team and cohesion?
2. What are the stages of the life course of a team and what are some of the specific stages suggested by Tuckman and by Drexler and Sibbet?
3. What is the nature of the relationship between cohesion and team performance?
4. What is the most commonly used cohesion assessment inventory, and what dimensions does it assess?
5. What general issues contribute to the cohesiveness of a team?

IV

Psychological Problems of Athletes

Part IV concludes *Applying Sport Psychology: Four Perspectives* with an in-depth exploration of some of the most serious challenges athletes face not only in their competitive lives but in the "real world" as well. Physical harm, responding to pressures to excel, and the sometimes abrupt ending of an athletic career can present athletes with difficulties that threaten their physical and mental health. A full understanding of these issues by researchers, consultants, coaches, and the athletes themselves is essential to ensure that athletes respond to these challenges in a constructive and life-enhancing way.

Chapter 12 discusses the ubiquitous problem of injuries among athletes. Athletic injuries are more than just a physical trauma. Rather, injuries have significant psychological, emotional, social, and career-related implications in the lives of athletes. Recovery from injury places substantial physical demands on athletes and has a powerful psychological component that can either hinder or facilitate the process. This chapter explores the kinds of reactions that athletes can have in response to injury and describes a variety of strategies to facilitate a healthy return to sport.

Chapter 13 describes the emotionally painful issue of eating disorders. In many sports in which athletes' weight affects their ability to perform, athletes can feel tremendous pressure, both internal and external, to lose or gain weight. Although some changes in weight can be beneficial, the emergence of an eating disorder can have life-threatening ramifications. This chapter looks at the most common eating disorders, how and why they develop, and how they can be treated.

Chapter 14 examines the equally difficult issue of substance abuse. In a culture where winning is everything, athletes at all levels can feel considerable pressure to do everything they can to maximize their performances. Some of athletes' efforts to respond to this pressure can include the use of illegal, performance-enhancing drugs to elevate performance or recreational drugs to escape from the pressure. This chapter discusses why substance abuse is on the rise in sports, the most commonly used drugs, and how consultants and coaches can help athletes avoid the temptation of drugs.

Chapter 15 ends the book by exploring the conclusion of athletic careers and athletes' transitions to life after sport. Considerable research and consulting experience indicate that a substantial number of athletes struggle with the ends of their careers. This chapter examines the most common causes of career transition, how athletes respond, and what consultants can do to smooth the transition to life beyond sport.

12
Injury

Edmund O'Connor, PhD—researcher
John Heil, PhD—consultant
Peter Harmer, PhD, ATC—certified athletic trainer
Iris Zimmerman—athlete

© Photodisc

The objectives of this chapter are

- to provide a comprehensive overview of the psychological influences on recovery from injury;
- to discuss the perception of rehabilitation as an athletic challenge in which athletes apply sport skills to the recovery process;
- to offer various perspectives on understanding the psychology of injury throughout the time line of rehabilitation;
- to provide an overview of the barriers to rehabilitation failure and how these hurdles can be avoided; and
- to describe the course of action necessary for athletes to achieve an optimal recovery.

njury is unfortunate but common in sports. It threatens athletes' career longevity and success. Some athletes are threatened by an injury, experience significant distress, and struggle with their recoveries. Ideally, athletes are able to view injury as another athletic challenge and can approach rehabilitation with the same tenacity and vigor that they display in the athletic arena. Athletes' reactions influence their recovery and return to sport participation.

Rehabilitation is a complex mixture of physical, psychological, emotional, and social influences. For athletes to make a complete recovery, these issues must be understood and addressed. "Hoping" to get better is not a method for success (Davis, 2003). Athletes must make a commitment to successful rehabilitation and return to sport performing as well as or better than before their injury.

Key Issues

A sport injury disrupts training and competition and challenges athletes physically and emotionally. During the recovery process, athletes experience negative emotions, such as anger and sadness, and positive feelings of optimism and hope. Typical roadblocks to successful rehabilitation include denial, pain, fear, doubt, and frustration. Education about injury and rehabilitation, goal setting, social support, and the use of mental skills are the foundations of the psychological rehabilitation of physical injury. Because the skills used in rehabilitation mimic those used in the athletic arena, athletes who learn to transfer these skills to rehabilitation recover most effectively. A small group of athletes so excel at rehabilitation that they show "remarkable recovery" and exceed their previous levels of competitive performance.

Chapter Purpose and Author Team

This chapter presents simple and clear concepts and practical strategies for the psychological rehabilitation of injury that are grounded in applied practice, consistent with the latest research, and of value to coaches and athletes. The researcher (Dr. Edmund O'Connor) integrates the latest scientific study on the psychology of injury into the applied issues presented by the consultant. The consultant (Dr. John Heil) describes the essential psychological issues that athletes face during the course of injury rehabilitation. The certified athletic trainer (ATC, Dr. Peter Harmer) offers his perspective on the struggle to return to high-level competitive performance. In the United States, ATCs are specialists in athletic medicine and may work with a team of healthcare professionals including orthopedic physicians (MD), psychologists (PhD), physical therapists (PT), and strength and conditioning specialists (CSCS). Finally, the athlete (Iris Zimmerman) discusses the challenges of recovering from an injury.

Trainer's Perspective

Elite athletes have highly structured lives. Their days are carefully laid out in precise measures of effort and recovery, focused on ultimate goals that are often years in the future. The apparent capriciousness of injury makes it difficult for athletes and coaches to be proactive in dealing with injury. How quickly and how well an athlete reacts to the changes caused by injury significantly influence the likelihood of success in rehabilitation. Athletes who make prompt, positive adjustments will fare much better than those who become mired in questions about why the disruption occurred. Similarly, in competition, the athlete who focuses on alternative strategies to overcome an opponent who is not reacting as expected will be more successful than the athlete who spends time wondering why the opponent is not behaving as anticipated.

■　　■　　■　　■

Athlete's Perspective

This chapter is right on. It helped me understand that I am not the only one who experiences injury. People who are most involved with the athlete's training—trainer, coach, therapist—must all communicate with the athlete about their expectations. After my injury I found it difficult to trust myself because of the loss of control I felt. If the people around me, especially the PT, had more clearly communicated their expectations, it would have helped me to focus on rehabilitation rather than feelings of mistrust and disappointment. I wish I had read this chapter when I was injured (and my coach too). I wish my coach had had insight into the psychological aspect of what I was going through as well as the physical aspect.

■　■　■　■

Patient As Athlete

The more I thought about it, the more cancer seemed like a race to me. Only the destination had changed. They shared grueling physical aspects, as well as a dependence on time, and progress reports every interval, with checkpoints and a slavish reliance on numbers . . . The idea was oddly restorative: winning my life back would be the biggest victory. (Armstrong, 2000, p. 89)

This quote from six-time Tour de France winner Lance Armstrong exemplifies the notion of "patient as athlete." During rehabilitation, patient-athletes are encouraged to continue to view themselves as athletes first and to use the mental skills they learned in sport to facilitate their recoveries. Reframing rehabilitation as an athletic challenge shifts athletes from a negative orientation of the injury to a positive one that emphasizes their strengths and gives them the tools to take control over their rehabilitation. Motivation, confidence, relaxation, and focus contribute to competitive success. Athletes can tap these areas to help them recover from their injuries in the most timely and effective way.

It is essential for athletes to see that the skills that they developed in sports can be transferred to their rehabilitation. Applying mental skills such as self-talk, relaxation, goal setting, and imagery to rehabilitation creates a mind-set that helps injured athletes bolster their rehabilitation (see chapters 2, 3, 7, and 8, respectively). This mind-set is characterized by personal responsibility, a strong goal orientation, intense and precise physical training, and a willingness to push physical and mental skills (Heil, Wakefield, and Reed, 1998).

Trainer's Perspective

In clinical sports medicine, the most effective rehabilitation protocols have evolved in large part from experience with noncompliant patients, often high-performing athletes, who are impatient with the pace of the prescribed rehabilitation program. For many years, rehabilitation of sport-related injuries (e.g., ligament reconstruction in the knee) was relatively conservative and built on the concept of uncomplicated recovery. Many athletes were better aware of their physical and mental resources than was their rehabilitation team and would push far ahead of the time lines that had been established for them. As more of these successful cases came to light, practitioners revised their expectations and developed new protocols that could accommodate the motivation and knowledge shown by successful athletes. Although failures occurred when athletes failed to exercise restraint, our understanding of resilience and recovery advanced quickly from the experiences of successful noncompliers. This, in turn, resulted in more realistic and productive rehabilitation strategies.

■　■　■　■

Athlete's Perspective

At first, I did not want to participate in physical therapy because I believed that the exercises were elementary. I thought, "I am a serious athlete and this person is giving me these simple exercises and not taking me seriously." For my coach, knowing how hard to push me was important: If he didn't push me hard enough, I felt like he didn't have confidence in me; if he pushed me a little too hard, I would reinjure myself, and we would both be disappointed. In the end, it was not about the MD, the PT, or the coach; it was about finding what I needed. For me this came down to overcoming the loss of my self-confidence.

■　■　■　■

Understanding the Psychological Factors of Injury and Rehabilitation

An estimated 17 million sport injuries occur yearly, with the severity varying from minor to catastrophic (Booth, 1987). The underlying causes appear to be a complex mix of physical, psychological, and sport-specific factors. Although considerable attention is directed toward helping athletes understand and maximize the physical aspects of their rehabilitation, little formal information may be offered to injured athletes on how they can overcome the psychological and emotional challenges of recovery from injury.

Trainer's Perspective

Contrary to popular mythology, ignorance is not bliss. When coupled with driving ambition, ignorance can be the cause of unimaginable, yet often unnecessary, distress for elite athletes. An incident that occurred while I was competing made the importance of understanding injury very clear and was an impetus for me to enter the sports medicine field. I was training in Japan and became very good friends with a young, talented, and dedicated American judo player. It was generally acknowledged, even by the Japanese coaches, that he had an exceptional competitive future. Unfortunately, while training at one of the premier clubs in Japan, he sustained a mild sprain of the ligaments in his left knee. This injury should have presented no more than a minor disruption to his training program. However, because of his commitment to making the U.S. national team that season, and the seemingly minor nature of the injury, he ignored advice to take time off to treat the injury. His knee became more problematic with each training session, but he thought that if he stopped he would lose ground in his quest to make the team. Within 2 weeks his knee had become so unstable that he was casted from his hip to his ankle and had to return to the United States for treatment. His season was lost because he refused to believe that he could not just "work through it." However, he did learn a valuable lesson and went on to win numerous international titles and make the Olympic team in the following quadrennium despite sustaining several more serious injuries. The difference was his willingness to listen to what the sports medicine personnel had to say.

■ ■ ■ ■ ■

Athlete's Perspective

Reading the text brings back some memories for me. I didn't want to believe I was injured and to accept my limits. I tried to ignore the pain. To say I was unhappy or even depressed doesn't capture the scope of the feeling. Unfortunately, there were a lot of negatives in the treatment of my injury. At times, I am afraid that this was passed on in my feelings and actions to others. It was all too easy to stay in a negative mood. It took time for me to mature enough to be able to deal with my injury. The biggest key for me was letting go and not being so hard on myself. That is easier said than done for most athletes at a high level.

■ ■ ■ ■ ■

Psychological Process of Injury

Just as athletes must progress through a physical healing process, they must also address the psychological consequences of injury such as loss of confidence, fear, and other negative emotions. Specific challenges within the medical stages of recovery may trigger emotional challenges that must be overcome to optimize rehabilitation.

Stage Perspectives

Initial attempts to understand the psychological process and its related time line of recovery underlying sport injury drew on the work of Kubler-Ross (1969), which explored the grieving process associated with death. She suggested that terminally ill patients move through a specific series of stages as they cope with their illness. The first stage is denial of the illness and isolation from others, followed by anger (e.g., "Why me?) and bargaining. The patient tries to make a deal with God to remove or change the illness in exchange for some "good" behavior. Depression follows and is characterized by mourning for losses. Acceptance is the final stage, often void of feelings as the patient realizes that death is inevitable. Kubler-Ross' approach has been applied to a broad range of conditions, including athletic injury. However, research has failed to demonstrate that either terminally ill patients or injured athletes consistently move through a predictable, sequential set of stages (Brewer, 1994). Rather, the recovery process is highly variable within and across individuals. The initial enthusiasm shown for this approach is probably more a reflection of the strong need felt by practitioners for a structure to explain psychological recovery from illness or injury than of its true utility.

Cognitive Models

Explanations of the psychological process of injury that focus on how athletes perceive their injuries have gained popularity (Udry, 1997; Wiese-Bjornstal, Smith, and La Mott, 1995). These perspectives suggest that how athletes respond to injury depends on their interpretation of the injury itself (i.e., its meaning to them) as well as situational factors (e.g., coping, social support) perceived to be either stressful or uplifting. These positive or negative appraisals determine athletes' emotional responses. Athletes may experience great distress if the injury is interpreted as career ending, if the pain is described as too great to handle, or if lack of communication with the coach is perceived as abandonment. On the other hand, perceiving rehabilitation as time off from intense sport training or an opportunity to focus on improving game strategy predicts good emotional adjustment. These emotions then influence the injured athlete's coping responses positively (e.g., optimism leading to increased effort in rehabilitation) or negatively (e.g., pessimism decreasing motivation to do a home exercise program). Social support mediates both the perceived severity and control over the injury and athletes' coping responses.

Affective Cycle of Injury

The affective cycle of injury (Heil, 1993) explains the psychological process of rehabilitation in a way that is both rigorous and of practical value. It assumes that emotional reactions to injury are stagelike but also cyclical and vary based on daily experiences that create stress or inspiration. The "engine of emotion" that drives the psychology of rehabilitation has three components: distress (e.g., anxiety, depression), denial (unacknowledged distress), and determined coping (vigorous, proactive, goal-driven behavior). This affective cycle maintains the emotional transformations of stage theories but is more flexible as it applies to the normal ups and downs throughout the physical stages of rehabilitation: immediate postinjury period, treatment decision and implementation, early postoperative or rehabilitation period, late postoperative or rehabilitation period, specificity, and return to play (Steadman, 1993).

Distress

Distress reflects the effects of injury on emotional equilibrium. It includes symptoms, such as anxiety, depression, fear, anger, guilt, and bargaining, for which athletes accept responsibility. Distress may also show itself in subtler, resistance-like behaviors such as redirected anger, complaining, and self-doubt. It is most frequently observed during the early stages of recovery but may appear at any time. Distress is almost always experienced during the immediate postinjury period, often described as a shocklike response or anxiety. Anticipatory anxiety during the treatment decision and implementation period is also common as athletes consider the consequences of treatment options. During the early and late stages of rehabilitation, physical limitations and treatment setbacks may trigger depressive symptoms characterized by a sense of helplessness. Athletes in the latter stages may also experience frustration and boredom with the rehabilitation process as well as a sense of urgency to return to play. As they move into the specificity and return to play periods, fear of reinjury and insecurity regarding the injured body part may be evident. The key elements to consider are the magnitude of the distress and how appropriate it is to the severity of injury. Social support and well-developed coping skills may buffer the distress. If they are lacking, the risk of distress is increased.

Early establishment of rapport and trust between injured athletes and the sports medi-

cine team is essential to minimize distress during the early phases of recovery. Education regarding the injury helps athletes perceive their recovery realistically, minimizing anxiety. Setting specific, short-term treatment goals keeps athletes focused on success, provides a reason for optimism, and minimizes depression and frustration. Each intervention is described in more detail later in this chapter.

Denial

Denial is unacknowledged distress. Injury-related stressors such as pain, feelings of loss, separation from teammates, and disruption of self-concept trigger distress, which goes unrecognized even as it drives behavior. Denial may be mild, often described as shock or disbelief that injury has occurred. More severe denial may be illustrated by athletes' lack of insight or difficulty acknowledging or minimizing the realistic challenges of injury and rehabilitation (e.g., avoiding a needed surgery). More profound denial occurs with athletes' outright failure to accept the severity of injury. These athletes can make poor rehabilitation decisions and risk greater harm. Conceptually, one might consider denial as one pole on a continuum that is anchored on the other pole by catastrophizing.

Denial is not identified simply from what athletes say but by how their comments may contradict other sources of information. Assessing denial in an applied setting involves judgments formed from in-depth personal contact with athletes and drawn from inconsistency in the words, emotions, and behavior of injured athletes and the feedback that is received from others close to them, such as ATCs, coaches, teammates, family, and friends. Athletes may exhibit denial regarding the severity of injury, level of psychological distress, prognosis for recovery, need for surgery or complex rehabilitation, and impact on athletic career. Given the specifics of its manifestation, denial may be either functional or dysfunctional, thereby facilitating or interfering with rehabilitation. Athletes' ability to remain positive and put distressing thoughts out of their minds is helpful when it protects them from being overwhelmed by negative emotions. However, denial is harmful when, for example, failure to recognize the severity of an injury results in poor compliance to the rehabilitation regimen.

Denial, like distress, typically occurs most often early in the recovery process. It is often adaptive during the immediate postinjury stage when athletes process what has just happened. There is typically no need to challenge this denial as long as it doesn't interfere with the athletes' safety. During the next treatment decision and implementation stage, denial should be minimized so that the injury facts can be considered and the best medical decisions made. Denial during the early and late rehabilitation stages can interfere with treatment and add to distress, such as when surgery is mistakenly expected to be a quick fix. On the other hand, denial of a prognosis involving physical limitations may facilitate a remarkable recovery in those athletes who understand that exceptional treatment effort is required. Although extraordinary gains may be made, treatment providers must be careful to manage the athletes' distress if treatment plateaus and more modest outcomes are expected or experienced. Denial of the injury's impact will be challenged by the sport environment itself in the specificity and return to play stages.

When denial interferes with treatment, education and goal setting are required to establish realistic expectations. Balancing the negative impact of injury with a time line and action plan for rehabilitation helps to move athletes into determined coping.

Determined Coping

Determined coping involves moving beyond a resigned sense of acceptance of the injury and a passive sense of waiting for the injury to heal. It includes exploration (looking for possibilities, clarifying goals, seeking resources, exploring alternatives, learning new skills) and commitment (new focus, vision, teamwork, cooperation, balance; Hanin, 2000). Determined coping involves applying the patient-as-athlete attitude to rehabilitation and is characterized by the channeling of knowledge, skill, and emotional energy to proactively meet the challenges of rehabilitation. Determined coping is generally more prevalent during the later stages of recovery but occurs during all stages. Education and goal setting move an athlete from distress and denial to determined coping. Social support facilitates emotional resilience and focus on the rehabilitation plan. In general, the more athletes adopt this emotional component, the greater their chances of a successful recovery. The skills that promote this reaction are described in a later section, "Path to Rehabilitation Success."

Embedded Cycles

The affective cycle of injury assumes that emotional recovery is not a simple linear process but rather is cyclical, varying over days and weeks and even within the course of a day (Yukelson and Heil, 1998). It is useful to envision a macrocycle (which spans the recovery process), minicycles (which are linked to the physical stages of rehabilitation), and microcycles (which reflect the ups and downs of daily life). In the macrocycle of recovery, athletes generally move from distress and denial to determined coping. Each distinct stage of rehabilitation presents new challenges and, as such, constitutes a minicycle. The microcycle recognizes shifts in emotional response among distress, denial, and determined coping that occur from the daily stresses of living with injury.

Even as one of the three components may predominate any given stage in rehabilitation, emotional responses will typically vary throughout the course of a day, so that even during periods of determined coping, denial or distress may appear briefly. For example, reviewing a game film that shows an injury may elicit distress. Setbacks in treatment and pain flare-ups are typical triggers of a shift from determined coping to distress or denial during a minicycle. To the extent that these situations cause athletes to believe (independent of their actual physical status) that they are not progressing, these situations will have a substantial impact on rehabilitation. Thus, the affective cycle facilitates awareness of and sensitivity to the specific psychological challenges of rehabilitation and provides indications of how athletes are responding to these challenges.

Path to Rehabilitation Failure

The potential negative impact of denial on rehabilitation was described previously. Pain, fear, and culpability are additional key psychological factors that can cause rehabilitation failure (Heil, 2000).

Trainer's Perspective

Normally rehabilitation may be considered to have "failed" if athletes return to activity more slowly or at a lower functional capacity than is typical, given that the injury is one for which returning to normal training is expected. Denial, pain, fear, and culpability are important underlying factors in rehabilitation problems. There are two particularly problematic mind-sets that are a complex manifestation of these factors—a "make me well" mentality, and injury as a face-saving exit strategy from sport. These present a significant challenge to the sports medicine team. Addressing this begins with teaching athletes that they are not merely patients whom medical personnel do things to. Injured athletes must also be provided a supportive, nonjudgmental environment where they can discuss fears of failure and rejection and other sensitive personal matters. Ultimately, athletes need to be willing to take responsibility for their own well-being and accept that they are in control of the outcomes of treatment. When they do so, the chance that rehabilitation will fail is greatly diminished.

■   ■   ■   ■   ■

Athlete's Perspective

Pain can be a trigger to the memory of being injured (especially after I was reinjured and had to have a second surgery). I would be afraid of being reinjured again, become upset, and then perform poorly. After being injured, I couldn't figure out what pain was good and what was bad. I needed a lot more communication and explanation on the possible types of pains that I might experience. I look back and feel as though there were times where I could have kept training but stopped and times when I needed to stop but didn't. Each time it made me feel helpless and lose confidence in my ability in the sport. If someone explained that I would feel these "pains" and that I could learn to differentiate among them, it would have saved me some anxiety. For a long time after, I couldn't count on my rear leg. I lacked confidence in it. This was not foremost in my mind but was always on my mind. Find-

ing a PT I could trust was very important. It helped me to push forward with confidence and deal with the fear of being reinjured.

■   ■   ■   ■   ■

Pain

The International Association for the Study of Pain (2002) defines pain as an unpleasant sensory and emotional experience associated with actual or potential tissue damage. Pain is a product of sensory processes, interpretations of what the pain means, emotions in response to this interpretation, reactive coping behaviors, and the social influences that shape the subsequent expression of pain (see "Guidelines for Pain Management" below).

The sensory process is most often (and sometimes exclusively) the pain component addressed. Biological variables that can cause pain (e.g., a broken bone) are assessed and treated. Various analgesic medications are prescribed to reduce the pain sensation. If treatment ends here, pain often will not be adequately controlled. Cognitive and emotional factors are unique and significant contributors to the pain experience that can result in performance limitations (Sullivan, Stanish, Waite, Sullivan, and Tripp, 1998). In some cases, these factors better account for the pain experience than the injury itself (e.g., Turner, Jensen, Warms, and Cardenas, 2002).

Guidelines for Pain Management

Only the athlete knows his or her pain. Do not assume that you know what the athlete is feeling.

Remember that pain is a sensory and an emotional experience. Help the athlete deal with both. Avoid thinking of and describing pain as either in the body or in the head. This leads to misunderstanding and mistrust.

Understand the difference between routine rehabilitation pain and dangerous pain. Share this knowledge with the athlete carefully and with a clear understanding of the limits of your own knowledge.

Arrange for the athlete to consult with a sports medicine specialist when pain is persistent or disrupts performance for whatever reason.

Avoid responding to complaints of pain by encouraging the athlete to be "tough." Instead, teach

skills to cope with pain. Then reward both toughness and skill.

Be aware that some athletes will attempt to mask dangerous pain if they feel it is not acceptable to express it. If necessary, ask the athlete about pain and then listen carefully to the response.

For some athletes, persistent pain and recurring injury may coincide with a loss of enthusiasm for sport. If need be, help them find a graceful way out of the situation.

Different types of pain present different challenges to the athlete. Be prepared to help the athlete meet these challenges as they occur.

When pain signals fear of reinjury, the athlete will have difficulty complying with rehabilitation or giving 100% at return to play. Be patient and understanding and provide persistent encouragement.

The impact of pain is not limited to the physical body. Pain affects the athlete's ability to participate in sport and life. As a result, the pain carries with it a specific meaning. Addison, Kremer, and Bell (1998) offered a continuum of pain experienced by athletes:

1. *Fatigue* and *discomfort* are normal or routine sensations associated with physical exercise, training, and rehabilitation.

2. *Positive training pain* is nonthreatening and typically occurs during endurance exercises. It is felt beyond fatigue but is understood and believed to be under the athlete's control.

3. *Negative training pain* is perceived as threatening when training has gone too far and is no longer thought to be beneficial.

4. *Negative warning pain* is similar to negative training pain but more serious and threatening. This may be a new sensation for the athlete, signaling potential injury. It is not a sudden pain; thus, the athlete can evaluate its cause and take appropriate action.

5. *Negative acute pain* is a sudden result of injury. It is perceived as intense and specific and is evaluated as catastrophic.

6. *Numbness* is identified as the absence of sensation and is interpreted as highly negative. It is uncommon relative to the other pains described and typically is a cause for concern.

Fatigue, discomfort, and positive training pain should be expected during rehabilitation and interpreted as encouraging signs of progress. Rehabilitation pain is ideally perceived as evidence that athletes are pushing themselves to higher levels of beneficial intensity. But when pain is not readily classifiable by athletes or is mistakenly believed to be negative acute pain, it may lead to distress and decreased compliance with rehabilitation, even if benign (Sullivan et al., 1998). Alternatively, when incorrectly interpreting training pain, athletes are at risk for treatment setbacks and reinjury.

Pain elicits strong emotional reactions that influence the experience of pain itself. If these emotions are negative, a vicious pain cycle develops where pain causes increased distress that in turn causes increased pain. Depression and anxiety increase pain perception directly through increased physiological arousal and interference with positive coping behaviors.

Athletes can choose their reaction to pain. Relaxation, exercise adherence, and good nutrition are positive choices that will facilitate healing. Catastrophizing is a cognitive coping strategy with emotional components (Jones, Rollman, White, Hill, and Brooke, 2003) that most consistently increases pain perception and disability compared with other maladaptive strategies. Unfortunately, catastrophic thinking (e.g., "the pain is killing me," "I can't go through another rehab") is a common reaction to athletic injury (e.g., Udry, Gould, Bridges, and Beck, 1997).

Catastrophizing is a thought process characterized by an excessive focus on pain sensations (rumination) with an exaggeration of threat (magnification) and the perception of not being able to cope with the pain situation (helplessness; Sullivan, Bishop, and Pivik, 1995). Nearly 100 studies have been published on catastrophizing and pain. This thinking style is associated with a more intense pain experience and increased psychological distress in general medical patients (Sullivan et al., 2001) and athletes (Sullivan, Tripp, Rodgers, and Standish, 2000). Catastrophizing increases an injured athlete's anxiety, which heightens the pain intensity by stimulating neural systems that produce increased sensitivity to pain (hyperalgesia; Grau and Meagher, 1999). Catastrophizing also increases muscle tension, further increasing pain intensity. When athletes catastrophize, their ability to make good treatment and coping decisions is impaired.

In addition to these factors that occur within the athlete, pain is experienced in a social context. Some sports may discourage the expression of pain and perceive athletes who communicate their pain as weak. The consequence of such expressions can damage relationships with coaches or teammates and create further isolation from them, prompting athletes to hide their pain. Treatment providers must carefully assess this pain scenario so that progress may be accurately measured and potential rehabilitation problems avoided. Toward the other extreme, pain may elicit excessive social support and attention from friends and family or allow athletes to avoid challenging workouts. These secondary gains can maintain pain. Such reinforcers must be carefully evaluated and addressed to minimize the potential negative impact of intended support.

Fear

Fear and the risk of injury are integral in sport. Each time one competes there is the risk, and perhaps fear, of failure. In high-risk sports (e.g., American football, alpine ski racing), as the risk of injury increases so can the fear of injury. Fear is not, however, necessarily an unhealthy reaction because it can cause athletes to develop a respect for the potential dangers and ensure sensible action. At the same time, fear that consumes athletes actually puts them at greater risk of injury by creating muscle tension and bracing, tentativeness in execution, and distraction from essential focus cues. Kathy Kreiner-Phillips (1990), 1976 Olympic skiing gold medalist, spoke candidly of fear that athletes must face and conquer in their quest for excellence, "Your mind is racing . . . you feel your heartbeat pounding in your chest . . . the image of you falling all the way to the bottom is foremost in your mind" (p. 114).

The sports medicine staff should pay careful attention to signs of fear from injured athletes (Shuer and Dietrich, 1997). Like pain, fear can be adaptive or maladaptive. Fear of injury (or reinjury) is common among athletes (Gould, Udry, Bridges, and Beck, 1997b; Mainwaring, 1999). Fear of reinjury can range from a routine concern, to a subclinical syndrome, to a diagnosable disorder. The critical task is determining whether fear is benign and simply a distraction or is an indication of a potential threat. Another test is whether the fear is reasonable and grounded in objective reality or irrational and inappropriate.

The physiological and psychological contributors to fear create a complex web of interacting influences. An example is illustrated in figure 12.1. Fear may diminish concentration and produce physiological changes. Awareness of these autonomic changes may further cause athletes to become distracted from their rehabilitation exercises, triggering a downward spiral that results in poor rehabilitation.

This interaction of physical and psychological influences inhibits coping and recovery in every phase of rehabilitation. Greater fear or distress delays healing (Kiecolt-Glaser, Page, Marucha, MacCallum, and Glaser, 1998) and is associated with longer hospital stays, more postoperative complications, and higher rates of hospital readmission following surgery (Glaser et al., 1999).

The reciprocal influence of pain and fear may cause athletes to experience muscular guarding. Also called bracing or splinting, muscular guarding is a natural protective response to injury that either isolates or decreases the mobility of the injured body part. This response is usually adaptive during the initial phase of injury because it protects the joint from trauma and facilitates

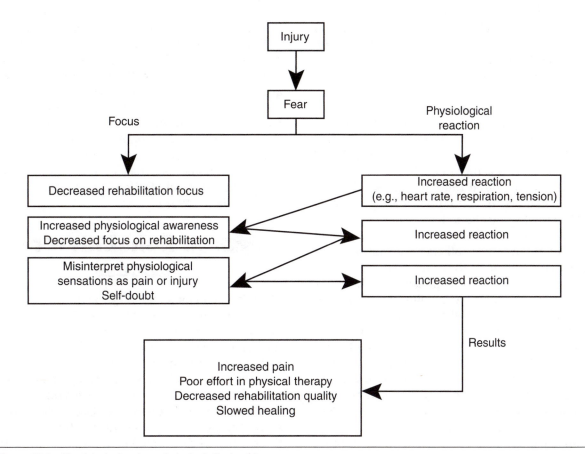

Figure 12.1 Physiological and psychological effects of fear.

healing. However, continued guarding can cause increased muscle tension locally and regionally, compensatory injuries, muscular and motoric imbalance, and improper body mechanics, and it can potentially increase the risk of reinjury.

If fear of reinjury persists as athletes return to sport participation, they may experience hesitancy, avoidance, or poor performance, all of which may increase the risk of reinjury. However, if athletes are engaged in a psychologically minded rehabilitation program, there is a gradual increase in their confidence and commensurate decrease in fear as they are able to successfully test the formerly injured area in training.

Culpability

Most injuries occur during the course of athletes' normal sport participation. When athletes are injured, most realize that it is a possible consequence of the risks inherent in sport, accept responsibility for it, and direct their energy into their recoveries. At the same time, it is reasonable for athletes to ask why the injury occurred. Determining the cause of an injury can help athletes understand what contributed to the injury and either give them a sense of control or show them that reinjury is highly unlikely. Some athletes may need to free themselves of the burden of guilt and blame for the injury so they can fully focus on healing and recovery.

Athletes are more likely to experience distress from an injury that is caused by an intentional, calculated action to do harm, especially when it occurs in conjunction with a rule violation or is otherwise seen as outside the bounds of fair play (Ford, 1983). The situation can be exacerbated when the rule-violating behavior of the athlete or coach who caused the injury goes relatively unpunished. In this situation, injured athletes will feel frustration about unfairness of the injury, anger toward the offending athlete or coach, and resentment toward the officials who allowed rule infraction that caused the injury to occur.

If injured athletes feel responsible for the injury or interpret the injury as a failure on their part, they may experience feelings of guilt and shame for allowing themselves to get injured. These feelings of guilt and shame may be exacerbated if athletes participate in a team sport because they may believe that they have let their team down. This reaction may be inadvertently triggered or worsened by significant others who have an investment in athletes' competitive successes (e.g., coaches, teammates, parents, fans). When athletes direct culpability toward themselves for an injury, the injury and the emotional pain of self-blame doubly victimize them.

When complications arise in rehabilitation or treatment does not proceed on course, culpability may also become an issue. The search for a solution to rehabilitation problems can lead the sports medicine staff to question the athlete's motivation and commitment to recovery and, in turn, athletes may question the adequacy of the medical care. Mutual respect and trust between the athlete and the sports medicine staff are essential to preventing these occurrences from harming the relationship or the progress of recovery (Petrie, 1993). Where personality conflicts arise around the question of responsibility for rehabilitation problems, treatment can be further undermined. Fortunately, such conflicts are the exception rather than the rule because there is usually a clear understanding that the sports medicine staff and the athletes share the common goal of a complete recovery and an effective and timely return to sport. Such problems are less likely to occur when the sports medicine staff takes a psychologically minded approach to treatment that includes clarification of athletes' (e.g., motivation, compliance, communication of concerns) and providers' (e.g., clear information about treatment, adequate pain control, participation in key decisions) roles in rehabilitation.

When the injury is particularly severe, athletes may ask, "Why me?" Some athletes may question the fairness of the world. With this mind-set, they are vulnerable to feelings of helplessness, hopelessness, depression, and a loss of responsibility and motivation in their rehabilitation. Research with general medical populations indicates that culpability is a risk factor related to increased pain, greater emotional disturbance, and less successful treatment outcomes (DeGood and Kiernan, 1997-1998; Williams, 1997).

Path to Rehabilitation Success

The mind is an important ally to injured athletes. Addressing the mental side of the injury can be beneficial in the following ways: It can facilitate the rehabilitation process, minimize emotional distress and maximize positive emotions, activate athletes' existing coping strategies, enhance athletes' mental readiness to return to sport, and maintain athletes' confidence (Heil, 1993). Four strategies can be used to help athletes maximize the quality of their rehabilitation and return to their sport in a timely fashion: education, goal setting, social support, and mental training (Heil, 1993).

Trainer's Perspective

It has become increasingly apparent over the past decade that physical and physiological characteristics do not differentiate elite athletes as significantly as in the past. Psychological skills are being recognized as increasingly critical. Psychological skills training is as vital to dealing with injuries as it is for competition, because physiologically rehabilitation is no different than training. Each represents a demand placed on the body, to which the body and mind must respond and adapt. If the demand is within the body's adaptive capacity, the body will improve its functional capacity and become stronger. The difference between rehabilitation and training is simply the magnitude of the demand. Injury diminishes the functional capacity of the injured structures, so rehabilitation entails lower loads. There are differing protocols but these are designed to reach the same end as training—improved performance. If they are to have successful athletic careers, then athletes must be equipped with the psychological skills that enable them to manage not only the challenges of training and competition but also those of injury and rehabilitation.

■ ■ ■ ■ ■

Athlete's Perspective

Coach and athlete both share the distress of injury and have difficulty understanding the myriad effects on themselves personally, on the other, and on their relationship. With this change in my relationship with my coach, my relationship with others became more important. My family was very helpful, and I found out who my true friends were.

The coaches, trainers, and whomever the athlete depends on for support must stay realistically positive. They need to be encouraging and know when to tell the athlete to slow down or stop. In retrospect, I realize that having clear goals was very important for me. I really like the breakdown by stages and the idea of an injury recovery time line, because of its link to short-term and long-term goals.

■ ■ ■ ■ ■

Education

Education helps the athlete understand the process of injury and rehabilitation. Understanding on the part of athletes of what they can expect during rehabilitation increases their ownership for their recoveries and fosters a sense of control and active participation. Once athletes understand what has happened, what they can expect, and what they need to do, they can then commit themselves to their recoveries and put optimal effort into rehabilitation. Research has shown that a clear understanding of what lies ahead is lacking in the recovery of many athletes (Mainwaring, 1999), particularly during the early stages of recovery (Quinn and Fallon, 1999).

Descriptions of the injury, with explanations of the anatomy, the healing process, and the course of rehabilitation, should be clear. The sports medicine staff is encouraged to identify a timetable of recovery and to clarify what is expected of the athletes in terms of time, energy, and commitment. Professional athletes have stated that having a realistic time line to full recovery is helpful in healing (Francis, Andersen, and Maley, 2000). A better understanding of the injury helps athletes make informed decisions regarding sport goals and personal safety when returning to play. In a recent study of professional ballet dancers (Macchi and Crossman, 1996), half of those sampled believed that their physicians did not provide enough information about their injury, and 28% returned to training before they were physically ready.

Athletes must be taught to differentiate between injury (dangerous) pain and rehabilitation (benign) pain and to use nonpharmacological methods of pain control. Athletes should be prepared for the emotional challenges they will face (e.g., periodic feelings of frustration, anger, sadness, and despair) related to the ups and downs of rehabilitation such as muscle soreness, pain flare-ups, and treatment plateaus. Athletes must be educated about the importance of strict compliance with the rehabilitation regimen and warned about the effects of either over- or underadherence on long-term healing and return to sport.

Goal Setting

Goal setting provides an action plan for rehabilitation. It enhances motivation, increases intensity, strengthens commitment, and offers direction to maximize recovery. It is one of the interventions that athletes prefer and respond to best (Durso Cupal, 1998), with some favoring it over medication (Maniar, Curry, Sommers-Flanagan, and Walsh, 2001). Clear goals and an awareness of progress provide a sense of control over rehabilitation, improve confidence, and reduce anxiety (Taylor and Taylor, 1997).

Faster rehabilitation with goal setting has been found in general medical populations such as stroke patients (Ponte-Allan and Giles, 1999) as well as in athletes (Ievela and Orlick, 1991). With athletes rehabilitating after reconstruction of the anterior cruciate ligament (ACL; the knee), goal setting was associated with increased home exercise compliance and physical therapists' ratings of athletes' intensity and adherence to directions in the clinic (Scherzer et al., 2001; see chapter 7 for details on developing a goal-setting program).

Social Support

During rehabilitation, athletes' social support network consists of the sport team, the sports medicine team, and family and friends. Support may be expressed by listening to the athlete, acknowledging good technical performance, providing emotional support, encouraging the achievement of physical performance goals, encouraging positive coping, and sharing experiences and opinions from which the athlete may benefit (Hardy, Burke, and Crace, 1999).

Social support has been widely researched in athletic injury. Connecting with other injured athletes, particularly those with similar injuries, has been found to be very helpful (Granito, 2001). Athletes sometimes report insufficient social support from sports medicine professionals (Mainwaring, 1999), especially at the beginning of rehabilitation (Johnston and Carroll, 2000). Athletes find emotional support to be particularly important when rehabilitation progress is slow, setbacks are experienced, or other life demands increase the athletes' sense of pressure (Evans, Hardy, and Fleming, 2000). For example, U.S. ski team athletes who did not recover from injury reported less attention and empathy from others and more negative relationships compared with those who recovered (Gould et al., 1997b).

Coaches have been viewed as less supportive than certified athletic trainers (Robbins and Rosenfeld, 2001) and were most frequently cited as having a negative influence during rehabilitation. Particular behaviors on the part of coaches that discourage the recovery process include being distant, being insensitive to the injury, and providing inappropriate or insufficient rehabilitation guidance (Udry, Gould, Bridges, and Tuffey, 1997). Injury also frequently separates athletes from their teammates and coaches (Mainwaring, 1999) and increases the athletes' sense of isolation and estrangement from the team. Social support combined with a sense of personal responsibility is associated with higher levels of physical therapist-rated adherence (Johnston and Carroll, 2000). Greater adherence likely leads to better outcomes and, when combined with mental training, fosters an effective and timely recovery and return to sport.

With healthy athletes, coaches typically provide support by acknowledging technical performance, progress toward performance goals, and coping with adversity. Often this does not continue during rehabilitation (Robbins and Rosenfeld, 2001). Speaking directly with athletes (instead of relying on certified athletic trainers' reports) demonstrates personal concern (Robbins and Rosenfeld, 2001). Coaches are encouraged to stay involved with the athlete and to provide alternative activities (such as developing special practice routines) so athletes can continue to participate in their sport during their rehabilitation. This ongoing involvement diminishes feelings of isolation from the team, offers consistent social support from teammates and coaches, allows athletes to continue to develop in their sport, reduces feelings that athletes are falling behind, and helps maintain confidence in their capabilities when they do return to their sport.

Mental Training

Mental training lies at the heart of applied sport psychology. Its value in enhancing athletic performance is supported by research and is an integral part of the work that sport psychologists do with athletes (Durso Cupal, 1998; Ross and Berger, 1996). The foundation skills of mental training include intensity regulation, concentration, self-talk, mental imagery, and performance routines. When athletes use mental skills during the course of rehabilitation, their physical recoveries are facilitated and psychological damage caused by the injury is minimized. Mental training during rehabilitation physically and mentally prepares athletes for a complete and healthy return to high performance in their sport (see chapter 8).

Relaxation

The stress, fear, and pain involved in injury and rehabilitation frequently activate the body's fight-or-flight response, a function of the autonomic nervous system that prepares the body for action through increased psychological and physiological intensity. Unfortunately, this reaction actually interferes with rather than benefits the recovery process. Overactivation undermines performance by taking athletes outside their "zone" (i.e., zone of optimal functioning; Hanin, 2000). This activation can increase feelings of stress, anxiety, fear, and pain and causes an array of negative effects, including muscle tension, increased heart rate, reduced respiration, vasoconstriction, decreased confidence, and poor concentration. Tense muscles are often a result of the body's natural tendency to tighten muscles as a way of isolating and protecting an injury. This muscular guarding is often counterproductive and can exacerbate pain and undermine healing. If left unchecked, guarding can become entrenched, slowing rehabilitation and causing a chronic injury pattern.

Relaxation training is a valuable tool for injured athletes to combat the fight-or-flight response. Relaxation techniques can be used to diminish physiological activation and reduce the negative effects of anxiety by decreasing tension, lowering heart rate, slowing breathing, and increasing blood flow. A literature review of relaxation studies found relaxation to reduce pain, insomnia, hypertension, anxiety, and medication use across multiple populations, diagnostic categories, and settings (Mandle, Jacobs, Arcari, and Domar, 1996; see chapter 3 for more on relaxation training).

Rehabilitation Imagery

Mental imagery may be the most powerful mental training tool that athletes have at their disposal. Mental imagery is akin to weight training because it can strengthen "mental muscles" including motivation, confidence, intensity, focus, and emotions. Imagery also has significant benefits in relation to injury. Used by healthy athletes, imagery can limit the risk of injury by inducing relaxation, reducing stress, enhancing confidence, improving technique, sharpening focus, and blocking out distraction (Green, 1992). A more in-depth discussion of mental imagery can be found in chapter 8.

Athletes are less likely to use imagery during rehabilitation than in training or competition. When imagery is used, the focus is generally on increasing motivation rather than on developing rehabilitation skills (Sordoni, Hall, and Forwell, 2000). As a result, imagery's benefits of performance enhancement, increased confidence, and intensity control (Martin, Moritz, and Hall, 1999) may not be maximized in the rehabilitation setting (Sordoni et al., 2000). Rehabilitation imagery can prepare athletes for the challenges of rehabilitation, including surgery, pain, setbacks, and return to sport. Athletes can imagine feeling calm and relaxed before surgery, being motivated and intense during physical therapy exercises, feeling confident when returning to the athletic arena, and performing aggressively with the recovered body part during competition. Rehabilitation imagery is a skill that develops with practice.

Taylor and Taylor (1997) offer specific guidelines to maximize rehabilitation imagery:

1. Use an imagery perspective that is most natural for you. This may be internal (i.e., viewing the image through your own eyes) or external (i.e., as if you were watching yourself perform, like watching a video).

2. Make the images vivid through the use of all senses (i.e., what you would see, hear, smell, taste, and feel). Watching actual videos of yourself and having a clear understanding of the healing process may enhance vividness.

3. Imagery control is essential. Spontaneous imagery replay of the injury may occur, creating negative emotions and making both the negative images and emotions more difficult to change. Immediately correct the image with a mental "remote control," where the image is stopped, rewound, positively edited, and played forward in slow motion. The speed may be gradually increased until the image is viewed with control in real time.

4. Imagine total performance, including all physiological and psychological aspects of rehabilitation. In addition to using all of your physical senses, you can rehearse emotions and thoughts.

5. Combine relaxation with imagery to enhance vividness and control (Greenspan and Feltz, 1989; Hellstedt, 1987).

6. Feel the imagery physically and emotionally to create strong positive associations with rehabilitation.

7. Use imagery to reestablish the good feeling necessary to maximize your physical therapy when you're "not feeling right."

For injured athletes, mental imagery aids the healing process, increases adherence, and can replace physical practice during recuperation (Jones and Stuth, 1997). Imagery was more frequently cited as a coping strategy among athletes who recovered successfully from injury compared with those athletes who were less successful in their recoveries (Gould, Udry, Bridges, and Beck, 1997a). Cupal and Brewer (2001) found greater gains in knee strength with greater reductions in pain and fear of reinjury with imagery. These recovery benefits may be attributable in part to the physiological changes that are triggered by imagery, such as reductions of stress hormones cortisol and β-endorphin in the blood (McKinney, Antoni, Kumar, Tims, and McCabe, 1997; McKinney, Tims, Kumar, and Kumar, 1997; see chapter 8 for more on the use of mental imagery and see "Imagery for Rehabilitation" below for examples of rehabilitation images).

• **Healing imagery.** Athletes can visualize the injured area and see the injury mending and returning to normal. Imagery has been found to stimulate muscle activity, blood flow, and the immune system (Achterberg, 1991; Sarno, 1984; Sheikh and Jordan, 1983). Although there is no clear evidence that imagery actually facilitates the physical healing process, there is enough support to believe that such a relationship does exist (Taylor and Taylor, 1997). Healing imagery also has psychological benefits including building confidence, reducing anxiety, and maintaining motivation. Imagery can create a positive mind-set and proactively counter feelings of helplessness and hopelessness. This process may be continued through rehabilitation to return to sport as a way of building confidence.

• **Imagery for relaxation.** Calming images such as lying on the beach can enhance relaxation and reduce pain. Early in the rehabilitation process, several soothing scenes should be identified and practiced (Taylor and Taylor, 1997). As a developed skill, these multisensory images can be an effective strategy to distract from pain and focus on more positive thoughts and feelings.

• **Pain imagery.** Sometimes, however, the pain may be too great to ignore. In these cases, an associative strategy can be more beneficial. Injured athletes are encouraged to imagine what is causing their pain using all senses. Athletes then address each sensation and gradually change the image in a way that that lessens the pain (see "Imagery for Rehabilitation"). This change must occur slowly because the body must have time to adjust to the image. For example, a burning sensation in the thigh may be visualized as red-hot muscles accompanied by the sound of a crackling fire. Application of ice may be imagined, changing the color of the muscles from red, to orange, to yellow, to a cool blue. The crackling fire sound may become gradually softer or gradually replaced by the sound of water flowing over rocks in a stream.

• **Performance imagery.** Injury is often misperceived as forced downtime from sport. Rehabilitation offers an opportunity to use performance imagery for improvements in technique, tactics, mental preparation, and competitive performance (Taylor and Taylor, 1997). Performance imagery also can be used to improve rehabilitation performance and coping through mental rehearsal of the physical skills necessary to succeed.

Imagery for Rehabilitation

Healing Images

- Ultrasound as creating a healing glow.
- Therapeutic application of ice as freezing up and shutting down pain receptors.
- Blood surging to the muscle and rebuilding it at an accelerated rate during resistance training.
- Nonsteroidal anti-inflammatory medication as sponges absorbing local tissue irritants.

Healed Images

- Ligaments as a combination of wound steel and rubber, strong but flexible.
- The meniscus as smooth as Teflon following knee surgery.

Pain Images

- A sharp, stabbing pain pictured as knife cutting into the affected area. Gradually the pain becomes duller as the blade becomes rounder and softer.
- Tight muscles as knotted ropes that loosen with each deep breath.

Relaxation Image   At the beach, watching and listening to the waves roll in, feeling the warm sun on your face, smelling suntan lotion, and tasting your favorite drink quenching your thirst.

Performance Images

- Reviewing the playbook and taking "mental reps" by imagining your performance for each play.
- First basketball game following ACL surgery and rehabilitation. Imagining quick reflexes and hard cuts on defense, trusting the strength and response of the rehabilitated knee.
- Visualizing the sport scenario that the injury occurred in, but performing with confidence, assertiveness, focus, and skill.
- Imagining the nervousness likely associated with return to sport (e.g., shallow breathing, rapid heart rate, worried thoughts), recognizing this reaction, and then imagining your improvement with deep breathing and realistically positive self-talk.

Focus

Focus involves thinking about the right thing, at the right time, in the right way. As challenging as focus is to healthy athletes, it is even more difficult for athletes who are injured because of the sometimes conflicting needs of performance and safety. Mastering this doubly complex focus challenge lies at the heart of understanding the difference between pain and injury (see chapter 4).

Research on long-distance runners has identified two focus strategies: association and dissociation (Heil, 1990; Morgan, 1978; Schomer, 1986). Association refers to athletes focusing on relevant performance cues. For example, runners would use association to be aware of their pace, rate of perceived exertion, fatigue, and pain. Dissociation involves the intentional use of distraction as a way of coping with the mental and physical demands of the sport. For instance, runners would listen to music, talk to another runner, or look at their surroundings to keep their mind off the discomfort. Overreliance on dissociation may both undermine performance and increase injury risk because athletes are not attending to important cues that might enable them to perform better or that warn of an impending injury. This research has indicated that elite distance runners rely more heavily on association and nonelite runners tend to use dissociation.

During rehabilitation from injury, athletes are constantly faced with pain. Both association and dissociation have a place in managing pain (Taylor and Taylor, 1997). Pain management involves athletes learning when to ignore the pain (dissociation) and when to focus on it and make necessary changes in response to the pain (association). The pain–sport attentional matrix (Heil, 1993) identi-

fies four focusing tasks athletes must master to perform effectively while maintaining safety:

- *Associating to both pain and sport* can be beneficial when pain signals proper technique. Changing movement patterns to avoid pain can backfire and result in compensatory injury.
- *Dissociating from both pain and sport* during performance is problematic because focus is sacrificed for the sake of pain management. This approach may be applied during natural breaks in activity as a way of getting some psychological downtime from the mental demands of sport.
- *Dissociating from pain while associating to sports performance* is appropriate when pain is understood as routine (or in medical terms, benign); otherwise pain becomes a distraction and undermines performance.
- *Associating to pain while dissociating from sport* is important in the management of overuse and chronic injuries. At times, sport performance can so fully absorb attention that pain sensations are suppressed to the detriment of athletes' physical well-being. This strategy can be used in breaks between activities to assess physical functioning. It can also be used as a check on muscular guarding. However, hyperawareness of pain can lead to negative self-talk and catastrophizing that hurt sport performance.

Self-Talk

The excessive focus on pain, and the exaggerated sense of threat associated with negative self-talk such as catastrophizing, can increase the perception of pain (Sullivan et al., 2000) and limit athletes' activity levels (Sullivan et al., 1998). Negative self-talk during rehabilitation includes thoughts such as, "I'll never recover," "I'm progressing too slowly," and "I can't get the pain out of my mind." The emotional distress associated with catastrophizing can inhibit athletes' motivation to remain committed to their rehabilitation programs. Negative self-talk and catastrophizing can become habitual when doubt, uncertainty, and fear guide athletes' thinking. Fortunately, negative thinking can be unlearned with conscious attention, frequent challenge, and replacement with realistically positive self-talk.

Individuals who are better able to minimize pain persist longer in painful activities, such as rehabilitation (Lysholm and Wiklander, 1987). Although positive self-talk can minimize pain and increase rehabilitation performance (Theodorakis et al., 1997), statements that are simply optimistic are not effective. Self-talk must be realistic and meaningful. An accurate injury assessment and medical facts about the injury and pain provide the evidence to counter negative self-talk and encourage "realistically positive" self-talk.

For example, a soccer player tears his ACL during a preseason game. His initial catastrophizing reaction is, "My career is over. I'm through." These thoughts increase anxiety, frustration, and pain. Compare this with the athlete who realistically assesses the situation and remains optimistic: "I'm injured and it's serious. I'll be out for a while, but let me wait to see what the doctor has to say. We've got a great sports medicine team. Maybe I can make it back for the playoffs" (see "Rehab Focusing Plan," below).

Rehab Focusing Plan

Jill is a fencer with residual knee pain after several surgeries and rehabilitations. The rehab focusing plan described next is designed to help her manage pain and the psychological consequences of longstanding injury.

Rebuild confidence in your body one day at a time.

I. Pain and injury are learning experiences.

- A. Build better body awareness.
    - Understand how your body works.
    - Know what is safe.
    - "Tune in" to your body when you need to.
    - Make adjustments as necessary.

- B. Boost refocusing skills.
    - Use mental skills (developed for competition) to manage pain and worry.
    - Learn when to "tune in" and when to "tune out" pain.

II. Break the pain–fear cycle.

- Avoid worry, which leads to fear and more pain.
- Avoid muscle tension, which leads to pain.

- A. Use body awareness to manage muscle tension.
    - Stretch after activity.
    - Do relaxation exercises.
    - Use ice as recommended by sports medicine staff.

- B. Focus to manage worry.
    - Use a "body check": When necessary tune in to your body (e.g., between bouts in competition or hard training), making adjustments via body awareness methods, and reassure yourself.
    - During day-to-day activities, tune out pain and focus on what you need to do.
    - During competition, trust your rehab and just fence!

Remarkable Recovery

Remarkable recovery defines the quest for competitive excellence in rehabilitation (Heil, 1993). Injury, although most often seen as a curse to athletes, can provide them with many benefits if they approach their injury and the subsequent recovery with the proper attitude and engage in their rehabilitation with sufficient commitment, determination, and vigor. Although injuries have ruined the careers of some athletes, for others, an injury can enable them to achieve new levels of performance by teaching them physical and mental skills that they then apply to their training and competitive efforts. These athletes become better athletes because during rehabilitation they learn to work hard, focus effectively, stay motivated and positive, adjust their intensity, control their emotions, manage pain, become more aware of their bodies, and gain a new appreciation for the role that sports play in their lives. Athletes who follow the previously described path to rehabilitation success (i.e., education, goal setting, social support, and mental training) and recover more quickly and efficiently relative to the norm, or those who return to sport at a higher level of performance than before injury, have made a remarkable recovery. Such a recovery is further characterized by benefits such as heightened body awareness, enhanced pain assessment, sharpened mental skills, emotional momentum, and a new perspective on sport.

Trainer's Perspective

K. was an exemplary two-sport athlete (track and soccer) with whom I worked for 5 years. The mainstay of the soccer team, she rewrote the university scoring record books, leading the team to the conference championship 4 years straight and to the national championship competition in her last two seasons. Although fast and talented, K. was slightly built and the target of brutal tackling by opposing teams. She endured numerous injuries that we were able to work through given her dedication and tenacity. In her final game she sustained an extraordinarily severe knee injury (an unfortunate result of a questionable tackle by the opposing keeper). She faced a poor prognosis—uncertain whether she would ever be able to walk normally again, with sports out of the question. However, K. moved relatively quickly through distress and some initial denial to determined coping. She drew on her previous injury experiences and subsequent successful recoveries to frame this new challenge. She launched her rehabilitation from a stable base consisting of a deep belief in her own strength and work ethic; a broad support system of family, teammates, and sports medicine staff; realistic but open-ended expectations; and life goals beyond competitive athletics. The goal of becoming a teacher served as an enduring point of focus, enabling her to avoid getting bogged down in the daily setbacks or advances that marked her rehabilitation. Within 2 years she had finished graduate school, was teaching at a local high school, and was coaching a youth team. And she had resumed playing soccer recreationally. Although K. never regained her previous physical prowess, her return to an active and fulfilling life was remarkable in the face of the severity, timing, and circumstances of her injury.

■　■　■　■　■

Athlete's Perspective

The MD and the PT guided me in seeing how the body works and how much stress it can take. I learned to be more careful about warm-up and stretching and smarter about body mechanics as well as rest and recovery. Over time I gained a better understanding of pain and how to rate it, and I even developed a better pain vocabulary. Since my injury, I am better able to focus and handle pressure. Before I worried more, whereas now I plan more. I am more resilient. When the chance to compete came again, I was grateful for the opportunity. I am happier and more positive now—before my injury there were more downs. I have gained momentum after my injury. I was just starting to fence again in late summer, and then I had my best result at World Championships in October, winning a bronze medal.

■　■　■　■　■

Heightened Body Awareness

Rehabilitation from injury forces athletes to revisit the fundamentals of physiology and conditioning. As the focus of their lives during their recovery from injury, rehabilitation brings a deeper level of scrutiny to the fundamentals of the human body and, with this exploration, greater awareness and knowledge of how the body works. Athletes meet sports medicine and conditioning professionals whose knowledge base complements that of coaches, giving athletes a broader understanding of physical health and training principles. Macchi and Crossman (1996) found that following injury, 42% of a sample of ballet dancers were more careful when dancing, paid better attention to proper technique, stretched more, and modified exercises to avoid reinjury. Nearly 50% of injured U.S. ski team athletes found that on their return to competition, they were skiing better technically (Udry, Gould, Bridges, and Beck, 1997). Athletes who commit themselves to making their rehabilitation positive learning experiences use their injury to become better, more complete athletes.

Enhanced Pain Management

The ability of athletes to better monitor, evaluate, and manage their pain is another benefit of injury rehabilitation that increases their ability to use pain as a tool to enhance their training and competitive efforts. Injury broadens the scope of athletes' pain experience, exposing them to pain that they may have never felt before. Athletes can emerge from rehabilitation with an improved ability to differentiate performance pain from injury pain and with a greater capacity to withstand the physical demands they place on themselves.

Pain decision making is a complex process that is poorly understood yet is an essential tool for athletes to maximize their sport performances. Pain is not simple sensory input but rather a multidimensional perceptual experience. Pain begins as an electrochemical process, which produces a subjective perception of pain, which in turn gains meaning (e.g., performance pain or injury pain). Meaning is the product of an interpretation, which incorporates multiple pieces of information, for example, memory of prior pain experiences, assessment of movement patterns, and emotional states. The meaning that athletes connect with the pain determines what decisions they make about the pain and how they respond to it.

Consider a distance runner who has the perception of a burning feeling in her legs as she climbs a hill. Evaluating this perception in comparison to prior experiences, she determines that the meaning of a "burning feeling" is routine performance pain. The likely action to follow is to continue running. Research by Peterson, Durtschi, and Murphy (1990) revealed that many elite runners relabel pain as exertion when describing the sensations associated with an intense running effort and thus evaluate this perception as a positive sign of good effort.

Consider another variation of the situation just described. Following perception of a burning feeling in his shoulder, a swimmer concludes that an injury is developing. The question then becomes, "Should the activity be stopped or is some alternate course of action acceptable?" To a swimmer, this pain might mean that an overuse injury is developing but can be corrected by a change in stroke mechanics.

Sharpened Mental Skills

Injury brings new challenges mentally as well as physically. Athletes must adapt to the change in lifestyle that injury brings and deal with the emotional demands of the injury and, if serious, the potentially long recovery. Even as rehabilitation presents a new and complex performance challenge, athletes may find the ordinary activities of daily living difficult as well because of physical limitations placed on them by the injury. For athletes who are motivated to return to competition at the same level as before they were injured, they will need to use every mental skill they have at their disposal. The French Olympic skiing champion, Jean-Claude Killy, tells of an injury that left him unable to train before an important race (Suinn, 1976). Because he was unable to actually train, Killy repeatedly imagined himself skiing the course as the race approached. To everyone's surprise given his injury, Killy won the race. As Ievleva and Orlick (1991) indicated, recovery comes best to athletes who systematically put their minds into the "game of rehab," identifying specific goals and envisioning success. The stress injury research (e.g. Williams and Roepke, 1993) shows the importance of coping skills in buffering the effects of stress on injury occurrence and by extension on the occurrence of reinjury during rehabilitation. Elite skiers whose rehabilitation was successful (compared with those who were unsuccessful) were more likely to identify managing thoughts and emotions as a coping strategy (Udry, Gould, Bridges, and Beck, 1997).

Emotional Momentum

Athletes who choose to confront the emotional challenges of rehabilitation with determination, intensity, and resourcefulness and decide to apply their mental skills in a committed and organized way can establish positive emotional momentum over the course of their recoveries. Consider Hanin's (2000) characterization of positive and negative affect as relatively independent dimensions. Injury increases the amount and intensity of negative affect that athletes must manage, particularly early in the recovery process. Yet, the ongoing quest for an effective and timely recovery demands a corresponding increase in positive affect to keep a relatively favorable emotional balance. Ideally, as recovery proceeds, positive affect increases and negative affect diminishes. Athletes who maintain a high level of positive affect experience a favorable balance of positive to negative affect. As positive affect increases during the course of rehabilitation, athletes will experience positive emotional momentum that carries them to the conclusion of rehabilitation and a higher level of performance.

New Perspective on Sport

Sport offers many benefits to athletes as well as presenting them with many challenges. Injury removes many of those benefits and increases the challenges athletes must face. Although an injury deprives athletes of the opportunity to compete and strive toward their goals, it has the paradoxical benefit of requiring athletes to look at their sport participation in a new light. An injury, particularly a serious one that might end their participation at that level, forces athletes to step back from their sport involvement and gain a new perspective on its meaning and the role it plays in their lives because that meaning and role may change. Deprived of this highly prized activity, athletes have a clearer sense of what they are missing and, from that sense of loss, can relearn how important their sport is to them. Either this new insight will lead athletes to realize that sports are not that meaningful to them and will provide the impetus to choose a new direction, or the injury will clarify for athletes the essential value of sports and strengthen their motivation and resolve to return in top form. Udry, Gould, Bridges and Beck (1997) found that more than 50% of injured U.S. ski team athletes gained a deepened appreciation for the opportunities their sport provided. Although adamantly opposed to being identified as disabled during their recovery, athletes recovering from serious knee injuries reported greater understanding and empathy for those who are disabled. Consider the words of Lance Armstrong (2000):

> To be afraid is a priceless education. Once you have been that scared, you know more about your frailty than most people, and I think that changes a man. I was brought low, and there was nothing to take refuge in but the philosophical: this disease would force me to ask more of myself as a person than I ever had before, and to seek out a different ethic. (p. 99)

Ten Keys to Remarkable Recovery

Ten keys to successful recovery from injury are identified as an intuitive guide to injured athletes (Heil, 1998).

1. **Know the game: "knowledge is power."** Proactive education about injury and rehabilitation is the cornerstone of successful recovery. Understanding the *what* and *why* of rehabilitation empowers the athlete and cultivates a sense of personal responsibility.

2. **Goal-directed thinking: "a road map to success."** Realistic short-term, intermediate, and long-term goals guide the day-to-day process of training and rehabilitation. Understanding the *how* of rehabilitation defines athletes' roles in recovery, shows them where they must go and how they can get there, and invests athletes in the rehabilitation process.

3. **Focused attention: "mental tenacity."** Focusing on the right thing, at the right time, in the right way, is as essential to successful rehabilitation as it is to sport performance. Pain, emotions, the complexity of rehabilitation, and normal life challenges, such as work, school, sleep, nutrition, and relationships, are potent distractions. The challenge of rehabilitation demands a consistent, task-oriented focus throughout the course of recovery.

4. **Controlled emotional intensity: "bringing heart to rehab."** Emotion is the fire that fuels athletes' drive to recovery and return to sport. Athletes must face and overcome negative emotions, such as fear, frustration, anger, and despair, and foster positive emotions, such as hope, excitement, pride, and joy. The channeling and control of emotion (positive and negative) are essential tools for rehabilitation.

5. **Precise skill execution: "goodness of form."** Precise execution of physical therapy exercises and progressive return of sport skills lead to steady gains in rehabilitation and regaining of technical form and performance when athletes return to their sport. Mastery begins with attention to fine detail and crystallizes as athletes are able to perform again on the injured area without thought.

6. **Training (rehabilitation) intensity: "overloading without overtraining."** A universal set of physical training principles that underlie sport conditioning can also be applied to rehabilitation of injury. Central to physiological conditioning, whether for sport or injury recovery, is appropriate intensity during exertion and thoughtful allocation of intensity over time. This principle ensures adequate overloading to maximize rehabilitation benefits without the dangers of overtraining.

7. **Performance over pain: "mastering the mind–body paradox**." Pain is inevitable as physical limits are pushed in the pursuit of excellence in sport performance and in recovery from injury.

Pain assessment and management are fundamental skills in sport and rehabilitation by which athletes differentiate performance pain and injury pain and can adjust their efforts accordingly.

8. Calculated risk taking: "playing the edge." To strive as athletes is to take risks of losing, failing, and suffering injury and reinjury. Calculated risk taking ensures athletes the greatest benefits from their efforts and, at the same time, guards them against injury from unnecessary risk. Effective decision making in how hard, how much, and how often to push is essential for a timely and effective recovery from injury.

9. Mental toughness: "courage in adversity." Overcoming the inevitable adversity athletes will face during rehabilitation begins with having the courage to face these challenges directly and focus on what they can control, namely, their thoughts, emotions, and actions. Mental toughness involves athletes' ability to remain positive, determined, and focused when they are tired, in pain, and dis-

couraged. Athletes develop mental toughness by applying the mental skills they learned as athletes to their rehabilitations. The critical challenge is ensuring that they experience more positive than negative emotions and build positive momentum as their recoveries progress.

10. Self-actualization: "striving for the zone." Taking performance to its highest level is a fundamental goal of sport competition. Self-actualization of athletic performance involves the personal growth and discovery that athletes experience in their efforts. For athletes recovering from injury, self-actualization means committing themselves fully to rehabilitation, meeting the emotional challenges of rehabilitation, learning how to become better athletes and people from the recovery process, and returning to sport better prepared to achieve their goals. As during sport competition, this realization process involves experiencing the supremely satisfying moments when the pursuit of excellence guides athletes into the zone.

Key Points

- Injury rehabilitation is best conceptualized as an athletic challenge in which athletes use their strengths of mental discipline, goal setting, and pain tolerance.
- The recovery time line best follows these medical stages (Steadman, 1993): (1) preinjury period, (2) immediate postinjury period, (3) treatment decision and implementation, (4) early postoperative or rehabilitation period, (5) late postoperative or rehabilitation period, (6) specificity, and (7) return to play.
- Within each of these stages, athletes will experience an affective cycle of injury that includes distress, denial, and determined coping.
- Rehabilitation failure is caused by maladaptive denial, unmanaged pain, fear, emotional distress, and unhealthy culpability that keep athletes from developing a positive attitude in response to the injury and the subsequent rehabilitation.
- Rehabilitation success comes from education about the injury and rehabilitation process; goal setting to provide an action plan for improvement; social support by athletes' sport team, sports medicine team, friends, and family; and mental training (i.e., relaxation, imagery, concentration, and realistically positive self-talk).
- Remarkable recovery, which involves a recovery and return to sport that are substantially faster and more complete than the norm, is characterized by heightened body awareness, enhanced pain management, sharpened mental skills, emotional momentum, and a new perspective on sport.

Review Questions

1. What sport skills are applied to rehabilitation?
2. What are two of the psychological perspectives for understanding the rehabilitation process?
3. What is the affective cycle of injury?
4. What are the four contributors to rehabilitation failure, and why do they interfere with progress?
5. What factors contribute to rehabilitation success, and how are they of benefit?
6. What is remarkable recovery, and how can it be achieved?
7. What are some of the benefits of sustaining an injury?

CHAPTER

13
Eating Disorders

Judy Goss, PhD—researcher
Susan Cooper, PhD, and Danny Stevens, MA, LPC—consultants
Sheilagh Croxon—coach
Nikki Dryden—athlete

© Sport the Library

The objectives of this chapter are

- to define and describe eating disorders both in the categories used by the *Diagnostic and Statistical Manual of Mental Disorders (DSM)-IV-TR* (APA, 2000) and also in additional subgroups of the athletic population;
- to describe the various associated medical and psychological problems that affect athletes;
- to discuss general causes of eating disorders as well as the particular reasons that athletes are susceptible; and
- to detail intervention and strategies for recovery from eating disorders, with a particular emphasis on prevention and early identification.

It is estimated that eating disorders affect several million people each year, with the most vulnerable being young women (Hoek, 1995). The commonly held stereotype of an eating-disordered person is an 18-year-old, white female who tries to be as thin as possible by starving herself or by vomiting after she eats. However, the extent and complexity of eating disorders extend well beyond the typical conceptions held by most people. Some people have full-blown eating disorders, whereas others suffer from disordered eating behaviors or patterns but do not meet the formal criteria for the eating disorder diagnoses.

The presence of eating disorders in the athletic population is even more extensive and problematic than in the general population. The culture of sport, where weight, body type, shape, and appearance are so important, both implicitly and explicitly encourages a preoccupation with eating and weight. When the physical, psychological, and emotional demands of sport are combined with pressure to lose, maintain, or gain weight, the results can be unhealthy, dramatic, and sometimes tragic.

Key Issues

Unfortunately, eating disorders are a common cultural phenomenon, particularly among women but also among men. Athletes seem to be especially prone because of the unique pressures of athleticism such as performance standards, personal perfectionism, pressure from coaches, and competition among peers. Symptoms such as starving, vomiting, use of laxatives, and compulsive exercise can cause serious medical consequences and also decrease athletic performance. Effective treatment approaches are available for most patients once the eating disorder is identified. Early detection and timely treatment are crucial to helping those athletes who develop an eating disorder.

Chapter Purpose and Author Team

The purpose of this chapter is to acquaint readers with the role that eating disorders often play in the lives of athletes and how they can recover. The researcher (Dr. Judy Goss) discusses theoretical and empirical findings that influence the development of an eating disorder and its symptom picture. Drawing on their clinical experience, the consultants (Dr. Susan Cooper and Danny Stevens) describe how eating disorders affect athletes psychologically, medically, and in terms of performance and how they can find their way to recovery. The coach (Sheilagh Croxon) offers her views on the development of eating disorders in synchronized swimming and the impact they have on athletes. Finally, the athlete (Nikki Dryden) presents the influence an eating disorder has had on her life and her athletic performance.

Coach's Perspective

I have had experience with athlete eating disorders every year of my coaching career. I may not have been aware of these problems at the beginning of my career, but as I look back, the signs and symptoms were there. I will speak specifically of one athlete, and although I did not personally coach this athlete until she reached the national team level, I have a general idea of her background as a developing athlete in the sport.

The athlete began synchronized swimming at a very young age (5 years). Primarily her mother coached her. The athlete experienced enormous success at a very young age, winning provincial titles in the 14-and-under age category from the age of 11 and national titles from the age of 12. Her technical proficiency was far beyond her years. It was apparent to other coaches and her teammates that her coach (her mother) was extremely hard on her. The athlete was often asked to leave the practice if she could not execute something perfectly or was simply experiencing an "off" day.

■ ■ ■ ■ ■

Athlete's Perspective

Bulimia crept into my life so stealthily that I did not know I had an eating disorder until I had recovered. My coach, who constantly stressed and was obsessed with my weight and that of my teammates and my competitors, planted the initial seed. That seed then grew into a weed that wrapped itself around my brain, strangling rational thought and replacing it with a desperate obsession about food.

■　■　■　■　■

Definitions of Eating Disorders

Eating disorders are extreme disturbances in an individual's thoughts, feelings, and behaviors related to weight, body image, and food. Eating disorders involve concerted attempts to lose or gain weight or achieve a particular physical appearance (Striegel-Moore, 1993). Negative attitudes and beliefs held by athletes about their bodies and food fuel behaviors that can be harmful and even life threatening. Such preoccupation and worry about food, body shape, weight, and food intake interfere with athletes' sporting lives, daily functioning, health, and happiness. Eating disorders may appear to be about food, weight, or body image, but they are often symptomatic of more fundamental psychosocial problems that athletes are unable to cope with effectively.

Coach's Perspective

An eating disorder is characterized by abnormal eating habits and a preoccupation with food, the scale, and body image. An athlete with an eating disorder is dominated by her need to be thin or desire to be at a certain body weight. This obsession consumes the athlete's thoughts and drives her behavior and decisions.

■　■　■　■　■

Athlete's Perspective

My whole life revolved around food. Every idle moment was spent thinking about what was I going to eat, when was I going to eat it, and how much of it I was going to eat. I weighed myself five times a day trying to insanely calculate the effects of a bowl of cereal on my overall weight. Then when the scale stopped showing me what I wanted to see, the bingeing and purging began.

Every Sunday night I would tell myself that things were going to change—I was going to be strong, diet properly, and lose weight. But my weeks would consist of one day skipping meals and the next day bingeing and purging. I used to come home from school and be alone in the house for 2 to 3 hours, and I would eat as much as I could before anyone came home. I would have these battles in my head with one voice

saying, "You are on a diet! You are only allowed to eat an apple! Your competitors wouldn't eat that!" and the other voice saying, "Come on, just eat, just pig out, it's only one day!" The first voice would win for about 15 minutes, and then I would gorge myself with bowl after bowl of cereal, yogurt, fruit, macaroni and cheese, or soup. All of it was healthy food, but I would just eat massive quantities of it.

The purging started when I learned about it from my teammates. I remember hearing about the older girls throwing up before a workout or eating prunes and drinking prune juice, and that was when I found a box of laxative in my parent's medicine cupboard and tried it for the first time.

For a younger swimmer on my high school team, whose eating disorder began shortly after I left the program, purging soon became her entire life. She described her purging as allowing her to eat whatever she wanted, whenever she wanted, because she would just throw it up. She spent day after day eating all the foods she had denied herself for so many years. She described her nightly ritual of coming home from swimming, eating as much as she could, going to her room, throwing up, brushing her teeth, and then getting ready for bed. She would then eat dessert, talk to her parents for a while, and go to bed. Every night she promised herself that she would not eat the next day so she would not have to throw up anymore.

■　■　■　■　■

Within the general category of eating disorders, the *DSM-IV-TR* (APA, 2000) has identified specific disorders with clearly defined symptoms. Three eating disorders have been categorized and detailed: anorexia nervosa, bulimia nervosa, and eating disorder not otherwise specified. In addition to these formally recognized eating disorders, two other conditions have recently been identified as prevalent in the athletic population: anorexia athletica and bigorexia.

Anorexia Nervosa

Anorexia nervosa is identified by drastic weight loss from extreme food restriction. *DSM-IV-TR* (APA, 2000, p. 589) defines anorexia nervosa as meeting three of the following criteria:

• Refusal to maintain body weight at or above a minimally normal weight for age and height, which is further described as weight loss leading to maintenance of body weight less than 85% of that expected, or failure to make expected weight gain during a period of growth, leading to body weight less than 85% of that expected.

- Intense fear of gaining weight or becoming fat, even though underweight. Disturbance in the way in which one's body weight or shape is experienced, undue influence of body weight or shape on self-evaluation, or denial of the seriousness of the current low body weight.

- In postmenarcheal females, the existence of amenorrhea, which is the absence of at least three consecutive menstrual cycles.

The *DSM-IV-TR* (APA, 2000, p. 589) sets out the following subtypes of anorexia nervosa:

- Restricting type: During the current episode of anorexia, the person has not regularly engaged in binge eating or purging behavior, for example, self-induced vomiting or misuse of laxatives, diuretics, or enemas. The weight loss is achieved by dieting, fasting, or excessive exercise.

- Binge eating/purging type: During the current episode of anorexia, the person has regularly engaged in binge eating or purging behavior, for example, self-induced vomiting or the misuse of laxatives, diuretics, or enemas. These behaviors are engaged in at least weekly.

Bulimia Nervosa

Bulimia nervosa is identified by frequent changes in weight, with periods of uncontrollable binge eating and purging. A binge is defined as eating a large amount of food in a small amount of time, which is then followed by some form of purging. Although an individual may not demonstrate each of the following symptoms, the *DSM-IV-TR* (APA, 2000, p. 594) defines bulimia nervosa as involving all of the following:

- Recurrent episodes of binge eating occur. An episode of binge eating is characterized by both of the following:

    —Eating, in a discrete period of time (e.g., within any 2-hour period), an amount of food that is definitely larger than most people would eat during a similar period of time and under similar circumstances.

    —Feeling a lack of control over eating during the episode (e.g., a feeling that one cannot stop eating or control what or how much one is eating).

- Engaging in recurrent inappropriate compensatory behavior to prevent weight gain, such as self-induced vomiting; misuse of laxatives, diuretics, enemas, or other medications; fasting; or excessive exercise.

- The binge eating and inappropriate compensatory behaviors both occur, on average, at least twice a week for 3 months.

- Self-evaluation is unduly influenced by body shape and weight.

- The disturbance does not occur exclusively during episodes of anorexia nervosa.

Eating Disorder Not Otherwise Specified

DSM-IV-TR (APA, 2000) has also identified a category termed eating disorder not otherwise specified (EDNOS), which refers to all eating disorders that do not meet the criteria for anorexia nervosa or bulimia nervosa. For example, some females may meet the criteria for anorexia but experience regular menses or an individual may use inappropriate compensatory behaviors after eating a small amount of food but maintain a normal body weight. The EDNOS category is an important advancement in the identification of eating disorders because many individuals do not meet the specific criteria for a formal diagnosis of anorexia nervosa or bulimia nervosa, but they do demonstrate eating patterns and behaviors that are unhealthy and require treatment. Having the ability to classify them as EDNOS provides a more accurate measure of the number of individuals with eating disorders and offers opportunities for treatment that might not otherwise be available. Included in EDNOS is the proposed category "binge eating disorder," which describes people who binge eat periodically but do not use a purging method and are usually overweight (Peterson and Mitchell, 1999).

Anorexia Athletica

Substantial research and anecdotal experience over the last 50 years have demonstrated the benefits of exercise for physical and mental health (Hays, 1999). However, excessive exercise in terms of frequency, duration, and intensity can be harmful. In recent years, another form of eating-disordered behavior, anorexia athletica, that involves excessive exercise, has been identified. Anorexia athletica refers to compulsive exercising that is aimed at controlling or reducing body weight but has serious health consequences (Sundgot-Borgen, 1993).

Individuals with this condition are obsessed with exercise; sacrifice work, school, and relationships to exercise; and are preoccupied with food, calories, and body shape. They are rarely satisfied with their efforts or accomplishments and justify their behavior by defining themselves as athletes striving to be their best. People suffering from anorexia athletica appear to be addicted to exercise in the same way as abusers of drugs, alcohol, and gambling (Prussin, Harvey, and DiGeronimo, 1992). Excessive exercise has several causes that need to be fully explored. For example, excessive exercise can be attributed to a distorted body image (Prussin et al., 1992). Dissatisfaction with body image is a growing problem, particularly among young women, because popular culture communicates an "ideal" and yet, for most, unattainable body shape (Garner, Garfinkel, Schwartz, and Thompson, 1980). Symptoms of anorexia athletica include a compulsive need to exercise, a drastic reduction in caloric intake, and the experience of anxiety when exercise is not possible (Sundgot-Borgen, 1993). Unlike bulimia nervosa, excessive exercise is the means by which calories are purged. To date, there is little research on this newly identified eating disorder.

Bigorexia

Bigorexia is a new term used to describe an eating disorder that is most commonly found in males (Pope, Phillips, and Olivardia, 2000). It has alternatively been labeled muscle dysmorphia, and it has been suggested that this condition belongs in the diagnostic manual as a category of male eating disorders (Olivardia, Pope, and Hudson, 2000). Bigorexia is similar to anorexia in that the individual has an extremely distorted body image, but men with bigorexia see themselves as too small. Bigorexia is common among bodybuilders and weightlifters, who live in a culture that admires heavily muscled physiques. Those with bigorexia express their eating disorder with a preoccupation with weight gain, muscularity, weightlifting, weight-gain supplements, and, often, illegal drugs such as steroids and human growth hormone (Pope et al., 2000)

Prevalence of Eating Disorders

The prevalence of eating disorders varies greatly depending on the specific disorder that is examined and the particular population sampled. It may be that the prevalence of eating disorders is underestimated because of the social unacceptability of eating disorders, leading individuals with eating disorders to deny that they have this problem.

Coach's Perspective

At the age of 15, the athlete qualified for the Olympic team. She was required to move away from home to centralize with the team for about 10 months in another part of the country. The average age of the team members was about 23 years. During this period, the athlete lived with a family in a supportive home environment. Around this time, the athlete experienced significant changes in her body shape and size. These changes were normal considering her body type and the fact that she had reached puberty. She mentioned to me that she was 14 pounds heavier than when she was junior national champion at age 14. Since she was only 5 feet, 2 inches tall, this was an obvious weight change and she was very bothered by it. Despite my attempts and other athletes' attempts to tell her that it was unwise to compare her body now with her body at the age of 14, she remained fixated on this fact. In addition to this, the head coach of the team at the time frequently made inappropriate comments about body shape and size to many of the athletes and often told this particular athlete that she needed to lose weight or simply confirmed the athlete's feelings that she needed to lose weight.

■　■　■　■　■

Athlete's Perspective

I was very successful at a young age, making the senior national team at 15. That first summer was the best and worst of my life. It was the start of an 8-year international swimming career and the start of my descent into bulimia.

After my breakthrough summer of racing, my club team went to Hawaii for a training camp. The goal of the camp was to maintain our fitness and keep us swimming through the last 2 weeks of summer. Traditionally this is a period when most swimmers take their only break all year, but that November, the World Championship Trials were being held and there was no time for a break. Usually training camps were the hardest training of the year, but this camp was meant to be somewhat fun. But in 2 weeks I gained 15 pounds from overeating and training only once a day.

I have always wondered whether my weight would have balanced itself out when I increased my training in the fall, had I been left alone. I have also wondered whether that weight gain or some of it was a necessary part of hitting puberty, getting stronger, or growing taller. Neither question will ever be answered because as soon as we returned from Hawaii, my coach came down on me, telling me I needed to lose all the weight. And that is when it all began; my adult male coach was able to manipulate me into thinking it was my decision and my goal to lose the weight.

So "we" created a goal weight that I needed to reach (which was lower than the weight I had been at when I made the national team) as well as target weights I had to hit along the way. If I did not hit the targets I would get yelled at and ridiculed, and on one occasion I was kicked out of the top group in our club for a week and sent to swim with the 12-year-olds. At 17, when I finally stopped growing, I was 6 feet 2 inches tall and weighed 150 pounds; never in my life have I been overweight or even close to being out of shape. But the pressure from my coach was relentless, and I lived my last 3 years of high school on a permanent diet trying to train 20 hours a week, all the time bingeing and purging to escape the possibility of gaining any weight. I was convinced that if I gained even a quarter of a pound, I would swim slowly.

For my younger teammate, life was even worse. She remembers going to the bathroom after a hard set that she had performed well in and making herself throw up anything that was in her stomach. She did it because she believed she was doing everything it would take to be the best swimmer. Most days, she threw up at least six times a day. However, she admits that on days when there was no one else in the house, she threw up 30 to 40 times a day. "I could spend the entire day eating and throwing up."

■ ■ ■ ■ ■

Prevalence Among Women

According to *DSM-IV-TR* (APA, 2000), the incidence of anorexia nervosa is approximately 0.5%, but other sources indicate it may be as high as 1.0% in populations at risk, for example, female dancers, female athletes in weight-conscious sports, and adolescent females (Garfinkel et al., 1996; Mitchell, 2001). Onset often occurs at the time of puberty but may also occur later in adolescence when young women enter college and fear gaining the "freshman 15." Young girls at puberty are susceptible for several reasons. First, they naturally gain weight as part of the maturation processes at a time when they feel growing pressure from popular culture, their peers, and sometimes their parents to be slim. Uncertainty and anxiety increase as they face numerous new stressors, such as establishing an adult identity and deal-

ing with their emerging sexuality and intimate relationships, new academic challenges, newly found freedom, and choices about their futures (Striegel-Moore, 1993).

Approximately 1% to 2% of women in the general population fit the diagnostic criteria for bulimia nervosa (Mitchell, 2001). Studies in the early 1980s that primarily examined college-age students reported bulimia prevalence ranging from 3.8% to 13% (Halmi, Falk, and Schwartz, 1981; Mitchell, Pyle, and Eckert, 1981), with 87% of these being women. The difference in recent statistics is partly due to more refined definitions of what constitutes bulimia nervosa. If prevalence rates include the occasional presence of bulimic behavior without a full diagnosis of bulimia nervosa or binge eating disorder, the percentage increases to between 50% and 70% of women, including adolescents (Mitchell, 2001).

Prevalence Among Men

Women appear to be more vulnerable than men to developing an eating disorder because of the current cultural standards of thinness impressed on women by Western popular culture (Andersen, Cohn, and Holbrook, 2000). However, men may be catching up in terms of those who have diagnosed eating disorders, those who diet excessively, and those who spend increasing amounts of money on cosmetic surgery (Andersen et al., 2000). Estimates comparing the number of men to women who have eating disorders range from 1 in 6 to 1 in 10, but these numbers may be underreported because many men may be unwilling to admit that they have a "woman's disease" (Andersen et al., 2000). In contrast, the percentage of men who are diagnosable with binge eating disorder is probably equal to that of women. Even though males may constitute 5% to 10% of people with anorexia nervosa, they are typically more concerned with having a muscular body, whereas women are more concerned about thinness (Mitchell, 2001). Unfortunately, because the categorization of bigorexia as an eating disorder is so recent, no studies of its prevalence have been published.

Prevalence Among Athletes

Adding the pressures of the sport culture to the causes of eating disorders in the general population increases the risks among athletes. Athletes may have a higher incidence than the general population because of characteristics associated with competitive sports, such as performance standards; perfectionism; coach, media, family, and community pressure; and peer influence (Sundgot-Borgen, 1993).

Research has estimated that approximately 63% of all female athletes develop symptoms of an eating disorder between 9th and 12th grade (American College of Sports Medicine, 1998). Although this finding does not mean that such a large percentage of athletes develop full-blown eating disorders, it is an indication of the serious impact of weight, body image and shape, and performance pressures on athletes. Although research limitations make it difficult to determine the exact prevalence of eating disorders in athletes, some studies have reported disordered eating behavior in 1% to 75% of female athletes and as high as 8% of elite male athletes (Brownell, 1995; Sundgot-Borgen, Skarderud, and Rodgers, 2003).

Eating disorders are most common among athletes who compete in three types of sport: weight-limit sports, aesthetic sports, and endurance sports. Sports that have objective weight limits, such as wrestling, boxing, rowing, and judo, often lead athletes to develop eating disorders. In an effort to "make weight" or to drop down to a lower weight class, athletes succumb to the pressure and engage in disordered eating behaviors. Some of these athletes resort to periodic purging of food to lose weight quickly. Others resume normal eating after the competitive season ends. Still others get caught in these unhealthy eating habits and develop a chronic eating disorder.

Aesthetic sports are those in which athletes are judged on their body shape and appearance, for example, figure skating, synchronized swimming, and gymnastics. Because skill level between athletes at a given level of competition is so close, the outcomes of these sports are often determined by how much an athlete's body shape coincides with the sport's aesthetic ideal. This issue is further exacerbated by the outfits in which many of these athletes must compete, such as swimsuits, leotards, and form-fitting costumes. Although often these outfits serve a functional purpose, they nevertheless emphasize athletes' physiques and can create extreme body consciousness in athletes.

Endurance sports, such as long-distance running, swimming, and triathlon, have propagated a misconception that "the thinner I am and the lower my body fat, the faster I will be." At times, an athlete will lose a few pounds and see an improvement in performance. This connection can lead athletes to believe that additional weight loss will lead to similar increases in performance. Often the opposite occurs and performance is hampered by further weight loss.

Symptoms of Eating Disorders Among Athletes

Eating disorders become evident as athletes begin to show a variety of physical, psychological, and behavioral symptoms. The number and frequency of these symptoms determine whether an athlete is diagnosed with a full-blown eating disorder or simply eating-disordered behaviors. The challenge for those who care about and care for athletes who demonstrate these symptoms is that the symptoms are often difficult to detect, easy to hide, or misinterpreted.

Coach's Perspective

The family was concerned that the athlete did not eat enough at mealtime and brought this to the attention of the team nutritionist. The family also expressed that often they would find large quantities of garbage and food in her room. The athlete rarely drank or ate snacks during training and when traveling with the team would eat next to nothing at meals. She claimed she was a vegetarian and could not eat meat. From time to time she would miss a couple of days of training claiming that she had the flu. As the year progressed the natural changes in her body became more pronounced and it was obvious that she was becoming increasingly self-conscious and unhappy about her body image. She mostly wore baggy clothes and always had a towel wrapped around her as soon as she got out of the water. On a tour following the Olympic Games, I remember hearing one of the other athletes comment that the athlete had eaten seven ice cream cones in one day.

■　■　■　■　■

Athlete's Perspective

I am very scared about my future. At age 12, I had anemia and that was a pre-eating disorder. I stopped drinking milk at dinner around age 15, replacing milk with water because I did not want the extra calories. It is only now at age 27 that my periods are regular, but I worry that I will have osteoporosis or other complications from my eating disorder.

I started purging by using laxatives because it was the first thing I could get my hands on. I also liked the control it gave me, I knew when I would be at my lightest weight, and I would time it so that I could be lightest in the mornings before we got weighed in. I tried several times to make myself throw up, but I spent the following hours coughing, and it kept giving me a sore throat and bloodshot eyes. So I stayed with laxatives, and when one dose stopped working, I would increase the number I took, until by the end I needed to take 12 doses at once.

I wish I had known that I was actually hurting my performance. There were times when I realized I was tired from lack of food or being dehydrated, but I was convinced that my body weight was the most critical factor to fast swimming. If I knew about the physiological or psychological effects of laxative abuse, I am certain I would have never started. I was constantly trying new vitamin, mineral, or herbal remedies to recover faster and train harder. I got plenty of sleep, drank lots of water, and ate healthy foods. I trained as hard as I could in the pool and in the weight room, pushing myself and demanding perfection. I was very health conscious, and that is what is so incredible; on the outside I appeared to be a perfectly healthy swimmer, but on the inside I was destroying any good I had done by bingeing and purging.

In high school I was depressed because of my waning popularity in school as I chose 9 p.m. bed times and weekends of swim meets over hanging with school friends. I suffered and still suffer from stomach problems, I got mononucleosis my last year of high school, and I developed cysts in my wrists that caused me to lose many hours of training. But what is most troubling is that by my third year of college I had tendinitis in both shoulders, an injury that haunted me the last 5 years of my swimming career and still bothers me today. I cannot say with any certainty whether these injuries and problems were related to my eating disorder, but I cannot say they weren't either.

■ ■ ■ ■ ■

Physical Symptoms

Many physical symptoms can indicate the presence of an eating disorder. Some of these symptoms are subtle, others can be misattributed to other causes, and still others are clear indications that an athlete may have an eating disorder. Awareness of the most common symptoms of eating disorders is essential for early detection and treatment. Physical symptoms can be broadly divided into two categories: musculoskeletal and immunological. Moreover, the symptoms of anorexia and bulimia can vary.

Musculoskeletal symptoms of anorexia include muscle weakness, overuse injuries, stress frac-tures, significant weight loss, and lanugo (fine hair growth). Immunological symptoms of anorexia consist of fatigue, intolerance to cold, dehydration, amenorrhea, and gastrointestinal problems. Musculoskeletal symptoms of bulimia include muscle weakness and cramps, tooth decay and gum disease, calluses on fingers from inducing vomiting, and frequent weight fluctuations. Immunological symptoms of bulimia are electrolyte abnormalities, swollen parotid glands, dehydration, menstrual irregularities, and gastrointestinal problems (Thompson and Sherman, 1993).

Psychological Symptoms

The psychological symptoms are more difficult to detect because they are evident in the thoughts and emotions of eating-disordered athletes. Like the physical symptoms, psychological symptoms differ between the two eating disorders. People with anorexia display an obsessive preoccupation with food and weight. They are also often diagnosed as either clinically depressed or suffering from anxiety (Thompson and Sherman, 1993).

Approximately 30% of patients with bulimia nervosa present a history of sexual abuse (Fallon and Wonderlick, 1997). It has also been estimated that half of the population suffering from bulimia nervosa have some type of personality disorder such as anxiety, affective, personality, and dissociative disorders (Wonderlick and Mitchell, 1998). This rate may appear high; however, there is not a single obvious pattern of symptoms and most often multiple symptoms should be considered (Tobin and Griffing, 1996).

Behavioral Symptoms

Noting behavioral symptoms of eating disorders provides the best chance of identifying athletes with an eating disorder. People with anorexia tend to withdraw from social situations, particularly during meals when they feel self-conscious about their eating habits. They engage in and rigidly adhere to rituals with food in which there is often contact with food but not ingestion such as moving food around the plate without eating a bite or spitting out food after chewing. Anorexic individuals often exercise well beyond what is healthy or beneficial to their sport. They also exercise while injured against the recommendations of sports medicine professionals. Those with anorexia weigh themselves often, looking for any evidence of weight loss. They also often appear restless and have difficulty sleeping (Thompson and Sherman, 1993).

Behaviors of people with bulimia are focused on concealing their binge-and-purge cycles. Those with bulimia binge alone and guard their secret closely. They act innocent when large amounts of food are missing. They make frequent and lengthy trips to the bathroom and often speak of having stomach upset to excuse those trips. People with bulimia are often agitated and can also be depressed, moody, and self-critical. They are often found with laxatives and diuretics. They may also exercise excessively and attempt to diet until their restraint fails and they engage in purging behavior (Hall and Cohn, 1992).

Female Athlete Triad

The female athlete triad is a syndrome that can affect females in any sport and often goes unrecognized. This triad refers to "three distinct yet interrelated disorders that are often seen in active women and girls: amenorrhea, osteoporosis and disordered eating" (Nattiv and Lynch, 1994, p. 60). The actual prevalence of the triad is not yet known, but anecdotal evidence suggests that it is a growing problem.

Amenorrhea occurs when a woman is not menstruating, has irregular menstrual periods, or has not had a menstrual period by the age of 16. Amenorrhea is a signal that estrogen in the body is dangerously low. Estrogen is essential to the preservation of normal calcium levels and bone density, and low levels of this hormone are associated with osteoporosis, a disease that is characterized by low bone mass and the premature weakening of bones. Athletes can develop stress fractures as a result of osteoporosis as well as skeletal problems later in life. Skeletal damage depends on the length and severity of the menstrual irregularity and the nature of the sport in which the athletes participate. Elevated cortisol levels from excessive physical training may also contribute to the bone loss (Grinspoon and Thomas, 2000).

For some female athletes with a previously normal menstrual cycle, a condition known as secondary amenorrhea may occur. Secondary amenorrhea has long been linked with physical training, occurs in 2% to 5% of the general female population, and has been found to occur in 3% to 66% of female athletes (Nattiv, Agostini, Drinkwater, and Yeager, 1994; Otis, 1992; Rosen and Hough, 1988; Shangold, Rebar, Wentz, and Schiff, 1990; Sundgot-Borgen, 1994). Although researchers have been studying this phenomenon for decades, there is still not a clear understanding of its cause (Wilmore and Costill, 2004). However, if the lack of menstrual cycles continues for a prolonged period of time, the level of estrogen and progesterone will be low and, as a result, the menstrual cycle will be disrupted. Women with amenorrhea may start to lose bone mineral density within a year. This loss of bone, if left untreated, appears to be partially irreversible, such that a young female athlete may end up with a bone mineral density comparable to that of a woman in her 50s (Drinkwater and Nilson, 1984).

Disordered eating, considered in the context of the female athlete triad, refers to a spectrum of abnormal eating patterns that may include bingeing and purging; fasting; use of laxatives, diuretics, or diet pills; excessive exercise; a preoccupation with food; dissatisfaction with body shape, weight, or size; fear of gaining weight, or a distorted body image. As a part of the female athlete triad, patterns of disordered eating pose a significant, long-term threat to the health of the female athlete.

Associated Health Problems

A multitude of health problems accompany disordered eating. No studies to date have determined the precise long-term effects of eating disorders, but there are immediate and significant effects on the athlete's body. Restrictive eating behaviors fail to balance the body's energy expenditures with intake. Thus, the restriction reduces the metabolic rate and causes changes in the musculoskeletal, cardiovascular, endocrine, and thermoregulatory systems (Mitchell, Pomeroy, and Adson, 1997).

Coach's Perspective

The team won a silver medal at the Olympic Games. The majority of the athletes retired at this point but naturally because of her youth this athlete planned to continue. The dissatisfaction with her postpubescent body continued and thus began a cycle of losing and gaining weight. At the next long-term training camp (3 months), the athlete missed approximately 2 months of training because of concussion-like symptoms encountered after she hurt her head and neck executing a team lift. After many tests and months of observation, the medical personnel concluded that there was no physical cause for the injury. The next summer during a 6-week training camp, the neck injury appeared again just days before the competition. Throughout the course of this training camp, the athlete appeared lethargic, often depressed, and emotionally detached from the team; exhibited poor endurance; and clearly did not have the physical energy required to handle the training load. She often missed training because of illness.

■ ■ ■ ■ ■

Athlete's Perspective

After quitting swimming, my young teammate finally asked for help when she was at the doctor's office complaining once again of a sore throat. She told her doctor how she could not stop herself from the cycle of eating and throwing up, so she was prescribed Prozac at the highest dose possible of 60 mg per day. She recalls that the day she left the office with the prescription in her hand, she already felt better. The Prozac, she said, helped her almost immediately, controlling the obsessive part of her bulimia. She was also more relaxed and less worried about her weight.

■ ■ ■ ■ ■

Physiological Effects of Anorexia Nervosa

One negative effect of starving is that it disrupts the musculoskeletal system. As the starvation begins, the body will burn fat. When all the fat stores have been exhausted, ketosis occurs, where muscle tissue is metabolized and burned as fuel. As a result, there is a decrease in the volume of cardiac muscle and an increase in cardiac arrhythmias, which together can lead to sudden death in people with anorexia (Crisp, Callender, Halek, and Hsu, 1992). The loss of fat and muscle mass also interferes with the body's ability to regulate body temperature, and, as a result, core and peripheral body temperature decrease as the body attempts to conserve resources (Drinkwater, Bruemner, and Chesnut, 1990). Finally, people with anorexia experience a loss of muscular strength attributable to the decrease in skeletal muscle mass (Isner, Roberts, Heymsfield, and Yager, 1985). Amenorrhea also occurs, which increases the risk of stress fractures and low bone density (Clark, Nelson, and Evans, 1988).

Blood chemistry is altered as a result of dehydration that primarily affects blood urea nitrogen and liver function. There is a decrease in white blood corpuscles, so that the effectiveness of the immune system declines and people with anorexia become more vulnerable to illness. The emergence of anemia is also an increased risk. Anorexics experience delayed gastric emptying, bloating, constipation, diarrhea, and swelling in the parotid gland (Geliebter et al., 1992; Kinzl, Biebl, and Herold, 1993).

Physiological Effects of Bulimia Nervosa

People with bulimia have a host of other health problems that must be considered. Foremost among them are digestive-gastrointestinal problems that arise from regular purging. Bulimic patients may report more physical complaints than anorexic patients even though their health is usually not as compromised (Mitchell, Pomeroy, and Adson, 1997). The most important of these effects are dehydration and electrolyte abnormalities. Fluid loss affects blood volume, which can reduce oxygen-carrying capacity, aerobic capacity, and endurance (U.S. Olympic Committee, 1987). Because the body is 60% to 70% water, no single nutrient deficiency can affect performance as much as insufficient water (Whitney and Hamilton, 1987).

Regular purging causes individuals to experience salivary gland and pancreatic inflammation, with an increase in serum amylase, esophageal and gastric erosion, and dysfunctional bowel. The consistent vomiting also erodes dental enamel and reduces thyroid metabolism (Mitchell, Pomeroy, and Adson, 1997).

Special Risks to Athletes

A few aspects of eating disorders can create special risks to athletes. The most important determinant of the impact of disordered eating on athletes is its length and severity. The effects can vary dramatically depending on the athlete's family history, the athlete's health status before the disorder, and the physical demands of the sport. As athletes fail to replenish their bodies with fuel, energy stores (muscle glycogen) are depleted, fatigue sets in, and performance and daily functioning become impaired. The muscles start to deteriorate, which leads to decreased strength, speed, and endurance; the emergence of overuse injuries; and slowed recovery from injury and illness. Without adequate fluid intake, dehydration occurs, which leads to earlier onset of physical fatigue and fluid and electrolyte imbalances (Garner, Vitousek, and Pike, 1997; Mitchell, Pyle, Eckert, Hatsukami, and Lents, 1983). As previously indicated, the heart and circulatory system can be significantly affected, which affects oxygen utilization as reflected in reduced blood volume and heart function (Isner et al., 1985; Perriello, 2001). Finally, athletes who starve their bodies of the essential nutrients experience a decline in mental acuity, in which thinking, focusing, information processing and analysis, and decision making are impaired. Eating-disordered athletes who perform in high-risk sports, because of the associated decrease in physical and mental functioning, put themselves and others in danger of injury or death.

Causes of Eating Disorders

Eating disorders are not caused by a single factor but by a combination of influences that can be difficult to identify. Biochemical imbalances, genetic predisposition, personality characteristics, cultural influences, and a dysfunctional family background are all associated with eating disorders (Garner and Garfinkel, 1980; Harvard Medical School, 1997; Jack, 2001; Kaye, 1995; Klump, Kaye, and Strober, 2001; Lock et al., 2001; Szabo, 1996; Vitousek and Manke, 1994; Wonderlich and Mitchell, 2001). The presence of one or several of these contributors, although not necessarily causally linked, can put athletes at a higher risk for developing an eating disorder.

Coach's Perspective

There seem to be a number of factors that cause eating disorders. I have found that athletes with very intense type A personalities are at risk. This type of personality coupled with being in an aesthetic, judged sport can often lead to disordered eating. Quite often, the athletes have an overweight mother or sister. Their desire "not to be like mom" can contribute to the development of an eating disorder. Sometimes when an athlete has gone through a difficult emotional experience, an eating disorder can develop. This is usually a cry for attention or help. The culture of the sport can contribute to the development of an eating disorder. For example, if younger athletes have role models who have disordered eating, there is a higher probability that the younger athletes will adopt similar behaviors.

■　■　■　■　■

Athlete's Perspective

When I look back on my teen years, there were signs that I was susceptible to an eating disorder. The summer I first qualified for the national team, the team sport psychologist conducted a profile of me, which I found while cleaning out my parents' attic. The profile measured my self-esteem as a swimmer and as a person, as well as a variety of other factors such as precompetition nerves. The sport psychologist noted that my self-esteem as a swimmer was off the charts, whereas my self-esteem as a person was extremely low, and he pointed out that it could be a problem if I continued to see myself as only a swimmer and did not improve my view of myself as a person.

Over the next 3 years of high school I thought I was ugly, fat, and unpopular, and as a result I was depressed and my low self-esteem contributed to the development of my eating disorder. But the difficulties of puberty only provided the foundation for the brainwashing that was to come from my coach and teammates.

I have a wonderful family who supported my swimming career with the perfect balance of encouragement and understanding. My parents and brother are extremely athletic and our family kitchen was always stocked with the healthiest foods. We never had any cookies or goodies in our house, so as a treat I would bake chocolate chip cookies sometimes. But at some point I took our healthy lifestyle a step too far. I stopped eating foods with any fat; I purchased diet shakes, which led to my secret purchase of diet pills and eventually to laxatives. Then, when I baked cookies I would eat the whole batch in 2 hours, eating half the dough before cooking and the rest after they were cooked. My parents were aware of my desire to stay slim, and they even gave me a scale when I asked for one for my birthday, but I began to hide the important signs of my problem, and it was not until I was 23, 4 years after I had last purged, that I finally told my parents.

■　■　■　■　■

Biochemistry and Genetics

Some theorists suggest that some eating disorders are linked to biochemical disturbances such as hypothalamic, pituitary, or limbic system dysfunction (Chowdhury et al., 2003; Kaye, 1995). In addition, individuals who have been diagnosed with an eating disorder are responsive to antidepressant medications, particularly selective serotonin reuptake inhibitors (SSRIs), such as Prozac, suggesting that serotonin dysregulation plays a role in the onset of an eating disorder (Garner and Needleman, 1997).

Recent twin and family studies suggest that more than 50% of the variance in eating disorders can be accounted for genetically (Klump et al., 2001). Recent research shows that people with anorexia may have inherited from their parents a longer form of DNA in the norepinephrine transporter gene, which makes them twice as likely to develop anorexia as those who inherited the shorter form of the DNA (Urwin and Beumont, 2002, cited in Sheldon, 2002). This genetic predisposition causes individuals with this type of DNA to supermetabolize norepinephrine, using up their supplies when dieting. The more they diet, the more depleted they become, and a vicious cycle is established. From this perspective, anorexia nervosa may be considered both a biochemical and a psychological disorder, because life events appear to trigger the genetic and biochemical predisposition.

Personality

The most prominent personality characteristic exhibited by anorexic people is obsessiveness associated with pronounced perfectionism (Karwautz, Troop, Rabe-Hasketh, Collier, and Treasure, 2003; Serpell and Troop, 2003; Sutandar-Pinnock, Woodside, Carter, Olmstead, and Kaplan, 2003). A portion of the obsessive behavior may be caused by the state of starvation, but some individuals with anorexia have stable obsessive personality traits such as extreme neatness, conscientiousness, rigidity, and preoccupation with doing things right (Serpell and Troop, 2003). These characteristics often precede the eating disorder and continue once the anorexic patient has recovered (Szabo, 1996; Vitousek and Manke, 1994). It may be that these personality traits enable people to be "successful" at starving themselves because of the constraint and persistence required to deny themselves food (Szabo, 1996). This perfectionism also leads to an attempt to establish total control over what appears to be a controllable area of life, in this case, intake of food and how the body appears. However, the rigid control actually causes the person with anorexia to be very out of control of health and wellness. Within the anorexic group, there is also a tendency to be low in novelty seeking, high in harm avoidance, and low in self-directedness (Karwautz et al., 2003). Anorexic persons can also be described as socially awkward and isolated and often suffer from avoidant personality disorders (Serpell and Troop, 2003; Walsh and Garner, 1997). Johnson (1990) summed up the personality of anorexics as cautious, shy, rejection-sensitive, inflexible, concrete in their thinking, and harsh in their self-evaluation.

Prototypical bulimic patients, on the other hand, are extroverted, impulsive, and chaotic; have volatile moods; are easily bored; and can be oppositional (Johnson, 2001). In addition, they are often self-critical and self-rejecting and, at the same time, have difficulty accepting themselves, nurturing themselves, and protecting themselves (Wonderlich, Klein, and Council, 1996). In fact, a negative self-concept has been found to be predictive of the onset of bulimia nervosa (Ruderman and Besbeas, 1992). Some bulimic people are as perfectionistic as those with anorexia, and anorexic people who are the binge–purge type are more like bulimic people in that they often show other impulse control problems such as substance abuse (Walsh and Garner, 1997).

Sociocultural Influence

Although anorexia nervosa has been reported for centuries in the medical annals (Silverman, 1997), its prevalence has increased dramatically over the last 20 years leading researchers to believe that we may be having an epidemic of eating disorders (Hoek, 1995; Wilfley and Rodin, 1995). In addition, we have witnessed the appearance of bulimia nervosa as a relatively new phenomenon since the 1970s. Why the sudden increase? Some researchers suggest it may be attributable to the emphasis in Western cultures, in particular, on the importance of an unrealistically slim appearance for beauty and acceptance (Brownell, 1995; Leitenberg, Rosen, Gross, Nudelman, and Vara, 1988; Striegel-Moore, Silberstein, and Rodin, 1993; Wilfley and Rodin, 1995). It is understandable, then, why models and athletes are at additional risk for the development of an eating disorder, because they experience additional demands on weight and shape on top of the media pressure experienced by every woman in this society (Wilfley and Rodin, 1995).

The images offered to women in magazines, on television, and in film as the "ideal" female appearance have pushed young women to deprive themselves of food and to use strategies such as vomiting, laxatives, and excessive exercise to achieve this new culturally accepted definition of beauty. This influence is particularly destructive for teenage girls, who not only are faced with these images in the media but also struggle with peer acceptance, attention from boys, low self-esteem, academic pressure, and struggles to become independent. If a particular girl is already at risk because of biological factors, personality, or family background, her drive to achieve this idealized look regardless of its unhealthy consequences may lead to an eating disorder. In fact, it is estimated that 61% of senior high school girls diet to improve their appearance (Jones, 1997). Of note is the discrepancy between the current cultural ideal and the biological realities that limit the degree to which a woman can control her weight and shape (Wilfley and Rodin, 1995). Therefore, women are driven to compromise their health by dieting or exercising excessively or even purging in an attempt to achieve this unrealistic ideal. Sadly, the majority of models, Playboy centerfolds, and Miss Americas are at least 15% below their expected weight, which qualifies them for a diagnosis of anorexia nervosa (Wilfley and Rodin, 1995).

Family Dynamics

Not all eating-disordered families are dysfunctional (Jack, 2001); however, family dynamics often play a role in the onset and maintenance of disordered eating. A major factor may be faulty attachment to the parents. Kenny and Hart (1992) found that women diagnosed with eating disorders reported an attachment to their parents characterized by anxiety and avoidance as well as high levels of conflict and negative emotions. These same women reported low levels of warmth, trust, support, and independence in their family units. Focusing on appearance and the desire to change may distract the young woman from the emotional pain associated with a negative attachment to her parents (Cole-Detke and Kobak, 1996). In terms of parenting styles, fathers of eating-disordered girls are often emotionally unavailable and disengaged, whereas their mothers either are overly involved and put pressure on their daughters to look a certain way or are underinvolved, causing the daughter to feel unloved (Maine, 1999). Girls who develop eating disorders are often caretakers in their families and focus on others' needs and feelings instead of on their own. Even their own desire for food can be obscured (Maine, 1999). In addition, poor communication and unresolved conflict are often present in eating-disordered families, leading to a general sense of helplessness and lack of control. Food and weight control, then, become compensations (Maine, 1999).

Families of individuals with anorexia tend to avoid conflict, pressure themselves and their children to achieve perfection, compete with each other, have control issues, and have difficulty expressing emotions directly, especially anger (Maine, 1999; Root, Fallon, and Friedruch, 1986). Families of those with bulimia may readily admit problems but never resolve them, so that the atmosphere remains chaotic (Maine, 1999).

In contrast to anorexic families, bulimic families are apt to have open conflict, display impulsivity, become involved in a myriad of compulsive behaviors, and behave in erratic ways. Individuals with bulimia often perceive their families as conflicted, disorganized, detached, and nonnurturing (Wonderlich et al., 1996). In particular, they experience discord with their mothers concerning food, body image, and identity as a woman.

Regardless of whether the family dynamics are pathological, an eating disorder places a huge burden on the family system, and its effects should be carefully assessed and treated (Yager et al., 2000).

Vulnerability in Adolescence

When girls approach puberty, they are faced with unfamiliar and uncomfortable physical changes as well as personal and social changes that challenge them psychologically and emotionally. Boys at puberty are similarly challenged but seem to negotiate these changes more easily (Striegel-Moore, 1993). In an attempt to circumnavigate this mine field that often includes unhealthy images from the media, peer pressure, and perfectionistic attitudes and behaviors modeled by mothers, teenage girls can get caught up in the "superwoman identity," (Striegel-Moore, 1993, p. 156). The result is the pursuit of perfection in every part of their lives—academics, sports, performing arts, peer relationships, and appearance. This pressure becomes an unbearable burden and creates fertile ground for the onset of disordered eating. By focusing on their eating and weight, girls are able to mask the real problems they face, relieve some of their stress, and gain some sense of control, self-esteem, and well-being—however unhealthy—from these efforts.

Sport-Specific Contributors to Eating Disorders

The nature and culture of sports exacerbate the challenges young people face in Western society, placing them at risk for eating disorders. The importance of sports in many cultures, their physical demands, and the win-at-all-cost attitude contribute to an environment in which young athletes can succumb to the pressure and take a road that may provide short-term benefits but also have long-term costs.

Coach's Perspective

Although the athlete continued to experience some individual success, it was obvious that the star quality of her youth was fading. Other athletes who had not been comparable at a young age were improving more rapidly and their body types appeared to be more suited to the international norm for the sport. Again, while away at competitions the athlete would avoid eating meals with the team and spend a great deal of time in her room, often hoarding food in her room.

It is obvious that being in a judged sport contributes to the prevalence of eating disorders in young women. Simple comments regarding costuming and performance can be construed to be about an athlete's body. "The suit looks great" or "the suit is not flattering" can easily reinforce an athlete's image that she looks thin or heavy.

Judges and officials are some of the biggest culprits in feeding an athlete's perception of how she looks. Quite often I hear officials commenting about athletes looking heavy, having lost weight, or looking much better. These judges do not realize the impact of their comments or the level of their inappropriateness.

As a young coach I did not have the experience or knowledge that I have today. In my early years as a coach I often would suggest that an athlete needed to work with a nutritionist to develop a leaner appearance. I think that many young, inexperienced coaches are guilty of the same thing. They do not realize the potential cycle that this can set in motion.

Athletes who are generally successful in synchronized swimming are well proportioned, lean, and gorgeous. This sends a strong message to any athlete having high expectations for performance success as to what is required to succeed. The trend in recent years in the sport is toward achieving more height out of the water in all movements. The less body weight one has, the easier it is to get high out of the water, further reinforcing the need to have as little body fat as possible.

■ ■ ■ ■ ■

Athlete's Perspective

When I was 14 I moved up into the top group in my club, and that is when I began to learn from my coach and my teammates that I had to be skinny or I would not swim fast. Every morning our entire team was herded across the pool deck and weighed like cattle. Every one of those weigh-ins was recorded in my coach's log book (and mine as well) and if we gained weight we would hear about it. We were never allowed to make excuses. If we were menstruating and were bloated, that was never factored into the equation.

For my teammate, as swimming became more stressful throughout the season she ate more, which meant she threw up more. She said it felt like it was the only thing she could control. Every morning when she was weighed she would hope to be less than the day before and when she was lighter she felt on top of the world and she got a lot of positive attention from her coaches. When she weighed more she was often ignored or put down in front of the other swimmers.

At swim meets or in training camps, when eating was crucial to replacing expended calories and renewing energy systems, we hated eating in front of our coach. At least during training we could eat in the privacy of our homes, but when our coach was around the guilt of eating anything other than salad was overwhelming.

My coach had a way of berating us in front of the entire team, so everyone knew you had gained weight. But it was a girl's problem, and the talk in the locker room before every workout was about how on earth we were going to make our weight. We would try to urinate, we would spit in the gutters, and we would stop drinking water. We would try anything to make our weight, and that attitude eventually led a majority of us to eating disorders. Of the 14 girls in my group, I believe at least 12 of them had some type of eating disorder, from bulimia to anorexia to a general disordered eating mentality that went through the entire team. Our behavior was so normal to us that I never even understood that it was a problem until I left the team and went to college. It was then that I realized how dysfunctional our team dynamics were.

■ ■ ■ ■ ■

Myths About Weight and Body Shape

Athletes can develop misconceptions about the relationship of food, body weight, body image, and sport performance. Although physical requirements are associated with many sports, they can often be exaggerated or distorted in a way that encourages a preoccupation with food and weight that can lead to disordered eating.

One such myth is "thin to win," which asserts that athletes in certain sports must be thin to be successful. Although there are some sports where a lean body has performance advantages (e.g., gymnastics and running), there is ample evidence that this rule is not as rigid as many people believe. Low weight has benefits in many sports, but only to a point, after which both strength and endurance are compromised with additional weight loss.

A related myth is that body fat will hurt performance. Although body fat is not conducive to performance in many sports, it is common in many sports, such as weightlifting, American football, baseball, and golf. Even in a sport like swimming, some body fat is beneficial because it provides buoyancy. Body fat is also necessary physiologically in endurance sports as an important source of fuel.

A third myth is that athletes must look a certain way in some sports to be successful. The so-called aesthetic sports, such as gymnastics and figure skating, promote the image that female athletes must be tall and lean to receive high marks. Yet, a careful examination of athletes in these sports reveals a much greater variety of body types than is stereotypically associated with them.

Social Influence

Parents and coaches have a tremendous influence on young athletes in the attitudes they adopt about all aspects of their sport, including eating issues. Comments from coaches and parents—"You're going to need to put on 15 pounds if you hope to start next season" or "Don't you think you need to watch your weight if you're going to compete against all of those skinny girls?"—however well intended, can cause young athletes to become preoccupied with food, body weight, and body shape. The media, fans, and others in a sports community can also exert significant—and sometimes public—pressure on athletes to be overly aware of food and weight issues (Ryan, 2000).

Performance Pressure

The pressure to succeed does not have to come from outside forces. By their very nature, athletes are highly competitive individuals who place great pressure on themselves to perform their best and achieve their goals. As a part of their drive for success, athletes may be willing to do whatever it takes to win. A powerful example of the lengths that athletes will go to succeed comes from a survey of current or aspiring U.S. Olympians (Sturm and Diorio, 1998). When asked if they would take a banned substance if they were guaranteed victory and would not get caught, 98% said yes.

When asked if they would take a banned substance if they were guaranteed to win and not get caught, but the substance would kill them within 5 years, 50% still stated they would take the drug. If athletes at this level of competition are willing to die for success, it is easy to see that many athletes choose to starve themselves, purge using vomiting or laxatives, or exercise beyond what is beneficial to achieve their goals.

Treatment of Eating Disorders

The first step in any recovery process is for athletes to recognize and admit that they have a problem. Sometimes recognizing an eating disorder is difficult because unhealthy dieting, the first step in virtually every eating disorder, is accepted as common practice in many parts of society, particularly in sports. Eating-disordered athletes also go to great lengths to hide their eating habits. Additionally, the physical signs of eating disorders are often not apparent until the eating disorder is well advanced.

Eating disorders are often first recognized by parents, coaches, teachers, or friends. Athletes may vehemently deny that they have a problem and may react defensively or angrily. Others may be relieved that they have been discovered, happy not to have to hide their secret any longer. Some may seek help on their own because the eating disorder begins to take a toll on their performance, health, and happiness. Athletes may find, to their frustration, that losing weight causes performance to deteriorate because of increased fatigue, muscle weakness, injury, and illness. These athletes' commitment to achieving their goals may provide sufficient impetus to address their problem.

Coach's Perspective

It is difficult to know what to do when you observe that an athlete is clearly dissatisfied with her body image and you suspect that she has an eating disorder. It is a difficult issue to raise with an athlete. Referring the athlete to a nutritionist does not address the true issue, and often a nutritionist may not know that she is dealing with a potential eating disorder. I find that the best thing is to get the athlete into psychological counseling and hope that the athlete feels confident enough with the therapist to discuss the issue. This often takes a long time, and in the meantime it leaves you feeling pretty helpless as a coach.

One of the most difficult challenges in breaking an athlete's cycle of gaining and losing weight is the athlete's perception that "this has always worked for me in the past." Quite often athletes will lose weight in a precompetition training camp believing that they will be more successful at the meet if they are thin.

Another challenge facing the coach is the notion that this can spread to other members of the team. If a role model on the team has disordered eating, this sets a dangerous precedent, which others may follow.

■ ■ ■ ■ ■

Athlete's Perspective

I was lucky, escaping my eating disorder by leaving home and going to college. The environment there was completely different for me, and my coach nurtured me as an athlete and a person, unlike in high school. I stopped bingeing immediately, and within months I was no longer purging. But over the years and many clubs I have trained with, some of my teammates have not recovered as easily. Every team I have swum with has had at least one anorexic person, let alone the handfuls of teammates with bulimia and other eating disorders. One college teammate suffered from anorexia and her story is still ongoing.

An Olympic silver medalist and world record holder, my college teammate was the perfect swimmer, student, daughter, and friend. But underneath the surface she was suffering greatly. Even at the Olympic Games in 1996 she was starving herself, losing 5 pounds in 3 days between her two races at the Games. After the Olympics, her world came crashing down and finally the team doctors and trainers stepped in, forcing her to go to counseling and eventually convincing her to enter an eating disorders clinic.

At the outset she hated the clinic. She was scared, and the daily schedule of the clinic was strict, where all meals were planned and counselors sat at each table to make sure everything was eaten. She was assigned a doctor, a nutritionist, a psychiatrist, and a psychologist. She spent her days in individual and group therapy sessions, and within a week of she began to love it. She told me about the support she received there and how she did not want to leave.

When she did leave she tried swimming again, but her recovery was not perfect, and there were times of relapse and renewed recovery and finally the end of her swimming career. She says the one big thing missing from her recovery was the education of her friends, family, and, most important, her coach.

For my young high school teammate, she too had to quit swimming to escape. By the end of her career she hated her coaches and she hated what she had become. She was also unhappy and hated swimming. It was just before the Olympic Trials in 1996 that she began to feel like she just wanted it all to be over. She says that she had never trained so hard in her life and yet she had never felt so underprepared for a race.

She had gained 4 pounds in the 8 days leading up to the team's departure for the meet because she had sprained her ankle and was unable to swim for 5 days. When she did finally get back in the pool, the team had begun to back off from hard training. She says that as her feet flipped onto the wall at the halfway mark of her race, she remembers saying to herself that she just wanted it to be over and that it was not worth it anymore.

After spending the previous 2 or 3 years wishing to be in an accident or hit by a car, she at least managed to maintain the understanding that those thoughts were not right. She finished her race, did not qualify for the Olympics, and was the happiest she had been for years. She spent the next 4 months exercising and throwing up without anyone ever knowing, before she finally found the courage to ask a doctor for help.

She began taking a prescription antidepressant, and she had weekly appointments with a psychiatrist and a nutritionist, who weighed her. She wrote in a food diary and still had the occasional episode, but for the most part she was doing better and stopped taking the antidepressant. She relapsed but knew right away that she needed to go back on medication, and she spent the next 4 years getting herself out of feeling fat and throwing up.

Six years later, her self-esteem is much better than it used to be; she has not had an episode for more than a year, and before that it was about 10 months. She has not taken antidepressants for almost 2 years and she feels good. She complains now of her teeth, which are in very bad shape, and she is certain she will have to have four of them pulled in the next couple of years. She also hopes that she has not done too much permanent harm to herself but acknowledges that only time will tell.

My college teammate best explained the difficulty of recovery: "The difference between alcoholics or other addicts and people recovering from eating disorders is that we have to face our demons three times a day. It is easier to stay out of bars when you are an alcoholic, but you have to eat . . . you have to eat every day to live."

■ ■ ■ ■ ■

Evaluation

If the problem has not reached the stage of a full-blown eating disorder, nutritional counseling and education about the effects of an eating disorder on performance and health may offer adequate incentive for athletes to stop the harmful behaviors. However, if the problem has become a physical or psychological threat to the athlete's health and well-being, a thorough physical and psychiatric evaluation should be conducted by a trained professional such as a physician, psychiatrist, psychologist, social worker, or professional counselor. This evaluation should involve a detailed examination of the presenting problem, the possible causes, and the physical and psychological effects of the eating disorder. The assessment provides the evaluating professionals with information about the most appropriate treatment of action.

Treatment Setting

An important part of the comprehensive evaluation involves choosing the most appropriate setting in which the athlete can receive the best treatment for his or her diagnosed problem. If the eating-disordered athlete is able to function in daily life, is not seriously compromised medically, can adhere to the prescribed treatment program, can control his or her eating behavior, and is not suicidal, outpatient therapy may be the optimal choice. The benefits of an outpatient program are that the athlete can maintain some semblance of normality (e.g., continued school, friends, and extracurricular activities), can rely on a previously established social support network, and may be able to continue participating in sport. The risks of outpatient treatment include lack of consistent supervision, an environment that fosters disordered eating habits, and the vulnerability of athletes to relapse into unhealthy attitudes and behavior.

If the athlete is at serious risk physically, psychologically, or behaviorally, an inpatient facility that specializes in treating eating disorders would be most suitable. An inpatient facility offers a safe and secure setting with consistent support directed entirely at helping patients overcome the disorder. The dangers of an inpatient setting include forced admission, feelings of isolation and confinement, unfamiliarity, and loss of readily accessible support.

Treatment Team

Because of the multifaceted nature of eating disorders, a treatment team is usually more effective than a therapist working alone with the athlete. A typical treatment team consists of professionals who can address the spectrum of physical and psychological issues that are presented by eating-disordered athletes. Because of the complexity and dangers of eating disorders, it is essential that all members of the team have specific education, training, and experience in treating eating disorders. A physician monitors overall physical health, as well as specific presenting problems, such as electrolyte and hormonal imbalances and heart condition. A psychiatrist assesses the presence of contributing psychological disorders, such as depression or anxiety and, if needed, prescribes medications for their treatment. A nutritionist or dietitian offers education to eating-disordered patients, monitors their food intake and purging behaviors, and provides eating plans to help the patients develop healthy eating practices.

The treatment team also includes a variety of mental health professionals who address the multifaceted psychological and emotional nature of eating disorders. These mental health professionals can be licensed psychologists, social workers, marriage and family therapists, or professional counselors. A psychotherapist provides individual counseling that focuses on the issues that underlie the eating disorder. Because eating disorders are often rooted in a dysfunctional family dynamic, a family therapist often works with the patient's family to uncover and treat parental and sibling contributors to the eating disorder. Eating-disordered patients often participate in group therapy with others with similar problems to foster shared experience, interpersonal growth, shame reduction, and improved self-esteem.

In severe cases of eating disorders, inpatient hospitalization may be required. These programs involve highly structured and controlled settings in which eating-disordered patients who are at extreme risk or who have life-threatening complications can be monitored and treated. A treatment team, such as the one just described, would be involved. Additionally, a nurse would typically supervise daily health concerns and consult regularly with the physician and psychiatrist. Other professionals may include a therapist who works on body image concerns, an educator who addresses cultural contributors, and specialists who administer complementary treatments, such as art therapy and recreation therapy.

Treatment Approach

Once the treatment setting has been decided on and the treatment team is in place, the individual therapist chooses a treatment approach that takes into account the eating-disordered athlete's unique issues and needs. The relationship between the therapist and the athlete is paramount because, regardless of the treatment modality selected, the comfort and trust that develop between the two will play an essential role in the athlete's recovery.

Research examining recovery from eating disorders indicates that regardless of the treatment approach taken, two thirds of individuals diagnosed with an eating disorder recover within the first 3 years of treatment and 90% within 7 years. The other 10% may have a strong and resistant genetic and biochemical predisposition to eating disorders or may suffer from debilitatingly low self-esteem. Unfortunately, these people do not recover and most of them die prematurely. These eating-disordered patients who are unresponsive to treatment are usually patients with anorexia who also engage in bingeing and purging (Johnson, 1995).

Nutritional Counseling

Used in conjunction with other treatment modalities, nutritional counseling is an essential contributor to the recovery process. Nutritional counseling first educates eating-disordered athletes about the influence of diet on health and athletic performance and the harm that continued eating-disordered behavior can cause. Dietary counseling then provides a structured eating plan that encourages a gradual return to a healthy diet and normal eating habits. This guidance is especially important during the "washout" phase when, early in the recovery, the body is adjusting to healthy eating and the absence of purging (if purging is a part of the disorder; MacKenzie and Harper-Guiffre, 1992).

It is not uncommon for eating-disordered athletes to be resistant to—and sometimes show hostility toward—the nutritional counselor as new nutritional requirements are placed on them and they attempt to cling to their familiar, unhealthy eating habits. A trusting relationship between the nutritional counselor and the athlete that combines compassion and firmness is important for new eating habits to be learned and recovery to take hold.

Psychoeducational Therapy

For those athletes who have minimal symptoms and have been identified early, a 6- to 10-week psychoeducational treatment program, often conducted in a group setting, may be sufficient to halt extreme food restriction or bulimic behavior (Olmstead et al., 1991; Ordman and Kirschenbaum, 1986). A typical psychoeducational program includes information about what the eating disorder entails, the medical consequences, the difference between normal eating and disordered eating, the dangers of dieting, new coping strategies to replace the starving or bingeing and purging, ways to improve body image, ways to develop a better relationship with one's body, and ways to prevent relapse (Davis et al., 1992).

Cognitive–Behavioral Therapy

Cognitive–behavioral therapy (CBT) has been the most frequently used and studied treatment for bulimia nervosa and has demonstrated the most conclusive benefits in the treatment of bulimia-related behavior (Wilson, Fairburn, and Agras, 1997). CBT targets the faulty behaviors and thinking patterns believed to cause and maintain the eating-disordered behavior (Peterson and Mitchell, 1999). According to Fairburn, Marcus, and Wilson (1993), the cycle begins with low self-esteem, which leads to a preoccupation with shape and weight followed by strict dieting. When restraint fails, the dieter has episodes of binge eating followed by purging to counter the effects of the binges. This cycle continues and is maintained by the belief that without purging behavior, weight will reach undesirable levels. In actuality, bulimic patients who stop purging usually stop bingeing because of the fear of weight gain and their weight usually stays the same (Rosen and Leitenberg, 1982). CBT encourages the development of new, more rational ways of thinking and behaving through the use of food diaries, the establishment of a regular schedule of healthy meals and snacks, weekly weighing, self-control strategies, the elimination of dieting, new problem-solving skills, changing irrational beliefs that maintain the binge-and-purge cycle, and strategies to prevent relapse (Wilson et al., 1997). Materials have been developed for the application of CBT in individual or group therapy or in a self-help format (Fairburn, 1995). Treatment is focused on symptoms and does not typically deal with the deeper psychological issues underlying the disorder (Peterson and Mitchell, 1996). Most CBT treatment programs are designed to last approximately 20 sessions (Wilson et al., 1997). Although CBT is less effective for anorexic individuals and those with binge eating disorders than for those with bulimia, it is still the most effective treatment to date for most eating-disordered individuals (Peterson and Mitchell, 1996; Waller and Kennerley, 2003;

Wilson et al., 1997). CBT may be less effective for those with anorexia and some with severe bulimia because their personality disturbances are long term, are entrenched, and therefore qualify them for personality disorder diagnoses that are notoriously hard to treat (Johnson, 1990). These people usually have difficulty regulating their behaviors and emotions and cannot establish mature relationships. A problem-focused approach to their difficulties is therefore not sufficient to treat the eating disorder at its core (Johnson, 1995).

Interpersonal Psychotherapy

In recent years, interpersonal psychotherapy (IPT), a form of therapy that focuses on how people with bulimia deal with interpersonal relationships, has been helpful to many individuals who suffer from bulimia nervosa or binge eating disorder (Fairburn, 1997; Marcus, 1997). The typical IPT treatment course for eating disorders lasts 15 to 20 sessions (Fairburn, 1997; Wilfley et al., 2003). Rather than targeting the eating behavior specifically, IPT helps identify and modify the interpersonal problems that can trigger disordered eating. Three phases characterize the IPT protocol and include the following: identifying the problem areas in relationships, working on change in relating based on the identified problems, and consolidating change and preparing the person for future success. The specific domains targeted in relationship areas are grief, interpersonal deficits, role disputes, and role transitions. For example, the eating-disordered person may have developed symptoms after the loss of a significant other (grief), may be socially isolated and therefore turn to food for nurturing (interpersonal deficit), may have a significant conflict with a coworker or family member (role dispute), and may have recently undergone a stressful divorce (role transition; Wilfley et al., 2003). Typical treatment techniques include evoking painful feelings, confrontation and clarification, communication analysis, and behavior change techniques. Improvement is brought about by gaining insight into these problems, developing a new perspective on them, and changing the relationships that may have triggered the disordered eating (Fairburn, 1997).

Family Therapy

The ways in which families function appear to play a significant role in the onset of both anorexia and bulimia (Sherman and Thompson, 1990). Therapists must assess the dynamics of the eating-disordered athlete's family and explore the specific ways in which the family dynamic may have contributed to the disordered eating. The therapist must then make family therapy a part of the eating-disordered athlete's treatment program. The purpose of family therapy in this context is to help family members gain insight into how the family dynamics may be affecting the eating-disordered athlete and how the family is negatively affected by the eating disorder (Jack, 2001). The therapeutic process involves reengineering the family dynamic (e.g., roles, boundaries, consequences, control, emotions) so that family interactions promote healthy change in the eating-disordered athlete.

Of particular importance is improvement in the family's patterns of communication. An eating disorder can be a symbolic way for athletes to communicate to their parents thoughts and emotions that, because of fear, doubt, or worry, the athletes cannot convey directly (Johnson, 1990). When athletes with an eating disorder have the courage and comfort to speak directly about their concerns and fears to their parents, the eating disorder often loses its grip.

In conjunction with other treatment strategies such as nutritional counseling, weight restoration, and individual and group psychotherapy, family therapy is a primary treatment choice for adolescents with eating disorders (Yager et al., 2000). The purpose of family therapy is to remove the eating disorder and the focus on food and eating from the center of family relationships so that family members can become truly intimate (Maine, 1999). Techniques aim to educate the family about the eating disorder, resolve parental overinvolvement, extract the eating-disordered person from her parents' marital problems, allow room for individuation and identity building, prevent overprotection, deal with conflict directly, enhance healthy communication, and loosen the rigidity in patterns of relating (Jack, 2001). In addition, both the eating-disordered person and the parents must be relieved of blame so that self-acceptance and self-worth can be enhanced (Maine, 1999; Lock, Le Grange, Agras, and Dare, 2001). Family therapy is sometimes a difficult, often painful, process that requires responsibility, commitment, and courage on the part of all family members. The willingness of family members, particularly parents, to acknowledge and confront the roles they may have played in the development of the eating disorder will often determine the outcome of the treatment and the long-term health and well-being of the athlete.

Psychodynamic Therapy

Psychodynamic psychotherapy is rarely used as a first-order treatment for anorexia or bulimia (Kaplan, Saddock, and Grebb, 1994). Other modalities such as CBT, IPT, and family therapy have been more fully researched and therefore their effectiveness is easier to establish than the potential effectiveness of psychodynamic therapy, which is notoriously difficult to measure as well as time consuming and expensive to deliver (Herzog, 1995). However, the psychodynamic approach to treating anorexia nervosa has a long history and warrants consideration especially when other treatment modalities have been tried without success. Psychodynamic psychotherapy refers to any long-term approach that focuses on early childhood relationship difficulties, the relationship between the therapist and client, and the developmental processes that may have become derailed in an individual's background (Herzog, 1995; Johnson, 1995). Anorexic and bulimic patients with significant pathology may benefit from a focus on early childhood relationships with parents and the process of individuating from these caregivers in adolescence (Kaplan et al., 1994).

Within the psychodynamic framework, symptoms can be viewed as "symbolic efforts to communicate the nature and extent of the individual's struggle" (Johnson, 1995, p. 350). According to Johnson, if the drive for thinness is a symbolic attempt to resist overcontrol from an intrusive parent, for example, then weight restoration would not last over time unless this underlying dynamic has been explored and new coping strategies have developed. Herzog (1995) contended that psychodynamic psychotherapy should be the primary treatment approach for anorexic individuals who have significant character pathology and should be used in conjunction with other therapies for those who have chronic symptoms. Johnson (1995) also advised the use of psychodynamic psychotherapy with bulimic patients who have pathology that does not respond to briefer treatment approaches.

Drug Treatment

Pharmacotherapy is not the treatment of choice for eating disorders but can be helpful as an adjunct to other treatments (Bruna and Fogteloo, 2003). Antidepressant medications of all kinds (tricyclics, SSRIs, monoamine oxidase inhibitors, and others) have been found to be beneficial in the treatment of bulimia (Agras, Dorian, Kirkley, Arnow, and Bachman, 1987; Garfinkel and Walsh, 1997; Goldenstein, Wilson, Thompson, Potvin, and Rampey, 1995; Walsh, Hadigan, Devlin, Gladis, and Roose, 1991). SSRIs are used most frequently, not because they are more effective but because they have fewer side effects than the other antidepressants. Even when the bulimic individual does not exhibit symptoms of depression, SSRIs are often helpful and should be considered (Bruna and Fogteloo, 2003). SSRIs have also been shown to decrease binge eating in patients with binge-eating disorder (Bruna and Fogteloo, 2003).

In anorexia nervosa, there are currently no benefits of antidepressants during the acute treatment phase and no established benefit after weight has been regained (Garfinkel and Walsh, 1997). A psychiatrist or primary-care physician will often medicate a coexisting psychiatric condition, such as depression or anxiety, that will respond to medication. Antidepressant medication can sometimes decrease obsessive thinking, lift mood, and reduce hunger, which can cause some patients to be less afraid to eat and more willing to gain weight (Mitchell, 2001). Because anxiety is a common component of anorexia, minor tranquilizers may be used 20 to 40 minutes before meals to make it easier to eat (Garfinkel and Walsh, 1997). Other drugs that may be of help in certain anorexic clients include appetite enhancers, drugs that speed up gastric emptying (because the stomach emptying is slow in many anorexic and bulimic patients), and estrogens to protect the bones from osteoporosis (Garfinkel and Walsh, 1997; Garfinkel et al., 1996; Vaccarino, Kennedy, Ralevski, and Black, 1994). Some antipsychotics have been tried with clients who have severe distorted body image but with mixed results (Bruna and Fogteloo, 2003; La Via, Gray, and Kaye, 2000).

Consequences of Severe Anorexia Nervosa

Treating anorexia nervosa can be more difficult than treating bulimia nervosa, because anorexia nervosa has a chronic and insidious course, the genetic and biochemical influence makes it more resistant to change, there are more significant health implications, and the risk of death exists (Isner et al., 1985). If an anorexic is of very low body weight and has serious medical complications, she may be unable to participate in certain treatment modalities. In severe cases of anorexia where basic health is at risk, the patient must be admitted to an inpatient program in which she is forced to gain weight before psychotherapeutic interventions can be initiated. Once the anorexic patient's health has been stabilized, early interventions must include overcoming her fear of eating and changing her beliefs about body weight, shape, and image. Later in treatment, deeper issues, such as self-esteem, family problems, perfectionism, emotions, and self-identity, must be addressed.

The likelihood of recovery from anorexia is modest at best. Many anorexic patients recover in terms of regaining weight but continue to have problems with body image distortion, disordered eating, and other psychiatric difficulties (Yager et al., 2000). Unfortunately, at least 5% die prematurely. Anorexic people can lose so much weight, have such entrenched and distorted ways of thinking about food and weight, and sustain such damage to their bodies from this self-abuse that they cannot save themselves and are beyond help. The anorexia overwhelms these people physically and psychologically, and the downward spiral cannot be stopped. When death occurs, it usually results from starvation, electrolyte imbalance, or illnesses caused by a compromised immune system.

Prevention of Eating Disorders

Prevention of eating disorders is a complex task that must begin at an early age. Effective education may be the most important preventive tool available to protect children from eating disorders. Preventive education should include nutritional counseling, an understanding of the causes of eating disorders, a clear explanation of their symptoms, and resources that athletes can turn to for help (Jones, 1997). Athletes must also learn that eating disorders are counterproductive to their athletic and life goals. Parents, teachers, and coaches must be educated to understand how they may contribute to the development of an eating disorder, to recognize children who are vulnerable to eating disorders, to be aware of the early warning signs of eating disorders, and to know the correct course of action when an eating disorder presents itself.

The power that coaches have over athletes with respect to eating disorders cannot be overestimated. Coaches must maintain and communicate a healthy perspective on the importance of sport and be sensitive to societal pressures that can put young athletes at risk. They need to be knowledgeable of research on nutrition, eating disorders, sport training, and stress management. Coaches must be able to talk about and model healthy attitudes and habits toward food and weight. Finally, they need the courage to act quickly and decisively when an athlete is at risk.

Coach's Perspective

Giving athletes more psychological training and support at a younger age could help in preventing eating disorders. Ongoing education for coaches and officials is also necessary to develop a greater awareness of how to be constructive versus destructive in giving feedback. Addressing the emotional and psychological well-being of athletes is a huge part of coaching and probably the most significant factor in creating well-rounded individuals with high self-esteem and self-acceptance.

■　■　■　■　■

Athlete's Perspective

Prevention is extremely important. If you do not catch a young athlete early enough, there seems no way to stop an eating disorder until she is ready to admit that she has one, which could be years down the road. Actually preventing an eating disorder, however, is a difficult challenge.

Once I started down the road of bulimia, it was like an avalanche and there seemed no way to stop. During training, your emotions become so tangled up with your goals and your priorities that it seems impossible to change your behavior despite knowing that it is wrong. My two teammates and I were all unable to admit we had eating disorders until the end of a swimming cycle, season, or even career.

The only thing that would have helped me is if I had never stepped on a scale. To this day I refuse to step on one, except for my yearly physical. My coach had his own scale that he carried around in his bag so that when he weighed us, he knew that the scale would always be accurate. That scale went everywhere with us: to meets and training camps and to every morning workout.

Although I did not learn how to binge and purge from my coach, I did learn from him that the only way I was going to lose weight was by eating less. When we were "overweight" we didn't get asked to do extra running or swimming, which would have made some sense. Instead we were often prevented from training, meaning that our only option was to diet. Then I learned how to purge from my teammates.

I remember some discussion about a nutritionist, but that wasn't my problem because I ate a perfectly balanced, healthy diet in the beginning. My problem was that I was told that I was fat and that being fat was going to make me swim slowly.

I think the only way to prevent eating disorders is through coach education. Male coaches dominate swimming, and some see "overweight" swimmers and think slow swimmers. (I use "overweight" ironically because at 6 feet 2 inches and 155 pounds, I was not overweight despite what my coach told me.) But if coaches were told about all the negative effects of eating disorders and were able to understand that a swimmer with an eating disorder really equals an unhealthy and therefore slow swimmer, then maybe it would change their coaching philosophy. That, coupled with early athlete education, may help stop the spread of eating disorders. I say *spread* because once one athlete on your team develops an eating disorder, it spreads like a wildfire through the team, especially when the atmosphere is ripe for it, as it was on my team.

But early education and prevention mean very early intervention. Whenever you think your child is ready for a conversation about eating disorders, it's probably too late. The seeds of these problems are planted before puberty, before weight becomes an issue, because older girls who are going through it surround us. Their behaviors are transferred to the younger girls, who adopt the attitudes and habits they see and hear.

■ ■ ■ ■ ■

Key Points

- Eating disorders affect millions of people each year, many of whom are athletes.
- Specific categories of eating disorders include anorexia nervosa, bulimia nervosa, EDNOS, anorexia athletica, and bigorexia.
- Eating disorders are found primarily among women but increasingly among men in the general and athletic populations.
- Eating disorders cause physical, psychological, social, and performance problems in athletes.
- Factors such as perfectionism, cultural pressures to be thin, family dynamics, and the special pressures created by the onset of puberty contribute to the development of eating disorders in the general population.
- Athletes are especially susceptible because of exposure to performance myths associated with thinness; the influence of coaches, parents, and peers; and the performance pressures inherent in sports.
- Recovery is enhanced by early detection and includes the appropriate choice of setting, a team of professionals, and treatment interventions matched to athletes' specific issues and needs.
- Prevention is the best means of dealing with eating disorders and requires a concerted effort by parents, coaches, educators, and others.

Review Questions

1. What are the five types of eating disorders discussed in the chapter?
2. What are some symptoms of each eating disorder?
3. What is the female athletic triad?
4. What are several of the physiological and psychological effects of eating disorders?
5. What are some causes of eating disorders?
6. Why are athletes particularly vulnerable to eating disorders?
7. What are the treatment interventions for eating disorders?
8. Who should be included in a treatment team?
9. What comprises an effective prevention program for eating disorders?

CHAPTER
14
Substance Abuse

Victoria L. Bacon, EdD—researcher

Bart S. Lerner, EdD—consultant*

Dave Trembley, MS—coach

Michael Seestedt, BA—athlete

The objectives of this chapter are

- to explore reasons why athletes take illegal or banned substances;
- to describe the types of drugs that are commonly taken and their impact on athletes;
- to examine treatment approaches, drug testing, and preventive programs; and
- to look at different mental health professionals who are trained to help athletes deal with substance use problems.

*Though Victoria Bacon, the researcher, is listed as the first author for this chapter to maintain consistency with the four perspectives highlighted in this book, the editors credit Bart Lerner, the consultant, as the lead contributor to this chapter.

Participation in sports offers athletes significant physical and psychological benefits. Sports are commonly associated with desirable values such as hard work, commitment, discipline, good sporting behavior, and determination. Those who participate in sport gain meaningful rewards, including physical health, enjoyment, mastery, social interaction, attention, and success.

Unfortunately, the win-at-all-costs attitude that pervades modern sport culture has, in many cases, taken precedence over the values and benefits of sports. This emphasis on results can cause athletes to lose perspective on their sport participation and make choices that may increase the chances of competitive success but at the cost of sacrificing honesty, integrity, fair play, and other healthy values and at the risk of paying a physical price, including injury, disease, and death. One such choice that many athletes are making is to use illegal drugs.

Key Issues

Athletes from all different sports and at all different levels of competition use and abuse drugs. Drugs are used for different reasons, such as to enhance performance, for recreation, and to manage pain and injury. Drugs commonly used to enhance performance are anabolic steroids, amphetamines, and caffeine. These drugs encourage muscle development, improve cardiovascular efficiency, maintain energy levels, or promote faster physiological recovery. Recreational drugs that act as either depressants or stimulants include alcohol, marijuana, cocaine, and tobacco. These drugs temporarily relieve stress and produce feelings of euphoria. As athletes feel pressure to continue to compete in the face of injury, they may turn to a variety of drugs, for example, antibacterial agents, analgesics, muscle relaxants, and anti-inflammatory medications, to help them mask the pain and allow them to compete while injured.

The treatment of substance abuse first requires athletes to admit that they have a problem. When athletes are committed to overcoming their dependency, a thorough physical and psychological assessment must be done to allow health care professionals to identify the best form of treatment for a particular athlete. Effective rehabilitation includes treatment of both the physical and psychological issues associated with substance abuse. With the use of various medications, athletes must first detoxify their bodies and reduce any health risks that may have arisen from the drug use. Then, psychological treatment must include individual and group therapy and support groups that encourage changes in the athlete's thoughts, emotions, and behavior.

Drug testing is implemented by the International Olympic Committee (IOC), the National Collegiate Athletic Association (NCAA), and most professional sports leagues. Although these organizations vary in their rigor, as a group they reduce the use of illegal or banned substances in their sports. Prevention and intervention programs are important steps in keeping athletes off of drugs and treating those who develop a substance abuse problem. Several elements are necessary for the development of an effective program, including an educational component, the availability of assessment and counseling services, support from the coaching staff, and integration of a mental health professional into the team setting. Finally, several types of mental health professionals may be qualified to treat substance-abusing athletes, including addiction counselors, licensed professional counselors, licensed psychologists, psychiatrists, and sport psychologists, Each of these professionals has different expertise and skills to treat drug abusers. Selecting the professional best trained to address the particular needs of an addicted athlete will require an extensive assessment of the athlete, including the type of drug being abused, why the athlete began taking the drug, and what physical and psychological problems have been presented.

Athletes are faced with many choices in their competitive lives that will determine the level of success they achieve. In today's sport culture, one of those decisions involves how far athletes are willing to go to accomplish their goals and whether they are willing to take illegal or banned substances to that end. Sport science researchers and applied sport psychology consultants must gain insight regarding substance abuse in the athletic arena. Similarly, coaches and athletes must recognize the physical, psychological, and performance risks that athletes take when they use drugs. With greater understanding, athletes can make better decisions about how they attempt to maximize performance and how their efforts affect their future health and well-being.

Chapter Purpose and Author Team

The purpose of this chapter is to introduce readers to the presence of substance abuse among athletes. The researcher (Dr. Victoria L. Bacon) incorporates the latest scientific literature related to addictive behavior and treatment options for athletes who abuse drugs. The consultant (Dr. Bart S. Lerner) describes the specific drugs used by athletes and suggests reasons why they use illegal or banned substances. The coach (Dave Trembley) discusses his views on the role and prevalence of drugs in sports. Last, the athlete (Michael Seestedt) provides an athlete's view on the difficult choices athletes face in a world where winning at all costs is highly valued.

Why Athletes Take Drugs

Athletes take drugs for a variety of reasons. Primarily, athletes use drugs to enhance performance, by building strength, combating fatigue, prolonging endurance, or facilitating recovery (e.g., steroids, amphetamines, and erythropoietin; Williams, 1998). Athletes also use substances for recreation, simply to give themselves a "high" (e.g., marijuana, cocaine, and alcohol; Inaba and Cohen, 1994). Drug use to alleviate pain (e.g., Percodan) is also common, enabling athletes to continue to compete while injured (Williams, 1998). Certain countries have promoted drug use to improve performance to further a particular political or nationalistic agenda (Anshel, 1991). Last, some athletes use drugs to self-medicate, attempting to control other unwanted psychological symptoms (Miller, Miller, Verhegge, Linville, and Pumariega, 2002).

The growing use of illegal or banned substances is correlated with increased acceptance in the sport culture. Because drug use is so widespread and implicitly accepted, athletes feel justified to use drugs just to stay competitive (Inaba and Cohen, 1994). In some cases, influential people in the sport community, for example, coaches, parents, officials, trainers, fans, or the media, subtly or actively encourage athletes to use substances to further their own selfish goals. Athletes can feel pressure from these outside forces to take substances to be accepted, to stay on a team, or

to receive support. Drug use is further exacerbated by the ready availability of drugs. Athletes can obtain drugs from many sources in local communities or on the Internet (Goldstein, 2001).

The benefits of athletic success at the Olympic and professional levels also provide athletes with significant impetus to take drugs, particularly those substances aimed at enhancing performance or enabling injured athletes to compete. Success at the highest levels of sport today provides athletes, many of whom come from simple means, with wealth, fame, respect, and power. These rewards, and the accompanying pressure to use drugs, have grown exponentially because of the dramatic commercialization of sports over the last 30 years (Leonard, 1998).

As the pressure on athletes to deliver consistent and outstanding results increases, either for financial or other reasons, they may feel compelled to take illegal or banned painkillers and healing agents to mask their pain and allow them to continue to compete. Although there are immediate benefits of reducing pain to a level that will enable athletes to perform while injured, the long-term costs can be significant. In the near term, when athletes continue to compete while injured, they do not allow their injuries to heal, thus prolonging the effects of the injury and causing compensatory problems around the site of the injury. In the long term, covering up pain prevents the injuries that cause the pain from healing, thereby increasing the risk of developing a chronic condition during the athletes' competitive years. In some cases, performing while injured can lead to a disability that severely limits the person's functioning after his or her athletic career has ended (Heil, 1993). For example, an athlete who has a back injury, is prescribed pain medication by the team physician, and returns to play sooner than he should could possibly suffer another back injury and even a disability. This in turn could force premature retirement from the sport and limit options for future employment or limit the opportunity to fully recover from the injury. The pain medication may propel the athlete back into competition before true rehabilitation has occurred.

Many countries have used illegal substances as a political tool to foster national pride. Former Eastern bloc countries, such as the USSR and East Germany, and China have used their athletic successes, which were driven by supervised governmental programs in the use of performance-enhancing drugs, to promote their political agendas. The results in international competition have been dramatic, but the physical repercussions for the athletes have been, in many cases, tragic. One repercussion of this is that 100 East German athletes filed suit for having been given "little blue pills" in the 1970s and 1980s as part of their training program. Now these athletes are suffering from a myriad of physical and emotional symptoms that require ongoing medical treatment. It is estimated that 10,000 German athletes were given steroids without their knowledge or consent (Swift, 2003).

Sadly, the problem of drug use among athletes is not exclusive to the highest level of sport. Drug use among youth and collegiate athletes has increased since 1997 (Nelson and Wechsler, 2001). The NCAA (2001) reported an increase in the use of amphetamines, anabolic steroids, and cocaine for student-athletes. It is difficult to estimate prevalence rates for elite and collegiate athletes before the mid-1990s given the dearth of scientific data (Peretti-Watel et al., 2003).

Coach's Perspective

The number one reason baseball players use drugs is to enhance performance. For example, baseball is a very long season, with spring training starting in February. For a minor league player, the regular season is 140 games in a 150-day playing season. For major league players, the season is actually 1 month longer (and 162 regular season games). Baseball players are constantly looking for an "edge," something to get them through the rigors of the schedule, travel, the

ups and downs of winning or losing, and being away from home.

However, the pressure to succeed might be the biggest factor in a player's decision to use performance-enhancing drugs. The game demands a high level of performance on a regular basis, and if one doesn't succeed he isn't going to be around too long in the minor league. The name of the game is to win, and some players will take any measure to ensure success, even though it comes with both physical and psychological risks.

■ ■ ■ ■

Athlete's Perspective

An athlete must work his way up the "corporate ladder" just like an individual in any other profession. All of the talented stars we watch on television had to start at the bottom. This progression to the top is most evident in the case of baseball players. Most begin their careers playing in the minor leagues. A player could spend years in the minor league system before even being considered for a spot on the major league roster.

Many believe that when an athlete starts using performance-enhancing drugs, he has essentially lost his perspective on sport participation and is sacrificing honesty, integrity, and fair play. In the case of professional ball players, playing baseball is not simply a sport; it is their job and livelihood.

A minor league baseball player, in most cases, makes only $850 to $2,500 per month for 5 months out of the year. This means that with no other form of employment, the average athlete playing in a farm system would bring home on average about $10,000 per year. Many ball players supplement their salary by finding off-season jobs, but even with a second job, most struggle to get by. The off-season job, although necessary to survive, takes valuable time that could be used to lift weights, run, and work on baseball skills that will help the player achieve his goal of becoming a major leaguer. When the athlete has a family, the challenges increase significantly. It is hard enough to support one person on a minor league salary, but supporting two or more is next to impossible.

After years of scraping by and spending 6 months of every year away from his family, a ball player comes to a turning point where he must decide to either keep striving for his goal or find a new profession. Some quit baseball and move on, but most believe that they have invested so much time and effort in the game that it would be a waste to quit if they have any chance at all. Most players in the minors demonstrate good stats year after year and have the skills necessary to be a successful major league player. What they come to realize, however, is that although they have what it takes to play major league baseball, they are lacking that "star quality" that helps them stand out and be recognized by scouts and upper management. When players discover that they cannot work any harder in the weight room or the batting cages and that their natural ability and talent have taken them as far as possible, and they couple this realization with the frustration of scraping by year to year and spending a large amount of time away from home, this is when ball players may turn to performance-enhancing drugs to carry them the extra distance.

Baseball players take a number of drugs for many specific reasons. The types of drugs most prominent in baseball are those that provide pain relief, combat fatigue, increase endurance, provide recreation, build strength, and enhance recovery.

■ ■ ■ ■ ■

Multiple Addictive Behaviors

Addiction is a complex behavior and a major health problem in American culture (Ajar, 1999). The challenges of treating an addiction are made worse when multiple addictive behaviors are present. As the name suggests, multiple addictive behaviors involve the presence of more than one addiction problem, which complicates the identification and treatment of the individual. Athletes with addictions are at high risk for affective disorders, criminal behavior, ethical misconduct, absenteeism, and problematic relationships (American Psychiatric Association, 2000). Collegiate student-athletes are thought to be at higher risk for academic and socially problematic behaviors than their nonathletic peers (Johnston, O'Malley, and Bachman, 1996). Recent research suggests that anabolic-androgenic steroid users are involved in other problematic behaviors such as abusing tobacco, alcohol, and other illicit substances; demonstrating aggressive and violent behaviors; and risk taking when driving motorcycles and automobiles (Miller, Barnes, Sabo, Melnick, and Farrell, 2002).

In the case of multiple addictive behaviors, most athletes do not meet the diagnostic criteria delineated in the *Diagnostic and Statistical Manual of Mental Disorders* (APA, 2000) for many problems. More often subclinical problems, for example, disordered eating, exist where unhealthy behaviors combine with addictive behavior to create a more challenging picture for diagnosis and treatment (Pope, Phillips, and Olivardia, 2000). (See chapter 13, Eating Disorders.)

Traditional approaches to addiction have considered the various addictive behaviors inde-pendently, with each having a well-defined set of symptoms and treatment protocols (Stevens and Smith, 2001). Contemporary approaches in addiction research, however, consider the addictive process as incorporating multiple addictive behaviors that are mutually reinforcing, a combination that makes prevention and treatment difficult (Shaffer, 1997). Treating one addictive behavior independently of another may only displace the underlying process of one addiction to another behavior. Considering addiction holistically shifts the perspective of addiction to a process where individuals display different behavior patterns. Shaffer (1997) suggested that individuals view addictive behaviors in cluster patterns.

Research among the athletic population indicates that multiple addictive behaviors are common. Several studies found multiple addictive behaviors among college athletes and found cluster patterns by gender: males with substance–gambling–alcohol problems and females falling into the eating and exercise cluster (Bacon and Lee, 1997; Bacon, Lee, and Calicchia, 1998; Rosen, McKeag, Hough, and Curley, 1986; Walsh and Garner, 1997). Martin (1998) found significantly less alcohol used in-season than out-of-season among NCAA Division I female basketball, softball, and volleyball players. When less alcohol was being used, there was an increase in disordered eating. Martin (1998) recommended using different types of prevention and intervention strategies depending on which addictive behavior was being used, based on whether the athletes were in-season or out-of-season.

Predictors of Substance Abuse

Understanding why some athletes abuse or become dependent on drugs is controversial at best. Attempting to theorize addiction in terms of biology or genetics has been with us since Jellinek's infamous book, *The Disease Concept of Alcoholism* in 1960 (Walters, 1999). This disease model suggests that an individual has a genetic predisposition to drugs and alcohol and that the disease is chronic and progressive. There are a number of psychological theories to understand addiction: drugs for self-medicating, addiction as a component of obsessive–compulsive spectrum, or the addictive personality. It also has been suggested that addiction is learned (Walters, 1999). Each theory contributes to understanding substance abuse, but no theory appears to have solved the mystery. Current research investigations are using a more integrative approach, combining elements from the various models.

Commonly Used Substances

A variety of drugs, legal and illegal, accepted and banned, are readily available to athletes. Drugs used by athletes fall into one of the following three categories: performance-enhancing drugs, mood-altering drugs, and drugs used to treat injuries or deaden pain. Each class of drugs includes specific substances that fulfill a particular function for athletes. The following is a description of the most commonly used drugs in the three categories.

Performance-Enhancing Drugs

Performance-enhancing drugs, also referred to as ergogenics, are used by athletes to improve their training and competitive efforts by manipulating some aspect of their physiology that is most relevant to their sport. Ergogenics typically influence one of four areas of sport training: muscle development, cardiovascular efficiency, maintenance of energy levels, or faster physiological recovery (Knopp, Wang, and Bach, 1997).

Anabolic Steroids

Anabolic steroids are considered to be the most abused performance-enhancing drug in sports today (Doweiko, 1999). Steroid use has been found in most sports that require weight and strength, for example, American football, weightlifting, track and field, baseball, wrestling, and boxing. Anabolic–androgenic steroids are used to increase weight, muscle mass, and strength and to enhance performance. Anabolic refers to the action of building muscle, and androgenic relates to producing masculine characteristics. Steroids are chemicals that resemble the male hormone testosterone. Anabolic–androgenic steroids are a form of testosterone and have two potential effects on the body: anabolic (tissue building) and androgenic (masculinizing by increasing protein synthesis; Knopp et al., 1997).

Unfortunately, anabolic steroids have clearly demonstrable benefits, which include increasing body mass and strength (Knopp et al., 1997). At the same time, the physical costs are significant. For males, risks include bloated appearance, baldness, swollen breasts, suppression of the body's own production of testosterone, shrinking testicles and penis, decreased sperm count, impotence, enlarged prostate, and decreased sex drive (Inaba and Cohen, 1994). For females, risks include facial and body hair, deepening of the voice, shrinking breasts, and menstrual irregularities (Inaba and Cohen, 1994). Males and females also share several adverse effects, such as severe acne, stunted growth, increased chance of cancer, increased chance of heart and liver disease, and high blood pressure (Inaba and Cohen, 1994).

Steroid use also has a variety of psychological and emotional side effects, including increased confidence and aggressiveness ("roid rage"), emotional instability, and irrational behaviors. High dosages and long-term use can produce withdrawal symptoms after discontinued use, such as fatigue, depression, restlessness, insomnia, decreased appetite, and decreased sex drive (Knopp et al., 1997). Steroid use has been documented in a variety of sports, such as track and field (Patrick, 2004), tennis ("Steroid Drug Testing," 2004), soccer ("English Soccer Blighted," 2004), and swimming (Rushall, 1998).

In recent years, major league baseball has received a great deal of attention concerning steroids. One major league baseball player believed that 25% to 40% of all major league baseball players use steroids, whereas another player stated that 50% of all players use steroids, and still another player reported that 85% of all players use steroids in baseball (Associated Press, 2003). A 1989 NCAA drug use survey reported that 1 out of every 20 student-athletes has used steroids; in particular, 1 out of every 10 football players and 1 out of every 25 male track-and-field student-athletes used steroids (NCAA, 2003b). Additionally, another survey examined use among 8th, 10th, and 12th graders, in which more than 43,000 students in 394 schools nationwide completed surveys. It was revealed that 2.5% of the 8th-grade students, 3.5% of the 10th-grade students, and 4.0% of the

12th-grade students had used steroids in their lifetime. Furthermore, 1.5% of the 8th-grade students, 2.2% of the 10th-grade students, and 2.5% of the 12th-grade students used steroids annually (NIDA, 2003). Although the use of steroids among high-level athletes appears to be common, these drugs are also finding their way into high school sports. One study surveyed 3,403 12th-grade boys and found that 6.6% had used anabolic steroids (Pope et al., 2000). There is also some evidence that a growing number of young males are using steroids simply to enhance their appearance (Doweiko, 1999). Steroid users have been reported to spend $200 to $400 per week, whereas professional athletes spend $20,000 to $50,000 per year, and the black market grosses $200 to $400 million per year (Inaba and Cohen, 1994).

An example of the benefits and costs of steroid use comes from Ken Caminiti, major league baseball's 1996 National League Most Valuable Player (MVP), who admitted to long-term steroid use to help him recover from an injury. During the 1996 season, he hit .326 and 40 home runs, with 130 runs batted in. Before and after that season, he never hit over .305, hit more than 30 home runs, or drove in more than 100 runs (Verducci, 2002). After returning to play, he continued using steroids beyond the recommended dosages and eventually incurred other injuries and side effects, such as damage to tendons and ligaments because they lacked the strength to support his added musculature. Additionally, his production of testosterone decreased, and Caminiti's career declined after his MVP year. He died in 2004 of a heart attack.

Lyle Alzado, another tragic example of steroid use, was a star defensive player for the Oakland Raiders of the National Football League. At the age of 42, he died of brain cancer that was believed to have been caused by years of steroid use. Alzado started using steroids in 1969 when he was 20 years old and continued use throughout his professional career (Buck, 1998).

Athlete's Perspective

Some of the main reasons athletes use drugs are endurance, building strength, and recovery. They are closely related, and athletes view each as critically important. In my experience, an athlete is most likely to cross ethical boundaries in regard to drug use because endurance, strength, and recovery time are the main components in being able to reach the next level. Improvement in these areas gives a player that

special "star quality" that baseball scouts and upper management are looking for. If a player is able to build strength, recover quickly to continue building strength, and then keep that strength throughout the course of a 6-month season, he will be noticed.

When an athlete realizes that weightlifting and supplements alone cannot help achieve his goal, he moves on to more effective means. Steroids and human growth hormone are used and accepted in professional baseball. Players and coaches know what the life of a minor league baseball player is like, and those in the sport believe that a player should make his own choices about performance-enhancing drugs. These drugs are viewed as an avenue for a player to stand out and be recognized.

■ ■ ■ ■ ■

Androstenedione

Androstenedione was made popular within the past few years by Mark McGwire, who used the drug during the 1998 major league baseball season when he hit 70 home runs, which broke the single-season record. Androstenedione, the immediate precursor to testosterone, is believed to elevate blood testosterone levels in both males and females and thus increase lean body mass (muscle mass) and physical strength (Porpora, 2003). Research has shown that androstenedione increased testosterone concentration by more than 300% in males and 600% in females and maintained elevated testosterone levels for about a week (Schnirring, 1998). An elevated testosterone level may cause the hypothalamus and the pituitary gland to suppress the body's natural production of testosterone, leading to testicular atrophy (United States Olympic Committee, 1998). However, to date, no studies have indicated that androstenedione has any ergogenic effects in humans regarding athletic performance (Porpora, 2003). Finally, the use of androstenedione is banned by the IOC, the National Football League, and the NCAA; it may be detectable in drug tests, but this depends on the specific test implemented (Schnirring, 1998).

Erythropoietin

Erythropoietin (EPO) is a naturally occurring hormone that stimulates the production of red blood cells. EPO is used by athletes to enhance performance by increasing stamina and energy levels, but its use in sport is illegal and it can be detected by drug tests (Institute of Child Health, 2003). Some of the potential side effects are high blood pressure, headaches, flulike symptoms (i.e., elevated temperature, lethargy, aching muscles and joints), and epileptic seizures. EPO's use has been documented within the cycling world ("Doping and Cycling," 2004).

Stimulants

Drugs that have a stimulating effect are used for both performance-enhancing and recreational purposes by athletes. The most common stimulants are caffeine, amphetamines, and cocaine. Caffeine is regulated by many sport governing bodies only in large quantities because of its performing-enhancing qualities. Amphetamines and cocaine are banned by the IOC and the NCAA (Conlee, 1991).

Athlete's Perspective

Fatigue is another major reason some athletes use substances. There are times in a baseball season when a player might play 25 games in 25 days. During this period, that player will spend 8 to 12 hours a day at the ballpark. With this type of schedule, it would be impossible for anyone not to get fatigued. An athlete, however, knows that it is his job to give his best performance every day, and sometimes he may need assistance with that. Ball players often turn to caffeine (coffee or pills), tobacco, ephedrine, and in some cases "beans" or amphetamines to combat the fatigue. With new bans on ephedrine inside and outside of baseball, the use of this substance has declined and the use of amphetamines is seen occasionally. Caffeine and tobacco use, however, is quite common. Players use these to stay alert and focused.

■ ■ ■ ■

Ephedra

Ephedra is categorized as a stimulant and has mainly been used by dieters and athletes because it stimulates the heart and central nervous system to lose weight, increase metabolism, and burn fat (Pedone, 2003). Ephedra is very dangerous for athletes because it can deplete the body of water and cause stimulant-like effects (e.g., increased blood pressure and heart rate). Currently, ephedra is not regulated because it is classified as a natural supplement. The Food and Drug Administration (FDA) has had difficulty obtaining reports of adverse effects because ephedra is protected under the Dietary Supplement Health and Education Act of 1994, which states that the FDA cannot regulate a dietary supplement unless it has been proven unsafe (Tiedt, 2003). The FDA has proposed new

warning labels, but the dietary supplement industry has blocked such action since 1997. FDA officials believe that putting warning labels on each bottle may limit or stop the sale of ephedra over the counter (Price, 2003). Research has shown that since 1994 ephedra has been linked to a number of deaths and many medical problems that range from insomnia and nervousness to severe heart arrhythmia, seizures, hepatitis, and stroke (Gugliotta and Shipley, 2003; Price, 2003). Its use has been documented in hockey (Yorio, 2004).

The NCAA has banned the use of ephedra since 1997, and the United States Olympic Committee and IOC have not allowed ephedra for more than 10 years. Additionally, in 2001, the National Football League (NFL) was the first professional sports league to ban ephedra, which stemmed from the deaths of Rashidi Wheeler, a Northwestern University football player, and Korey Stringer, an offensive lineman from the Minnesota Vikings. They both collapsed and died during team workouts after consuming ephedra products (Gugliotta and Shipley, 2003). In 2003, major league baseball banned the use of ephedra within the minor leagues, which was prompted by the death of Baltimore Orioles pitcher Steve Bechler after it was found that he took ephedra and died of heatstroke during the team's annual spring training practices (Price, 2003). One concern with the use of ephedra in weight loss and athletic performance is that the adverse effects can be augmented when combined with caffeine and aspirin (NCCAM, 2003). Finally, according to research, there is no evidence that ephedra can keep the weight off, and no studies have demonstrated that ephedra is beneficial to athletic performance (NCCAM, 2003). More research is needed to test the safety of ephedra.

Caffeine

Caffeine, a member of the chemical class alkaloids, is the most popular stimulant in the world (Doweiko, 1999). It is a legal substance found in coffee, tea, soft drinks, chocolate, and other popular foods and drinks. Caffeine is beneficial to athletes because it combats fatigue, increases energy, heightens alertness, prolongs endurance, and reduces appetite. It has been shown to be particularly useful for aerobic power and endurance events (Williams, 1998). Additionally, coffee has become such a popular part of Western culture that athletes drink it as part of their daily routines rather than for its performance-enhancing benefits.

Chronic overuse, known as "caffeinism," because of how it stimulates the central nervous system, results in habituation, tolerance, and withdrawal symptoms (Greden and Walters, 1997). Excessive use of caffeine can result in anxiety and increased risk of coronary disease, ulcers, diabetes, and liver disease. Caffeine can impede weight loss by stimulating the release of insulin, responsible for metabolizing sugar, and then reducing the level of sugar in the blood, which ultimately triggers hunger. Paradoxically, caffeine can also speed up metabolism and encourage weight loss, which is the reason it is contained in many diet pills. The specific effects on appetite and weight depend on the quantity of caffeine ingested, frequency of use, and whether it is combined with other substances or foods. Caffeine also acts as a diuretic, causing dehydration when used in excess (Williams, 1998). This last effect can have significant ramifications for athletes who compete in endurance sports or in extremely hot conditions (Williams, 1998).

Amphetamines

Amphetamines are artificial stimulants that can be injected, snorted, and smoked (e.g., Benzedrine and Dexedrine). They release "energy" chemicals known as norepinephrine and dopamine (Williams, 1998) that increase energy, alertness, and aggressiveness (Goldstein, 2001). In small doses, amphetamines increase heart rate, respiration, and blood pressure; facilitate the release of adrenaline; and decrease appetite. In larger doses or during extended use, they deplete energy stores and can produce lethargy, depression, anxiety, paranoia, hallucinations, decreased sleep, malnutrition, and decreased sex drive (Inaba and Cohen, 1994). Amphetamines are also highly addictive. Athletes use amphetamines to be more alert and focused so that they can sustain their endurance levels during competition.

Mood-Altering Drugs

Mood-altering drugs are used by athletes primarily for recreational purposes. These drugs not only are common within the athletic population but are also popular in many cultures. These substances may be legal or illegal, but because they are not seen as performance enhancing, they are not always banned by sport governing bodies (Williams, 1998).

Alcohol

Alcohol is one of the most widely used and abused drugs in sports (Doweiko, 1999). Its popularity is attributable largely to its legal status, availability, high degree of acceptance in society, and embedded place in many social situations. Athletes are drawn to alcohol because of its calming and disinhibiting effects (e.g., easing of social anxiety; Miller, Miller, et al., 2002).

Alcohol can relieve the stress that athletes may experience in their sporting lives. Common stressors found in the athletic culture include slumps, mistakes, losses, injuries, and pressure from family, friends, coaches, teammates, and the media. Alcohol allows athletes to temporarily escape these stresses. Alcohol is also seen as a viable means for dealing with negative emotions like frustration, anxiety, anger, and sadness (Goldstein, 2001).

Alcohol reduces neurological and physiological activity. Physical effects of alcohol include decreased motor coordination, dilation of the blood vessels (e.g., some individuals may have a flushed face or red nose when drinking), and reduced central nervous system activity. Small amounts of alcohol can have a stimulating effect, but larger quantities have a depressive influence on the body. Persistent, heavy drinking can lead to impairment of respiration and irritation of the stomach lining, which can result in ulcers and cirrhosis of the liver. Similarly, small amounts of alcohol can produce a euphoric effect in which drinkers feel confident, relaxed, and more at ease socially (Williams, 1998). Increased consumption of alcohol can reduce cognitive functioning (e.g., memory, focusing, information processing) and impair judgment (e.g., reasoning, decision making). Alcohol abuse can be caused by or can lead to depression or anxiety and can be addictive (Stevens and Smith, 2001).

Alcohol is classified as a depressant and has been used by athletes for mental toughness. Although some studies have found that athletes who used alcohol had reduced anxiety before an event, other studies have indicated that alcohol consumption may impair performance in both anaerobic and aerobic endurance performance (Williams, 1998).

Alcohol's impact on athletes is affected by a number of factors. Body size influences the amount of alcohol that athletes can consume. Larger individuals have greater blood volume in which the alcohol can be diluted in their systems, and, as a result, more alcohol is needed to produce deterioration in functioning (Daugherty and O'Bryan, 1995). For example, a 200-pound male would have a blood alcohol level (BAL) of .07 after drinking four 12-ounce beers in a 1-hour time span, whereas a 150-pound male would have a BAL of .09 after drinking the same within 1 hour, and a 100-pound female would have a BAL of .17 after consuming the same amount of alcohol within the same time period. Additionally, a 200-pound male would have a BAL of .05 after drinking three glasses of wine in a 1-hour time span, whereas a 150-pound male would have a BAL of .07 after drinking the same within 1 hour, and a 100-pound female would have a BAL of .13 after consuming the same amount of alcohol within the same time period (Daugherty and O'Bryan, 1995). Gender also plays a role, because men have more enzymes to break down and metabolize alcohol than women (Daugherty and O'Bryan, 1995). Elevation increases the effect of alcohol because of the lower proportion of oxygen available to metabolize the alcohol. The higher the elevation, the more quickly athletes will feel the effects of alcohol (Daugherty and O'Bryan, 1995). Concomitant use of drugs and alcohol can also heighten the influence of alcohol because of the chemical interaction of the two substances. Other factors that affect the impact of alcohol on functioning include food ingestion, fatigue, illness, and jetlag (Daugherty and O'Bryan, 1995). Finally, alcohol impairs athletic performance by reducing physiological activation, inhibiting motor skills, and impeding cognitive functioning (Daugherty and O'Bryan, 1995).

Recent cases of alcohol abuse by high-profile athletes have brought considerable attention to this issue in the media. For example, Oksana Baiul, the 1994 Olympic gold medalist in women's figure skating, admitted herself to a drug rehabilitation program after she was cited for an alcohol-related car accident (Eden, 2002). John Daly, a former British Open golf champion, admitted himself to an inpatient treatment program after a long history of drinking-related problems (Baddoo, 1999).

Marijuana

Marijuana may be the second most common recreational drug—after alcohol—among athletes (Inaba and Cohen, 1994). Its popularity stems from the feelings of relaxation and euphoria it causes (Williams, 1998). As Western culture has become more accepting of marijuana, its use by athletes has also increased. A 1997 *New York Times* poll indicated that 60% to 70% of athletes in the National Basketball Association smoke marijuana (Sind, 2001). Additionally, a 2001 national survey that included approximately 21,000 college student-athletes found that 27% of all athletes use marijuana in college (27.3% of football players, 26.9% of baseball athletes, and 23.6% of basketball players smoke marijuana; Higher Education Center for Alcohol and Other Drug Prevention, 2003). Also, among the athletes who smoke marijuana,

60% use it for recreational purposes, whereas 34% stated that it makes them feel better; 78.5% of the college athletes who use this drug started before college (Higher Education Center for Alcohol and Other Drug Prevention, 2003). Drug testing for marijuana in Olympic competition did not start until the Winter Games in Nagano, Japan, in 1998 (Love and Brookler, 1999).

Marijuana can act as either a stimulant or a depressant. Physical effects include increased heart rate, disruption of testosterone secretion, and an increase in anxiety and paranoia. Marijuana has been shown to slow learning and disrupt concentration. It can impair short-term memory, but no effects on long-term memory have been found (Inaba and Cohen, 1994). A lack of motivation (i.e., amotivational syndrome) can lead to apathy and a decline in interest and effort, which can hinder athletic performance that requires complex perceptual–motor abilities (Williams, 1998). Noticeable effects last for 4 to 5 hours after marijuana use, but its residual effects can last up to 6 months because of its storage in fat cells (Doweiko, 1999).

Tolerance increases rapidly with marijuana use. Withdrawal symptoms from chronic use include headaches, anxiety, depression, irritability, decreased sleep, restlessness, and aggressiveness (National Institute on Drug Abuse, 1999a). Because of its increased potency and chronic use in today's society, marijuana's addictive potential must be reevaluated. Its use has been documented in basketball ("Don't Risk Your Reputation," 2004).

Lamar Odom of the Los Angeles Clippers, the fourth-overall selection in the 1999 National Basketball Association (NBA) draft, was suspended in November 2001 for violating the NBA's antidrug policy for the second time in 8 months by using marijuana (Associated Press, 2001). Additionally, 3 days after winning the gold medal in the first Olympic snowboarding event held at the 1998 Winter Olympic Games in Nagano, Japan, Ross Rebagliati tested positive for marijuana and was stripped of his gold medal by the IOC. A subsequent court order forced the IOC to reinstate his medal because marijuana is a restricted, but not banned, substance (Love and Brookler, 1999).

Athlete's Perspective

Some drugs that athletes use have the opposite effect on performance than these athletes are looking for. Baseball and recreational drug use have been grouped together for nearly a century. Babe Ruth was known for his batting skill and his late nights on the town, Mickey

Mantle for his pregame drinks, and Darryl Strawberry for his highly publicized cocaine use; most recently, David Wells admitted that he was hung over when he pitched his perfect game. Baseball players, like any other athlete, feel a rush from competition that many times does not go away when the game ends. Many players satisfy that rush by partying. Although many ball players consume an occasional drink and are responsible with their alcohol use, there are just as many who abuse alcohol on a regular basis and some who even go further to use drugs like marijuana and ecstasy. But with random drug testing in effect in minor league baseball, the use of banned substances like pot is not as prominent as one may think. Some players do take a chance, but most, at least during the season, refrain from recreational drug use.

■　■　■　■　■

Cocaine

Cocaine use is considered a serious problem in the United States, with 7% of the population actively using (National Institute on Drug Abuse, 1999a) and a reported 3.2% of 8th graders having used crack (a refined and more potent form of cocaine) at least once (National Institute on Drug Abuse, 1999b). Cocaine increases energy and can act as an analgesic. Cocaine produces pleasure and stimulation, but it also releases neurochemicals, such as epinephrine (more commonly known as adrenaline), dopamine, and serotonin. Adrenaline is an endogenous opiate associated with the "fight or flight" response, which prepares people for emergencies with reactions that include increased heart rate and respiration, enhanced blood flow to essential parts of the body, and heightened alertness. Changes in serotonin levels resulting from cocaine use have been linked to disturbances such as insomnia, depression, and anxiety (Williams, 1998).

Common problems associated with cocaine use are withdrawal, overdose, and long-term risks. Cocaine withdrawal results in a decreased ability to experience pleasure, a lack of energy, and an intense craving for the drug. Overdose can injure the heart muscle and blood vessels, which can lead to death. Cocaine abuse causes an inverse tolerance, in which individuals develop greater rather than less sensitivity to the drug. Long-term dangers include increased risk of stroke and heart damage.

Len Bias died from a cocaine overdose 2 days after he was the second overall selection in the 1986 NBA draft (Harriston and Jenkins, 1986). This incident prompted government and institutional sanctions against athletes for drug use and more stringent drug-testing procedures for athletes by sport governing bodies and universities (Wilbon, 1987).

Tobacco

Tobacco, whose primary ingredient is nicotine, is recognized as the most widely used and dangerous drug available today (Doweiko, 1999). Although tobacco is legal in most countries, it is usually regulated by age. It is a psychoactive substance that affects the same areas of the brain as do cocaine and amphetamines. Nicotine provides an initial boost by stimulating glucose production, but as the glucose decreases in the body, it has a relaxing effect (National Institute on Drug Abuse, 1999c). Nicotine increases energy, decreases appetite, dulls the senses, and produces mild euphoria. It is theorized that nicotine may increase performance by improving reaction time, visual acuity, and vigilance, which would benefit athletes in baseball (Williams, 1998). Long-term use has significant health implications including heart and lung disease, cancer, and reduced life span. For example, a two-pack-a-day smoker lives, on average, 8 years less than a nonsmoker (Doweiko, 1999). Tolerance can begin within a few hours of smoking, and addiction to nicotine can develop within days. Withdrawal symptoms include headaches, irritability, inability to concentrate, agitation, and difficulty sleeping.

Another tobacco-related problem in sports is the popularity of smokeless tobacco in some sports, notably baseball and rodeo (Inaba and Cohen, 1994). Smokeless tobacco increases the risk of gum disease and throat, mouth, and esophageal cancer. Absorption takes longer with smokeless versus smoked tobacco, but more nicotine reaches the bloodstream, so the effects are felt more intensely.

Pain Relievers

Many athletes feel compelled to train and compete while injured even when their injuries demand rest, treatment, and rehabilitation. Some athletes continue to compete while injured because they are personally invested in their sport participation and putting their involvement on hold would cause them psychological and emotional harm. Other athletes who are injured may feel external pressure from coaches, family, teammates, the media, and fans to play hurt. Professional athletes have the added burden of having their livelihood depend on their continued participation. This need can lead some athletes to disregard their injuries and act contrary to their best long-term interests by turning to pain-killing medication to enable them to continue to perform (Taylor and Taylor, 1997) (see chapter 12).

One category of therapeutic drugs used to treat injuries is analgesics. The purpose of analgesics should be to facilitate healing and result in long-term and complete return to sport participation. Unfortunately, athletes, oftentimes supported by physicians and trainers, medicate for the singular purpose of masking the injury so the athlete can continue to perform without regard for the long-term ramifications.

Narcotic analgesics (e.g., morphine, Percodan, Vicodin) are intended to lessen pain associated with an injury. The problem with these drugs is that they mask pain without offering any healing benefit. Narcotic analgesics increase an athlete's pain threshold, so that the athlete fails to recognize injury and possibly suffers more injury. The most common use is to alleviate pain, although narcotic analgesics also have been used in the treatment of coughs (NCAA, 2003a). Side effects can include drowsiness, low blood pressure, and inability to urinate, and these drugs can ultimately lead to respiratory depression and arrest, coma, shock, and cardiac arrest. Narcotic analgesics can produce physical and psychological dependence (NCAA, 2003a).

Brett Favre, the NFL's Most Valuable Player in 1995, has experienced a number of painful conditions throughout his professional career (e.g., bruised and separated shoulder, arthritic hip, and sore low back). Favre began taking numbing injections and painkilling pills (i.e., Vicodin) early in his career to get through a game; he once took 13 Vicodin pills in the course of 1 day so that he could decrease his pain (King, 1996). Favre's addiction to pain killers was so extreme that it brought on seizures, which ultimately led to his voluntary enrollment into a drug rehabilitation center (King, 1996).

Athlete's Perspective

During the course of a 142-game minor league or a 162-game major league schedule, it is inevitable that an athlete will have some discomfort at some point. A ball player cannot simply decide to sit out because his arm hurts or knees are sore. Playing baseball is a profession, not a recreational activity. To compete at his top level every day, an athlete might take an over-the-counter or prescription pain reliever on occasion or even daily. There is a point at which treatment from an athletic trainer no longer works as well on pain and discomfort as does medicine. The most popular pain-relieving drugs include Advil, Aleve, Celebrex, and even muscle relaxants. Occasionally, a cortisone shot may be necessary to relieve constant elbow or knee soreness. Most of the time, these drugs are used as directed under the supervision of an athletic trainer or team doctor. Very rarely are they abused.

■ ■ ■ ■

Coach's Perspective

Drug use has changed over the years because drug testing is a major part of the program. At all levels of baseball there is mandatory drug testing. Both the player's team and major league baseball through the authority of the Baseball Commissioner's Office test randomly twice a year.

It used to be common to have "rip fuel" (ephedra) and various over-the-counter products (such as those one might purchase at GNC) very visible in most players' lockers. Players often took these without considering potential risks, simply wanting to improve their performance. However, with the recent death of Orioles pitcher Steve Bechler, those items are now nonexistent in the locker room. I think players still use these drugs but are not as open about it as in the past.

■ ■ ■ ■

Recognition, Prevention, and Intervention

Many different signs and symptoms are associated with substance use and abuse among athletes. Following are some common behaviors that may be considered warning signs.

Physical signs and symptoms

Acting intoxicated

Bloodshot or red eyes, droopy eyelids

Inaccurate eye movement

Wearing sunglasses at inappropriate times

Abnormally pale complexion

Impaired motor skills

Repressed physical development

Loss of or increased appetite

Emotional–cognitive signs and symptoms

Moodiness

Depression

Anxiety

Mood swings

Emotional outbursts

Irritability

Confusion

Denial that problem exists

Belief that individual is in control

Behavioral problems

Inappropriate overreaction to mild criticism

Decreased interaction and communication with others

Change in speech or vocabulary patterns

Preoccupation with self

Neglect of personal appearance

Loss of interest in sport

Loss of motivation and enthusiasm

Lethargy

Blackouts

Loss of ability to assume responsibility

Need for instant gratification

Changes in morals, values, and beliefs

Change in friends (peer groups)

If several of these signs and symptoms are present in an athlete's physical condition, emotional state, and behavior, coaches and consultants should consider guiding the athlete into a prevention or intervention program.

Several key components contribute to successful prevention and intervention programs. Effective programs begin with a multidisciplinary approach in which a full-time staff designs and administers all preventive and intervention services. This team consists of professionals in medicine, psychology, education, and coaching who have special training in the prevention and treatment of substance abuse.

These programs include a strong educational component in which athletes and coaches participate in an ongoing curriculum of drug education. This course of study, which often occurs during the preseason, addresses commonly used drugs in sports, their dangers, and the consequences associated with their use. Usually, a subcomponent of the educational portion of the program focuses on the coaching staff and their influence on drug use among their athletes.

Assessment services are also in place in which athletes at risk are noted and observed, and those who develop a substance abuse problem are identi-

fied early. Training the coaches, athletic trainers, and team physicians is essential to effective assessment. Counseling services are a necessary follow-up to education and assessment. These services must be easily accessible for the athletes, discrete, and confidential, and they must provide meaningful opportunities for substance-abusing athletes to overcome their dependencies.

The effectiveness of a prevention or intervention program depends largely on its endorsement and support by the coaching staff. If coaches buy into the value and use of the program, then athletes will be more likely to use its services. This commitment can be expressed in terms of mandatory education meetings, ongoing messages to athletes about the dangers of drugs, and prompt action when an athlete shows indications of substance abuse. Support from key athletes on the team, such as the team captains, long-term members of the team, or respected former team members, further reinforces the value of the program to the entire team. Finally, having a trained mental health professional integrated into the team increases the likelihood that athletes will reach out for help should concerns arise. Trust and comfort with such a professional can be fostered by having him or her involved in the education curriculum, included in coaches' meetings, and present at practices and competitions (Fitch and Robinson, 1998; Joy et al., 1997).

Coach's Perspective

Regular drug screening is held throughout the competitive season. Each team conducts urine testing of all players, coaches, and staff twice a year. This is usually done in the clubhouse immediately before a scheduled game or practice session. The team trainer is notified the morning that the test will be conducted, and all players must provide a urine sample before they are allowed onto the playing field. The security and administration of these procedures have changed over the years, making the testing much more precise. All players provide a sample one at a time while the trainer observes.

Major league baseball also conducts its own test twice a year, following the same procedures outlined for the team tests. As a coach, I never find out if a player has a problem with substance abuse. There is a high level of confidentiality, with all results going directly through the team physician, before the results are passed on to the player and team front office personnel. The coach is never involved.

■   ■   ■   ■   ■

Treatment for Substance Abuse

The treatment of and recovery from a drug addiction are long and often painful processes. Rehabilitation is further complicated by the multifaceted nature of substance abuse and its influence on so many aspects of athletes' lives. A drug addiction not only involves physical and psychological dependency but also affects athletes' self-esteem, identity, relationships, and livelihood. In addition to the physical addiction, the bonds that tie athletes to their drug of choice are also behavioral, social, habitual, and emotional.

A significant obstacle to effective treatment is the athletes' own denial that they have a drug problem. Denial is a powerful protection for substance abusers that often safeguards them from the very problem or motives that originally led to the abuse. Athletes have many reasons for denying their drug problem: The substance may be illegal or banned, treatment may have competitive or financial repercussions, others may reap benefits from the player's drug problem, or admitting a drug problem may threaten a player's self-perception. Getting athletes to admit that they have a problem is the first step in the treatment process because it allows them to take ownership of and responsibility for the problem, which also gives them the opportunity and the control to break their addiction. This may involve a coach, teammate, friend, or family member discussing the negative effects (i.e., mental and physical) that the drug is having on the athlete. The athlete himself or herself may experience a negative reaction (i.e., mental or physical) to the drug, which could cause a decrement in overall performance. This can lead the athlete to the realization that there is a problem.

An assessment by trained medical and mental health professionals is the next step in determining the best treatment for a substance abuse problem. The duration of use and abuse, causes, level of dependency, mitigating contributors, and physical and psychological presenting problems and risks must all be evaluated. Most treatment for substance abuse involves some combination of hospitalization, residential treatment, or outpatient care that includes medical intervention to help abusers break the physical addiction to the drug and counseling to address the psychological and emotional connections to the addiction (Stevens and Smith, 2001).

Treatment Options

There are numerous treatment options available for athletes, from minimal support to maximum support depending on the nature and severity of the drug problem.

In almost all cases, detoxification is an essential first step in treating the addiction. Detoxification involves a safe withdrawal from substances such as alcohol, barbiturates, hallucinogens, and heroin under proper medical care (Stevens and Smith, 2001). The difficulty of detoxification depends on the frequency and intensity of drug use, type of drug, and duration of the abuse. Detoxification is often an agonizing experience for abusers as their bodies are denied the substances they crave (Stevens and Smith, 2001). It also challenges abusers psychologically because of the emotional pain associated with acknowledging their problem and realizing the obstacles ahead of them and because of the strong compulsion to return to drug use. Therefore, programs that provide both detoxification and psychological support have shown beneficial results. These settings include the following (Perez, 2001):

- Dual-diagnosis inpatient hospital. Dual-diagnosis inpatient hospital settings are available for athletes with substance dependency along with a psychological condition (e.g., depression). These settings typically offer 7-, 14-, and 28-day programs that involve detoxification and psychological support such as individual and group counseling and Alcoholics Anonymous (AA) or Narcotics Anonymous (NA) meetings (Perez, 2001).

- Rehabilitation or residential program. Rehabilitation programs are based on a wellness model with a primary focus on change once the individual has successfully detoxified. Here athletes receive individual, group, and family counseling as well as education. Rehabilitation programs are dedicated to wellness and prepare individuals for success after leaving the facility (Borkman, 1998).

- Partial hospitalization. Partial hospitalization programs allow one to live at home while attending treatment during the day. These programs are for athletes without medical or psychological issues to get intensive psychological support; individual, group, and family counseling; as well as AA or NA meetings. Typical stay is 4 to 6 weeks (Frances, Wilson, and Wiegand, 1997).

- Halfway house. Halfway houses are a community-based treatment option for individuals after leaving a medical facility. This type of program requires the athlete to remain abstinent, be employed, attend a 12-step program, and probably undergo drug testing (Perez, 2001).

- Intensive outpatient substance abuse clinic. Intensive outpatient programs are available to the athlete once detoxified; these begin with an intensive day-long treatment and then move to weekly group therapy, family therapy, and AA or NA 12-step meetings. These programs usually last 90 to 120 days (Perez, 2001).

Psychological Treatment

As the physical concerns associated with a drug addiction are addressed through medication and detoxification, intensive counseling is essential for dealing with the psychological, emotional, social, and behavioral issues that initially led to the drug abuse. Individual counseling with a trained therapist allows rehabilitating substance abusers to gain insight into the causes of their addiction and to change the thoughts, emotions, and behaviors that led to the problem. Group counseling enables addicts to share their experiences, learn from others with similar problems, and gain support from others in their struggle for freedom from their addiction. Couples or marriage counseling helps the athlete to work on relational issues commonly associated with substance abuse (Stevens and Smith, 2001).

12-Step Programs

The 12-step program is not about addiction recovery; it began as Alcoholics Anonymous, a religious organization that binds its members together with fear of self-destruction, surrender of autonomy, prescribed meditations, and the promise of divine intervention (Benshoff and Janikowski, 2000). The 12 steps contain no suggestion that one actually quit drinking or using drugs or of how one might achieve this goal. The program expects its members only to desire to stop and achieve recovery through a personal commitment to abstinence (Benshoff and Janikowski, 2000). Recovery is not regarded as an immediate, individual responsibility but as a long-term, group project requiring intense support from others. There is no particular pattern of step completion, and many individuals continue to review and invest their time in the steps as a way of maintaining recovery.

The 12 steps incorporate important clinical issues, including problem recognition (Step 1), hope (Step 2), help seeking (Steps 3, 5, and 7), insight development (Steps 4, 6, and 10), restitution (Steps 8 and 9), stress reduction (Step 11), and adoption of a new consciousness and forms of behavior (Step 12; McCrady and Delaney, 1995). Unfortunately, little is documented concerning the treatment effectiveness of the 12-step program, mainly because of the unstructured nature of the program and the emphasis on anonymity (Benshoff and Janikowski, 2000). However, most people who are successful in this type of treatment option believe in what the 12 steps profess, which can ultimately lead to positive outcomes (Lewis, Dana, and Blevins, 1994).

Inpatient Programs

Inpatient programs (e.g., Betty Ford and Hazelden) offer services on a residential basis, which are typically known as 28-day programs because of the average length of stay. However, many programs have decreased their length of stay because of the lack of funding from organizations (Benshoff and Janikowski, 2000). Additionally, no research has shown that 28 days are adequate for the treatment of substance abuse (Benshoff and Janikowski, 2000). The general purpose of inpatient programs is to help people enhance their understanding of their specific problems and to prepare for long-term recovery (Lewis et al., 1994). Athletes should be able to develop personal goals for recovery, learn the skills needed to prevent relapse, and ultimately acquire a lifestyle without substances (McCrady, Dean, Dubreuil, and Swanson, 1985). Group therapy tends to be the mode of treatment, but individual counseling has been emphasized too. Because of the short duration of inpatient programs, they intended to be the starting point in the recovery process and therefore focus on short-term goals, whereas the long-term goals are addressed after the athlete's release (Benshoff and Janikowski, 2000).

Research has shown that inpatient programs are no more successful than outpatient programs (Fishbein and Pease, 1996). However, inpatient programs appear to be more effective for individuals who have failed at outpatient treatment centers, people with severe medical problems that require strict management, and individuals with limited support systems and poor motivation concerning recovery (Doweiko, 1999).

Cognitive–Behavioral Programs

Cognitive-behavioral treatments can be used in both group and individual sessions. Group sessions are designed to help athletes learn how to overcome their addiction and behavioral problems and strengthen their foundation for recovery. Individual sessions address, uncover, and resolve the underlying causes of the problem and ultimately change the thinking that has produced the dysfunctional behaviors. When thinking changes, behaviors change, which is the premise for cognitive–behavioral therapy (Benshoff and Janikowski, 2000). During this time, substance-abusing athletes must recognize the cues that trigger drug use. "Walk-throughs"—situations in which athletes had previously encountered and taken drugs—are an important self-control strategy. If athletes with a substance abuse problem continue to train and compete, it is likely that they will remain immersed in the culture that originally caused the drug use. Having the ability to recognize walk-throughs and develop alternative responses to the drug-related cues better enables athletes to resist future drug use (Azrin et al., 1994). This strategy ultimately allows athletes to remain in the sport environment that initially led to drug use, refuse the allure of drugs, and find positive solutions to the problems they faced in their sport and in their personal lives.

Individualized counseling focuses directly on reducing or stopping substance use. It can also address related areas of impaired functioning, on and off the field of play, such as employment status, family or social relations, and overall performance (McLellan, Arndt, Metzger, Woody, and O'Brien, 1993). This can help athletes develop coping strategies and tools for abstaining from substance use and then maintaining abstinence. Successful outcomes for this type of treatment depend on keeping the individual in counseling long enough to gain the full benefits of treatment, and therefore strategies for keeping an individual in the program are critical. Factors to consider include motivation to change the drug-using behavior, degree of support from friends and family, and whether there is pressure to stay in treatment from the organization (McLellan, Grisson, et al., 1993).

Relapse Prevention

Relapse prevention, a cognitive–behavioral therapy, is based on the theory that learning processes play a critical role in the development of maladaptive behavioral patterns (Carroll, Rounsaville, and Keller, 1991). In this type of program, individuals learn to identify and correct problematic behaviors by learning strategies to enhance self-control

(Carroll et al., 1991). Specific techniques include exploring the positive and negative consequences of continued use, self-monitoring to recognize drug cravings and to identify high-risk situations for use, and developing strategies for coping with and avoiding high-risk situations and the desire to use (Marlatt and Gordon, 1985). Research indicates that the skills individuals learn through relapse prevention therapy remain after the completion of the treatment process (Marlatt and Gordon, 1985).

Coach's Perspective

Each team has an Employee Assistance Program (EAP), 24-hour hot line, and bilingual counselors. All information is completely confidential, and the player's identity is protected. No financial penalties are levied against players who enter drug treatment. Once a player has successfully moved through the rehabilitation program, follow-up consultations are held on a regular basis throughout the year.

■　■　■　■

Athlete's Perspective

There is a large amount of legal and illegal drug use in baseball as well as other professional athletics. Many programs are offered by major league and minor league baseball as well as by individual organizations to combat drug use. Some of these programs include random drug testing, counseling, and hot lines, but none appear to possess a full and complete understanding of the athlete's point of view. There is not a full awareness of why and how drugs are being taken. For instance, a pitcher might have a case of tendinitis in his shoulder that will not go away. In order for him to pitch, he may need to take 12 to 16 Advil a day. If he does not take this medication, he will not be able to play and may lose a chance to be called up to the major leagues. As soon as the season is over, the pitcher will stop taking the Advil and give his arm time to rest and recuperate. What many programs fail to recognize is that the pitcher needs the Advil in order to play. Without it, his livelihood could be at stake, and once use is no longer necessary, it is discontinued. Most counseling programs only see that 16 Advil a day is above the recommended dosage and the player is abusing the drug. Although a system of prevention and intervention is necessary in baseball, there needs to be increased awareness and subsequent research regarding the true motivators behind drug use.

■　■　■　■

Drug Treatment Professionals

Finding mental health professionals who are qualified to assess and treat athletes with substance abuse problems is essential for athletes to overcome their addictions. Which professional is chosen to work with substance-abusing athletes depends on the nature of the problem and its identified cause. Several questions must be considered: What is the specific abuse? What is the purpose of the drug use? Are there other psychological problems, such as depression or anxiety? Is the athlete at significant risk physically or psychologically? A professional who is familiar with sports and their unique challenges can better understand how the substance abuse problem developed and also establish rapport and trust with an athlete. In selecting the proper professional to meet the needs of an athlete with a substance abuse problem, officials must consider the athlete's immediate and long-term health and well-being.

Addiction counselors typically earn a bachelor's degree (often in psychology) and then receive additional training and experience in the treatment of substance abuse. An addiction counselor deals specifically with concerns directly associated with substance abuse and is limited to its immediate treatment, usually under the supervision of a professional with a broader background in mental health, such as a psychiatrist or psychologist. Addiction counselors usually work at substance abuse treatment facilities.

A licensed professional counselor has a master's degree in mental health counseling and is licensed to practice independently in each state. To be qualified to treat substance abusers, counselors must also have additional education and training in drug treatment. Licensed professional counselors work in a variety of settings, including private practice, governmental agencies, residential drug treatment facilities, or colleges and universities.

A licensed psychologist has received a doctoral degree in counseling or clinical psychology, is licensed by the state, and is trained to deal with a wide range of psychological disorders that are identified in the *Diagnostic and Statistical Manual of Mental Disorders* (American Psychiatric Association, 2000). However, this training, which usually includes some exposure to substance abuse issues, is typically not sufficient to treat drug problems. A specific focus on substance abuse that involves practicum and supervision during either graduate school or postdoctoral fellowships is necessary for psychologists to ethically treat drug abusers. This blend of training is valuable because drug problems are often accompanied by psychological disorders, such as depression, anxiety, or posttraumatic stress disorder (Miller, Miller, et al., 2002). Licensed psychologists work in similar settings as licensed professional counselors as well as in hospitals, corporations, and other health care facilities and have admitting privileges to inpatient hospitals.

A psychiatrist has earned a medical degree, has completed a residency in psychiatry, and is licensed by the state. Psychiatrists are a beneficial part of a substance abuse treatment team because of several unique qualifications. First, they are trained to address both the physical and psychological aspects of the drug problem. Second, psychiatrists are trained to directly respond to the physical risks and problems associated with substance abuse. Third, they can readily arrange for hospitalization and medical care. Fourth, psychiatrists can prescribe relevant medications as part of the treatment protocol. Psychiatrists work in similar settings as psychologists.

A sport psychologist has received a doctoral degree in counseling or clinical psychology, is licensed to practice by the state, and has additional education, training, and experience in the field of applied sport psychology and other sport sciences. (Some professionals have doctoral degrees in sport science or a related field but cannot legally call themselves sport psychologists because the use of the title *psychologist* is regulated by state licensing boards; in addition, these people are not necessarily trained to address substance abuse issues.) Sport psychologists have demonstrable expertise in psychological assessment and intervention as well as extensive experience in sport. This combination of knowledge allows sport psychologists to understand not only the presenting problem but also the complex issues in sport that may have contributed to the development of the substance abuse problem. Sport psychologists work in similar settings as licensed psychologists as well as for sport governing bodies and athletic teams.

Drug Testing

Drug testing is a preventive and punitive strategy that has been increasingly implemented within many sports. The purpose of drug testing is, in essence, to scare athletes away from illegal or banned drug use by the threat of severe consequences, such as fines, suspension, mandatory counseling, and banishment from the sport. The IOC and its constituent member sports have organized drug-testing programs that consist of random testing at competitions and during the off-season ("The History of Drug Testing," 2002). Professional sport leagues in the United States, such as the National Basketball Association, National Football League, and Major League Baseball, also have some form of drug-testing programs; however, they are less effective because they do not include random testing and may not include all illegal or banned substances (FindLaw, 2002). The ineffectiveness of some of these programs is attributable in part to the influence of the players' unions, which exert significant control over intrusions into their members' professional and personal lives through the collective bargaining agreements negotiated between players and owners (FindLaw, 2002). Additionally, the technology for the detection of illegal or banned substances often lags behind the science of new performance-enhancing drugs and the means to make their use undetectable ("The History of Drug Testing," 2002). Moreover, drug testing is expensive and many sport organizations, particularly those that are not profit making, are reluctant to allocate money for these purposes (FindLaw, 2002). Despite these obstacles, drug-testing programs have proven to be of some value because athletes have been caught and punished, and more sports appear to be less tarnished by the presence of illegal drugs ("How Other Sports Handle Testing," 2002) (see "Drug Testing Programs," below).

Athlete's Perspective

There is no question that drug use is occurring in baseball as well as in other sports. Baseball players are using a variety of substances ranging from alcohol to human growth hormone. Better drugs are entering the market every day, and many athletes are willing to use them if they offer them a chance of achieving "star quality." This is a problem, but to say that this problem is occurring because of athletes' win-at-all-costs attitudes may not be accurate. The issue goes much further than just a will to win. Performance-enhancing drugs will help an athlete to compete better and help his or her team win, but a player takes drugs primarily to keep the career that he worked so hard for. Many athletes do not see the negative consequences of using drugs; they only see the positive outcomes for their careers, themselves, and their families. This is the issue that conflicts with the goals of many prevention and intervention programs. Will athletes ever want to discontinue drug use if the consequences of quitting outweigh the consequences of continuing?

■   ■   ■   ■   ■

Drug-Testing Programs

Minor League Baseball

Testing: All players are tested for amphetamines, cocaine, LSD, marijuana, opiates, PCP, ecstasy, alcohol, steroids, and androstenedione.

Punishment: First-time offenders are subject to education, treatment, and counseling and are placed in a program where there is more random testing. Repeat offenders are subject to various actions; five positive tests require a suspension.

NFL

Testing: All players are tested once during preseason for steroids, cocaine, marijuana, opiates, PCP, and ephedrine. Testing continues year-round with seven or eight players picked randomly from each team every week. There also are random off-season tests.

Punishment: A first-time offender is suspended for four games without pay. A second-time offender gets a six-game suspension without pay, and a third offense draws a year's suspension without pay.

NBA

Testing: Rookies get tested four times a year for amphetamines, cocaine, LSD, opiates, marijuana, PCP, and steroids.

U.S. Olympic Committee

Testing: Athletes are tested for steroids, diuretics, narcotics, peptide hormones (EPO), mimetics, analogs (e.g., human growth hormone and insulin-like growth factor-1), stimulants, blood doping, and plasma expanders. Also prohibited in certain circumstances (in competition, usually) are alcohol, β-blockers, marijuana, local anesthetics, and glucocorticosteroids. EPO is tested for at certain events, including the most recent Olympics in Sydney and Salt Lake City.

Punishment: Penalties vary by sport and by substance. First-time offenders can receive as little as a public warning or as much as a 2-year suspension. In 2001, a diver received a 2-month suspension for using ephedrine, a track athlete received a public warning for the same offense, and a cyclist received a 3-month suspension. All were first-time offenders who tested positive at events.

NCAA

Testing: A year-round, on-campus, random program tests for anabolic steroids in Division I football and track and field and Division II football and baseball. Every college player is tested at least once a year. Besides steroids and diuretics, stimulants and street drugs are tested for at NCAA championships and bowl games. A positive test results in loss of eligibility for 1 year.

USA Today, Retrieved on July 8, 2002 www.usatoday.com/usatonline/20020708/4253743s.htm

Key Points

- Athletes use drugs for a variety of reasons including to enhance performance, for recreation, and to manage injury and pain.
- Drugs used to enhance performance, including anabolic steroids, amphetamines, and caffeine, encourage muscle development, improve cardiovascular efficiency, maintain energy levels, or promote faster physiological recovery.
- Popular recreational drugs, such as alcohol, marijuana, cocaine, and tobacco, act as either depressants or stimulants on the body.
- Drugs used to manage injury and pain, including antibacterial agents, analgesics, muscle relaxants, and anti-inflammatory medications, mask pain and allow athletes to compete injured.
- It is common for athletes to have multiple addictive behaviors, for example, disordered eating and abuse of drugs.
- Treatment of substance abuse must address both the physical and psychological aspects of the addiction.
- Drug testing and prevention and intervention programs are two ways in which sport organizations attempt to curb the use and abuse of drugs among athletes.
- A variety of mental health professionals, such as addiction counselors, licensed professional counselors, licensed psychologists, psychiatrists, and sport psychologists, are trained to treat some aspect of a substance abuse problem.

Review Questions

1. What are the three primary reasons why athletes take drugs?
2. What are some specific reasons why drug use among athletes is growing?
3. What are the most common approaches for the treatment of substance abuse?
4. What are the strengths and weaknesses of drug-testing programs?
5. What are the key components of an effective prevention or intervention program?
6. What types of mental health professionals are suited to treat an athlete with a substance abuse problem?

15
Career Transitions

Mitchell A. Levy, PhD—researcher

Lauren Gordon, MSW—consultant

Roseann Wilson, MS—coach

Casey Barrett, BA—athlete

© Photodisc

The objectives of this chapter are

- to describe the different types and causes of career transitions;
- to discuss factors related to the quality of career transitions;
- to focus on the psychological, social, and coping skills and the multicultural variables that influence athletes' transition from sport; and
- to present a sample of intervention programs for career transition.

Because athletic careers start at a younger age and are considerably shorter than most other careers, athletes are confronted with career transition concerns much earlier than nonathletes. The ability of athletes to maintain high levels of performance, particularly at the Olympic and professional levels, is limited by injury, diminution of ability, and younger competition. These factors can abruptly end an athlete's career at any time. Athletes are often unprepared to transition from their athletic careers to new life paths. Frequently, athletes have little motivation, few resources to assist in preparation, and limited encouragement to consider the end of their competitive careers. The athletic culture has often discouraged athletes from considering life after sport, believing it would distract them from their competitive efforts. The unfortunate consequence is that athletes are often psychologically and vocationally ill equipped to shift career paths at an age when their peers have very often established and advanced their career and life plans.

Professional and scholarly interest in career transitions among athletes has been growing over the last 20 years. Before 1980, approximately 20 publications on career transitions in sport were written (Lavallee and Wylleman, 2000; McPherson, 1980). By 2000, 270 papers were published on this topic and, by 2002, at least another dozen references had emerged. The Professional Athletes Transition Institute was recently established at Quinnipiac University. The study of career transitions in other performance areas, including dance and business, has contributed to this growing body of knowledge (Patton and Ryan, 2000). Interest in career transition has occurred not only at the academic level. Applied sport psychology consultants often work with athletes during this sometimes difficult transition. Additionally, national governing bodies, universities, and professional leagues have implemented programs that offer vital career transition services to athletes during and at the conclusion of their careers.

Key Issues

Assisting athletes in making successful transitions to postathletic careers may be one of the most frequently encountered issues for applied sport psychology consultants (Murphy, 1995). Throughout the career span of an athlete, there will be ongoing opportunities to understand, prepare for, and assist in successful transitions from sport. Essential considerations that must be addressed include the notions that transitions are natural parts of development, that transition crises can be anticipated and prepared for, and that sport governing bodies and teams must support athletes' early attention to and preparation for career transitions. Additionally, organized career transition services must be available to athletes throughout and following their sports careers. Such services need to include self-exploration; peer, team, and institutional support; personal and career counseling; and career and life skills resources. To enhance the quality of career transitions, interventions must also focus on multicultural considerations, such as race, ethnicity, and gender. Diverse athlete populations that have not been studied need to be included in any new research, so specific interventions and models can be adapted to their individual as well as collective needs.

Chapter Purpose and Author Team

The purpose of this chapter is to provide an overview of the issues that influence the quality of career transitions among athletes and to explore how this shift in life path can be facilitated. Career transitions can be planned or unplanned, empowered or forced, and they can be best understood if considered as just one step in a lifelong process of development and growth. In addition, because the athletic community has become more diverse in terms of nationality, age, gender, disability, sexual identity, and racial or ethnic identity, more attention must be given to how these multicultural issues affect career transition. The researcher (Dr. Mitchell Levy) integrates the latest theory and research that attempt to explain and clarify career transition among athletes. The consultant (Lauren Gordon) introduces the essential issues that athletes face as they confront career transitions. Throughout the chapter, comments from Casey Barrett, a former Canadian Olympic swimmer, and Roseann Wilson, former U.S. Olympic Festival and Division I collegiate coach, will be interspersed to offer their personal experiences and perspectives.

Coach's Perspective

Although athletes may start to struggle in their ability to compete at a high level, many coaches will encourage them to remain focused on their athletic career, even when their confidence, ability, and motivation to compete begin to wane. I have seen coaches who will perpetuate (often falsely) athletes' dreams of athletic success. Unfortunately, this is done not to promote the athletes' well-being, but conversely, to serve the coach's and the team's needs. Often, rather than encouraging athletes to continue in their sport, coaches should start preparing athletes for the next phase of their lives.

I have noticed that those athletes who play an active role in the decision-making process throughout their athletic careers (including when to stop participation) tend to feel as though they are more in charge of their lives. Athletes who have had a domineering coach (or parent) are typically less confident in making choices, and this includes the decision to stop sport participation. They identify themselves as athletes, because that is what they have been told they are. As a result, it is difficult for them to quit being an athlete and to initiate this change on their own.

■ ■ ■ ■ ■

Athlete's Perspective

On March 28, 1998, I retired from swimming and went on a bender. For the next 3 weeks, I fled the lost demons of my athletic career and clouded my newfound freedom with large quantities of alcohol amid a string of very late nights. For the previous 14 years, I had arisen with the dawn and led a life entirely centered around my performance in the water. Now, the idea was to see the dawn from the other side, to charge through it without responsibility and collapse as the sun broke through—out of exhaustion of an entirely different kind. Fortunately, my stamina was better suited for healthier pursuits and I gradually lost this hunger for the night. But I was hardly alone in my reaction to retirement. Most of my friends and teammates found that the sudden loss of the greatest passion in our lives left a void that needed to be filled. In the short term, alcohol could do the trick; in the long-term, a positive life reassessment was in order.

■ ■ ■ ■ ■

Definitions of Career Transitions in Sports

The European Federation of Sports Psychology (FEPSAC), in its position statements 3 and 5 (1997) describes developmental stages in an athlete's career: the learning and choosing of specific sports; the adjustment to intensive training and increased competition; the attainment of most proficient status, which may be community team, club, or high school varsity; and intercollegiate participation, national or international competition, or professional status. Although recognizing these types of athletic career transitions, FEPSAC did not acknowledge the end of an athletic career as being a part of the process of athletic development. The sheer number of publications on the subject to date suggests that career transition should be added to this list as an essential—and inevitable—part of an athlete's life.

Sport psychology's emphasis on career retirement or career termination has often portrayed this process as being an abrupt and often negative experience (Alfermann, 2000; Cockerill and Edge, 1998; Lavallee, 2000; Taylor and Ogilvie, 1998). This chapter, however, focuses on a life span approach within which athletes' career transitions are viewed as a normal part of their sport participation as well as a small step in the larger progression of their lives. As a result, efforts to help athletes make transitions as smoothly as possible must include more than sport-related influences. These efforts must consider broader life issues, such as education and relationships, and multicultural variables such as gender and ethnicity that affect athletes' adaptation to the end of their careers and the start of a new career and life path.

Coach's Perspective

Career transition has a lot to do with keeping perspective, and this really starts in youth sports. Letting young athletes stay diversified in their sport choices and extracurricular activities will allow them to develop a variety of talents and interests. I have seen good coaches who encouraged multiple interests to develop a well-rounded individual, and I have unfortunately also witnessed the opposite. Most of the successful athletes with whom I have been involved made successful transitions to happy careers and lives after sports.

■ ■ ■ ■ ■

Social and Psychological Explanations of Career Transition

Early models of life transition arose from the field of social psychology. For example, McPherson (1980) was among the first to link sport transitions to social gerontology. Gerontology is a systemic analysis of aging, consisting of biology, sociology, and psychology subdivisions. Social gerontology integrates societal values with aging as developmental issues (Atchley, 1976). Rosenberg (1982) introduced the concepts of sports as a subculture in which career transitions can cause possible adjustment problems and these transitions can be viewed as a social death. He defined social death as loss of social roles, with possible isolation, rejection, or even ostracism. Gwen Verdon, a famous dancer, said, "A dancer dies twice, the first time at retirement." Many athletes have felt this way as well. Gordon (1995) adapted Kubler-Ross' (1969) model of death and dying to career transitions in sports, including the grief of the injury process. He saw athletes as leaving a subculture, not entering one. Kubler-Ross' model listed denial and isolation, anger, bargaining, depression, and acceptance as the five stages of death and dying. However, these models neither were sport specific nor addressed individual differences in how athletes experience transitions. These models view career transition negatively, focusing on endings and loss (Howe, Musselman, and Planella, 2000; Taylor and Ogilvie, 1998). These models also did not take into account cultural differences among athletes, such as sport, gender, age, race, coping skills, and family history, that might affect the quality of their career transition (Danish, Petitpas, and Hale, 1993; Pearson and Petitpas, 1990; Taylor and Ogilvie, 1993). In addition, these early models looked at career transition as a singular event rather than part of an ongoing process of development.

Developmental models that incorporate a life span perspective most accurately represent the dynamic nature of career transitions and take into account individual and cultural contributors to the experience. Wylleman (2003) noted that in the 1960s, athlete career endings were seen as a singular event; in the 1970s, athlete career termination was a transitional process; in the 1980s, athletes had career "transitions"; and in the 1990s to 2000s, athletes were studied and best assisted by understanding both their athletic and nonathletic transitions.

Developmental life span models reflect ongoing life transitions at cross-sections of age, personal and athletic mastery levels, psychosocial factors, and educational or career development that can be anticipated, planned for, adapted to, and moved on from (Levy, Hendricks, and Gordon, 2000; Wylleman, 2003). Lavallee (2000) cited Schlossberg (1981) who suggested that adaptations to transitions are influenced by personal and environmental variables such as individual factors (gender, age,

state of health, race, socioeconomic issues, values, and prior experiences in transitions); perception (role change, affect, onset, duration, degree of stress); and characteristics of pre- and posttransition environments (internal support, institutional support, and physical settings). Danish, Petitpas, and Hale (1992, 1993) and Taylor and Ogilvie (1994) took Schlossberg's (and Sinclair and Orlick's, 1993) model several steps further by emphasizing flexibility and multiple variables, allowing for both negative and positive adjustments. Taylor and Ogilvie (1998) integrated theoretical and empirical considerations and prior theories and used their own applied work to prepare a model of career transition. Lavallee (2000) listed the systemic steps of their model as causal, developmental, coping, quality of adjustment, and treatment issues. These steps are the basis for several intervention programs described later in this chapter.

One of the leading proponents of a life span approach to career development is Donald Super. Super (1990) believes that vocational preferences and competencies, the situations in which people live and work, and hence, their self-concepts, change with time and experience. Self-concepts, however, as products of social learning, are increasingly stable from late adolescence until later maturity, providing some continuity in choice and adjustment. Super (1990) wrote that the process of change may be summed up in a series of life stages. A "maxicycle" is characterized as a sequence of growth, exploration, establishment, maintenance, and decline. A small "minicycle" takes place from one stage to the next or each time an individual is destabilized by a reduction in force, changes in type of manpower needs, illness or injury, or other socioeconomic or personal events.

Feminist and multicultural approaches extend this dialogue even further. Sue (1991) stated that changing demographics are having a major impact on educational, economic, social, political, legal, and cultural systems. Feminism, which is rich in its layers of definition, is an encompassing world view and movement to end oppression, originally that of women (Oglesby, 2001.) This creates an inclusive viewpoint that has been continually expanded to include gender, race, class, and sexual identity diversity, among other multicultural variables (Gill, 2001a). Feminist sport psychology encompasses all areas of research, education, training, and practice in psychology. Worell and Johnson (1997) listed common themes of feminist sport psychology that include transformation and social change, diversity as a foundation of practice, analysis of power and oppression, promotion of empowerment, collaboration, and the value of diverse research methodologies. Gill (2001b), for example, argued that gender differences and homophobia (the fear of and oppression of other sexual identities; Gordon and Levy, 2001) are as important to our discussion as other contributors to the quality of career transition. For instance, because female athletes and all athletes of color have traditionally had fewer work opportunities beyond the playing field (Alfermann, 1995; Hall, 2001; Hastings, Kurth, and Meyer, 1989), the definitions of successful career transitions used by sport psychology consultants must take this discrepancy into consideration. Consequently, the definition of a successful career transition for a female athlete or athlete of color may be different than a successful career transition for a white male athlete. Therefore, sport psychology consultants must incorporate both feminist and multicultural awareness into career transition discussions with diverse populations of athletes.

Athlete's Perspective

For most athletes I know, the end of an athletic career seems to be dealt with through stubborn denial. Even those of us with wide and varied interests outside the sport often view other pursuits as merely hobbies. Admitting to more would be wavering in our commitment to the sport, to the true mission. Because of this inherent attitude, it seems essential that career transitions must be faced gradually—from a rookie season through the swan song. Other interests, skills, and, most of all, passions, should be discovered throughout a career, not in its final days.

One tragic consequence of true devotion to a sport is the gradual recession of other talents. I was often guilty of this shortsightedness, as were most of my teammates. When viewed next to our sport—in hours spent and attention given—our academic majors were usually our minors. Summer internships were generally put on hold in favor of serious training and travel to international competitions. Real-world experience was simply not considered.

■ ■ ■ ■ ■

Causes of Career Transitions

All athletes will have to end their sport career at some point in their lives, whether unexpectedly or of their own accord. This ending may come after high school, college, international, or professional competition. Regardless of the level athletes

achieve, leaving a sport can be a life-altering experience. There are many reasons why athletes' careers end, each cause having different implications in the quality and the outcome of the transition. Taylor and Ogilvie (1994) cited four primary causes of career transition: injury, age, deselection, and free choice. The first three causes of career transitions are involuntary and are believed to cause more distress than choosing to end one's career voluntarily (Ogilvie and Taylor, 1993).

Injury

In both the sports and performing arts literature, career termination caused by an injury is challenging and stressful for athletes (Lavallee, 2000; Ogilvie and Taylor, 1993a) and other performers (Patton and Ryan, 2000). Injury causes more adjustment problems than do other reasons for retirement (Webb, Nasco, Riley, and Headrick, 1998), particularly for those whose identities are highly connected with their participation (Brewer, 1994; Brewer, Van Raalte, and Petitpas, 2000; Kleiber and Brock, 1992). Ogilvie and Taylor (1993b) cited several studies indicating that severe injuries may result in a variety of psychological difficulties, including fear, anxiety, and loss of self esteem (Rotella and Heyman, 1986), as well as depression and substance abuse (Ogilvie and Howe, 1982). Tunick, Etzel, Leard, and Lerner (1996) stated that although there is a lack of consensus among researchers concerning the phases of adjustment regarding athletic injury, it is generally agreed that an injury can affect an athlete's psychological resources and coping mechanisms (see chapter 12).

Coach's Perspective

Injury at the prime of a career seems to be one of the most difficult things for athletes to deal with. Athletes know that, if not for the injury, they would be continuing their careers and enjoying success. Injuries are especially harmful to athletes whose self-identity is unhealthily invested in sport participation. Teaching athletes early that unfortunate circumstances can occur may help prepare them for the possibility of a career-threatening injury. Also, teaching athletes that they have talents and options outside of sport is important.

■ ■ ■ ■ ■

Age

Age is one of the most common reasons for career termination (Ogilvie and Taylor, 1993b). With age, the inevitable decline in physical capabilities can prevent athletes from competing at their highest level. The career-limiting effects of age have significant ramifications for both younger and older athletes. For example, the ages at which gymnasts and figure skaters reach the end of their careers versus baseball and soccer players relate to vastly different life stages. Taylor and Ogilvie (1998) stated that the impact that age has on career termination for athletes includes physiological, psychological, and social factors. Werthner and Orlick (1986) wrote that athletes often lose their motivation to train and compete because of increasing age. Additionally, Taylor and Ogilvie (1998), as well as Sinclair and Orlick (1993), identified the negative impact that loss of status attributable to age-diminished performance can have on career transitions.

Deselection

Involuntary transition attributable to deselection from teams or competitions—what Lavallee (2000) termed "athletic Darwinism"—can make the transition process even more difficult (Blinde and Stratta, 1992; Wheeler, Malone, Van-Vlack, Nelson, and Steadward, 1996). Deselection occurs at every level of competitive sport (see Petitpas, Champagne, Chartrand, Danish, and Murphy, 1997). Athletes who are deselected because of poor performance feel out of control, angry, unsupported, lacking in coping skills, and uncertain about their futures (Ogilvie and Taylor, 1993a, b; Sinclair and Hackfort, 2000). McInally, Cavin-Stice, and Knoth (1992) found that 27% of their sample were deselected from their teams, indicating that involuntary transition is a significant cause of career transition in sports.

Free Choice

The ideal way in which athletes should leave their sport is by their own choice and on their own terms. Many researchers believe that choice is an important determinant of the quality of the career transition (Coakely, 1983; Taylor and Ogilvie, 1994; Webb, Nasco, Riley, and Headrick, 1998). Athletes choose to leave sports for a variety of reasons including having accomplished their goals, having new priorities, and no longer finding enjoyment in their participation. These athletes often have set postcareer goals (Baillee, 1993), have a balanced self-identity (Grove, Lavallee, and Gordon, 1997), and feel well supported by significant others in their athletic and personal lives (Sinclair and Orlick, 1993). Athletes who choose to end their sport careers also have planned and prepared for

this moment (McGowan and Rail, 1996; Yallop, 1996), believe that they have many options available to them in their postathletic careers, and have considerable coping resources they can use (Sinclair and Hackfort, 2000) in the transition process. Although free choice does not guarantee a painless transition (Taylor and Ogilvie, 1998), because feelings of loss are a natural part of the process, athletes see the overall experience as positive.

Psychological Reactions to Career Transition

Significant negative psychological reactions are infrequent among high school and college athletes and more common among professional and world-class athletes during career transition (Lavallee, Nesti, Borkoles, Cockerill, and Edge, 2000). The Monster.com Olympian Career Survey (2001) found that 61% of former Olympians experienced emotional distress after Olympic competition. Svoboda and Vanek (1982) reported that 83% of the former Czech Olympian athletes they studied experienced some difficulties following retirement, whereas Werthner and Orlick (1986) found that 78.6% of Canada's elite athletes experienced some form of difficulty in transitioning out of competition. McInally and colleagues (1992) conducted a survey with retired professional football players and found that 88% of respondents found the overall career transition process to be extremely problematic. The following concerns were identified as causing moderate to severe problems for the retiring athletes: financial or occupational adjustment (31%), emotional adjustment (26%), and social adjustment (23%). Many athletes experience anxiety, denial, and depression as well as a loss of athletic identity, self-esteem, financial and social status, and social connectedness. Feelings of loss, adjustment difficulties, and heightened defenses are especially likely with athletes whose self-identity is heavily invested in their sport participation (Ball, 1976; Curtis and Ennis, 1988; Lavallee, Grove, Gordon, and Ford, 1988). Athletes who are forced to retire may experience depression and anger and may turn to alcohol, drugs, exercise, or other activities in excess to manage the stress and feelings that come from the transition (Alfermann and Gross, 1998). Additionally, athletes who feel unsupported by coaches or teammates can feel more bitter and isolated. One Canadian Olympic ice hockey player reported that after being cut from the Olympic team, she didn't hear from any of her teammates and did not feel welcome at team social events. Retiring athletes may also experience family conflict because the family structure has changed suddenly. Marital relations and child–parent bonds can be stressed as transitioning athletes struggle to establish themselves in their new life path.

Athletes are forced to confront the reduction of options, including financial perks, and the overwhelming landscape of new career choices. This uncertainty can create additional stress, particularly if athletes did not take active steps to prepare for a career transition. Ogilvie and Taylor (1993b) stated that career termination may be conceptualized as a complex interaction of stressors, and whether these stressors are financial, social, psychological, or physical, they may produce some form of trauma. Many researchers and practitioners, however, encourage athletes to view transitions as stressful yet positive life experiences (Allison and Meyer, 1988; Gordon, 1995). If athletes find enjoyment and fulfillment in the

sport itself and not only in terms of winning and losing, then their participation will play a positive role in their overall life satisfaction and will ease the transition process (Kern and Sayn, 2000). As can be seen in figure 15.1, the media has devoted increased attention to the issues facing athletes who are confronted with career termination. As these headlines attest, athletes face a myriad of challenges when they leave their sport.

Athlete's Perspective

The Olympic Village is often romanticized as a playground of pure competition and, after the events, a hedonistic community of liberated athletes. It is believed that, free from the extreme stress of 4 years of sacrifice, athletes can finally let go and revel in one another's accomplishments. Although the partying and inevitable "international affairs" are indeed a reality, the underlying current is often one of sadness and loss. Precompetition pressure gives way to a sudden

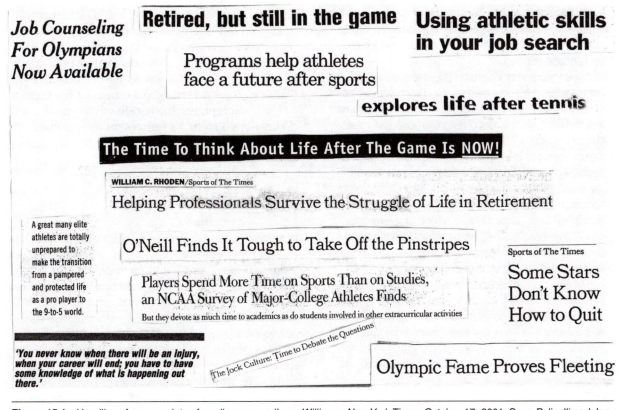

Figure 15.1 Headlines from a variety of media sources (Lena Williams, *New York Times*, October 17, 2001; Gene Policelli and Jennifer Rylery-Walsh, *University of Connecticut Newsletter*, Fall 1996; Carrie Mason-Draffen, *Newsday*, June 18, 2000; Mark Winters, *Tennisweek*, November 16, 2000; Advertisement for Professional Business and Financial Network in *Street and Smith's SportsBusiness Journal*, March 17, 2002; William C. Rhoden, *New York Times*, February 24, 2002; Robert Lipsyte, *New York Times Magazine*, November 30, 1986; Buster Olney, *New York Times*, November 2, 2001; William C. Rhoden, *New York Times*, March 2, 2002; Douglas Lederman, *The Chronicle of Higher Education*, December 7, 1998; Robert Lipsyte, *New York Times*, May 9, 1999; Amy Rosewater, *New York Times*, July 23, 2002).

realization that is best expressed as, "Well, what now?" Whether the athlete takes home gold or an ignoble last-place finish, an undeniable depression pervades the Village in the final days of the Games.

In 1996, I found myself, unexpectedly, in the midst of these conflicting emotions. I had placed 11th in the 200 butterfly—with a lifetime best time. Our Canadian team took home three medals, broke numerous national records, and had more than a few reasons to celebrate. But, although no one would admit it at the time, there was something missing. Something would never be the same, and even those of us who would continue competing could sense the loss. In retrospect, I recognize that feeling a mass career transition as a communal identity crisis shocked us all.

Regardless of the type of transition, the end of every athlete's career is truly a "little death." After the 2000 Games, Australian swimmer Susie O'Neill—a national icon and multiple Olympic gold medalist—was asked to share her feelings on her retirement. She replied, "The hardest part is knowing that I'll never be the best in the world at anything again." Although few athletes ever achieve the successes of O'Neill, her comment reflects the difficulties faced in even the most ideal circumstances. Here is a woman who was able to leave her sport on her own terms: at the top, in her home country, financially well off, and loaded with new opportunities. But everything that awaited her paled in comparison to sport.

I watched a very different "little death" a few years earlier when a friend experienced a transition far less ideal. Swimming the same event in many of the same international meets as O'Neill, she tore her rotator cuff at the age of 20. Four surgeries in 10 months followed—none of them effective. Less than a year after becoming an NCAA All-American, she was forced to retire in the middle of a promising college career. While I continued training, I watched as she became suddenly withdrawn from her once-close group of teammates. I don't think there was anything malicious in the team's alienation; the simple fact was that she no longer shared the core priority in their lives.

My own career transition was neither as perfect as O'Neill's nor as cruel as my friend's. It was an honest admission that my options were somewhat limited. I was 23 and at a level just steps away from sponsorships and prize money. I was good enough to scrape by until the next Olympic Games, but beyond that, few opportunities were available.

■ ■ ■ ■ ■

Coach's Perspective

Even the best-adjusted athletes will naturally feel a sense of loss once their career is over. This has been the main focus of their lives, probably for as long as they can remember. A certain amount of self-centeredness is required for athletic success. Everything, from eating to sleeping to training, has been oriented to one goal: athletic achievement. Suddenly, once this goal is accomplished or taken away, the best-intentioned person will feel a loss. The social status, sense of team, and self-esteem of the athlete can be very hard to replace.

■ ■ ■ ■ ■

Coping Factors Related to Quality of Career Transition

Athletes' ability to effectively cope with the many challenges they will face as their sport participation ends is essential to ensuring a smooth and effective transition from sport. How well athletes are able to cope with the new stressors depends on both internal and outside forces. The extent to which athletes are psychologically equipped to confront a career transition will, to a greater extent, determine their success (Alfermann, 1995; Lavallee, Gordon, and Grove, 1997). Athletes who possess a low degree of coping ability, when combined with deficient social support, will not have the resources necessary to deal with a potentially traumatic life event such as career termination (Tunick, Etzel, Leard, and Lerner, 1996). Having intrinsic capabilities, having effective support, and taking active steps as retirement approaches are all important factors contributing to the quality of athletes' career transition.

Self-Identity

The world of athletics has its own unique culture that influences athletes from their earliest participation. This culture has a set of well-established values, norms, and behavior that athletes adopt to become accepted and functioning members. For example, as Ferrante, Etzel, and Lantz (1996) indicated, many athletic departments see themselves and are perceived by others as autonomous entities, separated from the rest of the university. Remer, Tongate, and Watson (1978) described collegiate athletics as a self-perpetuating system that is difficult for outsiders to enter. From a positive standpoint, this insular, "circle the wagons" mentality can provide athletes with a sense of belonging and protection. However, Remer and colleagues concluded that although many student athletes are protected and supported by this system, they might not necessarily be optimally helped. Ferrante and colleagues stated that efforts to protect or control student-athletes, however well meaning, may in fact prevent athletes from learning to assume responsibility for their lives.

The athletic culture has a significant effect on the development of athletes' self-identities. When athletes' identities become too attached to their sport participation, they can be expected to resist attempts to develop alternate identities—life outside of and after sport—particularly as the end of their athletic career approaches. As defined by Brewer, Van Raalte, and Linder (1993), self-identity in the culture of athletics can be defined as the degree to which an individual identifies with the athletic role. Consequently, the influence of athletic identity has led to concern about how it affects athletes' career transitions (Brewer et al., 2000; Crook and Robertson, 1991; Gordon, 1995; Taylor and Ogilvie, 1994).

A limited self-identity may cause athletes to defend themselves against the threat of the end of their careers through denial. The role that an overly developed athletic identity plays in athletes' avoidance of the inevitable end to their careers needs to be understood and respected (Gordon and Levy, 2001; Thorenson and Kerr, 1978). If sport psychology consultants fail to address this issue when developing career transition interventions, the effectiveness of these efforts will be greatly compromised. According to Dimarco (1997), a lost sense of identity can cause people to lose confidence in their ability to make decisions and plan appropriately for the future. As athletes' identities narrow, their ability to develop in other domains of their life may be compromised (Finch and Gould, 1996; Heil, 1993; Parham, 1993; Pearson and Petitpas, 1990). Ogilvie and Taylor (1993b) indicated that athletes who become overly invested in their sport may be seen as "unidimensional people" (Ogilvie and Howe, 1986) and may be unhealthily dependent on their sport participation for self-validation (Pearson and Petitpas, 1990).

Coach's Perspective

The athletic culture is hard for nonathletes to understand. Often, athletes' attitudes, beliefs, and behaviors are influenced by this culture. Athletes grow up in this culture and seek comfort in its rules and norms. Suddenly, when their playing days are over, they are yanked out of this familiarity and placed in a different culture. The same rules often don't apply, and athletes can feel lonely, confused, and alienated. I think this is why so many athletes hang on to their athletic careers past their competitive prime or return after

an unsuccessful attempt to adjust to life outside the athletic culture.

This is why athletes should not live solely within the athletic culture and identify themselves solely as athletes. Their entire self-concept cannot be tied up in sports. There is more to all of us than simply our vocation, and we have many talents. Athletes need to have a life outside of athletics, so that when their careers end, they will have paths to follow. Part of their success resulted from the significant place sports had in their self-identity. But athletes who see themselves as many things, with athletics being only one part of their identity, have an easier time adjusting to career transition.

■ ■ ■ ■ ■

Social Support

Although athletes may be fortunate enough to have people who care for them and want to help them make a successful career transition, there is no guarantee that these individuals know how to support the athlete. Consequently, athletic departments and organizations must continue to develop career transition programs that address the myriad psychological, financial, social, and occupational concerns that arise for transitioning athletes.

Social support has been defined as "an exchange of resources between at least two individuals perceived by the provider or the recipient to be intended to enhance the well-being of the recipient" (Shumaker and Brownell, 1984, p. 13). As Lavallee (2000) indicated, the importance of social support networks among both active and injured athletes has been outlined in the literature (e.g., Ford and Gordon, 1999; Rosenfeld, Richman, and Hardy, 1989). Ogilvie and Taylor (1993b) wrote that social support is another resource that will facilitate the career termination process and that at least two means of support are important factors in dealing with this issue. First, emotional support from family and friends acts as a buffer against the stressors of termination (Coakley, 1983; Svoboda and Vanek, 1982). Evidence has shown that athletes who receive emotional support demonstrated less distress following career termination (Mihovilovic, 1968; Reynolds, 1981). Second, several investigators have reported that institutional support before, during, and after career termination was related to effective transition (Gorbett, 1985; Manion, 1976; Schlossberg, 1981). In their conceptual model of adaptation to career transition, Taylor and Ogilvie (1998) included social support and preretirement planning, in addition to coping strategies, as examples of the requisite resources that need to be available to athletes confronted with a career transition. Social support can come in many forms, including individual and group counseling that focuses on career transition issues, peer mentoring, continuing education, financial advisement, career counseling, and job placement assistance (Levy and Gordon, 2001).

Coach's Perspective

Sometimes the people who should support athletes during transition are the very ones who instead pressure them: parents who live vicariously through their child's athletic accomplishments, friends who enjoy the limelight of being with a successful athlete, and coaches who selfishly use the athlete. Not only must the athlete prepare for transition, but so must the significant others to whom the athlete will be turning for support.

■ ■ ■ ■ ■

Preretirement Planning

Preretirement planning is an effective tool for athletes to use as they approach the end of their careers (Alfermann, 2000; Gorbett, 1985; Lavallee, 2000). As Ogilvie and Taylor (1993b) stated, preretirement planning programs may include continued education, off-season job training, and financial planning. Additionally, these authors noted, "These preparations may ease the difficulties associated with career termination by broadening self and social identities and by enhancing the athletes' perceptions of control" (p. 361).

Sport psychology consultants can enhance their intervention repertoires by exploring the literature on career transitions for other types of performers, such as dancers. Patton and Ryan (2000) stated that early identification and commitment, as well as familiarity and commitment to a role, as identified by Baillie and Danish (1992) as likely stressors for dancers during a transition, are applicable to athletes. Patton and Ryan (2000) also wrote that Super's theory of career development, as discussed previously, with its life span approach, provides an excellent framework for facilitating productive career transitions for dancers as well as athletes. The incorporation of Super's (1980, 1992) theory into preretirement planning interventions for dancers and athletes allows consultants to view career transitions not as unique, solitary incidents but as points on a continuum of growth and change. For example,

the organization Career Transition for Dancers uses this approach by recognizing that dancers may need career counseling at any time in their careers—as student dancers, as active dancers, preretirement, and during retirement (see "Sample Programs From Dancer," page 265). As Malnig (1984) illustrated, many individuals who are successful in their careers did not necessarily prepare via a direct, planned path. Consequently, rather than viewing athletics, as well as dance, as a form of engagement that pulls participants away from considering other opportunities, we must continue to explore how such individuals can assess their values, goals, and interests via their performances to better prepare for eventual retirement.

Multicultural Considerations

The relevance of diversity issues in sports has increased in the past 20 years as minority participation has grown dramatically. Parham (1996) found that participation among student-athletes of color (e.g., African American, Asian Pacific Islander, Latino or Hispanic, and Native American) in college sports has risen significantly. He also noted increased participation by women of diverse multicultural backgrounds. Since the enactment of Title IX in 1972, young women's participation in sports in the United States has increased markedly at the high school, collegiate, and professional levels. There are more youth leagues and travel teams for girls, more athletic scholarships for women, and, in the last 10 years, a growth in professional sport opportunities, for example, in basketball, soccer, and softball leagues. However, women athletes are not a monolithic group, and their diversities must be examined as intersections of multiple identities, not as separate ones.

Ferrante and colleagues (1996) stated, "It is our belief that student-athletes comprise one of the most diverse groups of people on our college campuses today, particularly with regard to factors such as personal history, academic preparedness, life goals and expectations, physical skills, and developmental readiness. Consequently, to effectively 'reach out' to them as a group, factors related to their heterogeneity should never be underestimated or overlooked" (p. 4). To facilitate career transition for athletes, the influence of cultural factors (i.e., race, ethnicity, sexual identity, gender, religious affiliation, socioeconomic status, geography, education) must be addressed (Gordon and Levy, 2001; Sue, Arredondo, and McDavis, 1992; Wylleman, 2003). Each of these variables will influence how athletes view the world and consequently will affect their expectations regarding career choice, how they operationally define a successful career transition, and the extent to which they envision options outside of athletic competition. If career transition interventions are developed without an awareness of the impact that these cultural factors can have on occupational decision making, then the usefulness of these programs for a diverse population of athletes will be limited. As Brown (2003) wrote, "It is unethical to use Eurocentric models and approaches to career counseling, or any of the processes associated with them (e.g., assessment) when working with minority clients" (p. 111).

The importance of understanding cultural differences with respect to ethnicity, sexual orientation, gender, and socioeconomic status, among others factors, when developing counseling interventions for individuals has received considerable attention in the fields of counseling and clinical psychology and social work (Gordon and Levy, 2001). This interest has been reflected in more attention being devoted to education and training in multicultural issues for psychology professionals (Axelson, 1999; Carter and Querishi, 1995; D'Andrea and Daniels, 1995). Despite this importance, little attention is directed to training graduate sport psychology students to provide culturally sensitive services to the diverse clientele of athletes (Martens, Mobley, and Zizzi, 2000). Additionally, there is still a paucity of research on the influence of multicultural issues on the career transitions of athletes. As Brown (2003) wrote, "Unless the client's values and worldview are fully understood, the likelihood that career counseling is successful is greatly diminished" (p. 111).

Family Issues

Family expectations and involvement in athletes' careers play an important role in the quality of their career transitions. If an athlete's family has invested significant resources (e.g., time, energy, money) into the athlete's development or are dependent on the athlete's continued success, the family may hinder rather than facilitate the athlete's transition from sport by "enabling" (Beattie, 1989) a sense of denial.

In addition to the general concerns about the impact of familial factors on career transitions for athletes, multicultural awareness must be included in exploring the influence of the family on career transition. For example, Yost and Corbishley (1987) cited the following dysfunctional cognitions

as potentially impeding the career development process of culturally diverse people: "No one else in my family (my age, my sex) has ever done it, so I won't be able to either; men (women, old people) aren't supposed to do that sort of thing; it's against my upbringing; it will displease my husband (wife, parent)" (p. 29).

For instance, Asian Americans, Hispanic Americans, and Native Americans, who hold a collective social value, may have a different view of the career transition process than athletes from the majority culture, who make career decisions from a more personal, individualistic perspective (Brown, 2002; Leong, 1991). Lee (1991) stated that a collective social value is often manifested in a strong respect for and obedience to parents and family traditions. When a collective social value is seen as a very strong cultural priority for the athlete as well as the athlete's family, the values of the family members are likely to be the primary determinants of career choice (Sue and Sue, 1990; Yagi and Oh, 1995) and could affect the career path that athletes choose after they retire from their sport. Therefore, sport psychology consultants must be sensitive to the impact of the family on career decision making, especially with respect to those cultural variables that will influence athletes' ability to transition out of their current level of athletic competition.

Coach's Perspective

The athletes whose transitions are smoothest have parents who encourage a well-balanced child. The parents may be very focused on the child having success, but they expect success in the classroom and other areas as well. I have also seen athletes who can't make successful transitions, and their parents have difficulty in supporting and understanding their decisions to stop sport participation. Parents living through the success of their children seem to bring anguish on both themselves and their offspring when the athlete is unable or unwilling to continue competing.

■ ■ ■ ■ ■

Athlete's Perspective

I was lucky enough to have an extremely positive family support system—my family never lost sight of my life beyond the pool and continually brought me back to earth when I placed too much weight on my performance in the water. But I watched friends from different cultures—from Thailand to Sweden—who needed this guidance far more than I did. When an athlete suddenly becomes the hero of his or her small country, or when an entire family places its economic well-being on a son or daughter's accomplishment, these are the times when social support—or its absence—can influence an athlete during career transition.

■　■　■　■　■

Socioeconomic Status

Expectations regarding occupational attainment are positively correlated with socioeconomic status (Brown, 2002; Hotchkiss and Borow, 1996; Ponterotto and Casas, 1991; Sinha, 1990). Leung (1995) indicated that "current models of career development and counseling do not take into consideration the effects of social and economic barriers such as economic hardship, immigration disruption, and the effects of racial discrimination on the career behavior of ethnic minority individuals" (p. 550). Taylor and Ogilvie (1998) wrote that socioeconomic status might influence the adaptation process (Hare, 1971; Weinberg and Arond, 1952). They also stated, "these factors (i.e. gender and minority status) are likely to be most significant when interacting with socioeconomic status and pre-retirement planning" (Weinberg and Arond, 1952). Sport psychology consultants must continue to investigate the role that socioeconomic status has on athletes' readiness to engage in a positive, successful career transition.

Career Transition Interventions

Athletes are faced with significant psychological, social, and financial challenges in their transition to postathletic career and life. The most successful transitions from sport occur when athletes engage in a voluntary transition, have a balanced self-identity, have prepared over the course of their career, and are able to maintain fulfilling relationships. A successful transition can be facilitated by athletes having support for and access to education, counseling, psychological and social support, and career services. Fisher (2001) also reminded us of the influence of sport organizations in the career-transition process.

Numerous researchers and practitioners advocate early and ongoing career transition services for athletes (Baillie, 1993; Howe et al., 2000; Levy and Burke, 1986; Levy and Ehinger, 1996; Levy, Ehinger, and Whittaker, 1997; Levy et al., 2000; Petitpas et al., 1997; Taylor and Ogilvie, 1994). Applied sport psychology consultants can play an essential role in assisting athletes during their career transitions (Alfermann, 2000; Danish et al., 1993; Levy and Burke, 1986). Consultants can help athletes identify their values, skills, and interests through aptitude and skills assessments. They can assist athletes in obtaining the resources necessary for a smooth transition, for example, with Internet job searches, resume and cover letter preparation, and practice interviews. Consultants can provide athletes with outlets to address psychological, emotional, and social concerns. They can also help athletes create a positive and structured approach to their shift from sports to a new career path. For example, programs such as the Life After Sports Program (Levy and Burke, 1986) can offer athletes confidential, scheduled appointments with a sport psychology consultant to discuss various concerns and issues. In addition, as discussed by Levy and Gordon (2001), consultants can assist athletes in increasing their self-awareness with respect to career development and should introduce this intervention as early as possible into an athlete's educational experiences.

Athlete's Perspective

Like success in competition, a successful transition ultimately must come from within the athlete. However, there is a need for programs designed to help athletes through one of the most difficult times they'll ever face. When considering retirement, I received little guidance from the sport organizations that had once been so eager to facilitate every other aspect of my career. It's easy to see why. In sport, success is always judged in the present—with a time, a score, and a number next to the name. It is a world that makes sense. Those who live in this athletic culture are often reluctant to focus on what lies beyond the present. Also, when athletes retire, they are no longer under the purview of the governing body or team. With every athlete who leaves the sport, attention must now turn to the athlete taking his or her place. Unfortunately, retiring athletes are often left adrift to navigate the rough waters of their postathletic lives.

■　■　■　■　■

Successful transitions can be described in terms of occupational success and life satisfaction or adjustment (Alfermann, 1995; Perna, Zaichkowsky, and Bockner, 1996) or psychological readiness (Alfermann, 2000), but what defines a successful career transition is subjective, based on each athlete's expectations, needs, and values. As previously stated, to fully understand what comprises a successful transition for each athlete, multicultural factors must be taken into account. For example, one's gender or race may affect the options available to the individual. Consequently, a successful career transition for a female or nonwhite athlete may be defined differently than that of a white, male athlete, who may be offered different opportunities (Gordon and Levy, 2001).

Athlete's Perspective

Two months before the 1996 Olympic Games, our Canadian team received an intervention at the perfect moment. We were given a wide variety of personality tests, followed by individual meetings to discuss the results. As would be expected, few of us took a multiple-choice test seriously when we believed there were more important matters at hand. However, the process momentarily distracted us from the looming stress of competition and gave us an unexpected dose of perspective. The test ignored our specific talents in the pool and instead focused on our wider personality traits. From these results, an enthusiastic Russian psychologist led us through a variety of career options in which ("without a doubt," he told us) we could be successful later in life. In that brief window of time, it allowed the mind-set of the team to fall beyond the pressures of the Olympic Games. And later that afternoon—back in the water and again obsessed with our strokes—there was a slight sense of calm that hadn't been there before.

■　■　■　■　■

Life Skills Programs

Life skills programs have emerged at all levels of sports, including college programs, professional leagues, Olympic teams, and youth sports (Anderson, 1998; Danish et al., 1993; Levy et al., 2000; Petitpas et al., 1997). Life skills programs involve teaching athletes about the skills they will need during and after their athletic careers. Some of the life skills that are taught include study, social, and mental skills; time management; public speaking and presentation; and financial skills. Many programs include seminars on alcohol and drug use, sex education, and eating disorders (Iona College Promoting the Academic Success of Student-Athletes [PASS] Program; NCAA Challenging Athletes Minds for Personal Success (CHAMPS)/ Life Skills Program; NFL Player Development and Career Transition Program). Life skills programs also offer practical assistance on topics such as resume writing, interviewing, career exploration, college admissions, job training and placement, and mentoring (Athlete Career and Education [ACE] Program, Career Transition for Dancers, NCAA CHAMPS/Life Skills Program).

Personal Counseling

Career transition produces dramatic changes in athletes' lives that can result in uncertainty, upheaval, and strong emotional reactions. Athletes struggling with finding a new life path often feel emotions that include frustration, anger, sadness, and despair. Counseling can be a valuable resource for athletes as they face new psychological, emotional, and social challenges. It allows athletes to express their emotions in a supportive setting, receive useful feedback, problem solve, and develop essential skills to facilitate the transition. Proactive counseling can lead to prevention, earlier detection, and timely intervention for more serious difficulties, such as depression, substance abuse, and social withdrawal. Counseling often includes self and career assessments, cognitive and behavioral techniques, stress management, and emotional "working through." Counseling that is supported by and integrated into a team or school sport program, is readily accessible to athletes, is discrete and confidential, and focuses on the specific needs of athletes can be a significant asset during career transition.

Mentoring and Networking

Mentoring involves a close relationship between a trusted and experienced advisor and a protégé who is supported and guided in a particular area. Mentoring is gaining acceptance as a means of facilitating career transition in sports (Bloom, Durand-Bush, Schinke, and Salmela, 1998; Danish et al., 1993, Perna et al., 1996). The support, guidance, and feedback that mentors give athletes can help the athletes maintain perspective, allay concerns, and direct their efforts in a positive way (Lavallee et al., 2000; Werthner and Orlick, 1986), particularly after the transition to postsport life (Kane, 1988; Murphy, 1995).

Networking is the ongoing interchange or support among group members and can be a tenet of any career program (Lavallee et al., 2000). Networking can occur with peers, with mentors, within professional associations, and with educational, business, social, or other contacts. Examples of networking include alumni and player associations, business functions, and golf outings. The ACE Program, the Iona College PASS Program, TeamUSAnet, and Games Over (discussed in the "Sample Programs in Sport" section) include mentoring and networking among their interventions.

Family Involvement

Family involvement and support during career transition can play a significant role in the experience that retiring athletes have by influencing their perception of the external resources available. As stated previously, as an athlete transitions away from his or her "team and sport family" (Gordon and Levy, 2001), the support provided by family members may become even more critical. Many programs are beginning to recognize the impact of positive quality family support and are cultivating this. One program, Games Over, asks the athlete to identify a family member who will be part of the "team" for transition planning. The National Football League has a Family Assistance Unit to address the needs of the family as well as the player. The National Basketball Association has sanctioned the Mothers' Group, which publicly supports their sons and holds an annual conference that brings in financial, social, and spiritual advisors for the families. Athletes need to identify whom they consider family—whether blood relative, partner, or extended family. Young athletes who have coercive or abusive family involvement require protections including enlightened coaches and mentors, league or organization guidelines and sanctions, and psychological interventions. Consequently, more programs are also offering or mandating parent or coach good conduct education, both at the amateur and professional levels. Examples include the Positive Coaching Alliance and the National Alliance for Youth Sports.

Career Counseling

Many athletes, when their sport careers end, do not have a clear idea of the new path they want their lives to take. Some will need guidance to set educational goals before beginning a new career. Life After Hockey helps current and former National Hockey League players do this. Career counseling can also help in the transition process by assisting athletes in identifying the values and interests that might provide them with career direction as well as assessing their skills. One goal of career counseling is for athletes to recognize that the skills that enabled them to become successful in their sport can, in many cases, be transferred to other careers (Petitpas et al., 1997).

Identification of Skills

Many career counselors believe that skill identification and analysis are at the heart of career planning (Locke and Latham, 1984). Athletes in the midst of a career transition must view themselves as capable of achieving new career goals. Many authors have developed assessment instruments that can be used to assist athletes in identifying their skills (Arcieri and Green, 1999; Bolles, 2000; Ducat, 2002; Locke and Latham, 1984; Petitpas et al., 1997). For example, Campbell and Peterson (1992) developed the Campbell Interest and Skill Inventory (CISI), a systematic and comprehensive inventory that allows respondents to analyze their skills and identify activities they enjoy.

Identification of Interests and Values

A useful framework for identifying interests is for athletes to review and rank a list of skills that correspond to the seven career interest orientations identified by Campbell (1992): influencing, organizing, helping, creating, analyzing, producing, and adventuring. Athletes using this approach can analyze their skills while identifying various areas of interest. Assessments that identify values and interests are a beneficial supplement to personal and career counseling and mentoring and provide athletes with opportunities to better understand all aspects of themselves. Other instruments that are used for this purpose are the Self Directed Search (SDS; Holland, Powell, and Fritzsche, 1994) and *Athletes Guide to Career Planning* (Petitpas et al., 1997). The SDS incorporates Holland's typology, which categorizes both personality and occupations and allows clients to identify possible careers that correlate with their personality style.

Transfer of Skills

Many retiring athletes do not believe that they have skills to be successful outside of sport. Athletes must realize that many of the skills that made them successful in sports—motivation, confidence, focus, patience—will enable them to succeed in another career. As long as athletes are performing at a high level, they have little concerns for other life skills. Many athletes have spent so much time and energy focusing on their athletic careers that they have difficulty recognizing the extensive "toolbox" of skills they have available (Swain, 1991). As they approach the end of their sport careers, athletes become concerned about their ability to "make it" in the real world. Petitpas, Danish, McKelvain, and Murphy (1992) demonstrated that athletes respond positively when taught about transferable skills because this knowledge is somewhat reassuring. Guides such as *What Color Is Your Parachute* by Richard Bolles (annual editions) and *Athletes Guide to Career Planning* (Petitpas et al., 1997) are useful resources for helping transitioning athletes identify their transferable skills.

Sample Programs in Sport

For a long time, sport organizations had little concern for athletes who left the sport. "Historically, sport organizations have not paid the same attention to helping athletes exit from organizational structure as they have in helping them enter" (Sinclair and Hackfort, 2000, p. 132). In recent years, however, time and energy have been devoted to designing and implementing career transition programs for athletes. National governing bodies, universities, and professional leagues administer these programs aimed at helping athletes at the end of their careers transition to a new career and life path. Future research needs to identify underserved communities and service gaps that still exist. The following programs, both national and international in scope, address many of the issues that have been discussed in this chapter. (See "Sport Career Transition Resources" for a list of programs.)

The ACE Program, Australia

Viewed internationally as a unique service (Flanagan, 2001), the Athlete Career and Education (ACE) Program, administered under the auspices of the Australian Sports Commission under the Australian Institute of Sport, works with elite Australian amateur athletes to integrate educational and career planning from early in their careers through the conclusion. Established in 1995, this program comes closest to the systemic model advocated in this chapter that takes into account individual, developmental, psychosocial, and multicultural differences; promotes life skills; is backed by institutional support; and provides for interventions and services that balance sport performance with life goals. Approximately 3,000 athletes receive ACE services each year. Goals for the ACE program include (1) individual athlete assessment, (2) personal development plan, (3) educational and career planning, (4) establishment of business and community mentors, (5) continuity of career transition services, (6) transition counseling services, and (7) availability to professional athletes as fee for service. The success of the ACE program has resulted in its adoption by other countries, including Canada and Scotland (Anderson and Morris, 2000).

NCAA CHAMPS/Life Skills Program

A comprehensive development program for student athletes, the CHAMPS (Challenging Athletes Minds for Personal Success) Program was initiated by the NCAA in 1994 for student-athletes at U.S. universities. Currently, there are more than 465 CHAMPS programs at all levels of NCAA

Sport Career Transition Resources

The ACE Program, Australia: www.ais.org.au/ace/about.htm

NCAA CHAMPS/Life Skills Program: www.NCAA.org, phone 317-917-6222

U.S. Olympic Program, TeamUSAnet: http://teamusanet.monster.com

NFL Player Development and Career Transition Program: www.nflplayerdevelopment.com

Games Over: www.GamesOver.org

Life After Hockey: www.nhl.com

Professional Athletes Transition Institute: duncan.fletcher@quinnipiac.edu

Iona College PASS Program: mlevy@iona.edu, phone 914-633-2038

Career Transition for Dancers, the Caroline & Theodore Newhouse Center: www.careertransition.org or Lgordon@careertransition.org, phone 212-764-0172

40Plus of Washington: 40Plus@40Plus-DC.org, phone 202-387-1582

Powerplay, NYC: www.powerplaynyc.org

competition. Its objectives consist of fostering the following areas: (1) academic excellence (e.g., study skills, goal setting, time management); (2) athletic excellence (e.g., mental skills training); (3) personal development (e.g., nutrition, stress reduction, substance abuse prevention, depression awareness, finances, violence prevention); (4) community service (e.g., campus, community, spiritual); and (5) career development (e.g., freshmen–senior, postgraduates, agent issues, Alumni Career Network, and Life after Sports seminars). Programs are tailored to each university community, and some programs have more developed transition components than others. By 2002, the NCAA had established task forces that were looking at diversity issues, including women athletes and homophobia in collegiate sports.

Career Assistance Program for Athletes (CAPA)

In 1988, the United States Olympic Committee (USOC) initiated the Career Assistance Program for Athletes (CAPA) to assist Olympic athletes in making the transition out of active sport competition (Petitpas et al., 1992), based on a needs assessment sent to 1,800 Olympic and Pan-American Games athletes who competed from 1980 to 1988. A life span developmental model was used that placed athletes' careers in the context of a lifelong process. CAPA offered workshops related to career transition, including managing the emotional and social impact of transitions, increasing athletes' understanding and awareness of qualities relevant to coping with transitions and career development, and introducing information about the world of work. Although this program is no longer in existence because of funding cuts, it provided an excellent framework for program development and design, and many of its elements have been incorporated into other career transition programs, including its successor, TeamUSAnet. For further information, refer to Petitpas and colleagues (1992).

U.S. Olympic Program, TeamUSAnet

The USOC and Monster.com (an online career management service) launched TeamUSAnet, the first exclusive online transition program, in July 2001, with an initial preregistration of 220 Olympians. TeamUSAnet is currently available to the 2002 and 2004 U.S. Olympic teams free of charge to the athletes. As of June 2004, more than 1,900 eligible athletes had signed up. Services offered by TeamUSAnet include a private online forum for athletes, called Athletes Connected, to help athletes share experiences in sports, careers, or life issues; a career center with job search, cover letter, resume, and interviewing assistance and special USOC logos designating Olympian or Olympian hopeful; access to an alumni network; a mentor network from the USOC and volunteers from the business community; career counselor consultation through the USOC's Athletes Services Division; and Athlete Services Information, which provides information about health insurance, sport psychology, career services, and other resources on site at the USOC Training Centers.

Olympic Jobs Opportunities Program

Home Depot, the largest chain of home improvement stores in the United States, initiated the Olympic Jobs Opportunities Program. Home Depot is the largest employer of Olympic athletes in North America (116 employees were in the 2000 Sydney Games). Athletes are paid full salary and benefits to work 20 hours per week so they can train. Employee assessments of these athletes indicate that they are disciplined, prompt, and hard working. Other companies that sponsor jobs programs include McDonald's, Microsoft, and UPS.

National Football League Player Development Program, Career Transition Division, Games Over

American football's high rate of injury occurrence and brief career spans motivated the National Football League to create the Player Development Program. This program is among the most comprehensive in North American sports in assisting its players in career transition. Its mission statement is to challenge NFL players to be lifelong learners while pursuing continuous improvement in family relations, social interactions, personal growth, and career development during and beyond their careers. Established by Dr. Lem Burnham in 1991, the program offers active NFL and practice squad players and their families a range of services that include career development, athlete and family employee assistance, and life skills. More than 8,200 players and their families have taken part in this program. The Career Transition Division provides academic planning and continuing education for those players who did not graduate from college (often with special arrangements with universities near each NFL team), tutoring, internships, mentoring, and financial education and planning.

Recently, Games Over, a nonprofit, peer-run organization founded by a former NFL player, Ken Ruettgers, was established to extend these services to retired or released players. Services offered by Games Over include family counseling, financial counseling, transition planning, and networking with career counselors. Games Over has some unique features, such as offering a Personal Advisory Team consisting of a former professional athlete, a female mentor for players' spouses, and a financial mentor for investments, tax advice, and benefits eligibilities, as well as access to chaplains and physical trainers. All services are free, offered online, and provided by a large staff of volunteer specialists.

Iona College PASS

The Iona College (New York) Promoting the Academic Success of Student-Athletes (PASS) Program is a collaborative effort among the athletics department, counseling center, and academic resource center to support the holistic development of its student-athletes. Participating athletes receive assistance in the following areas: (1) academic development (new student-athlete orientation, academic skill workshops, tutoring, monthly monitoring of academic progress, and advocacy regarding special needs accommodations); (2) athletic development (performance enhancement counseling, stress management, visualization and relaxation training, and transferring practice skills to competitive situations); (3) team development (team building, leadership development, goal setting, and values clarification); and (4) social development (education and counseling for relationships, drugs and alcohol, gambling, eating disorders, learning disabilities, and consultation to team staff). From the inception of PASS in 1998 through the spring of 2004, more than 400 Iona College student-athletes attained a grade point average of 3.0 on a 4.0 scale, while winning many academic awards.

Sample Programs From Dance

Concurrent work in career transition has occurred in other settings including the performing arts and business. Although unique characteristics distinguish these populations from athletes (e.g., age, opportunities), the common ground is significant between athletes and dancers (e.g., physical abilities, length of training, effects of injury, core identity, adaptable and transferable skills, loss, deselection) and, as a result, lessons can be learned from these settings regarding career transition. As noted in other sections of this chapter, sport psychology and performance psychology share common roots and philosophies.

The Career Transition for Dancers (CTFD) program, a nonprofit organization, was founded in the United States in 1985 by former dancers Ann Barry, Alex Dubé, and Edward Weston. CTFD is a member of the International Organization for the Transition of Professional Dancers, whose purpose is to promote worldwide understanding, financial, and programmatic support for dancers. CTFD is funded by performing arts unions, grants, and private funds, providing free access to public forums and resource centers to all and career counseling and grants to eligible dancers. Recognizing the developmental aspects of transitions, CTFD provides professional dancers in the United States ongoing access to career transition services for their entire lives. Individual (in person or by long-distance telephone) and group career counseling sessions are offered, providing for a full range of career services that include educational and entrepreneurial grants, national outreach seminars, computer literacy training, and a national networking directory. To date, more than 2,700 dancers have received individual career counseling services through the New York City and Los Angeles chapters. Recent emphases include facilitating current and retired dancers' pursuits of higher education and early outreach to student and preprofessional dancers. CTFD is for all dance professions, employs a life span approach, uses both professional and peer–mentor–network career resources, recognizes the concept of an off-season, and can serve as a model for dedicated sport transition programs.

Athlete's Perspective

In the years since my last race as an elite swimmer, my own career transition is still in progress—and I believe it always will be. I deliberately distanced myself from sport and have gradually made my way back. I worked on the editorial staff at *Rolling Stone* magazine—as far removed as possible from a jock culture. I moved on to NBC television where I helped produce the swimming and diving competition at the 2000 Sydney Olympics, after which I was a producer for a tabloid television newsmagazine. Most recently, I've returned to my sport in an entirely new capacity—as the cofounder of a children's swimming school in New York City. I feel uncomfortable writing this brief bio as some sort of guideline for successful transitions. There are a million ways to bridge an athletic career with the wider working world, and all I can do is report my own experiences. An athlete's identity is supremely bound to his or her sport. After a certain point of achievement or commitment, one's character becomes defined by the sport. This is not necessarily a bad thing, but it can be dangerous. Without the right perspective—and the right guidance—sport (as well as successes or failures within it) can haunt everything you do for the rest of your life.

■   ■   ■   ■   ■

Key Points

- Career transition is an inevitable, although sometimes painful, part of the athletic world.
- Career transition has been an area of growing interest among sport psychology researchers and consultants.
- Athletic careers end for four primary reasons: age, injury, deselection, and free choice. The first three are the most difficult because they involve a diminution of the athlete's performance and are outside of the athlete's control. The optimum reasons for athletes to retire are because they have achieved their goals, changed their priorities, or lost their motivation to compete.
- Although psychological reactions to career transition vary, evidence has been found for the emergence of anxiety, denial, depression, and substance abuse as well as a loss of athletic identity, self-esteem, financial and social status, and social connectedness.
- Factors that influence the quality of adaptation to career transition include self-identity, social support, preretirement planning, family issues, and socioeconomic status. These considerations must be recognized and understood from a multicultural perspective.
- Theory and practice from career and life development, feminist psychology, and dance psychology continue to shape and inform sport psychology study and application.
- Components of career transition programs include life skills training, personal and career counseling, mentoring and networking, and the identification of skills, values, and interests. A number of formal programs offered by universities, national governing bodies, and professional sports leagues provide athletes with many services both early in their careers as well as when they approach retirement. The goal of these programs is to help athletes make the transition from sport to a new career as positive, constructive, and healthy as possible.

Review Questions

1. What are the primary causes of career transition?
2. What are some negative reactions that athletes may experience during career transition?
3. What are four multicultural variables that may affect career transition?
4. What factors affect the quality of career transition?
5. What are three career transition intervention strategies?

References

Preface

Bannister, R. (1981). *The Four Minute Mile.* New York: Lyons & Buford.

Counsilman, J.E. (1977). *Competitive swimming manual for coaches and swimmers.* Bloomington, IN: Council.

Part I

Taylor, J. (2001). *Prime sport: Triumph of the athlete mind.* New York: iUniverse.

Chapter 1

Abramson, L.Y., Seligman, M.E.P., & Teasdale, J.D. (1978). Learned helplessness in humans: Critique and reformulation. *Journal of Abnormal Psychology, 87,* 49-74.

Ames, C. (1992). Achievement goals, motivational climate, and motivational processes. In G.C. Roberts (Ed.), *Motivation in sport and exercise* (pp. 161-176). Champaign, IL: Human Kinetics.

Anderssen, N., & Wold, B. (1992). Parental and peer influences on leisure-time physical activity in young adolescents. *Research Quarterly for Exercise and Sport, 63,* 341-348.

Atkinson, J.W. (1957). Motivational determinants of risk-taking behavior. *Psychological Review, 6,* 359-372.

Babkes, M., & Weiss, M.R. (1999). Parental influences on children's cognitive and affective responses to competitive soccer participation. *Pediatric Exercise Science, 11,* 44-62.

Baker, A., Lewin, T., Reichler, H., Clancy, R., Carr, V., Garrett, R., et al. (2002). Evaluation of a motivational interview for substance use within psychiatric inpatient services. *Addiction, 97*(10), 1329-1337.

Bandura, A. (1986). *Social foundations of thought and action: A social cognitive theory.* Englewood Cliffs, NJ: Prentice-Hall.

Bandura, A. (1997). *Self-efficacy: The exercise of control.* New York: Freeman.

Biddle, S. (2001). Enhancing motivation in physical education. In G.C. Roberts (Ed.), *Advances in motivation in sport and exercise* (pp. 101-128). Champaign, IL: Human Kinetics.

Biddle, S., & Goudas, M. (1996). Analysis of children's physical activity and its association with adult encouragement and social cognitive variables. *Journal of School Health, 66,* 75-78.

Brennan, C. (1999). *Inside edge: A revealing journey into the secret world of figure skating.* New York: Scribner.

Briere, N.M., Vallerand, R.J., Blais, M.R., & Pelletier, L.G. (1996). Developpement et validation d'une mesure de mitvation intrinseque et extrinseque et d'amotivation en contexte sportif: L'Echelle de Motivation vis-à-vis les Sports (EMS) [Development and validation of a measure of intrinsic, extrinsic, and amotivation in sports: The Sport Motivation Scale (SMS)]. *Journal International Psychologie du Sport.*

Brustad, R.J. (1993). Who will go out and play? Parental and psychological influences on children's attraction to physical activity. *Pediatric Exercise Science, 5,* 210-223.

Brustad, R.J. (1996). Attraction to physical activity in urban schoolchildren: Parental socialization and gender influences. *Research Quarterly for Exercise and Sport, 67,* 316-323.

Cooperrider, D.L. (1995). Introduction to appreciative inquiry. *Organizational development* (5th ed.). Englewood Cliffs, NJ: Prentice Hall.

Csikszentmihalyi, M. (1996). *Flow: The psychology of optimal experience.* New York: HarperCollins.

Csikszentmihalyi, M. (2000). *Finding flow: The psychology of engagement with everyday life.* New York: Basic Books.

Deci, E.L. (1975). *Intrinsic motivation.* New York: Plenum Press.

Deci, E.L., Nezlek, J., & Sheinman, L. (1981). Characteristics of the rewarder and intrinsic motivation of the rewardee. *Journal of Personality and Social Psychology, 40,* 1-10.

Deci, E.L., & Ryan, R.M. (1985). *Intrinsic motivation and self-determination in human behavior.* New York: Plenum Press.

Deci, E.L., & Ryan, R.M. (1991). A motivational approach to self: Integration in personality. In R. Dientsbier (Ed.), *Nebraska symposium on motivation: Vol. 38. Perspectives on motivation* (pp. 237-288). Lincoln: University of Nebraska Press.

Dempsey, J.M., Kimiecik, J.C., & Horn, T.S. (1993). Parental influences on moderate to vigorous activity population: An expectancy-value approach. *Pediatric Exercise Science, 5,* 151-167.

Diener, E. (2000). Subjective well-being: The science of happiness and a proposal for a national index. *American Psychologist, 56*(3), 34-43.

Dowrick, P.W. (1983). Self-modeling. In P.W. Dowrick & S.J. Biggs (Eds.), *Using video: Psychological and social applications* (pp. 105-124). New York: Wiley.

Dowrick, P.W. (1991). *Practical guide to using video in the behavioral sciences.* New York: Wiley Interscience.

Dowrick, P.W. (1999). A review of self-modeling and related interventions. *Applied and Preventive Psychology, 8,* 23-29.

Dowrick, P.W., & Dove, C. (1980). The use of self-modeling to improve swimming performance of spina bifida children. *Journal of Applied Behavioral Analysis, 13,* 51-55.

Duda, J.L. (1989). Relationship between task and ego orientation and the perceived purpose of sport among high school athletes. *Journal of Sport and Exercise Psychology, 11,* 318-335.

Duda, J.L. (1992). Motivation in sport settings: A goal approach. In G.C. Roberts (Ed.), *Motivation in sport and exercise* (pp. 57-91). Champaign, IL: Human Kinetics.

Duda, J.L. (1993). Goals: A social-cognitive approach to the study of achievement in sport. In R.N. Singer, M. Murphey, & L.K. Tennant (Eds.), *Handbook of research on sport psychology* (pp. 421-436). New York: Macmillan.

Duda, J.L. (1997). Perpetuating myths: A response to Hardy's 1996 Coleman Griffith Address. *Journal of Applied Sport Psychology, 9,* 307-313.

Duda, J.L. (2001). Achievement goal research in sport: Pushing the boundaries and clarifying some misunderstandings. In G.C. Roberts (Ed.), *Advances in motivation in sport and exercise* (pp. 129-182). Champaign, IL: Human Kinetics.

Duda, J.L., & Whitehead, J. (1998). Measurement of goal perspectives in the physical domain. In J.L. Duda (Ed.), *Advances in sport and exercise psychology measures* (pp. 21-48). Morgantown, WV: Fitness Information Technology.

Feltz, D.L., & Lirgg, C.D. (1998). Perceived team and player efficacy in hockey. *Journal of Applied Sport Psychology, 83,* 557-564.

Foster, S. (2002). Enhancing peak potential in managers and leaders: Integrating knowledge and findings from sport psychology. In R.L. Lowman (Ed.) *Handbook of organizational consulting psychology* (pp. 176-221). San Francisco: Jossey-Bass.

Foster, S., & Prussack, T. (1999). *Skate your personal best.* San Francisco: Rudi.

Franks, I.M., & Maille, L.J. (1991). The use of video in sport skill acquisition. In P.W. Dowrick (Ed.), *Practical guide to using video in the behavioral sciences* (pp. 231-243). New York: Wiley.

Frederickson, B. (2000). Why positive emotions matter in organizations: Lessons from the broaden-and-build model. *Psychologist-Manager Journal, 4*(2), 131-142.

Frederickson, B. (2001). The role of emotions in positive psychology. *American Psychologist, 56*(3), 218-226.

Freud, S. (1950). *Beyond the pleasure principle.* New York: Liveright. (Original work published 1920)

Goleman, D., Boyatzis, R., & McKee, A. (2002). *Primal leadership.* Boston, MA: Harvard University Press.

Gottlieb, N.H., & Chen, M.S. (1985). Sociocultural correlates of childhood sporting activities: Their implications for heart health. *Social Science in Medicine, 21,* 533-539.

Green, T. (1997). *Dark side of the game: My life in the NFL.* New York: Warner Books.

Grolnick, W.S., Deci, E.L., & Ryan, R.M. (1997). Internalization within the family. In J.E. Grusec & L. Kuczynski (Eds.), *Parenting and children's internalization of values: A handbook of contemporary theory* (pp. 135-161). New York: Wiley.

Halliwell, W. (1990). Providing sport psychology consultant services in professional hockey. *The Sport Psychologist, 4,* 369-377.

Hanin, Y.L. (2000). Individual zones of optimal functioning (IOF) model: Emotions-performance relationships in sport. In Y.L. Hanin (Ed.), *Emotions in sport* (pp. 65-89). Champaign, IL: Human Kinetics.

Hardy, L. (1997). The Coleman Griffith Address: Three myths about applied consultancy work. *Journal of Applied Sport Psychology, 9,* 277-294.

Hardy, L. (1998). Responses to the reactants on three myths in applied consultancy work. *Journal of Applied Sport Psychology, 10,* 212-219.

Harter, J.K., Schmid, F.L., & Hayes, T.L. (2002). Business-unit-level relationship between employee satisfaction, employee engagement, and business outcomes: A meta-analysis. *Journal of Applied Psychology, 87*(2), 268-279.

Harter, S. (1978). Effectance motivation reconsidered. *Human Development, 21,* 34-64.

Harter, S. (1981). A model of intrinsic mastery motivation in children: Individual differences and developmental change.

In W.A. Collins (Ed.), *Minnesota Symposium on Child Psychology* (Vol. 14, pp. 215-255). Hillsdale, NJ: Erlbaum.

Harwood, C., Hardy, L., & Swain, A.B.L. (2000). Achievement goals in sport: A critique of conceptual and measurement issues. *Journal of Sport and Exercise Psychology, 22,* 235-255.

"Kostelic Beats Paerson in Slalom." (March 11, 2003). http://sportsillustrated.cnn.com/more/news/2003/03/08/alpine_women_ap/

Krane, V., Greenleaf, C.A., & Snow, J. (1997). Reaching for gold and the price of glory: A motivational case study of an elite gymnast. *The Sport Psychologist, 11,* 53-71.

Larson, R. (2000). Toward a psychology of positive youth development. *American Psychologist, 55*(19), 170-183.

Maehr, M.L., & Nicholls, J.G. (1980). Culture and achievement motivation: A second look. In N. Warren (Ed.), *Studies in cross-cultural psychology* (pp. 256-282). London: Academic Press.

McClelland, D.C. (1951). Measuring motivation in fantasy: The achievement motive. In H. Guetzkow (Ed.), *Groups, leadership, and men* (pp. 191-205). Pittsburgh, PA: Carnegie Press.

McClelland, D.C., Atkinson, J.W., Clark, R.A., & Lowell, E.L. (1953). *The achievement motive.* New York: Appleton-Century-Crofts.

McKenzie, D.C. (1999). Markers of excessive exercise. *Canadian Journal of Applied Psychology, 24,* 66-73.

Meyers, A.W., & Schleser, R.A. (1980). A cognitive-behavioral intervention for improving basketball performance. *Journal of Sport Psychology, 3,* 69-73.

Miller, W.R., Yahne, C.E., & Tonigan, J.S. (2003). Motivational interviewing in drug abuse services: A randomized trial. *Journal of Consulting and Clinical Psychology, 71*(4), 754-763.

Mowrer, O.H. (1960). *Learning theory and behavior.* New York: Wiley.

Nicholls, J.G. (1984). Achievement motivation: Conceptions of ability, subjective experience, task choice, and performance. *Psychological Review, 91,* 328-346.

Nicholls, J.G. (1989). *The competitive ethos and democratic education.* Cambridge, MA: Harvard University Press.

Pelletier, L.G., Fortier, M.S., Valerand, R.J., Tuson, K.M., Briere, N.M., & Blais, M.R. (1995). Toward a new measure of intrinsic motivation, extrinsic motivation, and amotivation in sports: The sport motivation scale (SMS). *Journal of Sport and Exercise Psychology, 17,* 35-53.

Roberts, G.C. (1984). Achievement motivation in children's sports. In J.G. Nicholls (Ed.), *Advances in motivation and achievement. Vol. 3. The development of achievement motivation* (pp. 251-281). Champaign, IL: Human Kinetics.

Roberts, G.C. (1992). Motivation in sport and exercise: Conceptual constraints and convergence. In G.C. Roberts (Ed.), *Motivation in sport and exercise* (pp. 3-29). Champaign, IL: Human Kinetics.

Roberts, G.C. (2001). Understanding the dynamics of motivation in physical activity: The influence of achievement goals on motivational processes. In G.C. Roberts (Ed.), *Advances in motivation in sport and exercise* (pp. 1-50). Champaign, IL: Human Kinetics.

Roberts, G.C., Treasure, D.C., & Balague, G. (1998). Achievement goals in sport: The development and validation of the Perception of Success Questionnaire. *Journal of Sports Sciences, 16,* 337-247.

Roberts, G.C., Treasure, D.C., & Kavussanu, M. (1996). Orthogonality of achievement goals and its relationship to beliefs about success and satisfaction in sport. *The Sport Psychologist, 10*(4), 398-408.

Roberts, G.C., Treasure, D.C., & Kavussanu, M. (1997). Motivation in physical activity contexts: An achievement goal perspective. In P. Pintrich & M. Maehr (Eds.), *Advances in motivation and achievement* (Vol. 10, pp. 413-447). Stamford, CT: JAI Press.

Ryan, J. (1995). *Little girls in pretty boxes.* New York: Doubleday.

Ryan, R.M., Connell, J.P., & Grolnick, W.S. (1990). When achievement is not intrinsically motivated: A theory of self-regulation in school. In A.K. Boggiano & T.S. Pittman (Eds.), *Achievement and motivation: A social-developmental perspective* (pp. 167-188). New York: Cambridge University Press.

Ryan, R.M., & Deci, E.L. (2000). Self-determination theory and the facilitation of intrinsic motivation, social development, and subjective well being. *American Psychologist, 55,* 68-78.

Ryan, R.M., & Grolnick, W.S. (1986). Origins and pawns in the classroom: Self-report and projective assessments of individual differences in children's perceptions. *Journal of Personality and Social Psychology, 50,* 550-558.

Schunk, D.H. (1987). Peer models and children's behavioral change. *Review of Educational Research, 57,* 149-174.

Schunk, D. H. (1988). Perceived Self-Efficacy and Related Social Cognitive Processes as Predictors of Student Academic Performance. Paper presented at the Annual Meeting of the American Educational Research Association, New Orleans, LA, April 5-9.

Shatte, A.J., Reivich, K., & Seligman, M.E.P. (2000). Promoting human strengths and corporate competencies: A cognitive training model. *Psychologist-Manager Journal, 4*(2), 183-196.

Singleton, D.A., & Feltz, D.L. (1999). *The effect of self-modeling on shooting performance and self-efficacy among intercollegiate hockey players.* Unpublished manuscript, Michigan State University, East Lansing.

Smith, R. E., & Smoll, F. L. (1990). Self-esteem and children's reactions to youth sport coaching behaviors: A field study of self enhancement processes. *Developmental Psychology, 26,* 987-993.

Standage, M., Treasure, D.C., Duda, J.L., & Prusak, K.A. (2003). Validity, reliability, and invariance of the Situational Motivation Scale (SIMS) across diverse physical activity contexts. *Journal of Sport and Exercise Science, 25*(1), 19-43.

Starek, J., & McCullagh, P. (1999). The effect of self-modeling on the performance of beginning swimmers. *The Sport Psychologist, 13,* 269-287.

Steinberg, G. (1996). *The effect of different goal strategies on achievement-related cognitions, affect, and behavior during the learning of a golf-putt.* Unpublished doctoral dissertation, University of Florida, Gainesville.

Taylor, W.C., Baranowski, T., & Sallis, J.F. (1994). Family determinants of childhood physical activity: A social-cognitive model. In R.K. Dishman (Ed.), *Advances in exercise adherence* (43-72). Champaign, IL: Human Kinetics.

Thorndike, E.L. (1935). *The psychology of wants, interest, and attitudes.* New York: Appleton-Century-Crofts.

Treasure, D.C. (2001). Enhancing young people's motivation in youth sport: An achievement goal approach. In G.C. Roberts (Ed.), *Advances in motivation in sport and exercise* (pp. 129-152). Champaign, IL: Human Kinetics.

Turman, P.D. (2003). Coaches and cohesion: The impact of coaching techniques on team cohesion in the small group sport setting. *Journal of Sport Behavior, 26*(1), 86-103.

Urdan, T.C., & Maehr, M.L. (1995). Beyond a two goal theory of motivation and achievement: A case for social goals. *Review of Educational Research, 65,* 213-243.

Valliant, G.E. (2000). Adaptive mental mechanisms: Their role in a positive psychology. *American Psychologist, 56*(3), 89-98.

Watkins, J.M., & Mohr, B.J. (2001). *Appreciative inquiry: Change at the speed of imagination.* San Francisco: Jossey Bass.

Weiss, M.R., McCullagh, P., Smith, A.L., & Berlant, A.R. (1998). Observational learning and the fearful child: Influence on peer models on swimming skill performance and psychological responses. *Research Quarterly for Exercise and Sport, 69*(4), 380-394.

Welk, G.J., Wood, K., & Morss, G. (2003). Parental influences on physical activity in children: An exploration of potential mechanisms. *Pediatric Exercise Science, 15,* 19-33.

White, R.W. (1959). Motivation reconsidered: The concept of competence. *Psychological Review, 66,* 297-333.

Chapter 2

Armstrong, L., & Jenkins, S. (2000). *It's not about the bike: My journey back to life.* New York: Putnam.

Bandura, A. (1986). *Social foundations of thought and action: A social cognitive theory.* Englewood Cliffs, NJ: Prentice-Hall.

Bandura, A. (1977). Self-efficacy: Toward a unifying theory of behavioral change. *Psychological Review, 84,* 191-215.

Bandura, A. (1997). *Self-efficacy: The exercise of personal control.* New York: Freeman.

Bandura, A., & Wood, R.E. (1989). Effects of perceived controllability and performance standards on self-regulation of complex decision-making. *Journal of Personality and Social Psychology, 56,* 805-814.

Biddle, S.J.H., Hanrahan, S.J., & Sellars, C. (2001). Attributions: Past, present and future. In R. Singer, H. Hausenblas, & C. Janelle (Eds.), *Handbook of sport psychology* (pp. 444-471). New York: Wiley.

Black, S.J., & Weiss, M.R. (1992). The relationship among perceived coaching behaviors, perceptions of ability, and motivation in competitive age-group swimmers. *Journal of Sport and Exercise Psychology, 14,* 130-145.

Butler, R.J., & Hardy, L. (1992). The performance profile: Theory and application. *The Sport Psychologist, 6,* 253-264.

Cook, D.L. (1992, October). *Understanding and enhancing confidence in athletes: From research to practice.* Paper presented at the annual meeting of the Association for the Advancement of Applied Sport Psychology, Colorado Springs, CO.

George, T.R., & Feltz, D.L. (1995). Motivation in sport from a collective efficacy perspective. *International Journal of Sport Psychology, 26,* 98-116.

Gould, D., Hodge, K., Peterson, K., & Giannini, J. (1989). An exploratory examination of strategies used by elite coaches to enhance self-efficacy in athletes. *Journal of Sport and Exercise Psychology, 11,* 128-140.

Graham, D., & Stabler, J. (1999). *The eight traits of champion golfers.* New York: Simon & Schuster.

Jackson, S.A. (1996). Toward a conceptual understanding of the flow experience in elite athletes. *Research Quarterly for Exercise and Sport, 67,* 76-90.

Jones, G., & Hardy, L (1990). Stress in sport: Experiences of some elite performers. In G. Jones & L. Hardy (Eds.), *Stress and performance in sport* (pp. 247-277). Chichester, UK: Wiley.

Lirgg, C.D., & Feltz, D.L. (1991). Teacher versus peer models revisited: Effects on motor performance. *Research Quarterly for Exercise and Sport, 62,* 217-224.

Lirgg, C.D., & Feltz, D.L. (1994). Relationship of individual and collective efficacy to team performance. *Journal of Sport and Exercise Psychology, 16*(Suppl.), S17.

Mahoney, M.J., & Avener, M. (1977). Psychology of the elite athlete: An exploratory study. *Cognitive Therapy and Research, 1,* 135-142.

Manzo, L.G., Silva, J.M., & Mink, R. (2001). The Carolina sport confidence inventory. *Journal of Applied Sport Psychology, 13,* 260-273.

Martens, R., Vealey, R.S., & Burton, B. (1990). *Competitive anxiety in sport.* Champaign, IL: Human Kinetics.

McAuley, E. (1985). Modeling and self-efficacy: A test of Bandura's model. *Journal of Sport Psychology, 7,* 283-295.

Murphy, S. (1996). *The achievement zone: An 8-step guide to peak performance in all areas of life.* New York: Berkley Books.

Peterson, C., Maier, S.F., & Seligman, M.E.P. (1993). *Learned helplessness: A theory for the age of control.* New York: Oxford University Press.

Ravizza, K. (1977). Peak experiences in sport. *Journal of Humanistic Psychology, 17,* 35-40.

Seligman, M.E.P. (1990). *Learned optimism.* New York: Pocket Books.

Seligman, M.E.P., Reivich, K., Jaycox, L., & Gillham, J. (1995). *The optimistic child: A revolutionary program that safeguards children against depression and builds lifelong resilience.* New York: Houghton Mifflin.

Taylor, J. (2001). *Prime sport: Triumph of the athlete mind.* New York: iUniverse.

Taylor, J., & Riess, M. (1989). A field experiment of "self-serving" attributions to valenced causal factors. *Personality and Social Psychology Bulletin, 15,* 337-348.

Taylor, J., & Wilson, G.S. (2002). Inensity regulation and athletic performance. In Van Raalte & Brewers (Eds.) *Exploring sport and exercise psychology.* Washington, D.C.: American Psychological Association, 99-130.

Tutko, T., & Tosi, U. (1976). *Sports psyching: Playing your best game all of the time.* New York: Penguin Putnam.

Vealey, R.S. (1986). Conceptualization of sport-confidence and competitive orientation: Preliminary investigation and instrument development. *Journal of Sport Psychology, 8,* 221-246.

Vealey, R.S. (2001). Understanding and enhancing self-confidence in athletes. In R. Singer, H. Hausenblas, & C. Janelle (Eds.), *Handbook of sport psychology* (pp. 540-565). New York: Wiley.

Weinberg, R. (2002). *Tennis and winning the mental game.* Oxford, OH: Robert Weinberg.

Wooden, J., & Jamison, S., (1997). *Wooden: A lifetime of observations and reflections on and off the court.* Chicago: Contemporary Books.

Zinsser, N., Bunker, L., & Williams, J.M. (2001). Cognitive techniques for building confidence and enhancing performance. In J.M. Williams (Ed.), *Applied sport psychology: Personal growth to peak performance* (pp. 284-311). Mountain View, CA: Mayfield.

Chapter 3

Carver, C.S., & Scheier, M.F. (1986). Functional and dysfunctional response to anxiety: The interaction between expectancies and self-focused attention. In R. Schwarts (Ed.), *Self-related cognitions in anxiety and motivation* (pp. 111-141). Hillsdale, NJ: Erlbaum.

Caudill, D., Weinberg, R., & Jackson, A. (1983). Psyching-up and track athletes. A preliminary investigation. *Journal of Sport Psychology, 5,* 231-235.

Cox, R.H. (1998). *Sport psychology: Concepts and applications* (4th ed.). Boston: McGraw-Hill.

Csikszentmihalyi, M. (1975). *Beyond boredom and anxiety.* San Francisco: Jossey-Bass.

Edwards, T., & Hardy, L. (1996). The interactive effects of intensity and direction of cognition and somatic anxiety and self-confidence upon performance. *Journal of Sport and Exercise Psychology, 18,* 296-312.

Elko, P.K., & Ostrow, A.C. (1991). Effects of a rational-emotive education program on heightened anxiety levels of female collegiate gymnasts. *The Sport Psychologist, 5,* 235-255.

Ellis, A. (1962). *Reason and emotion in psychotherapy.* New York: Stuart.

Eysenck, M.W. & Calvo, M.S. (1992). Anxiety and performance: The Processing Efficiency Theory. *Cognition and Emotions, 6,* 409-434.

Fazey, J., & Hardy, L. (1988). *The inverted-U hypothesis: A catastrophe for sport psychology?* (BASS Monograph 1). Leeds, UK: White Line Press.

Gould, D., & Krane, V. (1992). The arousal-athletic performance relationship: Current status and future directions. In T.S. Horn (Ed.), *Advances in sport psychology* (pp. 119-141). Champaign, IL: Human Kinetics.

Hamilton, S.A., & Fremouw, W.J. (1985). Cognitive-behavioral training for college basketball free-throw performance. *Cognitive Therapy and Research, 9,* 479-483.

Hanin, Y.L. (1986). State-trait research in sports in the USSR. In C.D. Spielberger & R. Diaz-Guerrero (Eds.), *Cross-cultural anxiety* (Vol. 3, pp. 45-64). Washington, DC: Hemisphere.

Hanin, Y.L. (2000). Individual zones of optimal functioning (IZOF) model: Emotions-performance relationships in sport. In Y.L. Hanin (Ed.), *Emotions in sport* (pp. 65-89). Champaign, IL: Human Kinetics.

Hanin, Y.L., & Syrja, P. (1995). Performance affect in soccer players: An application of the IZOF model. *International Journal of Sports Medicine, 16,* 260-265.

Hardy, L. (1990). A catastrophe model of performance in sport. In J.G. Jones & L. Hardy (Eds.), *Stress and performance in sport* (pp. 81-106). Chichester, UK: Wiley.

Hardy, L. (1996). Testing the predictions of the cusp catastrophe model of anxiety and performance. *The Sport Psychologist, 10,* 140-156.

Heyman, S.R. (1984). Cognitive interventions: Theories, applications, and cautions. In W.F. Straub & J.M. Williams (Eds.), *Cognitive sport psychology* (pp. 289-303). Lansing, NY: Sport Science Associates.

Jones, G. (1995). Competitive anxiety in sports. In S.J.H. Biddle (Ed.), *European perspectives on exercise and sport psychology* (pp. 128-153). Leeds, UK: Human Kinetics.

Kerr, J.H. (1989). Anxiety, arousal and sport performance: An application of reversal theory. In D. Hackfort & C.D. Spielberger (Eds.), *Anxiety in sports: An international perspective* (pp. 137-151). New York: Hemisphere.

Kerr, J.H (1997). *Motivation and emotion in sport: Reversal theory*. East Sussex, UK: Psychology Press.

Krohne, H.W. (1980). Parental child-rearing behavior and the development of anxiety and coping strategies in children. In I.G. Sarason & C.D. Spielberger (Eds.), *Stress and anxiety* (Vol. 7, pp. 243-272). Washington, DC: Hemisphere.

Landers, D.M., & Boutcher, S.H. (1986). Arousal-performance relationships. In J.M. Williams (Ed.), *Applied sport psychology: Personal growth to peak performance* (pp. 163-184). Palo Alto, CA: Mayfield.

McCann, S.C., Murphy, S.M., & Raedeke, T.D. (1992). The effect of performance setting and individual differences on the anxiety-performance relationship for elite cyclists. *Anxiety and Stress in Coping, 5,* 117-187.

Morgan, W.P., & Ellickson, K.A. (1989). Health, anxiety and physical exercise. In D. Hackfort & C.D. Spielberger (Eds.), *Anxiety in sports: An international perspective* (pp. 165-182). New York: Hemisphere.

Nideffer, R.M. (1989). Anxiety, attention, and performance in sports: Theoretical and practical considerations. In D. Hackfort & C.D. Spielberger (Eds.), *Anxiety in sports: An international perspective* (pp. 117-136). New York: Hemisphere.

Nideffer, R.M., & Sagal, M.S. (1998). Concentration and attentional control training. In J.M. Williams (Ed.), *Applied sport psychology: Personal growth to peak performance* (3rd ed., pp. 296-315). Mountain View, CA: Mayfield.

Oxendine, J.B. (1970). Emotional arousal and motor performance. *Quest, 13,* 23-30.

Passer, M.W. (1982). Psychological stress in youth sports. In R.A. Magill, M.J. Ash, & F.L. Smoll (Eds.), *Children in sport* (2nd ed., pp. 153-177). Champaign, IL: Human Kinetics.

Raglin, J.S., & Hanin, Y.L. (2000). Competitive anxiety. In Y.L. Hanin (Ed.), *Emotions in sport* (pp. 93-111). Champaign, IL. Human Kinetics.

Raglin, J.S., & Morris, M.J. (1994). Precompetition anxiety in women volleyball players. A test of ZOF theory in a team sport. *British Journal of Sports Medicine, 28,* 47-52.

Raglin, J.S., & Turner, P.E. (1992). Predicted, actual and optimal precompetition anxiety in adolescent track and field athletes. *Scandinavian Journal of Medicine and Science in Sports, 2,* 148-152.

Sanna, L. J. (1998). Defensive pessimism and optimism: The bittersweet influence of mood on performance and pre-factual and counterfactual thinking. *Cognition and emotion, 12,* 635-665.

Schmidt, R. A., & Wrisberg, C. A., (2000). *Motor learning and performance.* Champaign, IL: Human Kinetics

Silva, J.M., & Hardy, C.J. (1984). Precompetitive affect and athletic performance. In W.F. Straub & J.M. Williams (Eds.), *Cognitive sport psychology* (pp. 79-88). Lansing, NY: Sport Science Associates.

Spielberger, C. (1989). Stress and anxiety in sports. In D. Hackfort & C.D. Spielberger (Eds.), *Anxiety in sports: An international perspective* (pp. 3-17). New York: Hemisphere.

Taylor, J. (1995). A conceptual model of the integration of athletic needs and sport demands in the development of competitive mental preparation strategies. *The Sport Psychologist, 9,* 339-357.

Taylor, J. (2001). *Prime sport: Triumph of the athlete mind.* New York: Universe.

Weinberg, R.S., & Gould, D. (1999). *Foundations of sport and exercise psychology.* Champaign, IL: Human Kinetics.

Williams, J.M., & Harris, D.V. (1998). Relaxation and energizing techniques of regulation arousal. In J.M. Williams (Ed.), *Applied sport psychology: Personal growth to peak performance* (3rd ed., pp. 219-236). Mountain View, CA: Mayfield.

Wilson, G.S., & Raglin, J.S. (1997). Optimal and predicted anxiety in 9-12 year old track and field athletes. *Scandinavian Journal of Medicine and Science in Sports, 2,* 253-258.

Wilson, G.S., Raglin, J.S., & Pritchard, M.E. (2001). Optimism, pessimism, and precompetition anxiety in college athletes. *Personality and Individual Differences, 32,* 893-902.

Wilson, G.S., & Steinke, J.S. (2002). Cognitive orientation, precompetition and actual competition anxiety in collegiate softball players. *Research Quarterly for Exercise and Sport, 73,* 335-339.

Yerkes, R.M., & Dodson, J.D. (1908). The relation of strength of stimulus to rapidity of habit-formation. *Journal of Comparative Neurology and Psychology, 18,* 459-482.

Zaichkowsky, R.B., & Takenaka, K. (1993). Optimizing arousal level. In R.N. Singer, M. Murphy, & L.K. Tennant (Eds.), *Handbook of research on sport psychology* (pp. 511-527). New York: Macmillan.

Zajonc, R. B. (1985). Emotion and facial efference : A theory reclaimed. *Science, 228,* 15-21.

Chapter 4

Abernethy, B. (1999). The Coleman Roberts Griffith Address: Movement expertise: A juncture between psychology theory and practice. *Journal of Applied Sport Psychology, 11,* 126-141.

Abernethy, B., & Russell, D. (1987). Expert-novice differences in an applied selective attention task. *Journal of Sport Psychology, 9,* 326-345.

Allport, D., Antonis, B., & Reynolds, P. (1972). On the division of attention: A disproof of the single channel hypothesis. *Quarterly Journal of Experimental Psychology, 24,* 225-235.

Benson, H. (1977). *The relaxation response.* New York: William & Morrow.

Butler, L., & McKelvie, S.J. (1985). Processing of form: Further evidence for the necessity of attention. *Perceptual and Motor Skills, 61,* 215-221.

Csikszentmihalyi, M. (1990). *Flow: The psychology of optimal experience.* New York: Harper & Row.

Easterbrook, J. (1959). The effect of cue utilization and organization of behavior. *Psychological Review, 66,* 183-201.

Hebb, D. (1976). Physiological learning theory. *Journal of Abnormal Child Psychology, 4,* 309-314.

Huey, E.G. (1968). *The psychology and pedagogy of reading.* Cambridge, MA: MIT Press.

Jackson, S., & Csikszentmihalyi, M. (1999) *Flow in sports.* Champaign, IL: Human Kinetics.

Jacobson, E. (1930). *Progressive relaxation.* Chicago: University of Chicago.

Kahneman, D. (1973). *Attention and effort.* Englewood Cliffs, NJ: Prentice Hall.

Kauss, D. (2001). *Mastering your inner game.* Champaign, IL: Human Kinetics.

Keele, S. (1973). *Attention and human performance.* Pacific Palisades, CA: Goodyear.

Landers, D. (1980). The arousal-performance relationship revisited. *Research Quarterly for Exercise and Sport, 51,* 77-90.

Loehr, J.E. (1994). The development of a cognitive-behavioral between-point intervention strategy for tennis. In S. Sera, J. Alves, & V. Pataco (Eds.), *International perspectives on sport and exercise psychology* (pp. 219-233). Morgantown, WV: Fitness Information Technology.

Magill, R. (2001). *Motor learning concepts and applications* (6th ed.). New York: McGraw-Hill Higher Education.

Moran, A. (1996). *The psychology of concentration in sport performers.* East Sussex, UK: Psychology Press.

Nideffer, R.M. (1976). Test of attentional and interpersonal style. *Journal of Personality and Social Psychology, 34,* 394-404.

Nideffer, R.M. (1990). Use of the test of attentional and interpersonal style in sport. *The Sport Psychologist, 4,* 285-300.

Nideffer, R.M. (1992). *Psyched to win.* Champaign, IL: Leisure Press.

Nideffer, R. (1995). Preventing choking and downward performance cycles. *Student Sports Magazine, 5,* 13.

Nideffer, R.M., & Sagal, M-S. (2001). Concentration and attentional control training. In J.M. Williams (Ed.), *Applied sport psychology: Personal growth to peak performance* (pp. 312-332). Mountain View, CA: Mayfield.

Pacelli, J. (1997). Refocusing during sport downtime. *Self Help Magazine,* Sport Performance Section [Online]. Date accessed: 2-6-04. Available: http://selfhelpmagazine.com/articles/sports/refocus.html.

Pavlov, I.P. (1927). *Conditioned reflexes: An investigation of the physiological activity of the cerebral cortex.* New York: Dover.

Reeve, T.G. (1976). *Processing demands during the acquisition of motor skills requiring different feedback cues.* Denton: Texas A&M University College Press.

Schiffrin, R.M., & Schneider, W. (1997). Controlled and automatic human information processing, II: Perceptual learning, automatic attending, and general theory. *Psychological Review, 84,* 127-190.

Shea, C., Shebilske, W., & Worchel, S. (1993). *Motor learning and control.* Englewood Cliffs, NJ: Prentice Hall.

Taylor, J. (2001). *Prime sport: Triumph of the athlete mind.* New York: iUniverse.

Van Schyock, S.R., & Grasha, A.F. (1983). Attentional style variations and athletic ability: The advantage of a sport specific test. *Journal of Sport Psychology, 3,* 149-165.

Wegner, D.M. (1994). Ironic processes of mental control. *Psychological Review, 16,* 34-52.

Williams, J.M., & Krane, V. (2001). Psychological characteristics of peak performance. In J.M. Williams (Ed.), *Applied sport psychology: Personal growth to peak performance* (pp. 162-178). Mountain View, CA: Mayfield.

Wrisberg, C.A., & Shea, C.H. (1978). Shifts in attention demands and motor program utilization during motor learning. *Journal of Motor Behavior, 10,* 149-158.

Chapter 5

Bandura, A. (1997). *Self-efficacy: The exercise of control.* New York: Freeman.

Brunelle, J.P., Janelle, C.M., & Tennant, L.K. (1999). Controlling competitive anger among male soccer players. *Journal of Applied Sport Psychology, 11,* 283-297.

Cerin, E., Szabo, A., Hunt, N., & Williams, C. (2000). Temporal patterning of competitive emotions: A critical review. *Journal of Sports Sciences, 18,* 605-626.

Clore, G.L. (1994). Why emotions require cognition. In K.R. Scherer & P. Ekman (Eds.), *Approaches to emotions* (pp. 181-191). Hillsdale, NJ: Erlbaum.

Deci, E.L. (1980). *The psychology of self-determination.* Lexington, MA: Heath, Lexington.

D'Urso, V., Petrosso, A., & Robazza, C. (2002). Emotions, perceived qualities, and performance of rugby players. *The Sport Psychologist, 16,* 173-199.

Easterbrook, J.A. (1959). The effect of emotion on cue utilization and the organisation of behaviour. *Psychological Review, 66,* 183-201.

Eysenck, M.W., & Calvo, M.G. (1992). Anxiety and performance: The processing efficiency theory. *Cognition and Emotion, 6,* 409-434.

Goleman, D. (1995). *Emotional intelligence.* New York: Bantam.

Gould, D., Finch, L.M., & Jackson, S.A. (1993). Coping strategies used by national champion figure skaters. *Research Quarterly for Exercise and Sport, 64,* 453-468.

Hanin, Y.L. (2000a). Individual zones of optimal functioning (IZOF) model: Emotions-performance relationships in sport. In Y.L. Hanin (Ed.), *Emotions in sport* (pp. 65-89). Champaign, IL: Human Kinetics.

Hanin, Y.L. (2000b). Successful and poor performance emotions. In Y.L. Hanin (Ed.), *Emotions in sport* (pp. 157-187). Champaign, IL: Human Kinetics.

Hanin, Y., & Syrjä, P. (1995a). Performance affect in junior ice hockey players: An application of the individual zones of optimal functioning model. *The Sport Psychologist, 9,* 169-187.

Hanin, Y., & Syrjä, P. (1995b). Performance affect in soccer players: An application of the IZOF model. *International Journal of Sports Medicine, 16,* 264-269.

Hanin, Y., & Syrjä, P. (1996). Predicted, actual, and recalled affect in Olympic-level soccer players: Idiographic assessments on individualized scales. *Journal of Sport and Exercise Psychology, 18,* 325-335.

Jones, J.G. (1991). Recent developments and current issues in competitive state anxiety research. *The Psychologist, 4,* 152-155.

Jones, M.V. (2003). Controlling emotions in sport. *The Sport Psychologist, 17,* 471-486.

Jones, M.V., & Mace, R. (1998). A cognitive-behavioural intervention for emotional control during performance—A case study in golf. *Proceedings of the British Psychological Society, 6,* 109.

Jones, M.V., Mace, R.D., Bray, S.R., MacRae, A., & Stockbridge, C. (2002). The impact of motivational imagery on the emotional state and self-efficacy levels of novice climbers. *Journal of Sport Behavior, 25,* 57-73.

Jones, M.V., Mace, R.D., & Williams, S. (2000). Relationship between emotional state and performance during international field hockey matches. *Perceptual and Motor Skills, 90,* 691-701.

Kerr, J.H. (1997). *Motivation and emotion in sport.* East Sussex: Psychology Press.

Lazarus, R.S. (1991). *Emotion and adaptation.* Oxford, UK: Oxford University Press.

Lazarus, R.S. (1999). *Stress and emotion: A new syntheses*. New York: Springer.

Lazarus, R.S. (2000a). Cognitive-motivational-relational theory of emotion. In Y.L. Hanin (Ed.), *Emotions in sport* (pp. 39-63). Champaign, IL: Human Kinetics.

Lazarus, R.S. (2000b). How emotions influence performance in competitive sports. *The Sport Psychologist, 14,* 229-252.

Mace, R.D. (1990). Cognitive behavioural interventions in sport. In G. Jones & L. Hardy (Eds.), *Stress and performance in sport* (pp. 203-230). Chichester, UK: Wiley.

Martin, K.A,. Moritz, S.E., & Hall, C.R. (1999). Imagery use in sport: A literature review and applied model. *The Sport Psychologist, 13,* 245-268.

McGowan, R.W., & Shultz, B.B. (1989). Task complexity and affect in collegiate football. *Perceptual and Motor Skills. 69,* 671-674.

Munroe, K.J., Giacobbi, P.R., Hall, C., & Weinberg, R. (2000). The four Ws of imagery use: Where, when, why, and what. *The Sport Psychologist, 14,* 119-137.

Platt, J.J., Prout, M.F., & Metzger, D.S. (1986). Interpersonal cognitive problem-solving therapy (ICPS). In W. Dryden & W.L. Golden (Eds.), *Cognitive-behavioural approaches to psychotherapy* (pp. 261-289). London: Harper & Row.

Seligman, M.E.P. (1975). *Helplessness: On depression, development, and death*. San Francisco: Freeman.

Taylor, J. (2001). *Prime sport: Triumph of the athlete mind*. New York: iUniverse.

Terry, P.C. & Slade, A. (1995). Discriminant effectiveness of psychological state measures in predicting performance outcome in karate competition. *Perceptual & Motor Skills, 81,* 275-286.

Uphill, M., & Jones, M.V. (2004). Cognitive-Motivational-Relational-Theory as a framework for coping with emotions in sport. In D. Lavallee, J. Thatcher & M.V. Jones (Eds.) *Coping and emotion in sport* (pp. 75-89). Hauppauge, NY: Nova Science Publishers.

Vallerand, R.J. (1983). On emotion in sport: Theoretical and social psychological perspectives. *Journal of Sport Psychology, 5,* 197-215.

Vallerand, R.J. (1987). Antecedents of self-related affects in sport: Preliminary evidence on the intuitive-reflective appraisal model. *Journal of Sport Psychology, 9,* 161-182.

Vallerand, R.J., & Blanchard, C.M. (2000). The study of emotion in sport and exercise: Historical, definitional, and conceptual perspectives. In Y.L. Hanin (Ed.), *Emotions in sport* (pp. 3-37). Champaign, IL: Human Kinetics.

Zillmann, D. (1971). Excitation transfer in communication-mediated aggressive behavior. *Journal of Experimental Social Psychology, 7,* 419-434.

Chapter 6

Albrecht, R.R., & Feltz, D.L. (1987). Generality and specificity of attention related to competitive anxiety and sport performance. *Journal of Sport Psychology, 9,* 231-248.

Anshel, M.H., & Anderson, D.I. (2002). Coping with acute stress in sport: Linking athletes' coping style, coping strategies, affect, and motor performance. *Anxiety, Stress, and Coping, 15*(2), 193-209.

Berglund, B.H., & Säfström, H. (1994). Psychological monitoring and modulation of training load of world-class canoeists. *Medicine and Science in Sports and Exercise, 26,* 1036-1040.

Carron, A.V., Brawley, L.R., & Widmeyer, W.N. (1998). The measurement of cohesiveness in sport groups. In J.L. Duda (Ed.), *Advances in sport and exercise psychology measurement* (pp. 213-226). Morgantown, WV: Fitness Information Technology.

Carron, A.V., Colman, M.M., Wheeler, J., & Stevens, D. (2002). Cohesion and performance in sport: A meta analysis. *Journal of Sport and Exercise Psychology, 24,* 168-188.

Carron, A.V., Widmeyer, W.N., & Brawley, L.R. (1985). The development of an instrument to assess cohesion in sport teams: The Group Environment Questionnaire. *Journal of Sport Psychology, 7,* 244-266.

Chelladurai, P. (1990). Leadership in sports: A review. *International Journal of Sport Psychology, 21,* 328-354.

Chelladurai, P., & Saleh, S. D. (1980). Dimensions of leader behavior in sports: Development of a leadership scale. *Journal of Sport Psychology, 2,* 34-45.

Cox, R.H., Russell, W.D., & Robb, M. (1998). Development of a CSAI-2 short form for assessing competitive state anxiety during and immediately prior to competition. *Journal of Sport Behavior, 21,* 30-40.

Cox, R.H., Russell, W.D., & Robb, M. (1999). Comparative concurrent validity of the MRF-L and ARS competitive state anxiety rating scales for volleyball and basketball. *Journal of Sport Behavior, 22,* 310-320.

Curran, S.L., Andrykowski, M.A., & Studts, J.L. (1995). Short Form of the Profile of Mood States (POMS-SF): Psychometric information. *Psychological Assessment, 7,* 80-83.

Darst, P.W., Zakrajsek, D.B., & Mancini, V.H. (1989). *Analyzing physical education and sport instruction* (2nd ed.). Champaign, IL: Human Kinetics.

DeVellis, R.F. (1991). *Scale development: Theory and applications*. Newbury Park, CA: Sage.

Duda, J.L. (1989). The relationship between task and ego orientation and the perceived purpose of sport among male and female high school athletes. *Journal of Sport and Exercise Psychology, 11,* 318-335.

Duda, J.L. (1998). *Advances in sport and exercise psychology measurement*. Morgantown, WV: Fitness Information Technology.

Duda, J.L., & Hall, H. (2001). Achievement goal theory in sport. In R.N. Singer, H.A. Hausenblas, & C.M. Janelle (Eds.), *Handbook of sport psychology* (pp. 417-443). New York: Wiley.

Duda, J.L., & Tappe, M.K. (1989). The Personal Incentives for Exercise Questionnaire: Preliminary development. *Perceptual and Motor Skills, 68,* 1122.

Dunn, J.G.H., Dunn, J.C., Wilson, P., & Syrotuik, D.G. (2000). Reexamining the factorial composition and factor structure of the Sport Anxiety Scale. *Journal of Sport and Exercise Psychology, 22,* 183-193.

Durand-Bush, N. (1995). *Validity and reliability of the Ottawa Mental Skills Assessment Tool (OMSAT-3)*. Unpublished master's thesis, University of Ottawa, Ottawa, ON, Canada.

Durand-Bush, N., Salmela, J.H., & Green-Demers, I. (2001). The Ottawa Mental Skills Assessment Tool (OMSAT-3*). *The Sport Psychologist, 15,* 1-19.

Etzel, E.F., Jr. (1979). Validation of a conceptual model characterizing attention among international rifle shooters. *Journal of Sport Psychology, 1,* 281-290.

Fisher, A.C., & Taylor, A.H. (1980). Attentional style of soccer players [Abstract]. *Proceedings of the annual conference of the American Alliance for Health, Physical Education, Recreation, and Dance* (p. 71). Detroit: AAHPERD.

Ford, S.K., & Summers, J.J. (1992). The factorial validity of the TAIS attentional-style subscales. *Journal of Sport and Exercise Psychology, 14,* 283-297.

Gilbert, W., Trudel, P., & Haughian, L. (1999). Decision making process of ice hockey coaches during games. *Journal of Teaching in Physical Education, 18*(3), 290-312.

Glenn, S.D., & Horn, T.S. (1993). Psychological and personal predictors of leadership behavior in female soccer athletes. *Journal of Applied Sport Psychology, 5,* 17-34.

Gould, D., Tammen, V., Murphy, S., & May, J. (1989). An examination of U.S. Olympic sport psychology consultants and the services they provide. *The Sport Psychologist, 3,* 300-312.

Gruber, J.J., & Gray, G.R. (1981). Factor patterns of variables influencing cohesiveness at various levels of basketball competition. *Research Quarterly for Exercise and Sport, 52,* 19-30.

Guay, F., Vallerand, R.J., & Blanchard, C. (2000). On the assessment of situational intrinsic and extrinsic motivation: The Situational Motivation Scale (SIMS). *Motivation and Emotion, 24,* 175-213.

Hall, C.R., Pongrac, J., & Buckholz, E. (1985). The measurement of imagery ability. *Human Movement Science, 4,* 107-118.

Hall, C.R., Rodgers, W.M., & Barr, K.A. (1990). The use of imagery by athletes in selected sports. *The Sport Psychologist, 4,* 1-10.

Hanin, Y.L. (1999). *Emotions in Sport.* Champaign, IL: Human Kinetics, 315, 316.

Hanin, Y.L. (2000). Individual zones of optimal functioning (IZOF) model: Emotion-performance relationships in sport. In Y.L. Hanin (Ed.), *Emotions in sport* (pp. 65-90). Champaign, IL: Human Kinetics.

Hruby, P. (2000, May 1). Tests of character. *Washington Times* [Online]. Available: www.washingtontimes.com [October 31, 2003].

Ivey, A.E., & Ivey, M.B. (2003). *Intentional interviewing and counseling: Facilitating client development in a multicultural society* (5th ed.). Pacific Grove, CA: Thomson/Brooks/Cole.

Jones, J.G. (1991). Recent developments and current issues in competitive state anxiety research. *The Sport Psychologist, 4,* 152-155.

Jones, J.G. (1995). More than just a game: Research developments and issues in competitive anxiety in sport. *British Journal of Psychology, 86,* 449-478.

Jones, J.G., & Swain, A.B.J. (1992). Intensity and direction dimensions of competitive anxiety and relationships with competitiveness. *Perceptual and Motor Skills, 74,* 467-472.

Kallus, K.W., & Kellman, M. (2000). Burnout in athletes and coaches. In Y.L. Hanin (Ed.), *Emotions in sport* (pp. 209-230). Champaign, IL: Human Kinetics.

Kellman, M. (2002). Psychological assessment of underrecovery. In M. Kellman (Ed.), *Enhancing recovery: Preventing underperformance in athletes* (pp. 37-55). Champaign, IL: Human Kinetics.

Kellman, M., Altenburg, D., Lormes, W., & Steinacker, J. M. (2001). Assessing stress and recovery during preparation for the World Championships in rowing. *The Sport Psychologist, 15,* 151-167.

Kellman, M., Botterill, C., & Wilson, C. (1999). *Recovery-cue.* Unpublished manuscript, National Sport Centre, Calgary, Alberta, Canada.

Kellman, M., & Kallus, K. W. (2001). *Recovery-Stress Questionnaire for Athletes: User manual.* Champaign, IL: Human Kinetics.

Kellman, M., Kallus, K.W., & Kurz, H. (1996). Performance prediction by the Recovery-Stress-Questionnaire. *Journal of Applied Sport Psychology, 8*(Suppl.), S22.

Kellman, M., Patrick, T., Botterill, C., & Wilson, C. (2002). The Recovery-Cue and its use in applied settings: Practical suggestions regarding assessment and monitoring of recovery. In M. Kellman (Ed.), *Enhancing recovery: Preventing underperformance in athletes* (pp. 219-229). Champaign, IL: Human Kinetics.

Krane, V. (1994). The Mental Readiness Form as a measure of competitive state anxiety. *The Sport Psychologist, 8,* 189-202.

Lane, A.M., Sewell, D.F., Terry, P.C., Bartram, D., & Nesti, M.S. (1999). Confirmatory factor analysis of the Competitive State Anxiety Inventory-2. *Journal of Sports Sciences, 17,* 505-512.

Leffingwell, T.R., Rider, S.P., & Williams, J.M. (2001). Application of the Transtheoretical Model to psychological skills training. *The Sport Psychologist, 15,* 168-187.

Lloyd, R., & Trudel, P. (1999). Verbal interactions between eminent mental training consultant and elite level athletes: A case study. *The Sport Psychologist, 13,* 418-443.

Markland, D., & Hardy, L. (1993). The Exercise Motivations Inventory: Preliminary development and validity of a measure of individual's reasons for participation in regular physical exercise. *Personality and Individual Differences, 15,* 289-296.

Martens, R., Burton, D., Vealey, R.S., Bump, L.A., & Smith, D.A. (1990). Development and validation of the competitive sport anxiety inventory-2. In R. Martens, R.S. Vealey, & D. Burton (Eds.), *Competitive anxiety in sport* (pp. 117-126). Champaign, IL: Human Kinetics.

Martens, R., Vealey, R.S., & Burton, D. (1990). *Competitive anxiety in sport.* Champaign, IL: Human Kinetics.

Martin, D.T., Andersen, M.B., & Gates, W. (2000). Using Profile of Mood States (POMS) to monitor high-intensity training in cyclists: Group versus case studies. *The Sport Psychologist, 14,* 138-156.

McNair, D.M., Lorr, M., & Droppleman, L.F. (1971). *Profile of Mood States manual.* San Diego: Educational and Industrial Testing Service.

Merron, J. (2002, April 23). Taking your Wonderlics [Online]. Available: http://espn.go.com [April 23, 2002].

Morgan, W.P., Brown, D.R., Raglin, J.S., O'Connor, P.J., & Ellickson, K.A. (1987). Psychological monitoring of overtraining and staleness. *British Journal of Sports Medicine, 21,* 408-414.

Mullen, B., & Cooper, C. (1994). The relation between group cohesiveness and performance: An integration. *Psychological Bulletin, 115,* 210-227.

Murphy, S., & Tammen, V. (1998). In search of psychological skills. In J.L. Duda (Ed.), *Advances in sport and exercise psychology measurement* (pp. 195-209). Morgantown, WV: Fitness Information Technology.

Nideffer, R.M. (1976). Test of Attentional and Interpersonal Style. *Journal of Personality and Social Psychology, 34,* 397-404.

Nideffer, R.M., & Sagal, M. (2001). *Assessment in sport psychology.* Morgantown, WV: Fitness Information Technology.

Orlick, T. (1996). The wheel of excellence. *Journal of Performance Education, 1,* 3-18.

Pelletier, L.G., Fortier, M.S., Vallerand, R.J., Tuson, K.M., Brière, N.M., & Blais, M.R. (1995). Toward a new measure of intrinsic, extrinsic motivation, and amotivation in sports: The Sport Motivation Scale (SMS). *Journal of Sport and Exercise Psychology, 17,* 35-53.

Raglin, J.S. (1993). Overtraining and staleness: Psychometric monitoring of endurance athletes. In R.N. Singer, M. Murphey, & L.K. Tennant (Eds.), *Handbook of research on sport psychology* (pp. 840-850). New York: Macmillan.

Raglin, J.S., & Hanin, Y.L. (2000). Competitive anxiety. In Y.L. Hanin (Ed.), *Emotions in sport* (pp. 93-112). Champaign, IL: Human Kinetics.

Raglin, J.S., & Wilson, G.S. (2000). Overtraining in athletes. In Y.L. Hanin (Ed.), *Emotions in sport* (pp. 191-208). Champaign, IL: Human Kinetics.

Ravizza, K. (2001). Increasing awareness for sport performance. In J.M. Williams (Ed.), *Applied sport psychology: Personal growth to peak performance* (4th ed., pp. 179-189). Mayfield Publishing, Mountain View, CA.

Roberts, G.C., Treasure, D.C., & Balague, G. (1998). Achievement goals in sport: The development and validation of the Perception of Success Questionnaire. *Journal of Sports Sciences, 16,* 337-347.

Ryckman, R.M., Robbins, M.A., Thornton, B., & Cantrell, P. (1982). Development and validation of a Physical Self-Efficacy Scale. *Journal of Personality and Social Psychology, 42,* 891-900.

Shacham, S. (1983). A shortened version of the Profile of Mood States. *Journal of Personality Assessment, 47,* 305-306.

Smith, R.E., Schutz, R.W., Smoll, F.L. & Ptacek, J.T. (1995). Development and validation of a multidimensional measure of sport-specific psychological skills: The Athletic Coping Skills Inventory-28. *Journal of Sport and Exercise Psychology, 17,* 379-398.

Smith, R.E., Smoll, F.L., & Schutz, R.S. (1990). Measurement and correlates of sport-specific cognitive and somatic trait anxiety: The Sport Anxiety Scale. *Anxiety Research, 2,* 263-280.

Smith, R.E., Smoll, F.L., & Wiechman, S.A. (1998). Measurement of trait anxiety in sport. In J.L. Duda (Ed.), *Advances in sport and exercise psychology measurement* (pp. 105-127). Morgantown, WV: Fitness Information Technology.

Thomas, P.R., Murphy, S.M., & Hardy, L. (1999). Test of performance strategies: Development and preliminary validation of a comprehensive measure of athletes' psychological skills. *Journal of Sports Sciences, 17,* 697-711.

Trudel, P., Gilbert, W., & Tochon, F.V. (2001). The use of video to study pedagogical interactions in sport. *International Journal of Applied Semiotics, 2*(1-2), 89-112.

Vallerand, R.J., & Fortier, M.S. (1998). Measures of intrinsic and extrinsic motivation in sport and physical activity: A review and critique. In J.L. Duda (Ed.), *Advances in sport and exercise psychology measurement* (pp. 81-101). Morgantown, WV: Fitness Information Technology.

Van Schoyck, S.R., & Grasha, A.F. (1981). Attentional style variations and athletic ability: The advantages of a sports-specific test. *Journal of Sport Psychology, 3,* 149-165.

Vealey, R.S. (1986). Conceptualization of sport-confidence and competitive orientation: Preliminary investigation and instrument development. *Journal of Sport Psychology, 8,* 221-246.

Vealey, R.S., & Garner-Holman, M. (1998). Applied sport psychology: Measurement issues. In J.L. Duda (Ed.), *Advances in sport and exercise psychology measurement* (pp. 433-446). Morgantown, WV: Fitness Information Technology.

Vincent, W.J. (1999). *Statistics in kinesiology* (2nd ed.). Champaign, IL: Human Kinetics.

Williams, J.M. (2001). *Applied sport psychology: Personal growth to peak performance.* New York: McGraw-Hill.

Woodman, T., & Hardy, L. (2001). Stress and anxiety. In R.N. Singer, H.A. Hausenblas, & C.M. Janelle (Eds.), *Handbook of sport psychology* (pp. 290-318). New York: Wiley.

Yukelson, D., Weinberg, R., & Jackson, A. (1984). A multi-dimensional group cohesion instrument for intercollegiate basketball teams. *Journal of Sport Psychology, 6,* 103-117.

Chapter 7

Albrecht, J.L., & Adelman, M.B. (1984). Social support and life stress: New directions for communication research. *Human Communications Research, 2,* 3-22.

Burton, D. (1989). Winning isn't everything: Examining the impact of performance goals on collegiate swimmers' cognitions and performance. *The Sport Psychologist, 3,* 105-132.

Burton, D. (1992). The Jeckyll/Hyde nature of goals: Reconceptualizing goal setting in sport. In T. Horn (Ed.), *Advances in sport psychology* (pp. 267-297). Champaign, IL: Human Kinetics.

Burton, D. (1993). Goal setting in sport. In R.N. Singer, M. Murphey, & L.K. Tennant (Eds.), *Handbook of research on sport psychology* (pp. 467-491). New York: Macmillan.

Burton, D., Naylor, & Holliday (2001). Goal-setting in sport: Investigating the goal effectiveness paradox. In R.N. Singer, H.A. Hausenblas, & C.M. Janelle (Eds.), *Handbook of sport psychology* (2nd ed., pp. 497-528). New York: Wiley.

Burton, D., Weinberg, R.S., Yukelson, D., & D. Weigand. (1998). The goal effectiveness paradox in sport: Examining the goal practices of collegiate athletes. *The Sport Psychologist, 12,* 404-418.

Butler, R.J., & Hardy, L. (1992). The performance profile: Theory and application. *The Sport Psychologist, 6,* 253-264.

Chidester, J.S., & Grigsby, W.C. (1984). A meta-analysis of the goal setting performance literature. In A. Pearce & R.B. Robinson (Eds.), *Proceedings of the 44th annual meeting of the Academy of Management* (pp. 202-206). Ada, OH: Academy of Management.

Cleary, T.J., & Zimmerman, B.J. (2001). Self-regulation differences during athletic practice by experts, non-experts, and novices. *Journal of Applied Sport Psychology, 13,* 185-206.

Cohen, S. (1988). Psychosocial models of the role of social support in the etiology of physical disease. *Health Psychology, 7,* 269-297.

Covey, S.R. (1989). *The 7 habits of highly effective people: Powerful lessons in personal change.* New York: Fireside.

Ericsson, K.A. (1997). Deliberate practice and the acquisition of expert performance: An overview. In H. Jorgensen & A.C. Lehmann (Eds.), *Does practice make perfect?* (pp. 9-51). Stockholm: NIH Publikasjoner.

Ericsson, K.A. (2002). Attaining excellence through deliberate practice: Insights from the study of expert performance. In M. Ferrari (Ed.), *The pursuit of excellence through education* (pp. 21-55). Mahwah, NJ: Erlbaum.

Ericsson, K.A., Krampe, R.T., & Tesch-Romer, C. (1993). The role of deliberate practice in the acquisition of expert performance. *Psychological Review, 100,* 363-406.

Ericsson, K.A., & Lehmann, A.C. (1996). Expert and exceptional performance: Evidence of maximal adaptation to task constraints. *Annual Review of Psychology, 47,* 273-305.

Filby, C.D., Maynard, I.W., & Graydon, J.K. (1999). The effect of multiple-goal strategies on performance outcomes in training and competition. *Journal of Applied Sport Psychology, 11,* 230-246.

Gould, D. (1998). Goal setting for peak performance. In J.M. Williams (Ed.), *Applied sport psychology: Personal growth to peak performance* (pp. 182-196). Mountain View, CA: Mayfield.

Gould, D. (2001). Goal setting for peak performance. In J.M. Williams (Ed.). *Applied sport psychology: Personal growth to peak performance* (4th ed., pp. 190-228). Mountain View, CA: Mayfield.

Gould, D., Greenleaf, C., Guinan, D., & Chung, Y. (2002). A survey of US Olympic coaches: Variables perceived to have influenced athlete performance and coach effectiveness. *The Sport Psychologist, 16,* 229-250.

Gould, D., Tammen, V., Murphy, S., & May, J. (1989). An examination of U.S. Olympic sport psychology consultants and the services they provide. *The Sport Psychologist, 3,* 300-312.

Hall, H.K., & Byrne, A.T.J. (1988). Goal setting in sport: Clarifying recent anomalies. *Journal of Sport and Exercise Psychology, 10,* 184-189.

Hardy, C.V., Richman, J.M., & Rosenfeld, L.B. (1991). The role of social support in the life stress/injury relationship. *The Sport Psychologist, 5,* 128-139.

Hardy, L., Jones, G., & Gould, D. (1996). *Understanding psychological preparation for sport: Theory and practice of elite performance.* New York: Wiley.

Jones, G. (1993). The role of performance profiling in cognitive behavioral interventions in sport. *The Sport Psychologist, 7,* 160-172.

Kingston, K., & Hardy, L. (1997). Effects of different types of goals on processes that support performance. *The Sport Psychologist, 11,* 277-293.

Kitsantas, A., & Zimmerman, B.J. (2001). Comparing self-regulatory processes among novice, non-expert, and expert volleyball players: A microanalytic study. *Journal of Applied Sport Psychology, 14,* 91-105.

Kyllo, L.B., & Landers, D.M. (1995). Goal setting in sport and exercise: A research synthesis to solve the controversy. *Journal of Sport and Exercise Psychology, 17,* 117-137.

Locke, E.A. (1968). Toward a theory of task motivation incentives. *Organizational Behavior and Human Performance, 3,* 157-189.

Locke, E.A., & Latham, G.P. (1985). The application of goal setting to sports. *Journal of Sport Psychology, 7,* 205-222.

Locke, E.A. & Latham, G.P. (1990). *A theory of goal setting and task performance.* Englewood Cliffs, NJ: Prentice Hall.

Locke, E.A., Shaw, K.N., Saari, L.M., & Latham, G.P. (1981). Goal setting and task performance. *Psychological Bulletin, 90,* 125-152.

Mento, A.J., Steel, R.P., & Karren, R.J. (1987). A meta-analytic study of the effects of goal setting on task performance: 1966-1984. *Organizational Behavior and Human Decision Processes, 39,* 52-83.

Orlick, T., & Partington, J. (1988). Mental links to excellence. *The Sport Psychologist, 2,* 105-130.

Ravizza, K. (2001). Increasing awareness for sport performance. In J.M. Williams (Ed.), *Applied sport psychology: Personal growth to peak performance* (4th ed., pp. 179-189). Mayfield Publishing, Mountain View, CA.

Sullivan, P.A., & Nashman, H.W. (1998) Self-perceptions of the role of USOC sport psychologists in working with Olympic athletes. *The Sport Psychologist, 12,* 95-103.

Swain, A., & Jones, G. (1995). Effects of goal-setting interventions on selected basketball skills: A single subject design. *Research Quarterly for Exercise and Sport, 66,* 51–63.

Taylor, J. (1995). *The mental edge for alpine ski racing* (4th ed.). Denver: Minuteman Press.

Tubbs, M.E. (1991). Goal setting: A meta-analytic examination of the empirical evidence. *Journal of Applied Psychology, 71,* 474-483.

Weinberg, R.S., Burke, K., & Jackson, A.W. (1997). Coaches' and players' perceptions of goal setting in junior tennis: An exploratory investigation. *The Sport Psychologist, 11,* 426-439.

Weinberg, R.S., Burton, D., Yukelson, D., & Weigand, D. (1993). Goal setting in competitive sport: An exploratory investigation of practices of collegiate athletes. *The Sport Psychologist, 7,* 275-289.

Weinberg, R.S., Burton, D., Yukelson, D., & Weigand, D. (2000). Perceived goal setting practices of Olympic athletes: An exploratory investigation. *The Sport Psychologist, 14,* 280-296.

Weinberg, R.S., Butt, J., & Knight, B. (2000). High school coaches' perceptions of the process of goal setting. *The Sport Psychologist, 15,* 20-47.

Weinberg, R.S., Butt, J., Knight, B., & Perritt, N. (2001). Collegiate coaches' perceptions of their goal-setting practices: A qualitative investigation. *Journal of Applied Sport Psychology, 13,* 374-398.

Weinberg, R.S., Stitcher, T., & Richardson, P. (1994). Effects of a seasonal goal setting program on lacrosse performance. *The Sport Psychologist, 8,* 166-175.

Zimmerman, B.J. (2000). Attaining self-regulation: A social cognitive perspective. In M. Boekaerts, P.R. Pintrich, & M. Zeidner (Eds.), *Handbook of self-regulation* (pp. 13-39). San Diego: Academic Press.

Zimmerman, B.J. (2002). Becoming a self-regulated learner: An overview. *Theory Into Practice, 41,* 64-70.

Zimmerman, B.J., & Kitsantas, A. (1996). Self-regulated learning of a motoric skill: The role of goal-setting and self-monitoring. *Journal of Applied Sport Psychology, 8,* 60-75.

Zimmerman, B.J., & Kitsantas, A. (1997). Developmental phases of self-regulation: Shifting from process goals to outcome goals. *Journal of Educational Psychology, 89,* 29-36.

Chapter 8

Bakker, F.C., Boschker, M.S.J., & Chung, T. (1996). Changes in muscular activity while imagining weight lifting using stimulus and response propositions. *Journal of Sport and Exercise Psychology, 18,* 313-324.

Bonnet, M., Decety, J., Jeannerod, M., & Requin, J. (1997). Mental simulation of an action modulates the excitability of spinal reflex pathways in man. *Cognitive Brain Research, 5,* 221-228.

Bull, S.J. (1992). *Sport psychology: A self-help guide.* Marlborough, U.K.: Crowood Press.

Callow, N., & Hardy, L. (1997). Kinesthetic imagery and its interaction with visual imagery perspectives during the acquisition and retention of a short gymnastics sequence. *Journal of Sports Sciences, 15,* 75.

Callow, N., & Hardy, L. (2001). Types of imagery associated with sport confidence in netball players of varying skill levels. *Journal of Applied Sport Psychology, 13,* 1-17.

Collins, D.J., Smith, D., & Hale, B.D. (1998). Imagery perspective and karate performance. *Journal of Sports Sciences, 16,* 103-104.

Corbin, C.B. (1972). Mental practice. In W.D. Morgan (Ed.), *Ergogenic aids and muscular performance* (pp. 94-110). New York: Academic Press.

Decety, J., & Grezes, J. (1999). Neural mechanisms subserving the perception of human actions. *Trends in Cognitive Sciences, 3,* 172-178.

Driskell, J.E., Copper, C., & Moran, A. (1994). Does mental practice enhance performance? *Journal of Applied Psychology, 79,* 481-492.

Etnier, J.L., & Landers, D.M. (1996). The influence of procedural variables on the efficacy of mental practice. *The Sport Psychologist, 10,* 48-57.

Feltz, D.L., & Landers, D.M. (1983). The effects of mental practice on motor skill learning and performance: A meta-analysis. *Journal of Sport Psychology, 5,* 25-57.

Gould, D., & Damarjian, N. (1996). Imagery training for peak performance. In J.L. Van Hale, B. W. Brewer (ed.). *Exploring sport and exercise psychology* (pp. 25-50).Washington, DC: American Psychological Association.

Hale, B.D. (1982). The effects of internal and external imagery on muscular and ocular concomitants. *Journal of Sport Psychology, 4,* 379-387.

Hale, B.D. (1994). Imagery perspectives and learning in sports performance. In A. Sheikh & E. Korn (Eds.), *Imagery in sports and physical performance* (pp. 75-96). Farmingdale, NY: Baywood.

Hale, B.D. (1998). *Imagery training: A guide for sports coaches and performers.* Leeds, UK: National Coaching Foundation.

Hale, B.D., & Howe, B. (1999). Visualizing the perfect match. In B. Hale & D. Collins (Eds.), *Rugby tough* (p. 66). Champaign, IL: Human Kinetics.

Hardy, L., & Callow, N. (1999). Efficacy of external and internal visual imagery perspectives for the enhancement of performance on tasks in which form is important. *Journal of Sport and Exercise Psychology, 21,* 95-112.

Hardy, L., & Fazey, J. (1990). *Mental rehearsal.* Leeds, UK: National Coaching Foundation.

Hardy, L., Jones, G., & Gould, D. (1996). *Understanding psychological preparation for sport, theory and practice of elite performers.* New York: Wiley.

Hecker, J.E., & Kaczor, L.M. (1988). Application of imagery theory to sport psychology: Some preliminary findings. *Journal of Sport and Exercise Psychology, 10,* 363-373.

Hinshaw, K.E. (1991). The effects of mental practice on motor skill performance: Critical evaluation and meta-analysis. *Imagination, Cognition and Personality, 11,* 3-35.

Hird, J.S., Landers, D.M., Thomas, J.R., & Horan, J.J. (1991). Physical practice is superior to mental practice in enhancing cognitive and motor task performance. *Journal of Sport and Exercise Psychology, 12,* 281-293.

Holmes, P.S. (October, 1996). *Psychological support for elite pistol shooters.* Paper presented at the Annual Meeting of Great Britain Shooting Squads, Bisley, UK.

Holmes, P.S., & Collins, D.J. (2001). The PETTLEP approach to motor imagery: A functional equivalence model for sport psychologists. *Journal of Applied Sport Psychology, 13,* 60-83.

Holmes, P.S., Collins, D.J., & Saffery, G. (2000). *The representation of time in motor imagery.* Manuscript in preparation.

Jacobson, E. (1931). Electrical measurement of neuromuscular states during mental activities. *American Journal of Physiology, 94,* 115-121.

Jeannerod, M. (1997). *The cognitive neuroscience of action.* Oxford, UK: Blackwell.

Kohl, R.M., & Roenker, D.L. (1983). Mechanism involvement during skill imagery. *Journal of Motor Behavior, 15,* 179-190.

Landers, D.M., Arent, S.A., Lutz, R.S., Romero, D.H., Slade, J.M., McCullagh, P.D., & Ram, N. (2002). The effects of mental practice on performance: Problems and practical recommendations. Unpublished manuscript.

Lang, P.J. (1979). A bio-informational theory of emotional imagery. *Psychophysiology, 16,* 495-512.

Lutz, R., Landers, D.M, & Linder, D.E. (2001). Procedural variables and skill level influences on preperformance mental practice efficacy. *Journal of Mental Imagery, 25,* 111-130.

Mahoney, M.J., & Avener, M. (1977). Psychology of the elite athlete: An exploratory study. *Cognitive Therapy and Research, 1,* 135-141.

Martin, K.A., Moritz, S.E., & Hall, C.R. (1999). Imagery use in sport: A literature review and an applied model. *The Sport Psychologist, 13,* 245-268.

Miller, B. (1991). Mental preparation for competition. In S.J. Bull (Ed.), *Sport psychology: A self-help guide* (pp. 84-102). Marlborough, UK: Crowood Press.

Miller, S.L. (2001). *The complete player: The psychology of winning hockey.* Toronto: Stoddart.

Moritz, S.E., Hall, C.R., Martin, K.A., & Vadocz, E. (1996). What are confident athletes imagining? An examination of image content. *The Sport Psychologist, 10,* 171-179.

Murphy, S.M., & Jowdy, D. (1992). Imagery and mental practice. In T. S. Horn (Ed.), *Advances in sport psychology* (pp. 221-250). Champaign, IL: Human Kinetics.

Murphy, S.M., & Wookfolk, R. (1987). The effects of cognitive interventions on competitive anxiety and performance on a fine motor skill task. *International Journal of Sport Psychology, 18,* 152-166.

Orlick, T., & Partington, J. (1988). Mental links to excellence. *The Sport Psychologist, 2,* 105-130.

Paivio, A. (1985). Cognitive and motivational functions of imagery in human performance. *Canadian Journal of Applied Sport Science, 10,* 22-28.

Richardson, A. (1967). Mental practice: A review and discussion. Part 1. *Research Quarterly, 38,* 95-107.

Ryan, E.D., & Simons, J. (1983). What is learned in mental practice of motor skills: A test of cognitive-motor hypothesis. *Journal of Sport Psychology, 5,* 419-426.

Sackett, R.S. (1934). The influences of symbolic rehearsal upon the retention of a maze habit. *Journal of General Psychology, 13,* 113-128.

Slade, J.M, Landers, D.M., & Martin, P.F. (2002). Muscular activity during real and imagined movements: A test of inflow explanations. *Journal of Sport and Exercise Psychology, 24,* 151-167.

Smith, D., Collins, D.J., & Hale, B.D. (1998). Imagery perspectives and karate performance. *Journal of Sports Sciences, 16,* 98-99.

Smith, D., & Holmes, P.S. (2002). The effect of imagery modality on putting performance. In *Proceedings of the British Psychological Society* (pp. 75-76). Leicester: British Psychological Society.

Smith, D., Holmes, P.S., & Collins, D.J. (1998). The effect of mental practice on muscle strength and EMG activity. In *Proceedings of the British Psychological Society* (p. 22). Leicester: British Psychological Society.

Smith, D., Holmes, P., Whitemore, L., Collins, D., & Devonport, T. (2001). The effect of stimulus-laden and response-laden imagery scripts on field hockey performance. *Journal of Sport Behavior, 23,* 408-419.

Suinn, R.M. (1980). Psychology and sports performance principles and applications. In R. Suinn (Ed.), *Psychology of sports: Methods and applications* (pp. 26-36). Minneapolis: Burgess.

Taylor, J. (2001). *Prime sport: Triumph of the athlete mind.* New York: iUniverse.

Taylor, J., & Taylor, S. (1997). *Psychological approaches to sports injury rehabilitation.* Gaithersburg, MD: Aspen.

Vealey, R., & Greenleaf, C. (1998). Seeing is believing: Understanding and using imagery in sport. In J.M. Williams (Ed.), *Applied sport psychology: Personal growth to peak performance* (2nd ed., pp. 237-260). Mountain View, CA: Mayfield.

Vealey, R., & Walter, S. (1993). Imagery training for performance enhancement and personal development. In J.M. Williams (Ed.), *Applied sport psychology: Personal growth to peak performance* (2nd ed., pp. 220-224), Mountain View, CA: Mayfield.

Vogt, S. (1995). On relations between perceiving, imaging, and performing in the learning of cyclical movement sequences. *British Journal of Psychology, 86,* 191-216.

Washburn, M.F. (1916). *Movement and mental imagery.* Boston: Houghton Mifflin.

Williams, J.M. (1998). *Applied sport psychology: Personal growth to peak performance* (3rd ed.). Mountain View, CA: Mayfield.

Yue, G., & Cole, K.J. (1992). Strength increases from the motor program: Comparison of training with maximal voluntary and imagined muscle contraction. *Journal of Neurophysiology, 67,* 1114-1123.

Chapter 9

Adams, J.A. (1961). The second facet of forgetting: A review of warm-up decrement. *Psychological Bulletin, 58,* 257-273.

Bloom, G.A., Durand-Bush, N., & Salmela, J.H. (1997). Pre- and post-competition routines of expert coaches of team sports. *The Sport Psychologist, 11*(2), 127-141.

Boutcher, S.H. (1990). The role of performance routines in sport. In J.G. Jones & L. Hardy (Eds.), *Stress and performance in sport* (pp. 231-245). New York: Wiley.

Boutcher, S.H., & Zinsser, N. (1990). Cardiac deceleration of elite and beginning golfers during putting. *Journal of Sport and Exercise Psychology, 12,* 37-47.

Bunker, L.K., & Owens, N.D. (1985). *Golf: Better practice for better play.* West Point, NY: Leisure Press.

Bunker, L.K., & Rotella, R.J. (1982). *Mind, set and match.* Englewood Cliffs, NJ: Prentice Hall.

Caudill, D., Weinberg, R., & Jackson, A. (1983). Psyching-up and track athletes: A preliminary investigation. *Journal of Sport Psychology, 5,* 231-235.

Cohn, P.J. (1990). Pre-performance routines in sport: Theoretical support and practical applications. *The Sport Psychologist, 4*(3), 301-312.

Cohn, P.J., Rotella, R.J., & Lloyd, J.W. (1990). Effects of a cognitive-behavioral intervention on the preshot routine and performance in golf. *The Sport Psychologist, 4,* 33-47.

Crews, D.J., & Boutcher, S.H. (1986). Effects of structured preshot behaviors on beginning golf performance. *Perceptual and Motor Skills, 62,* 291-294.

Crews, D.J., & Boutcher, S.H. (1987). An observational analysis of professional female golfers during tournament play. *Journal of Sport Behavior, 9,* 51-58.

Heishman, M.F. (1989). *Pre-performance routines: A test of the schema theory versus the set hypothesis as an explanation for the efficacy of a pre-service routine in volleyball.* Unpublished doctoral dissertation, University of Virginia.

Highlen, P.S., & Bennett, B.B. (1983). Elite divers and wrestlers: a comparison between open- and closed-skill athletes. *Journal of Sport Psychology, 5,* 390-409.

Lobmeyer, D.L., & Wasserman, E.A. (1986). Preliminaries to free throw shooting: Superstitious behavior? *Journal of Sport Behavior, 9,* 70-78.

Mahoney, M.J., & Avener, M. (1977). Psychology of the elite athlete: An exploratory study. *Cognitive Therapy and Research, 1,* 135-141.

Moore, W.E. (1986). *Covert-overt service routines: The effects of a service routine training program on elite tennis players.* Unpublished doctoral dissertation, University of Virginia.

Ravizza, K., & Rotella, R.J. (1982). Cognitive somatic behavioral intervention in gymnastics. In L. Zaichkowsky & W. Sime (Eds.), *Stress management for sport* (pp. 25-35). Reston, VA: AAHPERD.

Rotella, R.J., & Bunker, L.K. (1981). *Mind mastery for winning golf.* Englewood Cliffs, NJ: Prentice Hall.

Schack, T. (1997). *Ängstliche Schüler im Sport—Interventionsverfahren zur Entwicklung der Handlungskontrolle.* Schorndorf, Germany: Hofmann.

Schack, T. (2002). Zur kognitiven Architektur von Bewegungshandlungen—modelltheoretischer Zugang und experimentelle Untersuchungen, Unpublished Habilitation, Department of Psychology, German Sports University, Cologne.

Schmidt, R.A. (1988). *Motor control and learning: A behavioral emphasis* (2nd ed.) Champaign, IL: Human Kinetics.

Schmidt, R.A., & Lee, T.D. (1998). *Motor control and learning. A behavioral emphasis.* Champaign, IL: Human Kinetics.

Shelton, T.O., & Mahoney, M.J. (1978). The content and the effect of "psyching-up" strategies in weight lifters. *Cognitive Therapy and Research, 2,* 275-284.

Taylor, J. (2001). *Prime sport: Triumph of the athlete mind.* New York: iUniverse.

Chapter 10

Argyle, M., & Henderson, M. (1984). The rules of friendship. *Journal of Social and Personal Relationships, 1,* 211-237.

Barrow, J.C. (1977). The variable of leadership: A review and conceptual framework. *Academy of Management Review, 2,* 231-251.

Bloom, G.A., Durand-Bush, N., & Salmela, J.H. (1997). Pre- and post-competition routines of expert coaches of team sports. *The Sport Psychologist, 11,* 127-141.

Brackenridge, C. (2001). *Spoilsports: Understanding and preventing sexual exploitation in sport.* London: Routledge.

Brewer, C.J., & Jones, R.L. (2002). A five-stage process for establishing contextually valid systematic observation instruments: The case study of rugby union. *The Sport Psychologist, 16,* 138-159.

Brustad, R.J. (1996). Parental and peer influence on children's psychological development through sport. In F.L. Smoll & R.E. Smith (Eds.), *Children and youth in sport: A biopsychosocial perspective* (pp. 112-124). Madison: Brown & Benchmark.

Carr, C., & Murphy, S.M. (1995). Alcohol and drugs in sport. In S.M. Murphy (Ed.), *Sport psychology interventions* (pp. 283-306). Champaign, IL: Human Kinetics.

Carron, A.V., & Bennett, B.B. (1977). Compatibility in the coach–athlete dyad. *Research Quarterly, 48,* 670-679.

Chelladurai, P. (1978). *A contingency model of leadership in athletics.* Unpublished doctoral dissertation, Department of Management Sciences, University of Waterloo, Canada.

Chelladurai, P. (1993). Leadership. In R.N. Singer, M. Murphey, & L.K. Tennant (Eds.), *Handbook on research on sport psychology* (pp. 647-671). New York: Macmillan.

Chelladurai, P., & Carron, A.V. (1978). *Leadership.* Monograph of the Canadian Association of Health, Physical Education and Recreation, Ottawa.

Chelladurai, P., & Carron, A.V. (1983). Athletic maturity and preferred leadership. *Journal of Sport Psychology, 5,* 371-380.

Chelladurai, P., & Riemer, H.A. (1998). Measurement of leadership in sport. In J.L. Duda (Ed.), *Advances in sport and exercise psychology measurement* (pp. 227-253). Morgantown, WV: Fitness Information Technology.

Chelladurai, P., & Saleh, S.D. (1978). Preferred leadership in sports. *Canadian Journal of Applied Sports Sciences, 3,* 85-92.

Chelladurai, P., & Saleh, S.D. (1980). Dimensions of leader behavior in sport: Development of a leadership scale. *Journal of Sport Psychology, 2,* 34-45.

Coppel, D.B. (1995). Relationship issues in sport: A marital therapy model. In S.M. Murphy (Ed.), *Sport psychology interventions* (pp. 193-204). Champaign, IL: Human Kinetics.

Deci, E.L., & Ryan, R.M. (2000). The "what" and "why" of goal pursuits: Human needs and the self-determination of behavior. *Psychological Inquiry, 11,* 227-268.

Douge, B. (1999, Summer). Coaching adolescents: To develop mutual respect. *Sports Coach,* 6-7.

Duda, J.L., & Hayashi, C.T. (1998). Measurement issues in cross-cultural research within sport and exercise psychology. In J.L. Duda (Ed.), *Advances in sport and exercise psychology measurement* (pp. 213-226). Morgantown, WV: Fitness Information Technology.

Dwyer, D. (2000). *Interpersonal relationships.* London: Routledge.

Ellis, R., & McClintock, A. (1990). *If you take my meaning: Theory into practice in human communication.* London: Edward Arnold.

Hellstedt, J.C. (1987). The coach/parent/athlete relationship. *The Sport Psychologist, 1,* 151-160.

Hellstedt, J.C. (1990). Early adolescent perceptions of parental pressure in the sport environment. *Journal of Sport Behavior, 13,* 135-144.

Hinde, R.A. (1997). *Relationships: A dialectical perspective.* London: Psychology Press.

Honeycutt, J.M., Woods, B.L., & Fontenot, K. (1993). The endorsement of communication conflict rules as a function of engagement, marriage, and marital ideology. *Journal of Social and Personal Relationships, 10,* 285-304.

Horn, T.S. (1992). Leadership in the sport domain. In T.S. Horn (Ed.), *Advances in sport psychology* (pp. 181-198). Champaign, IL: Human Kinetics.

Horne, T., & Carron, A.V. (1985). Compatibility in coach–athlete relationships. *Journal of Sport Psychology, 7,* 137-149.

Iso-Ahola, S.E. (1995). Intrapersonal and interpersonal factors in athletic performance. *Scandinavian Journal of Medicine and Science in Sports, 5,* 191-199.

Janssen, J., & Dale, G. (2002). *The seven secrets of successful coaches.* Tucson, AZ: The Mental Game.

Jowett, S. (2001). *The psychology of interpersonal relationships in sport: The coach–athlete relationship.* Unpublished doctoral dissertation. University of Exeter, UK.

Jowett, S. (2002). *The coach–athlete relationship questionnaire and dyad maps* (Research Monograph No. 1). Staffordshire, UK: Staffordshire University, School of Health.

Jowett, S. (2003). When the honeymoon is over: A case study of a coach–athlete dyad in crisis. *The Sport Psychologist, 17,* 444-460.

Jowett., S. (2005). On repairing and enhancing the coach–athlete relationship. In S. Jowett & M. Jones (Eds.), *The psychology of coaching* (pp. 14-26). Sport and Exercise Psychology Division. Leicester, UK: The British Psychological Society.

Jowett, S., & Cockerill, L. (2002). Incompatibility in the coach–athlete relationship. In I. Cockerill (Ed.), *Solutions in sport psychology* (pp. 16-31). Andover, UK: Thomson Learning.

Jowett, S., & Cockerill, I.M. (2003). Olympic medallists' perspective of the athlete-coach relationship. *Psychology of Sport and Exercise, 4,* 313-331.

Jowett, S., & Gale, E. (2002, July). *An exploratory study into the nature of the coach–athlete relationship in track and field athletics.* Presented at the Annual Conference of the British Association of Sport and Exercise Sciences, Manchester, UK.

Jowett, S., & Meek, G. (2000a). Coach–athlete relationships in married couples: An exploratory content analysis. *The Sport Psychologist, 14,* 157-175.

Jowett, S., & Meek, G.A. (2000b, May). *Outgrowing the family coach–athlete relationship: A case study.* Presentation at the International Conference on Sport Psychology organized by the Centre of Sports Science and Halmstad University, Sweden.

Jowett, S., & Meek, G. (2002). *Closeness, co-orientation, and complementarity in the "family" coach–athlete relationship: A case study.* Manuscript submitted for publication.

Jowett, S., & Ntoumanis, N. (2003). The Greek Coach–Athlete Relationship Questionnaire (GrCART-Q): Scale construction and validation. *International Journal of Sport Psychology, 34,* 101-124.

Jowett, S., & Ntoumanis, N. (2004). The Coach–Athlete Relationship Questionnaire (CART–Q): Development and initial validation. *Scandinavian Journal of Medicine and Science in Sports, 14,* 245-257.

Jowett, S., & Pearce, J. (2001, May/June). An exploration into the nature of the coach–athlete relationship in swimming. In A. Papaioannou, Y. Theodorakis, & M. Goudas (Eds.), *Proceedings of the 10th World Congress of Sport Psychology* (Vol. 3, pp. 227-229), Skiathos, Greece.

Kalinowski, A.G. (1985). The development of Olympic swimmers. In B.S. Bloom (Ed.), *Developing talent in young people* (pp. 139-192). New York: Balantine Books.

Kiesler, D.J. (1997). *Contemporary interpersonal theory research and personality, psychopathology, and psychotherapy.* New York: Wiley.

Laing, R.D., Phillipson, H., & Lee, A.R. (1966). *Interpersonal perception: A theory and a method of research.* New York: Harper & Row.

Lyle, J. (1999). Coaching philosophy and coaching behavior. In N. Cross & J. Lyle (Eds.), *The coaching process: Principles and practice for sport* (pp. 25-46). Oxford, UK: Butterworth-Heineman.

Newcomb, T.M. (1953). An approach to the study of communicative acts. *Psychological Review, 60,* 393-404.

Pensgaard A.M., & Duda J. L. (2002). If we work hard, we can do it: A tale from an Olympic (gold) medallist. *Journal of Applied Sport Psychology, 14,* 219-236.

Pensgaard, A.M., & Roberts, G.C. (2000) Elite athletes' experiences of the motivational climate: The coach matters. *Scandinavian Journal of Medicine & Science in Sports 12* (1), 54-59.

Poczwardowski, A., Sherman, C., & Henschen, K. (1998). A sport psychology service delivery heuristic: Building on theory and practice. *The Sport Psychologist, 12,* 192-208.

Rapaport, R. (1993). To build a winning team: An interview with a head coach Bill Walsh. *Harvard Business Review, 71,* 111-120.

Rees, T., Ingledew, D.K., & Hardy, L. (1999). Social support dimensions and components of performance in tennis. *Journal of Sports Sciences, 17,* 421-429.

Roloff, M.E., Soule, K.P., & Carey, C.M. (2001). Reasons for remaining in a relationship and responses to relational transgressions. *Journal of Social and Personal Relationships, 18,* 362-385.

Rosenblatt, P.C. (1977). Needed research on commitment in marriage. In G. Levinger & H.L. Rausch (Eds.), *Close relationships: Perspectives on the meaning of intimacy* (pp. 73-86). Amherst, MA: University of Massachusetts Press.

Salminen, S., & Liukkonen, J. (1996). Coach–athlete relationship and coaching behaviour in training sessions. *International Journal of Sport Psychology, 27,* 59-67.

Scanlan, T.K., Stein, G.L., & Ravizza, K. (1991). An in-depth study of former elite figure skaters: III. Sources of stress. *Journal of Sport and Exercise Psychology, 13,* 103-120.

Schutz, W. C. (1966). *The interpersonal underworld.* Palo Alto, CA: Science & Behavior Books.

Schutz, W.C. (1967). *The phenomology of the social world.* Evanston, IL: Northwestern University Press.

Smith, R.E., & Smoll, F.L. (1996). The coach as a focus of research and intervention in youth sports. In F.L. Smoll & R.E. Smith (Eds.), *Children and youth in sport: A biopsychosocial perspective* (pp. 125-141). Dubuque, IA: McGraw-Hill.

Smith, R.E., Smoll, F.L., & Curtis, B. (1978). Coaching behaviours in Little League baseball. In F.L. Smoll & R.E. Smith (Eds.), *Psychological perspectives in youth sports* (pp. 173-201). Washington, DC: Hemisphere.

Smith, R.E., Smoll, F.L., & Hunt, E.A. (1977). A system for the behavioral assessment of coaches. *Research Quarterly, 48,* 401-407.

Smoll, F.L. (1996). Improving the quality of coach-parent relationships in youth sport. In F.L. Smoll & R.E. Smith (Eds.), *Children and youth in sport: A biopsychosocial perspective* (pp. 63-73). Madison: Brown & Benchmark.

Smoll, F.L., & Smith, R.E. (1989). Leadership behaviors in sport: A theoretical model and research paradigm. *Journal of Applied Social Psychology, 19,* 1522-1551.

Smoll, F.L., Smith, R.E., Curtis, B., & Hunt, E. (1978). Towards a mediational model of coach–player relationships. *Research Quarterly, 49,* 528-541.

Stewart, I., & Joines, V.S. (1987). *TA today: A new introduction to transactional analysis.* Nottingham: Lifespace.

Sundgot-Borgen, J., Fasting, K., Klungland, M., Berlund, B., & Brackenridge, C. (in press). Sexual harassment and abuse in elite female athletes: A controlled study. *Medical Science of Sports and Exercise.*

Udry, E., Gould, D., Bridges, D., & Tuffey, S. (1997). People helping people? Examining the social ties of athletes coping with burnout and injury stress. *Journal of Sport and Exercise Psychology, 19,* 368-395.

Unger, R., & Crawford, M. (1992). *Women and gender: A feminist psychology.* New York: McGraw-Hill.

Vallerand, R. J. (2001). A hierarchical model of intrinsic and extrinsic motivation in sport and exercise. In G.C. Roberts (Ed.), *Advances in motivation in sport and exercise* (pp. 263-319). Champaign, IL: Human Kinetics.

Vergeer, I., (2000). Interpersonal relationships in sport: From nomology to idiography. *International Journal of Sport Psychology, 31,* 578-583.

Wylleman, P. (2000). Interpersonal relationships in sport: Uncharted territory in sport psychology research. *International Journal of Sport Psychology, 31,* 555-572.

Chapter 11

Alberda, J., & Murphy, P. (1997). Teambuilding. *The Coach, 1,* 22-27.

Brawley, L.R., Carron, A.V., & Widmeyer, W.N. (1987). Assessing the cohesion of teams: Validity of the Group Environment Questionnaire. *Journal of Sport Psychology, 4,* 275-294.

Carron, A.V. (1981). *Social psychology of sport: An experimental approach.* Ithaca, NY: Mouvement.

Carron, A.V. (1982). Cohesiveness in sport groups: Interpretations and considerations. *Journal of Sport Psychology, 4,* 123-138.

Carron, A.V. (1988). *Group dynamics in sport: Theoretical and practical issues.* London, ON: Sport Dynamics.

Carron, A.V. (1994). Group dynamics in sport. In S. Serpa, J. Alves, & V. Pataco (Eds.), *International perspectives on sport and exercise psychology* (pp. 79-101). Morgantown, WV: Fitness Information Technology.

Carron, A.V., Brawley, L.R., & Widmeyer, W.N. (1990). The impact of group size in an exercise setting. *Journal of Sport and Exercise Psychology, 12,* 376-387.

Carron, A.V., Brawley, L.R., & Widmeyer, W.N. (1998). The measurement of cohesiveness in sport groups. In J.L. Duda (Ed.), *Advances in sport and exercise psychology measurement* (pp. 213-226). Morgantown, WV: Fitness Information Technology.

Carron, A.V., & Chelladurai, P. (1981). Cohesiveness as a factor in sport performance. *International Review of Sport Sociology, 16,* 21-43.

Carron, A.V., & Hausenblas, H.A. (1998). *Group dynamics in sport* (2nd ed.). Morgantown, WV: Fitness Information Technology.

Carron, A.V., Hausenblas, H.A., & Mack, D. (1996). Social influence and exercise: A meta-analysis. *Journal of Sport and Exercise Psychology, 18,* 1-16.

Carron, A.V., & Spink, K.S. (1992). Internal consistency of the Group Environment Questionnaire modified for an exercise setting. *Perceptual and Motor Skills, 74,* 304-306.

Carron, A.V., & Spink, K.S. (1993). Team building in an exercise setting. *The Sport Psychologist, 7,* 8-18.

Carron, A.V., Widmeyer, W.N., & Brawley, L.R. (1985). The development of an instrument to assess cohesion in sport teams: The Group Environment Questionnaire. *Journal of Sport Psychology, 5,* 244-266.

Carron, A.V., Widmeyer, W.N., & Brawley, L.R. (1988). Group cohesion and individual adherence to physical activity. *Journal of Sport and Exercise Psychology, 10,* 127-138.

Covey, S.R. (1990). *The 7 habits of highly effective people.* New York: Simon & Schuster.

Drexler, A., Sibbet, D., & Forrester, R.H. (1998). The team performance model. In Reddy, W.B. & Jamison, K. (Eds.), Team building: Blueprints for productivity and satisfaction. NTL, Institute for Applied Behavioral Sciences, Alexandria, VA.

Gruber, A.G., & Gray, D.M. (1982). Multidimensional approach to a task and social cohesion: The Multidimensional Sport Cohesion Instrument. *International Review of Sport Psychology, 11,* 45-62.

MacKenzie, S.B., Podsakoff, P.M., & Rich, G.A. (2001). Transformational and transactional leadership and salesperson performance. *Journal of the Academy of Marketing Science, 29*(2), 115-134.

Martens, L.B. (1972). The Sport Cohesiveness Questionnaire: Attitude measurement with task and social emphasis. *The Sport Psychologist, 8,* 80-97.

McGuire, R.T. (1998). Team issues and considerations. In M.S. Thompson, R.A. Vernacchia, & W.E. Moore (Eds.), *Case studies in applied sport psychology* (pp. 139-156). Dubuque: Kendall/Hunt.

Podsakoff, P.M., MacKenzie, S.B., & Bommer, W.H. (1996). Transformational leader behaviors and substitutes for leadership and salesperson as determinants of employee satisfaction, commitment, trust and organizational citizenship behaviors. *Journal of Management, 22*(2), 259-298.

Rossum, J.V.A. van, & Murphy, P. (1994). The sporting group. *VolleyTech, 4,* 12-25.

Russell, G.W. (1993): *The social psychology of sport.* New York: Springer.

Schmidt, U., & Schleiffenbaum, E. (2000a). One for all—All for one? Differences in cohesion between business managers and athletes. In B.A. Carlsson, U. Johnson, & F. Wetterstrand (Eds.), *Proceedings of the Sport Psychology in the New Millennium Conference* (pp. 343-347). Halmstad, Sweden: Halmstad University Press.

Schmidt, U., & Schleiffenbaum, E. (2000b). Kohäsion in der Wirtschaft und im Sport—Eine Explorationsstudie bei Managern und Volleyballern [Cohesion in business and sport—An exploratory study between managers and volleyball-players]. In P. Kuhn & K. Langolf (Eds.), *Volleyball in Lehre und Forschung 1999. Schwerpunkt: Spiel- und Technikanalysen. 25. Symposium des Deutschen Volleyball-Verbandes 1999* (pp. 181-197). Hamburg, Germany: Czwalina.

Syer, J. (1986). *Teamspirit.* London: Kingswood Press.

Syer, J., & Connolly, C. (1984). *Sporting body—Sporting mind.* Cambridge, UK: University Press.

Tuckman, B.W. (1965). Development sequences in small groups. *Psychological Bulletin, 63,* 384-399.

Vernacchia, R.A., McGuire, R.T., & Cook, D.L. (1996*). Coaching mental excellence: It does matter whether you win or lose.* Portola, CA: Warde.

West, M.A. (Ed.) (1996). *Handbook of work group psychology.* New York: Wiley.

Widmeyer, W.N., Brawley, L.R., & Carron, A.V. (1985). *The measurement of cohesion in sport teams: The Group Environment Questionnaire.* London: Sport Dynamics.

Widmeyer, W.N., Brawley, L.R., & Carron, A.V (1992). Group dynamics in sport. In T.S. Horn (Ed.), *Advances in sport psychology* (pp. 163-180). Champaign, IL: Human Kinetics.

Widmeyer, W.N., Carron, A.V., & Brawley, L.R. (1992). Group cohesion in sport and exercise. In R.N. Singer, M. Murphy, & L.K. Tennant (Eds.), *Handbook of research on sport psychology* (pp. 672-692). New York: Macmillan.

Yukelson, F.J., Weinberg, T.O., & Jackson, R.V. (1984). The Multidimensional Sport Cohesion Inventory: The quality of teamwork according to attraction to group tasks. *Review of Sport Sociology, 5,* 20-52.

Zander, A. (1994). *Making groups effective* (2nd ed.). San Francisco: Jossey-Bass.

Chapter 12

Achterberg, J. (1991, May). *Enhancing immune function through imagery.* Paper presented at the Fourth World Congress on Imagery, Minneapolis, MN.

Addison, T., Kremer, J., & Bell, R. (1998). Understanding the psychology of pain in sport. *Irish Journal of Psychology, 19,* 486-503.

Armstrong. L. (2000). *It's not about the bike: My journey back to life.* New York: Putnam.

Booth, W. (1987, August 21). Arthritis Institute tackles sport. *Science, 237,* 846-847.

Brewer, B.W. (1994). Review and critique of models of psychological adjustment to athletic injury. *Journal of Applied Sport Psychology, 6,* 87-100.

Cupal, D.D., & Brewer, B.W. (2001). Effects of relaxation and guided imagery on knee strength, reinjury anxiety, and pain following anterior cruciate ligament reconstruction. *Rehabilitation Psychology, 46,* 28-43.

Davis, P. (2003, Winter). Hope is not a method. *Olympic Coach, 13*(1), 6-7.

DeGood, D.E., & Kiernan, B.D. (1997-1998). Pain related cognitions as predictors of pain treatment outcome. *Advances in Medical Psychotherapy, 9,* 73-90.

Durso Cupal, D. (1998). Psychological interventions in sport injury prevention and rehabilitation. *Journal of Applied Sport Psychology, 10,* 103-123.

Evans, L., Hardy, L., & Fleming, S. (2000). Intervention strategies with injured athletes: An action research study. *The Sport Psychologist, 14,* 188-206.

Ford, C.B. (1983). *The somatisizing disorders: Illness as a way of life.* New York: Elsevier Biomedical.

Francis, S.R., Andersen, M.B., & Maley, P. (2000). Physiotherapists and male professional athletes' views on psychological skills for rehabilitation. *Journal of Science and Medicine in Sport, 3*(1), 17-29.

Glaser, R., Kiecolt-Glaser, J.K., Marucha, P.T., MacCallum, R.C., Laskowski, B.F., & Malarkey, W.B. (1999). Stress-related changes in proinflammatory cytokine production in wounds. *Archives of General Psychiatry, 56*(5), 450-456.

Gould, D., Udry, E., Bridges, D., & Beck, L. (1997a). Coping with season-ending injuries. *The Sport Psychologist, 11,* 379-399.

Gould, D., Udry, E., Bridges, D., & Beck, L. (1997b). Stress sources encountered when rehabilitating from season-ending ski injuries. *The Sport Psychologist, 11,* 361-378.

Granito, V.J., Jr. (2001). Athletic injury experience: A qualitative focus group approach. *Journal of Sport Behavior, 24,* 63-82.

Grau, J.W., & Meagher, M.W. (1999, May/June). Pain modulation: It's a two-way street. *Psychological Science Agenda,* pp. 10-12.

Green, L.B. (1992). The use of imagery in the rehabilitation of injured athletes. *The Sport Psychologist, 6,* 416-428.

Greenspan, M.J., & Feltz, D.L. (1989). Psychological interventions with athletes in competitive situations: A review. *The Sport Psychologist, 3,* 219-236.

Hanin, Y.L. (Ed.) (2000). *Emotions in sport.* Champaign, IL: Human Kinetics.

Hardy, C.J., Burke, K.L., & Crace, R.K. (1999). Social support and injury: A framework for support-based interventions with injured athletes. In D. Pargman (Ed.), *Psychological bases of sport injuries* (2nd ed., pp. 175-198). Morgantown, WV: Fitness Information Technology.

Heil, J. (1990, October). *Association-dissociation: Clarifying the concept.* Paper presented at the Association for the Advancement of Applied Sport Psychology Annual Conference, San Antonio, TX.

Heil, J. (1993). *Psychology of sport injury.* Champaign, IL: Human Kinetics.

Heil, J. (1998, May). *Remarkable feats: Of pain tolerance, injury rehabilitation, and coping with adversity in sport.* Keynote presentation at the Second International Meeting of Psychology Applied to Sport and Exercise, Braga, Portugal.

Heil, J. (2000). The injured athlete. In Y.L. Hanin (Ed.), *Emotions in sport* (pp. 245-265). Champaign, IL: Human Kinetics.

Heil, J., Wakefield, C., & Reed, C. (1998). Patient as athlete: A metaphor for injury rehabilitation. *The Psychotherapy Patient, 10*(3/4), 21-39.

Hellstedt, J.C. (1987). Sport psychology at a ski academy: Teaching mental skills to young athletes. *The Sport Psychologist, 1,* 56-68.

Ievleva, L., & Orlick, T. (1991). Mental links to enhanced healing: An exploratory study. *The Sport Psychologist, 5,* 25-40.

International Association for the Study of Pain. (2002). IASP pain terminology [Online]. Available: www.iasp-pain.org/terms-p.html#Pain [February 6, 2004]

Johnston, L.H., & Carroll, D. (2000). Coping, social support, and injury: Changes over time and the effects of level of sports involvement. *Journal of Sport Rehabilitation, 9,* 290-303.

Jones, D.A., Rollman, G.B., White, K.P., Hill, M.L., & Brooke, R.I. (2003). The relationship between cognitive appraisal, affect, and catastrophizing in patients with chronic pain. *Journal of Pain, 4,* 267-277.

Jones, L., & Stuth, G. (1997). The uses of mental imagery in athletics: An overview. *Applied and Preventative Psychology, 6,* 101-115.

Kiecolt-Glaser, J.K., Page, G.G., Marucha, P.T., MacCallum, R.C., & Glaser, R. (1998). Psychological influences on surgical recovery: Perspectives from psychoneuroimmunology. *American Psychologist, 53,* 1209-1218.

Kreiner-Phillips, C. (1990, January). Psyche up for skiing. *Ski Canada,* pp. 111, 114.

Kubler-Ross, E. (1969). *On death and dying.* New York: Macmillan.

Lysholm, J., & Wiklander, J. (1987). Injuries in runners. *American Journal of Sports Medicine, 15,* 168-171.

Macchi, R., & Crossman, J. (1996). After the fall: Reflections of injured classical ballet dancers. *Journal of Sport Behavior, 19,* 221-234.

Mainwaring, L.M. (1999). Restoration of self: A model for the psychological response of athletes to severe knee injuries. *Canadian Journal of Rehabilitation, 12*(3), 143-154.

Mandle, C.L., Jacobs, S.C., Acari, P.M., & Domar, A.D. (1996). The efficacy of relaxation response interventions with adult patients: A review of the literature. *Journal of Cardiovascular Nursing, 10*(3), 4-26.

Maniar, S.D., Curry, L.A., Sommers-Flanagan, J., & Walsh, J.A. (2001). Student-athlete preferences in seeking help when confronted with sport performance problems. *The Sport Psychologist, 15,* 205-223.

Martin, K.A., Moritz, S.E., & Hall, C.R. (1999). Imagery use in sport: A literature review and applied model. *The Sport Psychologist, 13,* 245-268.

McKinney, C.H., Antoni, M.H., Kumar, M., Tims, F.C., & McCabe, P.M. (1997). Effects of guided imagery and music (GIM) therapy on mood and cortisol in healthy adults. *Health Psychology, 16,* 390-400.

McKinney, C.H., Tims, F.C., Kumar, A.M., & Kumar, M. (1997). The effect of selected classical music and spontaneous imagery on plasma β-endorphin. *Journal of Behavioral Medicine, 20,* 85-99.

Morgan, W.P. (1978, April). The mind of the marathoner. *Psychology Today,* pp. 38-40, 43, 45-46, 49.

Peterson, K., Durtschi, S., & Murphy, S. (1990, September). *Cognitive patterns and conceptual schemes of elite distance runners during sub-maximum and maximum running effort.* Paper presented at the annual meeting of the Association for the Advancement of Applied Sport Psychology, San Antonio, TX.

Petrie, G. (1993). Injury from the athlete's point of view. In J. Heil (Ed.), *Psychology of sport injury* (pp. 17-23). Champaign, IL: Human Kinetics.

Ponte-Allen, M., & Giles, G.M. (1999). Goal setting and functional outcomes in rehabilitation. *American Journal of Occupational Therapy, 53,* 646-649.

Quinn, A.M., & Fallon, B.J. (1999). The changes in psychological characteristics and reactions of elite athletes from injury onset until full recovery. *Journal of Applied Sport Psychology, 11,* 210-229.

Robbins, J.E., & Rosenfeld, L.B. (2001). Athletes' perceptions of social support provided by their head coach, assistant coach, and athletic trainer, pre-injury and during rehabilitation. *Journal of Sport Behavior, 24,* 277-297.

Ross, M.J., & Berger, R.S. (1996). Effects of stress inoculation training on athletes' postsurgical pain and rehabilitation after orthopedic injury. *Journal of Consulting and Clinical Psychology, 64,* 406-410.

Sarno, J. (1984). *Mind over pain.* New York: Morrow.

Scherzer, C.B., Brewer, B.W., Cornelius, A.E., Van Raalte, J.L., Petitpas, A.J., Sklar, J.H., et al. (2001). Psychological skills and adherence to rehabilitation after reconstruction of the anterior cruciate ligament. *Journal of Sport Rehabilitation, 10,* 165-172.

Schomer, H.H. (1986). Mental strategies and perception of effort in marathon runners. *International Journal of Sport Psychology, 17,* 41-49.

Sheikh, A.A., & Jordan, C.S. (1983). Clinical uses of mental imagery. In A.A. Sheikh (Ed.), *Imagery: Current theory, research, and applications* (pp. 391-435). New York: Wiley.

Shuer, M.L., & Dietrich, M.S. (1997). Psychological effects of chronic injury in elite athletes. *Western Journal of Medicine, 166,* 104-109.

Sordoni, C., Hall, C., & Forwell, L. (2000). The use of imagery by athletes during injury rehabilitation. *Journal of Sport Rehabilitation, 9,* 329-338.

Steadman, J.R. (1993). A physicians approach to the psychology of injury. In J. Heil (Ed.), *Psychology of sport injury* (pp. 25-32). Champaign, IL: Human Kinetics.

Suinn, R.M. (1976, July). Body thinking: Psychology for Olympic champs. *Psychology Today,* pp. 38-43.

Sullivan, M.J.L., Bishop, S.R., & Pivik, J. (1995). The pain catastrophizing scale: Development and validation. *Psychological Assessment, 7,* 524-532.

Sullivan, M.J.L., Stanish, W., Waite, H., Sullivan, M.E., & Tripp, D. (1998). Catastrophizing, pain, and disability in patients with soft tissue injuries. *Pain, 77,* 253-260.

Sullivan, M.J.L., Thorn, B., Haythornthwaite, J.A., Keefe, F., Martin, M., Bradley, L.A., & Lefebvre, J.C. (2001). Theoretical perspectives on the relation between catastrophizing and pain. *Clinical Journal of Pain, 17,* 52-64.

Sullivan, M.J.L., Tripp, D.A., Rodgers, W.M., & Standish, W. (2000). Catastrophizing and pain perception in sport participants. *Journal of Applied Sport Psychology, 12,* 151-167.

Taylor, J., & Taylor, S. (1997). *Psychological approaches to sports injury rehabilitation.* Gaithersburg, MD: Aspen.

Theodorakis, Y., Beneca, A., Malliou, P., Antoniou, P., Goudas, M., & Laparidis, K. (1997). The effect of a self-talk technique on injury rehabilitation. *Journal of Applied Sport Psychology, 9,* S164.

Turner, J.A., Jensen, M.P., Warms, C.A., & Cardenas, D.D. (2002). Catastrophizing is associated with pain intensity, psychological distress, and pain-related disability among individuals with chronic pain after spinal cord injury. *Pain, 98,* 127-134.

Udry, E. (1997). Coping and social support among injured athletes following surgery. *Journal of Sport and Exercise Psychology, 19,* 71-90.

Udry, E., Gould, D., Bridges, D., & Beck, L. (1997). Down but not out: Athlete responses to season-ending injuries. *Journal of Sport and Exercise Psychology, 19,* 229-248.

Udry, E., Gould, D., Bridges, D., & Tuffey, S. (1997). People helping people? Examining the social ties of athletes coping with burnout and injury stress. *Journal of Sport and Exercise Psychology, 19,* 368-395.

Wiese-Bjornstal, D.M., Smith, A.M., & La Mott, E.E. (1995). A model of psychological response to athletic injury and rehabilitation. *Athletic Training: Sports Health Care Perspectives, 1*(1), 17-30.

Williams, D.A. (1997, July/August). Acute procedural and postoperative pain: Patient-related factors in its under-management. *American Pain Society Bulletin,* pp. 8-9, 11.

Williams, J.M., & Roepke, N. (1993). Psychology of injury and injury rehabilitation. In R.M. Singer, M. Murphey, & L.K. Tennant (Eds.), *Handbook of research on sport psychology* (pp. 815-839). New York: Macmillan.

Yukelson, D., & Heil, J. (1998). Psychological considerations in working with injured athletes. In P. K. Canavan (Ed.), *Rehabilitation in sports medicine* (pp. 61-70). Stamford, CT: Appleton & Lange.

Chapter 13

Agras, W.S., Dorian, B., Kirkley, B.G., Arnow, B., & Bachman, J. (1987). Imipramine in the treatment of bulimia: A double-blind controlled study. *International Journal of Eating Disorders, 6,* 29-38.

American College of Sports Medicine Conference. (1998). Orlando, FL. June 2-5.

American Psychiatric Association. (2000). *Diagnostic and statistical manual of mental disorders* (4th ed., text revision). Washington, DC: Author.

Andersen, A., Cohn, L., & Holbrook, T. (2000). *Making weight.* Carlsbad, CA: Gurze Books.

Brownell, K.D. (1995). Eating disorders in athletes. In K.D. Brownell & C.G. Fairburn (Eds.), *Eating disorders and obesity* (pp. 177-187). New York: Guilford Press.

Bruna, T., & Fogteloo, J. (2003). Drug treatments. In J. Treasure, U. Schmidt, & E. Van Furth (Eds.), *Handbook of eating disorders* (2nd ed., pp. 252-274). West Sussex, UK: Wiley.

Chowdhury, U., Gordon, I., Lask, B., Watkins, B., Watt, H., & Christie, D. (2003). Early-onset anorexia nervosa: Is there evidence of limbic system imbalance? *International Journal of Eating Disorders, 33,* 388-396.

Clark, N., Nelson, M., & Evans, W. (1988). Nutrition education for elite female runners. *Physician and Sportsmedicine, 16,* 124-136.

Cole-Detke, H., & Kobak, R. (1996). Attachment processes in eating disorders and depression. *Journal of Consulting and Clinical Psychology, 64*(2), 282-290.

Crisp, A., Callender, J.S., Halek, C., & Hsu, L.K.G. (1992). Long-term mortality in anorexia nervosa. *British Journal of Psychiatry, 161,* 104-107.

Davis, R., Dearing, S., Faulkner, J., Jasper, K., Olmstead, M.P., Rice, C., & Rockert, W. (1992). The road to recovery: A manual for participants in the psychoeducation group for bulimia nervosa. In H. Harper-Giuffre & K.R. MacKenzie (Eds.), *Group psychotherapy for eating disorders* (pp. 281-341). Washington, DC: American Psychiatric Press.

Drinkwater, B.L., Bruemner, B., & Chesnut, C.H. (1990). Menstrual history as a determinant of current bone density in young athletes. *Journal of the American Medical Association, 263,* 545-548.

Drinkwater, B., & Nilson, K. (1984). Bone mineral content of amenorrheic and eumenorrheic athletes. *New England Journal of Medicine, 311,* 277-281.

Fairburn, C.G. (1995). *Overcoming binge eating.* New York: Guilford Press.

Fairburn, C.G. (1997). Interpersonal psychotherapy for bulimia nervosa. In M. Garner & P. Garfinkel (Eds.) *Handbook of treatment for eating disorders* (pp. 278-294). New York: Guilford Press.

Fairburn, C. G., Marcus, M.D., & Wilson, G. T. (1993). Cognitive-behavioral therapy for binge eating and bulimia nervosa: A comprehensive treatment manual. In C. G. Fairburn & G. T. Wilson (Eds.), Binge eating: Nature, assessment and treatment (pp. 361-404). New York: Guilford Press.

Fallon, P., & Wonderlick, S.A. (1997). Sexual abuse and other forms of trauma. In D.M. Garner & P.E. Garfinkel (Eds.), *Handbook of treatment for eating disorders* (2nd ed., pp. 394-414). New York: Guilford Press.

Garfinkel, P.E., Lin, E., Goering, P., Spegg, C., Goldbloom, D., Kennedy, S., et al. (1996). Should amenorrhea be necessary for the diagnosis of anorexia nervosa? *British Journal of Psychiatry, 168,* 500-506.

Garfinkel, P.E., & Walsh. (1997). Drug therapies. In D.M Garner & P.E. Garfinkel (Eds.), *Handbook of treatment for eating disorders* (2nd ed., pp. 372-382). New York: Guilford Press.

Garner, D.M., & Garfinkel, P.E. (1980). Socio-cultural factors in the development of anorexia nervosa. *Psychological Medicine, 10,* 647-656.

Garner, D.M., Garfinkel, P.E., Schwartz, D.M., & Thompson, M.M. (1980). Cultural expectations of thinness in women. *Psychological Reports, 47,* 483-491.

Garner, D.M., & Needleman, L.D. (1997). Sequencing and integration of treatments. In D.M. Garner & P.E. Garfinkel (Eds.), *Handbook of treatment for eating disorders* (2nd ed., pp. 50-66). New York: Guilford Press.

Garner, D.M., Vitousek, K.M., & Pike, K.M. (1997). Cognitive-behavioral therapy for bulimia nervosa. In D.M. Garner & P.E. Garfinkel (Eds.), *Handbook of treatment for eating disorders* (2nd ed., 67-93). New York: Guilford Press.

Geliebter, A., Melton, P.M., McCray, R.S., Gallagher, D.R., Gage, D., & Hashim, S.A. (1992). Gastric capacity, gastric emptying, and test-meal intake in normal and bulimic women. *American Journal of Clinical Nutrition, 56,* 656-661.

Goldenstein, D.J., Wilson, M.G., Thompson, V.L., Potvin, J.H., & Rampey, A.H., Jr. (1995). The Fluoxetine Bulimia Nervosa Research Group: Long-term fluoxetine treatment of bulimia nervosa. *British Journal of Psychiatry, 166,* 660-666.

Grinspoon, S., & Thomas, E. (2000). Bone loss in anorexia nervosa: Mechanisms and treatment options. *Eating Disorders Review, 16,* 21-29.

Hall, L., & Cohn, L. (1992). *Bulimia: A guide to recovery.* Carlsbad, CA: Gurze Books.

Halmi, K., Falk, J., & Schwartz, E. (1981). Binge-eating and vomiting: A survey of a college population. *Psychological Medicine, 11,* 697-706.

Harvard Medical School. (1997). Eating disorders—Part II. *Harvard Mental Health Letter, 14*(5), 1-2.

Hays, K. (1999). *Working it out: Using exercise in psychotherapy.* Washington, DC: American Psychological Association.

Herzog, D.B. (1995). Psychodynamic psychotherapy for anorexia nervosa, In Brownell, K.D., & Fairburn, C.G. (Eds.), *Eating Disorders and Obesity: a comprehensive handbook* (pp. 330-335). New York: Guilford.

Hoek, H.W. (1995). The distribution of eating disorders. In K.D. Brownell & C.G. Fairburn (Eds.), *Eating disorders and obesity* (pp. 199-206). New York: Guilford Press.

Isner, J.M., Roberts, W.C., Heymsfield, S.B., & Yager, J. (1985). Anorexia nervosa and sudden death. *Annals of Internal Medicine, 102,* 49-52.

Jack, S. (2001). Working with families. In J.E. Mitchell (Ed.), *The outpatient treatment of eating disorders.* Minneapolis: University of Minnesota Press.

Johnson, C. (1990). *Psychodynamic treatment of anorexia nervosa and bulimia.* New York: Guilford.

Johnson, C. (1995). Psychodynamic treatment of bulimia nervosa. In Brownell, K.D. and Fairburn, C.G. (Eds.) *Eating Disorders and Obesity.* New York: Guilford Press.

Johnson, C. (2001). Presentation: Recent advancements in the treatment of eating disorders. Eating Disorder Center of Denver opening. Denver, CO.

Jones, K. (1997). History and prevention of eating disorders. *The Prevention Researcher, 4*(3) 1-5.

Kaplan, H.I., Saddock, B.J., & Grebb, J.A. (1994). *Kaplan and Saddock's synopsis of psychiatry* (7th ed.). Baltimore: Williams & Wilkins.

Karwautz, A., Troop, N.A., Rabe-Hasketh, S., Collier, D.A., & Treasure, J.L. (2003). Personality disorders and personality dimensions in anorexia nervosa. *Journal of Personality Disorders, 17*(1), 73-85.

Kaye, W.H. (1995). Neurotransmitters and anorexia nervosa. In K.D. Brownell & C.G. Fairburn (Eds.), *Eating disorders and obesity* (pp.487-516). New York: Guilford Press.

Kenny, M.E., & Hart, K. (1992). Relationship between parental attachment and eating disorders in an inpatient and a college sample. *Journal of Counseling Psychology, 39*(4), 521-526.

Kinzl, J., Biebl, W., & Herold, M. (1993). Significance of vomiting for hyperamylasemia and siadalenosis in patients with eating disorders. *International Journal of Eating Disorders, 13,* 117-124.

Klump, K.L., Kaye, W.H., & Strober, M. (2001). The evolving genetic foundations of eating disorders. *Psychiatric Clinics of North America, 24,* 215-225.

La Via, M.C., Gray, N., & Kaye, W.H. (2000). Case reports of Olanzapine treatment of anorexia nervosa. *International Journal of Eating Disorders, 27,* 363-366.

Leitenberg, H., Rosen, J. C., Gross, J., Nudelman, S., & Vara, L. S. (1988). Exposure plus response prevention treatment of bulimia nervosa. *Journal of Consulting and Clinical Psychology, 56,* 535-541.

Lock, J., Le Grange, D., Agras, S.W., & Dare, C. (2001). *Treatment manual for Anorexia nervosa: A family-based approach.* New York: Guilford.

MacKenzie, K.R., & Harper-Guiffre, H. (1992). *Group psychotherapy for eating disorders.* Washington, DC: American Psychiatric Press.

Maine, M. (1999). The gap in treatment. *American Association for Marriage and Family Therapy,* (1)6, 1-5.

Marcus, M.D. (1997). Adapting treatment for patients with binge-eating disorder. In D.M. Garner & P.E. Garfinkel (Eds.), *Handbook of treatment for eating disorders* (2nd ed., pp. 484-500). New York: Guilford Press.

Mitchell, J.E. (2001). *The outpatient treatment of eating disorders.* Minneapolis: University of Minnesota Press.

Mitchell, J.E., Pomeroy, C., & Adson, D.E. (1997). Managing medical complications. In D.M. Garner & P.E. Garfinkel (Eds.), *Handbook of treatment for eating disorders* (2nd ed., pp. 383-393) New York: Guilford Press.

Mitchell, J.E., Pyle, R.L., & Eckert, E.D. (1981). Frequency and duration of binge-eating episodes in patients with bulimia. *American Journal of Psychiatry, 138,* 835-836.

Mitchell, J.E., Pyle, R.L., Eckert, E.D., Hatsukami, D., & Lentz, R. (1983). Electrolyte and other physiological abnormalities in patients with bulimia. *Psychiatric Medicine, 13,* 273-278.

Nattiv, A., Agostini, R., Drinkwater, B., & Yeager, K.K. (1994). The female athlete triad. The inter-relatedness of disordered eating, amenorrhea, and osteoporosis. *Clinical Sports Medicine, 13,* 405-418.

Nattiv, A., & Lynch, L. (1994). The female athlete triad—Managing an acute risk to long term health. *Physician and Sportsmedicine, 22,* 60-68.

Olivardia, R. Pope, H. & Hudson, J. (2000). Muscle dysmorphia in male weightlifters: A case-control study. *American Journal of Psychiatry 157,* 1291-1296

Olmstead, M.P., Davis, R., Garner, D.M., Rockert, W., Irvine, M.J., & Eagle, M. (1991). Efficacy of a brief group psychoeducational intervention for bulimia nervosa. *Behavioral Research and Therapy, 29,* 71-83.

Ordman, A.M., & Kirschenbaum, D.S. (1986). Bulimia: Assessment of eating, psychological adjustment, and familial characteristics. *International Journal of Eating Disorders, 5,* 865-878.

Otis, C.L. (1992). Exercise-associated amenorrhea. *Clinical Sports Medicine, 11,* 351-362.

Perriello, V.A. (2001). Aiming for healthy weight in wrestlers and other athletes. *Contemporary Pediatrics, 18*(9), 55-74.

Peterson, C.B., & Mitchell, J.E. (1996). Treatment of binge eating disorders in group cognitive behavioral therapy. In Werne, J. (Ed.) *Treating Eating Disorders.* San Francisco, CA: Jossey-Bass Publishers.

Peterson, C.B., & Mitchell, J. E. (1999). Psychosocial & pharmacological treatment of eating disorders: A review of research findings. *Journal of Clinical Psychology, 55*(6), 685-697.

Pope, H.G., Phillips, K.A., & Olivardia, R. (2000). *The Adonis complex: The secret crisis of male body obsession.* New York: Free Press.

Prussin, R., Harvey, P., & DiGeronimo, T.F. (1992). *Hooked on exercise—How to understand and manage exercise addiction.* New York: Fireside/Parkside Books.

Root, M.P., Fallon, P., & Friedruch, W.N. (1986). *Bulimia: A systems approach to treatment.* New York: Norton.

Rosen, J., & Leitenberg, H. (1982). Bulimia nervosa: Treatment with exposure and response prevention. *Behavior Therapy, 13,* 117-124.

Rosen, L.W., & Hough, D.O. (1988). Pathogenic weight-control behaviors of female college gymnasts. *Physician and Sportsmedicine, 16,* 79-84.

Ruderman, A.J., & Besbeas, M. (1992). Psychological characteristics of dieters and bulimics. *Journal of Abnormal Psychology, 101*(3), 383-390.

Ryan, J. (2000). *Little girls in pretty boxes: The making and breaking of elite gymnasts and figure skaters.* New York: Warner Books.

Serpell, L., & Troop, N. (2003). Psychological factors. In J. Treasure, U. Schmidt, & E. Van Furth (Eds.), *Handbook of eating disorders* (2nd ed.). West Sussex, UK: Wiley.

Shangold, M., Rebar, R.W., Wentz, A.C., & Schiff, I. (1990). Evaluation and management of menstrual dysfunction in athletes. *Journal of the American Medical Association, 263,* 1665-1669.

Sheldon, S. (2002, August 7). Researchers find anorexia gene. *UPI Science News,* 6.

Sherman, R. T., & Thompson, R. A. (1990*). Bulimia: A guide for family and friends.* San Francisco, CA: Jossey-Bass.

Silverman, J.A. (1997). Anorexia nervosa: Historical perspective on treatment. In D.M. Lamer & P.E. Garfinckel (Eds.), *Handbook of treatment for eating disorders* (2nd ed., pp. 3-10). New York: The Guilford Press.

Striegel-Moore, R.H. (1993). Etiology of binge eating: A developmental perspective. In C.G. Fairburn & G.T. Wilson (Eds.), *Binge eating: Nature, assessment, and treatment* . New York: Guilford Press.

Striegel-Moore, R. H., Silberstein, L. R., & Rodin, J. (1993). The social self in bulimia nervosa: public self-consciousness, social anxiety, and perceived fraudulence. *Journal of Abnormal Psychology, 102,* 297-303.

Sturm, J., & Diorio, D. (1998). Anabolic agents, sports pharmacology. *Clinics in Sports Medicine, 17,* 261-282.

Sundgot-Borgen, J. (1993). Prevalence of eating disorders in elite female athletes. *International Journal of Sport Nutrition, 3,* 29-40.

Sundgot-Borgen, J. (1994). Risk and trigger factors for the development of eating disorders in female elite athletes. *Medicine and Science in Sports and Exercise, 26,* 414-419.

Sundgot-Borgen, J., Skarderud, F., & Rodgers S. (2003). Athletes and dancers. In J. Treasure, U. Schmidt, & E. van Furth (Eds.), *Handbook of Eating Disorders* (2nd ed., pp. 105-131). Indianapolis, IN: Wiley.

Sutandar-Pinnock, K., Woodside, D.B., Carter, J.C., Olmstead, M.P., & Kaplan, A.S. (2003). Perfectionism in anorexia nervosa: A 6-24-month follow-up study. *International Journal of Eating Disorders, 33,* 225-229.

Szabo, C.P. (1996). Perfectionism in anorexia nervosa. *American Journal of Psychiatry, 154,* 132.

Thompson, R.A., & Sherman, R.T. (1993). Helping athletes with eating disorders. Champaign, IL: Human Kinetics.

Tobin, D.L., & Griffing, S.A. (1996). Coping, sexual abuse, and compensatory behavior. *International Journal of Eating Disorders, 20,* 143-148.

United States Olympic Committee. (1987). *Sports nutrition: Weight loss and sports performance.* Colorado Springs: U.S. Olympic Committee.

Vaccarino, F.J., Kennedy, S.H., Ralevski, E., & Black, R. (1994). The effects of growth hormone-releasing factor on food consumption in anorexia nervosa patients and normals. *Biological Psychiatry, 35,* 446-451.

Vitousek, K., & Manke, F. (1994). Personality variables and disorders in anorexia nervosa and bulimia nervosa. *Journal of Abnormal Psychology, 103,* 137-147.

Waller, G., & Kennerley, H. (2003). Cognitive-behavioural treatments. In J. Treasure, U. Schmidt, & E. van Furth (Eds.), *Handbook of eating disorders* (2nd ed.). West Sussex, UK: Wiley.

Walsh, B.T. & Garner, D.M. (1997). Diagnostic issues. In D.M. Garner & P.E. Garfinkel (Eds.), *Handbook for the Treatment of Eating Disorders* (pp. 25-33). New York: The Guilford Press.

Walsh, B.T., Hadigan, C.M., Devlin, M.J., Gladis, M., & Roose, S.P. (1991). Long-term outcome of antidepressant treatment for bulimia nervosa. *American Journal of Psychiatry, 148,* 1206-1212.

Whitney, E.N. & Hamilton, E.M. (1987). *Understanding nutrition* (4th ed.). Minneapolis: West Publishing.

Wilfley, D.E., & Rodin, D. (1995). Cultural influences on eating disorders. In K.D. Brownell, & C.G. Fairburn (Eds.), *Eating disorders and obesity: A comprehensive handbook* (pp. 79-82). New York: Guilford.

Wilfey, D.E., Wilson, G.T., & Agras, W.S. (2003). The clinical significance of binge eating disorder. *International Journal of Eating Disorders,* 34 (Supp), S96-S106.

Wilmore, J.H., & Costill, D.L. (2004). *Physiology of sport and exercise* (3rd ed.). Champaign, IL: Human Kinetics.

Wilson, G.T., Fairburn, C.G., & Agras, W.S. (1997). Cognitive-behavioral therapy for bulimia nervosa. In D.M. Garner & P.E. Garfinkel (Eds.), *Handbook of treatment for eating disorders,* (2nd ed., pp. 67-93). New York: Guilford Press.

Wonderlich, S., Klein, M.H., & Council, J.R. (1996). Relationship of social perceptions and self-concept in bulimia nervosa. *Journal of Consulting and Clinical Psychology, 64*(6), 1231-1237.

Wonderlich, S.A., & Mitchell, J.E. (1998). Eating disorders and comorbidity: Empirical, conceptual, and clinical implications. *Psychopharmacology Review, 33,* 381-390.

Wonderlich, S., & Mitchell, J.E. (2001). The role of personality in the onset of eating disorders and treatment implications. *Psychiatric Clinics of North America, 24,* 249-258.

Yager, J., Andersen, A., Devlin, M., Egger, H., Herzog, D., Mitchell, J., et al. (2000). Practice guidelines for the treatment of patients with eating disorders. *Practice guidelines for the treatment of psychiatric disorders compendium 2000* (2nd ed.). Washington: American Psychiatric Press.

Chapter 14

Ajar, B. (1999, January). New pieces filling in addiction puzzle. *American Psychological Association Monitor, 30*(1), 1, 15.

American Psychiatric Association. (2000). *Diagnostic and statistical manual of mental disorders* (3rd ed., text revised). Washington DC: Author.

Anshel, M.H. (1991). A survey of elite athletes on the perceived causes of using banned drugs in sport. *Journal of Sport Behavior, 14*(4), 283-308.

Associated Press. (2001). Odom breaks down while discussing suspension [Online]. Available: http://espn.go.com/nba/news/2001/1107/1274985.html [July 5, 2002].

Associated Press. (2003). Wells claims "25 to 40 percent" of players use steroids [Online]. Available: www.thesenetwork.com/Newsboards/Sports/headlines/48503911.shtml [July 6, 2002].

Azrin, N.H., McMahon, P.T., Donahue, B., Besalel, V., Lapinski, K.J., Kogan, E., et al. (1994). Behavioral therapy for drug abuse: A controlled treatment outcome study. *Behavioral Research and Therapy, 32*(8), 857-866.

Bacon, V.L., & Lee, K. (1997). *The Multiple Addictive Behaviors Questionnaire (MBAQ).* Unpublished instrument.

Bacon, V.L., Lee, K., & Calicchia, J.C. (1998). *A pilot study: An assessment of addictive behaviors in college athletes.* Bridgewater, MA: Bridgewater State College, Center for the Advancement of Research and Teaching.

Baddoo, T. (1999). A license to self-destruct [Online]. Available: http://sportsillustrated.cnn.com/inside_game/terry_baddoo/news/1999/09/24/baddoo_viewpoint/ [July 6, 2002].

Benshoff, J.J., & Janikowski, T.P. (2000). *The rehabilitation model of substance abuse counseling.* Belmont, CA: Wadsworth/Thomson Learning.

Borkman, T.J. (1998). Is recovery planning any different from treatment planning? *Journal of Substance Abuse Treatment, 15*(1), 37-42.

Buck, R. (1998). Steroids build NFL players up—and take them down too [Online]. Available: http://cbs.sportsline.com/u/page/covers/others/jul98/steroiddrug72398.htm [July 8, 2002].

Carroll, K., Rounsaville, B., & Keller, D. (1991). Relapse prevention strategies for the treatment of cocaine abuse. *American Journal of Drug and Alcohol Abuse, 17*(3), 249-265.

Conlee, R.K. (1991). Amphetamine, caffeine, and cocaine. In D.R. Lamb & M.H. Williams (Eds.), *Perspectives in exercise science and sports medicine, Vol. 4: Ergogenics—enhancement of performance in exercise and sport* (pp. 285-330). Ann Arbor, MI: Brown & Benchmark.

Daugherty, R., & O'Bryan, T. (1995). *On campus talking about alcohol.* Lexington, KY: Prevention Research Institute.

Don't risk your reputation or salary [Online]. (2004). Available: http://basketball-overseas.com/for_players/drugs-in-basketball.html [August 15, 2004].

Doping and cycling [Online]. (2004). Available: http://bicycling.about.com/library/weekly/aa022199.htm [August 15, 2004].

Doweiko, H.E. (1999). *Concepts of Chemical Dependency.* Belmont, CA: Brooks/Cole Publishing Co.

Eden, D. (2002). Oksana: Then and now [Online]. Available: www.viewzone.com/oksana.html [July 10, 2002].

English soccer blighted by drug-taking [Online]. (2004). www.passyourdrugtest.com/05-18-03.htm [August 15, 2004].

FindLaw. (2002). Drug use in sports [Online]. Available: http://news.findlaw.com/legalnews/sports/drugs/index.html [April 11, 2003].

Fishbein, D.H., & Pease, S.E. (1996). *The dynamics of drug abuse.* Boston: Allyn & Bacon.

Fitch, T.J., & Robinson, C.R. (1998, November/December). Counseling and development interventions with college athletes: A proposed model: *Journal of College Student Development, 39*(6), 623-627.

Frances, R.J., Wilson, E., & Wiegand, J.H. (1997). Hospital-based alcohol and drug treatment. In R.K. Schreter, S.S., Sharfstein, & A. Schreter (Eds.), *Managing care not dollars* (pp. 91-108). Washington DC: American Psychiatric Press.

Goldstein, A.G. (2001). *Addiction: From biology to drug policy* (2nd ed.). New York: Oxford University Press.

Greden, J.F., & Walters, A. (1997). Caffeine. In J.H. Lowinson, P. Ruiz, R.B. Millman, & J.G. Langrod (Eds.), *Substance abuse: A comprehensive textbook* (3rd ed., pp. 199-206). Baltimore: Williams & Wilkins.

Gugliotta, G., & Shipley, A. (2003). Ephedra controversy nothing new in sports: Dietary supplement linked to other deaths [Online]. Available: www.washingtonpost.com/ac2/wp-dyn?pagename=article&node=&contentId=A32497-2003Feb19&notFound=true [May 15, 2003].

Harriston, K., & Jenkins, S. (1986). Maryland basketball star Len Bias is dead at 22 [Online]. Available: www.washingtonpost.com/wp-srv/sports/longterm/memories/bias/bias1.htm [July 3, 2002].

Heil, J. (1993). *Psychology of sport injury.* Champaign, IL: Human Kinetics.

Higher Education Center for Alcohol and Other Drug Prevention. (2003). College athletes and alcohol and other drug use [Online]. Available: www.edc.org/hec/pubs/factsheets/fact_sheet3.pdf [May 10, 2003].

The history of drug testing in sports and how athletes beat the drug tests [Online]. (2002). Available: www.mesomorphosis.com/articles/anonymous/drug-testing-and-sports.htm [April 15, 2003].

How other sports handle testing. (2002). *USA Today* [Online]. Available: www.usatoday.com/usatonline/20020708/4253743s.htm [July 8, 2002].

Inaba, D.S., & Cohen, W.E. (1994). *Uppers, downers, all arounders* (2nd ed.). Ashland, OR: CNS Productions.

Institute of Child Health. (2003). Erythropoietin [Online]. Available: www.ich.ucl.ac.uk/factsheets/misc/erythropoietin_epo/ [April 17, 2003].

Johnston, L.D., O'Malley, P.M., & Bachman, J.G. (1996). *National survey results on drug use from the Monitoring the Future study, 1975-1994* (Vol. II). Washington, DC: National Institute on Drug Abuse.

Joy, E., Clark, N., Ireland, M.L., Martire, J., Nattiv, A., & Varechok, S. (1997). Team management of the female triad. *Physician and Sportsmedicine, 25*(4), 55-69.

King, P. (1996). Bitter pill [Online]. Available: http://sportsillustrated.cnn.com/football/nfl/features/favre/flashbacks/bitter_pill/ [April 18, 2003].

Knopp, W.D., Wang, T.W., & Bach, B.R. (1997, July). Ergogenic drugs in sports. *Clinics in Sports Medicine, 16*(3), 375-392.

Leonard, W.M. (1998). *A sociological perspective of sport* (5th ed.). Boston, MA: Allyn & Bacon.

Lewis, J.A., Dana, R.Q., & Blevins, G.A. (1994). *Substance abuse counseling: An individualized approach* (2nd ed.). Pacific Grove, CA: Brooks/Cole.

Love, S., & Brookler, B. (1999). Ross Rebagliati [Online]. Available: http://classic.mountainzone.com/snowboarding/99/features/rebagliati [July 12, 2002].

Marlatt, G., & Gordon, J.R. (Eds.) (1985). *Relapse prevention: Maintenance strategies in the treatment of addictive behaviors.* New York: Guilford Press.

Martin, M. (1998). The use of alcohol among NCAA Division I female College basketball, softball, and volleyball athletes. *Journal of Athletic Training, 33*(2), 163-167.

McCrady, B.S., Dean, L., Dubreuil, E., & Swanson, S. (1985). The problem drinkers' project: A programmatic application of social-learning-based treatment. In G.A. Marlatt & J.R. Gordon (Eds.), *Relapse prevention: Maintenance strategies in the treatment of addictive behaviors* (pp. 417-471). New York: Guilford Press.

McCrady, B.S., & Delaney, S.I. (1995). Self-help groups. In R.K. Hester & W.R. Miller (Eds.), *Handbook of alcoholism treatment approaches: Effective alternatives* (2nd ed., pp. 160-175). Needham Heights, MA: Allyn & Bacon.

McLellan, A.T., Arndt, I.O., Metzger, D.S., Woody, G.E., and O'Brien, C.P. (1993). The effect of psychosocial services in substance abuse treatment. *Journal of American Medical Association, 269* (15), 1953-1959.

McLellan, A.T., Grisson, G., Durell, J., Alterman, A.I., Brill, P., & O'Brien, C.P. (1993). Substance abuse treatment in the private setting: Are some programs more effective than others? *Journal of Substance Abuse Treatment, 10,* 243-254.

Miller, B.E., Miller, M.N., Verhegge, R., Linville, H.H., & Pumariega, A.J. (2002). Alcohol misuse among college athletes: Self-medication for psychiatric symptoms. *Journal of Drug Education, 32*(1), 41-52.

Miller, K.E., Barnes, G.M., Sabo, D.F., Melnick, M.J., & Farrell, M.P. (2002). Anabolic-androgenic steroid use and other adolescent problem behaviors: Rethinking the male athlete assumption. *Sociological Perspectives, 45*(4), 467-489.

National Institute on Drug Abuse. (1999a). Chronic marijuana users become aggressive during withdrawal [Online]. Available: www.nida.nih.gov/Med/adv/99/NR-420.html [April 16, 2003].

National Institute on Drug Abuse. (1999b). Cocaine use and addiction [Online]. Available: www.ida.nih.gov/Research/Reports/cocaine [April 16, 2003].

National Institute on Drug Abuse. (1999c). Cigarettes and other nicotine products [Online]. Available: www.ida.nih.gov/Infofax/tobacco [April 16, 2003].

NCAA. (2001, June). NCAA study of substance use habits of college student-athletes [Online]. Available: www.ncaa.org [May 26, 2003].

NCAA. (2003a). Drugs in sports: Over the counter drugs [Online]. Available: www.drugfreesport.com/choices/drugs/counter.html [April 22, 2003].

NCAA. (2003b). Expansion to year-round testing took program to efficient level [Online]. Available: www.ncaa.org/news/2002/20020930/active/3920n27.html [April 25, 2003].

NCCAM. (2003). NCCAM consumer advisory on ephedra [Online]. Available: http://nccam.nih.gov/health/alerts/ephedra/consumeradvisory.htm [May 14, 2003].

Nelson, T.F., & Wechsler, H. (2001). Alcohol and college athletes. *Medicine and Science in Sports and Exercise* [Online]. Available: www.acsm-msse.org [May 16, 2003].

NIDA (2003). High school and youth trends [Online]. Available: www.nida.nih.gov/Infofax/HSYouthtrends.html [May 11, 2003].

Patrick, D. (2004). Designer drug test flags US track stars [Online]. Available: www.usatoday.com/sports/olympics/summer/track/2003-10-16-drug-samples_x.htm [August 15, 2004].

Pedone, K. (2003). Lessons learned in fen-phen suits factor into ephedra cases [Online]. *[May 14, 2003]* Available: http://biz.yahoo.com/law/030415/4582cb409cc390d520450c58a2d132f_1.html [August 15, 2004].

Peretti-Watel, P., Guagliardo, V., Verger, P., Pruvost, J., Mignon, P., & Obadia, Y. (2003). Sporting activity and drug use: Alcohol, cigarette and cannabis use among elite student athletes. *Addiction, 98,* 1249-1256.

Perez, P.J. (2001). Treatment setting and treatment planning. In P. Stevens & R.L. Smith (Eds.), *Substance abuse counseling: Theory and practice* (pp. 151-176). Upper Saddle River, NJ: Merrill/Prentice Hall.

Pope, H.G., Phillips, K.A., & Olivardia, R. (2000). *The Adonis complex: How to identify, treat, and prevent body obsession in men and boys.* New York: Simon & Schuster.

Porpora, M. (2003). Creatine and androstenedione: The gray market of legal performance-enhancing drugs [Online]. Available: http://eserver.org/zine375/swallow.html [May 12, 2003].

Price, J.H. (2003). Athletes on ephedra risk death, FDA says [Online]. Available: www.washtimes.com/national/20030301-18137088.htm [May 13, 2003].

Rosen, L.W., McKeag, D.B., Hough, D.O., & Curley, V. (1986). Pathogenic weight-control behavior in female athletes. *Physician and Sportsmedicine, 14,* 79-86.

Rushall, B.S. (1998, March-April). A brief history of drugs in swimming. *Australian Swimming and Fitness,* pp. 40-44.

Schnirring, L. (1998). Androstenedione et al: Nonprescription steroids. *Physician and Sportsmedicine, 26,* 1-6.

Shaffer, H.J. (1997). *Sports gambling and the college campus.* Presentation cosponsored by the Center for Problem Gambling at Mount Auburn Hospital and the Massachusetts Council on Compulsive Gambling, Cambridge, MA, January 25, 1997.

Sind, B. (2001). Stoned sportsmen [Online]. Available: www.cannabisculture.com/articles/1951.html [May 5, 2003].

Steroid drug testing in tennis [Online]. (2004). Available: www.bdtzone.com/news_details.asp?id=54 [August 15, 2004].

Stevens, P., & Smith, R.L. (2001). *Substance abuse counseling: Theory and practice* (2nd ed.). Upper Saddle River, NJ: Merrill/Prentice Hall.

Swift, E.M. (2003). Bodies of evidence. *Sports Illustrated, 98*(15), 25.

Taylor, J., & Taylor, S.T. (1997). *Psychological approaches to sports injury rehabilitation.* Gaithersburg, MD: Aspen.

Tiedt, J.E. (2003). The ephedra injury page [Online]. Available: http://ephedrainjury.com/ [May 14, 2003].

United States Olympic Committee. (1998). Drug education control [Online]. Available: www.usoc.org.html [April 25, 2003].

USA Today, Retrieved on July 8, 2002. www.usatoday.com/usatodayonline/20020708/4253743s.htm

Verducci, T. (2002). Caminiti comes clean [Online]. Available: http://sportsillustrated .cnn.com/si_online/special_report/steroids [July 8, 2002].

Wilbon, M. (1987). Years after Bias' death, some unlearned lessons [Online]. Available: www.washingtonpost.com/wp-srv/sports/longterm/memories/bias/bias5.htm [July 11, 2002].

Walsh, B.T., & Garner, D.M. (1997). Diagnostic issues. In D.M. Garner & P.E. Garfinkel (Eds.), *Handbook of treatment for eating disorders* (2nd ed., pp. 25-33). New York: Guilford Press.

Walters, G.D. (1999). *The addiction concept: Working hypothesis of self-fulfilling prophesy?* Boston: Allyn & Bacon.

Williams, M.H. (1998). *The ergogenic edge: Pushing the limits of sports performance.* Champaign, IL: Human Kinetics.

Yorio, K. (2004). Hockey not immune to drug problem [Online]. Available: http://msnbc.msn.com/id/3745480 [August 15, 2004].

Chapter 15

Alfermann, D. (1995). Career transitions of elite athletes: Drop-out and retirement. In R. Vanfraechem-Raway & Y. Vanden Auweele (Eds.), *Proceedings of the 9th European Congress on Sport Psychology* (pp. 828-833). Brussels: European Federation of Sports Psychology.

Alfermann, D. (2000). Causes and consequences of sport career termination. In D. Lavallee & P. Wylleman (Eds.), *Career transitions in sport: International perspectives* (pp. 45-58). Morgantown, WV: Fitness Information Technology.

Alfermann, D., & Gross, A. (1998). How elite athletes perceive and cope with career termination. *Leistungssport, 28*(2), 45-48.

Allison, M.T., & Meyer, C. (1988). Career problems in retirement among elite athletes: The female tennis professional. *Sociology of Sport Journal, 5,* 212-222.

Anderson, D.K. (1998). *Lifeskill intervention and elite performances.* Unpublished master's thesis, Victoria University, Melbourne, Australia.

Anderson, D., & Morris, T. (2000). Athlete lifestyle programs. In D. Lavallee & P. Wylleman (Eds.), *Career transitions in sport: International perspectives* (pp. 59-80). Morgantown, WV: Fitness Information Technology.

Arcieri, A., & Green, M. (1999). *Majoring in success: Building your career while still in college.* Alexandria, VA: Octameron Associates.

Atchley, R.C. (1976). *The sociology of retirement.* Cambridge, MA: Schenkman.

Axelson, J. A. (1999). *Counseling and development in a multicultural society* (3rd ed.). Pacific Grove, CA: Brooks/Cole.

Baillie, P.H.F. (1993). Understanding retirement from sports: Therapeutic ideas for helping athletes in transition. *The Counseling Psychologist, 21,* 399-410.

Baillie, P.H., & Danish, S.J. (1992). Understanding the career transition of athletes. *The Sport Psychologist, 6,* 77-98.

Ball, D.W. (1976). Failure in sport. *American Sociological Review, 41,* 726-739.

Beattie, M. (1989). *Beyond codependency and getting better all the time.* San Francisco: Harper Collins.

Blinde, E.M., & Stratta, T.M. (1992). The "sport career death" of college athletes. *Journal of Sport Behavior, 15,* 3-20.

Bloom, G.A., Durand-Bush, N., Schinke, R.J., & Salmela, J.H. (1998). The importance of mentoring in the development of coaches and athletes. *International Journal of Sport Psychology, 29,* 267-281.

Bolles, R.N. (2000). *What color is your parachute? A practical manual for job hunters and career changers* (rev. ed.). Berkeley, CA: Ten Speed Press.

Brewer, B.W. (1994). Review and critique of models of psychological adjustment to athletic injury. *Journal of Applied Sport Psychology, 6,* 87-100.

Brewer, B., Van Raalte, J., & Linder, D.E. (1993). Athletic identity: Hercules' muscles or Achilles' heel? *International Journal of Sport Psychology, 24:* 237-254.

Brewer, B.W., Van Raalte, J.L., & Petitpas, A. (2000). Self-identity issues in sport career transitions. In D. Lavallee & P. Wylleman (Eds.), *Career transitions in sport: International perspectives* (pp. 29-43). Morgantown, WV: Fitness Information Technology.

Brown, D. (2002). The role of work and cultural values in occupational choice, satisfaction, and success: A theoretical statement. *Journal of Counseling and Development, 80,* 48-56.

Brown, D. (2003). *Career information, career counseling, and career development.* Boston: Allyn & Bacon.

Carter, R.T., & Querishi, A. (1995). A typology of philosophical assumptions in multicultural counseling and training. In J.G. Ponterotto, J.M. Casas, L.A. Suzuki, & C.A. Alexander (Eds.), *Handbook of multicultural counseling* (pp. 239-263). Thousand Oaks, CA: Sage.

Coakley, J.J. (1983). Leaving competitive sport: Retirement or rebirth? *Quest, 35,* 1-11.

Cockerill, I., & Edge, A. (1998). *A two stage approach to examining the effects of mentoring on disengagement from elite competition sport.* Unpublished manuscript, School of Sport and Exercise Sciences, University of Birmingham, UK.

Crook, J.M., & Robertson, S.E. (1991). Transitions out of elite sport. *International Journal of Sport Psychology, 22,* 115-127.

Curtis, J., & Ennis, R. (1988). Negative consequences of leaving competitive sport? Comparison findings for former elite hockey players. *Sociology of Sport Journal, 5,* 87-106.

D'Andrea, M., & Daniels, J. (1995). Promoting multiculturalism and organizational change in the counseling profession. In J.G. Ponterotto, J.M. Casas, L.A. Suzuki, & C.M. Alexander (Eds.), *Handbook of multicultural counseling* (pp. 17-34). Thousand Oaks, CA: Sage.

Danish, S.J., Petitpas, A.J., & Hale, B.D. (1992). A developmental-educational intervention model of sport psychology. *The Sport Psychologist, 6,* 403-415.

Danish, S.J., Petitpas, A.J., & Hale, B.D. (1993). Life development intervention for athletes: Life skills through sports. *The Counseling Psychologist, 21,* 352-385.

Dimarco, C. (1997). *Career transitions: A journey of survival and growth.* Scottsdale, AZ: Gorsuch Scarisbrick.

Ducat, D. (2002). *Turning points: The career guide for the new century.* Upper Saddle River, NJ: Prentice Hall.

FEPSAC Position Statement 3. (1997). *Sports career transitions.* Brussels, Belgium: European Federation of Sport Psychology.

FEPSAC Position Statement 5. (1997). *Sports career termination.* Brussels, Belgium: European Federation of Sport Psychology.

Ferrante, A.P., Etzel, E., & Lantz, C. (1996). Counseling college student athletes: The problem, the need. In E. Etzel, A.P. Ferrante, & J. W. Pinkney (Eds.), *Counseling college student athletes: Issues and interventions* (pp. 1-17). Morgantown, WV: Fitness Information Technology.

Finch, L.M., & Gould, D. (1996). Understanding and intervening with the student-athlete-to-be. In E. Etzel, A.P. Ferrante, & J. W. Pinkney (Eds.), *Counseling college student athletes: Issues and interventions* (pp. 1-17). Morgantown, WV: Fitness Information Technology.

Fisher, L.A. (2001). Review of Lavallee and Wylleman (2000). *The Sport Psychologist, 15,* 450-452.

Flanagan, J. (2001, June). *Athlete career transitions symposium.* Paper presented at the 10th World Congress of Sport Psychology, Skiathos, Greece.

Ford, I.W., & Gordon, S. (1999). Coping with sport injury: Resource loss and the role of social support. *Journal of Personal and Interpersonal Loss, 4,* 243-256.

Gill, D. (Ed.) (2001a). In search of feminist sport psychology: Then, now, and always. *The Sport Psychologist, 15,* 363-372.

Gill, D. (2001b). Feminist sport psychology: A guide for our journey. *The Sport Psychologist, 15,* 363-372.

Gorbett, F.J. (1985). Psycho-social adjustment of athletes to retirement. In L.K. Bunker, R.J. Rotella, & A. Reilly (Eds.), *Psychological considerations in maximizing sport performance* (pp. 288-294). Ithaca, NY: Mouvement.

Gordon, L., & Levy, M.A. (2001, September). *Assisting student athletes with retirement right from the beginning: A systematic approach.* Paper presented at Long Island University Institute on Counseling the Student Athlete: A Developmental and Multicultural Perspective. Brookville, NY

Gordon, S. (1995). Career transitions in competitive sport. In T. Morris & J. Summers (Eds.), *Sport psychology: Theory, applications and issues* (pp. 474-501). Brisbane: Jacaranda Wiley.

Grove, J.R., Lavallee, D., & Gordon, S. (1997). Coping with retirement from sport: The influence of athletic identity. *Journal of Applied Sport Psychology, 9,* 191-203.

Hall, R. (2001). Shaking the foundation: Women of color in sport. *The Sport Psychologist, 15,* 386-400.

Hare, N. (1971). A study of the black fighter. *The Black Scholar, 3,* 2-9.

Hastings, D.W., Kurth, S.B., & Meyer, J. (1989). Competitive swimming careers through the life course. *Sociology of Sport Journal, 6,* 278-284.

Heil, J. (1993). *Psychology of sport injury.* Champaign, IL: Human Kinetics.

Holland, J., Powell, A.B., & Fritzsche, B.A. (1994). *Self Directed Search professional users guide.* Odessa, FL: Psychological Assessment Resources.

Hotchkiss, L., & Borow, H. (1996). Sociological perspective on work and career development. In D. Brown & L. Brooks (Eds.), *Career choice and development* (3rd ed., pp. 281-334). San Francisco, CA: Jossey-Bass.

Howe, B., Musselman, D., & Planella, V. (2000, May 9). *Transition from elite sports: Two case studies. Connections* (University of Victoria)

Kane, M.J. (1988). The female athletic role as a status determinant within the social systems of high school adolescents. *Adolescence, 23,* 253-264.

Kern, G., & Dacyshyn, A. (2000). The retirement experience of elite female gymnasts. *Journal of Sport Psychology, 12,* 113-115.

Kleiber, D.A., & Brock, S.C. (1992). The effect of career ending injuries on the subsequent well-being of elite college athletes. *Sociology of Sport Journal, 9,* 70-75.

Kubler-Ross, E. (1969). *On death and dying.* New York: Scribner.

Lavallee, D. (2000). Theoretical perspectives on career transitions in sport. In D. Lavallee & P. Wylleman (Eds.), *Career transitions in sport: International perspectives* . Morgantown, WV: Fitness Information Technology.

Lavallee, D., Gordon, S., & Grove, J.R. (1997). Retirement from sport and the loss of athletic identity. *Journal of Personal and Interpersonal Loss, 2,* 129-147.

Lavallee, D., Grove, J.R., Gordon S., & Ford, I.W. (1988). The experience of loss in sport. In J. Harvey (Ed.), *Perspective on loss: A source book* (pp. 241-252). Philadelphia: Brunner/Mazel.

Lavallee, D., Nesti, M., Borkoles, E., Cockerill, I., & Edge, A. (2000). Intervention strategies for athletes in transition. In D. Lavallee & P. Wylleman (Eds.), *Career transitions in sport: International perspectives* (pp. 111-130). Morgantown, WV: Fitness Information Technology.

Lavallee, D., & Wylleman, P. (Eds.) (2000). *Career transitions in sport: International perspectives.* Morgantown, WV: Fitness Information Technology.

Lee, K.C. (1991). The problem of the appropriateness of the Rokeach Value Survey in Korea. *International Journal of Psychology, 26,* 299-310.

Leong, F.T.L. (1991). Career development attributes and occupational values of Asian American and White high school students. *Career Development Quarterly, 39,* 221-230.

Leung, S.A. (1995). Career development in counseling: A multicultural perspective. In J.G. Ponterotto, J.M. Casas, L.A. Suzuki, & C.M. Alexander (Eds.), *Handbook of multicultural counseling* (pp. 549-566). Thousand Oaks, CA: Sage.

Levy, M.A., & Burke, K. (1986). The life after sport clinic: A program proposal. *Journal of Applied Research in Coaching and Athletics, 1,* 212-225.

Levy, M.A., & Ehinger, G.E. (1996). *Student athlete development: Revising Chickering's model.* Paper presented at the New York Counseling Association 31st Annual Convention, Saratoga Springs, NY.

Levy, M.A., Ehinger, G. E., & Whittaker, W. (1997, May). *Understanding student athlete development: Preventing adverse behaviors.* Paper presented at the 14th Annual Conference on Counseling Athletes, Springfield, MA.

Levy, M.A., & Gordon, L. (2001, September). *Assisting student athletes with retirement right from the beginning: A systematic approach.* Paper presented at the Long Island University Institute on Counseling the Student Athlete: A Developmental and Multicultural Perspective, Brookville, NY.

Levy, M.A., Hendricks, G.E., & Gordon, L. (2000, May). *A systemic approach to career development programming for student athletes.* Paper presented at the 17th Annual Conference on Counseling Athletes, Springfield, MA.

Locke, E.A., & Latham, G.P. (1984). *Goal setting: A motivational tool that works.* Englewood Cliffs, NJ: Prentice Hall.

Malnig, L.R. (1984). *What can I do with a major in . . .* Ridgefield, NJ: Abbott Press.

Manion, U.V. (1976). Preretirement counseling: The need for a new approach. *Personnel and Guidance Journal, 55*, 119-121.

Martens, M.P., Mobley, M., & Zizzi, S.J. (2000). Multicultural training in applied sports psychology. *The Sport Psychologist, 14*, 81-97.

McGowan, E., & Rail, G. (1996). Up the creek without a paddle: Canadian women sprint canoeists retirement from international sport. *Avante, 2*, 18-126.

McInally, L., Cavin-Stice, J., & Knoth, R.L. (1992, August). *Adjustment following retirement from professional football.* Paper presented at the annual meeting of the American Psychological Association, Washington, DC.

McPherson, B.D. (1980). Retirement from professional sport: The process and problems of occupational and psychological adjustment. *Sociological Symposium, 30*, 126-143.

Mihovilovic, M. (1968). The status of the former sportsman. *International Review of Sport Sociology, 3*, 73-96.

Monster.com Olympian Career Survey. (2001). Data taken from TeamUSAnet Fact Sheet. www.Monster.com/olympiccareersurvey.html [June 16, 2003].

Murphy, S.M. (1995). Transition in competitive sport: Maximizing individual potential. In S.M. Murphy (Ed.), *Sport psychology interventions* (pp. 331-346). Champaign, IL: Human Kinetics.

Ogilvie, B.C., & Howe, M.A. (1982). Career crisis in sport. In T. Orlick, J.T. Partington, & J.H. Salmella (Eds.), *Mental training for coaches and athletes* (pp. 176-183). ISSP Fifth World Sport Psychology Conference, Coaching Association of Canada, Ontario, Canada.

Ogilvie, B.C., & Howe, M. (1986). The trauma of termination from athletics. In J.M. Williams (Ed.), *Applied sport psychology: Personal growth to peak performance* (pp. 365-382). Palo Alto, CA: Mayfield.

Ogilvie, B.C., & Taylor, J. (1993a). Career termination issues among elite athletes. In R.N. Singer, M. Murphy, & L.K. Tennant (Eds.), *Handbook of research on sport psychology* (pp. 761-775). New York: Macmillan.

Ogilvie, B.C., & Taylor, J. (1993b). Career termination in sports: When the dream dies. In J.M. Williams (Ed.), *Applied sport psychology: Personal growth to peak performance* (2nd ed., pp. 356-365). Mountain View, CA: Mayfield.

Oglesby, C. (2001). To unearth the legacy. *The Sport Psychologist, 15*, 373-385.

Parham, W. (1993). The intercollegiate athlete: A 1990's profile. *The Counseling Psychologist, 21*, 411-429.

Parham, W. (1996). Diversity within intercollegiate athletics: Current profiles and welcomed opportunities. In E. Etzel, A.P. Ferrante, & J. W. Pinkney (Eds.), *Counseling college student athletes: Issues and interventions* (pp. 1-17). Morgantown, WV: Fitness Information Technology.

Patton, W., & Ryan, S. (2000). Career transitions among dancers. In D. Lavallee & P. Wylleman (Eds.), *Career transitions in sport: International perspectives* (pp. 169-180). Morgantown, WV: Fitness Information Technology.

Pearson, R.E., & Petitpas, A.J. (1990). Transitions of athletes: Developmental and preventive perspectives. *Journal of Counseling and Development, 69*, 7-10.

Perna, F.M., Zaichkowsky, L., & Bockner, G. (1996). The association of mentoring with psychosocial development among male athletes at termination of college career. *Journal of Applied Sport Psychology, 8*, 76-88.

Petitpas, A., Champagne, D., Chartrand, J., Danish, S., & Murphy, S. (1997). *Athletes' guide to career planning: Keys to success from the playing field to professional life.* Champaign, IL: Human Kinetics.

Petitpas, A., Danish, S., McKelvain, R., & Murphy, S. (1992). A career assistance program for elite athletes. *Journal of Counseling and Development, 70*, 383-386.

Ponterotto, J.G., & Casas, J.M. (1991). *Handbook of racial/ethnic minority research.* Springfield, IL: Charles C Thomas.

Remer, R., Tongate, F., & Watson, J. (1978). Athletes: Counseling the overprivileged minority. *Personnel and Guidance Journal, 56*, 626-629.

Reynolds, M.J. (1981). The effects of sports retirement on the job satisfaction of the former football player. In S.L. Greendorfer & A. Yiannakis (Eds.), *Sociology of sport: Perspectives* (pp. 127-137). West Point, NY: Leisure Press.

Rosenberg, E. (1982). Athletic retirement as social death: Concepts and perspectives. In N. Theberge & P. Donnelly (Eds.), *Sport and sociology imagination* (pp. 245-258). Fort Worth: Texas Christian University Press.

Rosenfeld, L.B., Richman, J.M., & Hardy, C.J. (1989). Examining social support networks among athletes: Description and relationship to stress. *The Sport Psychologist, 3*, 23-33.

Rotella, R. J., & Heyman, S. R. (1986). Stress, injury, and the psychological rehabilitation of athletes. In J. M. Williams (Ed.), *Applied sport psychology: personal growth to peak performance* (pp. 343-364). Mayfield, California: Palo Alto.

Schlossberg, N.K. (1981). A model for analyzing human adaptation to transition. *The Counseling Psychologist, 9*, 2-18.

Shumaker, S. A., & Brownell, A. (1984). Toward a theory of social support: Closing conceptual gaps. *Journal of Social Issues, 40*(4), 11-36.

Sinclair, D.A., & Hackfort, D. (2000). The role of the sport organization in the career transition process. In D. Lavallee & P. Wylleman (Eds.), *Career transitions in sport: International perspectives* (pp. 131-142). Morgantown, WV: Fitness Information Technology.

Sinclair, D.A., & Orlick, T. (1993). Positive transitions from high performance sport. *The Sport Psychologist, 7*, 138-150.

Sinha, D. (1990). Interventions for development out of poverty. In R.W. Brislin (Ed.), *Applied cross cultural psychology* (pp. 77-97). Newbury Park, CA: Sage.

Sue, D.W. (1991). A conceptual model for cultural diversity training. *Journal of Counseling and Development, 70*, 99-105.

Sue, D.W., Arredondo, P., & McDavis, R.J. (1992). Multicultural counseling competencies and standards: A call to the profession. *Journal of Counseling and Development, 70,* 477-486.

Sue, D.W., & Sue, D. (1990). *Counseling the culturally different* (2nd ed.). New York: Wiley.

Super, D.E. (1980). A life-span, life-space approach to career development. *Journal of Vocational Behavior, 13,* 282-298.

Super, D.E. (1990). A life-span, life-space approach to career development. In D. Brown, L. Brook, & Associates (Eds.), *Career choice and development: Applying contemporary theories to practice* (2nd ed., pp. 197-261), San Francisco: Jossey-Bass.

Super, D.E. (1992). Toward a comprehensive theory of career development. In D. Montross & C. Shinkman (Eds.), *Career development: Theory and practice* (pp. 35-64). Springfield, IL: Charles C Thomas.

Svoboda, B., & Vanek, M. (1982). Retirement from high level competition. In T. Orlick, J.T. Partington, & J.H. Salmela (Eds.), *Proceedings of the Fifth World Conference of Sport Psychology* (pp. 166-175), Ottawa: Coaching Association of Canada.

Swain, D.A. (1991). Withdrawal from sport and Schlossberg's model of transitions. *Sociology of Sport Journal, 8,* 152-160.

Taylor, J., & Ogilvie, B.C. (1994). A conceptual model of adaptation to retirement among athletes. *Journal of Applied Sport Psychology, 6,* 1-20.

Taylor, J., & Ogilvie, B.C. (1998). Career transition among elite athletes: Is there life after sports? In J.M. Williams (Ed.), *Applied sport psychology: Personal growth to peak performance* (3rd ed., pp. 429-444). Mountain View, CA: Mayfield.

Thorenson, R.W., & Kerr, B.A. (1978). The stigmatizing aspects of severe disability: Strategies for change. *Journal of Applied Rehabilitation Counseling, 9,* 21-26.

Tunick, R., Etzel, E., Leard, J., & Lerner, B. (1996). Counseling injured and disabled student-athletes: A guide for understanding and intervention. In E. Etzel, A.P. Ferrante, & J. W. Pinkney (Eds.), *Counseling college student athletes: Issues and interventions* (pp. 1-17). Morgantown, WV: Fitness Information Technology.

Webb, W.M., Nasco, S.A., Riley, S., & Headrick, B. (1998). Athlete identity and reactions to retirement from sports. *Journal of Sports Behavior, 21,* 338-362.

Weinberg, K., & Arond, H. (1952). The occupational culture of the boxer. *American Journal of Sociology, 57,* 460-469.

Werthner, P., & Orlick, T. (1986). Retirement experiences of successful Olympic athletes. *Journal of Sport Psychology, 17,* 337-363.

Wheeler, G.D., Malone, L.A., Van-Vlack, S., Nelson, E.R., & Steadward, R.D. (1996). Retirement from disability sport: A pilot study. *Adapted Physical Activity Quarterly, 13,* 382-399.

Worell, J., & Johnson, N. G. (Eds.). (1997). *Shaping the future of feminist psychology: Education, research, and practice.* Washington, DC: American Psychological Association.

Wylleman, P. (2003, May). Developmental issues with elite athletes. Workshop presented at the 20th Annual Conference on Counseling Athletes, Springfield College, Springfield, MA.

Yagi, D.T., & Oh, M.Y. (1995). Counseling Asian American students. In C.C. Lee (Ed.), *Counseling for diversity* (pp. 61-84). Needham Heights, MA: Longwood.

Yallop, R. (1996, August 17-18). When athletes fall to earth. *Australian Magazine,* pp. 39-42.

Yost, E.B., & Corbishley, M.A. (1987). *Career counseling: A psychological approach.* San Francisco: Jossey-Bass.

Index

About the Editors

Jim Taylor, PhD, is a highly sought-after speaker and author in sport psychology. Dr. Taylor has 20 years of applied sport psychology experience in academic settings and in private consulting practice. The author of eight books and numerous publications in refereed journals, Dr. Taylor is a former world-ranked alpine ski racer, certified tennis coach, second-degree black belt in karate, marathon runner, and Ironman triathlete. He is an elected fellow and certified consultant for the Association for the Advancement of Applied Sport Psychology, and he has consulted extensively with world-class and professional athletes.

Gregory S. Wilson, PED, is an associate professor and chair of the department of human kinetics and sport studies at the University of Evansville in Indiana. He has coauthored six chapters for a variety of edited textbooks and has published numerous papers dealing with such topics as overtraining and staleness and the effects of precompetition anxiety on sport performance. A former track coach, he has coached an NCAA hurdles champion and a member of the U.S. Olympic and Pan American teams. Dr. Wilson is a member of the American College of Sports Medicine and the American Psychological Association.

About the Contributors

Victoria L. Bacon, EdD, is an associate professor and chair of the department of counselor education at Bridgewater State College, Bridgewater, Massachusetts. As a licensed clinical psychologist, she was trained to work with children, adolescents, and families with a focus on trauma and dual diagnoses. Dr. Bacon's current areas of clinical expertise, research, and writing include athletes and the physically active population involved with various addictive behaviors: gambling, substance abuse, disordered eating, and exercise addiction as well as critical incident stress debriefings with athletes and teams. In addition to training counselors, Dr. Bacon provides consultation and instruction to athletic trainers and sport nutritionists in the greater Boston area.

Casey Barrett was a member of the Canadian national team in 1995. His career culminated at the 1996 Atlanta Olympics, where he placed 11th in the 200 butterfly. Over the course of his career, Barrett trained under six different Olympic coaches on a variety of elite programs in Canada and the United States. In 1998 he worked for NBC in their Olympic coverage, where he worked in the Athlete Profiles Unit, focusing particularly on the swimmers and divers. At the Sydney Games, in addition to creating aquatic features, he served as writer and researcher for Rowdy Gaines, NBC's on-air analyst. Barrett currently works as an associate producer at the syndicated television program "Inside Edition" in New York.

Terry Brahm earned All-Ten and All-American honors in both track and cross country while at Indiana University. Brahm has been on numerous international teams and won the silver medal in the 5,000 meters at the Goodwill games. In 1988 he represented the United States in the 5,000 meters at the Seoul Olympics. Brahm, who has been inducted into the IU Athletic Hall of Fame, runs a running camp for children in the summer and teaches special education in Indianapolis.

Petra Cada is a member of the Canadian national table tennis team. Among her accomplishments, she has won the 2003 North American Doubles Championship, 2002 Commonwealth gold medal, 1995 Pan-Am Games gold medal, and 1993 Global Youth Champs bronze medal. She was also a member of the Canadian Olympic team at the 1996 Games in Atlanta.

Bobby Clark is the head men's soccer coach at the University of Notre Dame. Before coaching at Notre Dame, Coach Clark served as the director of men's and women's soccer at Stanford University. He has extensive coaching experience at the collegiate and international level and has been coaching for more than 40 years.

Susan Cooper, PhD, is the vice president of academic affairs and a member of the executive faculty at the Colorado School of Professional Psychology in Colorado Springs. In addition, Cooper is a licensed psychologist and a certified group psychotherapist who has specialized for 20 years in the treatment of eating disorders and group psychotherapy. She has also been a feedback coach at the Center for Creative Leadership in Colorado Springs since 1998. Cooper received a PhD in counseling psychology from the University of Denver, an MA in counseling psychology from Chapman University, and a BA in English from Dickinson College. Before becoming a psychologist, Sue taught secondary English in New York and Massachusetts.

Sheilagh Croxon helped guide Canada to two Olympic and two world championship synchronized swimming medals and also earned two Coaching Excellence Awards from the Coaching Association of Canada. She conceptualized some of the most memorable and original routines in the sport including the very popular Olympic Dreams, which earned Canada the bronze in the team event at the 2000 Olympics in Sydney.

Kim Cusimano, PhD, has consulted with athletes on both the collegiate and national levels, assisting them in optimizing their performance potential. Additionally, she has worked in hospitals and medical clinics helping to successfully integrate a mind–body philosophy to further rehabilitative potential and needed lifestyle change. Dr. Cusimano has published a number of articles and has spoken at various organizational conferences throughout the continental United States. Her specialty emphasizes the psychological challenges inherent to endurance sport. Dr. Cusimano works at UC, Davis Sports Medicine Center in Sacramento, California, as an interdisciplinary member of the sport performance team and as a private practitioner with issues related to personal and spiritual development. Dr. Cusimano has competed in collegiate and semiprofessional soccer, marathon running, and triathlons.

Mary Grigson Daubert, RN, secured a scholarship with the Australian Institute of Sport Mountain Bike program in 1995. For the next 4 years she represented Australia at international mountain bike events, while earning a top-10 world ranking. In January 2000, Daubert signed with American mountain bike team, Subaru/Gary Fisher. Over the next 4 years with this team, Daubert won two U.S. national titles, two World Cup events, and a 24-hour Solo World Championships, and she competed in two Olympic Games.

Scott Daubert earned his BA in English and communications from Fort Lewis College where he raced road and mountain bikes competitively. Daubert worked as a team mechanic, operations coordinator, and team manager for several professional cycling programs. He is currently the project leader for Trek bicycles in developing equipment supplied to the U.S. Postal Professional cycling team, working closely with Lance Armstrong.

Nicole DeBoom received her BA in sociology from Yale University where she was an All-Ivy League swimmer. She made her pro debut in 1999 by competing in the U.S. Triathlon Series (USTS) and in 2000 competed in her first Ironman event, finishing third. A former Olympic Trials qualifier in the breaststroke, DeBoom has won an impressive list of endurance events, including the Pike's Peak Triathlon, Memphis in May Triathlon, Shawnee Mission Triathlon, Mighty Hamptons Triathlon, the Vail Half Marathon, and 2004 Ironman Wisconsin.

Nikki Dryden is a two-time Olympic swimmer who has represented Canada in international competitions for the last 10 years. In addition to competing at the 1992 and 1996 Olympics, Dryden is a 21-time national champion, former Canadian and Commonwealth record holder, and a Pan American and Commonwealth Games medalist. She is a four-time SEC and three-time Ivy League champion and has competed on four conference-winning teams. She also competed in four NCAA championships where she earned nine All-America honors including a second place finish in the 500-yard freestyle as a sophomore. Dryden earned

her degree in international relations from Brown University after transferring from the University of Florida. She has media and journalism experience in television and radio broadcast, newsletter production, press operations, and magazine and Internet writing, most notably as a feature writer for *SwimNews Magazine.*

Natalie Durand-Bush, PhD, is an assistant professor in the School of Human Kinetics at the University of Ottawa. Her areas of interest and specialization include the development of expert performance and the role of resonance in the achievement of optimal performance and well-being. She is the coauthor of the Ottawa Mental Skills Assessment Tool (OMSAT-3*), an instrument developed to evaluate a variety of mental skills perceived to be important for consistent high-quality performance. Durand-Bush has presented her research and applied work at numerous international conferences and has also published several refereed articles as well as two chapters in books, one of which appears in the *Handbook of Sport Psychology, Second Edition.* She received the Young Scientist Award from the Canadian Society for Psychomotor Learning and Sport Psychology in 1998. Aside from academia, Durand-Bush has been working as a performance education consultant with many athletes of different levels, including athletes from Canadian national teams and university varsity teams. She has also developed a workbook to help athletes refine valuable mental and life skills.

Sandra Foster, PhD, is a performance enhancement psychologist and business coach who permanently relocated to Europe after many years' practice in San Francisco's financial district. She is among the first to publish about the application of sport psychology performance enhancement strategies in business coaching and consultation. She served on the faculty of Stanford University, where she received her doctorate and consulted for the fencing and gymnastics teams. Dr. Foster received the 2000 Francine Shapiro Award for Innovations in EMDR for her unique protocol using this trauma treatment for reducing performance anxiety with employees, musicians, actors, and athletes. She coauthored *Three-Shot Golf for Women,* combining instruction with sport psychology specifically for female players, and *Skate Your Personal Best,* which integrates performance enhancement strategies with fundamentals of technique. Dr. Foster is accredited by the International Coach Federation (PCC) and teaches peak performance and positive psychology courses for the College of Executive Coaching.

Lauren Gordon, MSW, a former student-athlete, has been in private practice in New York City as a psychotherapist and EAP consultant since 1986. Among her specialties are working with the sports and performing arts communities. Ms. Gordon is a career counselor at Career Transition for Dancers, a national service organization based in New York City, and conducts workshops and individual sessions on career issues at dance and theater companies. As a sports career counselor she has been the Career Week Coordinator for Starworks/Powerplay, a nonprofit organization for students, and was a panelist at the 2003 AAASP Annual Conference. With Dr. Mitchell Levy, Ms. Gordon has presented at the Conference on Counseling Athletes, Springfield College, and other settings. Ms. Gordon is a member of AAASP, Career Counselor Development Network, and the Women's Sports Foundation and is an advisor to the All American Girls Professional Baseball League.

Judy Goss received her PhD in sport psychology from the University of Maryland and is a certified consultant by the Association for the Advancement of Applied Sport Psychology. As an associate member of the American Association for Marriage and Family Therapy, she also is qualified in family and marriage counseling. Currently Goss is employed by the Canadian Sport Centre Ontario as an athlete services consultant developing programs and initiatives to enrich the general well-being of athletes and a sport psychology consultant working with national and Olympic team members in Ontario. She also maintains a private consulting practice working with athletes from a variety of sports, in particular the Canadian synchronized swimming team and the men's national wheelchair basketball team. Goss is also the athlete relations consultant for the Canadian Olympic Committee and has written numerous articles and presented at national and international conferences.

Brian Grawer is a 2001 magna cum laude graduate of the University of Missouri, where he was a 4-year letter winner as a point guard with the Tigers' nationally ranked men's basketball team. Team captain during his senior year, Grawer was consistently among the NCAA leaders in free throw and 3-point shooting percentage. Noted for his gritty competitiveness and always-hustling style of play, Grawer was the consummate model of a great team player and leader. He is currently a graduate assistant coach at Missouri, pursuing his master's degree in education.

Finn Gundersen has been a skier for 53 years, a competitive ski racer for 21 years, and a coach for 35 years. Gundersen is currently the United States Ski and Snowboard Association's director of alpine education, serving approximately 3,000 alpine coaches nationwide. He is a former World Cup and Olympic alpine coach for the U.S. ski team. He was headmaster of Burke Mountain Academy for 15 years, the first alpine ski academy and one of the first specialized sports academies in the nation.

Bruce D. Hale earned his PhD in 1981 from Penn State University in sport psychology in physical education. He is currently an associate professor of kinesiology at Penn State University, Berks-Lehigh Valley College. He is a certified consultant and fellow in the Association for the Advancement of Applied Sport Psychology. He was an accredited educational and research sport psychologist in the British Association for Sport and Exercise Sciences and on the USOC Registry for Sport Psychology Professionals. Hale has done performance enhancement consulting with hundreds of athletes in collegiate sports, several professional teams, and elite national teams such as USA Wrestling, British Biathlon, USA Rowing, TAC, and USA Rugby. In the area of mental imagery research, he completed his dissertation research on imagery perspectives and psychophysiological responses and has published one text and several book chapters. He is a coach of rugby and recently published *Rugby Tough,* a rugby mental preparation text, through Human Kinetics.

Peter Harmer, PhD, ATC, is a professor of exercise science at Willamette University, Salem, Oregon. He has been a certified athletic trainer since 1984 and was the athletic trainer for the USA Fencing team from 1989 to 2000. Currently he directs the sports medicine program for the United States Fencing Association national competitions. In 1998, at the World Fencing Championships in Switzerland, he received a special recognition award for services to the health care of international competitors and in 2000 became the first nonphysician ever elected to the 10-member medical commission of the International Fencing Federation. Professor Harmer has eclectic research interests including injury epidemiology in fencing and sumo, exercise in older adults, and ethics and has published broadly in journals such as *Research Quarterly for Exercise and Sport, Journal of Aging and Health, Journal of Exercise and Sport Psychology,* and the *Journal of the Philosophy of Sport.* He is a fellow of the Research Consortium of the American Alliance for Health, Physical Education, Recreation and Dance.

Robert J. Harmison, PhD, is the department head of the sport-exercise psychology program at Argosy University/Phoenix. He has a PhD in counseling psychology (University of North Texas) and an MS in exercise and sport science (University of Arizona). He completed his predoctoral internship in the Kansas State University Counseling Services, where he provided sport psychology services to university athletic teams, individual athletes, and coaches. He was a member of the U.S. Olympic Committee sport psychology staff from 1997 to 1999 and provided sport psychology services to athletes, coaches, and teams that trained at the Olympic Training Centers. He consulted with the 2002 U.S. Olympic snowboard team, currently provides services to U.S. Snowboarding in preparation for the 2006 Olympic Winter Games, and recently began working with minor league teams in the Kansas City Royals organization. His applied interests primarily consist of providing performance enhancement and counseling services to elite, collegiate, high school, and competitive recreational athletes.

Chuck Hartman has been the head baseball coach at Virginia Tech since 1979. Before coming to Virginia Tech, he coached 19 seasons at High Point College (now University). His 1,401 career wins rank him third among active Division I baseball coaches in victories. Hartman has been inducted into five halls of fame including the National Association of Intercollegiate Hall of Fame in 1989 and the American Baseball Coaches Association Hall of Fame in 2004.

John Heil, PhD, completed a master's degree in clinical psychology at St. Louis University, a doctorate in sport and health psychology at Lehigh University, and postdoctoral training in pain and behavioral medicine at the University of Utah Medical School. He is a licensed clinical psychologist and a certified consultant and fellow of the Association for the Advancement of Applied Sport Psychology, and he is included in the Sport Psychology Registry of the United States Olympic Committee. Dr. Heil is the author of the *Psychology of Sport Injury* as well as numerous papers on sport, pain, and injury rehabilitation. Dr. Heil has served as the director of sports medicine for the Virginia Commonwealth Games since 1991. He is the chair of sports medicine and science for U.S. Fencing.

Per Mathias Hoegmo is currently the manager of the Norwegian Premier League club Tromsö IL and also director of the Olympic Training Centre in Northern Norway. From 2000 to 2003 he was the head coach for the Under-21 national men's team in Norway. From 1996 to 2000 he was the head coach for the Norwegian female soccer team, which won gold medals in the Olympic Games in Sydney 2000. He also has extensive experience from coaching high-level league teams and junior national teams. He has the highest possible soccer coach certificate obtainable in Europe (the UEFA licence) and also has a master in sport sciences from the Norwegian University of Sport and PE. In addition, he has a broad background as a soccer player at both the national and international level. Mr. Hoegmo enjoys outdoor life and activities with his family when he is not involved in soccer activities.

Stacia Hookom has been a member of the U.S. alpine snow boarding team since its inception in 1994 and has been an integral part in shaping the U.S. alpine snowboarding program. With five U.S. Championship titles, a spot in five World Championship teams, and countless World Cup events on her resume, Hookom is still hungry for her first Olympics. Multiple injuries slowed her progression as an athlete, but her determined approach paid off in 2003 with the best results of her career. Hookom is also the 2003 Grand Prix Alpine champion, finished third in the 2000 Goodwill Games, and has had Nine Career World Cup Podiums. Off the snow, Hookom does her strength and conditioning at Athletes Performance in Tempe, Arizona, and attends the University of Colorado.

Sue Humphrey was the head U.S. women's track and field coach at the 2004 Olympics in Athens. Before being selected to this position, she served as an assistant coach for both the 1992 and 1996 U.S. Olympic teams. She has served as the women's assistant track and field coach at the University of Texas, Arizona State University, and Cal State-Long Beach and is the author of several acclaimed coaching manuals and videos. Currently, she is an assistant principal in Austin, Texas, and consults with postcollegiate jumpers.

Marc Jones, PhD, is currently a senior lecturer in sport and exercise psychology at Staffordshire University. Marc completed an undergraduate degree in applied psychology at Cardiff University and a PhD from Newman College, Birmingham, examining the role of emotion in sport performance. His main areas of research interest include the impact of emotions on performance levels, understanding how emotional control can be developed in athletes, and exploring factors that affect decision making in sport officials. As a sport psychology consultant, Jones has worked with a number of athletes across a range of sports, ages, and abilities. He is accredited by the British Association of Sport and Exercise Sciences (BASES) for providing sport psychology support and is a chartered psychologist with the British Psychological Society (BPS). Jones enjoys most sports with particular favorites including cricket, golf, and rugby.

Sophia Jowett, PhD, is a lecturer in sport and exercise psychology at Loughborough University. Her main research revolves around the affective, cognitive, and behavioral aspects of interpersonal relationships in sport (especially coach–athlete relationships, relationship rules, interpersonal perceptions, and social support). Current research projects are sponsored by the British Academy, the Nuffield Foundation, the J.F. Costopoulos Foundation, the Hellenic Olympic Committee, and the Hellenic Ministry of Culture and Sport. Dr. Jowett has presented her work at international conferences (British Psychological Society, European Federation of Sport Psychology); has published in refereed journals (*The Sport Psychologist, Psychology of Sport and Exercise, Journal of International Sport Psychology, Scandinavian Journal of Medicine and Science in Sports*); and has coauthored chapters in edited books. She serves as a member of the committee of the Sport and Exercise Psychology Section of the British Psychological Society (BPS). Dr. Jowett is a certified British Association Sport and Exercise Sciences (BASES) sport psychologist and a sport psychology consultant of the 2004 Greek Olympic team.

Thad R. Leffingwell, PhD, is an assistant professor in the department of psychology at Oklahoma State University. He earned his doctorate in clinical psychology (emphasis in sport psychology) at the University of Washington and a master's degree in sport and exercise psychology from the University of Arizona. During his doctoral training, Dr. Leffingwell was a consultant with Husky Sport Psychology Services in the department of intercollegiate athletics. Dr. Leffingwell's dissertation investigated the usefulness of psychological assessment feedback in applied sport psychology with intercollegiate athletes. His current research interests are focused on the behavior change process with high-risk health behaviors and brief interventions for encouraging behavior change.

Bart S. Lerner, EdD, is a member of the sport-exercise psychology faculty and is the department head of the MA professional counseling program at Argosy University in Phoenix. He is a licensed professional counselor in Arizona and an AAASP-certified consultant, in which his areas of interest include youth sport education, performance enhancement training (e.g., goal setting, imagery, performance anxiety), self-confidence, psychological aspects of injury and rehabilitation, substance abuse issues, supervision and training, and graduate training in sport psychology. Dr. Lerner has experience working with youth, high school, college, and professional athletes in the field of sport psychology for approximately 10 years. Dr. Lerner teaches courses in the exercise sciences (exercise physiology, motor learning and development, and sports medicine and rehabilitation) and statistics as well as counseling-related courses (basic intervention skills, life span development, and substance abuse).

Mitchell A. Levy, PhD, has more than 20 years experience in higher education. Currently, he is the assistant director and coordinator of training of the Iona College Counseling Center in New Rochelle, New York. Additionally, Dr. Levy is the consultant to the Iona College athletic department and the co-coordinator of the Iona College PASS (Promoting Academic Success of Student-athletes) program. Since the inception of the PASS program 5 years ago, the approximately 400 Iona College student athletes have averaged greater than a 3.0 grade point average every semester. Dr. Levy is also a member of the graduate faculty of Fordham University and Long Island University and has conducted a number of professional presentations in sport psychology with respect to multicultural counseling issues with student-athletes, career transitions for retiring athletes, preparing high school athletes for college success, and student–athlete personality development.

Luis G. Manzo, PhD, is a licensed psychologist and coordinator of alcohol and other drug treatment services at the University of Notre Dame's University Counseling Center. He received his doctorate in counseling psychology from Loyola University in 1999 and holds a master's degree in sport psychology from the University of North Carolina at Chapel Hill. He has given numerous workshops and lectures to coaches, athletes, and other professionals on confidence building, alcohol prevention strategies, and optimism building techniques. Manzo recently completed a research project funded by a USA Swimming Sport Sciences Grant to study the implementation of optimisim building techniques in youth swimmers. In 2002 he was awarded a Developing Leadership in Reducing Substance Abuse fellowship through the Robert Wood Johnson Foundation. He is a member of the Association for the Advancement of Applied Sport Psychology and the American Psychological Association (Divisions 17, 47, and 50).

E.J. McGuire is a former assistant coach with the Philadelphia Flyers of the National Hockey League. He was previously the head coach at the University of Brockport.

Rick McGuire, PhD, is the head track and field coach for men and women at the University of Missouri. He is also a graduate professor of sport psychology in the department of educational, school, and counseling psychology in the University's College of Education. During his tenure at Missouri, Dr. McGuire has led his teams and athletes to positions of prominence, producing Olympians, national champions, collegiate record holders, national and world rankings, and more than 100 All-American performers. He has chaired the sport psychology program for USA Track and Field since its inception in 1983, a program considered to be one of the finest sport psychology service delivery programs in the world today. Dr. McGuire has served on the staff for 11 U.S. national track and field teams, including the 1992 and 1996 Olympic Games. He has also worked as a consultant with the Chicago White Sox professional baseball organization, the Canadian national basketball teams, and with several PGA golfers.

Gregory W. Mondin, PhD, is a licensed psychologist in Boise, Idaho, who maintains a private practice specializing in health psychology, sport psychology, and individual counseling. After working as a psychiatric nurse for 10 years and competing as an amateur cyclist, he received his PhD in counseling psychology from the University of Wisconsin at Madison. Dr. Mondin then completed a postdoctoral fellowship in sport psychology at Ohio State University. He has worked with teams and individual athletes at the junior, university, and professional levels and has conducted clinics for

coaches, PGA instructors, sports medicine practitioners, and parents of young athletes. He has served as the sport psychology consultant to the U.S. women's rowing team since 1999. Dr. Mondin is also an adjunct faculty member at Boise State University, where he teaches classes in sport psychology and the psychology of athletic injury.

DeDee Nathan was a member of the USA 2000 Olympic track and field team. She was previously ranked as the number one heptathlete in the United States and has been on several World Championship, Pan Am, and Goodwill Games teams. She competed at Indiana University in track, where she gained All-Big Ten and All-American status. Nathan holds BS and MS degrees from Indiana University.

Edmund O'Connor, PhD, is the director and chief psychologist of the PEAK, Pain, & Headache Rehabilitation Programs at Rehabilitation Professionals in Grand Rapids, Michigan. He is also the sport psychologist for their sports medicine facility, GRSportsCenter.com. He is a member of the U.S. Olympic Committee Sport Psychology Registry and a certified consultant of the Association for the Advancement of Applied Sport Psychology (AAASP). Dr. O'Connor completed his undergraduate studies in psychology at Binghamton University and received his PhD in clinical psychology from the Illinois Institute of Technology. Previous experiences include clinical psychologist at the Pain & Rehabilitation Clinic of Chicago and biofeedback therapist at the Rehabilitation Institute of Chicago, Center for Pain Studies. His professional memberships include the American Psychological Association, Division of Sport & Exercise Psychology; AAASP; International Association for the Study of Pain; and Midwest Pain Society. Dr. O'Connor has numerous presentations and publications in the areas of pain and injury, rehabilitation, and performance enhancement.

Geoff Paull, PhD, is a consultant in performance enhancement in Perth, Western Australia. Dr. Paull is a registered psychologist and member of the College of Sport Psychologists of the Australian Psychological Society. Dr Paull's last university appointment was as principal lecturer in sport and exercise psychology at Staffordshire University in England. This position followed periods at Curtin University, Australia (School of Psychology), Florida State University (College of Health), and Arizona State University (department of exercise science and physical education). His areas of expertise include team and individual performance enhancement, elite coaching practice, program planning, and skill acquisition. These competencies are supported by having played and coached lacrosse, baseball, squash, and Australian football and by accreditation in the Australian National Coach Accreditation Scheme and the National Youth Sports Coaching Association (USA).

Anne Marte Pensgaard is currently director of sport psychology services at the Norwegian Olympic Training Centre and associate professor at the Norwegian University of Sport Sciences. Before this, she worked as a research fellow at the University of Birmingham, United Kingdom. Dr. Pensgaard has served as a sport psychology consultant for Olympic athletes since 1995 and was the sport psychologist for the Norwegian female soccer team in Sydney 2000 (gold medalists). Her main research interests are the process of coping with stress, the relationship of these processes to motivational factors, and understanding the meaning of the activity among participants in strenuous expeditions. She has written three textbooks about mental skills training that have been translated to Danish and Swedish as well as several chapters. Her main applied philosophy is to integrate mental training into physical training. She is also an experienced adventurer, participating on expeditions to Greenland and Spitsbergen, Svalbard.

Ron Pike is the head volleyball coach at Trinity Western University. He has served as the assistant coach for the Canadian team at the 2001 World University Games in Beijing and also for the Canadian junior team at the NORCEA Championship in Cuba in 2000. Previously he served as an assistant coach at the University of Calgary.

Chrissy Redden was the 2001 Pacific Sport Female Cyclist of the Year and in 1999 was named the Canadian Female cyclist of the year. She was a finalist for the 2000 Golden Horseshoe Athlete of the Year award and is a Guinness world record holder for the quickest ascent of tallest free-standing building in the world (CN Tower). In the 2000 Sydney Olympics she finished eighth in the cross-country mountain bike competition. She won the gold medal at the 2000 Commonwealth Games competition and has won numerous national competitions.

Hege Riise is currently assistant coach and player at Premier League club for women, Team Strömmen, Norway. She is one of the world's leading female soccer players—voted the best in the world in 1995—and from March 2001 until the fall of 2002 she played for the pro soccer team Carolina Courage in the United States. She started playing when she was 6 years old—with the boys!—and since then won the European Championship in 1993, the World Cup in 1995, and most recently the gold medal in the Sydney 2000 Olympic Games with the Norwegian national team, for which she is also the team captain. She has also organized and coached on several youth soccer camps in Norway. In addition to soccer, Hege also enjoys other sports like skiing, and she is interested in photography.

Ric Rosenkranz has a background as a professional triathlete and began his coaching career as a high school track coach in 1995. In 2001, he began working for USA Triathlon as talent identification and collegiate team coach. From 2002 to 2003, Ric worked as the USAT athlete development director at the National Training Center in Florida. He also served as Triathlon World Championship junior national coach in 2002 and 2003. At the end of 2003, he was named USOC developmental coach of the year for triathlon and became the USAT national select team junior coach and program coordinator. Ric is a USAT level II certified coach and a USA Cycling expert coach, and he maintains a small personal coaching business, TriaCoach.com. Ric holds a BA with honors in human development and psychology from the University of Kansas, a master's degree in psychology from the University of North Dakota, and a second master's in kinesiology from Kansas State University. Ric and his wife, Sara, and daughter, Ella, live in Colorado Springs, Colorado.

Thomas Schack, PhD, received his doctorate in 1996 for his research on mental training. He earned his MA in sport sciences and social science at the University in Zwickau in 1990 and finished a second master's degree in psychology at the University of Leipzig in 1999. Dr. Schack was a researcher and lecturer at the Technical University in Chemnitz and has been working at the Sports University in Köln since 1996. His main research interest concerns mental control, anxiety, and mental representation of complex movement. He has published more than 140 works and presented his research at various conferences in Asia, North America, and Europe. He was successful as an athlete in motocross sport, biathlon, and long-distance running (he ran the ultramarathon 15 times). Dr. Schack is also certified as a coach. As a consultant he works with the German women's volleyball national team and with the men's volleyball-paralympic team, winner of the gold medal in Sydney 2000.

Ulf Schmidt, PhD, studied teaching and social science in a master's program at the Georg-August-University in Göttingen. He also received, as a highly selected member of an international excellence program, his master of arts in educational psychology as well as in pedagogy at the Ludwig-Maximilians-University in Munich, Germany. With an Erasmus-scholarship, Ulf studied sport science at the University of Cheltenham and Gloucester in the United Kingdom. His dissertation at the University of the Federal Armed Forces in Munich focused on applying action theory in the domain of health, fitness, and well-being. His sport psychology research on the finalists of national and international Young Investigator's Awards is documented in more than 100 publications in national and international books and journals. Since 1996, Dr. Schmidt has worked as a researcher at the Institute of Sport Science and Sport at the University of the Federal Armed Forces in Munich and as a sport psychologist for the Olympic Training Center in Munich. In 1998, he was invited for an academic stay at the Wuhan Institute of Physical Education in China. In his free time Ulf is an active marathon runner.

Terri Schneider is a world-renowned adventure racer, triathlete, and ultrarunner. Schneider has been featured on the Discovery Channel, USA Network, high-profile talk shows, news segments, and popular outdoor publications highlighting her personal experiences and team dynamics relative to adventure racing, arguably the most grueling sport on the planet. She has competed internationally in seven Eco-Challenge Expedition Competitions, the Mild Seven Outdoor Quest in China, the ESPN X-Games Adventure Race, the Raid Gauloises in Tibet and Nepal, several 50- and 100-mile endurance runs, and 22 Ironman Triathlons, finishing in the top 5 three times in the Hawaii Ironman Triathlon World Championships. In addition to her 15 years of coaching endurance athletes, Schneider has completed her master's degree in sport psychology focusing her research on risk taking and team dynamics.

Michael Seestedt graduated from the University of Michigan in 1999 where he received his BA in communication studies. While at Michigan, Seestedt received Academic All-Big 10 honors as a catcher for the baseball team. He was drafted by the Baltimore Orioles and is currently playing in their minor league farm system.

Lynn Seiser, PhD, is a psychotherapist and author with more than 25 years of clinical experience in counseling offenders and victims of violence, trauma, and abuse. He is known for holistic recovery from addictions and an emphasis on healthy relationships. Dr. Seiser is a regular columnist in the *Long Beach Grunion Gazette* newspaper and *Awareness Magazine.* He is the coauthor of *Core Concepts in Psychotherapy: Interventions and Techniques* (Open University Press/McGraw Hill) and *Aikido Basics* (Tuttle Publishing). Dr. Seiser created *Aiki-Solutions,* a consulting business specializing in applied sports and performance psychology, tactical mental discipline, strategic performance enhancement, and nonviolent conflict prevention, management, and resolution. He is a lifelong student of the martial arts with more than 35 years of training. Dr. Seiser has completed marathons and triathlons.

Danny Stevens, MA, LPC, commits a large part of his time to working with athletes and their families. He specializes in working with athletes with eating disorders and performance issues. Stevens has developed numerous programs that are being implemented in schools, and he gives approximately 80 presentations a year to groups of all sizes on various topics in sport psychology.

Richard K. Stratton, PhD (Florida State University, 1977, movement science education), has been the motor learning and sport psychology specialist in the health promotion and physical education program at Virginia Tech since 1977. He earned a master's degree and a certificate of advanced graduate study in physical education from Georgia Southern University. In addition to his university experience, Dr. Stratton taught middle school physical education and coached football, boys' basketball, girls' basketball, and track and field. He has also coached swimming at the age group and college levels. His primary interests are the developmental aspects of information processing and motivation and stress in youth sport participants. He has also conducted research on motivation systems, stress, and mood states in collegiate athletes. As a service to youth sports, Dr. Stratton developed an Internet newsletter, *Coaching Youth Sports,* now in its seventh year of publication, which provides information to coaches, parents, and athletes.

Miyako Tanaka-Oulevey, MA, won a bronze medal in the synchronized swimming duet event in the 1988 Seoul Olympics. After retiring, she coached the Japanese and U.S. national teams. Tanaka-

Oulevey received an MA in Health, Physical Education, and Recreation and is currently working toward an MA in sport counseling. Now living in Japan, she teaches sport psychology classes at Nihon University in Tokyo and gives speeches in performance enhancement throughout Japan. Tanaka-Oulevey has also translated three health-related books from English to Japanese.

Dave Trembley is a coach with the Baltimore Orioles professional baseball organization. In 2001 he was selected by *Baseball America* as one of the top minor managers of the last 20 years and has been named minor league manager of the year on three different occasions. He has recorded more than 1,100 wins as a manager and holds BS and MS degrees in education from the State University of New York.

Brent Walker, PhD, is an assistant professor of sport psychology at Missouri Western State College and runs Play in the Zone consulting. He earned his MA degree from the University of North Carolina at Chapel Hill (1997) and his PhD from the University of Illinois (2002). His research focuses on the motivational experiences of youth sport participants, looking specifically at achievement goals and fear of failure. Besides consulting with athletes ranging from the youth to the professional ranks, he regularly provides clinics for coaches, athletes, and parents.

Robert S. Weinberg earned his PhD in psychology (specializing in sport and exercise psychology) at the University of California at Los Angeles in 1977. He is a professor in the department of physical education, health, and sport studies at Miami University in Ohio. Before coming to Miami University, Weinberg was a regents professor in the department of kinesiology at the University of North Texas. He was also voted one of the top 10 sport psychology specialists in North America by his peers. In addition to teaching undergraduate and graduate sport and exercise psychology for more than 25 years, Weinberg has published approximately 135 journal articles, contributed 20 book chapters, and published seven books as well as presenting more than 300 refereed and invited papers at sport and exercise psychology conferences. He has served as president of both the North American Society for the Psychology of Sport and Physical Activity and the Association for the Advancement of Applied Sport Psychology. He was the editor of the *Journal of Applied Sport Psychology* and is a certified consultant, member of the United States Olympic Committee

Sport Psychology Registry, and a fellow in the American Academy for Kinesiology and Physical Education.

Eric Weinrich is a defenseman for the Philadelphia Flyers of the National Hockey League. In 2003, he played in his 1,000th career NHL game, making him only the 190th player in NHL history to reach this mark. He was named to the All-NHL Rookie team his first season. Weinrich played for Team USA in eight World Championship tournaments (1991, 1993, 1997-2002) and was captain of the 1998 squad. He also played for Team USA at the 1988 Winter Olympic Games in Calgary and at the 1985 and 1986 World Junior Championship tournaments. Weinrich played collegiate hockey at the University of Maine.

Blair Whitmarsh, PhD, earned both his master's and doctoral degrees in physical education (sport psychology) from the University of Alberta in Edmonton. Dr. Whitmarsh is the chair of the department of human kinetics at Trinity Western University and has consulted with numerous provincial, national, and international athletes from the sports of ringette, hockey, baseball, volleyball, swimming, gymnastics, bodybuilding, and dance. Currently, he is a sport psychology consultant for the Canadian national ringette team and the Trinity Western University women's volleyball team. He is a regular contributor to *Muscle and Fitness* magazine and has been published in professional journals such as *The Sport Psychologist*.

George Williams is the head track-and-field coach at St. Augustine's College in Raleigh, North Carolina, where he also serves as the school's athletics director. Since he began coaching in 1976, his teams have won 24 NCAA Division II national championships and he personally has received 90 different Coach of the Year honors. Before being named the U.S. men's head track and field coach for the 2004 Olympics, he also served as the men's head coach for the 1999 World Outdoor Championships, the 1993 World Indoor Championships, and the 1992 IAAF World Cup and was an assistant coach at the 1996 Olympics.

Roseann Wilson, MS, is the former head women's track and cross country coach at Indiana University, where she was named Big 10 coach of the year in 1989. Previously, she was head coach at the University of Connecticut, where she was twice named Big East coach of the year as well as receiving NCAA district coaching honors. A distance runner, she captained the IU women's cross country team her senior year. She has coached numerous All-Americans and International team members in both track and cross country and served as an assistant coach at the U.S. Olympic Festival. She has taught physical education at both Erskine College and the University of Southern Indiana and is presently working as an elementary physical educator and junior high track, basketball, and soccer coach.

Dean Wurzberger, Husky coach, enters his 13th year at the helm of the University of Washington men's soccer program. Wurzberger has spent over a decade building the Husky program into one of the nation's finest fielding teams that annually compete for conference and national championships. The Huskies have appeared in the NCAA Tournament in eight of the last nine years. UW was one of only seven schools in the country to make seven straight NCAA trips from 1995-2001. His record in 12 seasons stands at 153-62-23 (.702).

Iris Zimmerman was captain of the fencing team at Stanford University. She represented the United States in foil fencing at the 2000 Olympics in Sydney.